Acquisitions Editor: *Rachel McCoy*
Publishing Coordinator: *Claudia Fernandes*
Senior Director of Market Development: *Kristine Suárez*
Development Editor: *Barbara Lyons*
Director of Editorial Development: *Julia Caballero*
Production Supervision: *Nancy Stevenson*
Project Manager: *Assunta Petrone*
Assistant Director of Production: *Mary Rottino*
Supplements Editor: *Meriel Martínez Moctezuma*
Media Editor: *Samantha Alducin*
Media Production Manager: *Roberto Fernandez*
Prepress and Manufacturing Buyer: *Brian Mackey*
Prepress and Manufacturing Assistant Manager:
    Mary Ann Gloriande

Interior Design: *Preparé Inc.*
Line Art Coordinator: *Maria Piper*
Illustrator: *Steve Mannion*
Director, Image Resource Center: *Melinda Reo*
Interior Image Specialist: *Beth Boyd Brenzel*
Manager, Rights & Permissions IRC: *Zina Arabia*
Photo Research: *Mary Ann Price*
Marketing Assistant: *William J. Bliss*
Publisher: *Phil Miller*

Cover images: *front*, John Miller / Robert Harding World
    Imagery; *back*, Terrance Klassen / AGE Fotostock
    America, Inc., Adalberto Rios / Photodisc Green / Getty
    Images, Inc., Craig Cranna / Index Stock Imagery, Inc.

Pearson Education LTD.
Pearson Education Australia PTY, Limited
Pearson Education Singapore, Pte. Ltd
Pearson Education North Asia Ltd

Pearson Education, Canada, Ltd
Pearson Educación de Mexico, S.A. de C.V.
Pearson Education—Japan
Pearson Education Malaysia, Pte. Ltd

Printed in the United States of America
10 9 8 7 6 5 4 3 2 1

Student text: **ISBN 0-13-192026-X**
Annotated Instructor's Edition: **ISBN 0-13-193076-1**

PEARSON
Prentice Hall

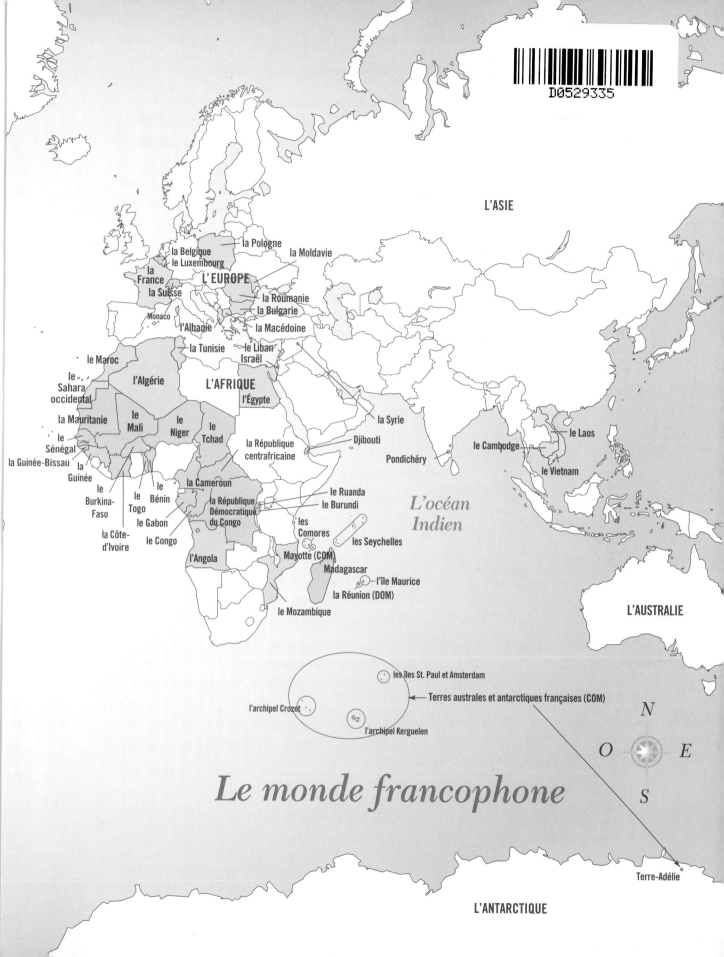

Le monde francophone

La France: les provinces
les départements

L'ANGLETERRE
LA BELGIQUE
L'ALLEMAGNE
LE LUX.
La Manche
LA SUISSE
L'ITALIE
L'océan Atlantique
La Mer
Méditerranée
L'ESPAGNE
L'ANDORRE
MONACO

Limite départementale
Limite provinciale
Gironde Nomme du département
CENTRE Nomme de la province
0 Kilomètres 200

ANNOTATED INSTRUCTOR'S EDITION

Chez nous

BRANCHÉ SUR LE MONDE FRANCOPHONE

Third Edition

Albert Valdman
Indiana University

Cathy Pons
University of North Carolina, Asheville

Mary Ellen Scullen
University of Maryland, College Park

PEARSON
Prentice
Hall

Upper Saddle River, New Jersey 07458

Brief Contents

Scope and Sequence

Preface

CHEZ NOUS, THIRD EDITION is a complete introductory French program designed for use at colleges and universities, over two or three terms/semesters, and is suitable for use in accelerated or intensive courses. Using a careful progression from skill-developing to skill-using activities and a mature treatment of Francophone culture, the text and its full complement of supplementary materials help students develop listening, reading, speaking, and writing skills as well as insights into other cultures by exposing them to authentic, contemporary French and encouraging them to express themselves on a variety of topics.

Building on the success of earlier editions, **CHEZ NOUS, THIRD EDITION** offers a richly nuanced focus on the Francophone world through a highly integrative and process-oriented approach to the development of language skills. This approach is consistent with the **National Standards for Foreign Language Learning for the 21st Century**, widely recognized as a set of desired outcomes for foreign language instruction. Rather than functioning as discrete and occasional influences on the text, the National Standards constitute an essential underlying principle of the program as a whole. The "Five C's," as defined by the National Standards, are directly embodied in essential aspects of the **CHEZ NOUS** program. The National Standards also constitute a subtext throughout the program—for example, many practice activities introduce cultural realities from across the French-speaking world, and culture is explored through skill-using activities and discovery methods of language learning. **CHEZ NOUS** addresses the National Standards by:

- Emphasizing **communication** developed through authentic language samples and tasks (**Points de départ**, **Formes et fonctions**, and in all skill-development exercises)
- Encouraging cultural **comparisons** (**Vie et culture** and **Venez chez nous !**)
- Presenting a broad cross section of French-speaking **communities** (**Points de départ**, **Vie et culture**, **Lisons**, **Écoutons**, and **Venez chez nous !**)
- Fostering **connections** by guiding students through a variety of disciplines, including history, geography, art, and literature (found in **Vie et culture**, **Venez chez nous !**, and **Lisons**)
- Promoting skill development within a distinctive **cultural** framework (found in **Vie et culture** and **Venez chez nous !**)

Hallmark features of **CHEZ NOUS** include:

- **Innovative treatment of grammar.** Structures are presented in the context of authentic communicative use of the language; i.e., the periphrastic future (**aller** plus the infinitive) is not the notional equivalent of the inflected future (**le futur simple**), and this distinction is clearly made in the presentation and in practice activities. Grammar treatments, reflecting the spoken language, make important generalizations about the structure of French. For example, the presentation of adjectives is based on the concept that the masculine form of variable adjectives is derived from the longer feminine form by dropping the final pronounced consonant (**grande/grand**). Similarly, students learn that verbs with two stems have a longer stem in the plural, from which the singular can be derived by this general rule of final consonant deletion (**partent/part**).

  Use of a cyclical syllabus also facilitates a focus on native speaker practice by enabling the instructor to focus on frequent and simpler language features first. Introduction of the conditional, for example, reflects the fact that this mood is most frequently used in polite requests. Additionally, the use of a cyclical syllabus allows complex structures—such as adjectives or the **passé composé**—to be presented, reviewed, and expanded upon gradually in a variety of contexts.

- **Process orientation to skills development.** The receptive skills (listening and reading) are developed using authentic materials that are just beyond students' productive skill level. Preview activities provide or activate background knowledge and introduce comprehension strategies; listening and reading activities guide and check comprehension as students encounter the material; and follow-up activities encourage them to reflect on what they have read or heard. The productive skills (speaking and writing) are likewise practiced via carefully sequenced activities that emphasize carrying out authentic tasks through a process approach. Pre-speaking and pre-writing preparation ready students to carry out the assigned tasks; frameworks for the actual speaking and writing assignments are provided; and thoughtful follow-up is encouraged. Through this process approach to development of the four skills, students gradually become confident and proficient at carrying out a wide variety of communicative tasks.

- **Pervasive and highly nuanced treatment of French and Francophone cultures.** Throughout each chapter, thematically interrelated lessons closely integrate the presentation of lexical and grammatical content within interesting and culturally authentic contexts. Nuanced cultural presentations also explicitly encompass the breadth and richness of the Francophone world, leading students to a deeper analysis and understanding of the diverse cultures of France and the French-speaking world. The cultural and thematic presentation of each chapter culminates in the final lesson, titled **Venez chez nous !**, which provides an in-depth and intellectually stimulating look at the chapter theme in the Francophone context. A rich pedagogical apparatus provides students with opportunities to further develop language skills while exploring the cultural topic and making cross-cultural comparisons.

- **Authentic texts and tasks.** Authentic texts and tasks form the basis for developing students' language skills in **CHEZ NOUS**. Listening activities and models for speaking reflect the everyday language of young people. Varied readings and writing tasks help students develop an awareness of appropriate style as they are exposed to a wide variety of Francophone writers and oral traditions. Throughout the textbook and supplements, practice of vocabulary and grammar is oriented toward real situations and authentic tasks.

What's New in CHEZ NOUS, THIRD EDITION?

1. **Further refinement of the cyclical scope and sequence.** Recent research and users' feedback has led to fine-tuning of the scope and sequence for enhanced linguistic effectiveness and flexibility in the classroom.

   - Recent research has guided revisions, ensuring that the most frequent and useful grammatical features are taught first, and that distinctions are made to reflect actual native speaker practice. As a result, the grammar presentation is practical and accessible but not unnecessarily detailed for beginning students.
   - The cyclical syllabus has been refined to allow for more flexible and efficient use of the **CHEZ NOUS** program over one to three terms/semesters. For example, a brief new preliminary chapter allows students to acquire quickly the basic elements needed to function in an all-French classroom. Past tenses are now presented earlier so that students can use present, past, and future time frames by the end of Chapter 5. The grammatical syllabus has been lightened at the end of the book to allow for additional recycling and integration of learning. We have maintained the same number of pages in the third edition as in the second edition so that we would not require instructors to increase the amount of time it takes to teach the entire text.

2. **Elaboration of the process orientation to skills development.** Better than any other first-year French textbook currently on the market, the third edition of **CHEZ NOUS** takes a process approach to the development of strategies for reading, listening, speaking, and writing.

   - The process orientation to skills development is further refined in **CHEZ NOUS, THIRD EDITION**, with a new focus on teaching explicit strategies for reading, writing, listening, and speaking. The process approach, in turn, has been unified and streamlined as strategies are put into practice, from preview to follow-up.

3. **Integration of an exciting new video.** The new video to accompany **CHEZ NOUS, THIRD EDITION**, is fully integrated into the program.

   - The exciting new video program introduces an engaging cast of French speakers from France, Belgium, Quebec, Haiti, Morocco, Benin, Congo, and Madagascar, who describe their homelands, families, work and leisure activities, their experiences, and their hopes for the future. They represent a variety of ages, living situations, and cultural backgrounds.
   - Complementary activities in the textbook, the new Video Manual, and on the Companion Website lead students to grasp and reflect on the linguistic and cultural content of each clip through pre-viewing, viewing, and post-viewing exercises.

4. **Interactive approach to discovering French and Francophone cultures.** More than any other first-year program, **CHEZ NOUS** leads students to a deeper analysis and understanding of the diverse cultures of France and the French-speaking world.

   - Cultural information is fully updated and now presented primarily through video, realia, and authentic texts, allowing students to "discover" elements of French and Francophone life as they discuss what they see, hear, and read. Related questions encourage students to make cross-cultural comparisons.

5. **Renewed emphasis on authentic texts and tasks.** The third edition includes a much wider variety of authentic texts and samples of authentic discourse.

   - Listening activities and models for speaking are derived primarily from unscripted samples of native speaker discourse.
   - A wide range of readings and writing tasks help students develop an awareness of appropriate style.
   - An increased number of literary texts in the third edition expose students to many periods, genres, and well-known Francophone writers. Folk tales, proverbs, and counting rhymes further enrich the cultural content.

6. **Increased flexibility and user-friendliness.** Designed for ease of use in a variety of classroom settings, the third edition increases user-friendliness.

   - The Instructor's Resource Manual provides more options for syllabus planning and additional sample lesson plans, as well as supplementary classroom activities, including information-gap activities for each chapter.
   - The **CHEZ NOUS** Testing Program has been completely revised to increase flexibility for users. Instructors have access to a wide variety of exercises for each chapter, which allows for customization of assessment instruments. The program includes formats for testing all language competencies as well as guidelines for grading. All listening comprehension exercises are recorded for the instructor's use.

7. **OneKey.** Powered by Blackboard, CourseCompass, or WebCT, this course management tool provides all instructor and student resources in one convenient place and adds to the ease of customization. This includes an electronic version of the Student Activities Manual, as well as the video, audio, and more.

Organization of the Textbook

CHEZ NOUS, THIRD EDITION consists of a brief introductory chapter plus twelve full-length chapters. Each is built around a cultural theme introduced by informative photographs, line drawings, and realia. The user-friendly organization in the third edition divides each chapter into three lessons that pair lexical and grammar presentations, and the concluding fourth **Venez chez nous !** cultural lesson. The first three lessons in each chapter typically include the following components:

Points de départ. Reflecting the chapter theme, this opening section presents situationally oriented vocabulary through varied and appealing visuals and exchanges representing authentic everyday contexts. All **Points de départ** language samples are recorded on the Text Audio CD. The **Points de départ** section includes extensive and updated cultural notes (now entitled **Vie et culture**) written initially in English, then (beginning in Chapter 7) in French. **Vie et culture** notes elaborate on the cultural references made in the vocabulary presentation. They incorporate photos and realia that students must analyze to discover features of French culture and make cross-cultural comparisons. Each **Points de départ** section offers a sequence of activities (**À vous la parole**) to be used in class to provide meaningful and personalized practice of the words and expressions through whole class, paired, and small group activities.

Sons et lettres. This section presents the main phonetic features and sound contrasts of French. It emphasizes the sound contrasts that determine differences in meaning, the major differences between French and English, and the relationship between sounds and spellings. Discrimination and oral practice exercises found in the text (**À vous la parole**) are also recorded on the Text Audio CDs.

Formes et fonctions. Clearly written grammar explanations in English focus on authentic usage and point out features of the spoken versus the written language. Numerous examples are provided and, where appropriate, color-coded charts summarize the forms. Similarly, verb conjugations are illustrated in charts whose color shadings indicate the number of spoken forms and show how forms are derived from the base. The **Formes et fonctions** section also includes class-friendly exercises that provide a full range of practice—from form-based to meaningful and personalized activities—incorporating the theme and the vocabulary of the lesson (**À vous la parole**). Icons clearly indicate pair and small group or whole class activities.

Lisons, Écoutons, Parlons, or Écrivons. Each of the first three chapter lessons concludes with one of these skill-oriented activities, allowing students to put into practice the vocabulary, grammar, and cultural knowledge acquired in the lesson. Through work with an authentic text or task in a reading, listening, speaking, or writing activity, students are guided in their development of receptive and productive skills.

Venez chez nous ! These newly revised and expanded cultural lessons allow students to explore the chapter theme in depth as it relates to a particular Francophone region or regions. Every **Venez chez nous !** lesson now includes substantive process-oriented activities that promote skill development while encouraging cultural analysis and cross-cultural comparisons. The new **Observons** activities draw on clips from the video to incorporate authentic listening practice with rich visual and cultural elements.

Vocabulaire. This section is found at the end of the chapter, and it summarizes the key vocabulary targeted for students' productive use. Words and phrases are grouped semantically by lesson, and English equivalents are provided. These new words and expressions are recorded on the Text Audio CDs.

Appendices. Located at the end of the text, these include presentations of the **plus-que-parfait**, the **futur antérieur**, and the **passé du conditionnel**, along with a sequence of practice activities; **verb charts** for regular and irregular verbs; **French-English** and **English-French glossaries**; the **International Phonetic Alphabet** with key words; and an **Index** of grammar, vocabulary, and cultural topics found in the book.

Finally, a series of colorful updated **maps** are included in the front and back of the book.

Other Program Components

Outstanding revised supplements provide additional opportunities for practicing lexical and grammatical features while extending the breadth and depth of the cultural presentation and the introduction to the Francophone world. Expanded electronic components extend the third edition's pedagogical and cultural presentations in interesting, creative ways through a new Video program and on-line Audio. A sophisticated Companion Website and OneKey provide additional opportunities for practice and carefully researched links that broaden students' access to information about the Francophone world. A new testing program allows instructors to customize tests for all language skills and culture.

Audio CDs to Accompany Text Each chapter's **Points de départ, Sons et lettres** and **Écoutons** segments as well as the end-of-chapter vocabulary lists can be found on the Text Audio CDs. Several poems and play excerpts from the **Lisons** sections have also been included.

Student Activities Manual (SAM), Answer Key, and Audio CD to Accompany the SAM. The new Student Activities Manual includes the Workbook, Lab Manual, and Video Manual.

Workbook exercises provide meaningful and communicative writing practice, incorporating the vocabulary and structures introduced in each chapter and offering additional skill-using activities. Each Workbook chapter concludes with a **Venez chez nous !** section that is closely tied to the chapter theme and allows students to delve deeper into the cultural focus of the **Venez chez nous !** lesson in the textbook through guided Web-based activities. The Lab Manual exercises provide listening practice that progresses from comprehension only to production based on what students hear. The exercises stress authentic speech and real-life tasks. Recordings corresponding to the Lab Manual activities feature native speakers of French. The Video Manual complements the listening practice provided in the textbook using additional video clips and expanded activities. A separately bound **Answer Key** is available for optional inclusion in course packages; it includes answers for all discrete and short answer exercises in the SAM. In addition, the Answer Key includes all of the answers to the textbook's **Observons** activities.

Video Program. The third edition includes a beautifully produced video, shot on location. This new video introduces native speakers from across the Francophone world who address the topics and themes of each chapter in varied settings and contexts. Carefully integrated with the **Vie et culture** sections and the **Venez chez nous !** lessons in the textbook, the video is easy to incorporate into daily lesson plans. The textbook's **Observons** exercises and the Video Manual activities take a process-oriented approach to the development of viewing skills.

Instructor's Resource Manual and Scripts. Included in the revised Instructor's Resource Manual (IRM) is an extensive introduction to the components of the **CHEZ NOUS, THIRD EDITION** program. Sample syllabi for two- and three-term course sequences are outlined, along with numerous sample lesson plans. The extensive cultural annotations are a unique feature of this IRM, providing further information about topics introduced in the textbook. Information-gap activities, ready for classroom use, are provided for each chapter. The IRM also provides the scripts for the Lab Manual and the Video Manual.

Image Resource CD. This will contain labeled and unlabeled versions of all of the line art images from the textbook. Instructors will be able to incorporate these images into presentation slides, worksheets, and transparencies as well as finding many other creative uses for them.

Testing Program and Audio to Accompany the Testing Program. A new and highly flexible testing program allows instructors to customize tests by selecting modules or exercises. This complete testing program, available in paper and electronic formats, includes quizzes, chapter tests, and comprehensive examinations that test listening, reading, and writing skills as well as cultural knowledge. Special formats to test listening and speaking skills are also included. All oral sections are recorded for the instructor's use in a classroom or laboratory setting. For all elements in the testing program, detailed grading guidelines are provided.

ON-LINE RESOURCES

Companion Website. The clearly designed and regularly updated Companion Website (CW) makes a wealth of material available to the student and instructor. Organized by chapter, the site offers automatically graded vocabulary and grammar practice, link-based activities for language and cultural learning, resources such as dictionaries and study manuals, the complete Audio program, and game activities. It now includes an extensive Instructor's Resource Center with the IRM and all the illustrations and charts found in the textbook. The instructor can use these illustrations to produce transparencies, presentation slides, and worksheets.

Instructor's Resource Center. The IRC is located on *www.prenhall.com* and provides instructor access to all the IRM resources as well as to the illustrations and charts found in the textbook which can be used to produce transparencies, presentation slides, and worksheets. This material is also available electronically for downloading.

OneKey. This new course management tool provides all of the instructor and student resources in one convenient place and adds to the ease of course customization. Components in OneKey include an electronic version of the SAM, the complete audio program, the **CHEZ NOUS** video, and a wide variety of Internet activities. The majority of exercises are machine gradable, and students' grades can be automatically placed in an electronic grade book for the instructor.

To the Student

Why did you choose to study French? Most students of French wish to develop basic language skills that they can put to practical use and to learn about how the lives of French-speaking peoples compare to their own. The **CHEZ NOUS, THIRD EDITION** program is designed to help you meet those goals. Specifically, with the aid of this textbook and the accompanying materials, you can expect to accomplish the following:

- Become familiar with many features of everyday life and culture in France and in the three dozen countries where French is spoken. You will have the opportunity to reflect on how your life in North America and your values compare with those of French speakers across the globe.

- Speak French well enough to get around in a country where French is spoken. You should be able to greet people, ask for directions, cope with everyday needs, give basic information about yourself, and talk about things that are important to you. You should also be able to assist French-speaking visitors in this country.

- Understand French well enough to get the main ideas and some details from a news broadcast, lecture, or conversation that you hear. You should understand French speakers quite well when they speak slowly about topics with which you are familiar.

- Read French Web sites as well as newspaper and magazine articles dealing with current events or other familiar topics. With the help of a dictionary, you should be able to read more specialized material in fields of interest. You should also be able to enjoy short and simple pieces of literature in French.
- Write French well enough to take notes, write messages and letters for various purposes, and fill out forms.
- Finally, you will gain an understanding of the structure of the French language: its pronunciation, grammar, and vocabulary. You will also gain insight into how languages function in societies. These insights may even help you to understand your native language better!

ASSURING YOUR SUCCESS

Whether or not you have already studied French, you bring some knowledge of that language to your study. Many words of French origin are used in English (**soufflé**, **croissant**, **détente**, and **diplomat,** for example). You also bring to the study of French your knowledge of the world in general and of specific events, which you can use to predict what you will read or hear. You can use your knowledge of a particular topic, as well as accompanying photos or titles, to predict what will come next. Finally, the reading and listening skills you have learned for your native language will also prove useful as you study a foreign language.

Many of the materials found in **CHEZ NOUS, THIRD EDITION** will seem challenging to you because you will not be able to understand every word you hear or read. That is to be expected—the readings in the textbook were written for native speakers, and listening exercises approximate native speech. The language used in **CHEZ NOUS, THIRD EDITION** is real and the topics current. You should use your background knowledge and prediction skills to make intelligent guesses about what you are hearing and reading. In this way, you can get the main ideas and some details, a good first step toward real communication in a foreign language.

Since access to native French speakers is limited in most parts of the United States, the classroom offers an important opportunity for you to practice your listening and speaking skills. Unless your instructor indicates otherwise, keep your book closed. Since what you are learning is explained in the textbook, you will not need to take notes during class. Instead, it is important that you *participate* as much as possible in classroom activities.

Adequate preparation is another key to success. Prepare each lesson as directed by your instructor before going to class. Be sure to complete assignments made by your instructor and review regularly, not just for an exam.

USING YOUR TEXTBOOK TO PREPARE

CHEZ NOUS, THIRD EDITION is made up of a brief introductory chapter plus twelve full-length chapters, each organized around a cultural situation that you are likely to encounter when you come into contact with native French speakers. Each chapter consists of three lessons that expand on this cultural situation. Each lesson includes the following sections:

The opening section called **Points de départ** provides a "point of departure" for the lesson by presenting vocabulary related to the chapter topic. The meaning of new words is conveyed through the use of art, photos, documents, dialogues, or brief descriptions in French. You can listen to these language samples on the Text Audio CDs. You should learn both the written and spoken forms of these words and expressions so that you can use them in your own speech and writing. Look over the exercises found under **À vous la parole**; many of these will be used in class. Your instructor may also assign additional practice from the Student Activities Manual (SAM) and the **CHEZ NOUS** Companion Website (CW) once you have dealt with the topic in class.

Vie et culture sections challenge you to discover aspects of Francophone life and culture and to make comparisons with your own culture as you examine photos and various types of documents. Language cannot be separated from the culture of its speakers, and the activities in **CHEZ NOUS, THIRD EDITION** provide a cultural context for your study of French.

Sons et lettres, "sounds and letters," focuses on important pronunciation features of French and differences between French and English. This section also provides guidance in spelling French words. Exercises in the textbook can be practiced using the Text Audio CDs. These exercises, plus those found in the Laboratory Manual, help you to first recognize, then produce, the French sounds.

Each lesson includes grammar presentations called **Formes et fonctions**. The forms taught can be combined with the lesson vocabulary to carry out specific tasks such as asking questions or ordering something to eat or drink. Read over the explanation in English and study the examples. Often a color-coded chart will summarize forms. Look for similarities with other structures you have already learned. Some new vocabulary may be found in these sections, for example, a list of verbs or negative expressions. Once the material has been practiced in class, your instructor may assign additional exercises from the SAM and CW.

The last section in each lesson is designed to help you put into practice the vocabulary, grammar, and cultural knowledge you have acquired in this and earlier lessons. Through the exercises called **Lisons**, **Écoutons**, **Parlons**, and **Écrivons**, you use your reading, listening, speaking, and writing skills to communicate in French with your instructor and with other class members.

At the end of each chapter you will find a colorful cultural lesson, **Venez chez nous !**, that allows you to examine the chapter theme in depth as it relates to the Francophone world and to make cross-cultural comparisons. These cultural lessons also include an activity, **Observons**, based on video clips from the exciting new video that accompanies **CHEZ NOUS, THIRD EDITION**. The **Venez chez nous !** activities found in your textbook are supplemented by exercises in the SAM and on the CW which features links to interesting sites related to the topic of the cultural lesson.

You will also want to familiarize yourself with the sections of your textbook designed to give you special help. Each chapter ends with **Vocabulaire**, a list of the words and expressions that you should be able to use in your own speech and writing. For each lesson, the words are grouped by meaning, and English equivalents are provided. These words and expressions are recorded on the Text Audio CDs, so that you can practice recognizing and pronouncing them on your own. The appendices of **CHEZ NOUS, THIRD EDITION** include verb conjugations for both regular and irregular verbs, a guide to pronunciation that uses simple key words and phonetic symbols, and colorful

maps of France and the Francophone world and a **Lexique** that allows you to look up a word in French or in English and find its equivalent in the other language. For vocabulary that you should be able to use in your speech or writing, chapter and lesson numbers indicate where a particular word or expression was first introduced. You will also find vocabulary used in readings, in directions, or in the **Vie et culture** sections that you should be able to recognize or guess from context. Finally, the **Index** lists vocabulary, grammar, and cultural topics alphabetically so that you can easily find the section you wish to read or review.

CHEZ NOUS, THIRD EDITION and its accompanying materials will provide you with opportunities to develop your French language skills—listening, reading, speaking, and writing—by exposing you to authentic French and encouraging you to express yourself on a variety of topics. It will also introduce you to Francophone cultures around the world and invite you to reflect on your own culture. As you begin this endeavor, we wish you « **Bon courage !** »

Acknowledgments

The publication of the third edition of **CHEZ NOUS** represents the culmination of two years of planning, field testing, and fine-tuning to which many instructors and students have contributed. We wish to thank our colleagues and students for their participation in this process, for their comments, and for their encouragement.

We extend our sincere thanks and appreciation to the colleagues who reviewed the manuscript at various stages of development. We gratefully acknowledge their participation and candor:

Ellen Abrams, Northern Essex Community College, MA
Hanna Albertson, University of Mississippi
Bruce Anderson, University of California-Davis
Eileen Angelini, Philadelphia University, PA
Julie A. Baker, University of Richmond, VA
Becky Baumann, Benedictine University, IL
Anatoli Boukhtiarov, University of North Carolina at Charlotte
Blake Carpenter, The University of Texas at Arlington
Sarah Chitwood, Virginia Western Community College
Linda Noreen Cochran, University of Central Oklahoma

Nathalie Dejoannis-Hulsmann, Auburn University, AL
Jean-Luc Desalvo, San José State University, CA
Chris De Ville, Pitt Community College, NC
Nathalie Dieu-Porter, Vanderbilt University, TN
Peter Dola, University of North Carolina at Greensboro
Annie Duménil, University of South Carolina
Catherine Dunand, Northeastern University, MA
Michelle Emanuel, University of Mississippi
Zakaria Fatih, George Mason University, VA
Carolyn Fay, Franklin & Marshall College, PA
Salvatore Federico, Thunderbird AGSIM, AZ
Christelle Fourmeaux, University of Mississippi
Carolyn Gascoigne, University of Nebraska at Omaha
Marjorie Hallett, Rockland Community College, NY
Alexander Hertich, St. Olaf College, MN
Joyce Johnston, Stephen F. Austin State University, TX
Theresa Anne Jordan, Wayne State University, MI
Carrie Klaus, DePauw University, IN
Cheryl Krueger, University of Virginia
Rose Marie Kuhn, California State University Fresno
Claude Lapeyre, Moraine Valley Community College, IL

Elizabeth Cavitch Lucia, The George Washington University, D.C.

Anne Lutkus, University of Rochester, NY

Chantal Maher, Palomar College, CA

Sandra Malicote, University of North Carolina at Asheville

Elfie Manning, Community College of Southern Nevada

Catherine Marachi, Saint Mary's College of California

Sharla Martin, The University of Texas at Arlington

Lee Mitchell, Henderson State University, AR

Jennifer Moody, Southern Union State Community College, AL

Perry Moon, Stephen F. Austin State University, TX

Ann Moore, Hampton University, VA

Katherine Mueller, University of Calgary, Canada

Shonu Nangia, Wayne State University, MI

Ida Nelson, SUNY College at Old Westbury

Daniel E. O'Sullivan, University of Mississippi

Katherine A. Paesani, Wayne State University, MI

Pamela Paine, Auburn University, AL

Barbara Place, Manchester Community College, CT

Hilary Raymond, University of Richmond, VA

Bernd Renner, Brooklyn College of CUNY

Angeliki Salamaleki, Wayne State University, MI

Kelly Sax, Indiana University

Jean Marie Schultz, University of California at Santa Barbara

Giovanna Summerfield, Auburn University, AL

Carole Verhelle, Wayne State University, MI

Martha Wallen, University of Wisconsin-Stout

Monique Watts, SUNY at Stony Brook, NY

Lynni Weibezahl, University of Nevada-Reno

Lawrence Williams, University of North Texas

Diana Zilberman, Baltimore City Community College, MD

We thank the following colleagues for their important contributions, without which the third edition would be incomplete: Virginie Cassidy of the University of Maryland, College Park, for the Lab Manual; Ellen Bailey of the University of North Carolina, Asheville, and Sandhya Mohan of the University of Maryland, College Park, for their outstanding work in revising the Companion Website originally developed by Virginie Cassidy; Kate Paesani of Wayne State University, for the Instructor's Resource Manual. We would like to thank P. Reychman and Michèle Dussaucy for their careful proofing of the textbook and Student Activities Manual manuscripts.

We offer a special thanks to our video participants, who graciously opened their homes and offices to us. Thanks also to Annette Brieger, who took many of the beautiful new photos and served as an impressive jack-of-all-trades on the shoot. Thanks to Laura, our tireless Parisian guide. And finally a special thanks to Jane Pittman, who did a superb job of directing, filming, and producing the finished project. *Merci*, Jane.

At the University of North Carolina, Asheville, we wish to thank supportive colleagues and cooperative students who tried out many of the new texts and activities and supplied helpful comments and enthusiastic encouragement.

At the University of Maryland, College Park, special thanks go to supportive colleagues and to the fabulous Graduate Teaching Assistants and other graduate students who answered questions, provided feedback, and made suggestions for improvement. And to those who responded to e-mail queries for help at all hours of the day and night, *un énorme merci*. Thanks should also go to the many undergraduate students who used the second edition and provided frank assessments of the material and suggestions for improvement.

We would also like to acknowledge the many people on the Prentice Hall team who contributed their ideas, talents, time, and publishing experience to this project. Thanks to Publisher for World Languages, Phil Miller, for his continuing support. Many thanks to Rachel McCoy, Acquisitions Editor, for her energy, enthusiasm, and willingness to try new things. Our special thanks go to our Development Editor, Barbara Lyons, who continued with us through the third edition and whose careful reading, suggestions, and moral support have been invaluable in virtually every aspect of the project. We cannot imagine having completed the revisions without her. Copy Editor, Karen Horner, did her usual excellent job of readying the manuscript for production and we greatly appreciate her eagle eye. We are indebted to the wonderful production crew both in Upper Saddle River and in Battipaglia. Mary Rottino, Assistant Director of Production, and Nancy Stevenson, Senior Production Editor, proved to be unflappable and always ready to solve yet another crisis. They worked overtime to keep us sane during a crazy time. Many thanks to Frank Weihening, Production Supervision and Assunta Petrone, Editor, of Emilcomp/Preparé who meticulously oversaw every detail to bring the third edition through production. *Grazie mille* especially to Assunta whose endless supply of patience, good humor, and language lessons were much appreciated at every stage of the production process.

We would also like to thank Samantha Alducin, Media Editor, for her enthusiastic support of the new video and for being constantly on call during the conception, shooting, and editing phases of this project. She was a tireless advocate for integrating new technologies into the third edition. Thanks also are owed to Meriel Martínez Moctezuma, Supplements Editor, for carefully overseeing the preparation of the revised Student Activities Manual, the Instructor's Resource Manual, and the Testing Program. We thank Claudia Fernandes, Publishing Coordinator, for handling the many small details in a timely fashion. Thanks also go to Mary Ann Price for her outstanding photo research and to Steve Mannion for his superb line art, which has greatly enriched the book.

And finally, we wish to thank our families, whose love, support, helping hands, and sacrifices made all the difference in bringing this project to a successful completion.

What does the photo tell you about where these French speakers are? What might their gestures tell you about their relationship?

Chapitre *Préliminaire*
Présentons-nous !

Leçon **1** *Je me présente*

Leçon **2** *Dans la salle de classe*

Venez chez nous !
Le français dans le monde

Leçon 1 *Je me présente*

POINTS DE DÉPART

Moi, je parle français

TEXT AUDIO

CHANTAL : Salut ! Je m'appelle Chantal. Et toi, comment tu t'appelles ?

ALAIN : Je m'appelle Alain.

CHANTAL : Tu es de Paris ?

ALAIN : Non, moi, je suis de Montréal.

LE PROF : Bonjour, mademoiselle, bonjour, monsieur.

CHANTAL ET ALAIN : Bonjour, madame.

LE PROF : Comment vous appelez-vous ?

CHANTAL : Je m'appelle Chantal Lafont.

LE PROF : Et vous ?

ALAIN : Roussel, Alain Roussel.

Additional practice activities for each **Points de départ** section are provided by:
- Student Activities Manual
- *Chez nous* Companion Website: **http://www.prenhall.com/cheznous**

Present material inductively by circulating around the room, shaking students' hands, greeting them, and introducing yourself using the expressions from L.1. You might consider preparing blank name tags for students to fill out. Include such phrases as *Bonjour, je m'appelle...* and *Je suis de...* on the name tags to help students respond to you.

Next, you may wish to show the dialogues and related drawings as you present them one by one (IRCD, Ch. Prélim.). Check comprehension and repeat key phrases. To conclude, show the illustrations without the dialogues and let students supply sample exchanges.

As you work through the exchanges, treat the cultural notes (**Vie et culture**) and have students 1) point out differences between the first two dialogues; 2) make a list of possible responses to the question *Comment ça va ?*; 3) make a list of ways to say "good-bye." Note that to say "good-bye," French Canadians often use *Bonjour* instead of *Au revoir*.

You might also use the opening montage of the *Chez nous* video to introduce students to the notion of the Francophone world as a focus of study; this is a colorful and exciting way to begin the course.

CHANTAL : Salut, Guy ! Comment ça va ?

GUY : Ça va. Et toi ?

CHANTAL : Pas mal.

GUY : Bonjour, madame. Comment allez-vous ?

LE PROF : Très bien, merci. Et vous ?

GUY : Bien aussi, merci.

CHANTAL : Madame, je vous présente Guy Davy. Guy, Madame Dupont.

GUY : Enchanté, madame.

LE PROF : Bonjour, Guy.

CHANTAL : Alain, voici mon ami Guy. Guy, je te présente mon camarade de classe, Alain.

ALAIN : Salut, Guy.

GUY : Salut.

GUY : Bon, au revoir, Chantal, au revoir, Alain.

CHANTAL : Salut, Guy.

ALAIN : À bientôt… Au revoir, madame.

LE PROF : Au revoir, Alain. À demain.

POUR SALUER ET RÉPONDRE

Comment ça va ?	*How are you?*
Très bien, merci.	*Very well, thanks.*
Ça va.	*Fine.*
Pas mal.	*Not bad.*
Comme ci, comme ça.	*So-so.*
Ça ne va pas.	*Things aren't going well.*

Vie et culture

Before going over **Vie et culture**, ask students to make inferences about the use of *tu* and *vous* based on the dialogues in the **Points de départ**. Test their understanding of the differences in usage by suggesting various people and letting students tell which form of address they would use. For example: a police officer; a pet; a grandparent; their best friend's mother, etc. Americans are generally considered very informal, but French speakers are also becoming less formal, using the first name and *tu* more frequently among colleagues and acquaintances.

Bonjour !

Look at the photos here and observe the corresponding video segment, *Bonjour*, in which people are greeting each other: what gestures and phrases do you notice?

When French people meet someone they know, or make contact with a stranger (for example, sales, office, or restaurant personnel), they always greet that person upon arriving and say good-bye when leaving. The greeting includes an appropriate title, and the last name is not used. Usually a woman is addressed as **madame** unless she is very young:

Bonjour, monsieur.
Bonsoir, madame.
Au revoir, mademoiselle.

Se serrer la main, faire la bise

When they meet or say good-bye, French people who know each other almost always shake hands, using the right hand (**se serrer la main**). Good friends and family members kiss each other lightly on each cheek (**faire la bise**). When talking together, the French stand or sit closer to each other than Americans do. A French person would be offended if you kept moving away as he or she attempted to maintain normal conversational distance.

Tu et vous

When addressing another person in French, you must choose between **tu** and **vous**, which both mean *you*. Use **tu** to address a family member, a close friend, or another student. Use **vous** to address someone with whom you have a more formal relationship or to whom you wish to show respect. For example, use **vous** with people you don't know well, with older people, and with those in a position of authority, such as your teachers. Always use **vous** also to address more than one person. Do the people in the video clip use **tu** or **vous**?

Et vous ?

1. Think of how you typically greet people each day. Although we don't make a distinction in English like the **tu/vous** distinction in French, how do we vary our forms of address?
2. What do the practices of shaking hands and kissing on the cheek tell you about the importance of close physical contact in French culture? Would you feel comfortable with these practices? Why or why not?
3. Compare your answers to these questions with those of your classmates. How would you explain any differences?
4. View the video segment again, paying close attention to the ways in which people greet each other; what can you conclude about their relationship in each case?

À vous la parole

P-1 Le mot juste. Give an appropriate response.

MODÈLE   Comment vous appelez-vous ?
➤ Roussel, Nicolas Roussel.

1. Bonjour, mademoiselle.
2. Comment tu t'appelles ?
3. Tu es de Montréal ?
4. Ça va ?
5. Comment allez-vous ?
6. Comment ça va ?
7. Voici mon ami David.
8. Je vous présente mon amie Claire.
9. Au revoir, monsieur.
10. Bon, à demain !

P-2 Présentez-vous. Get acquainted with some of your classmates and your instructor, following these suggestions.

MODÈLE   Greet your instructor.
➤ Bonjour, monsieur.
OU   ➤ Bonjour, madame.

(Your instructor responds.)
➤ Bonjour, mademoiselle.
OU   ➤ Bonjour, monsieur.

1. Greet and introduce yourself to a person sitting near you.
2. Ask a classmate what his or her name is, then introduce yourself.
3. Ask a classmate whether he or she is from your city.
4. Greet a classmate and ask how he or she is today.
5. Introduce two people whom you have met in class.
6. Greet your instructor and ask how he or she is today.
7. Introduce a classmate to your instructor.
8. Say good-bye to several classmates.
9. Say good-bye to your instructor.

P-3 Le savoir-faire. Do you know what to say and do in the situations described? Act out each one with classmates.

MODÈLE   You meet a very good friend.

É1   Salut, Anne ! Ça va ? (faire la bise)
É2   Ça va, et toi ?
É1   Pas mal.

P-3 Students can work in small groups to prepare exchanges, then act out their variations. You might also bring in photos/drawings of people greeting each other and have students create the dialogues. Use the photos in this lesson for the same purpose.

1. You and a friend run into your instructor on campus.
2. You sit down in class next to someone you do not know.
3. You are with your roommate when a new friend joins you.
4. You run into your friend's mother while doing errands.
5. You are standing near a new teacher who does not yet know your name.
6. Class is over, and you are saying good-bye to a close friend.
7. Class is over, and you are saying good-bye to your teacher.

P-4 Faisons connaissance. Imagine that you are at a party with your classmates. Greet and introduce yourself to as many guests as possible. Also, make introductions when other guests do not know each other.

MODÈLE   É1   Bonjour, je m'appelle David. Et toi ?
         É2   Je m'appelle Anne. Voici mon ami, Jérémie.
         É1   Salut, Jérémie.
         É3   Bonjour.

P-5 Tu es d'où ? You want to find out what city your classmates are from. First say what city you are from, then ask what city they are from.

MODÈLE   É1   Je suis de Chicago. Et toi ?
         É2   Moi, je suis de Lafayette.

FORMES ET FONCTIONS

1. *Les pronoms sujets et le verbe* être

Les pronoms sujets et le verbe être				
SINGULIER			**PLURIEL**	
je	**suis**	*I am*	nous	**sommes**	*we are*
tu	**es**	*you are*	vous	**êtes**	*you are*
il	**est**	*he is*	ils	**sont**	*they are*
elle		*she is*	elles		

● The verb **être** means *to be*. This form is called the *infinitive*; it is the form you find at the head of the dictionary listing for the verb. Notice that a specific form of **être** corresponds to each subject. Because these forms do not follow a regular pattern, **être** is called an *irregular verb*.

● A subject pronoun can be used in place of a noun as the subject of a sentence:

—**Alex** est de Paris ?   —*Alex is from Paris?*
—Non, **il** est de Montréal.   —*No, he's from Montreal.*

As you have learned, use **tu** with a person you know very well; otherwise use **vous**. Use **vous** also when speaking to more than one person, even if they are your friends. Pronounce the final **-s** of **vous** as /z/ if the word following it begins with a vowel sound, and link it to that word:

Olivier, **tu** es de Paris ?   *Olivier, are you from Paris?*
Madame, **vous**‿êtes de Lyon ?   *Madame, are you from Lyon?*
Audrey et Fred, **vous**‿êtes de Paris ?   *Audrey and Fred, are you from Paris?*

P-4 Use as a mixing activity at the end of class. Have students report back the names of people they met. You may wish to adapt this activity and use it a second time by passing out cards with French names written on them and having students introduce themselves to each other with their new identities.

Additional practice activities for each **Formes et fonctions** section are provided by:
● Student Activities Manual
● *Chez nous* Companion Website:
   http://www.prenhall.com/cheznous

Present inductively by questioning students about the city they are from: *Je suis de Chicago—et vous ? Vous êtes de… ? Elle est de … —et toi aussi ?* Model the various verb forms in this way, then ask students to summarize meaning and forms. Display the chart. Point out that subject-verb agreement takes place in English as well: *I am, she is, we are.* Explain the organization of the verb chart, with singular forms on the left and plural forms on the right, and the division into first/second/third-person forms. Ask students to provide the meanings for each form. Use the texbook examples to illustrate the various points as students help you explain.

Elles refers to more than one female person or to a group of feminine nouns.
Ils refers to more than one male person, to a group of masculine nouns, or to a group that includes both males and females or both masculine and feminine nouns.

Anne et Sophie, **elles** sont en forme.	*Anne and Sophie are fine.*
Jean-Luc et Rémi, **ils** sont stressés.	*Jean-Luc and Rémi are stressed out.*
Julie et David, **ils** sont occupés.	*Julie and David are busy.*

Adjective agreement will be treated in Ch. 1, L. 1. This treatment does not create a problem for oral practice, since the adjectives have identical masculine and feminine spoken forms. Have students repeat the expressions in the shaded box; these provide vocabulary for use with *être*.

● Use a form of the verb **être** in descriptions or to indicate a state of being.

Elle **est** occupée.	*She's busy.*
Tu **es** malade ?	*Are you sick?*
Je **suis** stressé.	*I'm stressed out.*

● The final **-t** of **est** and **sont** is usually pronounced before a word beginning with a vowel sound.

Il est‿en forme.	*He's fine.*
Il est malade.	*He's sick.*
Elles sont‿en forme.	*They're fine.*
Elles sont stressées.	*They're stressed out.*

COMMENT ÇA VA ?

Je suis en forme.	*I am fine.*
… fatigué/e.	*. . . tired.*
… stressé/e.	*. . . stressed.*
… très occupé/e.	*. . . very busy.*
… malade.	*. . . sick.*

Begin practice with a discrimination drill to ensure that students hear crucial distinctions: one or more than one? *Il est fatigué. Elles sont en forme. C'est un professeur. Ce sont des étudiants*, etc. Follow up with a simple substitution drill: *Je suis en forme ; nous → Nous sommes en forme*, etc. The spoken forms of these adjectives are identical, so students will never be wrong when they say these phrases. Exercises in the textbook with these adjectives should not be assigned as written work since students will not be able to produce the correct forms.

● Use **c'est** and **ce sont** to identify people and things:

C'est Madame Dupont ?	*That's Madame Dupont?*
C'est un ami, Kevin.	*This is a friend, Kevin.*
Ce sont M. et Mme Lafarges.	*This is Mr. and Mrs. Lafarges.*

À vous la parole

P-6 Comment ça va ? Tell how everyone is feeling today.

MODÈLE   Moi ? Fatigué/e.
> ➤ Je suis fatigué/e.

1. Mme Dupont ? En forme.
2. Toi ? Fatigué/e.
3. Adrien ? Très occupé.
4. Cécile ? Malade.

5. David et toi ? En forme.
6. Julien ? Stressé.
7. Nous ? Fatigués.
8. Vous ?

P-7 Vous êtes de... ? Based on the name of the country people live in, guess what city they come from. You may choose a city from the list, or provide another: **Bruxelles**, **Florence**, **Genève**, **Madrid**, **Mexico**, **Montréal**, **Nice**, **Paris**, **Washington**

MODÈLE   vous / en France
> ➤ Vous êtes de Paris ?

1. elle / au Mexique
2. Pierre / au Canada
3. Matthieu et Jonathan / en Belgique
4. nous / en Suisse
5. vous / en Italie
6. toi / aux États-Unis
7. moi / en Espagne
8. Mélanie et Caroline / en France

P-8 Qui est-ce ? Identify the people from the opening dialogues pictured below.

MODÈLE ➤ C'est Chantal.

1.   2.   3.   4.

5.   6.   7.

P-6 You may wish to point out that the verb *aller* is used in the questions *Ça va ?* and *Comment allez-vous ?* and that some answers to these questions would require using a form of *aller*, such as *Je vais bien* (that is, students cannot say, **Je suis bien*). The verb *aller* will be presented in Ch. 2, L. 3.

This can be cued with photos/drawings if you have some. This oral exercise does not require students to make written agreement of adjectives such as *occupé/e/s*.

P-7 Names of countries are for recognition only. Follow up by having students tell what their hometown is and then ask someone else.

P-8 You might allow students to look back at the **Points de départ** presentation as you display this exercise (IRCD, Ch. Prélim.).

P-9 Identité mystérieuse. Take on a new identity! Your instructor will give you a new name and city of origin. Circulate around the room and introduce yourself to at least three people. As a follow-up, you may have to introduce someone you met to the rest of the class!

MODÈLE   É1 Bonjour, je m'appelle Mathilde.
          É2 Tu es de Paris ?
          É1 Non, je suis de Québec. Et toi ?
          É2 Je m'appelle Louis-Jean, je suis de Port-au-Prince, à Haïti.

2. *Les pronoms disjoints*

● You know that subject pronouns can be used in place of a noun (for example, a person or an object) as the subject of a sentence. *Subject pronouns* appear with a *verb*:

—Adrien est de Paris ?   —*Is Adrien from Paris?*
—Non, **il** est de Montréal.   —*No, he's from Montreal.*

—Pierre et Mélanie sont occupés ?   —*Are Pierre and Mélanie busy?*
—Oui, **ils** sont occupés.   —*Yes, they are busy.*

● A different type of pronoun, a *stressed pronoun*, is used:

■ in short questions that have no verb:

Je m'appelle Claire, et **toi** ?   *My name is Claire, how about you?*
Ça va bien, et **vous** ?   *I'm fine, and you?*

■ where there are two subjects in a sentence, one of which is a pronoun:

Damien et **moi**, nous sommes   *Damien and I are tired.*
    fatigués.

■ to emphasize the subject of a sentence when providing a contrast:

Moi, je suis de Montréal,   ***I**'m from Montreal, but*
    mais **lui**, il est de Paris.   ***he**'s from Paris.*

■ after **c'est** and **ce sont**:

—C'est Pierre ?   —*Is that Pierre?*
—Oui, c'est **lui**.   —*Yes, it is he.*

—Ce sont M. et Mme Dulac ?   —*Is that Mr. and Mrs. Dulac?*
—Oui, ce sont **eux**.   —*Yes, it is they.*

Here are the stressed pronouns, shown with the corresponding subject pronouns:

moi	je	**nous**	nous
toi	tu	**vous**	vous
lui	il	**eux**	ils
elle	elle	**elles**	elles

À vous la parole

👥 P-10 C'est ça. With your partner, confirm who these people are.

MODÈLES É1 C'est toi ?

É2 Oui, c'est moi.

É1 Ce sont Marie et Hélène ?

É2 Oui, ce sont elles.

1. C'est Christophe ?
2. C'est Jessica ?
3. C'est toi ?
4. C'est Arnaud ?
5. Ce sont Adeline et Nathalie ?
6. C'est vous ?
7. Ce sont Simon et Maxime ?
8. Ce sont Vanessa et Laurent ?

P-10, **Variation:** Cue using the visuals from the introductions in the **Points de départ** (IRCD, Ch. Prélim.): *C'est Chantal ? —Oui, c'est elle ; C'est Guy ? —Oui, c'est lui,* etc.

👥👤 P-11 Et vous ? Interview each other in groups of three.

MODÈLE Je m'appelle… Et vous ?

É1 Je m'appelle Alex. Et vous ?

É2 Moi, je m'appelle…

É3 Et moi, je m'appelle…

1. Je m'appelle… Et vous ?
2. Moi, ça va. Et vous ?
3. Je suis de… Et vous ?

P-11 Model with two students before putting students into small groups to work. Follow up by having them tell what they learned about their partners, providing additional practice with the various forms: *Lui, il est de…, et elle, elle est de….*

👥👤 P-12 Présentez-vous ! Help out your forgetful instructor by identifying students in your classroom.

MODÈLE Lui, il s'appelle Matt ; elle, elle s'appelle Cindy.

P-12 Cue student responses by asking for the names of students or offering an incorrect name: *Lui, comment il s'appelle ? Et elle, elle s'appelle Nathalie ?*

Stratégie

Use your knowledge of the purpose of a text to figure out its content. Although you may not understand every word, pay attention to the kind of reading you are doing and make use of what you already know about the type of text you have before you.

Additional activities to develop the four skills are provided by:
- Student Activities Manual
- Text Audio
- *Chez nous* video
- *Chez nous* Companion Website: http://www.prenhall.com/cheznous

Avant de lire. We recommend that you treat this first reading in class to introduce students to the techniques used in this process approach. Be sure to explain the meaning of each subheading, because these will be used consistently throughout the textbook. Conduct this preliminary brainstorming activity with the class as a whole, putting the list up for all to see as it develops. Then ask students to match items in the list to actual information on the envelopes as you display them (IRCD, Ch. Prélim.).

En lisant. You might put students in pairs to complete this task, then have the class compare notes.

En regardant de plus près. This activity focuses on developing decoding techniques, so that students learn to rely on prior knowledge and contextual guessing rather than searching through a dictionary to discover the meaning of unfamiliar words and expressions. It is meant to build students' confidence. Work through the questions with them.

   Point out interesting cultural information such as the frequent use of capital letters for last names, cities, and countries; stamps, flags, and postmarks; the fact that the first two numbers in postal codes in France designate the *département*; CH as the abbreviation for *la Confédération Helvétique,* the official name for Switzerland (this last example is found in the **Après avoir lu**).

Après avoir lu. This may be completed as a whole-class activity, displaying the addresses for all to see. As an additional follow-up, ask students to give their own address as they would explain it to a French speaker.

Lisons

P-13 Des adresses en francophonie

A. Avant de lire. This reading asks you to look at envelopes and postcards addressed to various places in the Francophone world. Before looking at them, make a list of the information you expect to find on an addressed envelope.

B. En lisant. How does the list you made compare with what you actually see on the envelopes and postcards? Now, look more closely; you will find that you actually understand a number of words because their form and meaning are so similar in French and English. These words are called *cognates* (**des mots apparentés**). Examples in the addresses include **avenue** and **République**. Make a list of all the cognates that you find in the addresses and provide the English equivalent for each.

C. En regardant de plus près. Examine the following aspects of the text more closely.

1. Given the context and its similarity to English, what do you think the phrase **Boîte Postale** means?
2. Given the context, what do you think the word **rue** means?
3. Provide the full forms in French for the following abbreviations:

   M.   Mlle   Mme   B.P.

4. Although you do not see the phrase **code postal** in the addresses, most of them have one. What do you think the **code postal** is? What is the **code postal** for **Abidjan**, for **Tours**, for **Vieux-Québec**? What is different about the **code postal** for this last city?
5. Some of the envelopes include the words **destinataire** and **expéditeur**. What do you think those terms mean?

D. Après avoir lu. Now that you've studied the addresses, address an envelope to these two people.

1. Salut, je m'appelle Marie-Cécile. Je suis de Kinshasa. Mon adresse, c'est Boîte Postale 357. Il n'y a pas de code postal. Kinshasa est au Congo bien sûr.
2. Bonjour, je m'appelle Guy Leblanc. Je suis de Genève. Mon adresse, c'est Case Postale 1602. Le code postal, c'est CH-1211 Genève 1. Vous savez que Genève est en Suisse, n'est-ce pas ?

You may wish to divide the material in this section into two blocks. First, focus on classroom objects and the mini-dialogues. Continue with the **Vie et cultur**e notes and Ex. P-14 and P-15. In a subsequent class or later in the same period, present the classroom expressions and commands. Follow with Ex. P-16 and P-17. Describe the classroom, showing the labeled art (IRCD, Ch. Prélim.) or real objects in the classroom. You can also bring in a specially prepared backpack or bag filled with various items (i.e., *une règle, un stylo, une craie, un livre, une vidéocassette*). Use items in the bag to present the vocabulary or as an identification drill. Students can take turns reaching into the bag, drawing out an item and saying what it is. Using the unlabeled art (IRCD, Ch. Prélim.) or objects in the classroom, check comprehension by having students point to objects you name. Drill using either/or questions to practice pronunciation: *C'est une porte ou une fenêtre ?* Other simple drills: 1) draw one of the items and let others guess what it is; 2) find the "odd word out" in a list of three or four items: *une craie, un stylo, une règle, un crayon… (une règle)*; 3) Associations: What word do you associate with each of the following? *un professeur ?* — *un étudiant ; une craie ?* — *un tableau*, etc.

Leçon 2 *Dans la salle de classe*

POINTS DE DÉPART

La salle de classe

TEXT AUDIO

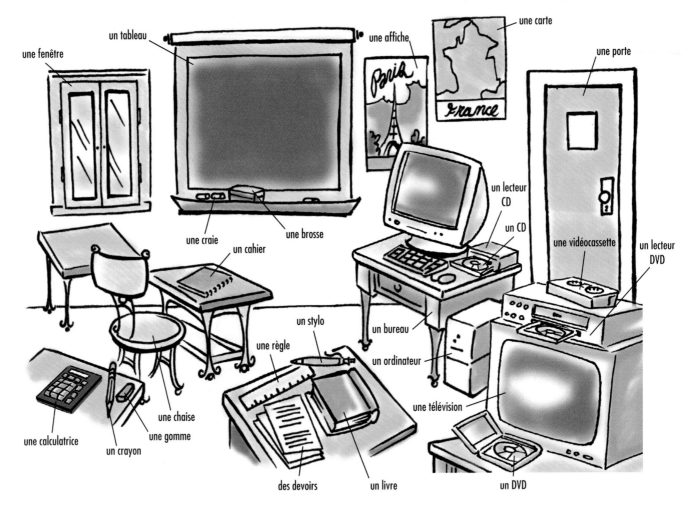

- une fenêtre
- un tableau
- une affiche
- une carte
- une porte
- une craie
- une brosse
- un lecteur CD
- un CD
- une vidéocassette
- un lecteur DVD
- un cahier
- un stylo
- un bureau
- un ordinateur
- une règle
- une télévision
- une calculatrice
- une chaise
- une gomme
- un crayon
- des devoirs
- un livre
- un DVD

Present the mini-dialogues, using examples of classroom objects; then move directly to the exercises. We avoid the traditional *voici/voilà* distinction because native speaker usage is highly variable. *Voilà* is the neutral term, acceptable in a wider variety of contexts. We present *voici* in Ch. Prélim., L. 1, in the context of introductions: *Voici mon ami Guy*, since native speakers are consistent in their use of *voici* in this context. *Il n'y a pas de* is taught here as a lexical item; negation is treated productively in Ch. 1, L. 3.

—Il y a un crayon sur le bureau ?

—Non, il n'y a pas de crayon, mais il y a un stylo. Voilà.

—Il y a des affiches dans la salle de classe ?

—Non, il n'y a pas d'affiches.

LE PROFESSEUR DIT :

Écoutez bien, s'il vous plaît !
Regardez le tableau !
Levez-vous !
Allez au tableau !
Allez à la porte !
Ouvrez la fenêtre !
Fermez le livre !
Montrez-moi votre livre !
Montrez Paris sur la carte !
Prenez un stylo !
Écrivez votre nom et votre prénom !
Lisez les mots au tableau !
Effacez le tableau !
Écoutez sans regarder le livre !
Répondez en français !
Donnez la craie à Marie-Laure !
Rendez-moi les devoirs !
Asseyez-vous !
Merci.

LES ÉTUDIANTS RÉPONDENT :

Pardon ? Je ne comprends pas.
Répétez, s'il vous plaît !
Parlez plus fort !
Comment dit-on « board » en français ?

Use the standard TPR (Total Physical Response) sequence to introduce and practice classroom commands: 1) demonstrate; 2) hesitate as students respond; 3) students perform alone; 4) introduce novel combinations and series of commands; finally, if you wish, 5) reverse roles, letting students give commands. For more information on TPR techniques, see the IRM. The goal of this treatment of commands is for students to be able to function in an all-French classroom and to follow basic classroom instructions; the forms of the imperative will be treated in Ch. 3, L. 1. We assume that the instructor will use the polite form with students. You may wish to introduce the familiar forms as well.

The Ch. 3 video segment, *Un peu d'histoire*, shows a Canadian speaker responding to *Merci !* with *Bienvenue !* Provide students with the opportunity to try out these expressions for themselves: Offer something to a classmate, let him/her thank you, and respond appropriately.

MODÈLE É1 Voilà (*and you hand over a pen*).
         É2 Merci !
         É1 De rien !

Vie et culture

Merci

In English, if someone says *Thank you* we frequently reply with *You're welcome*. In French it is much less common to reply to **Merci**. Sometimes, however, in more formal contexts, you may hear the reply **Je vous en prie** or **Je t'en prie**. In less formal contexts, a French speaker might say **De rien** or **Il n'y a pas de quoi**. In Canadian French the response to **Merci** is **Bienvenue**.

La rentrée

La rentrée for French school children generally takes place early in September and for university students early in October. A significant event for retailers and families, **la rentrée** marks the end of vacation and the change of seasons.

Look at the advertisement and notice what types of items are being sold. Which items can you name? Does this ad resemble back-to-school advertisements in your own area, or does it differ in some ways? Look at the highlighted sentence at the bottom—what is the main point being expressed?

Ma panoplie d'écolier pour moins de 24€

The goal of this activity is to begin to develop students' skills at analyzing authentic documents and making cross-cultural comparisons. Contribute your own ideas and insights to the discussion.

À vous la parole

P-14 Voilà ! As your instructor asks about various classroom objects, hand them over, point them out, or say there aren't any.

MODÈLES Donnez-moi un stylo, s'il vous plaît !
➤ Voilà (*and you hand over a pen*).

Montrez-moi une carte de France, s'il vous plaît !
➤ Voilà (*and you point to a map of France*).

Il y a des affiches ici ?
➤ Oui, voilà des affiches (*and you point to some posters*).
OU ➤ Non, il n'y a pas d'affiches.

P-15 Dans la salle de classe. Write down as many different classroom objects as you can see. Now compare your list with that of a classmate. Cross off the items that are common to both lists, then give yourself a point for each item on your list that your partner did not name. Who has the most points?

MODÈLE É1 un bureau, une fenêtre, un livre, une carte, une affiche, une télé
É2 un bureau, un tableau, une craie, une fenêtre, une porte, une carte, un cahier

É1 = 3 pts, É2 = 4 pts

P-16 C'est logique. With a partner, complete each command in as many logical ways as possible.

MODÈLE Ouvrez…
➤ Ouvrez la fenêtre.
OU ➤ Ouvrez le livre.

1. Regardez…
2. Écoutez…
3. Rendez-moi…
4. Montrez-moi…
5. Fermez…

6. Effacez…
7. Répondez…
8. Allez…
9. Écrivez…
10. Prenez…

P-17 Qu'est-ce que vous dites ? What could you say in each situation?

MODÈLE You want the teacher to speak up.
➤ Parlez plus fort, s'il vous plaît !

1. You want to interrupt the teacher.
2. You want the teacher to repeat.
3. You don't understand.
4. You ask how to say *door* in French.

5. You want to thank someone.
6. You can't hear what's being said.
7. You don't know how to say *please* in French.
8. Someone says **Merci !** to you.

Sons et lettres

L'alphabet et les accents

Here are the letters of the alphabet together with their pronunciation in French.

a	(a)	j	(ji)	s	(ès)
b	(bé)	k	(ka)	t	(té)
c	(sé)	l	(èl)	u	(u)
d	(dé)	m	(èm)	v	(vé)
e	(eu)	n	(èn)	w	(double vé)
f	(èf)	o	(o)	x	(iks)
g	(jé)	p	(pé)	y	(i grec)
h	(ach)	q	(ku)	z	(zèd)
i	(i)	r	(èr)		

Accents and other diacritical marks are an integral part of French spelling.

- **L'accent aigu** is used with **e** to represent the vowel /e/ of **stressé**:

  André   Québec   stressé   répétez

- **L'accent grave** is used with **e** to represent the vowel /ɛ/ of **la règle**:

  la règle   le modèle   très   Genève

  It is also used with **a** and **u** to differentiate words:

  la *the* vs. là *there*   ou *or* vs. où *where*

- **L'accent circonflexe** can be used with all five vowel letters. It often marks the loss of the sound /s/ at an earlier stage of French. The **s** is still present in English words borrowed from French before that loss occurred.

  être   s'il vous plaît   bientôt
  la hâte *haste*   l'hôpital *hospital*   coûter *to cost*

- **Le tréma** indicates that vowel letters in a group are pronounced individually:

  toi vs. Loïc /lo-ik/   Claire vs. Haïti /a-i-ti/

- **La cédille** indicates that **c** is to be pronounced as /s/ rather than /k/ before the vowel letters **a**, **o**, or **u**:

  ça   français   Françoise

Additional practice activities for each **Sons et lettres** section are provided by:
- Student Activities Manual
- Text Audio

This presentation focuses on orthography rather than pronunciation, so the International Phonetic Alphabet is not taught here. IPA symbols, along with key words in French, are provided in Appendix 7.

You may want to present the alphabet to your students in phonetic groups:

[e] : b c d g p t v w
[ɛ] : f l m n r s z
[i] : i j x y
[a] : a k h
[y] : q u
Ce qui reste : e, o

À vous la parole

First spell words and let students write them, then have students spell their name or another word that you provide. You may wish to teach students to say *deux èls*, etc., for double letters.

P-18 Les sigles. Match each French acronym with its full form and then provide the English equivalent.

1. l'ONU	a. l'Union Européenne
2. l'OEA	b. les États-Unis d'Amérique
3. l'OTAN	c. l'Organisation des Nations-Unis
4. l'UE	d. le Syndrome immunodéficitaire acquis
5. le SIDA	e. l'Organisation des États Américains
6. les USA	f. l'Organisation du Traité de l'Atlantique Nord

P-19 Key: 1) livre 2) carte 3) tableau 4) chaise 5) porte 6) devoirs 7) étudiante 8) craie

P-19 Qu'est-ce que c'est ? Reorder the letters to identify things you find in the classroom, and spell the correct word aloud.

MODÈLES LYSTO

➤ S-T-Y-L-O, stylo.

NORACY

➤ C-R-A-Y-O-N, crayon.

1. LERVI	3. LATAUBE	5. TROPE	7. DAUNITETÉ
2. TAREC	4. ICASHE	6. VISODER	8. CIERA

P-20 Les accents. Correct the following words or phrases by adding the missing accents and other diacritics, then spell each word aloud. (The asterisk indicates that these words are spelled incorrectly.)

1. le *francais	3. une *fenetre	5. *repondez	7. *repetez
2. une *regle	4. le verbe *etre	6. *bientot	8. *voila

FORMES ET FONCTIONS

1. *Le genre et les articles au singulier*

To present, begin with a series of either/or questions: *C'est un livre ou un cahier ? une affiche ou une carte ?*; then move to open-ended questions —*Qu'est-ce que c'est ?*—that require students to answer using familiar vocabulary and the indefinite article. Ask students how they decide whether to use *un* or *une* in their response. Their answers will help summarize the information provided in the textbook. Display the chart listing forms, and provide simple practice: *Un ou une ? livre, ordinateur, porte, bureau, fenêtre,* etc. Follow the same process in introducing the definite article.

All French nouns are assigned to one of two noun classes—*feminine* or *masculine*—and are therefore said to have a *gender*. The gender of a noun determines the form of other words that accompany it—for example, articles, and adjectives.

● **The indefinite article**

The indefinite articles **un** and **une** correspond to *a* or *an* in English. **Une** is used with feminine nouns and **un** with masculine nouns. **Un** or **une** can also mean *one*:

Voilà **un** bureau.	*Here's a desk.*
Donnez-moi **une** chaise.	*Give me a chair.*
Il y a **une** fenêtre dans la salle de classe.	*There's one window in the classroom.*

Before a vowel sound, **un** ends with an /n/ sound that is pronounced as if it were part of the next word: **un‿ami, un‿ordinateur.**

● **The definite article**

There are three forms of the singular definite article, corresponding to *the* in English: **la** is used with feminine nouns, **le** with masculine nouns, and **l'** with all nouns beginning with a vowel sound. As in English, the definite article is used to indicate a previously mentioned or specified noun.

Voilà **la** carte.	*Here's the map.*
C'est **le** professeur.	*That's the professor.*
Donnez-moi **l'**affiche.	*Give me the poster.*

In French the definite article also designates a noun used in a general or abstract sense. In such cases, no article is used in English.

J'aime **le** football.	*I like soccer.*
Ma sœur adore **la** musique.	*My sister loves music.*

LES ARTICLES

	masculin	féminin
indéfini	**un** cahier	**une** règle
	un ‿ordinateur	**une** affiche
défini	**le** cahier	**la** règle
	l'ordinateur	**l'**affiche

● **Predicting the gender of nouns**

Since the gender of a noun is not always predictable, it is a good idea to memorize the gender of each new word that you learn. For example, learn **une affiche** rather than **affiche** or **l'affiche**. The following guidelines will help you identify the gender of many nouns.

Although some students may have heard that nouns ending in **-e** are feminine, this is not necessarily the case. About half the nouns ending in **-e** are feminine, the other half are masculine.

■ Nouns designating females are usually feminine and nouns designating males are usually masculine:

la dame *the lady*	**le** monsieur *the man*
une étudiante *a (female) student*	**un** étudiant *a (male) student*

■ The names of languages are masculine:

le français *French*	**le** créole *Creole*

■ Words recently borrowed from other languages are generally masculine:

le marketing	**le** yoga	**le** rap	**le** tennis

■ Some endings are good predictors of the gender of nouns:

MASCULINE ENDINGS: **-eau, -o, -isme**

le tableau	**le** stylo	**le** socialisme

FEMININE ENDINGS: **-ion, -té**

la nation	**la** télévision	**la** liberté	**la** quantité

À vous la parole

Begin practice with a discrimination drill: *masculin ou féminin ? Voici un ordinateur ; une affiche ; un stylo*, etc. Do the same for the definite article.

Follow with substitution drills, having students change first from the indefinite to the definite article (*Voilà un stylo ; Voilà le stylo*, etc.), then from the definite to the indefinite (*Voilà le professeur ; Voilà un professeur*, etc.).

P-21 Dans la salle de classe. What can you name in this classroom?

MODÈLE ➤ Il y a un bureau,…

P-22 Be sure to bring some of the items to class and have them prominently displayed. To incorporate the idea of possession, place items on students' desks throughout the room.

P-22 Voilà ! Can you find the following objects in your classroom? If so, take turns with a partner indicating to whom they belong.

MODÈLE   un lecteur CD
➤ Voilà un lecteur CD ; c'est le lecteur CD de David.

1. un cahier
2. un crayon
3. une calculatrice
4. un livre

5. un stylo
6. un bureau
7. une règle
8. une gomme

P-23 Key: 1) le 2) le 3) le 4) la 5) la 6) le 7) le 8) le

P-23 Quel genre ? Can you guess the gender of these unfamiliar words?

MODÈLE   japonais
➤ le japonais

1. jet
2. rock
3. château
4. solution

5. beauté
6. métro
7. micro(phone)
8. communisme

2. Le nombre et les articles au pluriel

● Plurals of nouns

Most French nouns are made plural by adding a written letter **-s**:

un livre *a book*	deux livre**s** *two books*
une fenêtre *one window*	trois fenêtre**s** *three windows*

Singular nouns that end in a written -**s** do not change in the plural; nouns ending in -**eau** add the letter -**x**:

un cours *a course*	deux cours *two courses*
un bureau *one desk*	trois bureau**x** *three desks*

Although a letter -**s** or -**x** is added to written words to indicate the plural, it is not pronounced. You must listen for a preceding word, usually a number or an article, to tell whether a noun is plural or singular.

● Plurals of articles

The plural form of the definite article is always **les**, which is pronounced /le/:

le livre *the book*	**les** livres *the books*
la chaise *the chair*	**les** chaises *the chairs*

The plural form of the indefinite article is always **des**, which is pronounced /de/:

un cahier *a notebook*	**des** cahiers *notebooks, some notebooks*
une affiche *a poster*	**des** affiches *posters, some posters*

In English, plural nouns often appear without any article; in French, an article almost always accompanies the noun:

Il y a **des** livres ici.	*There are books here.*
J'aime **les** affiches.	*I like posters.*

Before a vowel sound, the -**s** of **les** and **des** is pronounced as /z/:

les chaises vs. **les** images   des bureaux vs. **des** ordinateurs
                /z/   /z/

Use written examples to elicit plural forms: *un livre, deux livre_ ? un bureau, deux bureau_ ? un cours, deux cours_ ?* Ask students to provide written plurals. Then contrast singular and plural forms to show that there is no difference in pronunciation of the noun, using first the noun alone, then the noun accompanied by a number or article: *bureau, bureaux; un bureau, trois bureaux; livre, livres; le livre, les livres.*

Stress the pronunciation of the full vowel of the article.

À vous la parole

👥 **P-24 Dans la salle de classe.** Ask a classmate whether each of the objects listed can be found in your classroom. He or she can respond by indicating to whom they belong.

MODÈLE   CD

> É1 Il y a des CD ?
> É2 Oui, voilà les CD de Vincent.

1. cahiers
2. livres
3. stylos
4. cartes
5. règles
6. devoirs
7. vidéocassettes
8. gommes
9. affiches

Begin practice with a discrimination drill: one, or more than one? *Voici une chaise, des ordinateurs, un crayon,* etc. Follow with a simple transformation drill, singular to plural: *Voici une chaise / Voici des chaises,* then plural to singular (which is more difficult since students will need to produce the appropriate gender).

P-25 Dans ta chambre. Ask a classmate questions to find out what objects are in his or her room.

MODÈLE   É1 Il y a des affiches ?

   É2 Oui, il y a trois affiches.

   OU Non, mais il y a des photos.

P-26 Sur mon bureau. In groups of three, compare what is on your desk at home by naming at least three items that are on it.

MODÈLE   É1 Sur mon bureau, il y a un ordinateur, des livres et une photo.

   É2 Et sur mon bureau, il y a…

   É3 Sur mon bureau, il y a…

TEXT AUDIO

P-27 Des francophones bien connus

Avant d'écouter. Allow students to make guesses about the individuals listed in the chart, but do not confirm or deny. You might pronounce each of the names in the chart before students listen to the descriptions, to ensure they will recognize the names when they hear them.

Script for *Écoutons*
C'est Jacques Chirac. Il est de Paris. C'est un homme politique. Il est élu président de la République française en 1995.

Elle, c'est Gabrielle Roy. Elle est du Manitoba au Canada. Elle est écrivain, donc elle a écrit des livres.

Voici Emmanuelle Béart. Elle est très élégante, non ? Elle est de Gassin. C'est une petite ville en France qui s'écrit G-A-S-S-I-N. C'est une actrice de cinéma. Elle joue dans le film « Manon des sources ».

Lui ? C'est M.C. Solaar. Il est de la ville de Dakar, au Sénégal, mais il habite Paris. Il est chanteur. En fait, il chante du rap, donc il est rappeur.

Après avoir écouté. Review the answers with students and find out what they listened for to determine the correct responses. Discuss the follow-up questions as a class.

A. Avant d'écouter. You will hear descriptions of four famous French-speaking people. Look at the chart below—do you recognize any of the names? Do you know anything about these individuals?

B. En écoutant. The first time you listen, fill in the first column of the chart with the city where each person was born. Next, listen again and try to determine why these people are famous. Write their profession in the second column. See whether any of your initial ideas are confirmed.

Nom	Ville d'origine	Profession
Jacques CHIRAC		
Gabrielle ROY		
Emmanuelle BÉART		
M.C. SOLAAR		

C. Après avoir écouté. Compare your answers with those of your classmates. Which of these people would you like most to learn more about? What would you like to learn about this person? Where would you go for more information?

Venez chez nous !
Le français dans le monde

P-28 Qui parle français ?

A. Avant de parler. What do you know about who speaks French, where, and for what purposes? Take the following quiz and see.

1. The French-speaking population of the world totals approximately…
   - **a.** 60 million
   - **b.** 110 million
   - **c.** 275 million
   - **d.** 450 million

2. In a Francophone country, everyone speaks French.
   - **a.** True
   - **b.** False

3. French is an official language in the United States.
   - **a.** True
   - **b.** False

4. In the 18th century, French was the Western world's major language of diplomacy and international affairs.
   - **a.** True
   - **b.** False

5. The world organization for countries where French is spoken is…
   - **a.** a political and economic federation, a kind of French commonwealth.
   - **b.** the only international organization based on a language.
   - **c.** a vehicle for recognizing the cultural diversity of French-speaking people.

B. En parlant. Now compare your answers with those of a partner to see how you did.

le Maroc

la Polynésie française

Additional activities to explore **Venez chez nous !** topics are provided by:
- Student Activities Manual
- *Chez nous* video
- *Chez nous* Companion Website: **http://www.prenhall.com/cheznous**

Unlike most **Parlons** sections, this activity is conducted in English.

The continent with the largest percentage of French speakers is Africa—11% of the total population. The regions with the highest percentages of French speakers (more than 15% of the total population) are the Maghreb, the Indian Ocean, and western Europe. The ten countries with the greatest number of French speakers are: France, Algeria, Canada, Morocco, Belgium, the Ivory Coast, Tunisia, Cameroon, the Republic of Congo, and Switzerland.

la Guadeloupe

le Sénégal

le Québec

Number 1

Did you answer . . . b. 110 million? You are correct. About 60 million of these people live in France; about 20 million live in countries where part of the population speaks French as an everyday language (Belgium, Canada, Switzerland); about 30 million are people who speak French and some other language(s) as vernaculars in countries where most of the population doesn't use French every day. The number of French-speaking people in the world has risen by almost 8% since 1990. Give yourself two points.

Number 2

The answer is False; give yourself two points if you answered correctly. In a Francophone country, not necessarily everyone speaks French. In some countries, French is both an official language (used in government and education) and a vernacular language (used in everyday communication). Belgium is an example of a country in which French is both an official and a vernacular language. In Haiti, on the other hand, French serves as one of two official languages, but is spoken by only about 15% of the population. The vernacular language of all Haitians is Haitian Creole.

Number 3

The answer is True; give yourself two points if you answered correctly. Since 1968, French and English have been declared official languages in Louisiana. About a quarter million speakers of Cajun French live in southwest Louisiana.

Number 4

Two points if you answered True. Philosophers such as Montesquieu, Voltaire, and Rousseau had a profound effect on the politics of the era. Both Benjamin Franklin and Thomas Jefferson spoke French and lived for a time in Paris, meeting many of the great French thinkers of the day. The influence of French philosophers is seen in our own United States Constitution: the notion of separation of executive, legislative, and judicial powers is an idea developed by Montesquieu in his work **L'Esprit des lois** (*The Spirit of Laws*).

Number 5

The answer is both B and C; give yourself two points for either, four points if you answered both! In 1970 several African nations joined to form an entity that would promote technology and culture across French-speaking countries. The current organization, **l'Agence intergouvernementale de la Francophonie (l'AIF)**, was founded after a series of developments: France disentangled itself from its last colony and became a champion of the Third World in the West; efforts began to counterbalance the predominance of American entertainment on the world's airwaves; Canada struggled with how to accommodate Quebec's reaffirmation of its French cultural roots without tearing the country apart. The first meeting of the organization took place in 1986, and more than fifty national delegations have attended the most recent meetings.

C. Après avoir parlé. How did you and your partner score? Did any of these answers surprise you? Why, or why not?

Total your points. If you earned . . .

10–12 points	**Bravo !** You're well informed about the Francophone world.
8 points	**Félicitations !** You're quite knowledgeable.
6 points	**Eh bien !** You've learned some new things today.
Less than 6 points	**Dommage !** But you'll learn more about French speakers in the upcoming chapters.

Lisons

P-29 Titres de journaux

A. Avant de lire. Here is a series of headlines from the French-language press. As you read them, you will find that you are able to grasp their general meaning because they include a number of cognates, For example, you can guess that the article entitled **Dossier Beauté : Écolo Cosméto** probably has to do with cosmetics and ecology because of the words **Écolo** and **Cosméto**. The subtitle contains other cognates that help to confirm this guess, including **cosmétologie**, **crèmes**, **plantes**, **aérosols**, and **fréon**.

B. En lisant. Watching for cognates, decide which headline/s deal/s with . . .

1. art
2. sports
3. politics/elections
4. cosmetics

5. medical news
6. the environment
7. international diplomacy

How did you make your decision in each case?

Stratégie

Look for cognates as you read a text. These are words whose form and meaning are very similar in French and English. Using them, you can grasp the general meaning of a text.

P-29 As you focus on the reading strategy, looking for cognates, ask why there are so many similar words in French and English. You may explain that after the arrival of William the Conquerer (*Guillaume le Conquérant*) in England in 1066, many of the English nobility and middle class began to use French as their everyday language. Gradually, many French words found their way into the English language.

As you work with the headlines, point out that students can also use context to guess the meaning of unfamiliar words. For example, in the phrase *aérosols sans fréon*, they might guess that the word *sans* means "without," since that would be an ecological improvement!

1.
Regards sur la ville aimée
Le musée de la Photographie à Charleroi présente une rétrospective de Gilbert De Keyser et une excellente cuvée de jeunes photographes.

Le Soir (Bruxelles)

2.
LE DOSSIER HAÏTI PASSE AUX NATIONS-UNIES
Résolution OEA

Haïti en marche (Miami)

3.
DOSSIER BEAUTÉ : ÉCOLO COSMÉTO
La cosmétologie se met à l'heure écolo. Shampooings biodégradables, crèmes aux plantes, aérosols sans fréon…

20 ans (Paris)

4.
Basketball/Première ligue Uni et Corcelles vont mal

L'Express (Neuchâtel)

5.
LA RÉFORME DU SYSTÈME ÉLECTORAL CANADIEN

Le Devoir (Montréal)

6.
La bombe d'Amsterdam
Sida : Un troisième virus?

Le Nouvel Observateur (Paris)

Show students how they use contextualized guessing in their native language, with examples such as the following: "Jancis, get the besom and sweep out my room a bit." "You did light a fire as will be hard to dout." In the first sentence, knowing what one does with a "besom" tells us what it must be: a broom. In the second, "dout" is something you do to a fire, clearly the opposite of "light." The examples are taken from *Precious Bane* by Mary Webb, which contains many examples of Welsh dialect that can be used to exemplify reading strategies for students.

Help students practice additional decoding strategies in item 2: b) *Uni* and *Corcelles* are proper names; remind students of the expressions *ça va, pas mal*, etc.; c) ask what type of group would pass a resolution; point out the juxtaposition of the noun and its modifier; d) point out word order; e) mention the tendency in French to abbreviate words— *métro(politain), restau(rant), McDo(nald's)*, focus on prepositions; f) show how *-ième* is a productive suffix.

Après avoir lu. These questions lead directly into the *Observons* exercise.

P-30 To prepare this activity, pronounce for the class the name of each of the people shown, then pronounce the place names and languages listed in French. The entire **Observons** clip introduces nine speakers; only the first six are treated here. The remaining speakers are introduced in the Video Manual. You might complete this exercise in class and assign the remaining introductions as homework, with students completing the activities in the Video Manual. Point out that these speakers will appear in other video clips.

C. En regardant de plus près. Now look more closely at these features of the headlines.

1. Point out at least one cognate in each headline.
2. Based on the context and use of cognates, indicate what the following words or expressions mean.

   a. Le musée de la Photographie (#1)
   b. Uni et Corcelles vont mal (#4)
   c. Résolution OEA (#2)
   d. Système électoral canadien (#5)
   e. Écolo cosméto ; crèmes aux plantes, aérosols sans fréon (#3)
   f. Troisième virus (#6)

D. Après avoir lu. For each headline, the source has been indicated. What does this tell you about where French is used in the world today? Can you explain why French is used all over the world?

 Observons

P-30 Je me présente

A. Avant de regarder. What information do people generally give when they introduce themselves? What expressions have you learned that people might use to provide this information in French?

B. En regardant. Watch and listen as the people shown introduce themselves, telling where they are from and what language(s) are spoken there. Match their photos with the places they come from and then find those places on the map inside the cover of your textbook. You can expect to listen more than once.

1. Vous avez compris ?

   a. Who is from . . .

le Bénin ?	Haïti ?
le Congo ?	le Maroc ?
la France ?	le Québec ?

Edouard FLEURIAU-CHÂTEAU Marie Éline LOUIS Fadoua BENNANI Bienvenu et Honorine AKPAKLA Marie-Julie KERHARO

b. How many people are from places where languages other than French are spoken?

2. Which of the following languages are mentioned?

_____ Arabic / l'arabe   _____ Fongbé / le fongbé

_____ Creole / le créole   _____ Spanish / l'espagnol

_____ English / l'anglais

C. Après avoir regardé. Discuss the following questions with your classmates.

1. What differences do you notice in the way these people look, dress, and speak?
2. What do these observations tell you about the Francophone world?

P-31 Voyages en francophonie

A. Avant d'écrire. On the inside cover of this textbook, a world map shows the Francophone countries/regions of the world. Take a look at this map.

B. En écrivant. On a separate sheet of paper, make two lists: (1) Francophone countries/regions that you have already visited (**J'ai déjà visité…**); (2) Francophone countries that you would like to visit in the future (**Je voudrais visiter…**).

MODÈLE   J'ai déjà visité :   Je voudrais visiter :

le Canada   la France

la Louisiane   le Maroc

etc.   etc.

C. Après avoir écrit. Compare your lists with those of other students in the class to see who has visited the most Francophone countries/regions. Talk about your experiences and why you'd like to visit the other places you named.

Script for *Observons*

EDOUARD :   Bonjour, je suis Edouard Fleuriau-Château. J'ai vingt-quatre ans, euh, je parle l'anglais, le français, l'espagnol… et bien sûr je suis français.

MARIE :   Bonjour, je m'appelle Marie Éline Louis. Je suis de Port-au-Prince, Haïti, mais j'habite ici aux États-Unis. À la maison, on parle créole. Je parle aussi français et anglais.

FADOUA :   Bonjour, je m'appelle Fadoua Bennani. J'ai vingt-cinq ans et j'habite à Nice. Mes parents vivent au Maroc. Euh, moi, je parle français et un peu arabe. Mon père il est marocain, donc lui il parle beaucoup plus arabe que moi, et ma mère est française.

BIENVENU :   Je m'appelle Bienvenu Akpakla. Je suis du Bénin. Je parle le français, ma langue maternelle fongbé et l'anglais. Voici mon épouse, elle se présente.

HONORINE :   Je m'appelle Honorine Akpakla, je viens du Congo. Je parle le français, ma langue maternelle et l'anglais.

MARIE-JULIE :   Alors, je m'appelle Marie-Julie Kerharo, je suis québecoise. Je suis originaire de Rimouski. J'habite les États-Unis depuis quelques années. Avant de venir ici, je parlais anglais, ce qui m'a aidé beaucoup.

En regardant. Play the sequence several times in class. Have students focus on each of the tasks separately. Pause after each speaker to give students time to find their responses.

You might also ask students to listen for expressions used to tell one's name: *je suis, je m'appelle*; to tell where you're from: *je suis de, j'habite, je suis né/e*; and to tell what language you speak: *je parle*. Regular *-er* verbs will be introduced in Ch. 1, L. 3.

Vocabulaire

Leçon 1

pour vous présenter — *to introduce yourself*

Comment tu t'appelles ?	*What is your name?*
Comment vous appelez-vous ?	*What is your name?*
Je m'appelle Chantal.	*My name is Chantal.*
Je te/vous présente Guy.	*I introduce/present Guy to you.*
Voici…	*Here is/are . . .*
Enchanté/e.	*Delighted.*
Je suis de Montréal.	*I am from Montreal.*

pour saluer — *to greet*

Bonjour.	*Hello.*
Bonsoir.	*Good evening.*
Comment allez-vous ?	*How are you?*
Très bien, merci.	*Very well, thank you.*
Bien aussi.	*Fine, also.*
Salut.	*Hi.*
Comment ça va ?	*How's it going?*
Ça va, et toi ? / et vous ?	*Fine, and you?*
Pas mal.	*Not bad.*
Comme ci, comme ça.	*So-so.*
Ça ne va pas.	*Things aren't going well.*

pour prendre congé — *to take leave*

Au revoir.	*Good-bye.*
À bientôt.	*See you soon.*
À demain.	*See you tomorrow.*
Salut.	*'Bye.*

des personnes — *people*

Madame (Mme)	*Mrs./ma'am/Ms.*
Mademoiselle (Mlle)	*Miss*
Monsieur (M.)	*Mr./sir*
un/e ami/e	*friend*
un/e camarade de classe	*classmate*
moi	*me*

quelques expressions avec le verbe être — *a few expressions with the verb to be*

être en forme	*to be fine*
être fatigué/e	*to be tired*
être malade	*to be sick*
être occupé/e	*to be busy*
être stressé/e	*to be stressed out*
c'est/ce sont…	*this is/these are . . .*

autres mots utiles — *other useful words*

oui	*yes*
non	*no*
ou	*or*

Leçon 2

dans la salle de classe — *in the classroom*

une affiche	*poster*
une brosse	*eraser (for chalk- or whiteboard)*
un bureau	*desk*
un cahier	*notebook*
une carte	*map*
une calculatrice	*calculator*
un CD	*CD, compact disk*
une chaise	*chair*
une craie	*piece of chalk*
un crayon	*pencil*
des devoirs (m.)	*homework*
un DVD	*DVD*
une fenêtre	*window*
une gomme	*eraser (for pencil)*
un lecteur CD	*CD player*
un lecteur DVD	*DVD player*
un livre	*book*
un magnétoscope	*videocassette player*
un ordinateur	*computer*
une porte	*door*

une règle	*ruler*
un stylo	*pen*
un tableau	*board*
une télé(vision)	*television (monitor)*
une vidéocassette	*videocassette*

pour donner des ordres — *to give orders*

Allez à la porte !	*Go to the door!*
Allez au tableau !	*Go to the board!*
Asseyez-vous !	*Sit down!*
Donnez la craie à Marie-Laure !	*Give the piece of chalk to Marie-Laure !*
Écoutez bien, s'il vous plaît !	*Listen carefully, please!*
Écoutez sans regarder le livre !	*Listen without looking at the book!*
Écrivez votre nom et votre prénom !	*Write down your last name and your first name!*
Effacez le tableau !	*Erase the board!*
Fermez le livre !	*Close the book!*
Levez-vous !	*Get up/stand up!*
Lisez les mots au tableau !	*Read the words on the board!*
Montrez-moi votre livre !	*Show me your book!*
Montrez Paris sur la carte !	*Point to Paris on the map!*
Ouvrez la fenêtre !	*Open the window!*
Prenez un stylo !	*Take a pen!*

Regardez le tableau !	*Look at the board!*
Rendez-moi les devoirs !	*Hand in your homework!*
Répondez en français !	*Answer in French!*

des expressions pour la salle de classe — *expressions for the classroom*

Pardon ?	*Excuse me?*
Je ne comprends pas.	*I don't understand.*
Répétez, s'il vous plaît.	*Repeat, please.*
Parlez plus fort !	*Speak louder.*
Comment dit-on « board » en français ?	*How do you say "board" in French?*
Voilà…	*Here/There is/are . . .*
Il y a… (Il n'y a pas de…)	*There is/are . . . (There isn't/aren't any . . .)*

pour remercier quelqu'un — *to thank someone*

Merci.	*Thank you.*
Je vous en prie./ Je t'en prie.	*Don't mention it.*
De rien.	*Not at all.*
Il n'y a pas de quoi.	*You're welcome.*

des personnes — *people*

un/e étudiant/e	*student*
un professeur	*teacher*
une dame	*lady*
un monsieur	*man*

What kind of occasion is shown here? Who are the people involved? Does this remind you of similar events you have attended?

Chapitre 1

Ma famille et moi

Leçon 1   *Voici ma famille*

Leçon 2   *Les dates importantes*

Leçon 3   *Nos activités*

*V*enez chez nous !
La famille dans le monde francophone

In this chapter:

- Talking about and describing family members
- Counting from 0 to 99 and telling how old someone is
- Describing activities
- Asking simple questions
- Describing families across the French-speaking world

Leçon 1 *Voici ma famille*

POINTS DE DÉPART

Ma famille

TEXT AUDIO

Salut, je m'appelle Éric Brunet. Voici ma famille :

D'abord il y a mes grands-parents Brunet—ce sont les parents de mon père. Mon père a une sœur ; elle s'appelle Annick Roy. Paul Roy est son mari. Ma tante est divorcée et remariée. Loïc est le fils de son premier mari mais Marie-Hélène est la fille de son deuxième mari, Paul Roy.

Ma mère est d'une famille nombreuse. Elle a deux frères et trois sœurs. Alors, j'ai beaucoup d'oncles, de tantes, de cousins et de cousines. Ma grand-mère Kerboul habite chez mon oncle ; mon grand-père Kerboul est décédé.

Ma grande sœur Fabienne est fiancée. J'ai aussi un petit frère, Stéphane. Chez nous il y a des animaux familiers. Nous avons un chien, César, deux chats, Minou et Cédille, et trois oiseaux.

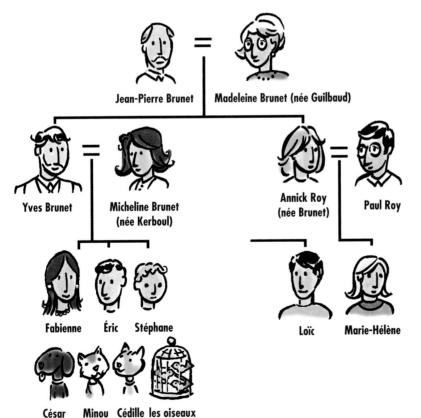

Additional practice activities for each **Points de départ** section are provided by:
- Student Activities Manual
- *Chez nous* Companion Website: **http://www.prenhall.com/cheznous**

Preview Ch. 1 by showing the video montage *La famille dans le monde francophone.* Ask students to guess what the various family relationships depicted might be. What do they notice about the interactions they observe?

Begin vocabulary presentation with Éric's description of his family, modeling a typical description and presenting some of the vocabulary inductively. Next present kinship terms more systematically, using the Brunet family tree (IRCD, Ch. 1). Test comprehension as you go along. First have students pronounce all the names. Then begin: *Voici Éric. La mère d'Éric s'appelle Micheline. Comment s'appelle la mère de Marie-Hélène ? la mère d'Annick ?,* etc. Not all terms need to be presented on the first day of the lesson.

Point out to students that the word *les parents* means both "parents" and "relatives." For example: *Mes parents habitent aux États-Unis* refers to the speaker's mother and father; *J'ai des parents au Canada* refers to other relatives.

LA FAMILLE

le mari	la femme		

les parents | | ### les grands-parents

le père	la mère	le grand-père	la grand-mère
le beau-père	la belle-mère		

les enfants | | ### les petits-enfants

le fils	la fille	le petit-fils	la petite-fille
le frère	la sœur		
le demi-frère	la demi-sœur		
le cousin	la cousine		
l'oncle	la tante		
le neveu	la nièce		

célibataire	fiancé/e	marié/e	divorcé/e	décédé/e

À vous la parole

1-1 Relations multiples. Describe the relationships among the various members of Éric's family.

MODÈLE   Paul Roy : Annick Roy, Éric
> ➤ C'est le mari d'Annick Roy ; c'est l'oncle d'Éric.

1. Loïc : Marie-Hélène, Éric
2. Annick Roy : Yves Brunet, Paul Roy
3. Annick Roy : Madeleine Brunet, Fabienne
4. Loïc : Yves Brunet, Jean-Pierre Brunet
5. Fabienne : Annick Roy, Marie-Hélène
6. Éric : Jean-Pierre et Madeleine Brunet, Yves Brunet
7. Madeleine Brunet : Yves Brunet, Marie-Hélène
8. Jean-Pierre Brunet : Annick Roy, Fabienne

1-2 Le mot juste. Complete the definitions of these family relationships.

MODÈLE   La mère de ma cousine est ma…
> ➤ La mère de ma cousine est ma tante.

1. Le père de ma mère est mon…
2. La sœur de mon père est ma…
3. La fille de mon oncle est ma…
4. Le frère de ma cousine est mon…
5. Le mari de ma tante est mon…
6. La mère de mon père est ma…
7. Le fils de mon frère est mon…
8. La fille de ma sœur est ma…

Vie et culture

According to the most recent U.S. census, the most common American names are: for men: James, John, Robert, Michael, William; for women: Mary, Patricia, Linda, Barbara, Elizabeth. The most popular names for children born in the past five years are: for boys: Jacob, Michael, Matthew, Joshua, Christopher; for girls: Emily, Hannah, Madison, Alexis, Ashley. Children are often named for family members, and sometimes for celebrities, in the U.S. Other common naming patterns include the use of *Junior* or a number to indicate a father's name passed down to the firstborn son. In the south, a son is sometimes given the mother's maiden name as a first name: *Parker, Tucker, Spencer.*

Je m'appelle…

In France, children are sometimes named for a relative or for the saint on whose day they are born; they may also be named for a celebrity. Naming customs follow trends, and certain names go in and out of fashion. In France today, the most common men's names are: **Jean**, **Michel**, **Pierre**, **Philippe**, and **André**. The most common women's names are: **Marie**, **Monique**, **Catherine**, **Françoise**, and **Isabelle**. The most fashionable names for boys are at present: **Lucas**, **Thomas**, **Théo**, **Hugo**, and **Maxime**. The most fashionable girls' names are: **Léa**, **Manon**, **Camille**, **Emma**, and **Océane**. It is also quite trendy to give children American names such as *Kevin* or *James* for boys and *Jennifer* or *Kelly* for girls.

What are the most common names in North America? the most fashionable? Is it trendy to give foreign names to children where you live? How do naming patterns compare with those in France?

Les animaux familiers

Look at the video segment, *Les animaux familiers*, and identify the types of animals you see and where you see them—are there any places that surprise you? How would you feel about dining in a restaurant where pets are regularly allowed under the tables? What does this custom suggest about differences in French and American attitudes toward public spaces?

Une famille nord-africaine

The French own approximately 9 million cats, 8 million dogs, 27 million fish, 7 million birds, and 2 million hamsters, rabbits, mice, etc. (statistics from Mermet, *Francoscopie*, 2003, p. 219). Ask students why they think cats outnumber dogs in France—it may be a function of urban living and smaller spaces.

Point out the frequent use of hyphenated names in French; most are composed with *Jean* or *Marie*. Explain that, as in English, some names can be either masculine or feminine: *Claude, Dominique, Pascal/e*. Other names have both a masculine and a feminine spoken form: *Simon, Simone; Jean, Jeanne; François, Françoise*. The popular name *Kevin* is pronounced either /kɛvin/ or /kevin/.

The most common names in Quebec for men: Michel, Pierre, André, Claude, Daniel. The most common names for women: Louise, Sylvie, Lise, Diane, Julie. The most popular names for newborn boys in 2002: William, Jérémie, Samuel, Gabriel, Xavier. The most popular names for newborn girls: Mégane, Laurie, Camille, Ariane, Sarah. Links to sites with this information can be found on the *Chez nous* Companion Website.

1-3 Portrait d'une famille. Here is a family portrait by the Post-Impressionist painter Henri Rousseau. The title of the painting is ***La noce*** and it depicts a wedding party. With a partner, identify the members of the wedding party.

MODÈLE Voilà le prêtre (*priest*), …

C. Jean / Reunion des Musées Nationaux / Art Resource, NY

1-4 This provides limited practice of the verb *avoir*, presented in Ch. 2, L. 2. You can also present *Je suis fils/fille unique.* You might ask students to bring in a photo of family members to use as a basis for conversation; be sensitive to the fact that some may not wish to do so; they might prefer sharing a photo of friends.

1-4 Et vous ? Tell your partner about your family and pets, using the outline below.

MODÈLE ➤ Je m'appelle Anne. Ma mère s'appelle Nancy et mon père s'appelle Rick. J'ai une sœur, elle s'appelle Christy. Je n'ai pas de frères. J'ai un chien, Rusty.

Je m'appelle…
Ma mère s'appelle…
Mon père s'appelle…

J'ai_____sœur/s, elle/s s'appelle/nt…   Je n'ai pas de…
J'ai_____frère/s, il/s s'appelle/nt…
J'ai_____chat/s_____chien/s,…

Sons et lettres

Additional practice activities for each **Sons et lettres** section are provided by:
• Student Activities Manual
• Text Audio

Les modes articulatoires du français : la tension et le rythme

The tension with which French vowels are pronounced and the rhythm of French speech are distinctive qualities of the spoken language.

- **Pronouncing French vowels**

At the end of a syllable, French vowels are pronounced with the lips and the jaws tense. French vowels are usually shorter than corresponding English vowels, and the lips and jaws do not move as they are produced. In contrast, when you pronounce English vowels, your chin often drops or your lips move, and a glided vowel results. When pronouncing French vowels, be sure that your lips and jaws do not change position.

- French /i/, as in **Mimi**, is pronounced with the lips spread and tense, as if you had a frozen, extreme smile. The sound produced is high-pitched.

- French /u/, as in **Doudou**, is pronounced with the lips very rounded, tense, and projected forward. The sound produced is a low-pitched, deep sound and very different from that of the vowel of English *do*, because for the French /u/ the tongue is also further back in the mouth.

- **Rhythm**

French speech is organized in rhythmic groups, short phrases usually two to six syllables long. Each syllable within a rhythmic group has the same strength; each receives the same degree of stress. The last syllable tends to be longer but not stronger than the others.

In English, in contrast, some syllables within words are stronger than others. Consider, for example, the pronunciation of the following words:

re**peat**   **li**sten   Chi**ca**go   Minne**a**polis

The syllables that are not stressed are usually short, and their vowel is a short, indistinct vowel like that found in the last syllable of the word *furnace* or *sofa*. In French, on the other hand, each syllable and therefore each vowel is pronounced evenly and distinctly.

Listen to the pronunciation of the following English and French words. Then, as you pronounce each French word yourself, count out the rhythm or tap it out with your finger.

1-2		1-2-3		1-2-3-4	
English	**French**	**English**	**French**	**English**	**French**
Phillip	Philippe	*Canada*	Canada	*Alabama*	Alabama
machine	machine	*alphabet*	alphabet	*francophony*	francophonie
madam	madame	*Isabel*	Isabelle	*introduction*	introduction

Before presenting this information, have students discriminate between equivalent names spoken in English and French (Phillip/*Philippe*, Alice/*Alice*, etc.). Ask students how they could tell which language was used. Usually students will mention stress/rhythm and vowel tenseness.

Have students compare the pronunciation of English "say" and French *c'est* with a hand under their chin; in the first case, the chin will drop; in the second, it should not, and the lips should be spread. Use the hand under the chin as a way of monitoring production of a tense, unglided vowel. To help students produce /i/ and /u/ correctly, use rising intonation with /i/, falling intonation with /u/.

À vous la parole

1-5 Les animaux familiers. At a pet show, owners are calling their cats. Repeat what they say, paying particular attention to the /u/ and /i/ sounds.

1. Ici (*here*), Mistigri !
2. Ici, Minouche !
3. Ici, Mimi !
4. Ici, Foufou !

5. Ici, Loulou !
6. Ici, Fifine !
7. Ici, Cachou !
8. Ici, Minette !

1-6 Slogan. In a French school zone you will find a sign urging motorists to drive slowly. Practice reading the warning aloud.

Pensez à nous ! Roulez tout doux !   *Think of us! Drive real slow!*

1-7 Répétez. Practice pronouncing the following sentences with even rhythm. Count out the rhythm of each rhythmic group. The last syllable of each rhythmic group is printed in boldface characters.

1. 1-2   1-2   Bon**jour** / ma**dame**.
2. 1-2   1-2-3   Voi**ci** / Fati**ma**.
3. 1-2-3   1-2   Il s'ap**pelle** / Pa**trick**.
4. 1-2-3-4   1-2-3-4   C'est mon am**ie** / Sylvie Da**vy**.

Additional practice activities for each **Formes et fonctions** section are provided by:
• Student Activities Manual
• *Chez nous* Companion Website:
  http://www.prenhall.com/cheznous

FORMES ET FONCTIONS

1. *Les adjectifs possessifs au singulier*

• Possessive adjectives indicate ownership or other types of relationships.

Voilà **ma** mère.   *There's my mother.*
C'est **ton** frère ?   *Is that your brother?*
Ce sont **tes** crayons ?   *Are these your pencils?*

singulier			pluriel
masculin *+ consonne*	*masc/fém* *+ voyelle*	*féminin* *+ consonne*	
mon frère	**mon**‿oncle	**ma** tante	**mes** cousins
ton père	**ton**‿ami/e	**ta** mère	**tes** parents
son cousin	**son**‿ami/e	**sa** sœur	**ses**‿amis

Present possessive forms inductively in class, using the Brunet family tree (IRCD, Ch. 1): *Voici Éric. Son père s'appelle Yves Brunet. Comment s'appelle son grand-père ? Sa sœur s'appelle Fabienne. Comment s'appelle sa mère ? Ma mère s'appelle Pauline. Et ta mère ?* Ask students to summarize the rules, then display the chart.

● The form of the possessive adjective depends on the gender and number of the noun that it modifies.

—C'est **le frère** de Sarah ? —Oui, c'est **son** frère. *Yes, it's her brother.*
—C'est **la tante** de Simon ? —Oui, c'est **sa** tante. *Yes, it's his aunt.*
—Voilà **les cousins** de Cédric. —Voilà **ses** cousins. *There are his cousins.*

● Use **mon**, **ton**, and **son** before any singular noun beginning with a vowel, and pronounce the liaison /n/:

C'est **mon**‿amie Sandrine. *This is my friend Sandrine.*
C'est **ton**‿oncle ? *Is that your uncle?*

● For plural nouns beginning with a vowel, pronounce the liaison /z/:

Voilà **ses**‿amies. *There are his/her friends.*
Ce sont **mes**‿oncles. *These are my uncles.*

À vous la parole

1-8 C'est qui ? Imagine you are at a family gathering with a friend. Answer his or her questions about the people you see.

MODÈLES É1 Ce sont tes cousins ?
  É2 Oui, ce sont mes cousins.

  É1 C'est le frère de ton père ?
  É2 Oui, c'est son frère.

1. C'est ta mère ?
2. Ce sont tes grands-parents ?
3. C'est ton frère ?
4. C'est ton oncle ?
5. Ce sont les enfants de ta sœur ?
6. C'est la sœur de ta mère ?
7. C'est le mari de ta sœur ?
8. Ce sont les parents de ton cousin ?

Begin practice with discrimination drills to ensure that students hear meaningful distinctions before having to produce them: is the form students hear masculine or feminine? singular or plural? Follow up with substitution (*Voilà ma cousine ; père. —Voilà mon père,* etc.) and transformation drills (*Voilà ma tante. —Voilà mes tantes,* and vice versa).

1-8 Point out that the masculine plural form, *mes neveux,* is used to indicate one's nieces and nephews, contrary to English usage. So, the response to #5, *Oui, ce sont mes neveux,* is ambiguous and could mean either "my nephews" or "my nieces and nephews."

1-9 Un arbre généalogique. Ask your partner questions so that you can draw his/her family tree.

MODÈLES É1 Paul, comment s'appellent tes grands-parents ?

É2 Mes grands-parents s'appellent Smith, ce sont les parents de ma mère.

É1 Et comment s'appelle ta mère ?

É2 Ma mère s'appelle Anne.

É1 Comment s'appelle ton père ?

É2 Mon père s'appelle David.

É1 Est-ce que tu as des frères ou des sœurs ?…

1-10 Qu'est-ce que vous prenez ? Imagine that your dorm/house/apartment is on fire, and you have time to take only three things. What would you take? Make a list and share it with your partner.

MODÈLE 1. les photos de ma famille et de mes amis
2. mes deux chats, Mickey et Minnie
3. mon ordinateur

2. Les adjectifs invariables

sympa(thique) ≠ **désagréable**

optimiste ≠ **pessimiste**

sociable ≠ **réservé/e**

dynamique ≠ timide

idéaliste ≠ réaliste

discipliné/e ≠ indiscipliné/e

conformiste ≠ individualiste

raisonnable ≠ têtu/e

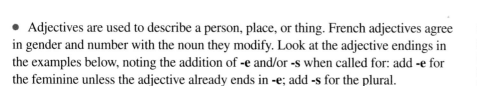

calme ≠ stressé/e

● Adjectives are used to describe a person, place, or thing. French adjectives agree in gender and number with the noun they modify. Look at the adjective endings in the examples below, noting the addition of **-e** and/or **-s** when called for: add **-e** for the feminine unless the adjective already ends in **-e**; add **-s** for the plural.

singulier	*f.*	Claire est	calme	et	réservé**e**.
	m.	Jordan est	calme	et	réservé.
pluriel	*f.*	Mes amies sont	calme**s**	et	réservé**es**.
	m.	Mes cousins sont	calme**s**	et	réservé**s**.

Present the adjectives using the labeled illustrations of opposite traits (IRCD, Ch. 1). Once several sets of opposites have been introduced, switch to the images without labels (IRCD, Ch. 1) to check students' comprehension: *Il est optimiste ?—Non, pessimiste.* or, *Nommez une personne qui est calme.* Follow comprehension checks with choral and individual repetitions of the vocabulary, then go on to the exercises in **À vous la parole**.

- All forms of adjectives like **calme** and **réservé**, whose masculine singular form ends in a vowel, are pronounced alike. Because they have only one spoken form, they are called *invariable*. The feminine ending **-e** and the plural ending **-s** show up only in the written forms.

- Most French adjectives follow the noun they modify.

Sarah est une étudiante **sociable**.	*Sarah is a friendly student.*
Damien est un enfant **raisonnable**.	*Damien is a reasonable child.*

Adjectives are also used in sentences with the verb **être**, where they modify the subject.

Laurent est **optimiste**.	*Laurent is optimistic.*
Marie-Louise est **calme**.	*Marie-Louise is calm.*

- With a mixed group of feminine and masculine nouns, the masculine plural form of the adjective is used.

Lucie et Marie sont **têtues**.	*Lucie and Marie are stubborn.*
Romain et Grégorie sont **réservés**.	*Romain and Gregory are reserved.*
Alexandre et Marine sont **disciplinés**.	*Alexander and Marine are disciplined.*

The French often express a negative trait or thought by using its opposite in a negative sentence:

Elle n'est pas très sympa !	*She's not very nice!*
instead of	
Elle est désagréable !	*She's disagreeable!*

À vous la parole

1-11 Le contraire. Answer each question using the opposite adjective.

MODÈLE   Ces étudiantes sont disciplinées ?
➤ Non, elles sont indisciplinées.

1. Ces femmes sont calmes ?
2. Ces professeurs sont idéalistes ?
3. Ces enfants sont sociables ?
4. Ces filles sont têtues ?
5. Ces familles sont conformistes ?
6. Ces étudiants sont pessimistes ?
7. Ces étudiantes sont timides ?

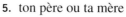 **1-12 Contrasts.** Compare your ideas with those of a classmate.

MODÈLE   le frère/la sœur idéal/e

   É1   Pour moi, le frère idéal est calme et réservé.

   É2   Pour moi, le frère idéal est calme aussi, mais il est sociable.

1-12, 1-13 Have students work in pairs and report back to the group. For 1-13, have students suggest other people to be described, perhaps members of the class or celebrities.

1. le frère/la sœur idéal/e
2. le père idéal
3. le professeur idéal
4. l'étudiant/e typique
5. le/la partenaire idéal/e

COMMENT PRÉCISER UNE DESCRIPTION

un peu (*a little*)   **assez** (*rather*)   **très** (*very*)   **vraiment** (*really*)   **trop** (*too*)

<——>

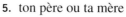 **1-13 Descriptions.** Describe each of the following people to a classmate.

MODÈLE   ton/ta camarade de classe

   ➤ Mon camarade de classe est un peu indiscipliné, mais il est très sympathique.

1. ton/ta camarade de classe
2. ton professeur préféré
3. ton/ta meilleur/e ami/e
4. ton frère ou ta sœur
5. ton père ou ta mère

Lisons

1-14 Faire-part de mariage

A. Avant de lire. On the following pages there are three very similar documents to look over.

1. For what purpose have they been designed?
2. What kinds of information do you expect to find as you read them? Choose from the list:

   _____ addresses   _____ places   _____ religion   _____ names

   _____ ages   _____ prices   _____ times   _____ relationships

   _____ dates   _____ professions   _____ weather

3. In documents such as these, the type of information provided, as well as the phrasing, is often highly predictable. Think of some common examples in English. Where would you expect to find such phrases as *request the pleasure of your company* or *are pleased to announce*? Anticipating the type of information and phrasing such texts are likely to contain will make your close reading of them much easier.

Stratégie

Certain types of documents—for example, announcements and invitations—are formulaic in nature. Your familiarity with such texts in English can help you anticipate and understand the content of similar texts in French.

Avant de lire. *In #3, request the pleasure of your company might be found in a dinner or wedding invitation; are pleased to announce would be commonly found in a birth or wedding announcement.*

B. En lisant. As you read, look for key information:

1. Fill in the following chart as completely as possible.

	1ᵉʳ faire-part	**2ᵉ faire-part**	**3ᵉ faire-part**
Couples' names:			
Parents' names:			
Date:			
Time:			

2. What information do you find in these documents that you expected to find? Is there any information that you did not expect?
3. Were you surprised by the style of the third document? How does it differ from that of the other two? What does it tell you about the people who created it?

Note the use of the 24-hour clock.

1.

Monsieur et Madame
André Lefranc

Monsieur et Madame
Dominique Santino

ont l'honneur de vous faire part du mariage de leurs enfants

Claudine et Patrice

La Cérémonie Religieuse sera célébrée le samedi 20 Mai 2006,
à 15 heures 40, en la Chapelle de l'Hautil, Route de l'Hautil - 78510 Triel

18, rue des Tournelles Pissefontaine
78510 Triel

127, rue de l'Ouest
75014 Paris

2.

Guillaume

a le plaisir de vous faire part du Mariage de ses parents

Nathalie   et   Bernard

La cérémonie se déroulera le Samedi 18 Juin 2005,
à 16 heures 30 à la Mairie d'Albi.

Un Vin d'Honneur sera servi à 17 heures 30,
à la salle des fêtes de Poulan-Pouzols.

Nathalie Duguai   et   Bernard Gaillard

19, rue Baptiste Marcet
81000 Albi
Tél : 05 63 64 30 52

3.

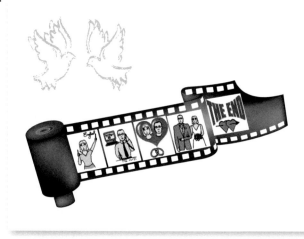

Moteur... On tourne...
À l'affiche, Samedi 19 juin 2004 :
« Les Mariés de l'An 04 »
avec, par ordre d'apparition :
Catherine : la mariée – Jan : le marié
le film sera projeté à 15 heures
en l'église St Pierre – Mons en Barœul.
La séance est suivie d'un vin d'honneur
à la salle du Trocadéro – Mons en Barœul.

Interprètes principaux:
Catherine Mariencourt & Jan Demol
adresse du fan club: 11, rue de la Viéwarde

59300 Valenciennes – Tél : 03.27.24.56.09

C. En regardant de plus près. Now look more closely at some features of these documents.

1. Two of them begin in a very similar way:

    M. et Mme André Lefranc et M. et Mme Dominique Santino ont l'honneur de vous faire part du mariage de leurs enfants.

    Guillaume a le plaisir de vous faire part du mariage de ses parents.

    Based on your familiarity with similar texts in English and on your knowledge of cognates, what do you think these first lines mean?

2. The location mentioned in one document is listed as **la chapelle** and in another as **l'église**. Given the context, what do you think is the meaning of these words?

3. In France, marriage is first of all an official act. Look at the text for Nathalie and Bernard. Their wedding will take place in **la Mairie d'Albi**. Looking at their address, you'll see that Albi is where they live. Given this information, what do you think is the meaning of the word **la mairie**?

4. **Le vin d'honneur** is a ceremony during which guests drink wine, often champagne, to celebrate a happy event. Which of these texts refer to a **vin d'honneur**, and when does it take place?

D. Après avoir lu. Compare your responses to the questions below with those of your classmates.

1. What do you generally do when you receive an announcement of this type?

2. Having seen these three examples, design a similar announcement for yourself, a family member, or a friend.

En regardant de plus près. Point out that the word *église* always designates a Catholic Church. Protestants would be married in *un temple*, Jews in *une synagogue*, Muslims in *une mosquée*. You may want to introduce some of these words as productive vocabulary.

Point out that one couple is having a civil service while the other two are having both a civil and a religious ceremony. Describe how, typically, the bride and groom go with their guests to the town hall for a civil ceremony. Afterwards, there may also be a religious ceremony in a church, synagogue, or elsewhere.

Note that in the case of Nathalie and Bernard, their son is taking the role of inviting people to the marriage since they have been living together as a family. This situation is not uncommon since many unmarried couples in France live together and have children. Students may also note that Catherine and Jan are already living together and that these two couples do not put their parents' names on the invitation. Marriage will be discussed in more detail in Ch. 7; the video for that chapter includes a segment with the mayor of a small town describing his role in officiating marriages.

Après avoir lu. Designing an announcement can be an in-class group writing activity.

Leçon **2** *Les dates importantes*

Present dates by showing the illustrations of holidays and pointing out the significance of each date: *la fête nationale ; Noël ; la fête du travail ; l'Armistice* (IRCD, Ch. 1). Use the calendar to continue practice with months (IRCD, Ch. 1).

POINTS DE DÉPART

Les fêtes et les anniversaires

C'est le quatorze juillet. C'est le vingt-cinq décembre. C'est le premier mai. C'est le onze novembre.

Days of the week are taught in L. 3 of this chapter; seasons in Ch. 5, L. 1. Liaison with numbers is treated in this lesson. Point out that months are not capitalized, and that the order day-month (*4/9, le quatre septembre*) is used in writing dates. Note the exception *le premier septembre* and that no elision is made before a date: *le onze novembre.*

LES MOIS DE L'ANNÉE

janvier	avril	juillet	octobre
février	mai	août	novembre
mars	juin	septembre	décembre

septembre

L	Ma	Me	J	V	S	D
					1	2
3	(4)	5	6	7	8	9
10	11	12	13	14	15	16
17	18	19	20	21	22	23
24	25	26	27	28	29	30

C'est le 4 septembre.   *It's September 4th.*

LES NOMBRES CARDINAUX DE 0 À 31

0	zéro	1	un	11	onze	21	vingt et un	31	trente et un

1	un	11	onze	21	vingt et un
2	deux	12	douze	22	vingt-deux
3	trois	13	treize	23	vingt-trois
4	quatre	14	quatorze	24	vingt-quatre
5	cinq	15	quinze	25	vingt-cinq
6	six	16	seize	26	vingt-six
7	sept	17	dix-sept	27	vingt-sept
8	huit	18	dix-huit	28	vingt-huit
9	neuf	19	dix-neuf	29	vingt-neuf
10	dix	20	vingt	30	trente

French speakers begin with their thumb when counting on their fingers. Show how the numbers 1–9 are typically written. Model pronunciation, then test comprehension: students write the number or date you say; they identify a) the higher or b) the lower of two numbers. Simple production drills: students say the number or date you write; count in even numbers *(les nombres pairs)*, odd numbers *(impairs)*, and backwards *(à rebours)*.

À vous la parole

1-15 Complétez la série. With a partner, take turns reading aloud each series of numbers and adding a number to complete it.

MODÈLE   2, 4, 6, …

      É1 deux, quatre, six, …

      É2 deux, quatre, six, huit

1. 1, 3, 5, …
2. 7, 14, 21, …
3. 6, 12, 18, …
4. 2, 4, 8, …

5. 5, 10, 15, …
6. 25, 27, 29, …
7. 31, 30, 29, …
8. 28, 26, 24, …

1-15 Have students provide additional groupings of numbers that form a series.

1-16 Cours de mathématiques. Create math problems to test your classmates!

MODÈLES É1 10 + 2 = ? (Dix et deux/Dix plus deux, ça fait combien ?)

        É2 Ça fait douze.

        É3 20 − 5 = ? (Vingt moins cinq, ça fait combien ?)

        É4 Ça fait quinze.

1-17 Associations. What number do you associate with the following?

MODÈLE   la superstition

    ➤ treize

1. le vote
2. une paire
3. l'alphabet
4. le premier

5. un imbécile
6. la chance
7. l'indépendance
8. Noël

1-16 Begin with addition and give several models. Have one student state the problem and designate another student to answer. You may have the second student write the problem on the board. The first student then judges the correctness of the response. When the student responds correctly, she/he then asks the next question. You might focus only on addition at first, then review and add problems using subtraction, multiplication, and division.

1-17, Possible answers: 1) 18 2) 2 3) 26 4) 1 5) 0 6) 2, 7, or 11 7) 4, 14, 18, or 21 8) 24 or 25

Vie et culture

Bon anniversaire et bonne fête !

Take a look at the French calendar shown below. How is it similar to the calendar you use? How is it different? Notice that some dates are highlighted in color. With a partner, make a list of these dates and try to determine the significance of each. Do some dates coincide with important dates on your own calendar? Also, note that a name is listed alongside most dates. Many French people celebrate two special days a year, their *birthday* (**Bon anniversaire !**) and their *saint's day* (**Bonne fête !**), the day associated in the Catholic tradition with the saint for whom they are named.

JANVIER			FÉVRIER			MARS			AVRIL			MAI			JUIN		
1	S	J. de l'An	1	M	Ella	1	M	Aubin	1	V	Hugues	1	D	F. du Travail	1	M	Justin
2	D	Basile	2	M	Présentation	2	M	Charles	2	S	Sandrine	2	L	Boris	2	J	Blandine
3	L	Geneviève	3	J	Blaise	3	J	Guénolé	3	D	Richard	3	M	Phil., Jacq.	3	V	Kevin
4	M	Odilon	4	V	Véronique	4	V	Véronique	4	L	Isidore	4	M	Sylvain	4	S	Clotilde
5	M	Edouard	5	S	Agathe	5	S	Olive	5	M	Irène	5	J	ASCENSION	5	D	Igor
6	J	Epiphanie	6	D	Gaston	6	D	Colette	6	M	Marcellin	6	V	Prudence	6	L	Norbert
7	V	Raimond	7	L	Eugénie	7	L	Félicité	7	J	Jean Bap. de la S.	7	S	Gisèle	7	M	Gilbert
8	S	Lucien	8	M	Mardi gras	8	M	Jean de Dieu	8	V	Julie	8	D	VICT. 1945	8	M	Médard
9	D	Alix	9	M	Cendres	9	M	Françoise	9	S	Gautier	9	L	Pacôme	9	J	Diane
10	L	Guillaume	10	J	Arnaud	10	J	Vivien	10	D	Fulbert	10	M	Solange	10	V	Landry
11	M	Paulin	11	V	N. D. Lourdes	11	V	Rosine	11	L	Stanislas	11	M	Estelle	11	S	Barnabé
12	M	Tatiana	12	S	Félix	12	S	Justine	12	M	Jules	12	J	Achille	12	D	F. des Pères
13	J	Yvette	13	D	Carême	13	D	Rodrigue	13	M	Ida	13	V	Rolande	13	L	Antoine de P.
14	V	Nina	14	L	Valentin	14	L	Mathilde	14	J	Maxime	14	S	Matthias	14	M	Elisée
15	S	Rémi	15	M	Claude	15	M	Louise de M.	15	V	Paterne	15	D	PENTECÔTE	15	M	Germaine
16	D	Marcel	16	M	Julienne	16	M	Bénédicte	16	S	Benoît-J.	16	L	Lundi de PENTECÔTE	16	J	J. F. Régis
17	L	Roseline	17	J	Alexis	17	J	Patrice	17	D	Anicet	17	M	Pascal	17	V	Hervé
18	M	Prisca	18	V	Bernadette	18	V	Cyrille	18	L	Parfait	18	M	Eric	18	S	Léonce
19	M	Marius	19	S	Gabin	19	S	Joseph	19	M	Emma	19	J	Yves	19	D	Romuald
20	J	Sébastien	20	D	Aimée	20	D	Rameaux	20	M	Odette	20	V	Bernardin			
21	V	Agnès	21	L	P. Damien	21	L	Clémence	21	J	Anselme	21	S	Constantin	20	L	Silvère
22	S	Vincent	22	M	Isabelle	22	M	Léa	22	V	Alexandre	22	D	Emile	21	M	ÉTÉ
23	D	Barnard	23	M	Lazare	23	M	Victorien	23	S	Georges				22	M	Alban
			24	J	Modeste	24	J	Cath. de Su.	24	D	Fidèle	23	L	Didier	23	J	Audrey
24	L	Fr. de Sales	25	V	Roméo	25	V	Marc				24	M	Donatien	24	V	Jean Bapt.
25	M	Conv. S. Paul	26	S	Nestor	26	S	Larissa	25	L	Marc	25	M	Sophie	25	S	Prosper
26	M	Paule	27	D	Honorine	27	D	PÂQUES	26	M	Alida	26	J	Bérenger	26	D	Anthelme
27	J	Angèle	28	L	Romain	28	L	DE PÂQUES	27	M	Zita	27	V	Augustin			
28	V	Th. d'Aquin				29	M	Gwladys	28	J	Valérie	28	S	Germain	27	L	Fernand
29	S	Gildas				30	M	Amédée	29	V	Catherine	29	D	F. des Mères	28	M	Irénée
30	D	Martine				31	J	Benjamin	30	S	Robert	30	L	Ferdinand	29	M	Pierre, Paul
31	L	Marcelle										31	M	Visitation	30	J	Martial

JUILLET			AOÛT			SEPTEMBRE			OCTOBRE			NOVEMBRE			DÉCEMBRE		
1	V	Thierry	1	L	Alphonse	1	J	Gilles	1	S	Th. de l'E.J.	1	M	Toussaint	1	J	Florence
2	S	Martinien	2	M	Julien-Ey.	2	V	Ingrid	2	D	Léger	2	M	Défunts	2	V	Viviane
3	D	Thomas	3	M	Lydie	3	S	Grégoire				3	J	Hubert	3	S	Xavier
			4	J	J.M. Vianney	4	D	Rosalie	3	L	Gérard	4	V	Charles	4	D	Barbara
4	L	Florent	5	V	Abel				4	M	Fr. d'Assise	5	S	Sylvie			
5	M	Antoine	6	S	Transfiguration	5	L	Raïssa	5	M	Fleur	6	D	Bertille	5	L	Gérald
6	M	Mariette	7	D	Gaétan	6	M	Bertrand	6	J	Bruno				6	M	Nicolas
7	J	Raoul				7	M	Reine	7	V	Serge	7	L	Carine	7	M	Ambroise
8	V	Thibaut	8	L	Dominique	8	J	Nativité N. D.	8	S	Pélagie	8	M	Geoffroy	8	J	I. Concept.
9	S	Armandine	9	M	Amour	9	V	Alain	9	D	Denis	9	M	Théodore	9	V	P. Fourier
10	D	Ulrich	10	M	Laurent	10	S	Inès				10	J	Léon	10	S	Romaric
			11	J	Claire	11	D	Adelphe	10	L	Ghislain	11	V	ARMISTICE 18	11	D	Daniel
11	L	Benoît	12	V	Clarisse				11	M	Firmin	12	S	Christian			
12	M	Olivier	13	S	Hippolyte	12	L	Apollinaire	12	M	Wilfried	13	D	Brice	12	L	Jeanne F.C.
13	M	Henri, Joël	14	D	Evrard	13	M	Aimé	13	J	Géraud				13	M	Lucie
14	J	F. NATIONALE				14	M	La Ste Croix	14	V	Juste	14	L	Sidoine	14	M	Odile
15	V	Donald	15	L	ASSOMPTION	15	J	Roland	15	S	Th. d'Avila	15	M	Albert	15	J	Ninon
16	S	N.D. Mt-Carmel	16	M	Armel	16	V	Edith	16	D	Edwige	16	M	Marguerite	16	V	Alice
17	D	Charlotte	17	M	Hyacinthe	17	S	Renaud				17	J	Elisabeth	17	S	Gaël
			18	J	Hélène	18	D	Nadège	17	L	Baudouin	18	V	Aude	18	D	Gatien
18	L	Frédéric	19	V	Jean Eudes				18	M	Luc	19	S	Tanguy			
19	M	Arsène	20	S	Bernard	19	L	Emilie	19	M	René	20	D	Edmond	19	L	Urbain
20	M	Marina	21	D	Christophe	20	M	Davy	20	J	Adeline				20	M	Abraham
21	J	Victor				21	M	Matthieu	21	V	Céline	21	L	Prés. de Marie	21	M	Pierre C.
22	V	Marie Mad.	22	L	Fabrice	22	J	Maurice	22	S	Elodie	22	M	Cécile	22	J	HIVER
23	S	Brigitte	23	M	Rose de L.	23	V	AUTOMNE	23	D	Jean de C.	23	M	Clément	23	V	Armand
24	D	Christine	24	M	Barthélemy	24	S	Thècle				24	J	Flora	24	S	Adèle
			25	J	Louis	25	D	Hermann	24	L	Florentin	25	V	Catherine L.	25	D	NOËL
25	L	Jacques	26	V	Natacha				25	M	Crépin	26	S	Delphine			
26	M	Anne, Joachim	27	S	Monique	26	L	Côme. Dam.	26	M	Dimitri	27	D	Avent	26	L	Etienne
27	M	Nathalie	28	D	Augustin	27	M	Vinc. de Paul	27	J	Emeline				27	M	Jean
28	J	Samson				28	M	Venceslas	28	V	Simon, Jude	28	L	Jacq. de la M.	28	M	Innocents
29	V	Marthe	29	L	Sabine	29	J	Michel	29	S	Narcisse	29	M	Saturnin	29	J	David
30	S	Juliette	30	M	Fiacre	30	V	Jérôme	30	D	Bienvenue	30	M	André	30	V	Roger
31	D	Ignace de L.	31	M	Aristide				31	L	Quentin				31	S	Sylvestre

À vous la parole

1-18 C'est quelle date ? What date corresponds to each holiday?

MODÈLE Noël
➤ C'est le 25 décembre.

1. le jour de l'An
2. la Saint-Valentin
3. la fête du travail
4. la fête nationale américaine
5. la fête nationale française
6. l'Armistice
7. la Toussaint

1-18 Expand by having students work with a calendar to find other holidays and saints' days.

1-19 Votre anniversaire et votre fête. Find a partner and ask each other when your birthday is and when your saint's day is. Share what you have learned about your partner with the class.

MODÈLE É1 Ton anniversaire, c'est quel jour ?
É2 C'est le 30 août. Et toi ?
É1 C'est le 9 mai.
É2 Et ta fête, Charles ?
É1 C'est le 2 mars. Et toi, Mandy ?
É2 Il n'y a pas de « Sainte Mandy ».

1-19 In a class of 20 students, the probability is high that two will share the same birthday. Some students will not have a saint's day. Follow up by having students report back and listing dates of birthdays and saints' days on the board. Also list names without a corresponding saint's day. Remind students of what they have learned about different naming practices in France and North America, and note that French first names are also greatly influenced by Catholic tradition.

Sons et lettres

TEXT AUDIO

La prononciation des chiffres

numeral alone	before a consonant	before a vowel
un	un jour	un‿an
une	une fille	une affiche
deux	deux cousins	deux‿amis /z/
trois	trois frères	trois‿oncles /z/
quatre	quatre profs	quatre étudiants
cinq	cinq filles	cinq‿enfants
six /sis/	six tantes	six‿oncles /z/
sept	sept livres	sept‿images
huit	huit cahiers	huit‿affiches
neuf	neuf cousines	neuf‿amies
dix /dis/	dix mois	dix‿ans /z/
vingt	vingt crayons	vingt‿affiches /z/

There is a tendency among native speakers to pronounce the final consonant of *cinq, huit, six,* and *dix* before a consonant in dates: *le huit /t/ mars.* This tendency is greatest with *cinq;* in fact, one may often hear *cinq /k/ filles.* In contrast, the final *t* of *quatre-vingt-un,* etc., is never pronounced. In normal conversational style, *quatre* is pronounced /kat/ before a consonant and in final position.

In general, final consonant letters are not pronounced in French, for example: **le chat, mes parents.**

Numbers 1–10 are exceptions. Their pronunciation depends on whether they occur by themselves, as in counting (**un**, **deux**, **trois**…), or whether they are followed by another word (**un_ami**, **deux_enfants**, **six chiens**).

Except for **quatre** and **sept**, all numbers have two or three spoken forms. **Neuf** has a special form before the words **ans** and **heures**; **f** is pronounced /v/:

Il a neuf ans.	*He is nine years old.*
Il est neuf heures.	*It's nine o'clock.*

À vous la parole

1-20 À la réunion de la famille Brunet. Repeat each expression.

Il y a…

un grand-père	un arrière-grand-père (*great-grandfather*)
trois tantes	trois oncles
dix filles	dix enfants
huit garçons	huit étudiants
cinq cousins	cinq animaux familiers

1-21 Une comptine. Repeat the following counting rhyme.

> Un, deux, trois, nous irons au bois,
> Quatre, cinq, six, cueillir des cerises.
> Sept, huit, neuf, dans mon panier neuf.
> Dix, onze, douze, elles seront toutes rouges.

FORMES ET FONCTIONS

1. Le verbe avoir *et l'âge*

● The irregular verb **avoir** (*to have*) is used to indicate possession and other relationships:

J'**ai** une sœur.	*I have a sister.*
Tu **as** un crayon ?	*Do you have a pencil?*

● **Avoir** is also used to indicate age:

Elle **a** vingt ans.	*She is 20 years old.*
Nous **avons** dix-huit ans.	*We're 18 years old.*

Begin practice with a discrimination drill. Give students a list of nouns and have them write in the number you call out (as if you were taking inventory). Begin student production with substitution drills, changing either the number or the noun: *Il a dix ans ; six.* — *Il a six ans*, etc.; *Elle a cinq frères ; oncles.* — *Elle a cinq oncles,* etc. To practice the isolation form, use the following exercise:

É1 Il a six euros.
É2 Combien ?
É1 Six.

For further practice with numbers, have students tell each other the number of people or animals there are in their families in the following categories: *grands-parents ; petits-enfants ; étudiants ; arrière-grands-parents ; garçons ; enfants ; cousins ; oncles ; chats ; chiens.* For example, — *Il y a deux grands-parents.* If there is no one in a given category, students should use the structure *Il n' y a pas de….* For example, — *Il n'y a pas de grands-parents.*

1-21 You may wish to point out that *nous irons au bois* means "we'll go to the woods;" *cueillir des cerises,* "gather cherries;" *dans mon panier neuf,* "in my new basket;" *elles seront toutes rouges,* "they'll all be red." Explain to students that *neuf* is a homonym which means "nine" and "new." Refer students to the Lab Manual for a French Canadian version of this counting rhyme.

Remind students that subject-verb agreement takes place in English as well: "I have," "she has." Remind them of the use of *avoir* in the idiomatic expression *il y a,* "there is/are." Point out that *je* becomes *j'* before a vowel.

In addition to the numbers you already know, the following numbers will be useful for talking about ages:

40	quarante	72	soixante-douze
50	cinquante	80	quatre-vingts
60	soixante	81	quatre-vingt-un
70	soixante-dix	90	quatre-vingt-dix
71	soixante et onze	91	quatre-vingt-onze

● Here are the forms of **avoir**, shown with the subject pronouns. Notice that the subject pronoun **je** becomes **j'** before a vowel. Liaison occurs before all the plural forms.

AVOIR _to have_					
SINGULIER			PLURIEL		
j'	**ai**	_I have_	nous‿	**avons**	_we have_
tu	**as**	_you have_	vous‿	**avez**	_you have_
il } elle }	**a**	_he/she/it has_	ils‿ } elles‿ }	**ont**	_they have_

● Use **ne ... pas de** to express the idea of _not having any_. Notice that both **ne** and **de** drop their final **-e** before a vowel sound.

Je **n'**ai **pas de** sœurs.	_I don't have any sisters._
Nous **n'**avons **pas d'**oncle.	_We don't have an uncle._

À vous la parole

👥 **1-22 Qu'est-ce que vous avez ?** Compare with a partner what you brought to class today, and report back to your classmates. See how many different items you can name.

MODÈLE ➤ Nous avons des cahiers. J'ai aussi un stylo et un livre.
Il/Elle a un crayon et un CD.

1-23 La famille Brunet. Tell how old each of the Brunet family members is.

Jean-Pierre Brunet (81) = Madeleine Brunet (77)

Yves Brunet (45) = Micheline Brunet (43)   Annick Roy (39) = Paul Roy (51)

Fabienne (21)   Éric (17)   Stéphane (14)   Loïc Leclerc (17)   Marie-Hélène Roy (12)

Quel âge ont les enfants de Jean-Pierre Brunet ?
➤ Yves Brunet a quarante-cinq ans et Annick Roy a trente-neuf ans.

1. Quel âge a la mère de Loïc ?
2. Quel âge a le père de Marie-Hélène ?
3. Quel âge a la sœur d'Éric ?
4. Quel âge ont les parents d'Yves Brunet ?
5. Quel âge ont les enfants d'Annick Roy ?
6. Quel âge a la femme d'Yves Brunet ?
7. Quel âge ont les neveux de Paul Roy ?

1-24 Et ta famille ? Ask a classmate how old various members of his or her family are.

MODÈLES ta mère ?

É1 Quel âge a ta mère ?
É2 Ma mère a quarante-huit ans.

tes frères ?

É1 Quel âge ont tes frères ?
É2 Mon frère Robert a douze ans. Mon frère Kevin a quinze ans.

1. ta mère ?
2. ton père ?
3. tes frères ?
4. tes sœurs ?
5. tes grands-parents ?
6. tes nièces ?
7. tes neveux ?
8. tes cousins ?

2. *Les adjectifs possessifs au pluriel*

- Corresponding to the subjects **nous**, **vous**, and **ils/elles** are the following possessive adjectives:

Voici **notre** père.	*Here's our father.*
C'est **votre** mère ?	*Is that your mother?*
C'est **leur** tante.	*That's their aunt.*

Remember that **vous/votre** can refer to one person (*formal*) or more than one.

- There is no distinction between masculine and feminine for **notre**, **votre**, and **leur**.

- For the plural forms, pronounce the liaison /z/ before a vowel:

Ce sont **nos** oncles.	*These are our uncles.*
Voici **vos** affiches.	*Here are your posters.*
Ce sont **leurs** amis.	*These are their friends.*

Review the singular-reference possessives, taught in Ch. 1, L. 1, before presenting the new forms. Use the Brunet family tree (IRCD, Ch.1) to present these forms inductively: *Voici Fabienne, Éric et Stéphane. Leur père s'appelle Yves Brunet. Comment s'appelle leur mère ?* Similarly, model the three children describing their family: *Notre mère s'appelle Micheline.* Summarize forms, using the chart that is part of this grammar presentation.

singulier			pluriel
masculin + consonne	*masc/fém + voyelle*	*féminin + consonne*	
mon frère	**mon** oncle	**ma** tante	**mes** cousins
ton père	**ton** ami/e	**ta** mère	**tes** parents
son cousin	**son** ami/e	**sa** sœur	**ses** amis
	notre mère		**nos** cousines
	votre oncle		**vos** amis
	leur père		**leurs** oncles

À vous la parole

1-25 C'est logique. Use the possessive to point out the person(s) indicated.

MODÈLE   Nous avons une fille.
> ➤ Voici notre fille.

1. Nous avons deux fils.
2. Vous avez un neveu.
3. Vous avez trois cousins.
4. Ils ont une nièce.
5. Ils ont trois enfants.
6. Nous avons une tante.
7. Nous avons deux oncles.

Begin practice with a transformation drill, singular → plural: *Voici notre tante → Voici nos tantes,* etc.

1-26 Décrivons la famille Brunet. With a partner, describe the family from the point of view indicated.

MODÈLE   pour Annick Roy

> É1 Ses parents s'appellent Jean-Pierre et Madeleine.
> É2 Sa nièce s'appelle Fabienne.

1. pour Fabienne Brunet
2. pour Jean-Pierre et Madeleine Brunet
3. pour Annick et Paul Roy
4. pour Loïc Leclerc et Marie-Hélène Roy
5. pour Yves Brunet
6. pour Fabienne, Éric et Stéphane Brunet

1-27 La famille étendue. Take turns asking and answering questions with a partner to describe your extended family.

MODÈLE   des tantes

> É1 Tu as des tantes ?
> É2 Oui, j'ai deux tantes.
> É1 Comment s'appellent tes tantes ?…

1. des tantes
2. des oncles
3. des cousines
4. des cousins
5. des nièces
6. des neveux

1-26 If this proves difficult for students, display the Brunet family tree (IRCD, Ch. 1).

At this point in the lesson, students generally know the Brunet family tree well. For a lively exercise using possessive adjectives, have class members take on the roles of various members of the Brunet family and test their memory of the family tree. Provide students with name tags and have them circulate in class asking each other questions such as [*à Fabienne, Éric et Stéphane Brunet*] : *Comment s'appelle votre mère ?* or *Comment s'appellent vos grands-parents ?* Students playing the role of these family members would respond: —*Notre mère s'appelle Micheline.* or —*Nos grands-parents s'appellent Jean-Pierre et Madeleine Brunet.* As an alternative, give students a card with their name on it, and have them circulate and ask questions to find their nuclear family: *Vous avez des enfants ? Combien ?* or *Je m'appelle Fabienne. Vous êtes ma mère ?*

Parlons

1-28 Trouvez quelqu'un qui...

Avant de parler. You may wish to complete this activity with the whole class. Students have only been exposed to asking questions with intonation and lexical phrases at this point. Questions with *est-ce que* are presented in L. 3 of this chapter. Possible questions include: *Ton anniversaire, c'est quel mois ? Ton anniversaire, c'est quelle date ? Ton anniversaire, c'est quand ? Tu as quel âge ? Tu as des frères et des sœurs ? Combien ? Tu as ton livre de français ?*

A. Avant de parler. Try to find people in your class who correspond to the descriptions below. To prepare, brainstorm with a partner to come up with a list of the questions you can ask in order to get the required information. For example, to find out if someone has a birthday in May, you could ask the general question: **Ton anniversaire, c'est en quel mois ?** (or, **Votre anniversaire, c'est en quel mois ?** if you are asking your instructor).

B. En parlant. Now circulate among your classmates and ask the questions you have prepared. You may have to speak to several people before finding someone who fits a particular description—keep moving! Your instructor will call time in just a few minutes.

MODÈLE ... a son anniversaire au mois de mai

        É1 Ton anniversaire, c'est en quel mois ?

        É2 C'est en décembre.

        (You ask someone else the same question.)

        É1 Ton anniversaire, c'est en quel mois ?

        É3 C'est en septembre.

        (You write this person's name down for #2.)

1. ... a son anniversaire au mois de mai
2. ... a son anniversaire au mois de septembre
3. ... a son anniversaire le même *(same)* jour que vous
4. ... a son anniversaire le même mois que vous
5. ... a le même âge que vous
6. ... a le même nombre de frères et de sœurs que vous
7. ... n'a pas de frères ou de sœurs
8. ... a son livre de français, son cahier d'activités et ses CDs
9. ... a un ordinateur
10. ... a des affiches de France

C. Après avoir parlé. Did you find someone who matched every description before time was called? If not, ask one of your questions to the class as a whole; perhaps someone else found a match!

MODÈLE ➤ Qui a son anniversaire au mois de mai ?

Leçon 3 *Nos activités*

POINTS DE DÉPART

Une semaine typique

TEXT AUDIO

C'est une semaine typique chez les Dupont. Le lundi matin, M. Dupont travaille normalement au bureau. Les enfants sont à l'école, et Mme Dupont travaille dans le jardin.

Aujourd'hui, c'est mardi. Mme Dupont parle au téléphone maintenant ; elle invite ses parents à déjeuner dimanche.

Le mercredi, il n'y a pas d'école. Les enfants restent à la maison. Le matin, Émilie joue du piano et elle prépare sa leçon de chant. L'après-midi, Simon joue au foot avec ses copains.

Le jeudi après-midi, M. Dupont joue souvent au golf ; il aime le sport.

Le vendredi soir, Simon ne travaille pas, il écoute de la musique ou regarde la télé.

Le samedi matin, il y a école, mais l'après-midi est libre.

Dimanche, les grands-parents arrivent, et la famille déjeune ensemble.

Present the vocabulary using the Dupont family's agenda (IRCD, Ch. 1). First describe the activities, then test students' comprehension: *Qui travaille dans le jardin ?*, etc. Have students repeat key expressions. Then ask them to provide more information: *Qu'est-ce qu'Émilie fait le mercredi matin ?* At this point, other visuals could be introduced, such as magazine photos. Contracted forms of *à* and *de* plus definite articles are presented here as lexical items for students to memorize. These forms will be treated in Ch. 2, L. 2.

Do not present forms of *-er* verbs, rather use the base form (*regarde/nt, joue/nt, écoute/nt*) with an appropriate subject to teach the lexical items. Model pronunciation, test comprehension by having students point to or mime the activity you describe, and have students pronounce new expressions. The conjugation of *-er* verbs will be presented in this lesson.

Let students examine the schedule and draw conclusions about the length of the school day in France and the length of the midday break; point out the use of the 24-hour clock. Make sure they notice the absence of classes on Wednesday and the Saturday morning schedule. Point out that parents may have a similar break at noon and may work until six o'clock. *Lycée* and university students typically have classes on Wednesday, but no class on Saturday.

Vie et culture

La semaine

Look at the weekly schedule for a middle school student. What do you notice about the times at which school begins and ends? the lunch break? the days on which there are classes? Many students devote the day on Wednesday to sports and cultural activites such as music or art lessons.

How does a typical week for young French students compare to that of North American students? What are the advantages and disadvantages of these varying schedules?

Mon emploi du temps

	LUNDI	MARDI	MERCREDI	JEUDI	VENDREDI	SAMEDI
8h30	français	français		français	maths	anglais
10h	maths	maths		maths	français	arts plastiques
11h30	déjeuner	déjeuner	pas d'école	déjeuner	déjeuner	sortie
13h30	théâtre	gym		théâtre	gym	/
15h	anglais	histoire		anglais	géographie	/
16h30	sortie	sortie		sortie	sortie	/

LES PARTIES DE LA JOURNÉE

le matin   l'après-midi   le soir

LES JOURS DE LA SEMAINE

lundi   mardi   mercredi   jeudi   vendredi   samedi   dimanche

DES ACTIVITÉS

arriver	déjeuner	écouter	inviter	jouer à/de	parler
préparer	regarder	rester	réviser	téléphoner	travailler

Using the text in the **Points de départ** (IRCD, Ch. 1), have students pick out which activities take place on a regular basis and which activities are one-time events. Make sure students notice that activities on a regular basis use *le*. Point out that in contrast to English, a preposition is never used with the days of the weeks or times: *le lundi* or *le soir*, in contrast to "*on* Monday(s), *in* the evening." Point out the use of *maintenant* to express an action occuring now.

The definite article **le** is used with days of the week or times of day to refer to an activity that always happens on that particular day of the week or at that particular time:

Le lundi, je travaille à la maison.   *Mondays, I work at home.*
Le samedi, on dîne au restaurant.   *On Saturdays, we eat out.*
Le soir, je regarde la télé.   *In the evening, I watch TV.*

Compare these examples with the sentences below, which do not use an article with the days of the week because they refer to specific, non-repeated activities.

Je joue au tennis avec des amis **mardi**.   *I'm playing tennis with friends on Tuesday.*
Dimanche, je dîne avec ma mère.   *Sunday, I'm having dinner with my mother.*

À vous la parole

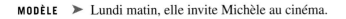 **1-29 Associations de mots.** What words do you associate with each of the verbs listed? Work with a partner to find as many answers as possible.

MODÈLE regarder
> ➤ la télé, un film, le tableau

1. écouter
2. jouer
3. rester
4. préparer

5. parler
6. travailler
7. aimer
8. inviter

1-30 L'agenda d'Émilie. Tell what Émilie has written in her pocket calendar each day of the week.

1-30 To prepare, have students repeat the names of the days of the week. Drill by having them name the day after *(mardi ?* —*mercredi)* or the day before *(vendredi ?* —*jeudi).* Then complete the exercise using Émilie's agenda (IRCD, Ch. 1). Students produce only the third-person form of *-er* verbs, which is the base form. Note use of the 24-hour clock. Time is presented only for receptive control here; students should merely recognize whether an activity takes place in the morning, afternoon, or evening. Telling time is treated in Ch. 4, L. 2.

Lundi **11**	Mardi **12**	Mercredi **13**	Jeudi **14**	Vendredi **15**	Samedi **16**	(09) SEPTEMBRE 2006
(09) SEPTEMBRE	(09) SEPTEMBRE	(09) SEPTEMBRE	(09) SEPTEMBRE	(09) SEPTEMBRE	(09) SEPTEMBRE	S L M M J V S D
S. Adelphe	S. Apollinaire	S. Aimé	La Ste Croix	S. Roland	S. Edith	35 1 2
						36 4 5 6 7 8 9 10
						37 11 12 13 14 15 16 17
						38 18 19 20 21 22 23 24
						39 25 26 27 28 29 30

Lundi: 9 *inviter Michèle au cinéma*

Mardi: 19 *préparer la leçon de chant*

Mercredi: 10 *préparer les leçons*

Jeudi: 16 *téléphoner à Grand-mère*

Vendredi: 20 *jouer au tennis avec Julie*

Samedi: 10-11 *travailler dans le jardin avec Maman*

(09) SEPTEMBRE 2006 column: TÉLÉPHONER, FAXER, @, VOIR – FAIRE, ÉCRIRE

Dimanche 17

(09) SEPTEMBRE   S. Renaud

Jeudi 14 *regarder un film avec Michèle*

MODÈLE ➤ Lundi matin, elle invite Michèle au cinéma.

1-31 Vary by asking what students are doing tonight.

1-31 Qu'est-ce que vous faites le samedi ? Use the elements from each column to tell a classmate what you typically do on Saturday.

MODÈLE   le matin / je révise / mes leçons
> Le matin je révise mes leçons.

	je travaille	le dîner
le matin	j'écoute	mes copains à dîner
l'après-midi	je joue	au tennis
le soir	je révise	la télé, un film
	je regarde	à la maison
	j'invite	de la musique
		mes leçons

FORMES ET FONCTIONS

1. Le présent des verbes en -er et la négation

Present the verb paradigm inductively using a personalized story: *Le week-end, je ne travaille pas à la fac. Avec ma fille, nous jouons au tennis et nous travaillons dans le jardin. Et vous, vous travaillez ou vous regardez la télé habituellement le week-end ?* etc. Ask students to provide the infinitive forms of verbs you have used, and to identify the various spoken forms. Remind students that English verbs also vary according to the subject: "I watch, s/he watches." Stress the fact that regular -er verbs in French have three spoken forms (and five written forms). These verbs show a boot pattern: the third-person plural form is pronounced the same as the three singular forms.

Regular French verbs are classified according to the ending of their infinitive. Most have an infinitive form that ends in **-er**. To form the present tense of an **-er** verb, drop the **-er** from the infinitive and add the appropriate endings according to the pattern shown.

REGARDER *to look at, to watch*			
SINGULIER		**PLURIEL**	
je	regard**e**	nous	regard**ons**
tu	regard**es**	vous	regard**ez**
il		ils	
elle }	regard**e**	elles }	regard**ent**
on			

• Verbs ending in **-er** have three spoken forms. All singular forms and the **ils/elles** plural forms are pronounced alike. Their endings are important written signals, but they are not pronounced. The only endings that represent sounds are **-ons** and **-ez**, which correspond to the subject pronouns **nous** and **vous**.

- When a verb begins with a consonant, there is no difference in the pronunciation of singular and plural for **il/s** and **elle/s.** Use the context to decide whether the speaker means one person, or more than one:

Mon cousin, il joue du piano.	*My cousin, he plays piano.*
Mes frères, ils jouent au foot.	*My brothers, they play soccer.*

- The liaison /z/ of the plural form allows you to distinguish the singular form from the plural when the verb begins with a vowel sound:

il aime vs. ils‿aiment	*he likes, they like*
elle habite vs. elles‿habitent	*she lives, they live*

- **On** is an indefinite pronoun that can mean *one, they,* or *people,* depending on the context. In conversational French, **on** is often used instead of **nous.**

On parle français ici.	*They speak French here.*
On joue au foot ?	*Shall we play soccer?*

- In French the present tense is used to talk about a state or an habitual action:

Je **parle** français.	*I speak French.*
Il **travaille** le week-end.	*He works on weekends.*

- It is also used to talk about an action taking place while one is speaking:

On **regarde** la télé.	*We're watching TV.*

- To make a sentence negative, put **ne** (or **n'**) before the verb and **pas** after it:

Je **ne** travaille **pas.**	*I'm not working.*
Nous **n'aimons pas** le golf.	*We don't like golf.*

Can you provide the missing form of **jouer** ?

À vous la parole

1-32 Une semaine chez les Dupont. Imagine that you're Mme Dupont, and describe your family's activities throughout the week.

MODÈLE lundi matin : Mme Dupont
> Je travaille dans le jardin.

1. lundi matin : M. Dupont, les enfants
2. mardi : Mme Dupont
3. mercredi après-midi : Émilie, Simon
4. jeudi après-midi : M. Dupont
5. vendredi soir : Simon
6. samedi matin : les enfants
7. dimanche : les grands-parents, la famille

Begin with a discrimination drill highlighting the presence or absence of liaison as a cue for number: one person, or more than one? *Ils habitent un appartement ; elle aime le rock,* etc. Follow with substitution drills: *Je joue au tennis ; nous. —Nous jouons au tennis,* etc. *J'aime la musique ; vous. —Vous aimez la musique,* etc.; *Je ne travaille pas ; nous. —Nous ne travaillons pas,* etc.

1-32 Display the Dupont family's agenda, used to present *-er* verb vocabulary (IRCD, Ch. 1).

1-33 Vos habitudes. With a partner, take turns explaining when you or the people you know typically do the things listed.

MODÈLES vous / regarder la télé
——Je regarde la télé le vendredi soir.

OU ——Je ne regarde pas la télé.

vos parents / téléphoner aux enfants
Ils téléphonent aux enfants le week-end.

1. votre camarade de chambre / préparer ses leçons
2. vous / regarder un film
3. vous et vos amis / jouer au tennis
4. votre père / préparer le dîner
5. vous / écouter la radio
6. votre frère ou sœur / téléphoner aux parents
7. vos parents / travailler
8. vous / rester à la maison

1-34 Cette semaine. With a classmate, take turns telling some of the things you'll be doing later this week.

MODÈLE ➤ Jeudi soir, je révise mes leçons ; vendredi soir, je regarde un film avec mes copains ; samedi, je parle au téléphone avec mes parents...

Then report back to the class what you learned about your partner.

2. Les questions

There are two types of questions in English and French: *yes-no questions*, which require confirmation or denial, and *information questions*, which contain words such as **qui** (*who*) or **comment** (*how*) and ask for specific information.

● The simplest way to form yes-no questions in French is to raise the pitch level of your voice at the end of the sentence. These questions are said to have a rising intonation:

Émilie est ta cousine ?   *Emily is your cousin?*

Tu t'appelles Anne ?   *Your name is Anne?*

Another way of asking a yes-no question is by putting **est-ce que/qu'** at the beginning of the sentence. These questions are usually pronounced with a falling voice pitch:

Est-ce que vous parlez français ?   *Do you speak French?*

Est-ce qu'il joue au foot ?   *Does he play soccer?*

- If a question is phrased in the negative, and you want to contradict it, use **si** in your response:

—Tu n'es pas mariée ?　　　　—*You're not married?*

—**Si,** voilà mon mari.　　　　—*Yes (I am), there's my husband.*

—Tu n'aimes pas le français ?　　—*You don't like French?*

—**Si,** j'aime le français.　　　—*Yes, I do like French.*

- When French speakers think they already know the answer to a question, they sometimes add **n'est-ce pas** to the end of the sentence for confirmation.

Vous êtes de Paris, **n'est-ce pas** ?　　*You're from Paris, aren't you?*

Ton père parle français, **n'est-ce pas** ?　*Your father speaks French, doesn't he?*

However, be careful. French speakers do not use **n'est-ce pas** as frequently as American speakers use tag questions such as *aren't you? doesn't he? didn't you?*

Drill the use of *si*; ask a series of questions and have students contradict you in every case, using *non* or *si*: *Vous jouez au foot ?* — *Non. Vous ne parlez pas francais ?* — *Si,* etc. Follow up using the family tree and asking questions that require the answers *oui/non/si*.

À vous la parole

1-35 Encore la famille Brunet ! Ask for confirmation from your classmates concerning the members of the Brunet family.

MODÈLE　La mère d'Éric s'appelle Micheline.

　　　　É1　Est-ce que la mère d'Éric s'appelle Micheline ?

　　ou　La mère d'Éric s'appelle Micheline ?

　　　　É2　Oui, sa mère s'appelle Micheline.

1. Éric a une sœur.
2. Sa sœur s'appelle Fabienne.
3. Il a deux cousins.
4. Ses grands-parents sont Jean-Pierre et Madeleine Brunet.
5. Il n'a pas de frère.
6. Sa tante est divorcée et remariée.
7. Elle a deux enfants.
8. La demi-sœur de Loïc s'appelle Marie-Hélène.
9. Annick Roy a un frère.
10. Le mari de Micheline s'appelle Yves.

1-35 You may use the Brunet family tree (IRCD, Ch. 1) to provide visual support; encourage students to invent other questions. Other visuals — the classroom (IRCD, Ch. Prélim.), the Dupont family's agenda (IRCD, Ch. 1) — can be used as a point of departure for students' questions.

1-36 C'est bien ça ? Draw a picture on the board. Your classmates will try to guess what it is.

MODÈLE　(Vous dessinez un crayon.)

　　　　É1　Est-ce que c'est un stylo ?

　　　　É2　C'est une craie ?

　　　　É3　Ah, c'est un crayon !

1-36 As a variation, common objects can be hidden in a bag (Kim's game).

For further practice use the following exercise as a mixing activity. Have students get up and circulate around the room, asking each person no more than two questions. When a person answers yes, his/her name is written down beside that activity. Give students about five minutes; they will probably not complete the list. As a follow-up, have them ask questions to complete their list: *Qui joue de la guitare ?* A student who found the response can then answer: *Jean joue de la guitare.* Other information can then be elicited: what type of music?, for example. At this point, treat the expressions *jouer de la guitare, jouer du piano, jouer au golf/tennis/foot* as lexical chunks for students to memorize. The distinction between *jouer à* and *jouer de* as well as contractions with these prepositions and the definite articles is treated in Ch. 2, L. 2.

Un remue-ménage ! Circulate around the classroom, asking your classmates questions to find out who does what. Limit your questions to two per person, write down your classmate's name when you get a positive response, and be ready to compare notes with the class as a whole.

MODÈLE : *jouer de la guitare É1 Tu joues de la guitare ? É2 Non, je joue du piano, mais pas de la guitare.* 1) jouer de la guitare ; 2) travailler le week-end ; 3) rester à la maison le week-end ; 4) préparer le dîner ; 5) danser la valse (waltz) ; 6) travailler dans le jardin ; 7) écouter de la musique classique ; 8) ne pas regarder la télé ; 9) ne pas écouter de rap ; 10) jouer au golf

Script for *Écoutons*

1. Salut. C'est Jennifer. Mercredi soir, il y a un bon film à la télé que je veux regarder. Je t'invite. On peut préparer du pop-corn. Téléphone-moi si tu veux le regarder avec moi. Allez, ciao !

2. Bonjour, c'est Jean-Pierre à l'appareil. Samedi matin, je joue au golf avec des copains. Tu veux jouer avec nous ? On a rendez-vous à 11 heures au parc. Appelle-moi si ça t'intéresse. Bon, au revoir !

3. C'est maman. Je t'invite à manger à la maison dimanche après-midi. Tes grands-parents, ton oncle Paul et tes cousins déjeunent avec nous. Téléphone-moi si tu es libre. On a envie de te voir. Allez, je t'embrasse !

4. Salut, c'est Annie. Vendredi soir, il y a un concert de piano à la fac. Je sais que tu aimes la musique classique. Appelle-moi si tu veux te joindre à nous. O.K., salut !

1-37 Une interview. Interview a member of your class that you do not know very well to find out more about him/her. Use the suggested topics, and report to the class something you have learned about your partner.

MODÈLE avoir des frères ou des sœurs

> É1 Est-ce que tu as des frères ou des sœurs ?
>
> É2 J'ai une sœur, mais je n'ai pas de frères.

1. avoir des enfants
2. avoir des animaux familiers
3. travailler beaucoup
4. jouer du piano ou de la guitare
5. jouer au football ou au tennis
6. regarder la télé
7. préparer le dîner
8. regarder des films
9. inviter des copains à dîner

1-37 You might arrange for another teacher or an advanced student to visit your class and be interviewed.

Écoutons

TEXT AUDIO

1-38 Le répondeur

A. Avant d'écouter. Fabienne has a lot of friends. Listen to the messages on her answering machine from people who are suggesting that she join them this week for various activities. Before you listen, think about the kinds of information you would expect to hear in a phone message.

B. En écoutant. As you listen, complete the first three columns of the chart below for each message.

	Who called?	Event suggested?	When?	Accept or refuse?
1.				
2.				
3.				
4.				

C. Après avoir écouté. Now, look over the chart again and decide which invitations you would accept and which invitations you would refuse if you were Fabienne. Fill in column four with this information, and discuss your responses with a classmate.

Venez chez nous!
La famille dans le monde francophone

The workbook reading contains an example of a couple announcing their *PACS*; generally couples refer to their relationship by saying, *Nous sommes pacsé/es.*

If you have not done so already, show the video montage *La famille dans le monde Francophone* to provide an overview of francophone families. You might pause and have students describe each family pictured. To encourage discussion and cross-cultural comparison after reading this section, you might ask students: How does the typical French family seem to compare to the typical North American family, and to your own? How would you characterize the role of family life in France? Is the role of family life in North America similar, in your opinion?

Stratégie

Use accompanying graphic elements to help understand a text. Often a graph or table, for example, will summarize at a glance the main points made in the text, serving as a useful point of reference both before and as you read.

LA FAMILLE EN FRANCE

The face of the family is changing in France. Today's couples tend to marry later and to have fewer children. Typically, French men get married for the first time at age 30 and French women at age 28.

Although divorce is less common than in the United States, the rate is rising; approximately one in three marriages ends in divorce. In addition, an estimated two and a half million unmarried French men and women live together. This represents almost one in every six couples. It is quite common for unmarried couples to have children together. In fact, more than half of all first-time births at the present time are to unmarried women. It is not unusual for couples to marry after the birth of one or more children. Since the creation of the **Pacte Civil de Solidarité (le PACS)** in 1999, unmarried couples living together, whether of the same or opposite sex, can legalize their union.

Although the family is changing, relations among family members still tend to be close and to have a strong influence in a French person's life. Young people, for example, have frequent contact with their extended family: grandparents, aunts, uncles, and cousins. Because of recent high unemployment rates, young people also tend to remain in their parents' home for longer periods of time. Typically French men leave home after age 24 and French women after age 22.

Avant de lire. The table does not duplicate the text information exactly. Display the table and work through it with students, using the questions provided; point out how large numbers and percentages are expressed, using spacing and commas. Note that the Canadian census is taken every five years, whereas in the U.S. it is every ten years. When students have developed their lists of preliminary conclusions, have them share these with the class as a whole.

1-39 La famille au Québec

A. Avant de lire. This reading about families in Quebec is accompanied by a table that presents census statistics about married and unmarried couples in the province. Examining the table beforehand can help you better understand the related text. Consider the following questions:

1. What types of family structure are referred to in the table? The key expressions here are: **avec enfants**, **sans enfants**, and **en union libre**.

Additional activities to explore the **Venez chez nous !** topics are provided by:
- Student Activities Manual
- *Chez nous* video
- *Chez nous* Companion Website: http://www.prenhall.com/cheznous

Can you explain the meaning of each? Notice that the footnotes provide additional information.

2. The far right column provides comparative data; what information is being compared?

3. What general conclusions might the statistics in the table lead you to make about the family in Québec? Work with a partner to make a list.

Couples selon la présence d'enfants, dans les ménages privés, chiffres de 2001, pour le Québec		
Structure de la famille :		**Variation 1996–2001 :**
Nombre total de couples	1 683 965	2,6 %
Couples mariés avec enfants[1]	594 990	−14,3 %
Couples mariés sans enfants[2]	580 445	6,3 %
Couples en union libre avec enfants[1, 3]	258 470	25,1 %
Couples en union libre sans enfants[2, 3]	250 050	29,2 %

[1] un couple avec au moins un enfant âgé de moins de 25 ans.

[2] un couple et enfants âgés de 25 ans et plus.

[3] En 2001, la catégorie comprend les couples en union libre formés de partenaires de sexe opposé ou de partenaires de même sexe.

Source: Recensement de la population de 2001

En lisant. You may wish to read the text aloud, asking students to circle the statistics. Do not ask students to read the text aloud, as it contains many unfamiliar words. Afterwards, review the statistics and have students explain their significance. Then address question #3, following up on the initial task and seeing whether students were able to draw correct conclusions.

B. En lisant. The essential information in this text, as in the preceding table, is statistical.

1. As you read, circle each statistic and focus on discovering its significance.

2. Which statistics are related to those in the preceding table?

3. Which of your preliminary conclusions based on analysis of the table can you now confirm?

Québec : le nombre d'unions libres continue de monter

Au Québec, un grand nombre de couples vivent[1] ensemble sans être mariés, selon le Recensement de 2001. De 1996 à 2001, le nombre d'unions libres a augmenté de 25 % au Québec pour atteindre[2] 508 520.

Les couples mariés représentent seulement[3] 58 % des familles comptées en 2001. C'est une baisse considérable par rapport à[4] la proportion de 64 % enregistrée[5] en 1996. Parallèlement, la proportion de couples vivant en union libre a augmenté, passant de 21 % à 25 %.

En 2001, seulement 3 familles sur 10 (29 %) au Québec sont des couples mariés avec des enfants de 24 ans et moins à la maison.

Le Recensement de 2001 est le premier à fournir[6] des données[7] sur les couples de même[8] sexe. Un total de 10 360 couples se sont identifiés comme étant[9] des couples de même sexe vivant en union libre, soit 30 % du total national de 34 200.

Adapté du Site Internet de Statistique Canada

[1]*habitent* [2]*reach* [3]*only* [4]*in comparison with* [5]*recorded* [6]*donner* [7]*facts* [8]*same* [9]*as being*

C. En regardant de plus près. Find the French words in the text corresponding to the following words and expressions in English:

1. according to the Census
2. to increase
3. a decline
4. living together without being married

D. Après avoir lu. Think about and then discuss the following questions with classmates.

1. What seems to be the primary trend in Quebec family life, as indicated by the statistics given in the text and illustrated by the related table? Based on what you have learned about current family life in France, is this trend similar to or different from what is happening in France? In what ways?
2. Are the trends similar in your own community? Explain your answer.

1-40 C'est ma famille

A. Avant d'écouter. You will see three short interviews in which people describe their family. Watch the video clip without sound. Try to determine which members of the family are being described by each speaker, and write down the relationships in French.

	without sound	with sound
Speaker(s)	relatives inferred	relatives described
Pauline :	*deux frères*	
Bruno, Diane et Claire :		
Marie-Julie :		

B. En regardant. Now listen and see if your list is correct and complete. Can you add to the list of family relationships based on what you hear?

C. Après avoir regardé. How are these francophone families similar to, or different from, American families? Can you draw at least a partial family tree for each speaker? What information is still missing? Work with a partner to draw the trees as completely as possible. What additional questions might you ask each speaker?

En regardant de plus près, Key:
1) *selon le Recensement* ; 2) *monter, augmenter* ; 3) *une baisse* ; 4) *vivant en union libre*

   Students may ask about the difference in meaning between *habiter* and *vivre. Habiter* generally is used to refer to physical location *(J'habite Paris, j'habite un appartement)*, while *vivre* refers more to personal and quality-of-life considerations *(Je vis avec mes parents, nous vivons en union libre).*

Observons This exercise treats the first three interviews in the clip. Additional interviews are treated in the Video Manual. You might ask students to complete those activities on their own.
Script for *Observons*

PAULINE: Toute ma famille habite à Paris. Euh, c'est-à-dire, euh, mes parents, mes frères, mes grands-parents, mes oncles, mes tantes, absolument tout le monde. Euh j'ai donc, euh, j'ai deux frères qui s'appellent Maxime et Clément. Ils sont plus jeunes que moi. Euh, moi, je suis née en 1976. J'ai vingt-sept ans donc, et mes frères, euh, ont vingt et un ans et vingt-trois ans.

BRUNO: Bonjour, je m'appelle Bruno. J'ai sept ans. Voici mes deux sœurs, Claire et Diane.

DIANE: Bonjour, je m'appelle Diane. J'ai onze ans et demi. Voici ma grande sœur et mon petit frère.

CLAIRE: Tandis que moi, je m'appelle Claire. J'ai treize ans et j'ai un petit frère et une petite sœur qui s'appellent Diane et Bruno. Donc je suis la plus grande de toute la famille. Voilà.

MARIE-JULIE: Je vous présente ma fille, Laura. Laura est québécoise, française et elle est née américaine. Et voici mon mari, Patrick. Il est français d'origine, à moitié breton, à moitié du Midi.

La famille en Afrique francophone

Families in Francophone Africa tend to be larger than European and North American families and to place more emphasis on the extended family and the obligation to help out family members. It is not uncommon for Africans studying and working in France to send money home to their families or to bring back books, school supplies, clothing, and household gifts when they return home for a visit. In many African societies, elderly people are greatly respected and they often live with their children and their families. Pensions and social security payments may be quite small or nonexistent, and older people rely on their children to provide for them.

Parlons

1-41 Des familles bien diverses

A. Avant de parler. Choose a photo from those shown here or in another part of this **Venez chez nous** lesson. You will describe this family to a partner, who will then have to decide which family you have chosen. Before you begin, make a list of the people you see in the picture, using words you have learned in this chapter (**la mère, la sœur** …). Next, decide how old each person might be and jot down a few adjectives to describe each person. You may also be able to say where they are or what they are doing (**Ils déjeunent ; Ils sont dans le jardin**).

B. En parlant. Now take turns describing the family in your photo and letting your partner guess which one you are talking about. Can either of you follow up by making suggestions to amplify your partner's description or otherwise to modify it? Conclude by presenting your description to the class as a whole while your partner points to each person you mention.

Écrivons

1-42 Une famille louisianaise

A. Avant d'écrire. Many North American families have roots in other parts of the world. Read this description of the origins of a Louisiana family. Amélie Ledet describes her great-great-great grandparents.

> Mon nom, c'est Amélie Ledet. J'ai 22 ans et j'habite à Montagut dans la paroisse Lafourche. Mon arrière-arrière-arrière-grand-père du côté de mon père s'appelle Jules Desormeaux. Il est né° à Grand Pré, en Acadie, en 1745 et il est décédé en 1806. Sa femme s'appelle Marie Landry. Mon arrière-arrière-arrière-grand-mère est née à Port-Royal, Acadie, en 1751 et elle est décédée en 1810. Du côté de ma mère, mon arrière-arrière-arrière-grand-père s'appelle Pierre Arceneaux. Il est né près de La Rochelle, en France, en 1772. Il est décédé en Acadie en 1840. Sa femme, Louise La Branche (Zweig), est née au Lac des Allemands, en Louisiane, en 1780. Elle est décédée en 1845.

was born

Based on her description, sketch the part of Amélie's family tree that she describes.

B. En écrivant. Now sketch your own family tree. Underneath, include a paragraph explaining where your (great-) grandparents are from. You may use Amélie's description as a model.

C. Après avoir écrit. Share your paragraph with your classmates to get a sense of the diversity within your own class.

Vocabulaire

Leçon 1

les relations familiales	family relations
un beau-père	stepfather, father-in-law
une belle-mère	stepmother, mother-in-law
un/e cousin/e	cousin
un enfant	child
une famille nombreuse	big family
une femme	wife, woman
une fille	daughter, girl
un fils	son
un frère	brother
un garçon	boy
une grand-mère	grandmother
un grand-père	grandfather
des grands-parents (m.)	grandparents
un mari	husband
une mère	mother
un neveu, des neveux	nephew, (nieces & nephews)
une nièce	niece
un oncle	uncle
des parents (m.)	parents, relatives
un père	father
une petite-fille, des petites-filles	granddaughter, granddaughters
un petit-fils, des petits-fils	grandson, grandsons
des petits-enfants (m.)	grandchildren
une sœur	sister
une tante	aunt

l'état civil	marital status
célibataire	single
décédé/e	deceased
divorcé/e	divorced
fiancé/e	engaged
marié/e	married
remarié/e	remarried

des animaux familiers	pets
un animal familier	pet
un chat	cat
un chien	dog
un oiseau	bird

le caractère	disposition, nature, character
calme	calm
conformiste	conformist
désagréable	disagreable
discipliné/e	disciplined
dynamique	dynamic
idéaliste	idealistic
indiscipliné/e	undisciplined
individualiste	individualistic
optimiste	optimistic
pessimiste	pessimistic
raisonnable	reasonable
réaliste	realistic
réservé/e	reserved
sociable	outgoing
stressé/e	stressed out
sympa(thique)	nice
têtu/e	stubborn
timide	shy

pour exprimer l'intensité	to express intensity
assez	rather
beaucoup	a lot
un peu	a little
très	very
trop	too much
vraiment	really

quelques mots divers	various words
chez	at the home of
chez nous	at our place
deuxième	second
un homme	man
mais	but
premier	first

Leçon 2

les mois (m.) de l'année (f.) — *the months of the year*

janvier	*January*
février	*February*
mars	*March*
avril	*April*
mai	*May*
juin	*June*
juillet	*July*
août	*August*
septembre	*September*
octobre	*October*
novembre	*November*
décembre	*December*
Quelle est la date	*What is the date*
… de ton anniversaire	*. . . of your birthday?*
(m.) ?	
C'est le premier mai.	*It's May 1.*
C'est le 4 septembre.	*It's September 4.*

l'âge (m.) — *age*

un an	*one year*
avoir	*to have*
Quel est ton/votre âge ?	*What is your age?*
Quel âge as-tu ?/	*How old are you?*
Quel âge avez-vous ?	
J'ai 39 ans.	*I am 39 years old.*

les nombres de 0 à 99
(see p. 45 for 0 to 31 and p. 49 for 40 to 99)

Leçon 3

pour dire quand — *to say when*

lundi	*Monday*
mardi	*Tuesday*
mercredi	*Wednesday*
jeudi	*Thursday*
vendredi	*Friday*
samedi	*Saturday*
dimanche	*Sunday*
aujourd'hui	*today*
la semaine	*week*
le week-end	*weekend*

le jour	*day*
le matin	*morning*
l'après-midi (m.)	*afternoon*
le soir	*evening*
maintenant	*now*

les activités — *activities*

aimer	*to like, to love*
arriver	*to arrive*
déjeuner	*to have breakfast/lunch*
dîner	*to have dinner*
écouter de la musique/	*to listen to music/*
la radio	*the radio*
habiter	*to live*
inviter	*to invite*
jouer au foot/du piano	*to play soccer/the piano*
ne … pas	*not (I'm not playing/*
(Je ne joue pas.)	*I don't play.)*
parler au téléphone	*to talk on the phone*
préparer le dîner	*to fix dinner*
regarder un film/	*to watch a movie/TV/*
la télé/ des photos	*look at photos*
rester à la maison	*to stay home*
réviser la leçon	*to review the lesson*
téléphoner à quelqu'un	*to call somebody*
travailler dans le jardin	*to work in the garden/yard*

quelques lieux — *some places*

au bureau	*at the office*
à l'école	*at school*
à la maison	*at home*

la musique — *music*

la musique classique	*classical music*
une guitare	*a guitar*

quelques sports — *some sports*

le foot(ball)	*soccer*
le golf	*golf*
le tennis	*tennis*

autres mots utiles — *other useful words*

avec	*with*
ensemble	*together*
une leçon de chant	*singing lesson*
si	*yes (after a negative question)*
typique	*typical*

Who are the people shown here, and what are they doing? Does this remind you of experiences you've had with people you know?

Chapitre 2 *Voici mes amis*

Leçon 1 *Mes amis et moi*

Leçon 2 *Nos loisirs*

Leçon 3 *Où est-ce qu'on va ce week-end ?*

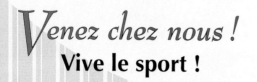
Venez chez nous !
 Vive le sport !

In this chapter:

- Describing appearance and personality
- Talking about leisure activities
- Asking for information
- Specifying dates and distances
- Understanding the notions of friendship and leisure across the French-speaking world

Leçon 1   *Mes amis et moi*

Provide an overview of the lesson by showing the Ch. 2 video segment *Les amis*. Have students listen and watch, then describe the activities friends are sharing. This video clip may also be shown in conjunction with the **Vie et culture** section.

POINTS DE DÉPART

Elles sont comment ?

Denise et Marie regardent un album de photos.

DENISE : C'est toi sur la photo là, avec le chapeau ?

MARIE : Bien sûr !

DENISE : Tu es jolie ! Qui sont les autres filles ?

MARIE : Ce sont mes amies du collège.

DENISE : Comment s'appelle l'autre fille avec un chapeau ?

MARIE : Ça c'est Diane ; elle est maintenant à la fac avec moi. C'est ma colocataire. Elle est très intelligente et ambitieuse. Mais elle est amusante aussi ; elle adore les histoires drôles.

DENISE : Et la grande fille mince et rousse ?

MARIE : C'est Clara. Elle est très élégante. Elle travaille dans une clinique ; c'est une fille gentille et généreuse.

DENISE : Et la blonde ?

MARIE : C'est Anne-Laure. Elle est super sportive et sociable ; pas du tout paresseuse, elle !

DENISE : Pas comme toi, donc !

MARIE : Arrête !

Additional practice activities for each **Points de départ** section are provided by:
- Student Activities Manual
- *Chez nous* Companion Website: **http://www.prenhall.com/cheznous**

Only feminine forms of variable adjectives are presented here, since in most cases the masculine spoken form can be easily derived from the feminine. This derivation rule will be taught in the **Formes et fonctions** section of this lesson. To present this vocabulary, use the girls' photo and the dialogue , as well as the boxed list of adjectives. Read or play the recorded dialogue, pointing out each person as she is described. Point out that *le collège* corresponds roughly to middle school, *la fac(ulté)* is the university. Test comprehension by asking *Qui est blonde ?*, etc., or by creating statements that students must identify as true or false. Next have students repeat key words, and then finally give their opposite. As follow-up, you may want to have students describe magazine photos of interesting-looking women.

POUR DÉCRIRE LES FEMMES

jeune	d'un certain âge	âgée	
belle	jolie	moche	
grande	de taille moyenne	petite	
mince	forte	grosse	
blonde	rousse	châtain	brune
élégante			
gentille		méchante	
généreuse		égoïste	
intelligente		bête	
ambitieuse	énergique	paresseuse	
sportive		pantouflarde	
sérieuse	drôle	amusante	

À vous la parole

2-1 En d'autres termes. Describe each young woman, using other words.

MODÈLE   Clara n'est pas égoïste.
➤ Clara est généreuse.

1. Clara n'est ni (*neither*) brune, ni rousse, ni châtain.
2. Clara n'est pas petite.
3. Clara n'est pas méchante.
4. Diane n'est pas très mince.
5. Diane n'est pas petite.
6. Diane n'est ni blonde, ni rousse, ni châtain.
7. Diane n'est pas bête.
8. Anne-Laure n'est pas paresseuse.
9. Anne-Laure n'est pas grande, mais elle n'est pas petite non plus.
10. Anne-Laure n'est pas très réservée.

2-2 Une personne connue. Describe a well-known girl or woman, real or imaginary, and have your classmates guess who it is.

MODÈLE   É1   Elle est très jeune ; elle a environ (*about*) douze ans. Elle est petite, mince et rousse. Elle n'a pas de parents, mais elle a un chien, Sandy.

É2   C'est Annie, la petite orpheline.

2-3 Voici une amie/mes amies. Bring in a photo of a female friend or friends to describe to a partner.

MODÈLE   ➤ Voici la photo d'une de mes amies. Elle s'appelle Julie. Elle est grande et blonde. Elle est intelligente et très énergique. Elle aime le tennis.

Vie et culture

Mon ami

While the term **un/e ami/e** means *a friend*, if you introduce someone as **mon ami/e** you are implicitly indicating that the person is your boyfriend/girlfriend. Another way to refer to a boyfriend/girlfriend is with the terms **mon petit ami/ma petite amie**, or **mon copain/ma copine**. If you want to introduce someone who is a friend, but not a boyfriend/girlfriend, you would say, for example, **Voici un de mes amis**, or **Voici une copine**.

Les amis

The nature of friendship varies from culture to culture. In France, friendships are often formed slowly, over years, but once established, they last a lifetime. American visitors and exchange students in France sometimes find it difficult to form friendships with French peers because of the brevity of their stays. French exchange students and visitors to the U.S., on the other hand, often report that Americans make friends very quickly and that they have many friends, but that these friendships seem superficial by French standards. Raymonde Carroll, a French anthropologist living in the United States, points out that the French use the word **ami** only for those people with whom a strong bond of friendship has been established. Americans, in contrast, use the term *friend* more loosely, in place of *acquaintance, classmate*, and even *co-worker*, as well as for close friends.

Et vous ?

1. What behaviors or features of American society might promote the perception among the French that friendships are formed quickly?
2. Would you generally characterize American friendships as "superficial?" Do you think that some deeper, lifetime friendships are also formed in the U.S., as in France? Explain your response.
3. Do you agree with Carroll's observation that Americans use the word *friend* rather loosely? What advantages and disadvantages are there to using *friend* to refer to a wide range of relationships?

Vie et culture If you have not yet shown it, use the Ch. 2 video segment *Les amis* to lead into this section or to follow up on discussion. As a follow-up, you might have students watch the clip and decide in each case whether use of *un/e ami/e* or *mon ami/e* would be more likely.

For more information, see Raymonde Carroll's chapter on friendship in her book *Évidences invisibles : Américains et Français au quotidien* (Éditions du Seuil, 1987); translated by Carol Volk as *Cultural Misunderstandings: The French-American Experience* (The University of Chicago Press, 1990).

Point out the tendency for Americans to use first names immediately on meeting someone, to invite people into their homes very soon after they have met, and even to hug or kiss business associates. Suggest to students that because Americans tend to change jobs and move frequently, often far from family and childhood friends, there is perhaps more of a necessity to form new friendships quickly.

Additional practice activities for each **Sons et lettres** section are provided by:
- Student Activities Manual
- Text Audio

Sons et lettres

La détente des consonnes finales

As a general rule, final consonant letters are not pronounced in French:

l'enfant   elle est   nous sommes   très jeunes   beaucoup

However, there are four final consonant letters that are generally pronounced: **-c**, **-r**, **-f**, and **-l**. To remember them, think of the English word *careful*.

la fac   pour   neuf   Daniel

An exception is the letter **-r** in the infinitive ending **-er** and in words ending in **-er** and **-ier**:

écouter   danser   le dîner   le premier   janvier

The letter **n** is seldom pronounced at the end of a word. Together with the preceding vowel letters it represents a nasal vowel sound:

mon copain   le chien   l'enfant

At the end of a word, one or more consonant letters followed by **-e** always stand for a pronounced consonant. These consonants must be clearly articulated, for they mark important grammatical distinctions such as feminine versus masculine forms of adjectives. The final **-e** doesn't represent any sound.

	Danielle est	intelligente	amusante	sérieuse
vs.	Daniel est	intelligent	amusant	sérieux

À vous la parole

2-4 Prononcer ou ne pas prononcer ? In which words should you pronounce the final consonant?

avec Robert	il aime danser	s'il vous plaît	pour ma sœur
neuf cahiers	le jour de Noël	le Québec	le singulier

2-5 Contrastes. Read each pair of sentences aloud and note the contrasts.

C'est Denise. / C'est Denis.

Voilà Françoise. / Voilà François.

Pascale est amusante. / Pascal est amusant.

Michèle est blonde. / Michel est blond.

FORMES ET FONCTIONS

1. Les adjectifs variables

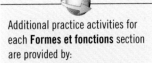

Additional practice activities for each **Formes et fonctions** section are provided by:
- Student Activities Manual
- *Chez nous* Companion Website:
  http://www.prenhall.com/cheznous

• You have learned that adjectives agree in gender and number with the noun they modify. *Invariable* adjectives have only one spoken form. The feminine ending **-e** and the plural ending **-s** show up only in the written forms.

Ma soeur est têtu**e**.   Mes amies sont têtu**es**.

Mon frère est têtu.   Mes amis sont têtu**s**.

Mon père est calme.   Mes parents sont calme**s**.

• *Variable* adjectives have masculine and feminine forms that differ in pronunciation. Their feminine form ends in a pronounced consonant. To pronounce the masculine, drop the final consonant sound. The written letter **-s** or **-x** at the end of plural adjectives is not generally pronounced.

singulier	*f.*	Claire est	amusan**te**	et	généreu**se**.
	m.	Jacques est	amusan**t**	et	généreu**x**.
pluriel	*f.*	Mes amies sont	amusan**tes**	et	généreu**ses**.
	m.	Mes copains sont	amusan**ts**	et	généreu**x**.

The feminine form of variable adjectives always ends in **-e**. The final **-e** is dropped in the masculine form; therefore, the final consonant sound, heard in the feminine form, is also dropped. Although some variable adjectives have spelling irregularities, this pronunciation rule still applies. For example, in the feminine form **généreuse** [ʒenerøz], the final consonant is pronounced, but it is dropped in the masculine form **généreux** [ʒenerø]. In the written form, the final **-e** is dropped in the masculine and the final **-s** is changed to **-x**. Such adjectives are fully regular in pronunciation but show an irregularity in the spelling. Other regular variable adjectives that show spelling changes include:

rou**sse** → rou**x**   gro**sse** → gro**s**   genti**lle** → genti**l**

• Adjectives whose masculine singular form ends in **-x** do not change in the masculine plural form.

Laurent est rou**x**.   Laurent et Matthieu sont rou**x**.

• As you have learned, with a mixed group of feminine and masculine nouns, the plural form of the adjective is always the masculine form.

Jessica et Laure sont **brunes**.   *Jessica and Laure are brunettes.*

Kevin et Benoît sont **blonds**.   *Kevin and Benoît are blonds.*

Max et Sylvie sont **roux**.   *Max and Sylvie are redheads.*

What we call *invariable* adjectives have a single spoken form, but some have distinct written masculine and feminine forms as well as distinct plural written forms. This presentation focuses on spoken forms and is reinforced by the **Sons et lettres** treatment. Workbook exercises provide students with written practice using both invariable and variable adjectives. To present, show examples of 1) invariable and 2) variable adjectives, and have students explain the written forms; then see whether students can give the rule for deriving the masculine spoken form from the feminine.

Point out that the irregularities involve changes in the final written consonant: -ss → -x; -ll → -l; etc.

Point out that *belle* and *brune* involve vowel changes (i.e., from [ɛ] to [o] for *belle-beau* and from [y] to [Ẽ] for *brune-brun*) as well as the loss of the final consonant; *sportive* shows a final consonant change from [v] to [f].

Point out that several frequently used adjectives precede the noun. These include *belle, grande, jeune, jolie,* and *petite,* all of which were presented in the **Points de départ**. A full treatment of the prenominal adjectives is found in Ch. 3, L. 1 and L. 2.

Begin with a discrimination drill, as in the **Sons et lettres**, so that students hear both masculine and feminine forms of adjectives: *Michel est amusant. Michèle est intelligente,* etc. Continue with a simple substitution exercise, such as the following: *Des jumeaux*. Pierre and Christelle are twins. Tell how they are alike: *Christelle est grande ; — Et Pierre est grand aussi ; elle est rousse ; elle est un peu forte ; elle est assez amusante ; elle est très intelligente ; elle est assez grande ; elle est vraiment gentille ; elle est très élégante ; elle est généreuse.*

Next reverse the direction of derivation by providing the masculine form and having students respond with the feminine. Stress the importance of overarticulating the final consonant since it contains the signal for the gender: *Pierre est très élégant. — Sa sœur est très élégante aussi.*

2-6 This reinforces the fact that adjectives used with *être* do not have a separate spoken plural form.

2-7 You may also bring large photos, such as those found in catalogs or magazines, into class. Put students into pairs to work out their description, then bring all the photos to the front of the class. As each pair describes their person, the other students try to guess to which photo the description corresponds.

● Note the following irregular forms:

féminin	masculin
belle	beau
brune	brun
sportive	sportif

À vous la parole

2-6 Pas mes amis ! Your friends are quite different from what your mother thinks; tell how.

MODÈLE Tes amies sont paresseuses !
➤ Ah non, elles sont énergiques.

1. Tes amis sont méchants !
2. Tes amis sont trop idéalistes !
3. Tes amies sont têtues !
4. Tes amis sont trop petits !
5. Tes amis sont trop bêtes !
6. Tes amis sont égoïstes !
7. Tes amies sont trop sérieuses !
8. Tes amis sont tous (*all*) pessimistes !

2-7 Les amis. Describe the friends in this photo.

MODÈLE ➤ Le garçon ici (*here*) est assez grand et brun.

2-8 Le monde idéal. Describe ideal people and pets, following the suggestions below. Compare in each case your ideal with that of a classmate, then with the class as a whole.

MODÈLE   le chien idéal

> É1   Pour moi, le chien idéal est petit, gentil et intelligent.
>
> É2   Pour moi aussi, le chien idéal est gentil et intelligent, mais il est grand.

1. la mère idéale
2. l'enfant idéal
3. le/la colocataire idéal/e
4. le professeur idéal
5. l'étudiant idéal
6. l'ami/e idéal/e
7. le/la partenaire idéal/e
8. le chat idéal

2. *Les adverbes interrogatifs*

Review formation of yes/no questions and the use of *si*, taught in Ch. 1, L. 3, before teaching this material; use exercises from those earlier sections. Present the new expressions using question and answer examples similar to those given here.

Remind students that they have learned to form some information questions using simply a question word without *est-ce que* or intonation: *Comment tu t'appelles ? Il a quel âge ?*, but that these are very informal ways of asking a question.

Questions using *quel* will be treated in Ch. 5, L. 2; *qui, que,* and *quoi* will be treated in Ch. 5, L. 3.

- To ask a question requesting specific information, it is necessary to use some type of interrogative word or expression. The interrogative word or expression usually comes at the beginning of the question and is usually followed by **est-ce que/qu'**:

Où est-ce que tes amis travaillent ?	*Where do your friends work?*
Quand est-ce que sa copine arrive ?	*When does his girlfriend arrive?*

Some of the words or expressions frequently used to ask questions are:

comment	*how*	**Comment est-ce que** tu t'appelles ?
où	*where*	**Où est-ce qu'** il travaille ?
quand	*when*	**Quand est-ce que** tu arrives ?
pourquoi	*why*	**Pourquoi est-ce que** tu ne travailles pas ?
combien de	*how many*	**Combien d'**étudiants **est-ce qu'**il y a ?

The question **pourquoi ?** can be answered in two ways:

—**Pourquoi est-ce que** tu aimes tes amis ?	—*Why do you like your friends?*
—**Parce qu'**ils sont très amusants.	—*Because they're lots of fun.*
—**Pourquoi est-ce que** tu téléphones ?	—*Why are you calling?*
—**Pour** inviter mes amis à dîner.	—*To invite my friends to dinner.*

When used to ask *how many*, **combien** is linked to the noun by **de/d'**:

Combien de frères est-ce que tu as ?	*How many brothers do you have?*
Combien d'enfants est-ce qu'ils ont ?	*How many children do they have?*

- Another question construction, called *inversion*, is used in writing, in formal conversation, and in a few fixed expressions. In questions with a pronoun subject using *inversion*, the subject follows the verb and is connected to it with a hyphen.

Notice that when the verb form ends in a vowel, the letter **-t-** is inserted before the pronoun and linked to it with a hyphen.

Comment **vas-tu** ?	*How are you?*
Comment **allez-vous** ?	*How are you?*
Quel âge **a-t-il** ?	*How old is he?*

Inversion is also more generally used with the verbs **aller** and **être** when the subject is a noun:

The verb *aller* is presented in L. 3 of this chapter.

Comment **vont tes parents** ?	*How are your parents?*
Où **est ta sœur** ?	*Where's your sister?*

À vous la parole

2-9 For further practice, repeat this exercise and have students provide the complete questions.

2-9 Pardon ? You can't quite hear all that your instructor says, so use a question word or expression to ask for the missing information.

MODÈLE   J'ai <u>cinq</u> cahiers.
  ➤ Combien ?

1. Nous travaillons <u>dans la salle de classe</u>.
2. Il y a un examen <u>mardi</u>.
3. Il y a <u>trois</u> étudiants français.
4. Jacques est absent <u>parce qu'il est malade</u>.
5. Elle s'appelle <u>Chloé</u>.
6. Elle a <u>deux</u> sœurs.
7. Nous ouvrons le livre <u>pour réviser un exercice</u>.

2-10 À propos de Thomas. Your friend is telling you about her new boyfriend Thomas and you want more details.

MODÈLE   Thomas a deux colocataires.
  ➤ Ah bon ? Comment est-ce qu'ils s'appellent ?
OU ➤ Ah bon ? Est-ce qu'ils sont aussi étudiants ?

1. Il est assez jeune.
2. Il n'habite pas dans la résidence (*dorm*).
3. Il est d'une famille nombreuse.
4. Il travaille le week-end.
5. Il arrive bientôt.
6. Il n'est pas en forme.
7. Il n'aime pas le sport.
8. Il a des chiens.

2-11 This is good preparation for playing the game called *Jeopardy!*, in which students earn points by providing the question that elicits the information given.

2-11 Au service des rencontres. Sandrine has called a dating service. As you listen in on her end of the phone conversation, imagine the questions she is being asked.

MODÈLE   Je m'appelle Sandrine Trembley.
  ➤ Comment vous appelez-vous, mademoiselle ?

1. J'ai vingt-deux ans.
2. Mon anniversaire, c'est le 20 janvier.
3. J'habite à Ottawa.
4. Oui, j'ai un chien.
5. Je travaille le samedi et le dimanche seulement (*only*).
6. Parce que je suis étudiante.
7. J'ai des cours (*classes*) le lundi, le mercredi et le vendredi.
8. Je travaille dans un bureau.

2-12 Questions indiscrètes ? Interview one of your classmates, asking him/her questions about the following subjects. Report back to the class what you learned about your partner.

MODÈLES la famille
➤ Est-ce que tu as des frères ou des sœurs ?
➤ Où est-ce qu'ils habitent ?…

la musique
➤ Est-ce que tu aimes la musique ?
➤ Quand est-ce que tu aimes écouter de la musique ?…

(*you report back*) Voici Ian. Il a un frère. Il habite à Baltimore. Ian n'aime pas la musique mais…

1. la famille
2. les animaux
3. les amis
4. la musique
5. le sport

2-12 You might offer to let students ask you any questions they wish, or bring in a visitor to be interviewed.

Lisons. If your students are not familiar with *Les Misérables*, there are many online resources for both the show and the novel. To prepare for the reading (and the **Après avoir lu**), you could have students look for the synopsis and some details about the main characters on the Web. See the *Chez nous* Companion Website for links. You may also wish to show a short excerpt from one of the many films made of *Les Misérables*. In particular, before completing **Avant de lire**, you might show the scene where Valjean arrives at the Bishop's house; ask students to describe the characters they see.

Avant de lire. You might have students work alone or in pairs. When everyone has come up with adjectives, lists could be compared in groups or though a whole-class discussion. Check to see whether some students are familiar with the story and know how these characters fit into the plot.

2-13 Les Misérables

A. Avant de lire. You are about to read an excerpt from the opening paragraphs of the novel ***Les Misérables*** by Victor Hugo, a well-known nineteenth-century French novelist, playwright, and poet. ***Les Misérables*** has been translated into many languages and has been a major musical for many years.

Three minor characters are introduced in the beginning of the novel, the Bishop of Digne and the two women in his household. Look at the illustrations of these three characters made by Georges Jeanniot for the first edition of ***Les Misérables***. Then make lists of adjectives you know in French that could be used to describe each person. Using the illustrations to make preliminary assumptions about these characters can help you to follow the author's descriptions, even if you cannot understand every word.

$\mathcal{S}tratégie$

Use illustrations to predict content. To anticipate and better understand an author's descriptions in the text, make preliminary assumptions by studying the illustrations.

Additional activities to develop the four skills are provided by:
• Student Activities Manual
• Text Audio
• *Chez nous* video
• *Chez nous* Companion Website:
  http://www.prenhall.com/cheznous

L'évêque

Mme Magloire, Mlle Baptistine, Jean Valjean et l'évêque

B. En lisant. As you read the descriptions of the Bishop, Mlle Baptistine, and Mme Magloire, focus on getting a general sense of the passage. You will note that the author incorporates a number of adjectives into his description of the two women and gives an indication of each person's age. Then look for the answers to the following specific questions:

1. How old is the Bishop, M. Myriel?
2. Knowing that **moins** means *less*, indicate how old his sister is.
3. What is the name of the Bishop's sister?
4. What is the name of their household servant?
5. Give two adjectives in English to describe each woman.

En 1815, M. Charles-Francois-Bienvenu Myriel était[1] évêque de Digne. C'était un vieillard[2] d'environ soixante-quinze ans…

M. Myriel était arrivé[3] à Digne accompagné d'une vieille fille[4], Mlle Baptistine, qui était sa sœur et qui avait[5] dix ans de moins que lui.

Ils avaient[6] pour tout domestique une servante appelée Mme Magloire.   5

Mlle Baptistine était une personne longue, pâle, mince, douce[7]. Elle n'avait jamais[8] été jolie…

Mme Magloire était une petite vieille, blanche, grasse, replète[9], affairée, toujours haletante, à cause de son activité d'abord, ensuite à cause   10
d'un asthme.

[1]*past tense of the verb* être   [2]*une personne âgée*   [3]*had arrived*   [4]*une femme d'un certain âge qui est célibataire*   [5]*past tense of the verb* avoir, sg.   [6]*past tense of the verb* avoir, pl.   [7]*gentle*   [8]*never*   [9]*grosse*

C. En regardant de plus près. Take a closer look at the following features of the text.

1. There are two words in the text that are synonyms and mean "household worker." What are they?
2. Look at the adjective **affairée**. This is an adjective used to describe a very busy person. Do you know any other adjectives in French that could be used to indicate the same idea?
3. Mme Magloire is described as **haletante**. The rest of the sentence explains why she is described in this way. Given this context, and the illustration of Mme Magloire, what do you think the adjective **haletante** means?

D. Après avoir lu. How successful are the author's brief descriptions in painting a portrait of each of the three characters? Look back at the lists of adjectives you drew up in preparation for reading. How closely do your predictions coincide with what you read? Is there anything you would change in the drawings, based on the descriptions in the text?

Leçon 2 *Nos loisirs*

POINTS DE DÉPART

Nos activités

TEXT AUDIO

Present this vocabulary by showing and describing the leisure activites (IRCD, Ch. 2). Test comprehension by showing the unlabeled images (IRCD, Ch. 2) and having students point to or mime the activity named. Have students repeat the new vocabulary, including the expressions in the boxed list. Then use visuals or miming (by the teacher or students) to get the class to identify activities. Use a quick substitution drill to review the forms of *-er* verbs like *jouer: Je joue au foot ; nous. — Nous jouons au foot,* etc.

Moi, je fais du sport ; je joue au foot avec des amis. Nous faisons un match tous les samedis.

Mes copains font de la musique. Ils jouent dans un groupe. Ils donnent un concert samedi soir. Mamadou joue de la guitare et Valentin joue du piano.

François et Léa organisent une fête. François fait les courses et Léa fait la cuisine.

Ma copine Amélie ne fait pas grand-chose ; elle reste à la résidence et elle regarde un film. Ses amies Vanessa et Anne-Laure jouent aux échecs.

Nathalie est super sportive ; elle fait de la natation. Elle fait du vélo aussi.

Benjamin fait du bricolage et son amie Élodie fait du jardinage.

Students have already seen the verb *faire* in expressions such as *Qu'est-ce qu'il fait ?* and *Deux et deux, ça fait quatre.* Limit use here to the singular forms, *fais/fait*; the complete paradigm for *faire* is treated in the **Formes et fonctions** for this lesson.

The forms *le football*, *le basket-ball*, and *le volley-ball* are often abbreviated to *le foot*, *le basket*, and *le volley*. This is frequent in spoken French, particularly among students.

DES LOISIRS

On fait…
    du sport
    de la natation, du vélo,
    du jogging

On joue…
    au football, au basket-ball, au tennis, au golf,
    au football américain, au rugby, au volley-ball,
    au hockey

On fait…
    de la musique

On joue…
    du piano, de la guitare, de l'harmonica,
    du saxophone, de la batterie
    de la musique classique, du jazz, du rock

On fait…
    des courses, la cuisine,
    du bricolage, du jardinage

On joue…
    aux cartes, aux échecs, au Scrabble, au loto,
    aux jeux de société

À vous la parole

2-14 You may wish to show the visual cues for this exercise (IRCD, Ch. 2).

2-14 On joue ? Based on the drawings, what is everyone doing this afternoon?

MODÈLE ➤ On joue au tennis.

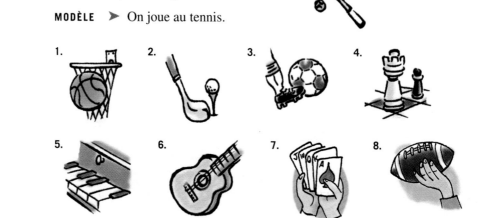

1.   2.   3.   4.

5.   6.   7.   8.

2-15 Chacun à ses goûts. Based on the descriptions, figure out with a partner what these friends probably do in their spare time.

MODÈLE   É1   Marie-Anne est très réservée.

           É2   Elle ne fait pas grand-chose ; elle reste à la maison et regarde un film.

1. Charlotte est très sociable.
2. Loïc est super sportif.
3. Delphine est une bonne musicienne.
4. Florian adore le cinéma.
5. Laurent est fanatique de jazz.
6. Céline aime préparer le dîner.
7. Alex préfère les jeux de société.
8. Rachid est très actif.
9. Anaïs est bricoleuse.

Vie et culture

Information adapted from *Francoscopie* by Gérard Mermet, based on a 1997 survey (Paris: Larousse, 2003).

Les loisirs des Français

The French devote one-third of their waking hours to leisure activities, about six hours per day on average. They now enjoy the shortest workweek of any European country, 35 hours, and have five weeks of paid vacation each year. Typically, about a quarter of the total household budget is used for leisure activities.

The chart indicates the percentage of French people over fifteen years old who participated in various leisure-time activities during a year's time. Examine the chart with a partner: How many activities can you identify? How do these activities compare with your own leisure activities and those of people you know? How do you think a chart drawn up for North Americans would differ from this one?

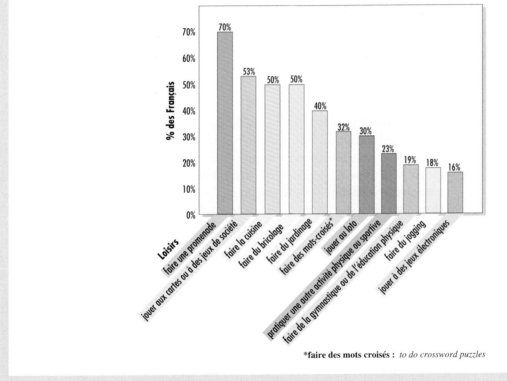

Une année de loisirs

% des Français

70% — faire une promenade
53% — jouer aux cartes ou à des jeux de société
50% — faire la cuisine
50% — faire du bricolage
40% — faire du jardinage
32% — faire des mots croisés*
30% — jouer au loto
23% — pratiquer une autre activité physique ou sportive
19% — faire de la gymnastique ou de l'éducation physique
18% — faire du jogging
16% — jouer à des jeux électroniques

Loisirs

*faire des mots croisés : *to do crossword puzzles*

2-16 Et toi ? With the person sitting beside you, take turns telling three things you typically do on the weekend. Use only words and expressions that you know. Then share with your classmates what you have learned about your partner.

MODÈLE É1 Le week-end, je travaille un peu, je joue au basket, et je fais la cuisine. Et toi ?
  É2 Je ne fais pas grand-chose ; je reste à la maison et je prépare mes cours.

2-17 Discuss whether class results resemble those of the French poll. Why might they differ? Are there any activities not included in the French poll that would probably figure prominently in a poll of American leisure activities?

2-17 Un sondage. Poll your classmates to find out what percentage participate in each of the activities included in the chart on the previous page. Designate one student in your group to ask the questions, and another to keep track of responses on the board. Compare your percentages with those presented for the French. What are your conclusions?

1. Posez des questions.

MODÈLES ➤ Qui joue aux cartes ? (*raise your hand if you do*)
         ➤ Qui fait du bricolage ? (*raise your hand if you do*)

2. Comptez les réponses.
3. Annoncez les résultats.

MODÈLES ➤ Cinq étudiants jouent aux cartes ; c'est 50 pour cent. (*if your group has 10 students*)
         Un étudiant bricole ; c'est 10 pour cent.

Sons et lettres

TEXT AUDIO

Les voyelles /e/ et /ɛ/

Treat this topic in conjunction with *Le verbe faire*.

In early stages, focus on the avoidance of glided vowels. For that reason, it is unwise to insist that student contrast /e/ and /ɛ/. Although that contrast is typical of Standard (Parisian) French (SF) and Canadian French speakers who differentiate between, for example, *le pré* (meadow) and *le prêt* (loan), it is not made by the majority of people in France. They follow what is called *la loi de position*: /e/ at the end of a word or syllable (open syllable); /ɛ/ before a consonant (closed syllable). This pronunciation is fully acceptable to SF speakers, who, in any case, exhibit a great deal of variation. You might want to follow this rule and use /e/ in *anglais, français, des, est*, and inside words in open syllables, for example, *intelligente*.

The vowels of **et** and **mère** differ by the degree of tension with which they are pronounced and where they occur in words. The vowel of **et**, /e/, must be pronounced with a lot of tension and without any glide; otherwise the vowel of the English word *day* is produced. To pronounce the French vowel, hold your hand under your chin to make sure it does not drop as you say **et**; your lips should stay in a smiling position and tense. The vowel /e/ occurs generally only at the end of words or syllables, and it is often written with **é**, or **e** followed by a silent consonant letter. It also occurs in the endings **-er**, **-ez**, and **-ier**.

la té**lé**   **et**   ass**ez**   janvi**er**   ré**pé**ter   écout**ez**

The vowel of **mère**, /ɛ/, is pronounced with less tension than /e/, but still without any glide. It usually occurs before a pronounced consonant and is spelled with **è**, **ê**, or **e** followed by a pronounced consonant. It is also spelled **ei** or **ai** in **seize** or **j'aime**, for example.

la m**è**re   b**ê**te   je préf**è**re   **elle**   il dét**e**ste

À vous la parole

Begin practice with a discrimination drill; have students indicate whether they hear the vowel /e/ or /ɛ/: *belle, les, mère, frère, janvier, et, elle, jouer*, etc.

2-18 Contrastes. Compare the pronunciation of each pair of words: the first word contains /e/ and the second /ɛ/.

anglais / anglaise	français / française	assez / seize
André / Daniel	préférer / je préfère	marié / célibataire

2-19 Des phrases. Read each of the sentences aloud. To avoid glides, hold the rounded, tense position of /e/ and do not move your lips or chin during its production.

1. Écoutez Hélène.
2. Hervé n'est pas bête.
3. Danielle est réservée.
4. Son père s'appelle André.
5. Sa grand-mère est âgée.

FORMES ET FONCTIONS

1. *Les prépositions* à *et* de

- The preposition **à** generally indicates location or destination and has several English equivalents.

Elle habite **à** Paris.	*She lives **in** Paris.*
Il est **à** la maison.	*He's **at** the house.*
Elle va **à** une fête.	*She's going **to** a party.*

As you've seen, the preposition **à** is also used in the expression **jouer à**, to play sports or games.

Nous jouons **au** tennis le lundi.	*We play tennis on Mondays.*
Ils jouent **aux** cartes le samedi soir.	*They play cards on Saturday evenings.*

With other verbs, **à** introduces the indirect object, usually a person who receives the action.

parler	Cédric **parle à** la petite fille.	*Cédric's speaking to the little girl.*
téléphoner	Nous **téléphonons à** nos amis.	*We're phoning our friends.*
donner	Elle **donne** la photo **à** son ami.	*She gives her boyfriend the photo.*

- **À** combines with the definite articles **le** and **les** to form contractions. There is no contraction with **la** or **l'**.

à + le → au	Il joue **au** tennis.	*He plays tennis.*
à + les → aux	Ils jouent **aux** cartes avec des amis.	*They play cards with friends.*
à + la → à la	Je reste **à la** maison vendredi soir.	*I'm staying home on Friday evening.*
à + l' → à l'	Je parle **à l'**oncle de Simon.	*I'm talking to Simon's uncle.*

- The preposition **de/d'** indicates where someone or something comes from.

Mon copain Jean est **de** Montréal.	*My boyfriend Jean is from Montreal.*
Elle arrive **de** France demain.	*She arrives from France tomorrow.*

To present this topic, provide examples such as those given in this section and ask students whether they can explain the rules.

Point out that French and English differ with regard to the types of objects used with verbs: *téléphoner à* (+ indirect object) vs. *écouter* (+ direct object). You might also want to contrast *parler à* and *parler de*.

As you've seen, **de** is also used in the expression **jouer de**, *to play* (*music or a musical instrument*).

Son ami joue **du** piano dans un groupe.	*Her friend plays piano in a group.*
Lui, il joue **de l'**harmonica.	*He plays the harmonica.*

De/d' also is used to indicate possession or other close relationships.

C'est le frère **du** professeur.	*It's the teacher's brother.*
Voilà le livre **de** Kelly.	*There's Kelly's book.*

● **De** combines with the definite articles **le** and **les** to form contractions. There is no contraction with **la** or **l'**.

de + le → du	Mon amie fait **du** jogging.	*My girlfriend goes jogging.*
de + les → des	On parle **des** projets pour le week-end.	*We're talking about plans for the weekend.*
de + la → de la	Moi, je joue **de la** guitare.	*I play the guitar.*
de + l' → de l'	Il joue **de l'**accordéon.	*He plays the accordion.*

À vous la parole

Begin practice with simple substitution drills: *Il joue au foot ; loto. — Il joue au loto,* etc. ; *Je joue du piano ; guitare. — Je joue de la guitare,* etc.

2-20 Ça cause. Tell what today's subjects of conversation are for Camille and her friends.

MODÈLE la copine de Bruno
➤ Elles parlent de la copine de Bruno.

1. le professeur de français
2. le match de basket le week-end dernier (*last*)
3. les problèmes du campus
4. la nouvelle (*new*) colocataire de Camille
5. l'oncle d'Antoine
6. les devoirs d'anglais
7. le dernier film de Spielberg

2-21 Have students suggest other famous athletes and musicians.

2-21 Des célébrités. What do these famous people do?

MODÈLE Shaquille O'Neal
➤ Il joue au basket-ball.

1. Eric Clapton
2. Lance Armstrong
3. Mia Hamm
4. Emeril Lagasse
5. Serena Williams
6. Elton John
7. Avril Lavigne
8. Tiger Woods

2-22 Trouvez une personne qui... Circulate in the classroom to find someone who does each of the things listed. When your instructor calls time, compare notes to see who came closest to completing the list.

MODÈLE   joue de l'harmonica

         É1 Tu joues de l'harmonica ?

         É2 Non. (*You ask another person.*)

         OU Oui. (*You write down this person's name.*)

1. fait du vélo
2. fait de la natation
3. est d'une grande ville, par exemple de Chicago ou de New York
4. joue au golf le week-end
5. joue du piano
6. téléphone à ses parents le week-end
7. parle au professeur en français
8. joue du saxophone
9. joue souvent (*often*) aux cartes
10. fait du jardinage

2-22 Use as a mixing activity; impose a time limit, then have students ask questions to get missing information: *Qui joue de l'harmonica ?* Ask follow-up questions: *Tu joues dans un groupe ?* etc. Since the verb *faire* has not been introduced in all its forms, you might delay this exercise, or else limit practice to the singular /fe/, which has been presented as a lexical item.

2. *Le verbe* faire

- The verb **faire** (*to make, to do*) is used in a wide variety of expressions. Here are the forms of this irregular verb.

FAIRE *to make, to do*		
SINGULIER	**PLURIEL**	
je fais	nous	**faisons**
tu fais	vous	**faites**
il	ils	
elle fait	elles	**font**
on		

Present the verb inductively through a short narrative: *Le week-end, je fais des courses et je fais du jardinage. Mon mari fait du bricolage ; les enfants font du sport,* etc. *Et vous, vous faites du sport ?* Ask students to summarize the forms. Remind students of where they have seen this verb before: in arithmetic problems and the question, *Qu'est-ce qu'il fait ?*, as well as in the lexical items taught in the **Points de départ**.

- A question using **faire** does not necessarily require using **faire** in the answer:

    —Qu'est-ce que tu **fais** samedi ?   —*What are you doing on Saturday?*

    —Je joue au golf.   —*I'm playing golf.*

- A form of the preposition **de** is used with the verb **faire** in some expressions.

    —Elle fait **du** sport.   —*She plays sports.*

    —Moi aussi, je fais **de la** natation.   —*Me too, I swim.*

- **Faire** is used in many idiomatic expressions related to everyday activities; it is one of the most common and useful French verbs.

Tu fais beaucoup de sport ?	*Do you do a lot of sports?*
Nous faisons une promenade.	*We're taking a walk.*
Elle aime faire la cuisine.	*She likes to cook.*
Il fait des courses.	*He's running errands.*
Ils font du jogging le matin.	*They jog in the morning.*
Vous faites de la danse ?	*Do you study dance?*
Je fais du français.	*I study French.*

À vous la parole

Begin practice with a discrimination drill: one person, or more than one? *Elle fait des courses ; Ils font une promenade ; Il fait de l'anglais*, etc. Follow up with a simple substitution drill: *Je fais du foot ; vous ; toi ; eux*, etc.

2-23 Suite logique. Based on their interests, what are these people doing in their spare time?

MODÈLE   Sylvie aime le ballet.
➤ Elle fait de la danse.

1. Nous arrivons au supermarché.
2. Florent et Hamid aiment la nature.
3. Tu adores préparer le dîner.
4. Vous êtes fanatique de jazz.
5. Ludovic aime travailler dans le jardin.
6. Hélène et Béa sont vraiment sportives.
7. J'aime travailler à la maison.
8. David et moi sommes très paresseux.

2-24 Point out the use of *pas de* in negative expressions, as shown in the model. Have students report back what they found out from their partner. Compare answers for all class members. As an additional exercise, put up a frequency scale and let students indicate how often they do the things you ask about.

2-24 Et vous ? Discuss with a partner your usual activities for each of the categories proposed.

MODÈLE   la musique

É1 Je ne fais pas de musique, mais j'ai un lecteur CD et beaucoup de CD ; j'aime le jazz.

É2 Je fais de la musique ; je joue du piano et de la guitare.

1. la musique
2. le sport
3. les jeux
4. la cuisine
5. des travaux à la maison

Écoutons

2-25 Des portraits d'athlètes

A. Avant d'écouter. Look at the photos of three Francophone athletes. Which sport does each play? Can you think of two or three adjectives to describe each athlete? Have you ever seen any of these athletes in person or on television?

Tony PARKER

Marinette PICHON

Donald AUDETTE

B. En écoutant. Listen to the descriptions of the three athletes and fill in the missing information in the chart below.

Name	Sport	Age	Appearance	Favorite Activities
Tony PARKER				
Marinette PICHON				
Donald AUDETTE				

C. Après avoir écouté. Now use the completed chart to summarize in a couple of sentences the information about the athlete who most appeals to you. Then add a sentence telling why this person is interesting to you.

MODÈLE ➤ Mon athlète préféré est… Je trouve cette personne intéressante parce qu'il/elle…

Script for *Écoutons*

Tony Parker est un Français qui joue au basket dans le NBA. Il est né en 1982 en Belgique. Il est brun et assez grand. Tony est très sportif. Il aime regarder le football, le hockey et le base-ball et il joue au tennis. Il aime bien la musique américaine et les fêtes entre amis et il adore les jeux électroniques.

Marinette Pichon est la première Française à jouer au football aux États-Unis. Elle fait partie de l'équipe féminine de France et de l'équipe de Philadelphie. Elle est née en 1975 à St-Memmie en France. Elle est assez petite, mince et très musclée. Elle aime regarder le base-ball et le football américain. Elle aime aussi écouter de la musique et aller au cinéma.

Donald Audette joue au hockey pour l'équipe des Canadiens. Il n'est pas très grand, mais il est très motivé. Il n'est pas très jeune. Il est né à Laval au Québec en 1969. Quand il ne joue pas, il travaille pour aider les enfants. Il est sympa et très généreux. Il aime aussi passer du temps avec sa femme et ses deux enfants.

Leçon 3 Où est-ce qu'on va ce week-end ?

POINTS DE DÉPART

Destinations diverses

Present the vocabulary showing the labeled drawing of the small town (IRCD, Ch. 2); read aloud or paraphrase the **Points de départ** text. Have students help describe in simple terms activities at each location, using *-er* verbs they know. Check comprehension by having students point to the places you name or describe. Have students repeat key words: (as you point to the drawing) *C'est la librairie ou la bibliothèque ?—C'est la librairie.* The Ch. 6 **Observons** video segment (*Visitons Seillans*) is a visit to the small town of *Seillans*; play this sequence without sound to allow students to see what a small town in France looks like. Point out that the verbs *manger* and *nager* have a spelling peculiarity in the first-person plural, reflecting the pronunciation :
nous mangeons,
nous nageons.

Le week-end, qu'est-ce que tu fais ? Tu aimes nager ? Alors tu vas probablement à la piscine. Tu pratiques un autre sport ? Alors tu vas probablement au stade, au gymnase, ou au parc. Tu aimes les activités culturelles ? Tu vas voir peut-être un film au cinéma ou une exposition au musée ; ou bien tu assistes à une pièce, un ballet ou un concert au théâtre. Tu cherches un livre ? Voilà la bibliothèque ou bien la librairie. Tu ne fais pas la cuisine ? Alors va au restaurant, au café ou chez un ami pour manger.

le stade · la piscine municipale · l'église · la mairie · le gymnase · LA PISCINE MUNICIPALE · le parc · le monument aux morts · la place · le cinéma · le théâtre · le musée · le marché · BIBLIOTHÈQUE MUNICIPALE · la bibliothèque municipale · LA GARE SNCF · Chez Pierrette · le café · la librairie · l'hôtel · la gare · le café · le restaurant

The presentation and the exercises that follow use only the singular forms of *aller*: *je vais, tu vas.* The complete paradigm is taught in the **Formes et fonctions** section of this lesson.

Vie et culture

Les petites et les grandes villes

Small towns in France have a traditional structure. At the center is the Catholic church; a square, often with a veterans' memorial, is nearby. This is usually the location for the open-air market. The town hall is also in a central location. Older towns and villages often still have small merchants clustered around this central area. In many cases, a train station and a modest hotel are also close to the town center.

Many smaller towns were transformed in the 1960's by the exodus of young people to cities to find jobs; shops closed, and entire villages became sites for second homes. Today, on the outskirts of larger cities, "bedroom communities" are developing. These still depend to a great extent on public transportation—the bus system—as well as personal cars.

Et vous ?

1. Is there a traditional structure for small towns in North America? Does this vary from region to region? Why do you think North American towns tended to evolve as they did? Compare your ideas with those of a partner.

2. What basic similarities and differences can you identify in the layout of traditional town centers in North America and France? How would you explain them?

3. Have residential patterns changed in the area where you grew up? If so, do the changes reflect social or economic changes, as is the case in France?

À vous la parole

2-26 Dans quel endroit ? Where would you hear people saying this?

Before beginning the exercises, review the preposition à using a quick substitution drill: Il est au café ; piscine. —Il est à la piscine, etc.

MODÈLE   Du rosbif, s'il vous plaît.
➤ au restaurant

1. Tu nages bien, toi !
2. Le match commence dans dix minutes.
3. Regarde, la mariée et le marié arrivent.
4. C'est mon ballet préféré.
5. Où sont les biographies, s'il vous plaît ?
6. On regarde la télé ce soir ?
7. La musique est excellente ce soir.
8. Encore un café ?
9. J'aime beaucoup cette statue.
10. C'est combien pour ces deux livres et un cahier ?

2-27 Votre itinéraire. With your partner, take turns telling where you're going and what you're doing this weekend. Then summarize your plans for your classmates.

MODÈLE   É1 Ce week-end, je vais au restaurant. Mon copain et moi, nous dînons ensemble. Et toi ?

            É2 Moi, je vais au musée. Il y a une exposition de photos.

2-28 Vos endroits préférés. Discuss with a partner your favorite place for each activity listed. How similar—or dissimilar—are your preferences?

MODÈLE   pour dîner ?

            É1 Moi, j'aime dîner chez ma mère. Et toi ?

            É2 Moi, j'aime dîner au restaurant.

1. pour dîner ?
2. pour travailler ?
3. pour regarder un film ?
4. pour rencontrer des amis ?
5. pour pratiquer un sport ?
6. pour écouter de la musique ?

FORMES ET FONCTIONS

1. *Le verbe* aller *et le futur proche*

• The irregular verb **aller** means *to go*.

| Je **vais** à la librairie. | *I'm going to the bookstore.* |
| Tu **vas** au ciné avec nous ? | *You're going to the movies with us?* |

• You have already used **aller** in greetings and commands.

Comment ça **va** ?	*How are things?*
Comment **allez**-vous ?	*How are you?*
Allez au tableau !	*Go to the board!*

ALLER *to go*	
SINGULIER	PLURIEL
je **vais**	nous‿**allons**
tu **vas**	vous‿**allez**
il	ils
elle } **va**	elles } **vont**
on	

- To express future actions that are intended or certain to take place, use the present tense of **aller** and an infinitive. This construction is called **le futur proche** (*the immediate future*). In negative sentences, place **ne ... pas** around the form of **aller**; the infinitive does not change.

Je **vais travailler** ce soir.	*I'm going to work this evening.*
Attention, tu **vas tomber** !	*Watch out, you're going to fall!*
Il **va téléphoner** à son père.	*He's going to call his father.*
Tu **ne vas pas danser** ?	*You're not going to dance?*

- To express a future action you may also simply use the present tense of a verb and an adverb referring to the future.

Mon copain arrive **demain**.	*My friend arrives tomorrow.*
Tu joues **ce soir** ?	*Are you playing tonight?*

Here are some useful expressions referring to the immediate future:

ce soir	*tonight*
demain	*tomorrow*
ce week-end	*this weekend*
bientôt	*soon*
la semaine prochaine	*next week*
le mois prochain	*next month*
l'été prochain	*next summer*
l'année prochaine	*next year*

À vous la parole

2-29 Où aller ? Based on their interests, where are these people probably going?

MODÈLE Anne adore nager.
➤ Elle va à la piscine.

1. Rémi aime le basket.
2. Nous aimons les films.
3. Tu désires manger des spaghettis.
4. M. et Mme Dupont aiment l'art moderne.
5. Vous adorez jouer au foot.
6. Sandrine aime les livres historiques.
7. J'aime beaucoup parler avec mes amis.
8. Sophie et Angélique adorent le café.

Begin practice with a discrimination drill: one person, or more than one? *Il va au ciné, Elles vont chez elles,* etc. Follow with a substitution drill: *Je vais bien ; vous. —Vous allez bien,* etc.

2-29 and 2-30 These exercises practice the present tense of *aller* and 2-31 and 2-32 provide practice with the *futur proche*.

2-30 Have students work in pairs or small groups to come up with imaginative responses, then compare notes.

👥 2-30 Les habitudes. Tell a partner where you usually go and why during the times indicated.

MODÈLE le samedi soir

    É1   Je vais au ciné avec mes amis pour voir un film.

    É2   Moi, je vais à une fête chez des amis pour manger et pour écouter de la musique.

1. le lundi matin
2. le vendredi soir
3. le jeudi après-midi
4. le mercredi soir
5. le dimanche matin
6. le samedi matin
7. le samedi après-midi

In the simple exercise below practicing the *futur proche*, students repeat subject and verb and add an infinitive. This more focused exercise will prepare students for 2-31.

Quoi faire? Based on where they're going, tell what these people are going to do.

MODÈLE *Je vais à la bibliothèque.*
    ➤ *Je vais travailler.*

1. Nous allons à la piscine.
2. Tu vas au stade ?
3. Elles vont au resto U.
4. Vous allez à la résidence.
5. Christine va au ciné.
6. Je vais au bureau du professeur.
7. Marc va au gymnase.
8. Jean et Louise vont à la librairie.

2-31 Les projets. What are these people likely to do this weekend, given the circumstances?

MODÈLE Marion révise ses leçons.
    ➤ Elle va travailler à la bibliothèque.

1. Christophe aime écouter de la musique.
2. Nous n'avons pas de devoirs.
3. Marine et Ludovic ont deux places (*tickets*) pour aller voir un ballet.
4. Jean-Thomas invite des amis.
5. Je travaille à la maison.
6. Amandine ne fait pas grand-chose ce week-end.
7. Vous faites du sport.
8. Tu regardes un film.

2-32 This can become an extended activity, or you may choose one or two items for students to discuss, then report back to the class as a whole.

👥 2-32 Vos projets. Interview a partner about his/her plans, and report back to the class what you have found out.

MODÈLE cet après-midi

    É1   Qu'est-ce que tu vas faire cet après-midi ?

    É2   Cet après-midi je vais travailler. Et toi ?

    É1   Mon camarade et moi, nous allons jouer au tennis.

1. cet après-midi
2. ce soir
3. demain
4. ce week-end
5. le semestre/trimestre prochain
6. l'été prochain
7. l'année prochaine

2. *Les nombres à partir de cent*

To express numbers larger than 100, use the following terms:

Review numbers up to 99 before treating this topic. In treating large numbers, we focus here on their use to express distances and dates. You might also practice numbers with prices, using euros and expanding on the travel theme.

101	cent un	700	sept cents
102	cent deux	750	sept cent cinquante
200	deux cents	900	neuf cents
201	deux cent un	999	neuf cent quatre-vingt-dix-neuf

1 000	mille	1 000 000	un million
2 000	deux mille	2 000 000	deux millions

1 000 000 000	un milliard	2 000 000 000	deux milliards

- As the examples above show, add **-s** after **cent**, **million**, and **milliard** in the plural. But when **cent** is followed by another number, do not add **-s**. No **-s** is ever added after **mille**.

- Dates can be expressed in either of two ways:

The spelling *mil* may also be used in dates.

La Révolution française commence en mille sept cent quatre-vingt-neuf (1789).

The French Revolution begins in 1789.

Les Américains vont sur la Lune en dix-neuf cent soixante-neuf (1969).

The Americans go to the Moon in 1969.

- A comma is used in French where we would use a decimal point.

Environ vingt-neuf virgule cinq pour cent (29,5 %) des Français jouent au loto.

About twenty-nine point five percent (29.5%) of the French play the lottery.

- Use a space to separate out thousands and other large numbers.

Periods are also sometimes used to separate thousands: 5.511 km.

De Paris à Montréal, ça fait 5 511 kilomètres.

From Paris to Montreal is 5,511 kilometers.

- Use **de/d'** after **million**:

Dans Paris intra-muros, il y a plus de 2 000 000 **d'**habitants.

The city of Paris has more than 2,000,000 inhabitants.

À vous la parole

Begin practice by having students write the number you say; say the number you write.

2-33 Use a map of France to show the location of each city.

👥 **2-33 Distances à parcourir.** Imagine you and a friend are taking a train from Paris to spend the weekend in another French city. With a partner, indicate the approximate distance and total number of kilometers traveled.

MODÈLE Paris – Toulouse / 600 km

      É1 De Paris à Toulouse, ça fait six cents kilomètres.

      É2 Donc, mille deux cents kilomètres pour le week-end !

1. Paris – Tours / 200 km
2. Paris – Strasbourg / 400 km
3. Paris – Bordeaux / 500 km
4. Paris – Nice / 700 km
5. Paris – Marseille / 650 km
6. Paris – Nantes / 350 km

2-34 Key: 1066 : les Normands... ; 1492 : Christophe Colomb... ; 1776 : Jefferson écrit... ; 1804 : les Haïtiens... ; 1860 : la Guerre de Sécession... ; 1914 : la Première Guerre Mondiale... ; 1939 : la Deuxième Guerre Mondiale... ; 1969 : les Américains vont sur la Lune.

2-34 Dates historiques. Match items in the two columns to tell what happened in the years listed.

MODÈLE 1804

    ➤ En mille huit cent quatre les Haïtiens déclarent leur indépendance.

1066	Les Haïtiens déclarent leur indépendance.
1492	La Révolution française commence.
1776	Les Normands arrivent en Angleterre.
1789	Les Américains vont sur la Lune.
1804	La Première Guerre Mondiale commence.
1860	Christophe Colomb découvre l'Amérique.
1914	La Deuxième Guerre Mondiale commence.
1939	La Guerre de Sécession commence.
1969	Jefferson écrit la Déclaration d'Indépendance américaine.

Point out that the French read phone numbers as a series of two numbers.

👥 **2-35 Chiffres importants.** Exchange the following information about yourself with a partner.

MODÈLES date de naissance (*birth*)

      É1 C'est le quatorze février, mille neuf cent quatre-vingt-sept. (14/02/1987)

    numéro de téléphone

      É2 C'est le cinq cent cinquante-cinq, zéro huit, trente-sept. (555-0837)

1. date de naissance
2. numéro de téléphone
3. code postal

Parlons

2-36 Jouons ensemble

A. Avant de parler. To prepare for this game, a form of bingo, think about the questions that you will need to ask in order to find people who do the activities shown in the squares.

B. Parlons. Now, circulate among your classmates, asking them questions with the aim of completing a row (up, down, across, or diagonally). The first person to fill in a classmate's name in each square of a row is the winner.

MODÈLES É1 Est-ce que tu travailles à la bibliothèque le soir ?
           É2 Non, je travaille chez moi. (*ask another student*)

           É1 Est-ce que tu travailles à la bibliothèque le soir ?
           É3 Oui, j'étudie à la Bibliothèque McKeldin le soir. (*write his or her name in the square*)

You may provide students with a printed out game board. Have students examine the game board and generate a few of the questions before beginning so that you are sure they can complete the activity successfully.

aller au gymnase deux fois (*times*) par semaine	travailler à la bibliothèque le soir	aller à l'église le dimanche soir	pratiquer un sport trois fois par semaine
jouer du saxophone	chercher des livres à la librairie une fois par mois	aller au musée le week-end	aller au cinéma le week-end
aller souvent chez des amis	aller au supermarché le samedi	nager à la piscine municipale	aller au stade le samedi après-midi
aller au théâtre une fois par mois	jouer au tennis le week-end	ne pas faire grand-chose le week-end	dîner au restaurant trois fois par semaine

C. Après avoir parlé. Who first called "bingo?" Have that person check his or her responses by telling the class whose name was filled in for each activity. Play another round!

Venez chez nous!
Vive le sport !

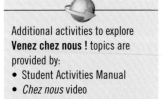

Additional activities to explore
Venez chez nous ! topics are
provided by:
- Student Activities Manual
- *Chez nous* video
- *Chez nous* Companion Website:
  http://www.prenhall.com/cheznous

Preview the lesson by finding out what
sports events in the Francophone world
students are already familiar with—have
any of them attended the World Cup, the
French Open, or the *Tour de France*? Show
the video montage (*Vive le sport !*); have
students identify the various sports being
practiced in this fast-paced segment.

LES SPORTS DANS LE MONDE FRANCOPHONE

From Marseille to Madagascar, from Martinique to Morocco, sports are a
unifying element in Francophone life. For example, in July, Europeans are glued
to the TV watching the international bike race **Le Tour de France**. Throughout
the year, you can find people all around the world listening to an exciting soccer
match on the radio. A win by a national team, such as the French victories in the
1998 World Soccer Cup, the 2000 European Soccer Cup, and the 2001 and 2003
Confederations Cups, fuels feelings of national honor and pride. Many people
believe that such victories also help to promote unity among Francophone people
generally, while dispelling nationalistic tendencies. The players on the French
soccer team are ethnically diverse, including Zinedine Zidane (of Algerian
descent), team captain Marcel Desailly (originally from Ghana), and Thierry
Henry (from the French Antilles). This diversity has been a source of team
strength as well as a buffer against intolerance.

Et vous ?

1. Are sports a unifying element in North America, as they are in Francophone
   countries? Are their victories a source of national pride?
2. In your opinion, do ethnically diverse teams function as a buffer against
   intolerance? Why or why not?
3. Are there sports and sporting events in North America whose popularity
   rivals that of soccer in the Francophone world? If so, which ones?

Lisons

2-37 Le cyclisme et le Tour de France

Cycling is a very popular sport in France, both to watch and to participate in. Many people of all ages join cycling clubs and train weekly. When the **Tour de France** or the shorter races such as the **Paris-Nice** take place, thousands of people line the streets to watch their favorite cyclists zip by at top speeds. The **Tour de France** takes place over a three-week period in June and/or July; it begins in the north and literally makes a tour of France, ending symbolically in Paris, on the Champs-Élysées. On July 25, 2004, the American cyclist Lance Armstrong made history when he became the only person to ever win the **Tour de France** six consecutive times.

A. Avant de lire. Examining this map of the 2004 **Tour de France** can help you better understand the following short description of this famous bicycle race. As you study the map, answer the following questions:

1. The year 2004 marked what year of the **Tour de France** competition?
2. What do you know about the geography of France? What geographical terms might you expect to see in a description of the race? How will distances be measured?
3. Notice the starting and ending points for the race. Is there anything that surprises you?
4. What symbols do you notice on the map? What do you think they might mean?

B. En lisant. As you read the text, check against the map and provide the following information:

Dates of the race:

Number of stages:

Number of mountain stages:

Number of days off:

Total distance:

The text itself also tells you:

Number of participating teams and individuals:

Total amount of prize money awarded, and the amount going to the overall winner:

Stratégie

Use accompanying graphics such as maps to help understand the content of a related text. Examine the titles; consider the meaning and purpose of the graphic elements and symbols that are used. Then refer to these elements as a continuing point of reference as you read the text.

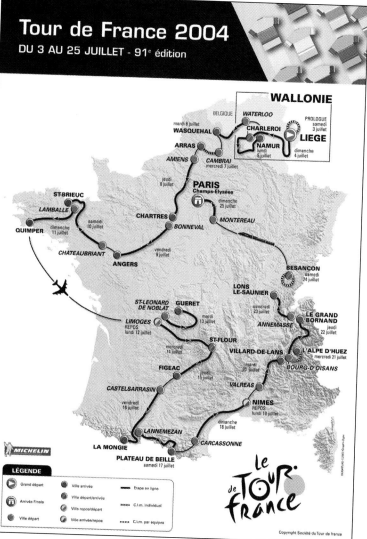

© A.S.O., 2004

Le Tour de France 2004 en bref

Le parcours

Du samedi 3 au dimanche 25 juillet, le Tour de France 2004 comprend un prologue et 20 étapes pour une distance totale d'environ 3 360 kilomètres.
Ces 20 étapes se décomposent comme suit :
11 étapes de plaine,
6 étapes de montagne,
2 étapes contre-la-montre individuel,
1 étape contre-la-montre par équipes.

Les particularités de l'épreuve

3 arrivées en altitude,
2 journées de repos,
75 kilomètres contre-la-montre individuel (dont 15 en ascension),
65 kilomètres contre-la-montre par équipes,
1 transfert en avion et 1 transfert en TGV

La participation

22 équipes de 9 coureurs sont invitées à participer au Tour de France 2004.

Les prix

Au total, 3 millions d'euros sont mis en jeu pour les équipes et les coureurs, dont 400 000 euros au vainqueur du classement général individuel.

© A.S.O., 2004

En regardant de plus près, Key:
1) 2 individual time-trial stages
2) 1 team time-trial stage 3) 3 mountain finishes 4) 2 rest days 5) 1 transfer by plane and 1 transfer by train (TGV)

C. En regardant de plus près. The text contains a few specialized racing terms. Can you explain the following?

1. 2 étapes contre-la-montre individuel
2. 1 étape contre-la-montre par équipes
3. 3 arrivées en altitude
4. 2 journées de repos
5. 1 transfert en avion et 1 transfert en TGV

D. Après avoir lu. Have you ever seen the **Tour de France** or a similar world-class biking event? Do you think such an event would generate great interest in North America? Why or why not?

Le Tour de France en Provence

Parlons

2-38 Un/e athlète célèbre

A. Avant de parler. Think about a Francophone or North American athlete whom you admire and would like to talk about. You may choose Tony Parker, Marinette Pinchon, Donald Audette, Zinedine Zidane, Thierry Henry, Marcel Desailly, or another athlete.

B. En parlant. What information would you like to convey about this athlete? You will probably include his or her name, sport, and nationality, and a physical description as well a description of the athlete's personality. Also, be sure to tell why you admire this person. Look at the brief description below, and use it as a model for your own. Can you show a picture of the athlete as you describe him or her to your classmates?

En parlant. You might also use one or more of the descriptions from the Ch. 2, L. 2 *Écoutons : Des portraits d'athlètes* as a model.

MODÈLE ➤ Lance Armstrong est un coureur (*racer*) cycliste. Il est américain. Lance est sérieux, motivé, ambitieux et très sportif. Il est assez grand et mince, et il est brun. J'admire Lance Armstrong parce qu'il est très discipliné et parce que c'est un champion.

Le Tour de force
de Lance Armstrong

En remportant son sixième Tour de France, le champion américain entre dans le légende du cyclisme.

© *La Croix,* 26 juillet 2004

C. Après avoir parlé. Listen as your classmates describe the athlete they most admire. What are the qualities you notice in their descriptions? Is it possible to make any generalizations about what we admire in famous athletes? Are certain individuals mentioned frequently?

Après avoir parlé. Have each student describe the athlete to the class. You might ask them to do this without telling who the athlete is. For example, students would begin with something like: *C'est un coureur cycliste.* Others can then try and guess who is being described. Whoever guesses correctly is the next person to give a description.

Écrivons

2-39 Les événements sportifs

le Championnat du Monde de pétanque

le Paris-Dakar

A. Avant d'écrire. Many international sporting events are hosted each year in the Francophone world, ranging from the world-famous **Tour de France** to lesser known events such as the World Championship for **pétanque**. Some of these events are shown here. Look at the photos and identify the sport in each one. Which would you most like to attend? Why?

B. En écrivant. Use information from the chart below to help you organize a brief description of one of these sporting events, or another similar event from the francophone world. Add a personal reaction to express your own ideas about the event you describe.

Quoi ?	Quand ?	Où ?	Description
le Rolland-Garros	mai–juin	au stade Rolland-Garros à Paris	des matchs internationaux de tennis
le Paris-Dakar	déc–janvier	de Paris à Dakar	une course internationale de voitures
le Tour de France	juin–juillet	en France	une course internationale de vélos
la Coupe du Monde de football	juin–juillet		le championnat mondial de football
les Jeux de la francophonie	2005	au Niger	une manifestation culturelle et sportive internationale

MODÈLE ➤ En 2005, au Niger, il y a les Jeux de la francophonie. C'est une manifestation culturelle et sportive internationale. Beaucoup d'artistes et d'athlètes du monde francophone participent aux jeux. C'est une occasion formidable pour fêter la francophonie, l'art et le sport.

C. Après avoir écrit. Read over your description and make sure that you have included all the relevant information. Look closely at your paragraph to be sure that you have spelled all words correctly, that subjects and verbs agree in number, and that nouns and adjectives agree in number and gender. Can you find a photo of your event? Share your description with classmates and learn about the wide variety of sporting events held in the Francophone world.

Observons

2-40 On fait du sport

A. Avant de regarder. In this clip, several speakers describe their sports and cultural activities. Look at the list below of activities that they mention; can you guess—in cases where you don't already know—what each of these activities might involve?

l'athlétisme   la danse classique   la danse orientale   le piano   le tennis

As you watch this video segment, look for any clues that might support your guesses about unfamiliar activities.

B. En regardant. Who does which activities? Each speaker is listed in order; fill in the activities each person mentions.

personne	activité/s	jour/s
Hervé-Thomas	_tennis_	
Caroline	1.	
	2.	
	3.	
Catherine (sa sœur)	1.	
	2.	
	3.	
	4.	
Fadoua		

Several of the speakers specify the days on which they do various activities; listen again and note those days on the chart.

C. Après avoir regardé. What is your impression of the types and number of activities in which these speakers are involved? How do their habits compare with your own habits and those of your family and friends?

Avant de regarder. Do not provide answers for the previewing activity; instead, let students make guesses and see whether they are confirmed by the clip. This activity is based on the first three interviews in the clip; two additional interviews are treated in the Video Manual.

Script for _Observons_
Note that the elements in brackets reflect standard usage and have been added to the written transcripts. They were not pronounced by the speaker(s) in question.

HERVÉ-THOMAS : Je suis professeur de littérature et d'histoire de France, mais j'aime aussi le sport. Je fais beaucoup de sport : je joue beaucoup au tennis. Euh, en général, je joue au tennis le lundi, le mercredi et le samedi.

CAROLINE : En dehors de l'école on a un emploi de [du] temps très chargé, exemple : le mercredi,... j'ai une heure et demie de piano...

CATHERINE : Et moi, c'est le lundi.

CAROLINE : Le vendredi, on a deux heures d'athlétisme... et voici nos maillots. On en est fières.

CATHERINE : Très fières.

CAROLINE : Le samedi, on fait une heure et demie de danse. Voici les... chaussons de danse... les pointes.

CATHERINE : Et le dimanche, moi, je fais du tennis avec mon grand-père quand je peux. Parce que des fois il pleut, mais la plupart du temps je fais avec lui.

FADOUA : Donc je fais [de] la danse orientale à la faculté de Nice. Donc on... nous avons un gymnase où on peut faire [de] la danse ; nous avons un professeur qui est d'origine algérienne. Elle s'appelle Yamina. En fait j'aime bien faire [de] la danse orientale parce que ça me permet d'avoir un [une] attache... à mon pays.

Vocabulaire

Leçon 1

le caractère	*disposition, nature, character*
ambitieux/-euse	*ambitious*
amusant/e	*funny*
bête	*stupid*
drôle	*amusing, funny*
égoïste	*selfish*
énergique	*energetic*
généreux/-euse	*generous, warm-hearted*
gentil/le	*kind, nice*
intelligent/e	*intelligent, smart*
méchant/e	*mean, naughty*
pantouflard/e	*homebody*
paresseux/-euse	*lazy*
sérieux/-euse	*serious*
sportif/-ive	*athletic*

le physique	*physical traits*
âgé/e	*aged, old*
beau/belle	*handsome, beautiful*
blond/e	*blond/e*
brun/e	*brunette*
châtain	*chestnut colored, auburn*
de taille moyenne	*of medium height*
d'un certain âge	*middle-aged*
élégant/e	*elegant*
fort/e	*strong, stout*
grand/e	*tall*
gros/se	*fat*
jeune	*young*
joli/e	*pretty*
mince	*thin, slender*
moche	*ugly*
petit/e	*short, little*
roux/-sse	*redhead, redheaded*

pour poser une question	*to ask questions*
combien de	*how many*
comment	*how*
où	*where*

parce que	*because*
pourquoi	*why*
quand	*when*
qui	*who*

en ville (f.)	*in the city*
une clinique	*private hospital*
un collège	*middle school*
une fac(ulté)	*college*

autres mots utiles	*other useful words*
adorer	*to adore, love*
arrête !	*stop it!*
autre	*other, another*
bien sûr	*of course*
un chapeau	*hat*
un/e coloc(ataire)	*roommate*
comme	*like, as*
un copain/une copine	*friend*
donc	*then, therefore, so*
une histoire drôle	*joke*
peut-être	*maybe*
une photo	*photo*
pour	*for, in order to*

Leçon 2

quelques sports (m.)	*some sports*
le basket(-ball)	*basketball*
le football américain	*football*
le *hockey	*hockey*
un match	*game (sports)*
le rugby	*rugby*
le volley(-ball)	*volleyball*
quelques jeux (m.)	*some games*
les cartes (f.)	*cards*
les échecs (m.)	*chess*
un jeu	*game, deck (of cards)*
un jeu de société	*board game*
le loto	*lottery*

la musique	*music*
le jazz	*jazz*
le rock	*rock*
une batterie	*percussion, drum set*
un concert	*concert*
un harmonica	*harmonica*
un saxophone	*saxophone*

d'autres activités	*other activities*
bricoler	*to do odd jobs, to tinker*
les loisirs (m.)	*leisure-time activities*
organiser une fête	*to plan a party*
rester à la résidence	*to stay in the dorm*

quelques expressions avec faire	*expressions using faire*
faire du bricolage	*to do odd jobs, to tinker*
faire des courses	*to run errands*
faire la cuisine	*to cook*
faire de la danse	*to dance, to study dance*
faire du français	*to study French*
faire du jardinage	*to garden*
faire du jogging	*to go jogging*
faire de la musique	*to play music*
faire de la natation	*to swim*
faire une promenade	*to take a walk*
faire du sport	*to play sports*
faire du vélo	*to go biking*
ne pas faire grand-chose	*to not do much*

Leçon 3

en ville	*in town*
une bibliothèque (municipale)	*(municipal) library*
un café	*café*
un cinéma	*movie theater*
une église	*Catholic church*
une gare	*train station*
un gymnase	*gym*
un hôtel	*hotel*
une librairie	*bookstore*
la mairie	*town hall*

un marché	*market*
un monument aux morts	*veterans' memorial*
un musée	*museum*
un parc	*park*
une piscine (municipale)	*swimming pool (municipal)*
une place	*square (in a town)*
un restaurant	*restaurant*
un stade	*stadium*
un théâtre	*theatre*

activités culturelles	*cultural activities*
assister à…	*to attend . . .*
un ballet	*a ballet*
un concert	*a concert*
voir…	*to see . . .*
une exposition	*exhibition*
une pièce	*a play (theater)*

pour parler de l'avenir	*to talk about the future*
aller (Je vais travailler.)	*to go (I'm going to study. /I will study.)*
l'année (f.) prochaine	*next year*
bientôt	*soon*
ce soir	*tonight*
ce week-end	*this weekend*
demain	*tomorrow*
l'été (m.) prochain	*next summer*
le mois prochain	*next month*
la semaine prochaine	*next week*

les nombres à partir de 100	*numbers from 100*
cent	*hundred*
mille	*thousand*
un million	*a million*
un milliard	*a billion*

autres mots utiles	*other useful words*
alors	*so*
chercher	*to look for*
une fois	*one time*
manger	*to eat*

Does this scene look familiar? Where do you imagine it is taking place?

Chapitre 3

Études et professions

 Leçon 1   *Nous allons à la fac*

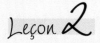 Leçon 2   *Une formation professionnelle*

Leçon 3   *Choix de carrière*

Venez chez nous !
Étudier et travailler au Canada

In this chapter:

- Talking about a university and courses of study
- Talking about jobs and the workplace
- Giving commands and making suggestions
- Expressing preferences
- Comparing education and the workplace in the U.S., France, and Canada

You may wish to present this vocabulary over two days. Present campus vocabulary on day 1 and do Ex. 3-1 and 3-2; review vocabulary and present the prepositions on day 2, completing Ex. 3-3. Present the vocabulary using the labeled campus map (IRCD, Ch. 3). Identify each location pictured, then have students help describe related activities, using verbs they know: *Dans le Centre étudiant ? —On regarde la télé, on mange, on parle avec des copains.* Check comprehension by having students point to the places you name or describe. Ask questions as you point to the visual: *C'est le centre informatique ou le labo de chimie ?*

Leçon 1   *Nous allons à la fac*

—*C'est le centre informatique.* Reinforce the distinction between *la librairie* and *la bibliothèque*. Note the abbreviated expressions *la bibli* and *la B.U.*, which are frequently used in France, as are *le resto U* and *la cafétéria*. Demonstrate each of the prepositions using the map. The chart organizes the prepositions as a list of opposites. Test comprehension by having students name the place you describe: *Qu'est-ce qui est derrière le Centre des sports ? —Ce sont les terrains de sport.* Provide further practice using the town map from Ch. 2, L. 3 (IRCD, Ch. 3); have students correct statements you make: *Est-ce que la mairie est loin de la place ? —Non, elle est près de la place.*

POINTS DE DÉPART

À la fac

Je m'appelle Julie et je suis en deuxième année d'études à l'Université de Montréal. Du lundi au vendredi, je vais à la fac. J'ai tous mes cours ici, et je travaille le week-end à la bibli. Après les cours, je retrouve mes amis au café dans le Centre étudiant. J'habite en ville, mais j'ai des amis qui habitent en résidence. On mange ensemble à la cafétéria et on fait du sport au Centre des sports.

Voici un plan du campus. Si vous arrivez à UdeM en voiture, le garage se trouve à droite du Pavillon principal. Si vous arrivez en métro, il y a une station juste en face du Pavillon principal. Dans le Pavillon principal, il y a une librairie et des bureaux administratifs. Les résidences se trouvent à gauche, et le Centre étudiant est juste à côté. Au Centre étudiant il y a un cinéma, un café, le bureau des inscriptions et des bureaux d'associations étudiantes. Le Centre des sports est tout près des résidences, et les terrains de sport sont juste derrière.

TEXT AUDIO

Additional practice activities for each **Points de départ** section are provided by:
- Student Activities Manual
- *Chez nous* Companion Website: http://www.prenhall.com/cheznous

Lead into the cultural content of Ch. 3 by talking about the use of French in Canada and discussing the reasons for the presence of French in Quebec. You might discuss how the universities of Quebec reflect its special situation as a French-speaking province in Canada. Ask students if there are examples of American universities that similarly reflect divergent cultural identities.

In Ch. 3 we begin to draw students' attention to regional differences in the French language. We focus on Quebec in the chapter on university studies, since the North American educational systems are more similar to each other than they are to the French system. In particular, the **Venez chez nous !** lesson presents Canadian French vocabulary and the **Observons** video segment includes a speaker with a Canadian accent.

PRÉPOSITIONS DE LIEU

à droite de	à gauche de
en face de	à côté de
dans	
près de	loin de
devant	derrière

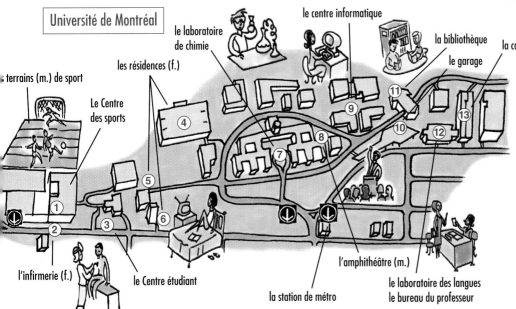

Université de Montréal

- les terrains (m.) de sport
- Le Centre des sports
- les résidences (f.)
- le laboratoire de chimie
- le centre informatique
- la bibliothèque
- le garage
- la cafétéria
- l'infirmerie (f.)
- le Centre étudiant
- la station de métro
- l'amphithéâtre (m.)
- le laboratoire des langues
- le bureau du professeur

1. Centre d'éducation physique et des sports (CEPSUM)
2. Pavillon 2101, boul. Édouard-Montpetit
3. Pavillon J.-A.-DeSève (Centre étudiant)
4. Résidence C (étudiants et étudiantes)
5. Résidence A (étudiants)
6. Résidence Thérèse-Casgrain (étudiantes)
7. Pavillon principal
8. Pavillon Claire-McNicoll
9. Pavillon André-Aisenstadt
10. Garage Louis-Colin
11. Pavillon Samuel-Bronfman
12. Pavillon Lionel-Groulx
13. Pavillon 3200, rue Jean-Brillant
Ⓛ Station de métro

À vous la parole

3-1 This exercise practices the key vocabulary used with the preposition à. Review, using a quick substitution drill: Il est au café ; piscine — Il est à la piscine, etc. You might also wish to review forms of aller; this can be practiced using a substitution drill and/or the campus visual (IRCD, Ch. 3).

As a brief personalized activity between Ex. 3-1 and 3-2, have students tell a partner where they are going after French class; compare notes.

3-1 Dans quel endroit ? Where would you be likely to hear people asking these questions or making these comments?

MODÈLE   Vous avez un permis (*permit*) pour votre voiture ?
> au garage

1. Voilà le bureau de l'association.
2. Le match commence dans dix minutes.
3. Listen and repeat: number one.
4. Écoute ! C'est une explosion !
5. Où sont les biographies, s'il vous plaît ?
6. On regarde la télé ce soir ?
7. Où est le docteur Martin ?
8. Désolé, Monsieur, je n'ai pas mes devoirs.
9. Tu as un autre CD ?
10. C'est combien pour ces deux livres et un cahier ?

3-2 Vos endroits préférés. Discuss with a partner your favorite place on campus for each activity listed. Then share your preferences with other classmates.

MODÈLE   pour dîner ?

É1 Moi, je préfère la cafétéria ; c'est très pratique. Et toi ?
É2 Moi, je préfère le café au Centre étudiant ; c'est plus calme.
É1 (*reporting back*) Pour dîner, je préfère la cafétéria, mais Anne préfère le café au Centre étudiant…

1. pour dîner ?
2. pour travailler ?
3. pour voir un film ?
4. pour parler avec des amis ?
5. pour pratiquer un sport ?
6. pour préparer un examen ?

3-3 For further practice, show the image of the UdeM campus map (IRCD, Ch. 3) and ask students to imagine that they are in the courtyard of the *Pavillon principal*. Have them take turns asking and indicating where the following places are located: *la station de métro ; le terrain de foot ; le garage ; la Résidence A ; un café ; la piscine ; une librairie ; le Centre étudiant.* For example,

É1 *la station de métro, s'il vous plaît ?*
É2 *Ce n'est pas loin ; c'est juste en face d'ici.*

Remind students of other ways to ask for directions: *Où se trouve… ? C'est loin / près d'ici… ? Je cherche…. C'est où… ?* As a follow-up, provide students with a map of your campus and have them work in pairs to label the map in French. This is good preparation for Ex. 3-3 and the **Parlons** activity at the end of this lesson.

As a follow-up, you might have students compare answers and have the class decide which is the best response.

3-3 Sur votre campus. Pick one place on your campus, then circulate among your classmates, asking where it is located. See the list below for some ideas. How many different responses do you get ?

MODÈLE   É1 C'est où, la résidence Denton ?
É2 La résidence Denton, c'est près des terrains de sport.
É1 La résidence Denton, s'il vous plaît ?
É3 C'est tout droit, en face du Centre étudiant.

1. la bibliothèque
2. les bureaux de l'administration
3. le Centre étudiant
4. la piscine
5. le bureau des inscriptions
6. le théâtre
7. la librairie
8. la cafétéria
9. la résidence X
10. les terrains de sport

Vie et culture

Le système éducatif au Québec

The educational system in the province of Quebec is organized somewhat differently from the system in the United States. Secondary school usually lasts five years; students normally graduate at 17 and then spend two years in a **CÉGEP (Collège d'enseignement général et professionnel)**. Afterwards, many continue at a university where they may complete **un baccalauréat (un bacc)**, **une maîtrise**, and **un doctorat**. These are equivalent to the American Bachelor's, Master's, and Ph.D. degrees respectively. As in American universities, students in Canadian universities may choose highly specialized degrees in one discipline or they may choose to have a major (**une majeure**) in one discipline and a minor (**une mineure**) in another.

L'Université de Montréal, the largest university in Canada, has an expansive campus located on the outskirts of town. It offers a wide range of majors and professional degrees.

La Sorbonne, l'Université de Paris IV, is at the heart of the busy Latin Quarter. Founded in 1253, it is surrounded today by cafés and bookstores that cater to the university clientele.

In Montreal there are four universities: two are French-speaking, *l'Université de Montréal (l'UdeM)* and *l'Université du Québec à Montréal (l'UQAM)*; and two are English-speaking, *McGill* and *Concordia University.*

Le campus de l'université française

Most French universities do not have a centralized campus. The different **facultés**, or schools, are often housed in buildings with historical significance that are scattered around town, usually in urban settings.

French students refer to their university as **la fac**; they say, for example, **Je vais à la fac**. To socialize and to study, students often go to a nearby café. Some French universities have residence halls located near classroom buildings, but if you are planning to study at the Sorbonne in Paris, the oldest and best-known French university, be prepared for a long **métro** ride to get to classes. The residence halls are at a significant distance from the **Quartier latin**, the neighborhood that is home to the Sorbonne, and they are largely filled with foreigners. Most French students, in Paris and elsewhere in France, live at home or rent a room in town.

Et vous ?

1. Does your region have any institutions comparable to the **CÉGEP** in Quebec?
2. How is your campus similar to a French campus, and how is it different? You might compare location, size, type of buildings, and general campus layout.
3. Are students' living arrangements at your university similar to or different from those of typical French students?

Point out that, whereas the *Québécois bacc* is equivalent to the American B.A. or B.S, the French *bac* is an examination that must be passed for graduation from the *lycée* and is a condition for admission to a university. The French *bac* is discussed further in the **Vie et culture** section of L. 2. Help students understand that the *CÉGEP* prepares Canadian students for university work and may account for a shorter time spent at university; recently, however, many Québécois universities have moved to a four-year *baccalauréat.*

Remind students that they have carried out commands in the classroom; ask them to provide some examples. Use TPR to review classroom commands, using first the *vous*-form; next, call on students individually and use the *tu*-form. Have students explain the difference in the two forms. Display examples of the imperative forms, and point out the written forms.

FORMES ET FONCTIONS

1. L'impératif

- To make a suggestion or a request, or to tell someone to do something, the *imperative* forms of a verb—without subject pronouns—may be used. For **-er** verbs, drop the infinitive ending, **-er**, and add:

  - **-e** when speaking to someone with whom you are on informal terms:

Ferm**e** la porte !	*Shut the door!*
Donn**e**-moi le cahier.	*Give me the notebook.*

  - **-ez** when speaking to more than one person or to someone with whom you are on formal terms:

Parl**ez** plus fort !	*Speak louder!*
Écout**ez**-moi !	*Listen to me!*

  - **-ons** to make suggestions to a group of which you are part:

Jou**ons** aux cartes.	*Let's play cards.*
Regard**ons** un film.	*Let's watch a film.*

- To be more polite, add **s'il te plaît** or **s'il vous plaît** as appropriate:

Ouvrez la fenêtre, **s'il vous plaît**.	*Open the window, please.*
Donne-moi la règle, **s'il te plaît**.	*Please give me the ruler.*

- To tell someone not to do something, put **ne (n')** before the verb and **pas** after it:

Ne regarde **pas** la télé !	*Don't watch TV!*
N'écoutons **pas** la radio.	*Let's not listen to the radio.*

À vous la parole

Begin practice with a discrimination drill: have students decide whether they hear a command to one person, to more than one person, or a suggestion: *Ferme la porte ! Parlons français ! Écoutez le professeur !*, etc. Follow with substitution drills; singular to plural: *Va au bureau ! —Allez au bureau !*; plural command to suggestion: *Allez au bureau ! —Allons au bureau !* In another simple exercise, have students associate verbs in the command form with nouns: *la fenêtre ? —Fermez la fenêtre ! Ouvrez la fenêtre !*

3-4 Impératifs. Use appropriate forms of the imperative to make requests to your friends and your instructor.

MODÈLE   Dites (*tell*) à un/e ami/e de ne pas regarder la télé.
> Ne regarde pas la télé !

Dites à un/e ami/e…

1. d'écouter
2. de fermer la porte
3. de ne pas parler anglais
4. de ne pas manger en classe

Demandez à votre professeur (n'oubliez pas [*don't forget*] d'être poli/e !)…

5. de répéter
6. de parler plus fort
7. de ne pas fermer la porte
8. de ne pas parler anglais

Proposez à vos amis…

9. de jouer au basket
10. d'écouter de la musique
11. d'aller au cinéma
12. de ne pas travailler

👥 **3-5 Pourquoi pas ?** You'd like to do something different in French class today. What can you suggest to your instructor? Choose from this list of possibilities and include some of your own ideas as well: **aller**, **jouer**, **faire**, **parler**, **écouter**, **regarder**.

MODÈLE   aller
➤ Allons au café.

👥 **3-6 Situations.** With a partner, give examples of a request or suggestion you'd be likely to hear in each situation. How many examples can you come up with?

MODÈLE   une mère à son enfant
➤ Écoute, mon chéri (*dear*).
ET   ➤ Mange tes carottes.

1. un professeur aux étudiants
2. une étudiante à un/e ami/e
3. un étudiant au professeur
4. un étudiant à son copain
5. un entraineur (*coach*) de basket à ses joueurs
6. votre professeur, à vous
7. vos parents, à vous

2. *Les adjectifs prénominaux au singulier*

● Most adjectives follow the noun in French. A few, however, are placed before the noun.

LES ADJECTIFS PRÉNOMINAUX

jolie/joli

belle/bel/beau

première/premier   dernière/dernier

jeune   vieille/vieil/vieux

nouvelle/nouvel/nouveau

bonne/bon   mauvaise/mauvais

petite/petit   grande/grand

                                grosse/gros

● In the singular, **jeune** and **joli/e** each have a single spoken form. For **joli**, add **-e** for the feminine written form: **jolie**.

une jeune étudiante   un jeune professeur
une joli**e** bibliothèque   un joli campus

3-5 Students can first work in pairs to come up with ideas. Variations: give advice to a fellow student who wants to improve his/her grade; give advice to someone who wants to relax over the weekend.

3-6 As a fun variation, sit down in a chair facing your class. Tell students that they should give you commands. Students enjoy turning the tables and having the teacher do the things that they are frequently asked to do.

Consistent with the presentation of variable adjectives in Ch. 2, L. 1, this presentation focuses on the spoken forms of adjectives and assumes the feminine as the base form, with a regular rule of final consonant deletion to derive the masculine. Plural forms are treated in L. 2 of this chapter.

To present, first show students contrasting examples illustrating the position of adjectives: *C'est un professeur raisonnable ; C'est un jeune professeur.*
    You might use the BRAGS mnemonic to introduce the meaning of these adjectives and help students remember them: "Beauty, Rank, Age, Goodness, Size." Point out that the boxed list of adjectives is arranged according to this mnemonic.
    Then display and read aloud the sentence examples for prenominal adjectives, asking students how many different spoken forms these adjectives have. Ask specifically what they notice about the pronunciation of the masculine form before a vowel sound, versus before a consonant sound. Point out differences in written forms as well.

● Most of the other adjectives that are placed before the noun have two spoken forms in the singular. Like other adjectives you know, the masculine form ends in a vowel sound and the feminine form ends in a pronounced consonant. However, the masculine form sounds just like the feminine form when followed by a word beginning in a vowel sound.

C'est une petite piscine.   C'est un peti**t** amphithéâtre.
C'est un peti~~t~~ laboratoire.

C'est une mauvaise bibli.   C'est un mauvais hôtel.
C'est un mauvai~~s~~ prof.

C'est la première librairie.   C'est le premie**r** ordinateur.
C'est le premie~~r~~ jour.

● **Belle**, **nouvelle**, and **vieille** also have two spoken forms in the singular. However, when followed by a consonant, the masculine form has a different vowel sound. Notice also the special written form of the masculine singular adjective before a word beginning with a vowel sound.

C'est une belle étudiante.   C'est un **bel** étudiant.
C'est un b**eau** garçon.

C'est une nouvelle étudiante.   C'est un **nouvel** étudiant.
C'est un nouv**eau** prof.

C'est une vieille amie.   C'est un **vieil** ami.
C'est un v**ieux** copain.

● The adjectives **grande** and **grosse** have three spoken forms in the singular. When followed by a word beginning with a vowel sound, the masculine form has a final consonant sound different from the feminine form.

C'est une gran**d**e piscine.   C'est un gran**d** amphithéâtre.
/d/   /t/
C'est un grand stade.

Regarde la gro**ss**e calculatrice !   Regarde le gro**s** ordinateur !
/s/   /z/
Regarde le gros stylo !

Une nouvelle résidence à l'Université de Nice

Begin practice with a discrimination drill, having students write or select the appropriate form of the adjective they hear: *Voilà un nouvel ordinateur ; une nouvelle étudiante ; un nouveau prof.* Point out the importance of the article in providing gender cues when the form of the adjective is ambiguous. Follow with simple substitution drills: *un bon ordinateur ; nouveau ; vieux,* etc.

À vous la parole

3-7 Tout à fait d'accord ! Indicate that you agree.

MODÈLE Le cours est bon ?

➤ Oui, c'est un bon cours.

1. Le prof est mauvais ?
2. La fac est nouvelle ?
3. L'hôtel est le premier ?
4. Le campus est grand ?
5. L'amphithéâtre est nouveau ?
6. Le stade est nouveau ?
7. L'ordinateur est beau ?
8. L'étudiante est jeune ?

3-7 Suggest additional emphatic statements: *Ah oui/Mais oui/C'est vrai, c'est un bon cours.*

3-8 Ce n'est pas vrai ! Contradict your partner!

MODÈLE É1 C'est un vieux professeur.

É2 Mais non, c'est un jeune professeur !

1. C'est un mauvais livre.
2. C'est un vieil ordinateur.
3. C'est le premier pavillon.
4. C'est une grande piscine.
5. C'est la dernière résidence.
6. C'est un petit ordinateur.
7. C'est un mauvais professeur.
8. C'est un nouvel amphithéâtre.

3-8 Suggest additional emphatic statements: *Ah non !/Au contraire, c'est un jeune prof.*

3-9 Trouvez une personne qui... Find someone in your class who . . .

MODÈLE a un bon prof de maths

É1 Est-ce que tu as un bon prof de maths ?

É2 Non, je n'ai pas de cours de maths. (*you ask another person*)

É1 Est-ce que tu as un bon prof de maths ?

É3 Oui, j'ai un bon prof ; il s'appelle M. McDonald. (*you write down the name of this student*)

1. a un bon prof de maths
2. a une bonne note en français
3. a un nouvel ordinateur
4. a son premier cours à 8 heures (*8 o'clock*) du matin
5. a un gros dictionnaire
6. prépare un grand examen
7. est en première année de fac
8. est en dernière année de fac
9. a un bon cours d'histoire
10. a un vieil ami sur le campus

3-9 Use as a mixing activity and have students report back what they learned. Expand on each item, for example, asking all students: *Qui a un bon prof ? C'est un prof de quoi ?,* etc.

Quelques étudiantes à la fac

Parlons

3-10 Visitons le campus !

A group of Francophone journalists is in town for a seminar and will be attending workshops on your campus. They may need help locating the things and places they need. Half of the class will play the role of journalists, the other half will be students working at the information desk in your student center.

A. Avant de parler. If you are a journalist, work with a partner to make a list of things and places to ask about, and practice formulating polite questions. If you are a student, brainstorm with a partner how you will indicate the location of various key places that your guests may ask about.

B. En parlant. Now take your places in front of or behind the information desk, asking questions or giving directions, as the case may be.

MODÈLE É1, JOURNALISTE Bonjour, nous cherchons un café.
        É2   Bonjour, monsieur. Ici dans le Centre étudiant il y a un petit restaurant et le café est très bon.
        É1   C'est où exactement ?
        É2   C'est à gauche, juste à côté de la librairie.
        É1   Merci bien !
        É2   Je vous en prie, monsieur.

C. Après avoir parlé. Were you able to answer all of your classmates' questions, and were they able to understand your directions? Did they accept your advice? Which questions and answers did you like best?

Voici le Centre des sports. C'est juste à côté de la résidence.

Leçon 2 *Une formation professionnelle*

POINTS DE DÉPART

Des programmes d'études et des cours

TEXT AUDIO

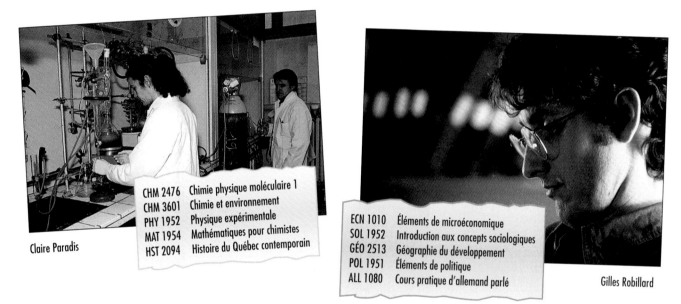

Claire Paradis

CHM 2476	Chimie physique moléculaire 1
CHM 3601	Chimie et environnement
PHY 1952	Physique expérimentale
MAT 1954	Mathématiques pour chimistes
HST 2094	Histoire du Québec contemporain

ECN 1010	Éléments de microéconomique
SOL 1952	Introduction aux concepts sociologiques
GÉO 2513	Géographie du développement
POL 1951	Éléments de politique
ALL 1080	Cours pratique d'allemand parlé

Gilles Robillard

Claire et Gilles, étudiants à l'Université de Montréal, parlent des cours qu'ils suivent :

GILLES : Qu'est-ce que tu as comme cours ce trimestre ?

CLAIRE : Deux cours de chimie, un cours de calcul, un cours de physique et un cours d'histoire.

GILLES : Tu aimes ton cours de calcul ?

CLAIRE : Non, c'est ennuyeux, mais c'est un cours obligatoire. Et ton cours de sciences politiques, ça va ?

GILLES : Ben, il est intéressant, ce cours, mais difficile.

CLAIRE : Il y a beaucoup d'examens ?

GILLES : Non, il y a un examen final, mais il y a deux devoirs à écrire. J'ai eu une note assez médiocre pour le premier devoir.

Begin presenting the vocabulary by describing the courses Gilles and Claire are taking. As a first test of comprehension, ask *Qui suit un cours de calcul ?*, etc.; see sample questions in Ex. 3-11 of **À vous la parole.** Have students listen to the dialogue, then check comprehension: pose questions that can be answered with the appropriate student's name: *Qui suit deux cours de chimie ? Qui a un cours de sciences politiques ?*

Show the course listings as you model pronunciation for the disciplines and courses, and provide explanation where necessary. Ask *Qui suit un cours de littérature ? C'est un cours de littérature américaine ou anglaise ?*, etc., to provide additional contextualization of the new words. As an early productive exercise, have students classify specific courses according to area of study: *la sociologie ? —C'est les sciences humaines.*

QU'EST-CE QUE VOUS ÉTUDIEZ ?

les lettres :	l'histoire, une langue étrangère, la littérature, la philosophie
les sciences humaines :	l'anthropologie, la psychologie, les sciences politiques, la sociologie
les sciences naturelles :	la biologie, la botanique, la physiologie, la zoologie
les sciences physiques :	l'astronomie, la chimie, la physique
les sciences économiques :	la comptabilité, l'économie, la gestion
les arts du spectacle :	le théâtre, la danse, le cinéma
les beaux-arts :	le dessin, la musique, la peinture, la sculpture, la photographie

l'informatique	le droit	la médecine
les mathématiques	le journalisme	les sciences de l'éducation

—Quels cours est-ce que vous suivez ?

—Je suis un cours de biologie, un cours d'économie, et un cours de maths.

Point out the forms of the verb *suivre*, treated here as a lexical item. *Suivre* is used idiomatically in this context; explain to students that English speakers "take" a course, but French students "follow" one. Regular -re verbs are presented in Ch. 5, L. 1.

SUIVRE   *to follow; to take (a course)*

SINGULIER		PLURIEL	
je	suis	nous	suivons
tu	suis	vous	suivez
il		ils	
elle	suit	elles	suivent
on			

C'est la faculté des lettres ou la faculté des sciences humaines ?

À vous la parole

3-11 Deux étudiants. Answer these questions about Gilles' and Claire's studies, based on the dialogue and the list of their current courses.

MODÈLE   Claire prépare un diplôme en sciences économiques ou en chimie ?
➤ Elle prépare un diplôme en chimie.

1. Sa mineure est en biologie ?
2. Et Gilles, quel diplôme est-ce qu'il prépare ?
3. Quelle est sa mineure ?
4. Ce trimestre, Claire suit un cours d'écologie ?
5. Pour quels cours est-ce qu'elle travaille au laboratoire ?
6. Elle suit un cours de maths ?
7. Gilles suit un cours de sciences humaines ce trimestre ?

3-11 Note that the term *une mineure* is used in Canada to refer to "a minor," *une majeure* is "a major." You may wish to point out to students that the concept of a minor does not exist in France, and that the term *une spécialisation* is used there to indicate one's major.

3-12 La majeure. Based on the courses they're taking, what are these Canadian students probably majoring in?

MODÈLE   Guillaume : Principes de chimie analytique ; Chimie physique moléculaire ; Mathématiques pour chimistes
➤ Il prépare sans doute (*no doubt*) un diplôme en chimie.

1. Cécile : L'Europe moderne ; Introduction à l'étude des États-Unis ; Histoire générale des sciences
2. Arnaud : Civilisation allemande ; Allemand écrit 1 ; Cours pratique d'allemand parlé
3. Romain : Introduction aux concepts sociologiques ; Communication et organisation ; Psychologie sociale
4. Jennifer : Théorie macroéconomique ; Éléments de microéconomique ; Statistique pour économistes
5. Ben : Histoire politique du Québec ; Éléments de politique ; Géographie du développement
6. Anne-Marie : Biologie expérimentale ; Principes d'écologie ; Introduction à la génétique
7. Aurélie : Systèmes éducatifs du Québec ; Philosophie de l'éducation ; Sociologie de l'école

3-12 The courses listed are actual course titles from the UdeM catalog.

3-13 Votre diplôme et vos cours. Compare your major and minor with a partner and discuss the courses you are taking this semester.

MODÈLE   É1   Je prépare un B.A. en sciences politiques. J'ai une mineure en espagnol. Et toi ?
    É2   Moi, je prépare un B.A. en mathématiques, mais je n'ai pas de mineure.
    É1   Ce semestre je suis deux cours d'histoire, un cours de sociologie et ce cours de français.
    É2   Bien sûr, je suis un cours de français et j'ai aussi trois cours de maths !

3-13 You may wish to have students make a chart with their partner's schedule. Create a sample schedule using the list of courses for Claire or Gilles. Provide blank schedule forms and have students report back to the class.

Vie et culture

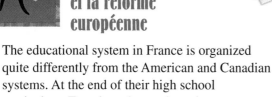

L'université française et la réforme européenne

The educational system in France is organized quite differently from the American and Canadian systems. At the end of their high school curriculum, French students take a rigorous national exam called **le baccalauréat (le bac)**. It is not uncommon for students to fail **le bac** on their first attempt and to repeat their last year of high school (**le lycée**) and retake **le bac**. Students who pass this exam are guaranteed entrance into the university system, or they can continue their

Un professeur à l'Université de Nice donne son cours dans un amphithéâtre.

The French government has set as an educational goal to have 80% of all high school students pass the *bac*. In 2002, 78.8% of candidates passed, as compared to the year 1982, when only 64.8% of students succeeded. Ask students to compare requirements for entrance into American universities with those for French universities. What are the advantages and disadvantages of each? Help students understand that the recent reforms are set up to allow students from one European country to move easily to another country to study, to complete an internship, or to work. Compare the North American system: Is it standardized? Is it easy to move from one place to another? What are the advantages of a standardized and a non-standardized system?

3-14 This can be completed first as a speaking activity with a partner; then students might make a tape recording about their university, to be graded.

3-14 Votre université et vous. Imagine you're going to send a tape to a French-speaking pen pal, telling him/her about your university and your studies. Prepare two or three short sentences on each suggested topic, then take turns practicing them with your partner. When you are ready, present your descriptions to the class as a whole.

MODÈLE votre université en général

> Notre université est très grande. Il y a plusieurs (*several*) facultés : une faculté des lettres et des sciences humaines, une faculté des sciences, une faculté de droit et une faculté de médecine.

1. votre université en général
2. votre campus (il est dans une ville ? il est grand ?)
3. votre faculté (quelle est votre faculté ? nommez [*name*] quelques départements)
4. votre diplôme (quelles sont votre majeure et mineure ? quels cours sont obligatoires ? nommez quelques cours que vous suivez)
5. votre cours de français (combien d'étudiants ? il est intéressant ? vous travaillez beaucoup ?)
6. vos professeurs (combien de professeurs différents ce semestre ? ils sont intéressants ? quel est votre professeur préféré ?)

studies in other, specialized institutions, such as schools of business or engineering. The most prestigious and competitive institutions of higher education in France are the **Grandes Écoles**, which are comparable to certain high-ranking graduate schools in North America. Many future politicians, business leaders, professors, and professionals are educated at the **Grandes Écoles**.

Recently France has been reforming its university system in concert with 32 other European countries. This reform involves reorganizing the university year into two semesters (instead of the traditional October to June year); the establishment of a common system of credits; and the awarding of diplomas based on a common progression from **une licence**, after three years of post-bac study, to **un master** after five years, and to **un doctorat** after eight years.

Look at the video clip *Je suis étudiant*, which was filmed at **l'Université de Nice**. Identify the places on campus you see and the subjects that each speaker studies (or teaches!).

Et vous ?

1. Comment on the **bac**. How would you feel about taking a rigorous national exam like this at the end of secondary school? How does it seem to compare to the exams you did take, such as the SATs and/or ACTs?
2. Think about the reforms of the French university system. What are likely to be some advantages and disadvantages of greater uniformity and transferability within Europe of university credits and diplomas?

Sons et lettres

TEXT AUDIO

Additional practice activities for each **Sons et lettres** section are provided by:
• Student Activities Manual
• Text Audio

Les voyelles /o/ et /ɔ/

The vowel of **beau**, /o/, is short and tense, in contrast to the longer, glided vowel of English *bow*. Hold your hand under your chin to make sure it does not drop as you say **beau**; your lips should stay rounded and tense. The vowel /o/ generally occurs at the end of words or of syllables, and it is written with **o**, **au/x**, **eau/x**, or combinations of **o** and silent consonants:

au resto U	**au**x bureaux	le mot	il est gros

The vowel of **sport**, /ɔ/, is pronounced with less tension than /o/, but still without any glide. It usually occurs before a pronounced consonant and is spelled **o**:

le prof	il est fort	Yvonne	il adore

In a few words, /o/ occurs before a pronounced consonant. In these cases, it may also be spelled **ô** or **au**:

le diplôme	les **au**tres	à g**au**che	elle est grosse

À vous la parole

Begin practice with a discrimination drill, reading a list of words and asking students to tell whether they hear the vowel of *beau* or that of *fort*.

3-15 Contrastes. Compare the pronunciation of each pair of words or phrases. The first has the /o/ sound; the second the /ɔ/ sound.

le stylo / la gomme	Bruno / Yvonne	la radio / la porte
le piano / la note	Mme Lebeau / M. Lefort	il est beau / elle est bonne

3-16 Les abréviations. French students use many abbreviations to talk about their courses and other aspects of university life. Many of these abbreviations end in /o/ as in the list below. With a partner, practice saying each abbreviation and match it to its full form.

1. le labo
2. le resto U
3. la compo
4. les sciences po
5. la psycho
6. la philo
7. la socio
8. le dico

a. le dictionnaire
b. le laboratoire
c. la philosophie
d. les sciences politiques
e. la sociologie
f. le restaurant universitaire
g. la composition
h. la psychologie

FORMES ET FONCTIONS

1. *Les verbes comme* préférer *et l'emploi de l'infinitif*

To present, display the verb chart and ask how this verb is similar to other *-er* verbs students have learned; you might draw a "shoe" to illustrate the fact that all the singular forms and the third-person plural are pronounced alike. Be sure that students notice accent changes, and point out that these reflect the pronunciation change discussed in the **Sons et lettres** of this lesson for the sounds /o/ and /ɔ/: /e/ in open syllables: *préférons*/pre fe rɔ̃/; /ɛ/ in closed syllables: *préfère*/pre fɛr/.

• For verbs conjugated like **préférer**, the singular forms and the third-person plural form of the present tense show the change from **é** /e/ to **è** /ɛ/. In all of these forms the endings are silent.

—Quel sport est-ce que vous préférez ?   —Nous, on préfère le football.
—Nous préférons le tennis.   —Eux, ils préfèrent le hockey.
—Vous préférez le rugby ?   —Non, moi, je préfère le golf.

PRÉFÉRER *to prefer*			
SINGULIER		**PLURIEL**	
je	préfère	nous	préférons
tu	préfères	vous	préférez
il / elle / on	préfère	ils / elles	préfèrent

- Other verbs that show the same type of change are **répéter** (*to repeat*) and **suggérer** (*to suggest*):

  Répétons après le professeur.   Répète après moi !
  Qu'est-ce que vous suggérez ?   Qu'est-ce que tu suggères ?

- **Préférer** may be followed by a noun or by an infinitive:

  Je préfère **le golf**.   *I prefer golf.*
  Il préfère **jouer** au tennis.   *He prefers to play tennis.*

- Use the following verbs to talk about likes and dislikes; all, like **préférer**, can be followed by a noun or an infinitive:

  détester   *to detest*
  aimer bien   *to like fairly well*
  aimer   *to like or to love*
  aimer beaucoup   *to like or love a lot*
  préférer   *to prefer*
  adorer   *to adore*

In addition to *répéter* (introduced in Ch. Prélim., L. 2) and *suggérer*, you might provide other verbs conjugated like *préférer*: *espérer, compléter*, only *préférer* will be practiced in this lesson. To practice *suggérer*, you might use:

  Suggestion : Qu'est-ce que tu suggères ?
  — Jouons aux cartes !
  — Non, moi, je préfère jouer au golf. ou Marie et moi, on préfère jouer au golf.

Remind students of the placement of the negative in infinitive constructions.

Begin practice with a discrimination drill: have students write the letter *è* or *é* based on the form they hear: *je préfère, nous préférons*, etc. Follow with a substitution drill: *Je préfère le jazz ; vous. — Vous préférez le jazz*, etc. Additional written practice is provided in the Workbook.

À vous la parole

3-17 Activités préférées. Everyone is supposed to be studying, but is instead thinking about his/her favorite activity! Tell what each person likes to do.

MODÈLE   Pauline aime jouer au tennis.

3-17 This is a good opportunity to recycle *faire* expressions and the difference between *jouer à* and *jouer de*. Vary the exercise by asking students what they like to do.

Pauline   Nicole   Grégory   Christine   Nicolas   Thomas

3-18 Items may have more than one logical response; encourage students to think of several.

3-18 Les vacances. Based on the descriptions, figure out with a partner what these people probably prefer to do during their vacation.

MODÈLE   Marie-Laure est très sociable.

      É1   Elle préfère organiser des fêtes.

  OU   É2   Elle préfère dîner avec ses amies.

1. Fred et ses amis adorent le sport.
2. Mathilde est très réservée.
3. Nous aimons la musique.
4. Le copain de Sabrina est très énergique.
5. Vous n'êtes pas très énergiques.
6. La mère de mon amie aime bien travailler dans la nature.
7. Je suis assez paresseuse.
8. Tu n'aimes pas beaucoup le sport.

For further practice, have students discuss in pairs and then share with the class what they love to do, and what they absolutely hate doing. Be sure to provide clear models:

adorer :

  É1   *Moi, j'adore travailler dans le jardin.*
  É2   *Moi non, j'adore surtout écouter de la musique.*

détester :

  É1   *Je déteste faire des courses le week-end.*
  É2   *Moi aussi, je déteste ça.*

To share with the class: *Moi, j'adore écouter de la musique, mais elle, elle adore travailler dans le jardin. Nous détestons faire des courses le week-end.*

3-19 Vos préférences. Discuss your preferences with a classmate, then summarize them for the class.

MODÈLE   les jeux : le Scrabble ou les échecs ?

      É1   Est-ce que tu préfères jouer au Scrabble ou aux échecs ?

      É2   Moi, je préfère jouer aux échecs, et toi ?

      É1   Moi, j'adore jouer au Scrabble.

      (*plus tard*) :

      É2   Moi, j'aime les échecs, mais lui, il préfère le Scrabble.

1. les jeux : le Scrabble ou les échecs ?
2. la musique : le rock ou le jazz ?
3. les sports : le football ou le basket ?
4. les cours : le français ou les mathématiques ?
5. les animaux : les chats ou les chiens ?

Les Français préfèrent les chats. Ils ont 9 millions de chats et 8 millions de chiens.

2. Les adjectifs prénominaux au pluriel

- You have learned that a few adjectives precede the noun in French. These include:

masc. sing.		masc. pl.	fem. sg.	fem. pl.
jeune		jeunes	jeune	jeunes
joli		jolis	jolie	jolies
petit		petits	petite	petites
grand		grands	grande	grandes
gros		gros	grosse	grosses
mauvais		mauvais	mauvaise	mauvaises
bon		bons	bonne	bonnes
premier		premiers	première	premières
dernier		derniers	dernière	dernières
+ consonne	**+ voyelle**			
beau	bel	beaux	belle	belles
nouveau	nouvel	nouveaux	nouvelle	nouvelles
vieux	vieil	vieux	vieille	vieilles

- The final letter of the plural form of these adjectives is usually not pronounced.

    des jolies filles   des jeunes filles

However, you hear the plural marker—usually a letter **-s** or **-x**—when these adjectives precede a plural noun beginning with a vowel sound.

    des beau**x**‿enfants   des jeune**s**‿amis

For **jeune** and **joli**, there are two spoken forms in the plural. For all the other prenominal adjectives you have learned, there are four spoken forms in the plural, for example:

    des grands labos   des grand**s**‿amphithéâtres
    des grandes piscines   des grande**s**‿universités

    des petits stades   des petit**s**‿amphithéâtres
    des petites librairies   des petite**s**‿affiches

For the plural forms before a word beginning with a vowel, add the liaison sound /z/ to the form used before a consonant.

Before presenting the new material, review adjective placement and singular prenominal adjective forms, taught in L. 1. To present, read a number of examples aloud and have students choose the appropriate form from a list, analyzing why they made the choice they did: *Voici des petits appartements : petit, petits, petites.* Summarize rules using the examples provided.

Remind students that although a letter -s or -x is generally added to written words to form the plural in French, this final letter is usually not pronounced. You must listen for a preceding word, usually a number or an article, to tell whether a noun is singular or plural. If the noun begins with a vowel, liaison can provide an additional clue:

    cinq étudiants
    des bureaux
    mes‿affiches

Stress the importance of articles and liaison in signaling gender and number, since, for example, /ptit/ is both masculine and feminine (before a vowel), singular and plural (feminine before a consonant).

Point out that *mauvais* and *gros* do not change spelling in the masculine plural. We are using the more frequent plural variant for the indefinite determiner: *des nouveaux étudiants* instead of *de nouveaux étudiants*, even though some conservative speakers might consider the latter form more "correct."

À vous la parole

Begin practice with a discrimination drill similar to that used for the presentation: *Voici des vieilles affiches : vieil, vieille, vieilles.* Follow up with substitution drills: *Voici des vieux musées ; résidences ; universités ; hôtels,* etc.

3-20 Décrivons l'université. Indicate that you agree.

MODÈLE   Les résidences sont nouvelles ?
> ➤ Oui, ce sont des nouvelles résidences.

1. Les amphithéâtres sont vieux ?
2. Les laboratoires sont bons ?
3. Les ordinateurs sont mauvais ?
4. Les examens sont les premiers ?
5. Les terrains de sport sont beaux ?
6. Les bureaux sont grands ?
7. Les affiches sont belles ?
8. Les piscines sont nouvelles ?

3-21 C'est le contraire ! Change the following narrative so that you express the opposite.

MODÈLE   Je suis étudiant dans une *petite* université.
> ➤ Je suis étudiant dans une *grande* université.

Je suis étudiant dans une *petite* université. Nous avons des *vieilles* résidences ; moi, j'ai une *grande* chambre au *premier* étage. Il y a des *nouveaux* terrains de sport juste derrière notre *petit* Centre étudiant. J'ai des *bons* cours et des *mauvais* cours. Dans mes cours, j'ai des *vieux* amis, et on travaille bien ensemble.

3-22 As a preview, you might have the class as a whole describe the town where your university is located. Then put students into pairs to describe their hometown. Have them report back and briefly describe some aspect of their partner's hometown.

3-22 Votre ville natale. Describe your hometown to a classmate, commenting on the features outlined below and using adjectives from the list: **jolie, belle, première, dernière, jeune, nouvelle, vieille, bonne, mauvaise, petite, grande, grosse.**

MODÈLE   des parcs
> ➤ Dans ma ville natale, il y a des jolis parcs…

1. une mairie
2. des parcs
3. des hôtels
4. des piscines municipales
5. des universités
6. des cinémas
7. des maisons
8. des appartements

3-23 Les devoirs ou le cinéma ?

A. Avant d'écouter. When you have a lot of work to do, how do you handle it? Do you tackle the most difficult task first? Do you pace yourself? Do you put off getting down to work?

B. En écoutant. Listen as Fanny and Nicolas discuss their plans for the evening. As you listen the first time, write down in French what academic work each of them has to do; listen again and note when it must be done.

	travail à faire	matière	pour quand ?
Nicolas	1. *examen*	1. *allemand*	1. *demain*
	2.	2.	2.
	3.	3.	3.
Fanny	1.	1.	1.
	2.	2.	2.

Now circle the letter of the most appropriate completion of each statement below.

1. Nicolas est probablement étudiant en…
   a. sciences politiques.
   b. lettres.
   c. sciences économiques.
2. Fanny est surprise parce que…
   a. Nicolas dit qu'il est malade.
   b. Nicolas est méchant avec elle.
   c. Nicolas a beaucoup de travail.
3. Finalement Nicolas décide…
   a. d'aller au cinéma.
   b. de travailler à la bibliothèque.
   c. de rester dans sa chambre.

C. Après avoir écouté. What do you think of the way Nicolas is using his time?

Script for *Écoutons*

FANNY : Bonjour Nicolas !

NICOLAS : Salut Fanny ! Comment ça va ?

F : Ça va bien, et toi ?

N : Oh, pas mal, mais j'ai beaucoup de travail. Un examen d'allemand demain et deux essais à rendre vendredi, l'un pour le prof de sciences éco et l'autre en marketing.

F : Mais dis donc, vous travaillez beaucoup à l'École de Commerce !

N : Et toi, à la fac des lettres, vous ne travaillez pas ?

F : Non, c'est pas ça. J'ai un examen de philo la semaine prochaine et un essai pour la semaine d'après en littérature américaine. Mais j'ai envie de me reposer un peu. Pas toi ?

N : Euh, oui, peut-être. Qu'est-ce que tu proposes ?

F : Eh bien, il y a un nouveau film de Wim Wenders qui passe au ciné Panthéon. Tu viens avec nous ? Ça t'aidera avec ton examen d'allemand !

N : Eh oui. Pourquoi pas ? J'adore les films allemands. C'est à quelle heure ?

F : Nous allons à la séance de 22 h 30. Donc, tu vas avoir du temps pour réviser ton cours avant.

N : Bon. Alors, à ce soir.

F : Au revoir. À plus tard !

Leçon **3** *Choix de carrière*

Use the opening questions and other similar ones to introduce the topic; *vouloir* is treated here as a lexical item. Present the names of places, job types, and occupations using the labeled groupings (IRCD, Ch. 3). Describe, in simple terms and using gestures, what each person does. Test comprehension by changing to the images without labels (IRCD, Ch. 3) and having students point out the person you name; then elicit repetitions with either/or questions: *C'est une pharmacienne ou une infirmière ?*

POINTS DE DÉPART

TEXT AUDIO

Qu'est-ce que vous voulez faire comme travail ?

Dans quel domaine est-ce que vous voulez travailler ? Est-ce que vous voulez aider les gens, comme les médecins, par exemple ? Est-ce que vous voulez voyager, comme certains journalistes ? Est-ce que vous êtes doué pour la mécanique, comme les mécaniciens ?

Point out that *la clinique* is a false cognate, referring to a private hospital. While *instituteur* and *institutrice* are traditional terms used to identify primary school teachers, recent educational reforms in France favor the use of *professeur des écoles*.

un/e pharmacien/ne · un/e dentiste · un/e technicien/ne · un/e assistant/e social/e · un/e comptable · un/e secrétaire · un/e avocat/e · un médecin · une infirmière · un infirmier · un/e architecte · un/e informaticien/ne · un/e journaliste

À l'hôpital ou à la clinique

Au bureau

un professeur des écoles

À l'école

un professeur

Au collège, au lycée ou à la fac

une ouvrière · un ouvrier · un/e mécanicien/ne · un ingénieur

À l'usine

un/e représentant/e de commerce
un vendeur
une vendeuse
une serveuse
un agent de police
un serveur

Les services

une actrice   un peintre   une chanteuse
un acteur
un/e musicien/ne   un chanteur
un écrivain

Les artistes

QU'EST-CE QUI VOUS INTÉRESSE ?

Je veux avoir…
    un bon salaire
    beaucoup de prestige
    beaucoup de responsabilités
    un contact avec le public
    un travail en plein air

Je cherche un travail où…
    on peut voyager
    on peut aider les gens
    on n'est pas trop stressé
    on est très autonome
    on gagne beaucoup d'argent

À vous la parole

3-24 Classez les métiers. Name some jobs or professions that have the features listed.

MODÈLE   On gagne beaucoup d'argent.
       ➤ Un avocat gagne beaucoup d'argent.
    OU ➤ Un acteur célèbre (*famous*) gagne beaucoup d'argent.

1. On est très autonome.
2. On travaille en plein air.
3. Un diplôme universitaire n'est pas nécessaire.
4. On n'est pas très stressé.
5. On a un contact avec le public.
6. On a beaucoup de prestige.
7. On peut travailler avec les enfants.
8. On peut voyager.

Some simple exercises: For each place named, tell which person would not work there: *un bureau : un avocat, un secrétaire, un serveur.* Recycle vocabulary dealing with college coursework: *Pour devenir médecin ? —Il faut étudier la biologie, la chimie, la médecine,* etc. Ask students what profession they associate with famous names: Pablo Picasso, Mikhail Baryshnikov, Georgia O'Keeffe, Marie Curie, Whoopi Goldberg, Albert Schweitzer, etc. Once they have been given a few examples, have students suggest others.

Once students are familiar with the names of professions, introduce the chart of job characteristics. Have students provide an example for each job characteristic: *Dans quelle profession est-ce qu'on a beaucoup de prestige ? —Un médecin a beaucoup de prestige,* etc.

You might include drills that focus on form as a clue to gender. Begin with a discrimination drill: *un homme ou une femme ? Michèle est informaticienne ; C'est un dentiste,* etc. Remind students of the rule that derives masculine variable adjectives from the feminine by loss of the final pronounced consonant. The same rule applies to some professions: *Elle est avocate* → *Il est avocat,* etc. Review the importance of a strong release of the final consonant for the feminine.

3-24 You can expand on or vary by including the opposites, for example, *on ne gagne pas beaucoup d'argent* or *un diplôme universitaire est nécessaire.*

You might ask students to generate additional examples of this trend in English, such as police officer, mail carrier, and sales associate.

To introduce further cultural information about the French and work, point out that relatively small numbers of high-school aged students in France hold part-time jobs (remind students of the heavy course schedule and long school day in France) and that most university students who work tend to focus on summer jobs. For example, many work as *moniteurs/monitrices* in summer camps or participate in *les vendanges* (grape harvests) during the month of September before returning to classes in October. Further interesting statistics about young people and work in France can be found in *Francoscopie 2003*, p. 296.

Vie et culture

La féminisation des noms de professions

Across the globe, women are making careers in professions that were once male dominated. Language reflects this. The trend in English is toward more gender-neutral terms: instead of *waiter/waitress*, we say *server*; instead of *fireman*, *firefighter*. The French language tends toward specifying gender with regard to profession. For some professions that lack a feminine form, such as **un professeur**, a female professional has traditionally been addressed as **Madame le Professeur**, and students talking about their professors would say, **Mon professeur de chimie est Madame Durand**. Canadian and Swiss students, however, routinely use the form **une professeure** and might say, for example, **Ma professeure de psychologie est Madame Laurent**.

Et vous ?

1. Based on what you have learned in the **Points de départ**, provide some examples to illustrate how names of professions in French may have:
   a. one form
   b. a variable article
   c. separate masculine and feminine forms

2. Why do you think that English speakers have opted for gender-neutral terms while in French-speaking countries the trend is toward gender-specific terms?

Examples might include:

a. one form: *un professeur, un écrivain, un médecin, un ingénieur*

b. a variable article: *un/e dentiste, un/e architecte, un/e journaliste*

c. separate masculine and feminine forms: *une avocate, un avocat ; une infirmière, un infirmier ; une musicienne, un musicien ; une vendeuse, un vendeur.*

It is interesting to note that Canadians have used the form *la professeure* for some time, while in France this form is frowned on. The French have no difficulty, however, using *la prof* in casual conversation. Additional feminine forms for professions include *une écrivaine, une ingénieure*. In countries like Switzerland and Canada, these terms have been officially accepted and are in use to some extent, especially among feminists and academics. Traditionalists however, tend to use the standard forms.

3-25 Offres d'emploi. Tell what kind of employee or professional the following people are probably looking for.

MODÈLE M. Loriot a un nouveau magasin (*store*).
➤ Il cherche des vendeurs ou des vendeuses.

1. Mlle Voltaire a un grand bureau.
2. Les Lopez désirent une nouvelle maison.
3. Le Dr Ségal est le directeur d'une nouvelle clinique.
4. Il y a beaucoup de crimes dans notre ville.
5. Il y a une nouvelle école primaire dans notre ville.
6. Mme Serres téléphone à la faculté de droit.
7. M. et Mme Duprès désirent un portrait de leurs enfants.

3-26 Aptitudes et goûts. Based on the descriptions, tell what each of these people will probably do for a living.

MODÈLE Rémy est sociable. Il aime aider les gens avec leurs problèmes.
➤ Il va être assistant social.

1. Lucie s'intéresse à la mécanique. Elle est très douée pour réparer les voitures et les motos (*motorcycles*).
2. Kevin aime le travail précis. Il est très bon en maths.
3. Stéphanie est énergique et sociable. Elle aime voyager, et elle aime le contact avec le public.
4. Camille s'intéresse à l'informatique et elle aime créer des programmes.

5. Nicolas est très doué pour les sciences ; il aime son travail au laboratoire de la clinique.
6. Nathalie adore la mode ; elle aime aider les clients au magasin.
7. Charline est douée pour le dessin ; elle aime dessiner (*to design*) des maisons et des appartements.
8. Grégorie aime travailler avec les enfants ; il est calme et patient.

3-27 Vos projets de carrière. In a group of three or four students, find out what career each person wants—and does not want—to pursue.

MODÈLE   É1   Toi, Mike, qu'est-ce que tu veux faire comme travail ?
          É2   Je veux être assistant social. J'aime travailler avec les gens.
          É1   Et toi, Margot, qu'est-ce que tu ne veux pas faire ?
          É3   Moi, je ne veux pas être avocate. On travaille trop et on est trop stressé.

3-27 Before completing in small groups, you might conduct a chain drill:
   S1   Qu'est-ce que tu veux faire ?
   S2   Je veux être dentiste. Et toi, qu'est-ce que tu veux faire ?
   S3   Je veux être architecte. Et toi ?, etc.

Vouloir (*veux*) is treated here as a lexical item. This exercise can serve as an inductive presentation to the verb, which is presented later in this lesson.

Sons et lettres

TEXT AUDIO

L'enchaînement et la liaison

In French, consonants that occur within a rhythmic group tend to be linked to the following syllable. This is called **enchaînement**. Because of this feature of French pronunciation, most syllables end in a vowel sound:

As you present this topic, review the notion of rhythmic groups.

   il a   /i la/   sept amis   /sɛ ta mi/   Alice arrive   /a li sa riv/

Some final consonants are almost always pronounced. If you recall, these include final **-c**, **-r**, **-f**, **-l**, and all consonants followed by **-e**:

   Éric   ma sœu**r**   neu**f**   l'éco**l**e   la no**t**e   sei**ze**   il ai**me**

Other final consonants are pronounced only when the following word begins with a vowel. These are called *liaison consonants*, and the process that links the liaison consonant to the beginning of the next syllable is called *liaison*. Liaison consonants are usually found in grammatical endings and words such as pronouns, articles, possessive adjectives, prepositions, and numbers. You have seen the following liaison consonants:

- **-s**, **-x**, **-z** (pronounced /z/): vous‿avez, les‿enfants, nos‿amis, aux‿échecs, très‿aimable, six‿ans, chez‿eux

- **-t**: c'est‿un stylo, elles sont‿énergiques

- **-n**: on‿a, un‿oncle, mon‿ami

Point out that liaison is never made with the final *-t* of the word *et*.

When you pronounce a liaison consonant, articulate it as part of the next word:

The asterisk in the examples is a linguistic convention used to show that this form is not part of a native speaker's repertoire.

   deux‿oncles /dø zɔ̃kl/   *not* */døz ɔ̃kl/
   on a /ɔ̃ na/   *not* */ɔ̃n a/
   il est‿ici /i le ti si/   *not* */il et i si/

À vous la parole

3-28 Contrastes : sans et avec enchaînement. Pronounce each pair of phrases. Be sure to link the final consonant of the first word to the following word when it begins with a vowel.

une classe	une université
pour Bertrand	pour Albert
Luc parle	Luc écoute
neuf dentistes	neuf actrices
quel cousin	quel oncle
elle préfère ça	elle aime ça

3-29 Liaisons. Pronounce the liaison consonants in the following phrases. Be sure to link the consonant with the following word.

nous‿allons	vous‿écoutez
on‿a	un‿an
ils‿arrivent	elles‿étudient
elles sont‿au labo	elles vont‿au resto U
son petit‿ami	il a vingt‿ans
ton‿amie	son‿enfant

FORMES ET FONCTIONS

1. C'est *et* il est

The functional difference between the two patterns is related to the notion of topic vs. comment. For example, if Julie has already been mentioned in the conversation, one is more likely to use the first pattern, *elle est musicienne*. If however Julie is being introduced into the conversation, one would be more likely to use *Julie, c'est une musicienne*. Display examples of the two patterns and explain usage.

- There are two ways to indicate someone's profession:

  - Use a form of **être** + the name of the profession, without an article:

Julie **est** musicienne.	*Julie is a musician.*
Son frère **est** acteur.	*Her brother is an actor.*
Nous **sommes** professeurs des écoles.	*We are schoolteachers.*

  - Use **c'est/ce sont** + the indefinite article + the name of the profession:

Julie, **c'est une** musicienne.	*Julie is a musician.*
Stéphane ? **C'est un** dentiste.	*Stéphane? He's a dentist.*
Leurs parents ? **Ce sont des** architectes.	*Their parents? They're architects.*

- When you include an adjective along with the name of a profession, you must use **c'est/ce sont** + the indefinite article. Compare:

Anne **est** musicienne.	*Anne is a musician.*
C'est une excellente musicienne.	*She's an excellent musician.*
Ils **sont** peintres.	*They're painters.*
Ce sont des peintres très doués.	*They're very talented painters.*

À vous la parole

3-30 Professions et traits de caractère. For each profession, specify a fitting character trait.

MODÈLE   Anne est infirmière.
➤ C'est une infirmière calme.

1. Delphine est avocate.
2. Rémi est assistant social.
3. Virginie est médecin.
4. Max est représentant de commerce.
5. Coralie est peintre.
6. Florian et Sylvie sont informaticiens.
7. Hugo et Jessica sont mécaniciens.
8. Sandra et Alex sont professeurs des écoles.

3-31 Identification. Identify the nationality and profession of each of the following famous people. Choose from: **américain/e**, **anglais/e**, or **français/e**.

MODÈLE   Jules Verne
➤ C'est un écrivain français.

1. Gustave Eiffel
2. Barbra Streisand
3. Gérard Depardieu
4. Charles Dickens
5. Stephen King
6. Leonard Bernstein
7. Victor Hugo
8. Toni Morrison

3-32 Quelle est leur profession ? With a partner, tell what some of the people you know well do for a living.

MODÈLE   votre mère
É1 Ma mère est technicienne de laboratoire.
É2 Ma mère travaille à la maison ; c'est une femme au foyer (*homemaker*).

1. votre mère
2. votre père
3. votre frère ou sœur
4. votre grand-père
5. votre oncle
6. votre tante

Begin practice using the unlabeled images of professions from the **Points de départ** (IRCD, Ch. 3). Have students identify the profession of each person shown: *C'est une infirmière*, etc.

3-30 Before beginning, review adjectives, brainstorming about what kind of people usually have what professions: *infirmière = gentille, généreuse ; avocat = sérieux, ambitieux ; peintre = individualiste*, etc.

3-31 Have students suggest additional possibilities; this could be structured as a game. Simplify by having students give the profession only: *Jules Verne ? C'est un écrivain.*

2. *Les verbes* devoir, pouvoir *et* vouloir

- The verbs **devoir**, **pouvoir**, and **vouloir** are irregular.

DEVOIR *must, to have to, to be supposed to*			
SINGULIER		PLURIEL	
je	dois	nous	dev**ons**
tu	dois	vous	dev**ez**
il		ils	
elle }	doit	elles }	doiv**ent**
on			

POUVOIR *can, to be able*			
SINGULIER		PLURIEL	
je	peux	nous	pouv**ons**
tu	peux	vous	pouv**ez**
il		ils	
elle }	peut	elles }	peuv**ent**
on			

VOULOIR *to want*			
SINGULIER		PLURIEL	
je	veux	nous	voul**ons**
tu	veux	vous	voul**ez**
il		ils	
elle }	veut	elles }	veul**ent**
on			

- These verbs are often used:
  - With an infinitive:

Tu **dois** travailler ?	*Do you have to work?*
Je **veux** arriver demain matin.	*I want to arrive tomorrow morning.*
Tu ne **peux** pas arriver ce soir ?	*Can't you arrive this evening?*

  - To soften commands and make suggestions. Compare:

Attendez ici !	*Wait here!*
Vous **devez** attendre ici.	*You must wait here.*
Vous **voulez** attendre ici, s'il vous plaît ?	*Will you wait here, please?*
Vous **pouvez** attendre ici.	*You can wait here.*

- The verb **devoir** also has the meaning *to owe*:

Il **doit** 50 € à mon frère.	*He owes my brother 50 euros.*
Combien est-ce que je vous **dois** ?	*How much do I owe you?*

- **Vouloir** is used in a number of useful expressions:

Tu **veux** aller avec nous au ciné ?	*You want to go to the movies with us?*
Je **veux** bien.	*OK.*
Qu'est-ce que vous **voulez** / tu **veux** dire ?	*What do you mean?*
Qu'est-ce que ça **veut** dire ?	*What does that mean?*

À vous la parole

3-33 Un peu de tact ! Caroline and Jean-Sébastien work in a department store. Caroline is speaking sharply to Jean-Sébastien. Give him the same instructions in a more tactful way.

MODÈLE   Va au bureau !
>   ➤ Tu veux aller au bureau ?
> OU ➤ Tu peux aller au bureau ?

1. Donne la calculatrice à Pierre !
2. Parle à cette dame !
3. Montre le lecteur CD au monsieur !
4. Change le DVD !
5. Va à la banque !
6. Téléphone au directeur !

Now change the orders given by the boss to both Caroline and Jean-Sébastien.

MODÈLE   Montrez les ordinateurs aux clients !
>   ➤ Vous voulez montrer les ordinateurs aux clients ?
> OU ➤ Vous pouvez montrer les ordinateurs aux clients ?

7. Fermez la porte du bureau !
8. Montrez ce magnétoscope au monsieur !
9. Allez au bureau du comptable !
10. Téléphonez au directeur !

3-34 Une future profession. What can these people do for a living? With a partner, suggest possibilities.

MODÈLE   Sarah veut gagner beaucoup d'argent, mais elle ne veut pas faire des études supérieures.

>   É1 Elle peut devenir (*become*) actrice de cinéma, par exemple.
>   É2 Elle peut aussi devenir chanteuse.

1. Adrien ne veut pas travailler dans un bureau ; il aime travailler en plein air.
2. Gaëlle et Alexandra veulent travailler avec les enfants.
3. Je veux voyager et je suis assez sociable.
4. Nous voulons un contact avec le public et nous préférons travailler le soir.
5. Jean-Baptiste veut aider les gens et il n'est pas doué pour les sciences.
6. Audrey est très douée pour la musique et très disciplinée.
7. Simon et David ne veulent pas un travail avec beaucoup de stress.

Begin practice with a discrimination drill: one person, or more than one? *Ils peuvent écouter ; elle veut dîner,* etc. Follow up with substitution drills for *vouloir* and *pouvoir : Je veux travailler ; nous. —Nous voulons travailler,* etc.

Next complete Ex. 3-33 through 3-35, which integrate practice of *vouloir* and *pouvoir*. To practice *devoir*, use Ex. 3-36 and the supplemental exercise on the IRCD (IRCD, Ch. 3):
Désirs et réalité. Based on the pictures, take turns with a partner telling what these people want to do and what they have to do.
MODÈLE   É1 Il veut regarder un match de foot à la télé, mais il ne peut pas;
         É2 Il doit travailler dans le jardin.

3-33 Expand by having students ask people in the classroom to do various things.

3-34 Have students describe their own interests, and let classmates suggest a suitable profession.

Qu'est-ce que vous faites dans la vie ? Do you remember the old TV show, "What's my line?" Here's a version students can play in French.
Avant de jouer. Divide into groups of five. One person in each group will be the "mystery guest" and the other four will be panelists. The mystery guest selects an occupation and writes it on a piece of a paper. Each panelist jots down a few questions aimed at finding out what the mystery guest does for a living. The mystery guest can respond with only "yes" or "no," so questions should be formed with *Est-ce que…*
En scène. The panelists take turns asking the mystery guest questions to find out what he or she does for a living. Remind the mystery guest to be mysterious and answer only with some variation of *oui* or *non*.
MODÈLES   Est-ce que vous travaillez avec les gens ?
          —Non, pas vraiment.
          Est-ce que vous aidez les gens ?
          —Oui, un peu.
          Est-ce que vous travaillez dans un garage ?
          —Bien sûr que non.

3-35 First brainstorm with the whole class some appropriate questions for each item. Examples:

1. Qu'est-ce que tu veux faire comme travail ?
2. Où est-ce que tu veux habiter ?
3. Où est-ce que tu veux voyager ?
4. Est-ce que tu veux avoir des enfants ? Combien ?
5. Est-ce que tu veux avoir beaucoup d'argent ?

Then put students in pairs to compare answers.

3-36 As a follow-up, have each student suggest an excuse, then vote on who has the most original/the most plausible/the most far-fetched excuse.

3-35 Vouloir, c'est pouvoir. What are your plans for the future? Compare your ideas with those of your partner.

MODÈLE   faire comme travail

    É1 Qu'est-ce que tu veux faire comme travail ?

    É2 Moi, je veux être médecin ou dentiste. Et toi ?

    É1 Moi, je ne veux pas être médecin ni (*nor*) dentiste ; je veux être architecte.

1. faire comme travail
2. habiter
3. voyager
4. avoir des enfants
5. avoir de l'argent

3-36 Trouvez une excuse. You don't want to go out (*sortir*) with your classmate's friend, so you must come up with a good excuse!

MODÈLE   ➤ Je ne peux pas sortir ce soir avec ton ami/e ; je dois préparer un examen et aller chez mes parents.

Stratégie

Scan a text by searching quickly to locate specific information that you need. Then, when you find the desired information, focus on it and read it carefully.

3-37 Petites annonces

A. Avant de lire. The text below consists of several job ads from a newspaper. When you read ads like these, you typically will be looking for specific pieces of information. You may want to know, for example, if any of the ads is for a teaching position or if your bilingual skills would be an asset in any of the positions advertised. The reading skill you use to search a text quickly for specific information of this sort is scanning. You can scan the text—assisted by the design and layout—to find relevant ads, then focus more intensively on information of interest.

En lisant, Key: 1) a. CÉGEP ; b. Fruits & Parfums , Comptable ; c. hygiéniste dentaire ; d. comptable ; e. Fruits & Parfums   2) Tous les emplois annoncés s'adressent aux hommes et aux femmes ; for women: Hygiéniste Dentaire demandée ; for both men and women: enseignant(e), conseiller(ère), pharmacien(ne)   3) comptable
4) pharmacien(ne) ; une fin de semaine

B. En lisant. Scan the ads to find the answers to the following questions.

1. Find an ad:
   a. for a teaching job
   b. for a full-time permanent position
   c. for a temporary position
   d. for an office job
   e. for which you need to speak two languages

2. Find a sentence that indicates that all jobs are offered to both men and women. In spite of this, one ad is clearly written with women in mind. Which ad is it? Which ad(s) make(s) it clear that both men and women are encouraged to apply?

3. One job requires knowledge of computers. You can find it by looking for names of computer programs. Which ad is it?

4. One job specifies that working some weekends is required. Which one? The expression used to express "weekend" is different from the word used in France, **le week-end**. How is this expressed in Canadian French?

carrières

Pour faire paraître vos annonces dans cette section composez 868-0237 ou écrivez à carrières et professions

Tous les emplois annoncés s'adressent aux hommes et aux femmes.

CÉGEP

de St-Philippe

Le Cégep de Saint-Philippe requiert les services d'enseignant(e) afin de dispenser les charges de cours suivant :

CH-2006-04 Charge temps partiel en mathématiques

Exigence : baccalauréat en mathématiques

L'expérience en psychopédagogie et en enseignement est souhaitable. Les personnes intéressées doivent faire parvenir leur curriculum vitae *au plus tard le 7 mai 2006 à 17 h* à l'adresse suivante :

Cégep de Saint-Philippe
Service des ressources humaines
Saint-Philippe (Québec) G2R 8K2
Télécopieur : (418) 261-9796

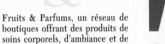

Fruits & Parfums

Fruits & Parfums, un réseau de boutiques offrant des produits de soins corporels, d'ambiance et de gourmet est à la recherche d'un(e)

CONSEILLER(ÈRE) AUX VENTES (temps plein)

– Vous avez un sens de la vente.
– Vous détenez un diplôme d'études secondaires.
– Vous êtes bilingue.

Si vous êtes un(e) passionné(e) de fragrances enivrantes, veuillez faire parvenir votre curriculum vitae au plus tard le 30 avril prochain, par télécopieur au (418) 296-2080, par courriel au *emploi@fruits-parfums.com* ou en vous présentant directement à la boutique située dans le Vieux-Québec.

CONSTRUCTION QUÉBÉCOISE

Entrepreneur général en construction résidentielle recherche un(e)

COMPTABLE

Connaissance du système Acomba et des applications Excel et Word nécessaire.

Expérience en construction serait un atout. Bonne formation et quelques années d'expérience pertinente souhaitables.

S.V.P. faire parvenir curriculum vitae à l'attention de Gilles Lamontagne

**CONSTRUCTION QUÉBÉCOISE
4500, boul. de la Couronne
Québec (QC) G2F 2B9**

HYGIÉNISTE DENTAIRE

demandée à Lac-Saint-Martin

Temps plein en remplacement d'un congé de maternité, 18 à 24 mois

Tél : **489-4271**

Pharmacien(ne)

Ville de Québec
(quartier Petit Champlain)
33 heures/semaine
Une (1) fin de semaine sur quatre (4)
Horaire flexible

**Appeler Alain Paradis
459-3025**

C. En regardant de plus près. Now that you have located particular pieces of information in the ads, focus on the following features.

1. Look more closely at the ad for a teaching job: Is this a full-time position? What qualifications are required, and what experience is desirable?

2. Based on their ad, what type of business is **Fruits & Parfums**?

3. If you wanted to apply for the job at **Fruits & Parfums**, what options do you have?

D. Après avoir lu. Now discuss the following questions with your classmates.

1. Would you be qualified for any of the jobs listed? Explain why or why not. Do you find any of the jobs particularly interesting? Why?

2. Are these ads in any way different from ads for the same types of jobs in your own local newspaper?

En regardant de plus près, Key:
1) the teaching job is a part-time position, requiring a *bacc* in the area taught, with pedagogical training and teaching experience desirable   2) a retail store offering luxury skin care, and home and gourmet products   3) one can apply by fax, by e-mail, or in person at the boutique.

Après avoir lu. One difference between similar ads in French and English is the need in French to make clear that jobs are for men and women by changing the ending of words.

Venez chez nous !
Étudier et travailler au Canada

Additional activities to explore the
Venez chez nous ! topics are
provided by:
• Student Activities Manual
• *Chez nous* video
• *Chez nous* Companion Website:
  http://www.prenhall.com/cheznous

Show the video montage *Étudier et
travailler au Canada* to provide a brief
introduction to the lesson. In Canada, all
government documents are published in
both English and French. This does not
mean that all Canadians are bilingual,
however.

LES FRANCOPHONES AU CANADA

Canada is officially bilingual,
and almost seven million of
the country's 30 million
citizens speak French as
their native language. Most
French Canadians live in
the province of Quebec,
where approximately 85%
of the population is
French-speaking.
Montreal is the second
largest Francophone city
in the world, after Paris.
In this lesson we will
review some of the
history of French
speakers in Canada and
explore what it is like
to live, study, and work
there today.

Le Château Frontenac à Québec

Le vieux Montréal

Observons

3-38 Un peu d'histoire

A. Avant de regarder. You are about to listen in on a conversation between Marie, a university student, and Marie-Julie, a professor at the same university. Marie is writing a paper on the history of Quebec and she is asking her knowledgeable friend some questions. Naturally, since they are talking about historical events, both often use the past tense. Take a look at the following words and expressions from their conversation and see if, drawing on your familiarity with cognates as well as your knowledge of history, you can determine what they mean.

1. Verrazzano a découvert le territoire
2. Jacques Cartier en a pris possession au nom du roi de France
3. Samuel de Champlain a fondé la première colonie
4. la Nouvelle-France a été cédée à l'Angleterre après une longue guerre

You will, of course, also hear references to important dates throughout the discussion of Quebec's history. Remember that in general, dates in French are given in three parts: the thousands (**mille/mil**), the hundreds (**cinq cents**), and the rest. So 1524 is: **mil cinq cent vingt-quatre.**

B. En regardant. As you watch the video clip, indicate where each event mentioned fits on the time line by writing the number of the event under the proper year.

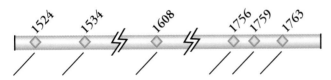

1. La Nouvelle-France est cédée à l'Angleterre.
2. Verrazzano découvre le territoire et le nomme la Nouvelle-France.
3. Jacques Cartier prend possession de la Nouvelle-France au nom du roi.
4. Samuel de Champlain fonde une colonie en Nouvelle-France.
5. Il y a 65 000 colons français et 1 500 000 colons anglais.

C. Après avoir regardé. Now discuss the following questions with classmates.

1. What name is given to **la Nouvelle-France** now?
2. Can you think of place-names in North America that include this idea of "new?" How did these places come to have these names?

Après avoir regardé. Possible answers for #2 include New England, New Hampshire, New Jersey, New York (all from England), New Orleans, and New Mexico.

Additional activities related to the **Observons** can be found in the Video Manual. Go over the examples in **Avant de regarder** with students, focusing on cognates, and make sure they have grasped the basic meaning of the sentences. There is no need to explain the *passé composé.*

Script for *Observons*

MARIE : Bonjour Marie-Julie.

MARIE-JULIE : Ah, Bonjour Marie. Viens t'asseoir.

MARIE : Merci. Je dois préparer un rapport sur l'histoire du Québec pour mon cours d'histoire. Pouvez-vous m'aider un peu ?

MARIE-JULIE : Bien sûr que oui.

MARIE : À l'origine le Québec était français. Pourquoi il est… il n'est pas toujours français ?

MARIE-JULIE : Eh bien, le Québec parle français, mais depuis 1763 le Québec a été ou plutôt la Nouvelle-France a été cédée à l'Angleterre après une longue guerre de sept ans.

MARIE : Je ne comprends pas. Vous dites la Nouvelle-France et Québec. Pourquoi les deux noms ?

MARIE-JULIE : Alors, maintenant ça s'appelle le Québec mais avant 1763 la colonie était française. C'est Verrazzano en 1524 qui a découvert le territoire et l'a nommé et Jacques Cartier en a pris possession en 1534 au nom du roi de France, François Ier.

MARIE : Donc, c'est Jacques Cartier qui a fondé la première colonie en Nouvelle-France ?

MARIE-JULIE : À vrai dire, non. C'est Samuel de Champlain en 1608 qui a fondé officiellement la première colonie en Nouvelle-France. Alors entre cette époque 1608 et la cession en 1763 on comptait environ 65 000 colons français contre 1 500 000 de colons dans les colonies anglaises.

MARIE : Attends, je note : 65 000 colons français et 1 500 000 colons anglais en 1756. C'est bon ?

MARIE-JULIE : C'est bien ça.

MARIE : C'est bon. Je crois que mon rapport va être intéressant. Merci.

MARIE-JULIE : Bienvenue.

La Révolution tranquille et la Loi 101

Around 1960, Quebec experienced the "Quiet revolution" (**la Révolution tranquille**). The provincial government began to encourage wider participation by the Francophone majority in industry and commerce while it promoted Québécois culture through music, theater, film, and literature. In 1977, the provincial legislature made French the sole official language of Quebec with Bill 101 (**la Loi 101**). All official documents, however, have continued to be published in English and French, and the rights of Anglophone minorities who are Canadian citizens are protected.

The preamble to **la Loi 101** outlines its rationale and lists the five areas, in addition to the legal system, in which French will be used:

Charte de la langue française

[Sanctionnée le 26 août 1977]

Préambule

Langue distinctive d'un peuple majoritairement francophone, la langue française permet au peuple québécois d'exprimer son identité.

L'Assemblée nationale reconnaît la volonté des Québécois d'assurer la qualité et le rayonnement de la langue française. Elle est donc résolue à faire du français la langue de l'État et de la Loi aussi bien que la langue normale et habituelle du travail, de l'enseignement, des communications, du commerce et des affaires.

Lisons

Stratégie

3-39 Le français au Québec

A. Avant de lire. This excerpt is from an informational magazine called **Emménager à Montréal** (*Moving to Montreal*), which is a guide for people who are relocating to Montreal. This particular passage is concerned with the use of the French language. Thinking about what you have just learned about **la Loi 101** in Quebec can help you to understand this text. What is the intent of this law and what do you think the implications are likely to be for English-speaking people who move to Montreal?

B. En lisant. As you read, look for the following information.

1. What language is commonly used by most people in Quebec?
2. According to the article, name three things for which French is used most often.
3. The law requires that two things be done mostly in French. What are they?
4. How could you learn French if you were moving to Quebec?

Le français au Québec

Le Québec se caractérise par un taux de bilinguisme élevé[1], dans une société où le français est la langue publique commune. C'est la langue que l'on utilise le plus souvent[2] en recherche et développement dans les milieux[3] de travail, les communications, le commerce et les affaires.

Le Québec tient à[4] préserver et à promouvoir sa langue officielle. Le français représente non seulement[5] un instrument de communication essentiel, mais aussi un symbole commun d'appartenance à la société québécoise. La réglementation de la Loi 101 prévoit[6] donc que l'affichage et la publicité doivent être présentés majoritairement en français.

Le ministère des Relations avec les citoyens et de l'Immigration du Québec offre aux immigrants toute une gamme[7] de cours de français GRATUITS, le jour ou le soir, à temps plein ou à temps partiel, dans les écoles spécialisées ou en milieu de travail. (514) 864-9191.

Source: *Emménager à Montréal, 2000/2001*

[1]*a high rate* [2]*the most often* [3]*the context* [4]*is determined to* [5]*not only* [6]*requires* [7]*a wide range*

C. En regardant de plus près. Focusing on the context and your own background knowledge, can you provide an English equivalent for each of the highlighted words?

1. … préserver et **promouvoir** la langue officielle.
2. … un symbole… d'**appartenance** à la société québécoise.
3. … l'**affichage** et la publicité doivent être présentés… en français.
4. … cours de français **gratuits**,…

D. Après avoir lu. Discuss the following questions with your classmates.

1. What is your opinion of the provisions of **la Loi 101** mentioned in this excerpt? Do you think they are necessary and appropriate? How do you think you would feel about this law and its provisions if you were going to be living in Quebec?

2. At this time, there is no national law specifying that English is the official language of the United States, although some groups have expressed support for such a law. Do you think an English-only law is necessary or would be beneficial? Why or why not?

Le Carnaval de Québec

Parlons

3-40 Une langue bien de chez nous

A. Avant de parler. Consider how the following brief French-Canadian conversation differs from a conversation in Standard French, the French you are learning. Are there words and turns of phrase that you are not familiar with?

ALEX : Allô Julie. Ça va ?

JULIE : C'est pas pire.

ALEX : Je te présente ma blonde, Sabrina.

JULIE : Salut, Sabrina.

SABRINA : Salut, Julie.

ALEX : Excuse-nous, Julie, on ne peut pas jaser, on doit travailler à la bibli.

JULIE : O.K., c'est beau. Moi, je vais dîner à la cafétéria. Bonjour Alex, bonjour Sabrina.

SABRINA : Salut. À prochaine.

French spoken in Quebec is not exactly like Parisian French. French speakers in Quebec have their own accent and use some words differently. As the well-known Québécois singer Michel Rivard sings in **Le cœur de ma vie : C'est une langue de France, Aux accents d'Amérique…**

Here are some common expressions in Québécois French:

au Québec	en France
allô	bonjour
c'est pas pire	c'est pas mal
c'est le fun	c'est amusant
ma blonde	ma petite amie
mon chum	mon petit ami
la fin de semaine	le week-end
jaser	discuter
une job	un job
O.K. c'est beau	d'accord, c'est bon
bienvenue	je vous en prie
à prochaine	à la prochaine
bonjour	au revoir

B. En parlant. Use some of the Québécois words and expressions listed above to create a dialogue with one or two classmates. Choose from the scenarios suggested below, or create your own. Act out your dialogue for the class.

1. You run into a friend on campus and introduce him/her to your boyfriend/girlfriend.
2. You call a friend and invite him/her to do something fun. Your friend wants to come, but there is a problem…
3. You run into a former girlfriend/boyfriend and try to impress him/her.

C. Après avoir parlé. Can you think of some examples of regional differences in your native language? Why might regional language differences exist?

En parlant. Encourage students to develop their conversations orally, without writing down a script. Then have each group perform their dialogue—and let the class decide who did the best job!

Après avoir parlé. Some typical regional differences in English include 1) pronunciation of merry/marry/Mary 2) usage of the words soda/pop/soft drink; students can probably add many more examples.

Écrivons

3-41 Les universités au Canada

You may have the opportunity to travel to or study in Canada. Explore whether you might like to spend a semester or a year at a Canadian university, then write a brief paragraph about your conclusions.

A. Avant d'écrire

Refer students to the *Chez nous* Companion Website for links to several Canadian universities.

1. Choose a Canadian university that you would like to know more about. Here are some possibilities:

   Concordia University

   McGill University

   Université de Montréal (UdeM)

   Université de Québec à Montréal (UQAM)

   University of Ottawa

   University of Toronto

2. Next, search at the library or on the Web to find the information needed to complete the chart below in French.

Nom de l'université : _____

La langue des cours : _____

Nombre d'étudiants : _____

Nombre d'étudiants étrangers : _____

Quelques majeures (une liste de 2 ou 3) : _____

Quelques associations d'étudiants (une liste de 2 ou 3) : _____

_____

Équipes sportives : _____

B. En écrivant

1. Begin your paragraph by stating why you have decided you might like to study at the institution you chose:

   MODÈLE ➤ Je veux étudier à UdeM parce que…

2. Continue your paragraph by mentioning what elements you like and what you do not like about the university.

   MODÈLE ➤ UdeM est située à Montréal, et c'est une grande ville. J'aime beaucoup les grandes villes. Mais je n'aime pas…

3. Decide whether it would be beneficial to you to study at this university in Canada, and conclude your paragraph with a summary statement.

   MODÈLE ➤ Je veux travailler comme avocate internationale, donc (*therefore*) je pense que c'est important de passer un semestre à UdeM. Après un semestre au Québec, je vais parler assez bien le français !

C. Après avoir écrit

1. Review your first draft to make sure you have clearly addressed the major points.

2. Once you are satisfied with the content of your paragraph, proofread it for errors in spelling and grammar. Share your paragraph with the class. Which schools are most often mentioned, and why?

Vocabulaire

Leçon 1

à l'université, à la fac(ulté)	***at the university, the school***
un amphithéâtre	*lecture hall*
des associations (f.) étudiantes	*student organizations*
la bibliothèque universitaire (la BU)	*university library*
des bureaux (m.) administratifs	*administrative offices*
le bureau des inscriptions	*registrar's office*
le bureau du professeur	*professor's office*
la cafétéria	*cafeteria*
le centre des sports	*sports complex*
le centre étudiant	*student center*
un centre informatique	*computer center*
un garage	*garage*
une infirmerie	*health center*
un labo(ratoire) de chimie	*chemistry lab*
un labo(ratoire) de langues	*language lab*
un pavillon	*building*
le pavillon principal	*main building*
un plan du campus	*campus map*
la résidence	*residence hall*
le restaurant universitaire (le resto U)	*dining hall*
une station de métro	*subway, metro stop*
un terrain de sport	*playing field, court*

prépositions de lieu	***prepositions***
à côté de	*next to, beside*
à droite de	*to the right of*
à gauche de	*to the left of*
dans	*in, inside*
derrière	*behind*
devant	*in front of*
en face de	*across from*
loin de	*far from*
près de	*close to, near*

adjectifs prénominaux	***adjectives that precede the noun***
beau/bel/belle	*beautiful, handsome*
bon/bonne	*good*
dernier/dernière	*last*
grand/e	*tall*
gros/se	*big, fat*
jeune	*young*
joli/e	*pretty*
mauvais/e	*bad*
nouveau/nouvel/ nouvelle	*new*
petit/e	*small, short*
premier/première	*first*
vieux/vieil/vieille	*old*

autres mots utiles	***other useful words***
après	*after*
un cours	*course*
ici	*here*
retrouver quelqu'un	*to meet someone*
tous (m. pl.)	*all*
se trouver	*to be located*
une voiture	*car*

Leçon 2

des cours (m.)	***courses***
l'allemand (m.)	*German*
l'anglais (m.)	*English*
l'anthropologie (f.)	*anthropology*
l'astronomie	*astronomy*
la biologie	*biology*
la botanique	*botany*
le calcul	*calculus*
la chimie	*chemistry*
la comptabilité	*accounting*
la danse	*dance*
le dessin	*drawing*
l'économie (f.)	*economics*
l'espagnol (m.)	*Spanish*
le français	*French*

l'histoire (f.)	*history*
l'informatique (f.)	*computer science*
une langue étrangère	*foreign language*
la littérature	*literature*
les mathématiques (f.) (les maths)	*mathematics*
la musique	*music*
la peinture	*painting*
la philosophie	*philosophy*
la physiologie	*physiology*
la physique	*physics*
la psychologie	*psychology*
les sciences (f.) politiques	*political science*
la sculpture	*sculpture*
la sociologie	*sociology*
le théâtre	*theater*
la zoologie	*zoology*

les facultés (f.)   *colleges*

les beaux-arts (m.)	*fine arts*
le droit	*law*
la gestion	*business*
le journalisme	*journalism*
les lettres (f.)	*humanities*
la médecine	*medicine*
les sciences de l'éducation (f.)	*education*
les sciences économiques	*economics*
les sciences humaines	*social sciences*
les sciences naturelles	*natural sciences*
les sciences physiques	*physical sciences*

pour parler des études (f.)   *to talk about studies*

un bacc(alauréat) (en sciences économiques)	*B.A or B.S. degree (Can.) (in economics)*
une composition	*in-class essay exam*
un devoir	*essay*
des devoirs	*homework*
un dictionnaire	*dictionary*
un diplôme (en beaux-arts)	*degree (in fine arts)*
un examen (préparer un examen)	*exam (to study for an exam)*
une majeure (en sociologie)	*major (Can.) (in sociology)*
une mineure (en français)	*minor (Can.) (in French)*

une note (avoir une note)	*grade (to have/receive a grade)*
préparer un diplôme (en chimie)	*to do a degree (in chemistry)*
un semestre	*semester*
une spécialisation (en français)	*major (in French)*
suivre un cours	*to take a course*
un trimestre	*trimester, quarter*

pour décrire les cours, les examens, les notes   *to describe courses, tests, grades*

difficile	*difficult*
ennuyeux/ennuyeuse	*boring, tedious*
facile	*easy*
final/e	*final*
intéressant/e	*interesting*
médiocre	*mediocre*
obligatoire	*required*

pour exprimer les préférences   *to express preferences*

adorer	*to adore*
aimer	*to like or to love*
aimer beaucoup	*to like or love a lot*
aimer bien	*to like fairly well*
détester	*to detest*
préférer	*to prefer*

verbes conjugués comme préférer   *verbs conjugated like préférer*

répéter	*to repeat*
suggérer	*to suggest*

Leçon 3

où on travaille   *where people work*

un bureau	*office*
une clinique	*private hospital*
un collège	*middle school*
une école	*elementary school*
une fac(ulté)/ une université	*college, university*
un hôpital	*public hospital*
un lycée	*high school*
un magasin	*store*
une usine	*factory*

des métiers (m.) et des professions (f.)	*jobs and professions*
un acteur/une actrice	*actor/actress*
un agent de police	*police officer*
un/e architecte	*architect*
un/e artiste	*artist*
un/e assistant/e social/e	*social worker*
un/e avocat/e	*lawyer*
un chanteur/ une chanteuse	*singer*
un/e comptable	*accountant*
un/e dentiste	*dentist*
un écrivain	*writer*
un infirmier/ une infirmière	*nurse*
un/e informaticien/ne	*programmer*
un ingénieur	*engineer*
un/e journaliste	*journalist*
un/e mécanicien/ne	*mechanic*
un médecin	*physician*
un/e musicien/ne	*musician*
un ouvrier/une ouvrière	*factory worker*
un peintre	*painter*
un/e pharmacien/ne	*pharmacist*
un/e professeur/e	*professor (f., Can.)*
un professeur des écoles	*elementary school teacher*
un/e représentant/e de commerce	*sales representative*
un/e secrétaire	*secretary*

un serveur/une serveuse	*server*
un/e technicien/ne	*lab technician*
un vendeur/ une vendeuse	*sales clerk*

quelques mots utiles	*some useful words*
l'argent (m.)	*money*
autonome	*independent*
une carrière	*career*
être doué/e	*to be talented*
les gens (m.)	*people*
en plein air	*outdoors*
le prestige	*prestige*
le public (un contact avec le public)	*the public (contact with the public)*
la responsabilité	*responsibility*
un salaire	*salary*
les services (m.)	*the service sector*
le travail	*work*

quelques verbes	*some verbs*
aider les gens	*to help people*
chercher	*to look for*
devoir	*must, to have to, should*
gagner (de l'argent)	*to earn, to win (money)*
s'intéresser à	*to be interested in*
pouvoir	*to be able to*
vouloir	*to want, to wish*
voyager	*to travel*

Where are these people and where are they going, in your opinion? How do they seem to be feeling?

Chapitre 4 *Métro, boulot, dodo*

Leçon 1   *La routine de la journée*

Leçon 2   *À quelle heure ?*

Leçon 3   *Qu'est-ce qu'on met ?*

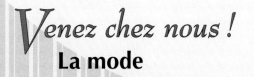

Venez chez nous !
La mode

In this chapter:

- Talking about your daily routine
- Telling time
- Making comparisons
- Describing clothing
- Comparing daily routines and fashion in places where French is spoken

Leçon 1   *La routine de la journée*

POINTS DE DÉPART

La routine du matin

TEXT AUDIO

Il est huit heures du matin. La journée commence !

Chez les Bouchard, Thomas se réveille ; il va bientôt se lever.

Sa petite sœur Vanessa est déjà debout ; elle se coiffe. Monsieur Bouchard est en train de se raser. Il va bientôt prendre une douche.

Madame Bouchard se maquille et elle s'habille pour aller au travail. Le bébé s'endort de nouveau.

Dans son appartement, Caroline se dépêche ; elle va bientôt à la fac. Elle se lave les mains et la figure et elle se brosse les dents.

Chez les Morin, Madame Morin se douche et se lave les cheveux ; après, elle s'essuie. Son mari rentre à la maison. Lui, il travaille tard la nuit, donc il rentre tôt le matin pour se coucher. Il se déshabille et il se couche.

Use the cross section of the apartment building (IRCD, Ch. 4) to present the new vocabulary. Describe the activities pictured, using the textbook description as a model. Test comprehension by having students tell who is doing what: *Qui se lave la figure ?*, etc. Have students repeat key phrases, then mime, or have students mime, activities while others guess what's being done.

Additional practice activities for each **Points de départ** section are provided by:
- **Student Activities Manual**
- *Chez nous* Companion Website:
  http://www.prenhall.com/cheznous

Bring in items to illustrate toiletries; for example, show toothpaste and shampoo containers with labels in French, and an actual *gant de toilette*. Use the visual of toiletry items (IRCD, Ch. 4) to present additional items and test comprehension: have students point to items you name, then repeat by identifying items: *C'est un peigne ou une brosse à dents ?* Associate each item with an activity: *avec un rasoir ? — On se rase ;* or, *Qu'est-ce qu'il faut : pour se raser ? — un rasoir,* etc. Note that native speakers use the expressions *se doucher/prendre une douche, se laver/se brosser les dents* interchangeably. The only forms practiced here are the third-person singular and the infinitive; the focus is on learning the meaning of the vocabulary. The forms of reflexive verbs are treated in the **Formes et fonctions** for this lesson.

Use the video clip *La routine du matin* to help introduce or reinforce some of the new vocabulary; note that we incorporate it below in the **Vie et culture**. Alternatively, the video can serve as an inductive presentation for **Formes et fonctions 1**. Note that in this segment, the two sisters use the form *nous nous levons*, etc., to describe their morning routine.

du maquillage

du shampooing

une brosse à dents

une brosse à cheveux

un peigne

du dentifrice

un lavabo

un savon

un rasoir

un gant de toilette

une serviette de toilette

Les articles de toilette

Vie et culture

Métro, boulot, dodo

The expression **métro, boulot, dodo** epitomizes the daily routine of most Parisians—in fact, of people who live in any big city. In the morning, many Parisians take the **métro** (the highly efficient Paris subway), go to their **boulot** (a slang word for **un job/un travail**), then at night they return home and crawl into bed to **faire dodo** (a child's expression for **se coucher/dormir**). In English, we often call this routine *the daily grind*.

What does the expression **métro, boulot, dodo** lead you to believe about life in Paris? Describe a person whose daily routine could be summarized by this expression. Would this expression apply also to the daily routine of North Americans who live in big cities? Would it apply to life in your hometown?

Now watch the video clip *La routine du matin* as two girls describe their morning routine. Make a list of their activities, for example: *Elles se réveillent.* Is there anything that surprises you about their routine, or does it seem very familiar and logical?

À vous la parole

4-1 Ordre logique.
In what order do most people complete the following activities?

Ex. 4-1 to 4-3 can serve as an inductive presentation of pronominal verbs, treated in this lesson. Verbs in -ir like dormir, partir, and sortir are treated in Ch. 4, L. 2.

MODÈLE   on se coiffe, on se douche
> ➤ On se douche, et puis on se coiffe.

1. on se lave, on s'habille
2. on se lave les cheveux, on se coiffe
3. on se lève, on se réveille
4. on se déshabille, on se couche
5. on mange, on se brosse les dents
6. on se couche, on se brosse les dents
7. on se couche, on s'endort
8. on s'essuie, on se lave

4-2 Suite logique.
Tell what these people are going to do next, choosing a verb from the list.

se coiffer	s'essuyer	se laver les cheveux
se coucher	s'habiller	se lever
s'endormir	se laver	se raser

MODÈLE   Margaux a un tee-shirt et un jean.
> ➤ Elle va s'habiller.

1. Adrien a un rasoir.
2. Olivier va dans sa chambre.
3. Julie cherche le shampooing.
4. Fanny est très fatiguée.
5. Damien entend sa mère qui dit, « Allez, debout ! »
6. Grégory va prendre une douche.
7. Delphine termine sa douche.
8. Sandrine a un peigne.

4-3 Un questionnaire.
Do you pay attention to how you look? A little? Too much? Not enough? Ask your partner the following questions and then add up the points. What are your conclusions?

1. Vous prenez une douche ou un bain tous les jours ?	**oui**	**non**
2. Vous vous lavez les cheveux tous les jours ?	**oui**	**non**
3. Vous vous brossez les dents après chaque repas ?	**oui**	**non**
4. Vous vous coiffez trois ou quatre fois pendant la journée ?	**oui**	**non**
5. Vous vous habillez différemment chaque jour ?	**oui**	**non**
6. Vous vous maquillez/vous vous rasez tous les jours ?	**oui**	**non**
7. Vous vous mettez du parfum/de l'eau de Cologne ?	**oui**	**non**
8. Vous faites très attention de ne jamais grossir (gain weight) ?	**oui**	**non**

Maintenant, marquez un point pour les réponses « oui », zéro pour les réponses « non » et ensuite additionnez vos points :

■ Si vous avez 7 ou 8 points, vous vous intéressez peut-être un peu trop à votre apparence physique. Pensez un peu aux choses plus sérieuses.

■ Si vous avez de 3 à 6 points, c'est bien. Vous faites attention à votre présentation, mais vous n'exagérez pas.

■ Si vous avez moins de 3 points, attention ! Vous risquez de vous négliger.

Sons et lettres

La voyelle /y/

The vowel /y/, as in **tu**, is generally spelled with **u**. To pronounce /y/, your tongue must be forward and your lips rounded, protruding, and tense. As you pronounce /y/, think of the vowel /i/ of **ici**. It is important to make a distinction between /y/ and the /u/ of **tout**, as many words are distinguished by these two vowels.

4-4 Imitation. Be careful to round your lips when pronouncing /y/!

tu   du   zut   Luc   Jules   Bruno   Lucie   Suzanne

4-5 Contrastes. Be careful to distinguish between /y/ (spelled *u*) and /u/ (spelled *ou*).

tu	tout	bout	bu
du	doux	poux	pu
zut	tous	début	debout

4-6 Salutations. Practice greetings, using the following names.

MODÈLES Bruno
➤ Salut, Bruno.

Mme Dupont
➤ Bonjour, Madame Dupont.

1. Bruno
2. Lucie
3. Suzanne
4. Mme Dumont
5. M. Dumas
6. Mme Camus

FORMES ET FONCTIONS

1. Les verbes pronominaux et les pronoms réfléchis

• Verbs like **s'essuyer** (*to dry oneself off*) and **se laver** (*to wash up*) include a reflexive pronoun as part of the verb: this pronoun indicates that the action is reflected on the subject. In English, the word *-self* is sometimes used to express this idea.

Je **m'essuie**.	*I'm drying myself off.*
On **se lave**.	*We're washing up.*
Tu **te lèves** ?	*Are you getting up?*

Here are the reflexive pronouns, shown with the verb **se laver**.

SE LAVER	*to wash*				
SINGULIER			PLURIEL		
je	**me**	lave	nous	**nous**	lav**ons**
tu	**te**	lav**es**	vous	**vous**	lav**ez**
il elle on	**se**	lave	ils elles	**se**	lav**ent**

- Before a vowel sound, **me**, **te**, and **se** become **m'**, **t'**, **s'**.

  Je **m'**essuie les mains.   *I'm drying my hands.*
  Tu **t'**habilles ?   *Are you getting dressed?*
  Il **s'**essuie la figure.   *He wipes his face.*

- Note that reflexive pronouns always maintain their position near the verb, even in the negative and the immediate future.

  Il ne **se** lave pas.   *He's not washing up.*
  Je ne vais pas **m'**habiller.   *I'm not going to get dressed.*

- When a part of the body is specified, the definite article is used, since the reflexive pronoun already indicates whose body part is affected.

  Elle se lave **la** figure.   *She's washing her face.*
  Ils se brossent **les** dents.   *They're brushing their teeth.*

- In an affirmative command, the reflexive pronoun follows the verb and is connected to it by a hyphen. Note the use of the stressed form **toi**. In negative commands, the reflexive pronoun precedes the verb.

  Lave-**toi** la figure !   Ne **te** lave pas la figure !
  Dépêchez-**vous** !   Ne **vous** dépêchez pas !

À vous la parole

4-7 Qu'est-ce qu'on fait ? Explain how people use the objects mentioned.

MODÈLE   Moi, le shampooing ?
➤ Je me lave les cheveux.

1. Les enfants, le savon et un gant de toilette ?
2. Jules, son rasoir ?
3. Vous, la serviette de toilette ?
4. Toi, le pull-over ?
5. Moi, le dentifrice ?
6. Nous, le peigne ?
7. Julie, le maquillage ?

Remind students that they have seen reflexive pronouns used with the verb *s'appeler*. Although this presentation does not treat forms of the verbs used reciprocally, you might wish to introduce here the notion of reciprocal pronominal verbs, corresponding to English "each other:" *Ils s'embrassent, Ils se téléphonent, Ils se parlent souvent*, etc. Idiomatic pronominal verbs, such as *se fâcher* and *s'entendre* will be presented in Ch. 7, L. 3. You may also wish to use the video segment *La routine du matin* as you present this topic.

Point out the following irregularities: *lever/lève, essuyer/essuie* (the latter with loss of stem-final /į/). Full conjugations can be found in Appendix 4.

To help students remember to use the definite article, you may want to recount the anecdote of a French speaker who has a hard time remembering to use the possessive in English because after all, "Whose face would I wash? Mine of course!"

You may wish to delay presentation of the imperative forms and the accompanying Ex. 4-8 until day 2 of the lesson, so students can assimilate and practice verbs with reflexive pronouns before being confronted with the syntactic changes in the imperative.

Begin practice with a substitution drill: *Je me lave ; nous.* —*Nous nous lavons*, etc. Provide additional drills for the negative and *futur proche*.

Begin practice of command forms with simple transformation drills: (1) singular to plural, and vice versa: *Réveille-toi !* —*Réveillez-vous !*; (2) affirmative to negative, and vice versa: *Réveille-toi !* —*Ne te réveille pas !*

👥 **4-8 Fais ta toilette !** Your partner always has an excuse! Take turns asking and answering questions and making comments about grooming.

MODÈLE se raser

> É1 Tu te rases ?
>
> É2 Non, je n'ai pas de rasoir.
>
> É1 Tiens, voilà un rasoir ; rase-toi donc !

1. se laver les mains
2. se laver la figure
3. s'essuyer les mains
4. se laver les cheveux
5. se brosser les dents
6. se coiffer

👥 **4-9 La routine chez vous.** At your house or in your family, who does the following things? Compare your answers with those of a partner.

MODÈLE se lève en premier ?

> É1 Qui se lève en premier chez toi ?
>
> É2 Ma mère se lève en premier. Et chez toi ?
>
> É1 Moi, je me lève en premier.

1. se lève en premier ?
2. se douche en premier ?
3. se maquille tous les jours ?
4. s'habille avec beaucoup d'attention ?
5. se lave les cheveux tous les jours ?
6. se couche tard le soir ?
7. se réveille facilement le matin ?

👥 **4-10 Mes journées.** Describe these three types of days to a partner.

MODÈLE une journée typique

> É1 Décris une journée typique.
>
> É2 Je me lève pour aller à mes cours. Je me lave et je m'habille, et je vais en classe. Ensuite (then), je vais au resto U pour manger. Après, je me brosse les dents… Et toi ?

1. une journée typique
2. une journée idéale
3. une journée horrible

2. Les adverbes : intensité, fréquence, quantité

- The adverbs listed below indicate to what degree something occurs.

trop	Elle se maquille **trop**.	*She wears too much makeup.*
beaucoup	Elle travaille **beaucoup**.	*She works a lot.*
assez	Nous mangeons **assez**.	*We eat enough.*
un peu	Je me dépêche **un peu**.	*I hurry a little.*
ne ... pas	Il **ne** se rase **pas**.	*He doesn't shave.*

- These same adverbs, followed by **de/d'** plus a noun, indicate quantities.

trop de	Il prend **trop de** douches.	*He takes too many showers.*
beaucoup de	Elle a **beaucoup d'**amis.	*She has lots of friends.*
assez de	Vous avez **assez d'**argent ?	*Do you have enough money?*
peu de	J'ai **peu de** maquillage chez moi.	*I don't have much makeup at my house.*
ne ... pas de	Tu **n'**as **pas de** rasoir ?	*Don't you have a razor?*

- Other adverbs indicate frequency, how often something is done. Notice that these adverbs follow the verb, like those you learned in the first section above.

tous les...	Je me lave les cheveux **tous les** jours.	*I wash my hair every day.*
toutes les...	Nous avons un match **toutes les** semaines.	*We have a game every week.*
toujours	Je me lève **toujours** en premier.	*I always get up first.*
souvent	Il prend **souvent** le métro.	*He often takes the metro.*
quelquefois	Tu travailles **quelquefois** ici ?	*Do you work here sometimes?*
rarement	Elle se maquille **rarement**.	*She rarely wears makeup.*
ne ... jamais	Il **ne** se coiffe **jamais**.	*He never combs his hair.*

Point out that longer adverbs such as *quelquefois* and those ending in *-ment* can also be placed at the beginning or end of a sentence: *Tu travailles ici quelquefois ? Normalement il travaille chez lui.*

À vous la parole

To assist students, show the scales from the first and third points as they complete Ex. 4-11; show the scale from the second point for Ex. 4-12.

▲▲ 4-11 Vos habitudes. Be precise! Compare your habits with those of your partner.

MODÈLE travailler le week-end

     É1 Moi, je travaille beaucoup le week-end.

     É2 Par contre, moi, je travaille rarement le week-end.

1. travailler le week-end
2. se réveiller tôt le matin
3. se brosser les dents
4. parler français
5. jouer au tennis
6. regarder la télé
7. aider les gens
8. se coucher de bonne heure (tôt)

▲▲ 4-12 Combien ? How much or how many do you have? Compare your responses with those of your partner.

MODÈLE des livres

     É1 J'ai beaucoup de livres.

     É2 Moi, j'ai peu de livres.

1. des livres
2. des CD
3. des rasoirs
4. des serviettes
5. des peignes
6. du maquillage
7. des amis
8. de l'argent
9. des problèmes

4-13 You might also ask students to generate additional examples.

4-13 Stéréotypes et réalité. What is the stereotype, and what is the reality? Compare ideas with your partner.

MODÈLE É1 les Américains : manger au McDo ?

           É2 Les Américains mangent très souvent au McDo.

           É1 Mais moi, je ne mange jamais au McDo.

1. les Américains : manger dans des fast-foods ?
2. les Américains : se dépêcher ?
3. les Africains : être décontractés (*relaxed*) ?
4. les Suisses : avoir beaucoup d'argent ?
5. les Français : jouer au football ?
6. les Français : manger de la quiche ?
7. les étudiants : se coucher tard ?
8. les étudiants : travailler ?
9. les professeurs : se lever tôt ?
10. les professeurs : donner des devoirs ?

Lisons

4-14 Familiale

A. Avant de lire. Jacques Prévert (1900–1977) has probably been the most popular and widely read French poet since Victor Hugo. Prévert's first book of poetry, **Paroles** (*Lyrics*), appeared in late 1945 just as World War II was ending. The poem you are about to read is taken from that collection.

In **Familiale**, Prévert uses the simple language of everyday life to make a profound statement about war and loss. He indicates in a matter-of-fact way what the three members of a family do:

La mère fait du tricot. / Elle tricote.	*The mother knits.*
Le père fait des affaires.	*The father does business.*
Le fils fait la guerre.	*The son wages war.*

As the poem reaches its climax, the poet's simple statements about the family members' lives are interrupted. The rhythm changes and verbs ultimately disappear from the narrative. Consider, as you read the poem, how these structural changes help to evoke and reinforce the poet's troubling message.

B. En lisant. As you read the poem on the following page, answer these questions.

1. What is the nature of the characters' everyday life as conveyed in the first nine lines of the poem?
2. Like a play or a film, the poem builds to a climax. What is that climax? What happens afterward?

C. En regardant de plus près. Now look more closely at the structure of the poem.

1. The poem uses repetition to produce an effect and to convey meaning. For example, with what repeated phrase does Prévert suggest the characters' attitude toward their daily life? When this phrase recurs the third time, it has taken on new meaning and become associated with a terrible irony. Why? Can you point out some other instances of repetition that are significant in the poem?
2. What verb is used most frequently in the poem? What effect does this produce, and what is the effect when another verb is used instead? At what point do verbs disappear altogether?
3. Poetry is often characterized by a rhyme scheme. How would you describe the rhyme scheme in this poem? What might this type of rhyme scheme symbolize?
4. Look at the final line of the poem. How would you explain the seeming contradiction of the poet's reference to « La vie avec le cimetière » ?

FAMILIALE°

Family Life

La mère fait du tricot
Le fils fait la guerre
thinks   Elle trouve° ça tout naturel la mère
Et le père qu'est-ce qu'il fait le père ?   5
Il fait des affaires
Sa femme fait du tricot
Son fils la guerre
Lui des affaires
Il trouve ça tout naturel le père   10
Et le fils et le fils
Qu'est-ce qu'il trouve le fils ?
nothing   Il ne trouve rien° absolument rien le fils
Le fils sa mère fait du tricot son père des affaires lui la
    guerre   15
finishes   Quand il aura fini° la guerre
will do   Il fera° des affaires avec son père
La guerre continue la mère continue elle tricote
Le père continue il fait des affaires
killed; no longer   Le fils est tué° il ne continue plus°   20
Le père et la mère vont au cimetière
Ils trouvent ça naturel le père et la mère
La vie continue la vie avec le tricot la guerre les
    affaires
Les affaires la guerre le tricot la guerre   25
Les affaires les affaires et les affaires
La vie avec le cimetière.

Jacques Prévert, *Paroles.*
© Éditions Gallimard

D. Après avoir lu. Now discuss the following questions with your classmates.

1. Poetry is meant to be read aloud. With a partner, or with your class as a whole, practice reading aloud ***Familiale***. Does this help you to appreciate Prévert's efforts to convey meaning through the form and rhythm of his poem as well as through the words themselves?

2. Work with a partner to translate the poem. How can you use the structure and rhythm of the poem in English to convey the same message Prévert is trying to convey?

3. Good literature has a timeless quality; readers in many different contexts can relate it to their circumstances. Do you believe Prévert's poem has this quality?

Leçon *2* *À quelle heure ?*

Point out the expressions *Super !, Zut (alors) !, Mince !* You might provide other examples of appropriate use of these expressions, and encourage students to use them as well when appropriate.

POINTS DE DÉPART

Je n'arrête pas de courir !

Present the vocabulary by describing Delphine's day, using the illustrations (IRCD, Ch. 4). Drill the main divisions of the hour using a clock face with moveable hands, or the multiple images (IRCD, Ch. 4). Describe your own daily activities, incorporating each of the time expressions. At the end of the narrative, summarize expressions. Then test student comprehension by having them draw (for an analog) or write (for a digital clock) the times you give.

Point out that *commencer,* like *manger* and *nager,* has a spelling change in the first-person plural: *nous commençons.* Explain that this change reflects the pronunciation. Full conjugations can be found in Appendix 4.

TEXT AUDIO

Delphine parle de sa journée :
Mon radio-réveil sonne à sept heures du matin. Mon premier cours commence à neuf heures, alors je quitte ma chambre à huit heures et demie pour aller à la fac.

J'arrive en classe à neuf heures moins le quart. Super ! je suis en avance ; je vais trouver une bonne place.

Le professeur arrive toujours à l'heure ; il entre dans la classe à neuf heures moins cinq et il commence à parler.

À dix heures et quart, je regarde ma montre. Zut alors ! encore un quart d'heure !

À onze heures moins vingt je vais au café. Je parle avec des camarades de classe pendant vingt minutes. Je regarde l'horloge. Mince, je suis en retard ! J'arrive au deuxième cours à onze heures dix. J'ai dix minutes de retard.

Entre midi et une heure de l'après-midi, je déjeune au resto U avec un ami, Jean-Baptiste.

L'après-midi, nous allons voir le nouveau film de Gérard Depardieu. On va à la séance (*show*) de 14h55. C'est moins cher (*expensive*), et ça fait une petite pause dans une journée mouvementée. Ouf !

Vous avez l'heure ?

Demie is written with a final *e* in all time expressions except *midi et demi, minuit et demi*. In the other forms, *demie* is an adjective modifying the feminine *heure*.

Il est deux heures et quart de l'après-midi.
(Il est quatorze heures quinze.)

Il est neuf heures et demie du soir.
(Il est vingt et une heures trente.)

Il est minuit moins le quart.
(Il est vingt-trois heures quarante-cinq.)

Il est minuit.
(Il est zéro heure.)

Il est deux heures moins le quart du matin.
(Il est une heure quarante-cinq.)

jeudi 15
(10) OCTOBRE   Th. d'Avila

8
9 cours de littérature
10 h 45 rendez-vous avec prof d'anglais
11 h 30 manger au resto U avec Lucie
12
13
14 travailler à la B.U.
15
16 h 30 tennis avec Jean-Claude
17
18
19
20 dîner avec Maman
21 travailler chez Christine

4-15 Ask students to convert to the informal system of telling time.

À vous la parole

4-15 Une journée bien mouvementée. Look at Sophie's agenda and tell what she is doing today.

MODÈLE ➤ À neuf heures du matin, elle a son cours de littérature.

4-16 Dans le monde francophone. Look at the map below showing world time zones and tell what time it is in each of the Francophone cities shown. Then, based on the time, indicate what people are most likely to be doing.

MODÈLE   À Paris. On mange ou on se couche ?
         ➤ À Paris il est midi. On mange.

1. À La Nouvelle-Orléans. On se lève ou on travaille ?
2. À Cayenne. Les étudiants vont en classe ou ils rentrent chez eux ?
3. À Dakar. On va bientôt déjeuner ou on va bientôt dîner ?
4. À Marseille. On rentre à la maison pour manger ou on travaille ?
5. À Djibouti. On fait la sieste ou on mange ?
6. À Mahé. On nage ou on rentre à la maison pour dormir ?
7. À Nouméa. On se couche ou on joue au football ?

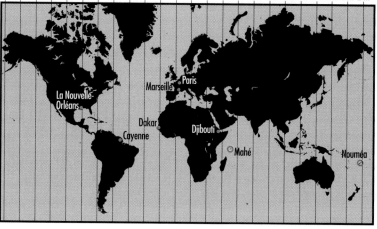

156 *cent cinquante-six*   **CHAPITRE 4** ◆ **MÉTRO, BOULOT, DODO**

Vie et culture

Le système des 24 heures

In this lesson you have already seen examples of the 24-hour clock (sometimes called *military time* in English). In many countries, the 24-hour clock is used to avoid ambiguity in published schedules for classes, transportation, television programming, and public events. The expressions **et quart**, **et demie**, and **moins le quart** are not used when reporting times using the 24-hour clock. Instead, give the exact number of minutes after the hour: for example, **15 h 15** is read as **quinze heures quinze**.

Find examples of the 24-hour clock in the photos. Can you restate the equivalents in conventional time? What can you learn about typical business hours in France from these photos? In what ways are these hours similar to and different from business hours in North America? Which system do you prefer and why?

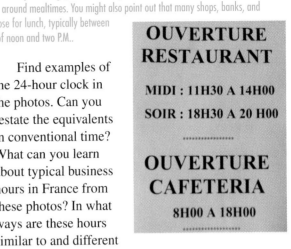

OUVERTURE RESTAURANT

MIDI : 11H30 A 14H00

SOIR : 18H30 A 20 H00

••••••••••••••••

OUVERTURE CAFETERIA

8H00 A 18H00

••••••••••••••••

fnac.com

HORAIRES D'OUVERTURE

le lundi de 13h00 à 19h00
du mardi au vendredi
de 10h00 à 19h00
le samedi
de 9h30 à 19h00

↳ www.fnac.com

MARCHÉ PLUS

OUVERT

Du lundi au samedi

de 7H à 21H

le Dimanche

de 9H à 13H

4-17 You could use this as a means of finding out how "compatible" partners are: could they function as roommates? If not, have them circulate to try to find a more compatible partner.

4-17 Votre journée typique. What do you typically do at the times specified below? Share your responses with a partner, using some of the boxed suggestions. How similar—or dissimilar—are your responses?

se lever	se coucher
aller en cours de/au labo de…	regarder la télé
faire…	téléphoner à…
jouer à…	travailler
manger…	parler à…

MODÈLE   à huit heures du matin

É1   Normalement, à huit heures du matin, je me lève. Et toi ?
É2   Moi, à huit heures, je vais au resto U.

1. à huit heures du matin
2. à dix heures du matin
3. à midi et demi
4. à quatre heures de l'après-midi

5. à six heures du soir
6. à huit heures du soir
7. à minuit
8. à deux heures du matin

FORMES ET FONCTIONS

1. Les verbes en -ir comme dormir, sortir, partir

Before presenting this topic, review -er verbs to highlight the differences. Stress the importance of a clear articulation of the final consonant in the third-person plural; it is this final consonant that distinguishes the singular from the plural in speech. Note that *courir* does not have the same pattern as *dormir*, since *courir* has only three spoken forms in the present tense. The conjugation for *courir* can be found in Appendix 4.

- You have learned that regular **-er** verbs have one stem and three spoken forms in the present indicative. Unless the verb begins with a vowel sound, you must use the context to tell the difference between the third-person singular and plural:

Mon frère ? **Il regarde** la télé.	*My brother, he's watching TV.*
Mes amis ? **Ils regardent** le match de foot.	*My friends, they are watching the soccer game.*
Ma sœur ? **Elle écoute** la radio.	*My sister, she's listening to the radio.*
Ses amies ? **Elles‿écoutent** un CD. /z/	*Her friends, they are listening to a CD.*

- Verbs like **dormir** (*to sleep*) have two stems and four spoken forms. Their singular endings are **-s, -s, -t**; these letters are usually silent. The stem for the plural forms contains the consonant heard in the infinitive.

dormir (*to sleep*)	Ils dorment tard.	Il dort debout.
sortir (*to go out*)	Elles sortent souvent.	Elle sort le week-end.

DORMIR *to sleep*		
SINGULIER	**PLURIEL**	
je dor**s**	nous dorm**ons**	
tu dor**s**	vous dorm**ez**	
il	ils	
elle } dor**t**	elles } dorm**ent**	
on		

IMPÉRATIF : Dor**s** bien ! Dorm**ez** tard ! Dorm**ons** ici !

- Here is a list of verbs conjugated like **dormir**, along with the prepositions often used with some of these verbs.

dormir jusqu'à	Je **dors jusqu'à** 8 heures.	*I sleep until 8 o'clock.*
s'endormir	Ils **s'endorment** tout de suite.	*They go to sleep right away.*
partir avec	Je **pars avec** mes parents.	*I'm leaving with my parents.*
de	Nous **partons de** Montréal.	*We're leaving from Montreal.*
pour	Vous **partez pour** la France ?	*Are you going to France?*
sortir avec	Elle **sort avec** ses amies.	*She goes out with her girlfriends.*
	Elle **sort avec** David.	*She's dating David.*
de	Les étudiants **sortent du** labo.	*The students are leaving the lab.*
servir	Qu'est-ce qu'on **sert** ce soir ?	*What are they serving tonight?*

À vous la parole

4-18 C'est fini le boulot ! These people are leaving their place of work; identify their workplace.

MODÈLE Mlle Morin est pharmacienne.
> ➤ Elle sort de la pharmacie.

1. Nous sommes vendeurs.
2. Florian est comptable.
3. Vous êtes mécanicien.
4. Je suis actrice.
5. Jérémy et Audrey sont professeurs des écoles.
6. Tu es ingénieur.
7. Claire et Marine sont serveuses.

Begin practice with a discrimination drill: one person, or more than one? *Ils dorment très tard ; Elle sert du café ; Elles partent demain,* etc. Follow up with a simple substitution drill. Start first with the contrast third-person plural vs. third-person singular by visual cuing: *Ils partent ce soir ;* (show one finger) —*Il part ce soir.* Then proceed with the other forms. *Nous partons demain ; je.* —*Je pars demain.*

4-18 This recycles professions and places of work from Ch. 3, L. 3.

4-19 Since students need to use inference to choose among the -ir verbs, it is best to complete this as a group activity. To begin, either list the possible -ir verbs on the board or on a transparency or ask students to brainstorm to come up with this list before beginning. After an item is answered correctly, provide a variant to practice other forms of the verb; for example for #1: *Anne et Marie travaillent toujours ? — Non, elles dorment.*

4-20 Have students interview each other and report back what they learned about their partner.

For further practice use the following mixing activity. Have students circulate, asking each person no more than two questions. They should write down the name of the person each time they get an affirmative response. Compare notes at the end, and ask follow-up questions, many of which can be related to time expressions. **Nos habitudes.** Try to find someone who does each of the things listed. When your instructor calls time, compare notes with classmates.

MODÈLE *dormir l'après-midi*

    É1 *Est-ce que tu dors l'après-midi ?*

    É2 *Oui, je dors quelquefois l'après-midi.*

1. s'endormir pendant les cours ;
2. sortir pendant la semaine ;
3. partir pour le week-end ;
4. servir le dîner dans un restaurant ;
5. dormir très tard le matin ;
6. sortir avec un groupe de gens ;
7. partir de chez lui/elle très tôt le matin ;
8. dormir l'après-midi ;
9. sortir avec ses parents ;
10. partir en vacances ;
11. servir du café quand il/elle a des invités.

The comparison and superlative of adjectives are treated in Ch. 4, L. 3.

4-19 Notre routine. Gaëlle is describing her family and friends. Use a logical verb in **-ir** to complete each description.

MODÈLE   Mon frère, il n'est pas énergique. Le samedi matin…

    ➤ Le samedi matin, il dort très tard.

1. Maman travaille tout le temps ? Non, …
2. Gilles et toi, vous travaillez dans un café ; vous…
3. Mes amis et moi travaillons pendant la semaine. Mais le samedi soir…
4. Mes copains travaillent dans un bureau à Paris. Le matin…
5. Karine est serveuse dans un restaurant, alors elle…
6. Tu vas au cinéma ce soir ? Oui, …
7. Mireille arrive ? Non, elle…

4-20 Je n'arrête pas de courir. Compare your weekly routine with your partner's. Then tell the class what you've learned.

MODÈLE   Pendant la semaine, je dors jusqu'à…

    É1 Moi, pendant la semaine, je dors jusqu'à 7 h.

    É2 Moi, je dors jusqu'à 8 h 30 ; mon premier cours commence à 9 h.

1. Pendant la semaine, je dors jusqu'à…
2. Le week-end, je dors jusqu'à…
3. Le matin, je pars pour mon premier cours…
4. Le week-end, je pars souvent pour…
5. Je sors avec mes amis…
6. Je ne sors pas quand…
7. Le soir, je m'endors vers (*around*) …

2. *Le comparatif et le superlatif des adverbes*

- You have learned to use adverbs to make your descriptions more precise.

Elle dort.	*She's sleeping.*
Elle dort **tard**.	*She sleeps late.*
Elle dort **bien**.	*She sleeps well.*
Elle dort **souvent** en classe.	*She often sleeps in class.*

- The expressions **plus … que** (*more than*), **moins … que** (*less than*) and **aussi … que** (*as much as*) can be used with adverbs to make comparisons.

plus … que	Je dors **plus** tard **que** mon frère.	*I sleep later than my brother.*
aussi … que	Tu joues **aussi** bien **que** Stéphane.	*You play as well as Stéphane.*
moins … que	Il sort **moins** souvent **que** moi.	*He goes out less often than I do.*

When a pronoun follows **que** in a comparison, it must be a stressed pronoun.

- The adverb **bien** has an irregular comparative form **mieux**, as shown below:

Je chante bien.	*I sing well.*
Je chante aussi bien que toi.	*I sing as well as you do.*
Je chante moins bien que lui.	*I don't sing as well as he does.*
Tu chantes **mieux que** nous.	*You sing **better** than we do.*

- When comparing amounts, **plus**, **moins**, and **autant** are followed by **de** and a noun:

plus de … que	Elle a **plus de** travail **que** nous.	*She has more work than we do.*
moins de … que	Il a **moins de** devoirs **que** vous.	*He has less homework than you.*
autant de … que	J'ai **autant d'**amis **que** vous.	*I have as many friends as you.*

- To express a superlative, use the definite article **le** and **plus**, **moins**, or **mieux**:

Elle sort **le moins souvent**.	*She goes out the least often.*
Il a **le plus d'**amis.	*He has the most friends.*
Tu chantes **le mieux**.	*You sing the best.*

À vous la parole

4-21 Comparaisons. Who does better? Compare your answers with those of your partner.

4-21 This exercise focuses on *mieux*, the most frequent comparative adverb.

MODÈLE   Qui chante mieux, vous ou votre mère ?

        É1   Ma mère chante mieux que moi.

        É2   Moi aussi, je chante moins bien que ma mère.

1. Qui chante mieux, vous ou votre mère ?
2. Qui travaille mieux, vous ou votre meilleur/e ami/e ?
3. Qui danse mieux, vous ou votre ami/e ?
4. Qui parle mieux le français, vous ou votre professeur ?
5. Qui mange mieux, vous ou votre père ?
6. Qui joue mieux au basket, vous ou votre frère/votre sœur ?
7. Qui s'habille mieux, vous ou votre meilleur/e ami/e ?

4-22 Plus ou moins ? Look in your backpack or book bag, and compare what you have with what your partner has.

4-22 Have students work in pairs and report back to the class.

MODÈLE   Qui a le plus de stylos ?

     ➤ Moi, j'ai le plus de stylos ; j'ai trois stylos, et toi, tu as deux stylos.

  OU ➤ Tu as moins de stylos que moi.

  OU ➤ J'ai plus de stylos que toi.

1. Qui a le plus de stylos ?
2. Qui a le plus de livres ?
3. Qui a le plus de cahiers ?
4. Qui a le plus de crayons ?
5. Qui a le plus de devoirs ?
6. Qui a le plus d'argent ?
7. Qui a le plus de photos ?

4-23 Distribution des prix. In your French class, who excels in each of the following categories? Ask your classmates questions to find out. Can you get them to demonstrate their talents?

MODÈLE chanter

　　É1 Qui chante le mieux ?

　　É2 Cindy chante le mieux.

1. chanter
2. parler français
3. travailler
4. danser
5. s'habiller
6. parler espagnol
7. écrire

Parlons

4-24 Une journée typique

A. Avant de parler. Chose a photo and imagine what a typical day in the life of one of the people shown would be like. You may want to jot down a few notes.

B. En parlant. In a group of four or five people, share your description. What similarities or differences do you notice in each person's description?

MODÈLE ➤ Je suis en vacances à Aix-en-Provence, alors je dors assez tard le matin. Je me lève en général à dix heures et je vais au marché. L'après-midi, je visite la ville jusqu'à quatre heures et demie. Le soir, je sors dans des bars…

C. Après avoir parlé. Whose day would you prefer? Why? Whose day is the most like your own?

Le marché aux fleurs à Aix-en-Provence

Dans une petite rue à Marrakech

Leçon *3* Qu'est-ce qu'on met ?

POINTS DE DÉPART

Les vêtements et les couleurs

TEXT AUDIO

une jupe un chemisier

un foulard un tailleur un collant

une robe en soie un sac en cuir

des chaussures (f.) à talons

Vêtements pour femmes

Deux amies regardent des vêtements dans la vitrine d'un grand magasin :

—J'ai envie d'acheter la belle robe noire.

—Dis donc, elle est chère ; regarde le prix !

—Ah oui ; en plus, elle est un peu démodée, tu ne penses pas ?

—Si, mais regarde la jupe bleue ; elle est moins chère.

une chemise en coton

un costume en laine

SOLDES

une cravate

des mocassins (m.)

Vêtements pour hommes

This vocabulary is divided into small groups for ease in initial presentation. This is best presented over two days. You might, for example, present women's and men's, clothing on day one along with colors and the accompanying cultural notes. Review and present sportswear and outerwear on day two. You might bring in a suitcase filled with interesting clothing items, or encourage your students to "dress up" in interesting ways. For the initial presentation, describe the articles of clothing using visuals (IRCD, Ch. 4). Present only a few items at a time before checking students' comprehension: have them come up to the overhead and point to the article that you name, using the unlabeled visual (IRCD, Ch. 4) ; you may also ask, *Qui porte un tee-shirt ?*, etc.

To further test comprehension, use *la chasse à l'intrus : quel mot ne va pas avec les autres ?* un chemisier, un jean, un pantalon ; des chaussettes, des chaussures, des gants ; un manteau, un imperméable, un collant, etc.

To provide simple productive practice on day one, ask *Qui porte du rouge ?* and have students respond with, for example: *Moi, je porte un polo rouge.* Go over the dialogues and use them as the basis for simple role-play using the visuals or actual articles of clothing you have brought in. You may also use variants of Ex. 4-25, 4-26, and 4-27, but be careful not to introduce items not yet taught. All of the exercises can be used on day two.

Have students listen to the mini-dialogues. Point out the expression *avoir envie de* and ask students for a synonym in French (*vouloir, désirer*). Mention that it can be followed by a noun or a verb. (*J'ai envie d'une belle robe noire. J'ai envie d'acheter cette robe.*)

LEÇON 3 ◆ QU'EST-CE QU'ON MET ? *cent soixante-trois* **163**

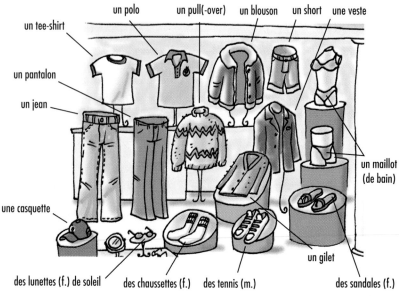

un tee-shirt
un polo
un pull(-over)
un blouson
un short
une veste
un pantalon
un jean
un maillot (de bain)
une casquette
un gilet
des lunettes (f.) de soleil
des chaussettes (f.)
des tennis (m.)
des sandales (f.)

Vêtements de sport et de loisirs

Un vendeur parle au monsieur :

—Vous désirez, monsieur ?

—Je voudrais une chemise en coton.

—Tenez, voici une belle chemise jaune.

—Je n'aime pas le jaune ; vous avez ce même modèle en bleu ?

—Bien sûr, monsieur. Voilà.

Point out that when a color is paired with a noun, agreement is made, but when used alone, the color name takes the masculine form: *J'aime le vert* = "I like the color green" or "I like the green one." *Marron* and *orange* are unlike other color names. They are derived from the name of the fruit, *une orange,* and the nut, *un marron,* "chestnut." These two adjectives never vary in spelling. Point out the idiosyncratic spelling for *blanche*; the masculine oral form is derived in normal fashion from the feminine, i.e., by the loss of the final consonant sound. Model pronunciation for the colors, then test comprehension; ask, *Qu'est-ce qui est bleu ?* Students can name an item of clothing from the visuals or something in the classroom.

To further practice colors, have students name the colors for: *le drapeau américain ; le drapeau français ; un pingouin ; une tulipe ; une banane ; une craie ; un éléphant ; un océan ; une plante ; un tigre ; un zèbre.*

un parapluie
un imper(méable)
une écharpe
des gants (m.)
un manteau
un chapeau
un anorak
des bottes (f.)

Vêtements d'extérieur

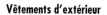
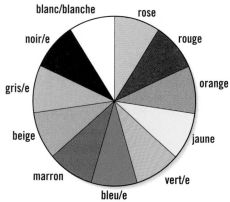

blanc/blanche
rose
noir/e
rouge
gris/e
orange
beige
jaune
marron
vert/e
bleu/e

Vie et culture

Les compliments

The French do not usually compliment people they do not know well on their personal appearance. Among friends, the compliments and responses below are typical. What do you notice about the nature of the response in each case? How do you typically respond to compliments? Would you feel comfortable responding to compliments as the French do?

—Il est chic, ton pantalon !

—Tu trouves ?

—Elle est très jolie, ta robe !

—Oh, elle n'est pas un peu démodée ?

—Tu parles très bien le français.

—Ah ! pas toujours !

—*Your pants are really stylish!*

—*Do you think so?*

—*Your dress is very pretty!*

—*Oh, isn't it a little old-fashioned?*

—*You speak French really well.*

—*Oh! not always!*

La mode et les jeunes Français

The French have long been associated with chic personal style. However, it has become difficult to define French style because people—especially the young—increasingly resist uniformity in favor of creating individual looks. The adoption in many offices of **le casual everyday** also has encouraged individualism. Nonetheless, some trends can be noted for both men and women: underwear has become an important fashion statement; people are spending more money on shoes, particularly shoes used for sports; jewelry and accessories (hats, bags, and belts, for example) are critical to achieving a personal style.

Consider these photos of French young people. Can you particularly identify with one of the styles shown? Why, or why not?

Un jeune « skater »

Un jeune couple, style classique

4-25 As a variation, have students explain how their choices might differ from those of their parents.

Play the following game with students. Instruct them by saying:
Find a partner, and take a minute to look at each other. Now stand back-to-back with your partner. (Wait until they have complied before continuing.) Describe what the other person is wearing today; no looking allowed!

MODÈLE   É1   Tu portes un chemisier bleu et blanc ?

          É2   Oui.

          É1   Et un pantalon noir ?

          É2   Non, mon pantalon est gris.

Here are two variations you may also want to consider: first, as students close their eyes, describe someone in the class by the clothes that s/he is wearing and have the class guess who you are describing. Alternatively, ask one student to leave the classroom and stand out in the hallway. While that person is gone, ask his or her classmates to describe what s/he is wearing. Bring the student back and compare the actual outfit to the students' recollections.

4-25 Comment s'habiller ? What do you normally wear for each of the following occasions?

MODÈLE   pour aller en classe
➤ Pour aller en classe, je porte un jean, un polo et des tennis.

1. pour aller à un mariage
2. pour courir dans un marathon
3. pour manger dans un restaurant élégant
4. pour travailler dans le jardin
5. pour faire du ski
6. pour nager
7. pour aller au théâtre
8. pour sortir avec des amis

4-26 Marier les vêtements. What goes well with each of the items mentioned? Work with a partner to decide.

MODÈLE   avec une robe bleue en soie ?

É1   Avec une robe bleue en soie, on peut porter un foulard bleu et vert.
É2   Et des chaussures à talons.
É1   Oui, c'est bien.

1. avec une mini-jupe rouge
2. avec un costume bleu marine
3. avec une chemise rose
4. avec un short vert et jaune
5. avec un beau chemisier blanc en soie
6. avec un gros manteau vert
7. avec un chemisier bleu en coton
8. avec un pantalon noir en cuir

4-27 Students can work in pairs or small groups to create their list. As a variation, have students prepare and read their lists, letting classmates guess their probable destination (a list of possible destinations can be provided).

4-27 Préparez la valise. Imagine that you have just won a trip to the destination indicated. Work with a partner to decide what items you will pack, and make a list.

MODÈLE   huit jours à Tahiti
➤ trois maillots de bain, deux paires de sandales, des tennis, cinq shorts, sept tee-shirts, des lunettes de soleil

1. un long week-end à Québec, en février
2. quatre jours à Lafayette, en Louisiane, en juillet
3. huit jours à Grenoble, dans les Alpes, en janvier
4. trois jours à Haïti
5. cinq jours à Dakar, au Sénégal
6. huit jours à Paris, en avril

Sons et lettres

Les voyelles /ø/ et /œ/

To pronounce the vowel /ø/ of **deux**, start from the position of /e/ as in **des** and round the lips. The lips should also be tense and moved forward. It is important to lengthen the sound while continuing to keep the lips rounded, protruded, and tense. Typically, /ø/ occurs at the end of words and syllables and before the consonant /z/: **deux**, **jeu**, **peu**, **sérieuse**, **vendeuse**. When it is pronounced, the *mute e* (in words like **le**, **me**, **ce**, and **vendredi**) is usually pronounced with the vowel /ø/ of **deux**.

To pronounce the vowel /œ/ of **leur**, start from the position of /ø/ and relax the lips somewhat. Both vowels are usually spelled as **eu**. The vowel /œ/ is also spelled as **œu**, as in **sœur**. The vowel /œ/ of **leur** occurs before a pronounced consonant, except for /z/ as mentioned above.

This vowel distinction is often difficult for speakers of English to perceive and produce in isolation. You may wish to use the text audio CD to practice this distinction with your class. Stress the distribution facts, namely that [œ] occurs before a consonant and [ø] in open syllables.

/ø/	/œ/
bl**eu**	la coul**eu**r
il p**eu**t	ils p**eu**vent
la vend**eu**se	le vend**eu**r
vendredi	une h**eu**re

À vous la parole

4-28 Contrastes. Compare the vowels in each pair of words.

/y/ vs /ø/	/ø/ vs /œ/
du / deux	ne / neuf
lu / le	eux / sœurs
du jus / deux jeux	la chanteuse / le chanteur

Begin practice with a discrimination drill; have students tell which of the two vowels they hear (the vowel of *deux* or that of *leur*) for words you read aloud such as *lieu, veulent, tailleur, bleu, jeudi, couleur, fleur, peu, vendeuse, ennuyeuse, sœur, neuf, monsieur.*

4-29 Au féminin. Provide the appropriate feminine form.

MODÈLE   le vendeur
> la vendeuse

1. le chanteur
2. le chercheur
3. il est généreux
4. ils sont malheureux
5. il est paresseux

4-30 Phrases. Read each sentence aloud.

1. Des cheveux bleus ! Ce n'est pas sérieux !
2. Le neveu de Monsieur Meunier sort de l'immeuble à neuf heures.
3. La sœur de Madame Francœur porte un tailleur à fleurs bleues.
4. Le vendeur suggère ces deux couleurs.
5. Depardieu est un acteur ; Montesquieu, un auteur.

FORMES ET FONCTIONS

1. Le comparatif et le superlatif des adjectifs

Before presenting this material, review the comparative of adverbs and nouns, treated in Ch. 4, L. 2.

- In the previous lesson, you learned to use the expressions **plus ... que**, **moins ... que**, and **aussi ... que** with adverbs to make comparisons.

Je dors **plus** tard **que** lui.	*I sleep later than he does.*
Tu joues **aussi** bien **que** moi.	*You play as well as I do.*
Il sort **moins** souvent **que** toi.	*He goes out less often than you do.*

Comparatives and superlatives can be presented inductively in class using appropriate visuals, or by having various students stand up, and then comparing them: *Sarah est plus grande que Julie*, etc. Be attentive, however, to students' sensitivity about their looks and especially with regard to their weight.

- To compare the qualities of two people or things, use these same expressions with an adjective. The adjective you use agrees with the first noun.

La robe est **plus** élégante **que** le tailleur.	*The dress is more elegant than the suit.*
Le pantalon est **moins** cher **que** la jupe.	*The pants are less expensive than the skirt.*
Les bottes noires sont **aussi** larges **que** les bottes marron.	*The black boots are as roomy as the brown boots.*

POUR DÉCRIRE LES VÊTEMENTS

long, longue	court/e
large	petit/e
à la mode	démodé/e
fin/e	
cher, chère	bon marché

- When comparing people, remember to use stressed pronouns after **que**:

Christiane est plus grande que **moi**.	*Christiane is taller than I am.*
Vous êtes moins sociables qu'**eux**.	*You are not as outgoing as they are.*
Je suis aussi grand que **lui**.	*I'm as tall as he is.*

- The adjective **bon** has an irregular comparative form **meilleur/e**, as shown below:

La qualité de cette robe est bonne.	*The quality of this dress is good.*
En fait, la robe est **meilleure** que la jupe.	*In fact, the dress is better than the skirt.*
La qualité de la jupe est moins bonne.	*The quality of the skirt is less good.*

- To express the superlative, use the definite article **le**, **la**, or **les** with **plus**, **moins**, or **meilleur/e**:

La jupe rose est **la moins** chère.   *The pink skirt is the least expensive.*

Les bottes marron sont **les plus** élégantes.   *The brown boots are the most elegant.*

Le sac noir en cuir est le **meilleur**.   *The black leather bag is the best.*

À vous la parole

4-31 Comparez les vêtements. Answer the questions, referring to the illustrations.

MODÈLE   Quel pantalon est le plus long ?
> Le pantalon bleu est plus long que le pantalon noir.

1. Quelle robe est la plus élégante ?
2. Quel blouson est le plus large ?
3. Quelle jupe est la plus courte ?
4. Quelles chaussures sont les plus fines ?
5. Quelle chemise est la plus à la mode ?

First test comprehension using a visual (a photo, image, or actual students) and questions to which students respond with a name: *Qui est moins grand, Brigitte ou Pauline ? —Brigitte. Qui est plus âgé, le prof ou Tom ?*, etc. Using names of famous people, you can also have students make simple comparisons using *plus* and *moins*; you might also suggest possible adjectives.

4-31 This can be completed using the illustrations of clothing (IRCD, Ch. 4). For each item, ask which is better for a specific context: *Quel pantalon est le meilleur pour l'hiver ? Quelle robe est la meilleure pour un mariage ?*

1.   2.   3.

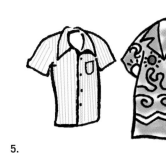

4.   5.

4-32 As a follow-up, have students compare their height and age with that of their partner. Provide students with the means of measuring their height in meters and centimeters before they move to Ex. 4-33, and have them switch partners.

4-32 **Comparaisons.** Work with a partner to compare these students' height and age.

nom	taille		âge
Christelle	1 m 60	(5′3″)	18 ans
Alexandre	1 m 80	(6′)	21 ans
Pauline	1 m 75	(5′9″)	21 ans
Laura	1 m 80	(6′)	19 ans
Sébastien	1 m 85	(6′3″)	23 ans
Vincent	1 m 65	(5′5″)	23 ans
Marine	1 m 60	(5′3″)	20 ans
Fabien	1 m 95	(6′5″)	17 ans

MODÈLES Christelle / Fabien

    É1 Christelle est moins grande que Fabien.

    É2 Mais elle est plus âgée que lui.

Christelle / Fabien / Sébastien

    É1 Fabien est le plus grand.

    É2 Et Sébastien est le plus âgé.

1. Christelle / Laura
2. Alexandre / Sébastien
3. Laura / Vincent
4. Vincent / Fabien
5. Marine / Pauline / Christelle
6. Fabien / Alexandre / Vincent
7. Marine / Sébastien / Laura

4-33 Follow up and practice the superlative by asking the class to name the tallest, etc., student in the class.

For an additional pair activity, perhaps for review:

Comparez-vous ! Tell your partner how you compare to each of the people listed.

MODÈLE votre mère et vous

    É1 Ma mère est plus âgée que moi, mais je suis plus grand que ma mère. Elle est plus patiente et plus généreuse que moi.

    É2 Ma mère est beaucoup plus âgée que moi, et elle est plus grande. Elle est plus amusante, mais moins sportive que moi.

1. votre mère et vous
2. votre père et vous
3. votre frère ou votre sœur et vous
4. votre ami/e et vous
5. votre colocataire et vous
6. votre professeur et vous

4-33 **Distribution des prix.** Compare yourself to your partner. Who is . . .

MODÈLE le plus grand ?

    É1 Qui est le plus grand, toi ou moi ?

    É2 Moi, je fais 1 m 75.

    É1 Et moi, 1 m 80.

    É1 Alors, je suis plus grand que toi.

1. le plus grand ?
2. le moins âgé ?
3. le moins sérieux ?
4. le plus sociable ?
5. le plus élégant ?
6. le moins doué pour le sport ?
7. le plus doué pour le français ?
8. le meilleur chanteur ?
9. le meilleur musicien ?
10. le meilleur étudiant en français ?

2. *Le verbe mettre*

- The verb **mettre** (*to put, to put on*) has a wide range of meanings.

Mettez vos manteaux dans l'armoire !	*Put your coats in the wardrobe!*
Tu **mets** un pull-over ?	*Are you putting on a sweater?*
Tu peux **mettre** la table ?	*Can you set the table?*
Nous **mettons** une heure pour arriver là.	*It takes us one hour to get there.*

- Here are the forms of the verb **mettre**.

Present this verb inductively by modeling numerous examples, using the familiar clothing vocabulary and activities: *Pour jouer au tennis, nous mettons un short et un tee-shirt. Pour aller au restaurant, qu'est-ce que vous mettez habituellement ? Pour faire du ski, je mets toujours…*, etc. Ask students the meaning of the verb, and how many spoken forms they hear. See whether they can conjugate the forms orally. Then display the verb paradigm and examples to illustrate the various meanings of *mettre*.

Other verbs whose pattern follows *mettre* (*promettre, permettre, remettre,* and *transmettre*) are not introduced because they generally occur in constructions with indirect objects.

METTRE	*to put, to put on*		
SINGULIER		**PLURIEL**	
je	mets	nous	mett**ons**
tu	mets	vous	mett**ez**
il elle on	met	ils elles	mett**ent**

IMPÉRATIF : Mets la table ! Mett**ez** un pull ! Mett**ons** nos livres là !

- As is the case for all two-stem verbs, you can tell if someone is talking about one person or more than one person since the plural form ends in a pronounced consonant.

Ils me**tt**ent des gants. Elle me**t** son pull-over.

À vous la parole

4-34 Bien s'habiller. Tell what people typically wear in each situation.

MODÈLE C'est le mois de mars et on va en ville. On…
➤ On met un imperméable ou un blouson.

1. C'est le mois de juillet et je joue au base-ball. Je…
2. Vous allez à la montagne pour faire du ski. Vous…
3. C'est le mois d'octobre et ils travaillent dans le jardin. Ils…
4. On dîne dans un restaurant élégant ce soir. Tu…
5. C'est bientôt Noël et elle fait du shopping. Elle…
6. Nous allons à la piscine pour nager. Nous…
7. Il va en classe. Il…

Begin practice with a discrimination drill: one person, or more than one? *Elle met un chapeau. Elles mettent des gants. Ils mettent une heure. Elle met la table. Elles mettent un pull. Ils mettent des lunettes de soleil. Il met une veste. Elles mettent deux heures.* etc. Follow with a simple substitution drill: *Je mets un pull ; vous.* —*Vous mettez un pull,* etc.

4-35 Ask students to summarize; this will allow them to use more verb forms: *Moi, je mets… Lui, il met… Nous, nous mettons…*

👥 4-35 Où est-ce que vous mettez ça ? Tell your partner where you normally put the items listed: **dans votre chambre, dans votre sac à dos** (*back pack*) ou **dans la voiture** ?

MODÈLE   tes lunettes de soleil

      É1   Où est-ce que tu mets tes lunettes de soleil ?

      É2   Je mets mes lunettes dans la voiture.

1. ton CD préféré
2. ton dictionnaire
3. ton manuel de français
4. un plan de la ville
5. ton pull préféré
6. ton lecteur CD
7. ton agenda

4-36 Survey the class and compare responses given by students.

👥👤 4-36 Vous mettez combien de temps ? In groups of three, ask your partners how much time it takes them for the trips listed: **quinze minutes ? deux heures ?** Then, compare your responses; are they similar or different?

MODÈLE   É1   Combien de temps est-ce que vous mettez pour aller à la fac le matin ?

      É2   Je mets quinze minutes pour aller à la fac. Et toi ?

      É3   Moi, je mets trente minutes.

      É1   Et moi aussi, trente minutes.

      É3   Nous deux, nous mettons trente minutes, mais lui, il met quinze minutes.

1. pour aller à la fac le matin
2. pour aller à la bibliothèque
3. pour aller en ville
4. pour rentrer chez vous le soir
5. pour aller chez vos parents

TEXT AUDIO

Information about Oumou Sy can be found on the Web; see the *Chez nous* Companion Website for a link. She has also been featured in several magazine articles, for example, in *Afrique Magazine*, v. 136, *Entre Imaginaire et réalité.*

4-37 Dans la boutique d'Oumou Sy

Oumou Sy is a well-known Senagalese fashion designer who lives and works in Dakar. Her creations are sold in boutiques in Paris, London, Geneva, and Dakar and can also be ordered directly from the designer. Imagine that you work for the company that ensures quality control for the operators who sell Oumou Sy's line of clothes. Listen in on the following conversations to determine if they are performing their jobs properly.

A. Avant d'écouter. Before listening, answer the following questions.

1. Think about when you've ordered something on the phone. What did you say? What did the operator ask you? With a partner, make a list of expressions in French that one would likely hear in a conversation of this type.
2. You will hear the conversations of two clients who are looking for information or placing an order for clothes designed by an African designer.

   a. What kinds of questions do you think they will ask?
   b. Look at the photos and make a list of the type of clothes they may wish to order.

B. En écoutant. Listen to the two conversations and answer the following questions.

1. In the first call, what does the woman order?
   a. une veste
   b. une robe pagne
   c. un boubou brodé

2. How much is she going to pay?
   a. 95 euros
   b. 85 euros
   c. 115 euros

3. In the second call, what does the man wish to buy?
   a. une cravate et une chemise
   b. un costume
   c. un pantalon et une chemise

4. How much does the shirt cost?
   a. 53 euros
   b. 63 euros
   c. 43 euros

5. Look again at the photos and decide which corresponds to:
   a. un pagne
   b. un boubou
   c. une chemise batik

C. Après avoir écouté. Now discuss these questions with classmates.

1. Did the two operators perform satisfactorily? Why or why not?
2. Would you be interested in buying something designed by Oumou Sy? Why or why not?

A *boubou* is a long tunic worn by African men over pants. It is also a large, flowing dress worn by African women, often with fancy stitching.

Script for *Écoutons*

Appel 1

STANDARDISTE : Magasin CSAO, bonjour.

CLIENTE : Bonjour, madame. Je voudrais acheter une robe africaine. J'ai une amie qui a visité le Sénégal, où elle a acheté de très beaux vêtements.

S : Oui, Madame, voulez-vous une jupe, une robe pagne ou un boubou ?

C : Oh là là ! Je ne sais pas du tout. Un boubou, c'est quoi exactement ?

S : C'est une robe large à la mode africaine, parfois avec de la broderie.

C : Non, ce n'est pas ça. Ma copine a une robe en batik avec un grand carré de tissu de la même couleur qu'elle porte en chapeau. Je voudrais une robe comme ça.

S : Oh, je vois. Je crois que vous parlez d'une robe avec un pagne.

C : Un pagne ?

S : Oui, c'est un grand carré de tissu, souvent en batik, que les femmes africaines portent autour de la taille ou autour de la tête comme coiffe.

C : Ça doit être ça. Je voudrais une robe comme ça dans des couleurs très vives.

S : J'ai exactement ce qu'il vous faut. Une robe rouge, orange et jaune avec un joli pagne qui l'accompagne. Ça fait 95 euros.

C : C'est en batik ?

S : Bien sûr, madame.

Appel 2

STANDARDISTE : Allô.

CLIENT : Je voudrais acheter une chemise et un pantalon dans le style africain.

S : Oui ?

C : Est-ce que vous vendez des vêtements comme ça ?

S : Oui.

C : Ça coûte combien ?

S : Monsieur, je ne peux pas vous dire sans plus de précisions. Voulez-vous une chemise en coton, en soie ou en batik, par exemple ?

C : En coton batik.

S : Une chemise ça fait 53 euros.

C : Et le pantalon ?

S : Un pantalon pagne coûte 64 euros. Alors, vous allez commander quelque chose ?

Venez chez nous!
La mode

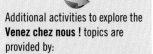
To provide an overview of the lesson, show the video montage *La mode*, which includes many clothing styles and leads into the reading since it shows many examples of stores owned by well-known French fashion designers. See how many of these students recognize as they watch the clip.

Women's fashion magazines, many men's magazines, and department store sales flyers will carry ads by some of the designers shown in the video montage and named in the introduction here. Bring ads to class, or ask your students to bring them, to enrich the presentation visually. You might also link to designers' Websites for additional visuals. Ask students to provide examples of fashion terms used in English but which have a French origin; they may mention, for example, *prêt-à-porter, couturier, bateau neckline, décolleté, plissé.*

Stratégie

Familiarize yourself with key subject-related vocabulary before you read. Knowing essential specialized terms greatly enhances your ability to understand and enjoy a text.

LA MODE VESTIMENTAIRE

Paris has long been an international fashion center with worldwide influence. The impact of major French designers on seasonal trends within many Francophone countries and throughout the world has been significant for more than 150 years.

Un défilé de mode à Paris, la haute couture

Lisons

4-38 Qu'est-ce que la haute couture ?

A. Avant de lire. The topic of French fashion brings immediately to mind such great designers as Coco Chanel, Pierre Cardin, and Christian Lacroix. You might also think of luxurious materials, sometimes outrageous styles, and high prices. Because the fashion industry has its own vocabulary, learning some of the specialized terms will help you better understand the text below, an introduction to high fashion in France.

Before reading the text, link each of the words below to its definition.

Avant de lire, Key: 1) c 2) g 3) h 4) f 5) b 6) e 7) d 8) a

1. la haute couture
2. l'artisanat
3. une maison de couture
4. un mannequin
5. un défilé de mode
6. le prêt-à-porter
7. le tissu
8. les accessoires

a. les sacs, les foulards, les chaussures, etc.
b. une succession de personnes qui portent et qui présentent des vêtements de stylistes
c. les vêtements les plus à la mode et les plus chers
d. la matière utilisée pour faire des vêtements — le coton, la soie, le nylon, etc.
e. les vêtements fabriqués et vendus en masse au public
f. une personne qui porte et présente les vêtements d'un styliste
g. la fabrication d'objets à la main, par l'individu
h. une entreprise qui emploie un personnel assez important pour fabriquer des vêtements

B. En lisant. As you read, answer the following questions.

1. How does the first paragraph define **la haute couture**?
2. Why is Charles Worth important in the history of French fashion?
3. The second paragraph describes the presentation of the Paris designers' collections. Explain:
   a. when the shows take place
   b. who typically attends
   c. where the shows are held
   d. what elements contribute to the dazzling effect of the shows

En lisant, Key: 1) it is defined as "know-how" linked to craftsmanship 2) Worth was the first designer to establish his business in Paris (still located on the *rue de la Paix*) and the first to hold a fashion show with live models 3) a) in January (for spring collections) and July (for fall); b) international journalists, celebrities, wealthy American women (who make up 60% of attendees); c) in the finest hotels and new galleries of the Louvre; d) the fine fabrics, sumptuous accessories, and the staging. You might tell students that in France today there are 18 *maisons de haute couture*: Balmain, Pierre Cardin, Carven, Chanel, Christian Dior, Louis Féraud, Givenchy, Lecoanet Henant, Christian Lacroix, Lapidus, Guy Laroche, Hanae Mori, Paco Rabanne, Nina Ricci, Yves Saint Laurent, Jean-Louis Scherrer, Torrente, Emanuel Ungaro.

Qu'est-ce que la haute couture ?

Qu'est-ce que la haute couture ? C'est d'abord un savoir-faire[1], lié à[2] un artisanat qui existe depuis[3] près de cent cinquante ans : l'origine de la haute couture remonte[4] à Charles Frédéric Worth, un Britannique qui crée, en 1858, à Paris, la première maison de haute couture. Worth a l'idée de présenter ses créations à ses clientes en les faisant porter par des mannequins vivants[5]. Le défilé de mode, inséparable aujourd'hui de
5 l'idée de collection, est né[6].

En janvier et en juillet, ce sont près de 1 000 journalistes internationaux (ils sont 2 000 pour le prêt-à-porter) qui assistent aux[7] collections de haute couture, qui se déroulent[8] — tradition oblige — dans les grands palaces parisiens, comme l'hôtel Intercontinental, le Ritz, le Grand Hôtel et quelquefois dans les nouvelles salles[9] du Carrousel du Louvre, qui accueille[10] surtout le prêt-à-porter. Il y a là une ambiance très particulière,
10 où l'éclat[11] des tissus, la somptuosité des accessoires, la mise en scène[12] de chaque apparition, donnent à chaque mannequin la présence d'une déesse[13]. Au premier rang[14], les clientes et les célébrités prennent[15] des notes : Paloma Picasso chez Christian Lacroix, Catherine Deneuve chez Yves Saint Laurent, et, autour[16], les riches Américaines (60 % de la clientèle) venues[17] respirer[18] l'air frais à Paris, l'air de la perfection.

Adapté des articles de Laurence Benaïm & Jean-Louis Arnaud pour ***Label France***.

[1]*know-how* [2]*linked to* [3]*for* [4]*goes back* [5]*living* [6]*is born* [7]*attend* [8]*take place* [9]*galleries* [10]*hosts* [11]*shine, glitter* [12]*staging* [13]*goddess*
[14]*row* [15]*take* [16]*around* [17]*who have come* [18]*to breathe*

C. En regardant de plus près. Now examine the following features of the text.

1. The word **la couture** is used in the text: what might be the meaning of each of the following related words?
   a. le couturier :   model   designer   customer
   b. coudre :   to sew   to model   to display

2. The verb **créer**, found in the text, is related to the other words below; provide the meaning for each.
   a. une création   b. le créateur

D. Après avoir lu. Discuss the following questions with classmates.

1. What names do you identify with high fashion in North America? Are these American designers as influential as their French counterparts? Explain your answer.

2. Does **la haute couture** have an influence on fashion where you live? if so, in what way(s)? if not, why not?

Des créations d'Oumou Sy

Visit the *Chez nous* Companion Website for links to *le Festival International de la Mode Africaine*. Interesting photos and posters of the events can be found on-line. An exercise in the Workbook also guides students to these web sites and leads them to discover more about *FIMA*.

La haute couture en Afrique

La haute couture is not limited to Europe or North America. Since 1998, FIMA (**le Festival International de la Mode Africaine**) has been held in Niger and features the largest fashion shows of African designers. In Senegal, **la haute couture** takes center stage during SIMOD (**la Semaine Internationale de la Mode de Dakar**). Fashion shows present the creations of designers such as Monsieur Alphadi, Madame Dieng Diouma, and Madame Oumou Sy, who showcase traditional African styles alongside more European styles.

Et vous ?

1. African fashion designers are not well known in North America. Why do you think this is so?
2. In Africa, the way one dresses can also be seen as a social or political statement. What message might a businessman in Senegal convey by wearing a traditional **boubou** to work? What message might a female politician in Nigeria convey by wearing a suit designed by Yves Saint Laurent?

Observons

Avant de regarder. Accessories are the easiest items with which to personalize your dress: jewelry, hats, belts, scarves. See the Video Manual for activities related to two additional speakers from Morocco and Quebec who describe typical clothing.

4-39 Mon style personnel

A. Avant de regarder. In this video clip, watch as two people describe the ways in which they personalize their wardrobe. With what elements of everyday dress can you most easily make a personal statement? Make a list in French of those items of clothing.

B. En regardant. As you watch, look for answers to the following questions.

1. For what items of clothing does Pauline demonstrate various uses?
2. How can she wear each item?
3. She claims that she is not trying to be stylish, but rather she often . . .
   a. has nothing to wear   b. gets cold   c. loses her accessories
4. What colors does she say she frequently wears?
5. Honorine and her friend model typical women's clothing from Bénin. She specifies that women dressed like this are . . .
   a. stared at   b. imitated   c. respected
6. In her country, women do not typically wear . . .
7. She demonstrates how to use an item of clothing called . . .
   a. un pagne   b. un boubou   c. une chemise batik

Script for *Observons*
Note that the elements in brackets reflect standard usage and have been added to the written transcripts. They were not pronounced by the speaker(s) in question.

PAULINE : Donc, voilà, ici c'est ma chambre euh avec mon lit, là, mes affaires, c'est là que je range mes habits... Ce sont, donc, les foulards. Euh les foulards, en fait, c'est parce que j'ai très souvent froid, donc, je mets des foulards pour sortir dans la rue. C'est pas pour être chic, c'est juste parce que j'ai froid. Mais je l'utilise aussi, quand il fait plus chaud, et à ce moment-là, le foulard va devenir ma jupe. Alors c'est très facile, je le mets autour de moi, et puis je l'attache à la taille, et voilà, ça devient ma jupe. Bon, normalement c'est un peu mieux que ça, parce que j'ai pas une jupe dessous, mais voilà... Mais... j'aime beaucoup les... tout ce qui est écharpe et foulard, en général. Là, j'en ai une autre, une autre écharpe qui est un peu dans les mêmes tons, euh vert, gris. Et que pareil, soit je peux mettre, si je dois être un peu plus habillée, pour aller à une fête ou quelque chose, je le* mettrai juste comme ça, ou bien, quand je suis dans la rue, avec mon manteau, pour me réchauffer, et je vais le* mettre juste autour du cou. Donc, voilà.

*Note that the speaker should have used the direct-object pronoun *la* to refer to *l'écharpe*.

HONORINE : Et si on sort comme ça, on est [plus] respecté que de porter [des] pantalons comme ici, chez nous, on ne [les] porte pas. Les femmes ne portent pas [de] pantalon, c'est comme ça que nous nous habillons. Ici sur la tête, c'est un autre morceau de de ce pagne, là. On a beaucoup de manières pour [l']attacher. Voilà, je peux faire comme ça. Ça dépend de ce que tu veux. Voilà. C'est comme ça que nous nous habillons chez nous.

En regardant. Note that many native speakers distinguish between *un foulard*, made of more delicate material such as silk, and *une écharpe*, which can be made of any material, often heavy.

C. Après avoir regardé. Now discuss the following questions with your classmates.

The corresponding English proverb is "Clothes make the man," which expresses the opposite idea. Students may also think of "First impressions are lasting ones," since this can be related to appearance.

1. In this video clip you see Pauline and Honorine model and talk about their clothing. Does either woman also make a personal statement through her clothing? How?
2. If you saw Honorine or Pauline on the street in your town, you might guess from their clothing that they are not from your region. Can North Americans be identified in a similar way by their style of dress? What items in particular are typical of your region?
3. In French there is a proverb, **L'habit ne fait pas le moine** (*monk*). Do you know a similar proverb in English? How is it different from the French example?

Parlons

4-40 Où acheter ses vêtements ?

Avant de parler. Many of the stores listed here have a Website; illustrations from Websites or catalogues will enrich this presentation. Check to see whether students understand the main differences between the various options by supplying examples of similar types of shopping venues in North America. Note that many popular stores from North America are represented in France: Gap, Banana Republic, for example.

A. Avant de parler. Not everyone can shop in the **boutiques des grands couturiers !** The word **boutique** in French, however, does not imply only an exclusive shop, but is used to describe any specialized store, so that one might shop in **une boutique de fleurs** as well as **la boutique Lanvin**. The French have many shopping options; here are a few. What types of North American shopping locales do these correspond to?

des grands magasins	Les Galeries Lafayette, Le Printemps, La Samaritaine
des grandes surfaces	Leclerc, Carrefour, Prisunic, Monoprix
achats par catalogue	La Redoute
vêtements « recyclés »	Les puces

La Samaritaine, un grand magasin à Paris.

Carrefour, une grande surface

Une boutique à Paris

Un marché aux puces

B. En parlant. With a partner, describe . . .

1. the various shopping options you see here;

MODÈLE ➤ Voilà un grand magasin ; c'est peut-être…

2. what types of clothing you find in each place;

MODÈLE ➤ Dans les grands magasins, on trouve habituellement…

3. where you prefer to buy your own clothing, and why.

MODÈLE ➤ Habituellement, j'achète mes vêtements… parce que c'est plus pratique/moins cher, etc.

C. Après avoir parlé. How do you think the two women in the video, Pauline et Honorine, would answer the third question above: Where do you prefer to buy your own clothing, and why? Compare your answers, and those of your partner, with the answers of the class as a whole.

4-41 La mode dans les îles

In Martinique and Guadeloupe, you will find people who choose to dress in a variety of ways.

Avant d'écrire. Discuss the opening questions with the class as a whole, then put students into pairs to continue the activity. Have students share their compositions with the class so that others get an idea of how their classmates handled the topic.

A. Avant d'écrire

1. Look at the pictures. For each one, make a list of the clothes and the colors that you see.
2. Look carefully at the pictures again and note the setting: where are the people? What are they doing? What kind of events are going on around them? Think about the influence this might have on their choice of clothing.

B. En écrivant. Write one or two paragraphs that compare the traditional dress of the Caribbean with the every day style of young people in the region.

1. Begin with a description of the two styles of clothing. Continue by discussing the similarities and differences between the two styles. Then conclude by telling which style you prefer and why.

2. To make your descriptions more colorful and interesting, don't forget to use adjectives and adverbs. For example, compare the following two sentences. Which is more colorful? more interesting?

    a. Les femmes en Martinique portent des jupes.
    b. Avec le costume traditionnel, les femmes en Martinique portent souvent des longues jupes rouges et jaunes.

3. Remember that comparatives and superlatives could be useful in your comparison.

C. Après avoir écrit. Re-read your paragraph. Is there something else you would like to add? Look closely at your text. Do the adjectives you've used agree with the nouns they modify (**masculin**, **féminin**, **singulier**, **pluriel**)? Are all the verbs conjugated correctly? Make the necessary corrections before handing in your composition.

Des vêtements pour hommes dans une boutique parisienne

Vocabulaire

Leçon 1

la routine de la journée	the daily routine
être debout	to be up
prendre une douche	to take a shower
se brosser les dents	to brush one's teeth
se coiffer	to fix one's hair
se coucher	to go to bed
se dépêcher	to hurry
se déshabiller	to undress
se doucher	to shower
s'endormir	to fall asleep
s'essuyer	to dry off, towel off
s'habiller	to get dressed
se laver (les cheveux, la figure, les mains)	to wash (one's hair, one's face, one's hands)
se lever	to get up
se maquiller	to put on makeup
se raser	to shave
se réveiller	to wake up
rentrer	to return home

les articles de toilette	toiletries
une brosse à dents/ à cheveux	toothbrush/ hairbrush
du dentifrice	toothpaste
un gant de toilette	wash mitt
du maquillage	makeup
un peigne	comb
un rasoir	razor
un savon	bar soap
une serviette de toilette	towel
du shampooing	shampoo

pour exprimer la fréquence	to express frequency
toujours	always, still
tous les…/toutes les…	every . . .
souvent	often
quelquefois	sometimes
rarement	rarely
ne … jamais	never

autres mots utiles	other useful words
déjà	already
de nouveau	again
être en train de (+ infinitif)	to be busy (doing something)
une journée	day
le lavabo	bathroom sink
la nuit	at night
tôt	early
tard	late
assez	enough

Leçon 2

pour parler de l'heure	to talk about the time
une horloge	clock
une montre	watch
un (radio) réveil	alarm clock (clock radio)
être à l'heure	to be on time
être en avance	to be early
être en retard	to be late
Vous avez l'heure ?	What time is it?
pendant	during, for
jusqu'à	until
encore (un quart d'heure)	another (quarter of an hour)
entre	between
Il est une heure, huit heures.	It is one o'clock, eight o'clock.
et quart	00:15
et demi/e	00:30
moins vingt	00:40
moins le quart	00:45
du matin	in the morning, A.M.
de l'après-midi	in the afternoon, P.M.
du soir	in the evening, P.M.
midi	noon
minuit	midnight

quelques expressions utiles	some useful expressions
Mince !	Shoot!
Super !	Great !
Ouf !	Whew!
Zut (alors) !	Darn!

quelques verbes utiles	some useful verbs
chanter	to sing
commencer	to begin
courir	to run
dormir	to sleep
partir	to leave
quitter (ma chambre)	to leave (my room)
servir	to serve
sonner	to ring, to alarm
sortir	to go out
trouver	to find

pour comparer	to compare
aussi … que	as … as
autant de … que	as many … as
moins (de) … que	less … than
plus (de) … que	more … than
mieux que	better than
le mieux	the best

Leçon 3

les vêtements (m.) pour femmes	women's clothing
des chaussures (f.) à talons	high-heeled shoes
un chemisier	blouse
un collant	pantyhose
un foulard	silk scarf
une jupe	skirt
une robe	dress
un sac	purse
un tailleur	woman's suit

les vêtements pour hommes	men's clothing
une chemise	man's shirt
un costume	man's suit
une cravate	tie
des mocassins (m.)	loafers

les tissus (m.) et les matières (f.)	fabrics and materials
le coton	cotton
le cuir	leather
la laine	wool
la soie	silk

les vêtements de sport et de loisirs	sportswear
un blouson	heavy jacket

une casquette	baseball cap
des chaussettes (f.)	socks
un gilet	cardigan sweater
un jean	jeans
des lunettes (f.) (de soleil)	(sun)glasses
un maillot (de bain)	swimsuit
un pantalon	slacks
un polo	polo shirt
un pull(-over)	pull-over sweater
des sandales (f.)	sandals
un short	shorts
un tee-shirt	T-shirt
des tennis (m.)	tennis shoes
une veste	jacket, suit coat

les vêtements d'extérieur	outerwear
un anorak	parka (with hood)
des bottes (f.)	boots
une écharpe	scarf
des gants (m.)	gloves
un imper(méable)	raincoat
un manteau	overcoat
un parapluie	umbrella

les couleurs (voir page 164)	colors

au (grand) magasin	at the (department) store
avoir envie de (+ nom, + infinitif)	to want (something, to do something)
ce modèle	this style
mettre	to put, to put on
porter (une robe)	to wear (a dress)
le prix	price
les soldes (f.)	sales
Tenez…	Here …
la vitrine	display window

pour décrire les vêtements	to describe clothing
à la mode	stylish, fashionable
bon marché	cheap
cher/chère	expensive
court/e	short
démodé/e	old-fashioned, out-of-date
fin/e	thin, elegant
large	big, large, roomy
long/ue	long
même	same
(le/la) meilleur/e	better (the best)

Regardez ces deux personnes : où sont-ils, à votre avis ? Qu'est-ce qu'ils vont probablement faire aujourd'hui ?

Chapitre 5

Activités par tous les temps

 Leçon 1 *Il fait quel temps ?*

Leçon 2 *On part en vacances !*

Leçon 3 *Je vous invite*

Venez chez nous !
Vive les vacances !

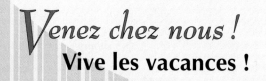

In this chapter:

- Talking about the weather
- Telling about past actions or events
- Talking about vacation and cultural activities
- Asking questions
- Extending, accepting, and refusing invitations
- Identifying vacation spots and activities in places where French is spoken

Il fait quel temps ?

You might provide an overview of this chapter by showing the video montage *Vive les vacances !* See whether students can identify the various places, activities, and seasons. Use the weather visuals (IRCD, Ch. 5) and brief descriptions to present the new vocabulary. Once you have presented a few items, show an image without labels (IRCD, Ch. 5) and test comprehension by having students point to a picture that illustrates the weather you describe. Next, have students repeat key expressions. Emphasize the use of *il fait* for most expressions, except for *il pleut* and *il neige*. Point out that the pronoun *il* is used in an

POINTS DE DÉPART

Additional practice activities for each **Points de départ** section are provided by:
• Student Activities Manual
• *Chez nous* Companion Website:
  http://www.prenhall.com/cheznous

Le temps à toutes les saisons

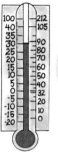

En été, il fait chaud et lourd.

Il fait beau. Il y a du soleil et le ciel est bleu.

Le ciel est couvert ; il y a des nuages. Il va pleuvoir.

impersonal way and does not refer to a person. Point out near-equivalent expressions, for example, *il y a des nuages/le ciel est couvert*.

Finally, treat the **Vie et culture** notes and check comprehension: *Il fait 30° C. —Il fait très chaud.* We suggest that you review this new vocabulary on day 2 of the lesson and then present the seasons, continuing with the exercises that follow.

Au printemps, il fait frais et il y a du vent.

En automne, il fait mauvais. Il pleut et il y a du brouillard.

Il y a un orage : il y a des éclairs et du tonnerre.

En hiver, il gèle ; il y a du verglas.

Il fait froid et il neige.

To indicate that a person feels cold or hot, use the verb **avoir**:

Il fait 30°C ; j'**ai** très **chaud**.   *It's 87 degrees; I'm very hot.*

Il commence à neiger ; nous **avons froid**.   *It's starting to snow; we're cold.*

Vie et culture

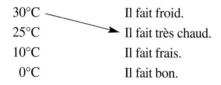

En avril, ne te découvre pas d'un fil

Gare aux geléès tardives. Des records de froid ont été battus en raison de l'arrivée d'une masse d'air froid venue de Scandinavie

Michel BARELLI, *Nice-Matin*, 9 avril 2003, p. 30

Mesurer la température

In Francophone countries and throughout much of the world, temperature is measured in degrees Celsius. To make things easy, just remember a few key expressions that correspond to certain temperatures. For example, look at the thermometer to match each temperature with the most appropriate expression:

30°C   Il fait froid.
25°C   Il fait très chaud.
10°C   Il fait frais.
0°C   Il fait bon.

Proverbes

This headline from the newspaper **Nice-Matin** uses a proverb to introduce a story about the weather. Most languages have proverbs that refer to the weather, but like many other aspects of language, proverbs cannot be translated literally. To understand this one, look at the context. In which month did the headline appear? Look at the text in bold under the headline and pick out words that indicate what kind of weather is anticipated. Putting these pieces of information together, can you guess the meaning of the proverb?

In addition to understanding the literal meaning of proverbs, try also to understand their message. For example, another common proverb evoking the weather is: **Après la pluie, le beau temps**. This saying suggests that after each hardship there will be easier times ahead. To some extent, we could convey the message of this proverb with a similar, though not identical, English proverb: *Every cloud has a silver lining*. How is the English proverb similar to the French one? How is it different? Why do you think weather proverbs are common in both French and English?

À vous la parole

5-1 Quel temps fait-il ?

D'après le journal, dites quel temps il fait dans ces villes francophones.

MODÈLE   Paris
➤ À Paris, il fait assez frais et le ciel est couvert.

1. Paris
2. Alger
3. Dakar
4. Montréal
5. Nice
6. La Nouvelle-Orléans
7. Papeete
8. Fort-de-France
9. Tunis

PRÉVISIONS POUR LE 2 AVRIL

Ville par ville, les minima/maxima de température et l'état du ciel.
S : soleil ; C : couvert ; P : pluie ; V : vent fort ; O : orages ; N : neige

AMÉRIQUES		
BRASILIA	19/28	S
CHICAGO	7/21	S
MEXICO	10/24	S
MONTRÉAL	−6/0	N
NEW YORK	5/14	C
LA NOUVELLE-ORLÉANS	10/26	S
TORONTO	2/13	C

FRANCE métropole		
AJACCIO	9/19	S
BIARRITZ	8/16	P
CAEN	3/10	C
LILLE	3/11	C
NICE	9/16	S,V
PARIS	3/12	C

FRANCE d'outre-mer		
CAYENNE	23/27	P
FORT-DE-FR.	23/28	S
PAPEETE	25/31	P

AFRIQUE		
ALGER	13/21	S
DAKAR	20/26	O
KINSHASA	23/29	P
LE CAIRE	16/27	S
TUNIS	15/26	P

(margin note)
5-1 Use a map (for example, IRCD Maps) to show the location of cities. You may also wish to show the weather forecast (IRCD, Ch. 5). To expand and review, have students describe what clothing they would wear in each city.

5-2 Prévisions météorologiques.

Voilà le temps qu'on annonce pour la France. Demandez à votre partenaire quel temps il va faire et la température.

MODÈLE   à Lyon

É1   Quel temps est-ce qu'il va faire à Lyon ?
É2   À Lyon, il va pleuvoir.
É1   Et la température ?
É2   Il va faire onze degrés, donc il va faire assez frais.

1. à Paris
2. à Bordeaux
3. à Perpignan
4. à Brest
5. à Nice
6. dans les Alpes
7. à Lille
8. à Strasbourg
9. à Bastia

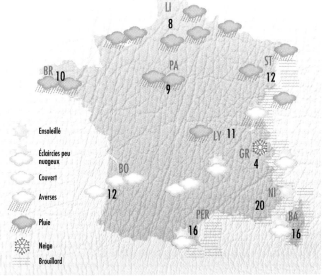

(margin note)
5-2 Show the weather map (IRCD, Ch. 5) and go over the city codes and weather symbols before completing the exercise.

As an alternative to Ex. 5-2, have students (in pairs or small groups) describe the weather in famous paintings you display as posters or slides. Some examples of good paintings to use include: *Rue de Paris, jour de pluie*; *Toits sous la neige, Paris*, Gustave Caillebotte; *La neige à Louveciennes*; *Printemps aux environs de Paris, pommiers en fleurs*, Alfred Sisley; *Coquelicots*; *Promenade près d'Argenteuil*; *Effet de vent, série des Peupliers*; *Le Déjeuner*, Claude Monet; *Les Boulevards extérieurs, effet de neige*; *Arbres en fleurs*, Pissarro; *La Méridienne ou La Sieste* (*d'après Millet*), Vincent Van Gogh; *Les parapluies*, Renoir.

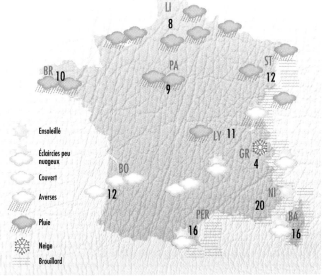
Map legend:
Ensoleillé
Éclaircies peu nuageux
Couvert
Averses
Pluie
Neige
Brouillard

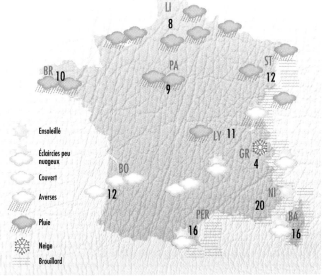
City markers on map:
LI 8
BR 10
PA 9
ST 12
LY 11
GR 4
BO 12
NI 20
PER 16
BA 16

5-3 Follow up by having the class compare responses for each item.

👥👥 **5-3 Vos préférences.** Avec un/e partenaire, posez les questions suivantes pour découvrir quand votre partenaire préfère faire ces activités. Ensuite, comparez vos réponses avec celles de vos camarades de classe.

MODÈLE   É1   Quand est-ce que tu n'aimes pas aller en classe ?

           É2   Je n'aime pas aller en classe quand il neige beaucoup ou quand il y a un orage.

1. Quand est-ce que tu aimes rester dans le jardin ?
2. Quand est-ce que tu n'aimes pas faire du shopping ?
3. Quand est-ce que tu aimes faire du sport ?
4. Quand est-ce que tu préfères rester chez toi ?
5. Quand est-ce que tu aimes aller au cinéma ?
6. Quand est-ce que tu n'aimes pas voyager ?

You may wish to present this vocabulary on day 2. Have students describe the weather in each photo. Ask what month they think it is, and present the seasons. Point out that the preposition *en* is used with all months of the year and all seasons except *le printemps* (*au printemps*).

LES SAISONS DE L'ANNÉE

**le printemps
(au printemps)
mars
avril
mai**

**l'été
(en été)
juin
juillet
août**

**l'hiver
(en hiver)
décembre
janvier
février**

**l'automne
(en automne)
septembre
octobre
novembre**

👥👥 **5-4 Nous sommes en quelle saison ?** Pour chaque phrase, décidez avec un/e partenaire de quelle saison on parle.

MODÈLE   En Bretagne le ciel est souvent couvert, il y a souvent de la pluie mais il fait bon. On peut jouer au tennis ou au golf.

      É1   C'est le printemps ou peut-être l'automne.

      É2   Je pense que c'est le printemps parce qu'il y a beaucoup de pluie.

1. En France, on célèbre la fête nationale. Mais c'est la saison des orages : il y a des éclairs et du tonnerre.
2. Il y a souvent du brouillard en Bourgogne. Il gèle et il y a du verglas.
3. À Paris, c'est la rentrée et le temps est variable. Souvent, il y a du vent et le ciel est gris.
4. À la Martinique, il fait très chaud et lourd et il y a des nuages. Il pleut souvent.
5. On est sûr d'avoir du soleil et un temps chaud en France. Voilà pourquoi les Français partent en vacances.
6. Il y a beaucoup de soleil à Tahiti. On porte un maillot de bain.
7. Partout en France c'est la belle saison. Le ciel est bleu et il fait très beau. Mais les étudiants sont stressés parce que les examens vont bientôt commencer.
8. Il fait très beau à la Guadeloupe. Il ne fait pas trop chaud et le temps est sec (*dry*). C'est le temps parfait pour travailler dans le jardin.

👥👥 **5-5 Quel est le climat chez vous ?** Posez des questions à votre partenaire pour découvrir quel temps il fait d'habitude chez elle/lui et chez les membres de sa famille, pendant la saison indiquée.

MODÈLE   en hiver, chez ses parents

      É1   Quel temps fait-il en hiver chez tes parents ?

      É2   Chez mes parents, en Louisiane, il fait assez frais et le ciel est souvent couvert en hiver.

1. en été, chez elle/lui
2. en hiver, chez elle/lui
3. au printemps, chez ses parents
4. en automne, chez ses grands-parents

L'été en Bretagne. Il fait chaud et il y a du soleil.

Quel temps fait-il ? Téléphonez pour savoir !

5-4, Key: *l'automne* = 3, 4 ; *l'hiver* = 2, 6 (from the point of view of the northern hemisphere) ; *le printemps* = 7, 8 ; *l'été* = 1, 5.

Ask students to give specific months when appropriate 1 = *juillet*, 3 = *septembre/octobre*, 5 = *juillet/août*, 7 = *mai/juin*. This exercise introduces cultural information and additional useful vocabulary; explain unfamiliar terms. Remind students that seasons are relative to the hemisphere; southern and northern hemispheres experience seasons at opposite times of the year. As a personalized follow-up, ask students *Quelle saison préférez-vous ? pourquoi ?*

5-5 Conclude by having students tell what type of climate they prefer and why.

Examine the poster and have students look at the weather symbols and read the sequences out loud to discover what they mean: *Il fait beau ? Il (ne) fait pas beau ?* What can one do in France to hear the weather report? -call 32-50.

Sons et lettres

Les voyelles nasales

Additional practice activities for each **Sons et lettres** section are provided by:
- Student Activities Manual
- Text Audio

Both English and French have nasal vowels. In English, any vowel followed by a nasal consonant is automatically nasalized, as in *man*, *pen*, *song*. In French, whether the vowel is nasal or not can make a difference in meaning. For example:

beau	/bo/	*handsome*	vs.	bon	/bɔ̃/	*good*
ça	/sa/	*that*	vs.	cent	/sɑ̃/	*a hundred*
sec	/sɛk/	*dry*	vs.	cinq	/sɛ̃k/	*five*

There are four nasal vowels in French. Use this phrase to remember them:

| un /œ̃/ | bon /bɔ̃/ | vin /vɛ̃/ | blanc /blɑ̃/ | *a good white wine* |

Nasal vowels are always written with a vowel letter followed by a nasal consonant (**m** or **n**), but that consonant is not usually pronounced: **mon, dans, cinq**.

- The vowel /ɔ̃/ is usually spelled **on**: **l'oncle**
- The vowel /ɑ̃/ is spelled **an** or **en**: **janvier, le vent**
- For /ɛ̃/ there are several spellings: **vingt, le chien, l'examen, la main**
- The vowel /œ̃/, which is rare and often pronounced like /ɛ̃/, is spelled **un**: **brun, lundi**
- Before **b** and **p**, all nasal vowels are spelled with **m**: **combien, le temps, impossible**

Note this exception: **le bonbon**

The distinction between /œ̃/ and /ɛ̃/ is not generally made by speakers in the region of Paris, who tend to use /ɛ̃/ only. Because of that, and because /œ̃/ occurs in few words (*un, chacun, quelqu'un, lundi, parfum*) it not useful to insist that students make this distinction.

À vous la parole

Begin practice with a discrimination drill. Have students raise their hand when they hear words with a nasal vowel: *bon, l'eau, chanter, Jeanne*, etc.

5-6 Contrastes. Répétez et faites bien entendre les différences de prononciation.

| beau / bon | allô / allons | sec / cinq |
| fine / fin | Jeanne / Jean | américaine / américain |

In another discrimination exercise, write the three vowels on the board as in *an on*, and have students indicate which you have pronounced: *Jean, blond, vingt*, etc.

5-7 Quelle voyelle nasale ? Faites attention à bien faire entendre les différences de prononciation entre ces voyelles nasales.

1. le vin / le vent
2. cent pages / cinq pages
3. c'est long / c'est lent
4. il vend / ils vont
5. la langue / elle est longue

5-8 Phrases. Répétez chaque phrase.

1. Allons, allons ! Voyons ! Voyons !
2. En septembre, il y a souvent du vent.
3. Alain et Colin vont à Lyon par le train.
4. On annonce une température de vingt-cinq degrés.

FORMES ET FONCTIONS

1. *Les verbes en* -re *comme* vendre

Additional practice activities for
each **Formes et fonctions** section
are provided by:
- Student Activities Manual
- *Chez nous* Companion Website:
  http://www.prenhall.com/cheznous

- Verbs ending in **-re** differ from the **-er** verbs you have already learned in two ways:

  - The singular forms have different written endings. Note that the final consonants in these singular forms are never pronounced.

    j'attend**s** (*I wait*)   tu entend**s** (*you hear*)   il répon**d** (*he answers*)

  - With these verbs, you can always tell whether someone is talking about one person, or more than one, because the **-d** is pronounced in the plural forms.

    elles répon**d**ent   vs.   elle répon**d**

Before presenting this topic, review -er *and* -ir *verbs to highlight the differences in the number of stems and spoken forms. Stress the importance of a clear articulation of the final consonant in the third-person plural for both* -ir *and* -re *verbs; it is this final consonant that distinguishes the singular from the plural in speech.*

ATTENDRE *to wait for*	
SINGULIER	PLURIEL
j' attend**s**	nous attend**ons**
tu attend**s**	vous attend**ez**
il	ils
elle } attend	elles } attend**ent**
on	

IMPÉRATIF : Attend**s** ! Attend**ons** ici.
Attend**ez** un moment !

- Here are the most common verbs ending in **-re**.

attendre	*to wait for*	Ils **attendent** le professeur.
descendre (à)	*to go down*	Je **descends au** labo.
de	*to get off*	Elle **descend du** bus.
en ville	*to go downtown*	Vous **descendez en ville** ?
entendre	*to hear*	Tu **entends** cette musique ?
perdre	*to lose*	Il **perd** toujours ses cahiers.
rendre à	*to give back*	Le prof **rend** les essais **aux** étudiants.
rendre visite à	*to visit someone*	Nous **rendons visite à** nos parents.
répondre à	*to answer*	Vous **répondez à** sa lettre ?
en		Elle **répond en** anglais.
vendre	*to sell*	Ils **vendent** des magazines.

Be sure to stress that rendre visite à *is the equivalent of the English verb "to visit," when a person is involved. Make sure students understand that the cognate* visiter *can only be used with places (e.g.,* Je rends visite à mes grands-parents. On visite le musée du Louvre).*

- Remember that English and French often differ in the use of prepositions with verbs:

  J'attends le métro.   *I'm waiting **for** the subway.*
  Il répond **au** professeur.   *He's answering the professor.*
  Elle rend visite **à** sa mère.   *She's visiting her mother.*

5-9 C'est logique. Complétez chaque phrase de manière logique en utilisant un verbe en **-re**.

MODÈLE   nous / le métro
> Nous attendons le métro.

1. le professeur / en anglais en classe
2. l'étudiante / ses devoirs au professeur
3. nous / des livres à la bibliothèque
4. moi / mes parents à Québec
5. vous / du train ?
6. toi / le téléphone ?
7. elle / son foulard
8. Marc / le week-end pour sortir avec des amis

5-10 Réponses personnelles. Posez les questions suivantes à votre partenaire, puis partagez avec le reste de la classe ce que vous avez appris.

MODÈLE   À qui est-ce que tu rends visite le week-end ?
> Je rends visite à mes parents.
OU > Je rends visite à mes amis.

1. À qui est-ce que tu rends visite le week-end ?
2. Est-ce que tu perds souvent tes vêtements ? si oui, comment ?
3. Est-ce que tu revends tes livres à la fin du semestre ? pourquoi ?
4. Est-ce que tu réponds rapidement à tes lettres ?
5. Quand est-ce que tu descends en ville, et pourquoi ?

2. Le passé composé avec avoir

- To express an action completed in the past, use the **passé composé**. The **passé composé** is composed of an auxiliary, or helping verb, and the past participle of the verb that expresses the action. Usually, the present tense of **avoir** is the helping verb.

J'**ai travaillé** hier.	*I worked yesterday.*
Tu **as mangé** ?	*Did you eat?*
Il **a fait** beau ce week-end.	*The weather was nice this weekend.*
Nous **avons écouté** la météo à la radio.	*We listened to the weather forecast on the radio.*
Vous **avez regardé** la météo à la télé.	*They watched the weather forecast on TV.*
Ils **ont annoncé** du beau temps à la radio.	*They predicted nice weather on the radio.*

Sidebar notes (left margin):

Begin practice with a discrimination drill: one person, or more than one? *Ils attendent le prof ; Elle entend le téléphone ; Elles vendent la maison,* etc. Follow up with a simple substitution drill. Start first with the contrast third-person plural vs. third-person singular by visual cuing: *Elles descendent en ville.* (Show one finger) — *Elle descend en ville.* Then proceed with the other forms: *Nous descendons en ville ; je. — Je descends en ville.*

5-10 Have students compare their responses.

This topic can be presented inductively in class. Begin by describing your own activities during, for example, the past weekend. Then ask students questions about their own weekend, using yes/no, either/or, and short-answer questions. Then ask students to tell you what time frame you are talking about, and whether they can tell how to form the *passé composé.* For students who are visual learners, you could display the text of your weekend activities on a transparency or PowerPoint slide with the forms in the *passé composé* highlighted.

- The specific meaning of the **passé composé** depends on the verb and on the context.

Hier on **a montré** un film à la télé.   *Yesterday they showed a film on TV.*
Mais j'**ai** déjà **préparé** les devoirs !   *But I have already done the homework!*
L'hiver dernier il **a fait** très froid.   *Last winter it was very cold.*
Mais j'**ai** beaucoup **travaillé** !   *But I did work a lot!*

- To form the past participle . . .

  - for **-er** verbs, add **-é** to the base (the infinitive form minus the **-er** ending):
  quitt**er**   J'ai quitt**é** la maison à huit heures.   *I left home at eight o'clock.*

  - for **-ir** verbs, add **-i** to the base (the infinitive form minus the **-ir** ending):
  dorm**ir**   Tu as dorm**i** pendant le concert ?   *You slept during the concert?*

  - for **-re** verbs, add **-u** to the base (the infinitive form minus the **-re** ending):
  attend**re**   Ils ont attend**u** devant le café.   *They waited in front of the café.*

- Here are past participles for irregular verbs that you know.

avoir	J'ai **eu** froid.	*I was cold.*
devoir	Il a **dû** travailler hier soir.	*He had to work last night.*
être	On a **été** supris.	*We were surprised.*
faire	Il a **fait** beau.	*It was nice weather.*
mettre	J'ai **mis** un chapeau.	*I put on a hat.*
pleuvoir	Il a **plu** hier.	*It rained yesterday.*
pouvoir	J'ai **pu** sortir.	*I was able to go out.*
vouloir	Elles n'ont pas **voulu** partir.	*They refused to leave.*

- In negative sentences, place **ne** and **pas** around the conjugated auxiliary verb.

Il **n'**a **pas** fait beau hier.   *The weather wasn't nice yesterday.*
Nos parents **n'**ont **pas** téléphoné.   *Our parents didn't call.*

You might point out that short adverbs such as *déjà* and *beaucoup* are placed after the helping verb.

The following expressions are useful for referring to the past.

hier	*yesterday*
avant-hier	*the day before yesterday*
samedi dernier	*last Saturday*
l'année dernière	*last year*
il y a longtemps	*a long time ago*
il y a deux jours	*two days ago*
ce jour-là	*that day*
à ce moment-là	*at that moment*

5-11 La météo d'hier. Regardez la carte météorologique et dites quel temps il a fait hier au Canada et en Nouvelle-Angleterre.

MODÈLE au Nouveau-Brunswick
➤ Au Nouveau-Brunswick il y a eu du verglas et il a plu.

1. à Chicoutimi
2. à Montréal
3. en Nouvelle-Angleterre
4. à Ottawa
5. à Gaspé
6. à Sherbrooke

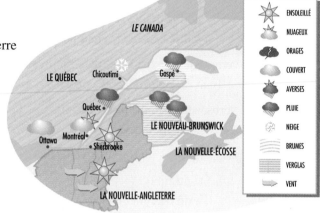

5-12 Mais c'est logique ! Avec un/e partenaire, imaginez ce que ces gens ont fait à l'endroit mentionné. Combien de possibilités est-ce que vous pouvez trouver ?

MODÈLE Qu'est-ce que Julie a fait dans le magasin hier ?
➤ Elle a acheté une jolie robe.
OU ➤ Elle a travaillé ; c'est une vendeuse.

1. Qu'est-ce que vous avez fait au labo de langues ce matin ?
2. Qu'est-ce que les Brunet ont fait à la piscine l'été dernier ?
3. Qu'est-ce que tu as fait à la bibliothèque hier ?
4. Qu'est ce que nous avons fait au gymnase hier soir ?
5. Qu'est-ce que tu as fait chez toi hier soir ?
6. Qu'est-ce que David a fait au stade avant-hier ?
7. Qu'est-ce que vos camarades ont fait chez eux le week-end dernier ?
8. Qu'est-ce que le prof a fait dans son bureau ce matin ?

5-13 Normalement, mais... Racontez à votre partenaire vos habitudes et aussi les exceptions !

MODÈLE dormir
➤ Normalement, je dors jusqu'à sept heures, mais samedi dernier j'ai dormi jusqu'à dix heures.

1. dormir
2. manger
3. quitter la maison
4. travailler à la bibliothèque
5. jouer
6. regarder la télé
7. passer l'été

5-14 Quelle sorte de journée ? Vous êtes normalement très actif/active, assez actif/active ou sédentaire ? Vos camarades de classe vont juger. En groupes de trois, racontez vos activités d'hier matin, après-midi et soir. Vos camarades vont prendre des notes, et ensuite ils vont décider si vous avez passé une journée plutôt active ou calme.

MODÈLE   É1 **le matin** : J'ai mangé au resto U. J'ai assisté au cours de français.
J'ai travaillé au labo.

l'après-midi : J'ai joué au tennis. J'ai préparé le dîner.

le soir : J'ai joué au basket. J'ai regardé la télé.

É2 Cette personne a passé une journée assez active.

5-14 Have students list a certain number of activities, then give a score for each activity (i.e., 1 for sedentary, 3 for very active); the total score can then be judged. Point out that note-taking does not require full sentences; the emphasis here is on listening and speaking.

Lisons

TEXT AUDIO

5-15 Il pleure dans mon cœur

A. Avant de lire. The poet Paul Verlaine (1844–1896) believed that the music of language is more important than the actual words, and that suggestion is more important than statement. The effect of his poetry is like that of Impressionist art or music, and his poems are often compared with the paintings of Claude Monet or the music of Claude Debussy (who set sixteen of Verlaine's poems to music).

Verlaine often used free verse (that is, unrhymed lines of unequal length) and the sounds and rhythms of French to create richly musical poems, like **Il pleure dans mon cœur**, which even listeners who do not know French can appreciate. Listen as the poem is read aloud and think about how its sounds and rhythm suggest the poet's melancholy sadness on a rainy day. Next, read the poem and complete the related work.

Ce tableau de Claude Monet, « Impression : soleil levant », a donné son nom au mouvement impressionniste.

B. En lisant. As you read, look for answers to the following questions.

1. In Verlaine's poem, nature reflects his own feelings. How is this the case?
2. In the first two verses, the poet alternates between references to the weather outside and his own feelings. How does he do this?
3. In the last two verses, the poet focuses on his own feelings. What point does he seem to want to make about his feelings of sadness?
4. Is there a "plot" to this poem? How might you summarize what happens?

Stratégie

Discover by reading aloud how sounds and rhythm affect the musicality of a poem. Consider in turn what the music of language may be suggesting about a poem's meaning, and what the impact is on your own reactions.

In his *Art poétique*, Verlaine proclaimed, « *De la musique avant toute chose* ». Emphasize to students that the message of Verlaine's poem is conveyed largely through its sounds and its rhythm. The reference to Rimbaud is a reprise of a line written by this fellow poet, with whom Verlaine had an unhappy romantic relationship. Be sure to point out to students that the Monet painting shown here was the source of the name for the Impressionist movement, which was much ridiculed when these artists began to show their work. You might show students additional examples of Monet's paintings and play part of Debussy's *Après-midi d'une faune* to illustrate Impressionism in art and music.

Have students listen as you read aloud or play the recording of the poem.

Additional activities to develop the four skills are provided by:
• Student Activities Manual
• Text Audio
• *Chez nous* video
• *Chez nous* Companion Website: http://www.prenhall.com/cheznous

En lisant, Key: 1) The falling rain is like tears falling   2) he contrasts the phrases *il pleut/il pleure*   3) that he does not know the reason for his sadness   4) it rains, and the poet is sad.

IL PLEURE DANS MON CŒUR...

Il pleut doucement sur la ville.
Arthur Rimbaud

It's crying; heart

Il pleure° dans mon cœur°
Comme il pleut sur la ville ;
Quelle est cette langueur
Qui pénètre mon cœur ?

soft sound
ground; roofs
is troubled
song

Ô bruit doux° de la pluie   5
Par terre° et sur les toits° !
Pour un cœur qui s'ennuie°
Ô le chant° de la pluie !

is discouraged
no betrayal
sadness

Il pleure sans raison
Dans ce cœur qui s'écœure.°   10
Quoi ! nulle trahison° ?...
Ce deuil° est sans raison.

worst pain
not knowing
hate
so much

C'est bien la pire peine°
De ne savoir° pourquoi
Sans amour et sans haine°   15
Mon cœur a tant de° peine !

Paul Verlaine

C. En regardant de plus près. Now look more closely at the following features of the text.

1. Find two repeated phrases in the poem that are almost identical in pronunciation and that are somewhat related in meaning—how do they help convey the poet's message?
2. The effect of a French poem is closely related to the number of syllables in each line and the rhythm this establishes. How many syllables are there in each line of this poem? What is the rhyme scheme?
3. Notice the repetition of certain sounds in the poem, most notably the vowel in **cœur.** Find all the words containing that sound; how important are these words to the rhyme scheme? What kind of mood does the repetition of this long vowel produce? You might want to listen to the poem once more.

D. Après avoir lu. Discuss these questions with your classmates.

1. Look at the painting by Monet shown on the previous page. Are there ways in which Monet's painting seems similar to Verlaine's poem? Do both, for example, suggest a mood or impression? Are the artist's and poet's approaches to their subject matter delicate or heavy-handed?
2. What features of music can produce a melancholy effect similar to that produced by Verlaine's poem?

Leçon 2 On part en vacances !

POINTS DE DÉPART

Des activités par tous les temps

À la plage, on peut faire…
du ski nautique
du surf
de la voile
de la planche à voile

À la campagne, on peut faire…
des pique-niques
du cheval
du vélo

You might show the video montage for **Venez chez nous !** (*Vive les vacances !*) at the beginning of L. 2, as it provides examples of vacation activities at different times of the year. Ask students to identify locations (*la plage, la montagne, la ville*), seasons, weather, and activities that they see. The video clip *La Côte d'Azur : destination de rêve* can also be used in L. 2. In this clip, a young woman describes attractions of the *Côte d'Azur*. See the Video Manual for a complete treatment.

Show the vacation activities (IRCD, Ch. 5) to present the new vocabulary. Describe each scene briefly; display each image without labels (IRCD, Ch. 5), and test comprehension by having students point to the activity you name. As a prelude to Ex. 5-16, have students associate each activity with a place, a season, and weather conditions. Have students repeat the new vocabulary, using either/or questions: *on fait du ski nautique ou de la voile ?*, etc. You may wish to present as additional vocabulary *aller à la mer* and *se bronzer*. Complete Ex. 5-16 before presenting the dialogue.

À la montagne, on peut faire...
du camping
de l'alpinisme
des randonnées
du ski
du surf des neiges

En ville, on peut faire...
du tourisme
un tour dans le quartier
un tour au parc
des courses
des achats
et on peut visiter des musées
et des monuments

The locations mentioned in the dialogue—*les Antilles, Tahiti, les Seychelles*—are either *départements* or *collectivités d'outre-mer* (former French colonies), so all are logical choices for a French family. Locate each place on a map. The **Venez chez nous !** lesson provides more information on the these territories.

This dialogue introduces some typical exclamations used in French. In normal conversational style, negative *ne/n'* is usually dropped by native speakers of French. However, point out that it is better for students learning French to pronounce the *ne/n'*, as its loss by non-native speakers is perceived negatively by many French speakers. Thus, students should say *Ce n'est pas vrai !* Have students listen to the dialogue. Check comprehension by having students pick out the preferred activities of each person. You can use this exchange as a point of departure for discussing *les vacances de février.* Follow up with Ex. 5-17 through 5-19.

Projets de vacances

TEXT AUDIO

M. KELLER : Cette année nous n'allons pas aux sports d'hiver.

MAX : Ah, non, c'est pas vrai ! Zut alors !

M. KELLER : Si, cette année vous n'allez pas faire du ski en février, mais du ski nautique.

CAROLINE : Chouette ! Alors nous allons aux Antilles ? À Tahiti ?

M. KELLER : Pas tout à fait, ma grande. J'ai des billets d'avion pour aller aux Seychelles, dans l'Océan Indien.

MAX : Bravo ! Vive les Seychelles !

CAROLINE : Et la voile, la planche à voile !

M. KELLER : Et vive la pêche et le repos !

À vous la parole

5-16 Qu'est-ce qu'on peut faire ? Avec un/e partenaire, suggérez des activités logiques.

MODÈLE   Qu'est-ce qu'on peut faire à la montagne, quand il y a de la neige ?

      É1   On peut faire du ski.

      É2   On peut faire du surf des neiges.

1. à la plage, en été ?
2. à la campagne, quand il fait beau ?
3. au gymnase, même (*even*) quand il fait mauvais ?
4. à la montagne, quand il fait beau ?
5. au stade, en automne ?
6. à la piscine, quand il fait chaud ?
7. en ville, quand il fait beau ?
8. en ville, quand il fait mauvais ?

5-17 Suggestions. Proposez une activité à votre partenaire; il/elle va donner sa réaction.

MODÈLE   Vous êtes à la montagne.

      É1   Nous allons faire une randonnée.

      É2   Super ! J'adore la nature !

      OU   Zut alors ! Je n'ai pas de bonnes chaussures !

1. Vous êtes à la montagne.
2. Vous êtes à la plage.
3. Vous êtes à la campagne.
4. Vous êtes en ville.

5-17 Let students take turns suggesting an activity. Note that the reactions come from the dialogue *Projets de vacances.*

5-18 À l'Office de Tourisme. En parlant avec un/e partenaire, expliquez ce que les vacanciers peuvent faire dans votre région.

MODÈLE   É1   J'habite à Asheville, en Caroline du Nord. Nous sommes à la montagne. Il fait beau en été et on peut faire du camping et des randonnées. En hiver, il neige et on peut faire du ski. Et toi ?

      É2   Moi, j'habite à Baltimore, dans le Maryland. C'est près de l'océan. Il y a un port et un grand aquarium, …

5-19 Les vacances idéales. Demandez à un/e camarade quelles sont ses vacances idéales, et ensuite dites ce que vous préférez.

MODÈLE   É1   Moi, je préfère aller à la plage, où il fait chaud. J'aime bien nager et jouer au volley-ball. Et toi ?

      É2   Pour moi, les vacances idéales, c'est la montagne en hiver. J'adore faire du ski et du surf des neiges.

5-19 Follow up by having students report back on their ideal vacations.

Vie et culture

Use the school calendar to review important cultural concepts such as *la rentrée* and holiday periods in France. Establishing zones makes it possible to avoid major traffic difficulties when everyone leaves on vacation and overcrowding at the most popular destinations.

Les vacances des Français

Look at the calendar to identify the various holiday periods for French school children. Notice that France is divided into three zones for two of the vacation periods; the map shows the location of each zone. Can you explain this division into zones? Think about when these vacation periods take place, what French people might do and where they would most likely go during these times.

Since 1982, all salaried workers in France have had the right to five weeks of paid vacation each year. With the advent of the 35-hour workweek, the French are beginning to take more frequent, and shorter, vacations, often opting for long weekend trips. Throughout France, however, it is still not unusual to see businesses (restaurants, hairdressers, small shops, bakeries, etc.) closed for several weeks in the months of July or August.

Et vous ?

1. How many weeks of paid vacation are typical in the United States? How does this situation compare with that of France, and what factors might account for any differences?
2. The right to longer paid vacations has often been a factor in labor negotiations in France. Knowing this, and that many businesses shut down for weeks at a time for vacation, what conclusions can you draw about the value the French place on vacation? Are vacations valued in a similar way in North America?

VACANCES SCOLAIRES

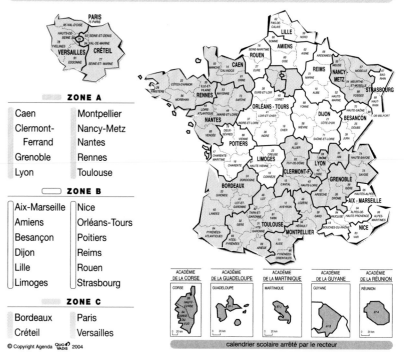

ZONE A
Caen   Montpellier
Clermont-   Nancy-Metz
 Ferrand   Nantes
Grenoble   Rennes
Lyon   Toulouse

ZONE B
Aix-Marseille Nice
Amiens   Orléans-Tours
Besançon   Poitiers
Dijon   Reims
Lille   Rouen
Limoges   Strasbourg

ZONE C
Bordeaux   Paris
Créteil   Versailles

© Copyright Agenda QUO VADIS 2004

calendrier scolaire arrêté par le recteur

ZONE A
Caen, Clermont-Ferrand, Grenoble, Lyon, Montpellier, Nancy-Metz, Nantes, Rennes, Toulouse

Rentrée scolaire des élèves	Toussaint	Noël	Hiver	Printemps	Début des vacances d'été*
le lundi [04-09-06]	du mercredi [25-10-06] au lundi [06-11-06]	du samedi [23-12-06] au lundi [08-01-07]	du samedi [10-02-07] au lundi [26-02-07]	du samedi [31-03-07] au lundi [16-04-07]	le mercredi [04-07-07]

ZONE B
Aix-Marseille, Amiens, Besançon, Dijon, Lille, Limoges, Nice, Orléans-Tours, Poitiers, Reims, Rouen, Strasbourg

Rentrée scolaire des élèves	Toussaint	Noël	Hiver	Printemps	Début des vacances d'été*
le lundi [04-09-06]	du mercredi [25-10-06] au lundi [06-11-06]	du samedi [23-12-06] au lundi [08-01-07]	du samedi [24-02-07] au lundi [12-03-07]	du samedi [14-04-07] au mercredi [02-05-07]	le mercredi [04-07-07]

ZONE C
Bordeaux, Créteil, Paris, Versailles

Rentrée scolaire des élèves	Toussaint	Noël	Hiver	Printemps	Début des vacances d'été*
le lundi [04-09-06]	du mercredi [25-10-06] au lundi [06-11-06]	du samedi [23-12-06] au lundi [08-01-07]	du samedi [17-02-07] au lundi [05-03-07]	du samedi [07-04-07] au lundi [23-04-07]	le mercredi [04-07-07]

Le départ en vacances a lieu après la classe, la reprise des cours le matin des jours indiqués.

You may want to discuss the following quote from *Francoscopie 2003* about changing patterns in French vacation practices as another source of cross-cultural comparisons:
... on pourrait... parler des trois D : détente, divertissement, développement. Si les Français cherchent évidemment à se reposer et à se faire plaisir, beaucoup profitent en effet des vacances pour développer leurs connaissances et leurs capacités physiques ou intellectuelles. (p. 497) How does this vision of vacation compare to the typical American one?

Sons et lettres

TEXT AUDIO

Les voyelles nasales et les voyelles orales plus consonne nasale

Compare the following pairs of words; the first ends with a final pronounced consonant (**-n** or **-m**) and the second ends in a nasal vowel. Only the second word contains a nasal vowel; notice the difference as you repeat after your instructor.

Demonstrate for students a careful articulation of the final /n/ for words in the left-hand column. To practice other pairs, use *Jeanne/Jean, Adrienne/Adrien, Yvonne/Yvon.*

bonne /bɔn/	bon /bɔ̃/
Simone /simɔn/ (*woman's name*)	Simon /simɔ̃/ (*man's name*)
ma cousine /kuzin/	mon cousin /kuzɛ̃/
l'année /lane/	l'an /lɑ̃/

For words containing a nasal vowel, pronounce each syllable slowly, and do not pronounce **-m** or **-n** when it follows the nasal vowel:

le camp	le cam-ping	la cam-pagne
mon	mon-ter	la mon-tagne

À vous la parole

5-20 Les groupes de mots. Attention de bien insister sur les voyelles nasales.

1. mon   mon-tagne
2. sans   san-té (*health*)
3. camp   cam-ping
4. un   in-dien
5. franc   fran-çaise
6. l'un   lun-di

Begin with an exercise that requires a change from masculine to feminine, and vice versa: *Il est bon. —Elle est bonne ; Il est brun ; Ils sont canadiens ; Il est américain ; C'est Jean ; mon cousin ; mes voisins ; Voilà Simon ; Ils sont bons.*

5-20 Have students pronounce the second word syllable by syllable several times, and then as a word: *mon, mon tagne, montagne.* Additional words with *n*: *rentrer, penser, chanter, randonnée*; with *m*: *combien, la campagne, impossible.*

5-21 Les phrases. Lisez chaque phrase.

1. Il fait bon en automne.
2. Mettons notre blouson et nos gants.
3. Jean et Jeanne vont en Bourgogne en juin.
4. Au printemps, Marianne va en Louisiane chez son oncle.
5. Lundi, nous faisons une randonnée à la montagne avec nos parents.

5-22 Poème. Répétez ces deux vers de Verlaine.

5-22 Students should recognize that the repetition of nasal vowels in the Verlaine poem helps produce a melancholic mood. Verlaine was 18 years old when he wrote this poem; you might read it in its entirety for students.

> Les sanglots° longs des violons de l'automne   *sobbing*
> Blessent° mon cœur d'une langueur monotone.   *strike*
>
> —Extrait de Paul Verlaine, « *Chanson d'automne* »

FORMES ET FONCTIONS

1. *Le passé composé avec* être

You might show contrasts like *Je suis allé/e à la bibliothèque* vs. *J'ai trouvé le livre de Simenon* and ask students what type of expression follows the verb. Point out that verbs that form the *passé composé* with *être* do not take a direct object, only adverbial complements. In fact, if a direct object does follow, the verb *avoir* must be used: *Je suis sorti ce matin* vs. *J'ai sorti le chien ; Il est monté au bureau* vs. *Il a monté les ordinateurs au bureau.* Also, not all verbs of motion form the *passé composé* with *être: J'ai marché une heure ; nous avons traversé la rue ; tu as quitté l'université ?*

• To tell what you did in the past, you have already learned that most French verbs form the **passé composé** with the present tense of **avoir**. However, some verbs use the present tense forms of **être** as an auxiliary. These are usually verbs of motion:

aller	*to go*	Tu **es allé** à la plage ce week-end ?
arriver	*to arrive*	Je **suis arrivé** en ville vers 10 heures du matin.
venir	*to come*	Il **est venu** à la campagne avec nous pour un pique-nique.
revenir	*to return*	Elle **est revenue** à l'Office de Tourisme hier matin.
devenir	*to become*	Elle **est devenue** médecin.
entrer	*to go/come in*	Anne **est entrée** dans le magasin.
rentrer	*to go/come back*	Nous **sommes rentrés** tard après une journée de ski.
retourner	*to go back*	Il **est retourné** en France.
partir	*to leave*	Ses amies **sont parties** ensemble à la montagne.
sortir	*to go out*	Rémy **est sorti** en ville avec Juliette pour faire du tourisme.
passer	*to go/come by*	On **est passé** chez toi hier.
rester	*to stay*	Ils **sont restés** à la plage tout l'après-midi.
tomber	*to fall*	Elle **est tombée** dans la rue (*street*).
monter	*to go up*	Lucie **est montée** dans sa chambre.
descendre	*to go down*	Nous **sommes descendues** en ville pour dîner.
naître	*to be born*	Elle **est née** en 1988.
mourir	*to die*	Il **est mort** l'été dernier.

• For verbs that form the **passé composé** with **être**, the past participle agrees in gender and number with the subject.

Mon frère est arrivé hier.	*My brother arrived yesterday.*
Ma sœur est arrivé**e** ce matin.	*My sister arrived this morning.*
Ses cousins sont allé**s** au musée.	*Her cousins went to the museum.*
Ses cousines sont descendu**es** en ville aussi.	*Her cousins went downtown too.*

• Pronominal verbs also use **être** in the **passé composé**. Note, however, that when a noun follows the verb, no past participle agreement is made.

Il s'est endormi.	*He fell asleep.*
Ils se sont couché**s**.	*They went to bed.*
Elle s'est lavé**e**.	*She washed up.*
Elle s'est lavé les cheveux.	*She washed her hair.*

À vous la parole

5-23 L'après-midi de M. Dumont.
Racontez l'après-midi de M. Dumont au passé.

Cet après-midi M. Dumont va sortir faire une promenade. Sa femme va rester à la maison pour préparer le dîner. Alors, M. Dumont va sortir avec son chien, Castor. Ils vont partir vers (*around*) trois heures, et ils vont passer chez un ami de M. Dumont. Ensuite (*then*) ils vont aller au parc, et ils vont entrer au zoo. Finalement, ils vont descendre par l'avenue principale et ils vont rentrer à la maison vers cinq heures.

MODÈLE Hier après-midi, M. Dumont est sorti faire une promenade.

Begin practice with a discrimination drill: tell a story in the past and have students raise their hands when they hear a verb conjugated with *être*: *Nous avons décidé de préparer une fête. J'ai téléphoné à Alain. Il est venu chez moi*, etc. Review the forms of *être* with simple substitution drills: *Je suis parti ; nous ; eux*, etc. ; *Je me suis réveillé ; toi ; vous*, etc. Follow with a transformation drill, present to past: *Je voyage. —J'ai voyagé ; Je pars. —Je suis parti/e.*

5-24 Jeu de détective.
D'après les indications, déduisez ce que tout le monde a dû faire hier. Répondez en utilisant une expression qui convient parmi cette liste.

aller à la plage, à la montagne, à la campagne
se coucher très tard
sortir en ville
rester chez elle
(ne pas) partir en vacances

MODÈLE J'ai dormi jusqu'à dix heures.
➤ Tu t'es couché très tard hier soir.

1. Anne a un examen aujourd'hui.
2. Cédric parle du surf des neiges.
3. Mes filles sont très fatiguées.
4. Nous avons mangé en plein air.
5. Mes parents n'ont pas répondu au téléphone.
6. J'ai visité un musée extraordinaire.
7. Ma mère a beaucoup de travail.

5-25 Le samedi de Guillaume.
Racontez comment Guillaume a passé la journée samedi. Utilisez les expressions ci-dessous pour faire un récit.

5-25 To prepare for the narrative, introduce the useful adverbs *d'abord, ensuite, après, puis, enfin,* and have students first narrate in the present tense. You might have students work in pairs. You may also ask them to go beyond the pictures and imagine other logical activities. As a follow-up, have several pairs read their narratives and have the class vote on the best one.

POUR FAIRE UN RÉCIT

d'abord	ensuite	après	puis	enfin
first	*next*	*after*	*then*	*finally*

MODÈLE D'abord, Guillaume a quitté sa chambre à huit heures. Ensuite, il…

OU ➤ D'abord, Guillaume est sorti à huit heures. Après, il…

5-26 Vary by having students tell about last weekend, last summer, etc.

5-26 Et vous ? Qu'est-ce que vous avez fait hier ? Où est-ce que vous êtes allé/e ? Avec qui ? Qu'est-ce que vous avez fait ? Racontez à un/e partenaire.

MODÈLE ➤ Hier, dimanche, je ne suis pas allé/e à la fac. J'ai quitté mon appartement vers neuf heures, et ensuite…

You might use this as an opportunity to review question formation and prepare for the interrogative forms to be presented in L. 3. Use a communicative activity from Ch. 2, L. 1 to review, Ex. 2-12, for example. To present *quel,* use the sentence examples and ask students to explain the differences in spelling; point out *enchaînement* and *liaison* before nouns beginning with a vowel, in the singular and plural, respectively. Written practice is provided in the Workbook.

2. *Les questions avec* quel

● The interrogative word **quel** is used to ask *which?* or *what?* Although **quel** agrees in number and gender with the noun it modifies, it is always pronounced the same, unless a plural form, **quels** or **quelles**, modifies a noun beginning with a vowel.

Quel écrivain est-ce que tu préfères ?	*Which writer do you prefer?*
Quelle musique est-ce qu'il préfère ?	*What type of music does he prefer?*
Quels cours est-ce que tu suis ?	*Which courses are you taking?*
Quelles affiches est-ce que tu vas acheter ?	*Which posters will you buy?*

- **Quel** is used in a number of fixed interrogative expressions:

  Quel temps fait-il ?   *What's the weather like?*
  Quelle heure est-il ?   *What time is it?*
  Quelle est la date aujourd'hui ?   *What's today's date?*
  Quel âge est-ce que tu as ?   *How old are you?*

Since many of these examples involve inversion, students will first learn them as fixed phrases; do not teach inversion here.

- **Quel** can also be used before a form of the verb **être**, followed by the noun it modifies:

  Quel est ton cours préféré ?   *What's your favorite course?*
  Quelles sont les meilleures   *Which are the best residence halls?*
    résidences ?

À vous la parole

👥 **5-27 Petite épreuve.** Posez des questions à un/e partenaire, qui doit répondre correctement !

Begin practice with a quick drill: *Tu vois le lac ? —Quel lac ? ; Tu vois le monsieur ? les enfants ? le cheval ? les vélos ? la montagne ? les skis ? les billets ?*

MODÈLE   les jours de la semaine

       É1 Quels sont les jours de la semaine ?
       É2 Lundi, mardi,…

1. les jours de la semaine
2. les mois de l'année
3. les saisons de l'année
4. la date de la fête nationale française
5. la date de ton anniversaire
6. ta saison préférée

5-28 Précisez, s'il vous plaît ! Demandez à votre partenaire de préciser, en utilisant une question avec **quel**.

5-28 If you wish for students to have written practice, you might ask them to write out their questions. Additional written practice is provided in the Workbook.

MODÈLE   la saison

       É1 Quelle saison est-ce que tu préfères ?
       É2 Je préfère l'automne.

1. la saison
2. la ville
3. l'artiste
4. les acteurs
5. le sport
6. la musique
7. les écrivains

Écrivons

5-29 Have students write on an actual postcard or on one of their own design. This will impose a limit on the amount written. Postcards can be exchanged among class members or with another class. This activity can also be completed as a group writing project.

5-29 Une carte postale

A. Avant d'écrire. Quand vous êtes en vacances, est-ce que vous écrivez des cartes postales ? À qui est-ce que vous écrivez ? Qu'est-ce que vous décrivez ? Faites une liste de trois ou quatre choses que vous écrivez normalement sur une carte postale.

B. En écrivant. Choisissez quelqu'un dans votre classe à qui vous allez envoyer votre carte postale et puis regardez le modèle. Dans votre carte postale, dites :

1. où vous passez les vacances
2. le temps qu'il fait
3. les endroits (*places*) visités, vos activités
4. la date de votre retour

Fort-de-France, le 12 février

Chère Nicole,

Je passe des vacances magnifiques à la Martinique. Ici, il fait très beau, avec tous les jours un ciel bleu et des températures entre 20 et 25 degrés.

Aujourd'hui, on va à la plage et demain on va à la montagne pour faire une randonnée. J'espère aussi visiter Pointe du Bout et la ville de Saint-Pierre. Je rentre à Paris le 18, avec beaucoup de photos et de souvenirs !

Amitiés,

Suzanne

Mlle LEFRANC Nicole
38, rue d'Assas
75 006   PARIS

C. Après avoir écrit. Avant de donner votre carte postale à votre camarade de classe (ou au professeur), vérifiez que vous avez inclus tous les éléments requis. Ensuite, lisez-la encore une fois pour vous assurer qu'il n'y a pas de fautes d'orthographe ni de grammaire. Puis, « envoyez » votre carte postale. Si vous avez de la chance, vous allez recevoir une carte postale aussi. Lisez-la et écrivez une courte réponse.

Leçon 3 *Je vous invite*

POINTS DE DÉPART

Qu'est-ce qu'on propose ?

TEXT AUDIO

—On organise une petite fête
 samedi soir ; tu es libre ?
—Non, désolée, je ne peux pas.

Display the cultural activities (IRCD, Ch. 5) and describe them; ask for examples of ballets, plays, concerts, and exhibitions; use the mini-dialogues to introduce formulas for inviting, accepting, and refusing. Test students' comprehension of these items by asking them to point to the activity you describe, using the unlabelled illustrations (IRCD, Ch. 5). Find out which of these cultural activities your students prefer, using either/or questions, so that students repeat key vocabulary.

—Vous êtes libres samedi ? J'ai des
 places pour un ballet, « Coppélia »
 de Delibes.
—Ah oui, c'est très gentil à vous !

—On ne joue pas au tennis à cause de la
 pluie, alors, je peux t'accompagner à
 l'exposition.
—Super ; on se retrouve devant le musée ?

—Alors, rendez-vous au Palais des
 Congrès pour voir le concert de rock ?
—Oui, à 19 h 30.

—Tu veux nous accompagner au théâtre ?
 On va voir une pièce de Molière.
—Volontiers ! J'adore le théâtre.

—Il pleut, donc qu'est-ce qu'on fait cet après-midi ?
—Il y a un bon film à la Cinémathèque.
—Super ! On y va ensemble ?

—On va passer une soirée tranquille chez nous.
—Je regrette, je ne peux pas venir. Je dois
 travailler.

POUR INVITER QUELQU'UN

Tu es/vous êtes libre/s ?

On y va ensemble ?

Tu veux m'accompagner ?/Vous voulez nous accompagner ?

POUR ACCEPTER UNE INVITATION

Oui, je suis libre.

(J'accepte) Avec plaisir.

C'est gentil à toi/vous.

Je suis ravi/e.

Volontiers.

POUR REFUSER UNE INVITATION

Je suis désolé/e...   je ne suis pas libre.

Je regrette...   je suis pris/e.

C'est dommage,...   j'ai déjà un rendez-vous.

Vie et culture

Les pratiques culturelles

The chart shown here, based on a survey by the French Ministry of Culture, indicates the percentages of French people participating in various leisure activities over a period of twelve months. According to these statistics, what are the most popular activities? If you were to construct a similar chart for your friends and family, how might it resemble or differ from what you see here? It is common for the French to go with friends and family to concerts, movies, and museums, and often such activities are included in a family's vacation plans.

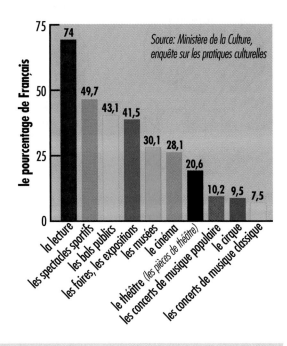

Source: Ministère de la Culture, enquête sur les pratiques culturelles

le pourcentage de Français

- la lecture — 74
- les spectacles sportifs — 49,7
- les bals publics — 43,1
- les foires, les expositions — 41,5
- les musées — 30,1
- le cinéma — 28,1
- le théâtre (les pièces de théâtre) — 20,6
- les concerts de musique populaire — 10,2
- le cirque — 9,5
- les concerts de musique classique — 7,5

Students may be surprised to learn that a Ministry of Culture exists in France. To test comprehension of the graph, ask the class to rank these activities in popularity on a scale from 1 to 10, paraphrasing where appropriate, e.g., *lire des livres ; aller voir un match de football ; aller danser*, etc.

À vous la parole

5-30 Treat the schedule on the following page first as a short reading; have students identify the main categories of activities taking place, then describe some of the specific events. Note that guided tours are in English and French, etc. Once students are familiar with the schedule, go on to complete the exercise.

5-30 Qu'est-ce qu'on peut faire ? Le Centre Pompidou est un musée à Paris qui a aussi des salles de cinéma, de conférences et de spectacles. Avec un/e partenaire, regardez le programme à la page suivante et décrivez les activités possibles.

MODÈLE   É1   Le onze mars, il y a un spectacle de danse.

              É2   Et regarde, du 5 au 14 mars, il y a un festival de films.

👥 **5-31 Oui ou non ?** Avec un/e camarade de classe, imaginez les situations suivantes. Qu'est-ce que vous allez dire ?

MODÈLE   On vous invite à aller au musée demain. Vous ne voulez pas y aller.

        É1   Tu veux aller au musée avec moi ? Il y a une bonne exposition.

        É2   Je regrette (OU Désolé), je ne suis pas libre.

1. On vous invite à un concert. Vous êtes ravi/e d'y aller.
2. On vous invite à aller au théâtre. Vous demandez quelle pièce on joue.
3. On vous invite à faire une randonnée, mais vous n'aimez pas les promenades.
4. On cherche quelqu'un pour jouer au bridge. Vous aimez ce jeu.
5. On a des places pour un concert de rock. Vous aimez ce type de musique, mais vous avez un rendez-vous ce jour-là.
6. On a deux places pour un ballet. Vous demandez, « C'est pour quel soir ? », et puis vous acceptez.

👥👥 **5-32 Les distractions du week-end dernier.**
Découvrez comment vos camarades de classe ont passé le week-end dernier. Faites le tour de la classe pour obtenir les renseignements suivants et essayez d'obtenir quelques détails supplémentaires. Après, faites un compte-rendu.

MODÈLE   organiser une fête

        É1   Est-ce que tu as organisé une fête ?

        É2   Oui, j'ai organisé une fête avec ma colocataire.

        É1   Tu as invité beaucoup de personnes ?

        É2   Seulement cinq ou six amis.

plus tard :

        É1   Julie a organisé une petite fête avec sa colocataire. Elle a invité quelques amis…

1. aller à un concert ou au théâtre
2. faire une randonnée ou du camping
3. aller à un événement sportif
4. aller au musée ou aller voir une exposition
5. inviter quelqu'un
6. organiser ou aller à une fête

AGENDA
TOUTES LES MANIFESTATIONS
CENTRE POMPIDOU – Art, culture, musée, expositions, cinémas, conférences, débats, spectacles, concerts.

EXPOSITIONS
Sophie Calle, M'as-tu vue
Installations, photographies, récits.
19 novembre – 15 mars
11h00 – 21h00
Galerie 2 Niveau 6

VISITES COMMENTÉES
Les visites commentées des collections du Musée
Le samedi et le dimanche à 16 h.
En anglais le samedi à 15 h.
6 mars – 27 juin
16 h 00
Entrée du Musée

CINÉMAS
Cinéma du réel, 26e festival international
5 – 14 mars

CONFÉRENCES-DÉBATS
Création et technologies, Conférences du lundi soir
Décrire la relation entre une idée artistique et sa réalisation utilisant les nouvelles technologies…
29 septembre – 31 mars

SPECTACLES-CONCERTS
Neptune, **Musique Philippe Manoury**
Chorégraphie Marion Ballester
11 mars

ACTIVITÉS POUR ENFANTS
De l'Atelier au Musée le mercredi
Les enfants explorent pendant trois séances la démarche d'un artiste, ses thèmes, ses matériaux.
Cycles de trois mercredis à 14 h 30.
7 janvier – 17 mars
14 h 30 – 16 h 30
Espace éducatif

5-31 The brief exchanges prepare students for the more exetended and open-ended activities in Ex. 5-32 and 5-33.

5-32 Use as a mixing activity. Impose a time limit, and tell students to ask no more than two questions of any one person before moving on. When time is up, have students ask questions about the items they did not find: *Qui a organisé une fête ?*

5-33 Have students work individually to prepare their lists of people to invite and activities to suggest. Once students have their lists prepared, they should circulate and everyone should invite three people in the class. You can follow up by asking students who they invited and if anyone accepted.

5-33 Des invitations. Vous allez inviter des camarades de classe. Ils vont accepter ou refuser selon leurs préférences.

1. D'abord, faites une liste de trois activités que vous voulez proposer et une liste de trois personnes que vous voulez inviter. N'oubliez pas le professeur !
2. Ensuite, proposez vos activités à trois personnes différentes qui vont accepter ou refuser vos invitations selon leurs préférences. Bien sûr, vos camarades de classe vont vous inviter aussi et vous devez accepter ou refuser à votre tour.
3. Pour terminer : Qui est-ce que vous avez invité ? Pour quelle activité ? Est-ce qu'on a accepté ou refusé ?

FORMES ET FONCTIONS

1. *Les verbes comme* acheter *et* appeler

Review regular -er verbs and verbs like *préférer* before treating this section: use quick substitution drills and have students summarize the number of spoken forms. Remind them of the alternation /e/ vs. /ɛ/ presented in Ch. 2, L. 2, and link this to the nature of the syllable: open syllables end in /e/, closed syllables in /ɛ/; this is the same alternation they will observe in the new verbs. Emphasize pattern similarities and the link to what students already know.

• You have learned that for verbs like **préférer** (*to prefer*), the second vowel in the singular forms and the third-person plural form of the present tense are spelled and pronounced like the **è** in **mère**:

Je préfère le cinéma.   Ils préfèrent le théâtre.

• Verbs like **acheter** (*to buy*) and **appeler** (*to call*) similarly show changes in the singular forms and in the third-person plural. The final vowel in these forms is also pronounced like the /ɛ/ in **mère**.

   ■ This pronunciation change is reflected in the spelling by the use of the **accent grave** in verbs like **acheter**.

acheter	*to buy*	Qu'est-ce que tu **achètes** ?
amener	*to bring a person*	Ils **amènent** leurs enfants au théâtre.
lever	*to raise*	Elle ne **lève** jamais le doigt (*finger*).

   ■ Verbs like **appeler** reflect the pronunciation change by doubling the final consonant of the base in the singular and the third-person plural forms:

appeler	*to call*	J'**appelle** le théâtre pour avoir des places ?
épeler	*to spell*	Il **épelle** son nom.
jeter	*to throw* (*out*)	Elle ne **jette** pas les billets des spectacles qu'elle a vus.

• The **nous** and **vous** forms for these verbs are two syllables long:

nous achetons   vous appelez

ACHETER *to buy*		
SINGULIER	PLURIEL	
j' ach**è**te	nous achetons	
tu ach**è**tes	vous achetez	
il elle ach**è**te on	ils elles ach**è**tent	

IMPÉRATIF : **Achète** ce foulard !
Achetez cette belle robe !
Achetons des jeans !

APPELER *to call*		
SINGULIER	PLURIEL	
j' app**elle**	nous appelons	
tu app**elles**	vous appelez	
il elle app**elle** on	ils elles app**ell**ent	

IMPÉRATIF : **Appelle** le dentiste !
Appelez le médecin !
Appelons le mécanicien !

À vous la parole

5-34 Des achats. Quels vêtements est-ce qu'on achète ?

MODÈLE Je dois aller à un mariage.
➤ J'achète un costume bleu marine.

1. Nous allons à Tahiti pour les vacances.
2. Mes amis vont à un concert de rock.
3. David va voir un ballet.
4. Maryse passe ses vacances à la plage.
5. Vous aimez faire du cheval.
6. Christiane est très élégante quand elle va au théâtre.
7. Nous aimons les vêtements très décontractés (*relaxed*) pour les vacances.
8. Je n'ai pas beaucoup d'argent.

5-35 Mais pourquoi ? Imaginez que vous avez un/e colocataire impossible. Demandez-lui pourquoi il/elle fait les choses suivantes.

MODÈLE jeter mon affiche préférée

É1 Pourquoi est-ce que tu jettes mon affiche préférée ?

É2 Je n'aime pas ton affiche. Elle est moche.

1. acheter tous ces magazines
2. ne pas appeler tes parents
3. porter mon beau pull rouge
4. ne pas épeler correctement mon nom
5. acheter toujours des chips et du chocolat
6. jeter mon CD préféré
7. appeler tous tes amis

Begin practice with a discrimination drill; have students write out the verb form they hear in sentences: Il appelle son chien ; Nous jetons les billets ; Elles amènent les enfants ; Vous appelez le théâtre ? ; Tu achètes un programme ? Since pronunciation differences are reflected in the spelling, written practice is appropriate. Follow with simple substitution drills to practice correct pronunciation: J'appelle le chien ; nous ? —Nous appelons le chien, etc.

5-35 Vary the form used by having students imagine they are speaking to more than one co-renter.

5-36 As a follow up, have students tell something they learned about their partner.

5-36 Une interview. Interviewez un/e partenaire pour apprendre s'il/si elle...

MODÈLE ne jette jamais ses vieux tickets de concerts

      É1 Tu ne jettes jamais tes vieux tickets de concerts ?

      É2 Si, je jette mes vieux tickets de concerts.

1. appelle ses parents tous les week-ends
2. n'appelle jamais ses parents
3. achète beaucoup de CD
4. n'achète jamais de magazines
5. se lève toujours avant huit heures
6. ne jette jamais ses vieux tickets de concerts
7. jette toujours ses devoirs et examens corrigés
8. amène toujours des amis quand il/elle est invité/e à une fête

2. Les questions avec les pronoms interrogatifs : qui, que, quoi

Review question formation from Ch. 2, L. 1 and Ch. 5, L. 2. Ask questions using the new expressions and have students answer logically. Then present the new information using examples.

- To ask *what*, use **qu'est-ce qui** and **qu'est-ce que**:
  - **Qu'est-ce qui** is used as the subject of a question and is followed by a verb:

Qu'est-ce qui se passe ?	*What's happening?*
Qu'est-ce qui est sur la photo ?	*What's in the photo?*

  - **Qu'est-ce que** is used as the direct object and is followed by the subject of the sentence:

Qu'est-ce que vous faites ?	*What are you doing?*
Qu'est-ce que tu as mis dans la valise ?	*What did you put in the suitcase?*

- To ask *who* or *whom*, use **qui**:
  - When **qui** is the subject, it is followed directly by the verb:

Qui va au cinéma ?	*Who's going to the movies?*
Qui n'aime pas les fêtes ?	*Who doesn't like parties?*

  - When **qui** is the direct object, use **est-ce que** before the subject of the sentence:

Qui est-ce que tu aimes ?	*Who do you like?*
Qui est-ce qu'ils regardent ?	*Who are they looking at?*

  - When a verb requires a preposition, that preposition precedes **qui**:

À qui est-ce que tu parles ?	*Who are you talking to?*
Avec qui est-ce que tu vas au musée ?	*Who are you going to the museum with?*

- After prepositions, use **quoi** to ask *what*:

Avec quoi est-ce qu'on écrit ?	*What are we writing with?*
De quoi est-ce qu'il va parler ?	*What is he going to speak about?*

À vous la parole

5-37 Projets de vacances. La famille Dupont va partir en vacances. Mme Dupont est très anxieuse et n'arrête pas de poser des questions pour avoir tous les détails. Avec un/e partenaire, suivez le modèle et jouez les rôles de Mme Dupont et de son mari.

MODÈLES
É1 Dis, chéri, *Georges* va acheter les billets ?
É2 Mais non.
É1 Alors, *qui* va acheter les billets ?

É2 Dis, chéri, nous allons laisser (*leave*) le chat *chez les Michaud* ?
É1 Mais non, ma chérie.
É2 Alors, *chez qui est-ce que* nous allons laisser le chat ?

1. Nous allons demander *à Suzanne* de garder (*keep*) le chien ?
2. *Georges* va porter nos sacs ?
3. Stéphane va amener *sa fiancée* ?
4. Nous allons acheter *des cartes postales* comme souvenirs ?
5. Nous allons faire *du vélo* ?
6. *Ta secrétaire* va téléphoner à l'hôtel ?
7. Nous allons payer *avec la carte de crédit* ?

5-38 Jéopardy ! Avec deux partenaires, jouez au Jéopardy. La première personne va donner une réponse au hasard. Les deux autres vont consulter la liste des verbes pour pouvoir poser une question logique. La première à poser sa question peut donner la réponse suivante.

admirer   écouter   manger   parler   regarder   réviser   téléphoner

MODÈLES
É1 de la musique classique
É2 Qu'est-ce que vous écoutez ?
É1 C'est bon. Alors, c'est à toi.
É2 à mes parents
É3 À qui est-ce que tu téléphones ?
É2 Oui, à toi alors !

la télévision   la sociologie
Mère Teresa   le manuel de français
de la pizza   de politique
à mon copain   Madonna

Begin practice by showing examples of *qui, qui est-ce que,* and *qu'est-ce qui* in minimal pairs: *Qu'est-ce qui est sur la photo ? / Qui est sur la photo ? ; Qu'est-ce que vous attendez ? / Qui est-ce que vous attendez ?* You can stress the difference between questions using *qui* or *quoi* with the following questions and answers: *Avec **qui** est-ce que tu joues au tennis ? — Avec ma sœur. Avec **quoi** est-ce que tu joues au tennis ? — Avec ma nouvelle raquette.* Use the following drill to help students learn to recognize and understand the forms rather than to produce questions. Ask students to tell you if each of the following questions is asking about a person (*une personne*) or a thing (*une chose*). *Qu'est-ce que tu fais ? — On parle d'une chose. Qu'est-ce que tu as préparé ? Qui est-ce que tu as invité ? Avec quoi est-ce que vous allez faire ça ? Chez qui est-ce que nous allons ? Qu'est-ce qu'elle a entendu ? Qu'est-ce qu'ils ont fait ? De quoi est-ce que vous allez parler ? Qu'est-ce qui est dans ton sac ? Qu'est-ce qu'ils vont regarder ?*

5-38 Put students on teams to play this popular game.

5-39 On va tout savoir. Interviewez un/e partenaire pour connaître tous les détails de sa vie universitaire.

MODÈLES habiter

➤ Où est-ce que tu habites ? Avec qui est-ce que tu habites ?

faire comme études

➤ Qu'est-ce que tu fais comme études ?

1. habiter
2. faire comme études
3. manger
4. préférer
5. faire le week-end

En écoutant. Remind students that it is normal to listen to answering machine messages more than once, even in one's native language, to get all the details. Encourage them to complete the chart progressively by listening to the messages several times.

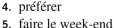

5-40 Des invitations

Aurélie a beaucoup d'amis et elle sort beaucoup. Écoutez les messages sur son répondeur.

A. Avant d'écouter. Quand vous écoutez vos messages sur le répondeur, quel type d'informations est-ce que vous pensez entendre ?

B. En écoutant. Complétez le tableau avec les détails importants de chaque message.

1. La première fois que vous écoutez ces messages, décidez pourquoi chaque personne a appelé : **pour inviter Aurélie**, **pour accepter une invitation**, **pour refuser une invitation**.
2. Écoutez encore et notez les détails pour **Activité**, **Quand** et **Où**.
3. Écoutez une dernière fois et notez d'autres détails importants pour chaque message.

Qui	Sylvain	Cécile	Florian	Maman
Pourquoi	*pour inviter*		*pour confirmer*	
Activité				
Quand				
Où	*chez Patrick et Delphine*			
D'autres détails importants				

C. Après avoir écouté. Imaginez que vous êtes Aurélie. À qui est-ce que vous allez téléphoner d'abord ? Pourquoi ? Et ensuite ? Comparez vos réponses avec les réponses de vos camarades de classe.

Venez chez nous!
Vive les vacances !

La Réunion, un département d'outre-mer. Regardez la carte du monde francophone au début de votre livre et trouvez les quatre départements et les six collectivités d'outre-mer.

Additional activities to explore the **Venez chez nous !** topics are provided by:
- Student Activities Manual
- *Chez nous* video
- *Chez nous* Companion Website: **http://www.prenhall.com/cheznous**

LES DÉPARTEMENTS ET LES COLLECTIVITÉS D'OUTRE-MER

« Où va le Père Noël après le 25 décembre ? » La bonne réponse n'est probablement pas « sur la Côte d'Azur » car[1] en hiver dans le Midi[2] de la France il ne fait pas assez chaud pour se bronzer à la plage ou nager dans la mer. Une meilleure réponse, c'est « aux Antilles, aux Seychelles, à l'île Maurice ou à Tahiti ». Ce sont des bonnes destinations touristiques si vous voulez trouver le soleil en hiver et des plages, et si vous voulez entendre parler français !

Certains de ces territoires sont des **départements d'outre-mer** (**D.O.M.**) et d'autres sont des **collectivités d'outre-mer**. Ce sont des anciennes[3] colonies françaises qui continuent à être associées administrativement et politiquement à la France. Depuis 1946, les D.O.M. ont la même organisation administrative que les départements de la France métropolitaine, et leurs habitants sont des citoyens français. Dans la plupart[4] des D.O.M., on parle créole et français. Depuis 2003, les autres territoires d'outre-mer ont une plus grande autonomie administrative, et on les nomme les collectivités d'outre-mer.

[1]parce que [2]*South of France* [3]*former* [4]la majorité

Ask students to locate the D.O.M. and *les collectivités d'outre-mer* on a map (IRCD, Maps) and speculate about what the climate would be like—*Quel temps fait-il à la Martinique ? Il fait chaud ?*—and what activities would be likely. Finally, ask students to find out what languages are spoken in these regions. Then complete the questions in *Et vous ?* in small groups or as a whole class activity. D.O.M. = la Guadeloupe, la Martinique, la Réunion, la Guyane française; C.O.M. = la Mayotte, St. Pierre-et-Miquelon, Wallis-et-Futuna, la Polynésie française (including Tahiti) and la Nouvelle-Calédonie and les Terres australes et antarctiques françaises (TAFF). The status of these last two territories is bit more complicated. Until the constitutional revision in March 2003 and corresponding legislation passed in July 2003, the *collectivités d'outre-mer* were referred to as *les T.O.M. (territoires d'outre mer)*. For more information, visit the *Chez nous* Companion Website for links to the *Ministère de l'Outre-mer*.

Et vous ?

Compare D.O.M. and *collectivités d'outre-mer* with the status of Puerto Rico and the American Virgin Islands. Note the influences of colonial practices and the slave trade in the history of France.

1. Est-ce que les États-Unis possèdent des territoires comme les D.O.M. et les collectivités d'outre-mer ?
2. Comme vous l'avez remarqué sur la carte, la France a des territoires partout (*everywhere*) dans le monde. Est-ce que c'est un avantage pour la France ? Expliquez.
3. Est-ce que c'est un avantage pour les départements et les collectivités d'outre-mer ? Expliquez.
4. Pour quelles raisons historiques est-ce que la France a développé des liens (*ties*) avec ces territoires ?

Lisons

Stratégie

Use the title and subtitles of a text as clues to understanding its focus and organization. You can learn what kind of information is likely to be included and what the major subdivisions are. With this approach, you will know a great deal about the content even before you read the passage as a whole.

5-41 Martinique : Guide pratique

La baie de St-Pierre et le volcan, Mont Pélée, à la Martinique

Avant de lire, Key: 1) the intended audience is those who are planning to travel there; brainstorm a list with students; this might include: information about visas, climate, what to visit and so forth   2) general information and practical concerns   3) students' answers will vary, but should include the main topics listed in the subheadings

A. Avant de lire. The following passage is excerpted from a travel guide written by **l'Office Départemental du Tourisme de la Martinique**. Before reading, look at the title and the various subtitles to get a sense of the focus and organization of this passage.

1. The title of the booklet is **Martinique : Guide pratique**. Who do you think is the intended audience for a **Guide pratique** ? What kind of information would you expect to be included in a "practical guide?"
2. Now look at the two major subtitles that appear in red type. They set up the two major divisions of this text. What is the focus of each?
3. Finally, look at the seven black subheadings. These indicate the topic of each paragraph. Considering these subheadings together with what you have determined about the focus and organization of the text, summarize what you know already about its content.

B. En lisant. As you read each section, look for the following information.

1. What is the capital of Martinique?
2. How far is Martinique from France?
3. What is the climate like?
4. Name three natural resources of Martinique.
5. Which languages are spoken and understood in Martinique?
6. As a North American, do you need a visa to enter Martinique? What is required?
7. What type of clothes would you need to bring to visit Martinique?

En lisant, Key: 1) Fort-de-France 2) 7,000 kilometers 3) warm comfortable climate, not too hot, around 26°C (or about 79° F) 4) rum, sugar, bananas 5) French, Creole, English in tourist regions 6) No visa is required for a stay of under three months; proof of identity is required 7) casual summer clothes, sweaters for evening, sunglasses

---

Martinique : Guide pratique

Informations générales

Histoire et administration
Christophe Colomb débarqua à la Martinique en 1502 et depuis 1635, excepté de courtes périodes d'occupation anglaise, elle partage[1] les destinées de la France. Département français depuis 1946, sa structure administrative et politique est identique à celle des départements de la métropole. Siège[2] de la préfecture, Fort-de-France est la capitale administrative, commerciale et culturelle de la Martinique.

Géographie
La Martinique fait partie du groupe des petites Antilles ou « Îles au vent ». Elle est baignée à l'Ouest par la Mer des Antilles et à l'Est par l'Océan Atlantique. Elle se trouve à environ 7.000 km de la France et 440 km du continent américain.

Climat
Le climat est relativement doux à la Martinique et la chaleur n'y est jamais insupportable. La température moyenne se situe aux environs de 26°C, mais sur les hauteurs, il fait plus frais. De l'Est et du Nord-est, des brises régulières, les alizés, rafraîchissent l'atmosphère.

Ressources économiques
Principales ressources naturelles de l'île : le rhum, le sucre, l'ananas, la banane. La Martinique produit également des conserves de fruits, des confitures et des jus de fruits locaux. Le tourisme connaît un essor[3] remarquable et tend à devenir le secteur économique de pointe.

Langue
Le français est parlé et compris par toute la population mais on entend beaucoup le créole. Bien entendu, l'anglais est également parlé surtout dans les lieux touristiques.

Informations pratiques

Formalités d'entrée
Les Français peuvent entrer en Martinique avec leur carte nationale d'identité ou leur passeport. Les ressortissants des États-Unis et du Canada sont admis sans visa pour un séjour inférieur à trois mois. Une pièce d'identité est toutefois requise.

Conseils vestimentaires
Au pays de l'éternel été, vous porterez des vêtements légers et décontractés pour vos excursions : maillot de bain, short et sandales pour la plage. Les femmes s'habillent généralement le soir davantage[4] que les messieurs pour lesquels veste et cravates ne sont exigés que[5] rarement. Toutefois n'oubliez pas un lainage et vos lunettes de soleil.

[1]*shares* [2]*Seat* [3]*development* [4]*more* [5]*are only required*

C. En regardant de plus près.
Now that you understand the focus and general content of this text, examine the following elements closely.

1. In the section on climate, look at the phrase **mais sur les hauteurs**, **il fait plus frais**. Given the context and the fact that the word **hauteurs** is related to the adjective **haut/e** (*high*), can you provide a synonym in French for **les hauteurs**?

2. Look at the noun **les ressortissants** in the section **Formalités d'entrée**. Can you see an **-ir** verb in the noun? Which one? Given the meaning of that verb and the context, what does the word **ressortissants** mean?

3. The word **vestimentaires** in the section **Conseils vestimentaires** is related to another French word you know. Given the context, what do you think this adjective means?

4. In the same section, you see the noun **un lainage**. If you know that the word **laine** means *wool* and given the context, what do you think **un lainage** is?

D. Après avoir lu.
Discuss the following questions with your classmates.

1. How well did your initial summary of the content of this guide correspond with the specific information that actually was provided?

2. What information, if any, do you think is missing for potential visitors to Martinique?

3. Based on the information provided above, would you be interested in visiting Martinique? Why or why not?

Observons

5-42 Des superbes vacances

A. Avant de regarder.
Dans cette séquence vidéo, Corinne et Édouard parlent de leurs superbes vacances. D'après les phrases et expressions suivantes, où est-ce qu'ils sont allés ? Qu'est-ce qu'ils ont fait ?

Corinne :

J'ai pu voir des crocodiles…

… ils ont un beau hamac.

… j'en ai profité pour faire des photos avec Mickey, Daisy, Donald…

Édouard :

… je suis parti en croisière en bateau à voile.

… on a découvert… toutes les îles italiennes

B. En regardant. Regardez et écoutez la séquence pour répondre aux questions suivantes.

1. Pour chaque personne, indiquez les endroits mentionnés :

Corinne :

_____ la Californie _____ les États-Unis _____ les Everglades _____ la Floride

_____ Miami _____ New York _____ Orlando _____ Paris

Édouard :

_____ Antibes _____ la Corse _____ a France _____ la Grèce

_____ l'île Maurice _____ Naples _____ Nice _____ Rome

2. Avec qui est-ce que Corinne et Édouard ont passé leurs vacances ?
3. Qu'est-ce qu'ils ont vu pendant leur voyage ?

C. Après avoir regardé. Discutez de ces questions avec vos camarades de classe.

1. Pourquoi, à votre avis, est-ce que Corinne et Édouard considèrent que ce sont des superbes vacances ?
2. Est-ce que vous avez visité les endroits mentionnés par Corinne ou Édouard ? Si oui, qu'est-ce que vous avez vu et qu'est-ce que vous avez fait ?
3. Pour vous personnellement, qu'est-ce que c'est des superbes vacances ?

5-43 Les vacances d'hiver

A. Avant de parler. Comme vous le savez, beaucoup de Français prennent des vacances d'une ou deux semaines au mois de février. Imaginez que vous avez des vacances vous aussi en février. Où est-ce que vous voudriez aller ? Pensez à vos vacances idéales et partagez vos idées avec un/e partenaire. Regardez les images pour avoir des idées.

On fait du ski à Chamonix dans les Alpes françaises.

Script for *Observons*

CORINNE : En septembre 2001, j'étais aux États-Unis en Floride chez ma famille. Et ils m'ont fait un petit peu visiter euh le la la région. Donc, ils m'ont amenée aux Everglades. J'ai pu voir des crocodiles et euh… cette photo me plaît beaucoup parce que… la première fois que je tenais un petit crocodile qui a failli me manger les doigts d'ailleurs.

Et sinon, les familles ont des belles villas avec des très beaux jardins ce que je n'ai pas la chance d'avoir ici. Et ils ont un beau hamac. J'étais très contente de pouvoir… poser dedans avec mes petites cousines et mes petits cousins.

Évidemment j'ai pas… je suis allée à Orlando je pouvais pas éviter. J'adore Disney donc vu que je connaissais celui en France je voulais absolument voir le Walt Disney américain et donc j'en ai profité pour faire des photos avec Mickey, Daisy, Donald et visiter tout le parc.

ÉDOUARD : Donc cet été j'ai eu un été très sympathique puisque je suis parti en croisière euh en bateau euh… à voile. Je suis parti de… Antibes euh jusqu'à Naples durant trois semaines avec trois autres amis euh et on a découvert euh la Corse, euh euh toutes les îles italiennes jusqu'à arriver à Naples euh où je suis resté trois jours et je suis revenu en train en France. Et c'est vraiment des vraiment des vacances très très bonnes.

Parlons. As an alternative, have each student (or small group of students) chose a vacation spot in the Francophone world and prepare a small exposé on it, presenting the climate, activities, clothes one should bring, and languages spoken there. This allows students to practice the presentational mode of the *National Standards*. As each student (or group) presents, the others can guess which spot is being described and/or vote on the destination that sounds the most interesting.

On visite le Musée d'Orsay à Paris.

Musée D'Orsay, Paris, interior, main floor. Gae Aluenti architect, 1986. John Brooks/
Liaison Agency, Inc./Getty Images

On fait du bateau à l'île Curieuse aux Seychelles.

B. En parlant. En groupes de quatre ou cinq personnes, parlez de vos vacances d'hiver idéales. Expliquez aux membres de votre groupe le climat que vous préférez, les vêtements que vous voulez porter et les activités que vous voulez faire. Les autres vont vous suggérer des endroits possibles pour ce voyage dans le monde francophone ?

C. Après avoir parlé. Comparez les vacances proposées dans votre groupe avec les autres groupes dans la classe. Est-ce que vous voulez tous aller au même endroit ou est-ce que vous avez des camarades de classes qui veulent aller partout dans le monde francophone ?

Écrivons

5-44 Mes meilleurs souvenirs de vacances

A. Avant d'écrire. Racontez des vacances mémorables que vous avez passées. Répondez à ces questions avant d'écrire.

1. Où est-ce que vous êtes allé/e ? Avec qui ?
2. Qu'est-ce que vous avez fait ?
3. Est-ce qu'il a fait beau ?
4. Pourquoi est-ce que vous avez aimé ce voyage ou ces vacances ?

B. En écrivant. Rédigez un ou deux paragraphes pour décrire vos vacances. N'oubliez pas d'utiliser le passé composé.

C. Après avoir écrit. Relisez d'abord votre description et vérifiez que vous avez employé les formes correctes du passé composé et que vous avez fait un bon choix entre les auxiliaires **être** et **avoir**. Puis, échangez votre travail avec vos camarades de classe. Qui a passé les vacances les plus intéressantes ?

Écrivons. As a follow-up, have students exchange their descriptions, read silently, then summarize the trip they read about in two or three sentences.

On fait un tour de Paris. Il fait beau aujourd'hui !

Vocabulaire

Leçon 1

le temps à toutes les saisons (f.) — *the weather in all seasons*

Quel temps fait-il ? — *What's the weather like?*
Il fait beau. — *It's beautiful weather.*
Il y a du soleil. — *It's sunny.*
Le ciel est bleu. — *The sky is blue.*
Il y a du brouillard. — *It's foggy.*
Il y a des nuages. (m.) — *It's cloudy.*
Le ciel est couvert. — *The sky is overcast.*
Le ciel est gris. — *The sky is gray.*
Il y a du vent. — *It's windy.*
Il fait mauvais. — *The weather's bad.*
Il fait lourd. — *It's humid.*
Il neige. (neiger) — *It's snowing. (to snow)*
Il y a du verglas. — *It's icy, slippery.*
Il y a un orage. — *There is a (thunder)storm.*
Il y a des éclairs. (m.) — *There is lightning.*
Il y a du tonnerre. — *There is thunder.*
Il pleut. (pleuvoir) (la pluie) — *It's raining. (to rain) (rain)*

pour parler de la température — *to talk about the temperature*

Il fait 10 degrés. (m.) — *It's 10 degrees.*
Il fait chaud. — *It's hot (weather).*
Il fait bon. — *It's warm (weather).*
Il fait frais. — *It's cool (weather).*
Il fait froid. — *It's cold (weather).*
Il gèle. (geler) — *It's freezing. (to freeze)*
J'ai chaud/froid. — *I'm hot/cold.*
la météo(rologie) — *weather, weather report*

les saisons (f.) — *the seasons*

au printemps (m.) — *in the spring*
en été (m.) — *in the summer*
en automne (m.) — *in the fall*
en hiver (m.) — *in the winter*

verbes en -re — *-re verbs*

attendre — *to wait for*
descendre — *to go down*

entendre — *to hear*
perdre — *to lose*
rendre à — *to give back*
rendre visite à — *to visit someone*
répondre à — *to answer*
vendre — *to sell*

pour parler du passé — *to talk about the past*

hier — *yesterday*
avant-hier — *the day before yesterday*
samedi dernier — *last Saturday*
l'année dernière — *last year*
il y a longtemps — *a long time ago*
il y a deux jours — *two days ago*
ce jour-là — *that day*
à ce moment-là — *at that moment*

Leçon 2

les vacances (f. pl.) — *vacation*

partir en vacances — *to go on vacation*
un billet (d'avion) — *(plane) ticket*
une carte postale — *postcard*
des destinations (f.) — *destinations*
  la campagne — *countryside*
  la mer — *sea*
  la montagne — *mountains*
  la plage — *beach*
  la ville — *city*
la pêche (aller à la pêche) — *fishing (to go fishing)*
des projets de vacances (m.) — *vacation plans*
le repos — *rest*
les sports d'hiver (m.) — *winter sports*

des activités (f.) — *activities*

faire…
  des achats (m.) — *to shop*
  de l'alpinisme (m.) — *to go mountain climbing*
  du camping — *to camp, to go camping*
  du cheval — *to go horseback riding*
  un pique-nique — *to picnic*

de la planche à voile	*to windsurf*
une randonnée	*to take a hike*
du ski	*to ski*
du ski nautique	*to water ski*
du surf	*to go surfing*
du surf des neiges	*to go snowboarding*
un tour dans	*to tour the*
le quartier/au parc	*neighborhood/park*
du tourisme	*to go touring,*
	to go sightseeing
de la voile	*to go sailing*
visiter des musées ou	*to visit museums*
des monuments	*or monuments*

quelques expressions utiles — *some useful expressions*

Bravo !	*Great! Well done!*
C'est pas vrai !	*It can't be!*
Chouette !	*Neat!*
Pas tout à fait !	*Not quite!*
quel/le	*which*
Vive… (les Seychelles) !	*Hurray for. . .*
	(the Seychelles)!

quelques verbes conjugués avec être au passé composé — *some verbs conjugated with être in the passé composé*

devenir	*to become*
entrer	*to go/come in*
monter	*to go up*
mourir	*to die*
naître	*to be born*
passer	*to go/come by, to spend (time)*
rentrer	*to go/come back*
retourner	*to go back*
revenir	*to return*
tomber	*to fall*
venir	*to come*

pour faire un récit — *to construct a narrative*

d'abord	*first*
ensuite	*next*
après	*after, after that*
puis	*then*
enfin	*finally*

Leçon 3

pour inviter quelqu'un — *to invite someone*

Tu es/Vous êtes libre(s) ?	*Are you free?*
On y va ensemble ?	*Shall we go (there) together?*
Tu veux/Vous voulez m'accompagner ?	*Would you like to come with me?*

pour accepter une invitation — *to accept an invitation*

Oui, je suis libre.	*Yes, I am free.*
(J'accepte) Avec plaisir.	*(I accept) With pleasure.*
C'est gentil à toi/vous.	*That's kind (of you).*
Je suis ravi/e.	*I am delighted.*
Volontiers.	*With pleasure, gladly.*

pour refuser une invitation — *to refuse an invitation*

Je suis désolé/e…	*I am sorry . . .*
C'est dommage…	*It's too bad . . .*
Je regrette…	*I'm sorry . . .*
Je ne suis pas libre.	*I'm not free.*
Je suis pris/e.	*I'm busy.*
J'ai déjà un rendez-vous.	*I already have a meeting/ date/appointment.*

des distractions (f.) — *amusements/diversions*

aller à un concert	*to go to a concert*
voir/jouer une pièce	*to watch/perform a play*
passer une soirée tranquille	*to spend a quiet evening*
une place	*seat, place*
se retrouver	*to meet*

quelques verbes utiles — *some useful verbs*

acheter	*to buy*
amener	*to bring (a person)*
appeler	*to call*
épeler	*to spell*
jeter	*to throw, to throw away*
lever	*to raise*

pour poser une question — *to ask a question*

qu'est-ce que/qui… ?	*what . . .?*
qui ?	*who?*
quoi ?	*what?*

une expression utile — *a useful expression*

à cause de	*because of*

Est-ce que cette maison est semblable aux maisons où vous habitez ? Pourquoi ?

Chapitre **6** *Nous sommes chez nous*

Leçon **1** *La vie en ville*

Leçon **2** *Je suis chez moi*

Leçon **3** *La vie à la campagne*

Venez chez nous !
**À la découverte de la France :
les provinces**

Leçon 1 · *La vie en ville*

POINTS DE DÉPART

Chez les Santini

TEXT AUDIO

Additional practice activities for each **Points de départ** section are provided by:
- Student Activities Manual
- *Chez nous* Companion Website: **http://www.prenhall.com/cheznous**

Les Santini habitent à Paris dans le dix-huitième arrondissement, près de Montmartre. M. et Mme Santini ont deux enfants, Nicolas et Véronique. Ils habitent un bel immeuble dans une rue tranquille d'un quartier résidentiel.

L'appartement des Santini est au sixième étage — on peut prendre les escaliers ou l'ascenseur. C'est un cinq-pièces, avec une grande salle de séjour, une salle à manger et trois chambres. Chaque enfant a sa propre chambre. Il y a aussi une salle de bains, des toilettes (des W.-C.) et une grande cuisine. L'appartement a un grand balcon qui donne sur la rue, et dans la chambre de M. et Mme Santini il y a même un petit balcon qui donne sur la cour. Au sous-sol, il y a un garage où les Santini garent leur voiture. Ils ont des voisins sympathiques au cinquième étage.

Use the photo and line drawings (IRCD, Ch. 6) to present the vocabulary. Read the narrative aloud as you show the visuals, elaborating where appropriate. Explain that Paris is divided into 20 *arrondissements* or neighborhoods. Explain the distinction between *salle de bains/toilettes, W.-C.* (from English *water closet*). In France, the kitchen and bath are not included when counting the number of rooms. Test comprehension by having students point to the feature you name, using the unlabeled art (IRCD, Ch. 6) or by having them describe activities: *Dans la cuisine ? —On prépare le dîner, on mange,* etc. Next have students repeat key words and phrases: *C'est la cuisine ou le séjour ? —C'est le séjour,* etc.

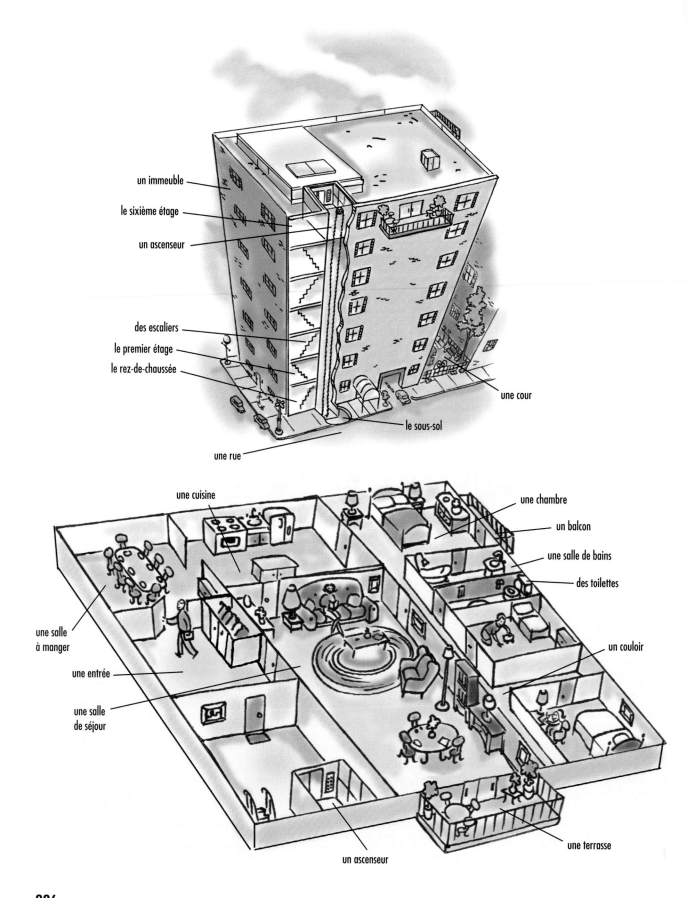

un immeuble

le sixième étage

un ascenseur

des escaliers

le premier étage

le rez-de-chaussée

une cour

le sous-sol

une rue

une cuisine

une chambre

un balcon

une salle de bains

des toilettes

une salle
à manger

un couloir

une entrée

une salle
de séjour

un ascenseur

une terrasse

À vous la parole

6-1 Où est-ce qu'ils sont ? Expliquez où sont ces gens.

MODÈLE   Nicolas fait ses devoirs.
>   ➤ Il est dans sa chambre.

1. Mme Santini prépare le dîner pour la famille.
2. Véronique met la table.
3. M. Santini regarde un film à la télé.
4. Nicolas se douche.
5. Les enfants jouent aux cartes.
6. M. Santini regarde les voitures qui passent.
7. Le voisin frappe (*knocks*) à la porte.
8. M. Santini prépare le café.
9. Véronique fait la sieste.
10. Mme Santini gare la voiture.

6-2 Où allez-vous ? Où est-ce que vous préférez faire les choses suivantes ? Comparez vos préférences avec celles de vos camarades de classe.

MODÈLE   faire la sieste

>   É1   J'aime aller dans ma chambre pour faire la sieste.
>   É2   Je préfère faire la sieste dans la salle de séjour, devant la télé.
>   É3   J'aime aller sur la terrasse.

1. faire la sieste
2. regarder un film
3. faire les devoirs
4. dîner
5. écouter de la musique
6. jouer à des jeux sur l'ordinateur
7. parler avec des amis

6-2 Have students report back to the class on their preferences and the preferences of their classmates. Ask follow-up questions such as *Pourquoi est-ce que vous préférez faire la sieste dans la salle de séjour ?*

6-3 C'est où exactement ? Avec un/e partenaire, dites où se trouvent ces choses dans le bâtiment où vous avez votre cours de français.

MODÈLE   des téléphones
>   ➤ Il y a des téléphones au rez-de-chaussée.
> OU   ➤ Il n'y a pas de téléphones dans notre bâtiment.

1. un snack-bar
2. un amphithéâtre
3. une bibliothèque
4. un centre informatique
5. un laboratoire
6. des bureaux
7. des salles de classe

6-3 Treat *à quel étage* in the *Vie et culture* before doing this activity which recycles campus vocabulary; vary it by suggesting other places in familiar campus buildings.

Vie et culture

Use the photo to describe home construction in France and compare it with construction in North America. Homes in France are generally constructed of stone, brick, or block, considered more durable than wood. Students should notice the presence of a wall and grill surrounding the house, and the tiled roof.

Où habitent les Français ?

Environ[1] 56 % des familles en France habitent une maison individuelle, mais dans les centres urbains les appartements sont plus nombreux. La majorité des Français (55 %) sont propriétaires de leur maison ou appartement ; 41 % sont locataires, c'est-à-dire qu'ils paient un loyer chaque mois. Quelquefois les charges (l'électricité et le gaz) sont comprises[2] dans le loyer et quelquefois c'est en supplément.

Dans les grandes villes, il y a beaucoup de quartiers résidentiels, et beaucoup de familles habitent un appartement dans un grand immeuble. En France, le nombre de pièces (sans compter la cuisine, la salle de bains ou les toilettes) détermine la classification des appartements et des maisons. Un studio est un appartement avec une seule pièce (plus éventuellement[3] cuisine, salle de bains et toilettes). Est-ce que la majorité des Américains habitent des maisons individuelles ou des appartements ? Comment est-ce qu'on détermine la classification des appartements et des maisons en Amérique du Nord ?

[1]*approximately* [2]*included* [3]peut-être

Voici une maison typique en France. Est-ce qu'elle est semblable aux maisons de chez vous, ou est-ce qu'elle est très différente ?

À quel étage ?

In English, we often call the ground floor of a building the *first floor* and the floor above it the *second floor*. In French, however, the ground floor of a building is called **le rez-de-chaussée**, and the floor above it **le premier étage**, followed by **le deuxième**, **le troisième**, etc. The basement is called **le sous-sol**.

RdeCh	rez-de-chaussée	11e	onzième
1er	premier	12e	douzième
2e	deuxième	…	
3e	troisième	20e	vingtième
…		21e	vingt et unième

As students read the cultural note, ask them to discover: the meaning of the various percentages, and the meaning of key words such as *loyer*, *charges*, *comprises*, using cognates and context. Concepts like *propriétaire* and *locataire* will be used in the exercises below, and students should add them to their productive vocabulary. Students may be unfamiliar with the notion of buying an apartment, but this can be compared to condominium or co-op housing. You may wish to introduce the phrase *habiter en banlieue* (to live in the suburbs) to allow students to describe their living situation. Note that the expression *la banlieue* in French has a rather negative connotation and often refers to poorer neighborhoods, filled with subsidized housing, and in *la banlieue parisienne*, with immigrants.

According to the 2000 U.S. Census, the majority of householders in each of the four census regions owned their homes: Midwest, 70.2%; South, 68.4%; Northeast, 62.4%; and West, 61.5%. In North America, apartments (and homes) are advertised based on the number of bedrooms. A two-bedroom apartment in the U.S. would be equivalent to *un appartement trois-pièces* in France.

Point out the special forms *premier/première, second/e* (the latter term used when there are only two items in a series). You may wish to provide your students with a full list of ordinals to complement the examples given here. Practice by having students write down the ordinal you say: *treizième, vingt et unième*, etc. (Students write: 13e, 21e, etc.) Next have students read the ordinals you write.

6-4 Une comparaison. Avec un/e partenaire, comparez l'endroit (*place*) où vous habitez avec l'appartement des Santini.

MODÈLE Les Santini habitent un appartement de cinq pièces.

> É1 Moi, j'habite un deux-pièces.
>
> É2 Moi, j'ai une chambre à la résidence.

1. Les Santini habitent une grande ville.
2. Ils habitent un quartier tranquille.
3. Ils habitent un bel immeuble.
4. Ils sont propriétaires.
5. Ils habitent au sixième étage.
6. Il y a un ascenseur et aussi des escaliers dans l'immeuble.
7. Les Santini habitent un appartement de cinq pièces.
8. Chez les Santini, il y a une grande cuisine.
9. Il y a trois chambres chez eux.
10. Ils ont deux balcons.

6-5 Quatre appartements. Voici quatre appartements. Avec un/e partenaire, décrivez chaque appartement et choisissez l'appartement que vous préférez.

6-5 As a follow-up, have students draw and describe their current home or apartment; their ideal apartment.

MODÈLE ➤ Le premier appartement est un deux-pièces. Il y a une petite chambre et un séjour. Il y a une terrasse, etc.… Je préfère…, parce que…

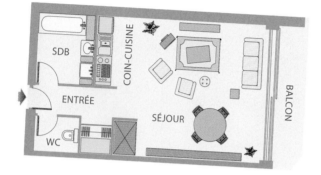

Additional practice activities for
each **Sons et lettres** section are
provided by:
• Student Activities Manual
• Text Audio

Sons et lettres

TEXT AUDIO

La consonne *l*

Say the English word *little*. Notice how your tongue moves from the front to the
back of your mouth. In English, we have two ways of producing the consonant **l**:
a front **l**, with the tongue against the upper front teeth and a final **l**, pronounced
with the tongue pulled back. To pronounce a French **l**, however, always keep
your tongue against your upper front teeth, just like the English front *l*. Compare
the differences in pronunciation of a final **-l** in English and French:

English	French
ill	il
bell	belle
bowl	bol

La prononciation de *-ill-*

The combination of letters **-ill-** has two pronunciations: with the /l/ sound of **il** or
the /j/ sound at the end of **travail**. It is difficult to predict how that combination
is to be pronounced in a given word; the pronunciation of individual words must
be memorized. Compare:

/l/		/j/	
mille	un million	la fille	la famille
la ville	le village	se maquiller	elle se maquille
tranquille		s'habiller	il s'habille

À vous la parole

6-6 Répétitions. Répétez les mots et les groupes de mots suivants après votre professeur.

le ciel	un cheval	la salle	la ville
il gèle	elle épelle	tranquille	Jules
une ville calme	dans quelle salle	le journal idéal	

Begin practice with a discrimination drill: *anglais ou français ?* Levez le doigt pour le français : bell, *belle*, tell, *telle*, ill, *il*, *cool*, cool, ball, *balle*, *Paul*, Paul, pull, *pull*.

6-7 Qui habite au premier ? Avec un/e partenaire, posez des questions et répondez.

MODÈLE au premier : Loïc et Michèle Martel

É1 Qui habite au premier étage ?

É2 Loïc et Michèle Martel.

1. au cinquième : Cyril et Nicole Blondel
2. au quatrième : Clément Lemont et Gaëlle LeBrun
3. au troisième : Sylvain et Charlotte Roussel et leurs enfants : Claire, Lucie, Daniel
4. au deuxième : Paul et Amélie Lalonde
5. au premier : Loïc et Michèle Martel

6-8 La lettre « L ». Voici un petit poème du livre *Comptines en forme d'alphabet* de Jo Hoestlandt. Répétez cette strophe après votre professeur.

6-8 The van Gogh painting suggests strong emotion and a swirling Milky Way. Translation of the poem:

> What Beauty of the night in anger
> Has thrown her pearl necklace up there,
> Her celestial necklace of stars
> In the Milky Way?

Quelle Belle de nuit en colère
A lancé son collier de perles là-haut,
Son céleste collier d'étoiles
Dans la Voie lactée ?

Vincent van Gogh (1853-1890), « La nuit étoilée » 1889.
Oil on canvas, 29 × 36 1/4" (73.7 × 92.1 cm). Acquired through the Lillie P. Bliss Bequest. (472.1941). The Museum of Modern Art, NY, U.S.A. Digital Image © The Museum of Modern Art/Licensed de Vincent Van Gogh

Review -er, -ir, and -re verbs as an introduction to this topic. Remind students that for all two-stem verbs, the spoken singular forms are derived by dropping the final consonant sound of the third-person plural form; see whether they can derive the forms for *choisir*, then for other verbs in the list.

Other verbs in -ir/-iss- correspond to English verbs in "-ish:" *finir, punir, établir, démolir.*

FORMES ET FONCTIONS

1. Les verbes en -ir comme choisir

• Like other **-ir** verbs, verbs like **choisir** have four spoken forms. The final /s/ of the plural form is dropped in the singular.

    ils **choisissent** /ʃwazis/ le deux-pièces   il **choisit** /ʃwazi/ le studio

To form the present indicative of verbs like **choisir**, add **-iss-** to the base for the plural forms: **chois ir → chois -iss-**.

CHOISIR *to choose*		
SINGULIER		**PLURIEL**
je choisi**s**		nous choisi**ssons**
tu choisi**s**		vous choisi**ssez**
il		ils
elle } choisi**t**		elles } choisi**ssent**
on		

IMPÉRATIF : Ne **choisis** pas ça ! **Choisissez** le studio ! **Choisissons** un appartement !

PASSÉ COMPOSÉ : J'ai déjà **choisi**.

• Some **-ir/-iss-** verbs are derived from common adjectives. They express the meaning that someone or something is becoming more like the adjective:

maigre	*thin, skinny*	**maigrir**	*to lose weight*
grosse	*large, fat*	**grossir**	*to gain weight*
grande	*large, tall*	**grandir**	*to grow taller, to grow up (for children)*
rouge	*red*	**rougir**	*to blush*
pâle	*pale*	**pâlir**	*to become pale*

• Some other common verbs conjugated like **choisir** are:

finir	*to finish*	Tu **as fini** la visite de l'appartement ?
obéir à	*to obey*	**Obéis** à ta mère ! Pas de chocolat dans le séjour !
désobéir à	*to disobey*	Ces enfants **désobéissent** toujours **à** leur père.
punir	*to punish*	Tu **punis** ton fils parce qu'il n'a pas bien garé la voiture ?
réfléchir à	*to think*	Je **réfléchis à** l'appartement que je préfère.
réussir à	*to succeed*	Elle ne **réussit** pas **à** appeler l'ascenseur.
	to pass	Il **a** bien **réussi à** son examen de maths. (OU, Il **a réussi** son examen de maths.)

À vous la parole

6-9 Des enfants modèles ? Est-ce que ces enfants obéissent ou désobéissent à leurs parents ?

MODÈLE   Delphine ne s'essuie pas quand elle sort de la douche.
> ➤ Elle désobéit à ses parents.

1. Fabien mange du chocolat dans sa chambre.
2. Laetitia et Fabien font leurs devoirs devant la télé.
3. Tu manges bien tous les matins avant d'aller à l'école.
4. Fabien et Delphine jouent au basket sur la terrasse.
5. Laetitia ne mange jamais dans sa chambre.
6. Vous ne sortez pas quand vous avez un examen à préparer.
7. Delphine et vous, vous mettez la télévision très fort.
8. J'aide mes parents à préparer le dîner.

Begin practice with a discrimination drill: one person, or more than one? *Elle grandit ; Ils maigrissent ; Ils finissent ; Elle obéit ; Elle choisit bien ; Ils rougissent ; Il réussit ; Elles réfléchissent* ; etc. Follow with one or two simple substitution drills: *Je maigris ; nous ; lui,* etc. You might also include a transformation drill, present to past or vice versa: *Nous choisissons un studio. — Nous avons choisi un studio,* etc.

6-10 Le choix est à vous ! Qu'est-ce que vous choisissez ? En groupes de trois ou quatre, comparez votre réponse avec la réponse de vos partenaires.

MODÈLE   entre un appartement au rez-de-chaussée et un appartement au cinquième étage

> É1 Moi, je choisis l'appartement au rez-de-chaussée ; c'est pratique pour sortir.
> É2 Pas moi ! Je choisis l'appartement au cinquième, j'aime avoir une belle vue.
> É3 Moi aussi, donc toi et moi, nous choisissons l'appartement au cinquième.

1. entre un appartement en centre-ville et un appartement dans un quartier tranquille
2. entre un studio et un deux-pièces
3. entre l'ascenseur et les escaliers
4. entre une grande cuisine et une grande salle de bains
5. entre une belle terrasse qui donne sur la rue et un petit balcon qui donne sur la cour
6. entre un appartement avec une grande chambre et un appartement avec deux petites chambres
7. entre un appartement avec un jardin et un appartement avec un garage

6-10 After completing, have students report back what they and their partners decided.

6-11 Trouvez une personne. Dans votre salle de classe, trouvez une personne qui…

MODÈLE finit toujours ses devoirs avant d'arriver en classe

> É1 Est-ce que tu finis toujours tes devoirs avant d'arriver en classe ?
>
> É2 Non, je ne finis pas toujours mes devoirs avant d'arriver en classe.
>
> OU Oui, je finis toujours mes devoirs avant d'arriver en classe.

1. rougit toujours quand il/elle parle devant un groupe
2. finit toujours ses devoirs avant d'arriver en classe
3. grossit toujours en hiver
4. grandit toujours (*still*)
5. réfléchit toujours avant de répondre
6. réussit toujours à ses examens
7. maigrit quand il/elle est stressé/e
8. grossit quand il/elle est stressé/e
9. ne désobéit jamais à ses parents

2. *Les pronoms compléments d'objet direct* le, la, l', les

● A direct object receives the action of a verb, answering the question *who* or *what*. For example, **un appartement** is the direct object in the following sentence: **Ils habitent un appartement**. A direct-object pronoun can replace a direct-object noun indicating a person or thing; it agrees in gender and number with the noun it replaces.

Elle gare **la voiture** ?	Oui, elle **la** gare.	*Yes, she is parking it.*
Elle regarde **le voisin** ?	Oui, elle **le** regarde.	*Yes, she is looking at him.*
Elle achète **l'appartement** ?	Oui, elle **l'**achète.	*Yes, she is buying it.*
Elle aime bien **les voisins** ?	Oui, elle **les** aime bien. /z/	*Yes, she likes them.*

● Here are the forms of the direct-object pronouns. In the plural, liaison /z/ is pronounced before a vowel.

	singulier	pluriel
masc	le	les
m/f + voyelle	l'	les /z/
fém	la	les

- To point out people or objects, the direct-object pronouns precede **voilà**.

Sylvie ? **La** voilà. *Sylvie? There she is.*

Mes CD ? **Les** voilà. *My CDs? There they are.*

- In most other cases, direct-object pronouns precede the conjugated verb:

—Vous aimez l'appartement en centre-ville ? —*Do you like the downtown apartment?*

—Nous ne **l'**aimons pas. C'est trop cher. —*We don't like it. It's too expensive.*

—Où sont les escaliers ? —*Where are the stairs?*

—Je ne sais pas, je ne **les** ai pas remarqués. —*I don't know, I didn't notice them.*

—Tu vas payer les charges ? —*Are you going to pay the utilities?*

—Mais bien sûr, je vais **les** payer. —*Well, of course I'm going to pay them.*

The negative **ne** never comes between an object pronoun and verb:

Les voisins, nous ne **les** appelons jamais. *. . . we never call them.*

L'appartement, je ne **l'**ai pas acheté. *. . . I didn't buy it.*

La voiture, je ne vais pas **la** garer. *. . . I'm not going to park it.*

- In negative commands, an object pronoun is placed before the conjugated verb:

Cet appartement ? Ne **le** montrez pas ! *. . . Don't show it!*

In affirmative commands, an object pronoun is placed after the conjugated verb and joined to it by a hyphen.

Le nouveau studio ? Montrez-**le** à Susan ! *. . . Show it to Susan!*

- In the **passé composé**, the past participle agrees in gender and number with a preceding direct-object pronoun:

J'ai donné **le CD** à Karine. Je **l'**ai donné à Karine.

J'ai donné **la lampe** à Ludovic. Je **l'**ai donnée à Ludovic.

J'ai donné **les livres** à Gaëlle. Je **les** ai donnés à Gaëlle.

J'ai donné **les affiches** à Rémy. Je **les** ai données à Rémy.

In French you cannot emphasize a word by adding stress to it, as in English: "Did you see *John* or *Bill*?" "I saw *John*." One way to emphasize a word or phrase in French is to place it at the very beginning of the sentence, and put a pronoun equivalent in its place: **Les voisins**, tu **les** aimes ?

Past participle agreement affects only the pronunciation of participles that end with a consonant. The addition of the feminine marker -e causes the consonant to be pronounced. Compare Le livre, je l'ai pris ; La lettre, je l'ai prise ; Les lettres, je les ai prises with Ce livre, je l'ai donné à Paul ; Cette lettre, je l'ai donnée à Karine ; Ces lettres, je les ai données au musée. For that reason, past participle agreement is presented largely for recognition. You may also provide appropriate written practice. As this agreement is largely a spelling convention, it is no surprise that native speakers often omit it in writing or in casual speech.

Dislocation is a frequent and useful conversational feature in spoken French and is practiced in Ex. 6-12.

À vous la parole

Begin practice with a discrimination drill: have students raise their hand when they hear a sentence with a direct-object pronoun: *Où est la télé ? ; La voilà ; Je l'ai mise dans le séjour ; Elle préfère le deux-pièces ; Nous achetons l'appartement ; Le voilà ; Il l'a visité hier ; Je les ai jetés.* etc. Follow up with identification of number and gender: *Je la mets ; Elle les choisit ; Vous le faites bien ; Tu l'as acheté où ? ; Ils le choisissent chaque fois ; Nous la voulons ; Je les appelle le dimanche après-midi ; Elle l'a bien épelé pour une fois ; Tu l'as mise où ?* Next, have students supply possible nouns for pronoun substitutes: *Je l'ai regardé à la télé. — Le film ; Elle l'a acheté en ville ; Nous allons le choisir demain ; Il l'appelle le soir ; Ils la regardent beaucoup ; Tu la gares toujours au parking ? ; Je les trouve très chers ; Vous le préparez ? ; Elles les portent tous les jours.* Use simple substitution drills to practice forms: *Le crayon ? — Le voilà ; Les devoirs ? — Les voilà ; Le tableau ? La porte ? Les fenêtres ? Le professeur ? Les livres ? Les cahiers ? L'examen ? L'affiche ? La cassette ? Le stylo ?* etc. This leads into Ex. 6-13.

6-12 Les opinions sont partagées ! Décidez avec un/e partenaire si vous êtes d'accord ou non.

MODÈLE On les aime : les films ? les examens ?

       É1 Les films, on les aime.

       É2 Les examens, on ne les aime pas.

1. On l'aime beaucoup : la danse ? le théâtre ?
2. On l'aime bien : le golf ? le football ?
3. On les écoute toujours : les parents ? les professeurs ?
4. On les déteste : les jours de pluie ? les jours d'orage ?
5. On les regarde souvent : les films ? les documentaires ?
6. On la visite souvent : la ville de New York ? la France ?
7. On l'adore : le français ? la musique ?
8. On les aime : les pique-niques ? les vacances ?

6-13 Où est-ce que c'est rangé ? David s'installe dans un nouvel appartement, mais il ne trouve plus rien ! Jouez les rôles de David et de son copain avec un/e partenaire.

MODÈLE É1 Où sont mes casseroles (*pots*) ?

       É2 Les voilà dans la cuisine.

1. Où est ma télé ?
2. Où sont mes livres ?
3. Où est mon manteau ?
4. Où sont mes CD ?
5. Où est mon mixer ?
6. Où sont mes photos ?
7. Où est mon ordinateur ?
8. Où est mon affiche de la France ?

6-14 Expand by having students state how often they do each activity:

    É1 *Tu aimes faire la cuisine ?*

    É2 *Oui, j'aime la faire ; je la fais souvent. Et toi ?*

    É3 *Non, moi, je n'aime pas la faire ; je la fais rarement.*

Simplify by providing students with a scale of frequency adverbs : *ne … jamais ; rarement ; quelquefois ; souvent ; toujours.*

6-14 Les occupations et les loisirs. Quels sont les occupations et les loisirs de vos camarades de classe ? Posez des questions à deux camarades, et ensuite comparez les réponses.

MODÈLE faire la cuisine

      É1 Tu aimes faire la cuisine ?

      É2 Oui, j'aime la faire. Et toi ?

      É3 Non, je n'aime pas la faire.

1. faire la cuisine
2. faire les courses
3. mettre la table
4. faire les devoirs
5. inviter tes amis
6. préparer les repas
7. regarder la télé pendant le dîner

6-15 Deux appartements

A. Avant d'écouter. Imaginez que vous cherchez un appartement. Faites une liste de vos critères de sélection, c'est-à-dire, ce que vous voulez trouver dans l'appartement.

B. En écoutant. Maintenant, écoutez Ben qui décrit deux appartements qu'il a visités.

1. Pour chaque appartement, cochez les critères qu'il mentionne.

	Appartement n° 1	**Appartement n° 2**
en centre-ville		
deux pièces		
cuisine équipée		
salle de bains		
W.-C.		
balcon		
parking		

2. Écoutez une deuxième fois pour vérifier que vous avez coché tous les détails que Ben a mentionnés.

C. Après avoir écouté. Discutez de ces questions avec vos camarades de classe.

1. D'après la description des deux appartements, est-ce que Ben devrait louer le premier ou le second ? Pourquoi ?
2. Est-ce que Ben a les mêmes critères que vous pour un appartement ?
3. Et vous, quel appartement est-ce que vous préférez ? Pourquoi ?

Additional activities to develop the four skills are provided by:
• Student Activities Manual
• Text Audio
• *Chez nous* video
• *Chez nous* Companion Website: http://www.prenhall.com/cheznous

Avant d'écouter To prepare this activity, give students time to write their lists in French and then have them compare their ideas.

Script for *Écoutons*
Le premier appartement se trouve en centre-ville. C'est un très beau deux-pièces rénové, avec un grand séjour et une grande chambre. Il y a aussi une petite cuisine, des W.-C. et une douche dans la salle de bains. Au sous-sol, il y a un parking pour les habitants de l'immeuble.

Le deuxième appartement est à l'extérieur de la ville, mais avec le train, je serai à une demi-heure seulement du centre-ville. J'aime cet appartement ; c'est un grand studio avec un petit balcon et une vue magnifique sur le parc. C'est un appartement neuf avec un coin cuisine très moderne, une petite salle de bains et des W.-C. L'inconvénient, c'est qu'il n'y a pas d'endroit pour garer ma voiture.

LEÇON 1 ◆ LA VIE EN VILLE *deux cent trente-sept* **237**

Leçon 2 *Je suis chez moi*

Read the description aloud as you use the photo and the labeled drawing of Christelle's room (IRCD, Ch. 6) to present this vocabulary. Test comprehension by having students point to items you name as you show the unlabelled room (IRCD, Ch. 6), or ask what various items are used for: *Un lit ? — C'est pour dormir*, etc. Next have students repeat key terms and group descriptive words as opposites: *abîmée/neuve; ancienne/moderne*, etc. All the prepositions are familiar except for *sous* and *sur*.

POINTS DE DÉPART

Chez Christelle

TEXT AUDIO

Voici l'immeuble où se trouve le studio de Christelle.

Christelle habite un vieil immeuble rénové dans le centre-ville de Nice. Son studio se trouve sous les toits : il n'est pas très chic, mais il est agréable. En plus, il n'est pas cher : son loyer est de seulement 400 euros par mois. Le studio est meublé : il y a une belle armoire ancienne pour ranger ses vêtements et des rideaux neufs. Par terre il y a un beau tapis. Les autres meubles sont un peu abîmés, mais ils sont confortables, surtout le lit et le fauteuil. Il y a des affiches aux murs. Le coin cuisine est petit mais bien équipé : il y a un petit réfrigérateur à côté de l'évier, une cuisinière avec un petit four. Il y a aussi des grands placards — c'est très pratique pour mettre ses affaires. Il y a aussi une salle de bains moderne et des W.-C.

Vie et culture

Le quartier

Dans les grandes villes, c'est le quartier qui donne un aspect plus personnel à la vie urbaine souvent trop impersonnelle. Chaque quartier est comme une petite communauté : il y a le café du coin[1] et les petits commerçants[2]. On peut faire les courses tous les jours. Il y a souvent un marché certains jours de la semaine.

Regardez la séquence vidéo, *Mon quartier*, où une jeune Parisienne décrit son quartier. Quels aspects de son quartier est-ce qu'elle aime en particulier ? Et vous, est-ce que vous habitez aussi dans un quartier ? Est-ce que vous avez aussi le sentiment de faire partie d'une petite communauté ? Pourquoi ?

[1]*corner*   [2]*merchants*

It is becoming more common for students or young professionals in France to share an apartment or house without being in a romantic relationship or having a family connection. This is referred to as *la colocation*. Visit the *Chez nous* website for links to sites with ads for people seeking *des colocataires* that you could use in class to practice key vocabulary linked to housing.

À vous la parole

6-16 Chez Christelle. Décrivez l'appartement où habite Christelle en choisissant un adjectif approprié.

MODÈLE   L'immeuble est neuf ou vieux ?
➤ L'immeuble est vieux.

1. Le studio est spacieux ou petit ?
2. Le loyer est cher ou pas cher ?
3. Le fauteuil est confortable ou pas confortable ?
4. La salle de bains est ancienne ou moderne ?
5. L'armoire est neuve ou ancienne ?
6. Les rideaux sont neufs ou vieux ?
7. Le tapis est abîmé ou beau ?
8. La cuisine est bien équipée ou mal équipée ?

6-16 To provide review of prenominal adjective forms, have students reply with: *C'est un vieil immeuble.* Note that the adjective *neuf/neuve* is irregular in its formation.

6-17 Before completing, review the prepositions students learned in Ch. 3, L. 1 and the contracted forms of the prepositions *à* and *de*. Point out that *sur* is used to talk about things placed on horizontal surfaces. Use the preposition *à* for items on vertical surfaces, for example, *L'affiche est au mur.* You might also have students indicate what is *not* in the room, e.g., *Il n'y a pas de tapis,* etc.

As a follow-up, use other famous paintings of interiors to practice this vocabulary; allow students to work in pairs or groups.

6-17 La chambre de Van Gogh. Van Gogh (1853–1890), un artiste néerlandais bien connu, a habité en France. Voici un de ses tableaux ; c'est sa chambre en Provence. Décrivez cette chambre en cinq ou six phrases.

MODÈLE ➤ Dans cette chambre, il y a un petit lit. À côté du lit, il y a…

Vincent Van Gogh, « La chambre de Van Gogh à Arles », 1889.
Oil on canvas. 57.5 × 74 cm. Musée d'Orsay, Paris, France. Erich Lessing/Art Resource, NY.

6-18 Modify by having one student describe his/her room while the partner tries to draw it.

6-18 Ma chambre. Avec un/e partenaire, décrivez votre chambre à la résidence, dans votre maison ou votre appartement, ou chez vos parents.

MODÈLE ➤ Dans ma chambre, il y a deux fenêtres avec des rideaux. Il y a un grand lit, …

6-19 C'est bien chez moi. Vous habitez la résidence ou un appartement meublé ? C'est quelquefois un peu triste. Qu'est-ce que vous pouvez faire ou qu'est-ce que vous avez déjà fait pour rendre votre environnement plus personnel ? Discutez avec un/e partenaire.

Des suggestions : Qu'est-ce qu'il y a aux murs ? par terre ?

Quels objets personnels — des photos, des plantes — est-ce qu'il y a ?

Quelles couleurs est-ce que tu as mises dans ta chambre ?

MODÈLE É1 J'habite la résidence universitaire dans une petite chambre.

É2 Moi aussi. Qu'est-ce que tu as fait pour la rendre plus personnelle ?

É1 J'ai mis des plantes ; j'adore les plantes. Et toi ?

É2 Moi j'ai mis un beau tapis par terre et beaucoup d'affiches aux murs. C'est très bien chez moi.

Sons et lettres

La consonne *r*

The French /R/ has no equivalent sound in English. To pronounce /R/ in French, begin by saying **aga**; then move your tongue up and back until you pronounce a continuous sound: **ara**. Practice by alternating the two sounds: **aga/ara**, **aga/ara**, etc.

Note the pronunciation of /R/ in **liaison** and linking across words (**enchaînement**).

Liaison:	le premier‿étage	le dernier‿immeuble
Enchaînement:	un séjour‿agréable	Il sort‿avec moi.

> The American *r* is a retroflex *r*; the tongue curves back. Tell students not to roll their tongue to produce the French R.
>
> Point out that liaison also involves *enchaînement*. Liaison is the pronunciation of a liaison (or latent) consonant before a vowel; *enchaînement* is the pronunciation of any consonant—whether latent or always pronounced—before words beginning with a vowel. The consonant is pronounced as if it were part of the next word.

À vous la parole

6-20 Répétitions. Répétez les mots après votre professeur.

la **r**ue	la **r**oute	la **r**ose	la te**rr**asse	a**rr**iver
Pa**r**is	la ga**r**e	p**r**emière	se**r**vir	maig**r**ir

> Begin practice with a discrimination drill: *anglais ou français ? roux, rue, Robert, rat, Richard, terrasse,* etc.

6-21 La forme correcte. Donnez les formes de la troisième personne (singulier et pluriel) du présent de l'indicatif des verbes suivants.

MODÈLE servir
> ➤ elle sert, elles servent

sortir	partir	dormir	maigrir	servir

6-22 Phrases. Répétez chaque phrase.

1. La te**rr**asse donne su**r** la **r**ue.
2. L'ascenseu**r** s'a**rr**ête au de**r**nie**r** étage.
3. Ma**r**ie achète l'aut**r**e appartement.

FORMES ET FONCTIONS

1. *Les pronoms compléments d'objet indirect* lui *et* leur

- You have learned that nouns that function as direct objects answer the question *who?* or *what?*; they follow the verb directly and can be replaced by a direct-object pronoun.

Tu prends **cet appartement** ?	—Oui, je **le** prends.
Elle attend **le propriétaire** ?	—Oui, elle **l'**attend.
Vous aimez **ces appartements** ?	—Non, nous ne **les** aimons pas.

> Review the forms of the direct-object pronouns with a transformation drill before introducing the indirect-object pronouns: *Je regarde la télé. —Je la regarde ; les voisins —Je les regarde ; le toit ; les fenêtres ; l'ascenseur ; la cuisinière ; le balcon,* etc. To present the new forms, give students numerous written or oral examples, perhaps in a narrative, and see whether they can explain usage; for example: *Aujourd'hui, j'ai rendez-vous avec un collègue ; je lui téléphone pour vérifier. J'ai cours avec mes étudiants à 10 h ; je leur rends les devoirs. Je déjeune avec une amie ; c'est son anniversaire, et je lui offre un cadeau,* etc.

- In French, nouns that function as indirect objects are generally introduced by the preposition **à**; they often answer the question *to whom?* and always refer to a person:

> Je donne le loyer **à la propriétaire**.   *I'm giving the rent **to the landlady**.*
>   (or, *I'm giving **the landlady** the rent.*)
>
> Tu as répondu **à tes parents** ?   *Did you answer **your parents**?*

In the above sentences, the indirect-object pronouns **lui** (*to him, to her*) and **leur** (*to them*) can be substituted for **à la propriétaire** and **à tes parents**.

> Je **lui** donne le loyer.   *I'm giving the rent **to him/her**.*
> Tu **leur** as répondu ?   *Did you answer **them**?*

Students should be able to summarize placement rules on their own, since this is review. You may wish to point out that in the *passé composé*, the past participle never agrees with a preceding indirect-object pronoun.

- Like other object pronouns, **lui** and **leur** are placed immediately before the conjugated verb, unless there is an infinitive. If there is an infinitive in the sentence, **lui** and **leur** precede the infinitive.

> Je **lui** parle au sujet du loyer.   *I'm speaking **to him/her** about the rent.*
> Nous **leur** avons téléphoné.   *We called **them** up.*
> Tu vas **lui** donner l'argent pour les charges ?   *Are you going to give **him/her** the money for utilities?*
> Elle peut **leur** expliquer combien ça coûte par mois.   *She can explain **to them** how much it costs per month.*

- In negative commands, **lui** and **leur** are placed immediately before the conjugated verb:

> Ne **lui** prête pas l'appartement.   *Don't loan the apartment to him/her.*

In affirmative commands, **lui** and **leur** are placed immediately after the verb and joined to it by a hyphen:

> Donne-**lui** ton nouvel adresse.   *Give her/him your new address.*
> Téléphone-**leur** à propos de l'appartement.   *Call them about the apartment.*

The irregular verbs *dire* and *écrire* will be presented in Ch. 7, L. 1.

- Two main groups of verbs take indirect objects.

  - Verbs of communication:

demander	*to ask*	On va **leur** demander l'adresse.
expliquer	*to explain*	Tu peux **lui** expliquer le problème ?
montrer	*to show*	Qui va **lui** montrer la chambre ?
parler	*to speak*	Je **leur** parle souvent au téléphone.
répondre	*to answer*	Elle ne **leur** a pas répondu.
téléphoner	*to phone*	Nous **leur** avons téléphoné hier.

- Verbs of transfer:

acheter	to buy	Je **leur** ai acheté un petit appartement.
apporter	to bring	La propriétaire **lui** a apporté la lettre.
donner	to give	On peut **leur** donner l'adresse.
emprunter	to borrow	Je **lui** emprunte la voiture.
offrir	to give (a gift)	Elle **lui** offre un cadeau pour son anniversaire.
prêter	to lend	Tu **leur** prêtes ton appartement ?
remettre	to hand in/over	Nous **lui** avons remis le loyer.
rendre	to give back	Je **lui** ai rendu le livre.

Note that this construction is ambiguous for the verb *acheter: Je lui achète un livre* (I'm buying a book for/from him). For greater clarity: *J'achète un livre pour mon frère.* Point out to students that *offrir*, like *ouvrir*, takes *-er* verb endings. A full conjugation can be found in Appendix 4.

À vous la parole

👥 **6-23 De quoi est-ce qu'on parle ?** Avec un/e partenaire, trouvez au moins deux possibilités logiques pour chaque phrase.

MODÈLE   Je lui offre souvent des cadeaux.
> ➤ J'offre souvent des cadeaux à mon petit frère.
OU   ➤ J'offre souvent des cadeaux à mon copain.

1. Je leur téléphone souvent le week-end.
2. Je lui ai rendu visite l'été passé.
3. Je voudrais lui donner mon adresse.
4. J'aime leur parler.
5. Je lui prête mes affaires.
6. Je leur explique mes problèmes.
7. Je peux lui demander de l'argent.
8. Je leur offre des cadeaux.

6-24 Qu'est-ce qu'on peut offrir ? Les personnes suivantes ont acheté un nouvel appartement. D'après les indications, qu'est-ce qu'on pourrait leur offrir comme cadeau ?

MODÈLE   Ma sœur n'a pas grand-chose aux murs.
> ➤ Je lui offre une belle affiche.

1. Mes parents ont un nouveau lecteur DVD.
2. Mon oncle adore faire la cuisine.
3. Ma tante adore les plantes et les fleurs (*flowers*).
4. Ma cousine aime les livres.
5. Mes grands-parents aiment la musique.
6. Mon cousin n'a pas de colocataire.
7. Mes amis ont une belle terrasse.

Begin practice with a discrimination drill: one person or more than one? *Je lui téléphone le week-end ; Je leur remets la lettre ; Je leur donne un cadeau ; Je lui prête ma voiture ; Je lui remets le loyer ; Je leur rends la vidéocassette ; Je peux leur expliquer la situation ; Je lui parle tout le temps ; Je leur ai montré le studio ; Je lui ai répondu hier ;* etc. Use a wide variety of verbs, but do not vary the subject. Follow with a simple substitution drill: *Je réponds au prof —Je lui réponds ; à mes parents ; à Suzanne ; à mes amis ; à mon frère ; à mes colocataires ; au serveur ; à mon meilleur ami ; à mes cousins.*

6-23 This focuses on the meaning of the indirect-object pronouns and the use of the preposition *à* with noun phrases. Students' answers can be personalized.

6-24 This can be personalized by asking students about the interests of their family and friends and having others suggest suitable gifts.

6-25 Follow up by having students report back what they learned.

6-25 Rarement, souvent ou jamais ? Interviewez un/e camarade de classe pour savoir avec quelle fréquence il/elle fait les choses suivantes : **rarement**, **souvent** ou **jamais** ?

MODÈLE   prêtes tes vêtements à ta/ton colocataire

   É1   Est-ce que tu prêtes tes vêtements à ta colocataire ?

   É2   Non, je ne lui prête jamais mes vêtements.

   OU   Oui, je lui prête souvent mes pull-overs.

1. rends toujours les devoirs au professeur
2. expliques tes problèmes à tes parents
3. parles souvent à tes parents
4. offres des cadeaux à tes amis
5. demandes souvent de l'argent à tes parents
6. empruntes souvent des vêtements à tes amis
7. achètes des bonbons pour tes nièces et tes neveux
8. empruntes de l'argent à tes amis

2. Les pronoms compléments d'objet me, te, nous, vous

Before treating this topic, use substitution drills to review direct- and indirect-object pronouns in the third person: *le, la, l', les* (Ch. 6, L. 1); *lui, leur* (this lesson). Present the new information using numerous examples and having students summarize rules.

• The pronouns **me/m'**, **te/t'**, **nous**, and **vous** function as direct-object pronouns, corresponding to **le**, **la**, **l'**, and **les**. They also serve as indirect-object pronouns, corresponding to **lui** and **leur**.

Direct-object pronouns

Tu **m'**attends devant l'immeuble ?	*Will you wait for me in front of the building?*
Attention ! On **te** regarde.	*Watch out. They're looking at you.*
Elles **nous** ont invités chez elles.	*They invited us to their place.*
Je vais **vous** inviter à dîner.	*I'm going to invite you to dinner.*

Indirect-object pronouns

Je **te** téléphone tout de suite.	*I'll call you right away.*
Vous **me** parlez ?	*Are you talking to me?*
Il **nous** a montré des photos de sa maison.	*He showed us pictures of his house.*
Qui **vous** a dit que l'appartement est à louer ?	*Who told you that the apartment is for rent?*

- Here is a summary of object pronouns:

	personne		direct	indirect
singulier	1ère		me/m'	me/m'
	2^e		te/t'	te/t'
	3^e	*m.*	le/l'	lui
		f.	la/l'	lui
pluriel	1ère		nous	nous
	2^e		vous	vous
	3^e		les	leur

À vous la parole

6-26 Esprit de contradiction ou pas ? Vous allez proposer quelque chose. Un/e de vos partenaires va donner son accord, l'autre va refuser.

MODÈLE   É1 Tu m'attends ?
            É2 Oui, je t'attends.
            É3 Non, je ne t'attends pas.

1. Tu m'aides à ranger l'appartement ?
2. Tu me téléphones ?
3. Tu m'invites chez toi ?
4. Tu me prêtes ton studio à Paris ?
5. Tu vas me répondre ?
6. Tu vas me montrer ta chambre ?
7. Tu vas m'accompagner à l'agence immobilière (*real estate agency*) ?

6-27 Du chantage. Répondez que vous êtes d'accord.

MODÈLE   Je t'invite à dîner si tu me prêtes de l'argent.
            ➤ Alors, je te prête de l'argent.

1. Je te réponds si tu me donnes ton adresse.
2. Je te téléphone si tu me donnes ton numéro de téléphone.
3. Nous t'accompagnons au musée si tu nous invites à ta fête.
4. Nous t'offrons le dessert si tu nous aides à ranger le garage.
5. Je t'amène au cinéma si tu me prêtes ta voiture demain.
6. Je répare ton vélo si tu m'expliques le problème de maths.
7. Nous te prêtons de l'argent si tu nous accompagnes à la bibliothèque.

Begin practice with substitution drills: *Il les regarde ; nous, toi*, etc. *Elle lui parle ; vous, eux*, etc.

6-26 Modify to practice plural forms: *Vous nous aidez ?* etc.

6-28 Qu'est-ce qu'ils font ? Qu'est-ce que ces gens font pour vous ?

Parlez-en avec un/e camarade, et ensuite comparez vos réponses avec celles des autres étudiants.

MODÈLE   vos parents

> É1   Qu'est-ce que tes parents font pour toi ?
>
> É2   Ils me téléphonent le week-end ; ils me prêtent de l'argent pour payer mes études ; ils m'offrent des cadeaux.

1. votre frère ou sœur
2. votre colocataire
3. votre meilleur/e ami/e
4. votre copain/copine ou votre mari/femme
5. vos professeurs
6. vos parents

Parlons

6-29 À la recherche d'un appartement

A. Avant de parler. Imaginez que vous cherchez un appartement. Quelles sont les questions que vous voudriez poser à un agent immobilier (*real estate agent*) à propos d'un appartement à louer ? Si vous étiez un agent immobilier, comment persuader un/e client/e de prendre l'appartement ? D'abord, créez une liste de questions pour le/la client/e et une liste de commentaires possibles pour l'agent immobilier.

B. En parlant. Maintenant, jouez avec un/e partenaire l'un ou l'autre des deux rôles : client/e ou agent immobilier.

MODÈLE   AGENT IMMOBILIER :   J'ai un très bel appartement au cinquième étage.

CLIENT/E :   Il a combien de pièces ? Je voudrais un deux-pièces…

Ensuite, échangez les rôles.

C. Après avoir parlé. Présentez votre dialogue aux autres.

Leçon 3 *La vie à la campagne*

POINTS DE DÉPART

Tout près de la nature

TEXT AUDIO

Les Santini possèdent une petite villa qui se trouve loin de la ville. Ils ont passé le week-end dernier là-bas. M. Santini en parle avec son collègue M. Deleuze.

Cette résidence secondaire est une vieille ferme ; les propriétaires peuvent bricoler et faire du jardinage le week-end et pendant les vacances.

M. DELEUZE :	Qu'est-ce que vous avez fait le week-end dernier ?
M. SANTINI :	Nous sommes allés à la campagne où nous avons une petite maison.
M. DELEUZE :	C'était bien ?
M. SANTINI :	Formidable ! C'était calme, j'ai bricolé, je suis allé à la pêche et avec les enfants, nous nous sommes promenés dans le bois. Comme il a fait très beau, on a même fait un pique-nique au bord du lac.
M. DELEUZE :	Vous avez un jardin aussi ?
M. SANTINI :	Oh, nous avons un petit potager et quelques arbres fruitiers, c'est tout. C'est ma femme qui s'occupe de tout cela.
M. DELEUZE :	Alors, il me semble que vous avez passé un week-end agréable.
M. SANTINI :	En effet, on se détend toujours quand on est à la campagne.

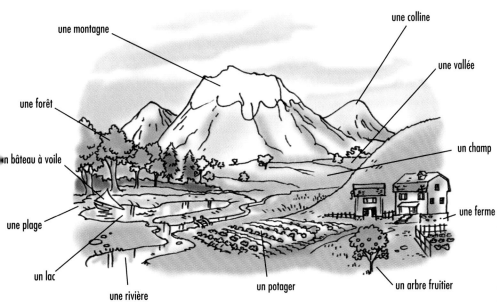

une montagne

une colline

une vallée

une forêt

un bâteau à voile

un champ

une ferme

une plage

un arbre fruitier

un lac

un potager

une rivière

Vie et culture

Le bleu et le vert des vacances

Où vont les Français quand ils veulent se détendre ? Regardez le tableau pour trouver leurs cinq destinations préférées. Où est-ce que les Français voyagent le plus ? Où est-ce qu'ils passent les plus longs séjours, en nombre de nuits ? Selon[1] le tableau, est-ce que les Français se limitent toujours à une seule destination ?

Quand les Français voyagent à l'intérieur du pays[2], ils ne restent pas forcément dans un hôtel. Ils sont logés le plus souvent chez des parents, chez des amis, ou chez eux, dans leur résidence secondaire. La moitié (50 %) de ces résidences sont situées à la campagne, le reste à la mer ou à la montagne. Quelles sont les destinations préférées des Nord-Américains qui cherchent à se détendre ? Est-ce qu'ils préfèrent rester à l'hôtel, ou chez des amis et de la famille ?

[1]*according to* [2]*country*

Point out the title of this cultural note as a clue to the main point of the text. The heading on the chart also summarizes the major point; have students explain how the statistics illustrate this. Using context and word families, students should be able to understand the categories.
Hotels represent only about 10% of overnight stays when the French travel within France: 44% stay with family; 13%, with friends; and about 10%, in their *résidence secondaire*.

Plus de séjours à la campagne, plus de temps à la mer

	En % de séjours	En % de nuitées
Mer	27,9	39,7
Montagne	14,3	18,3
Campagne	35,8	32,2
Lac	4,1	5,3
Ville	33,2	26,0

Le total est supérieur à 100%, plusieurs espaces pouvant être fréquentés au cours d'un même séjour.

Source : enquête SDT Direction du Tourisme/SOFRES

À vous la parole

6-30 Où est-ce que c'est ? D'après la conversation, quel est l'endroit décrit ?

MODÈLE Pour avoir une meilleure vue sur la vallée, il faut monter.
➤ C'est la montagne.

1. Il n'y a pas assez de vent pour faire du bateau à voile.
2. Il y a beaucoup de grands arbres anciens ici !
3. Tu veux traverser (*cross*) ici ? L'eau n'est pas trop profonde.
4. Il y a un petit potager, et voilà les champs pour les animaux.
5. Tu veux nager un peu ?
6. Quand est-ce qu'on va arriver au sommet ?
7. C'est un bon endroit; il y a beaucoup de poissons (*fish*) ici !
8. Voilà les carottes, et ici, ce sont mes belles tomates.
9. Mettons la tente ici, sous un arbre.

6-31 Projets pour une sortie.
Avec deux ou trois camarades de classe, faites des projets pour une sortie. Imaginez qu'il fait beau et que vous avez une journée de libre. Choisissez une destination et des activités.

MODÈLE É1 On va à la montagne ?

É2 Je préfère aller au bord d'un lac.

É3 Moi aussi. On peut nager…

6-31 Put students into small groups to plan. You might impose certain constraints—time of year, distance they may travel, amount of money they may spend, etc.

6-32 Plaisirs de la ville, plaisirs de la campagne.
Vous préférez habiter la ville ou la campagne ? Pourquoi ? Discutez votre préférence avec un/e partenaire et dressez une liste des avantages et des inconvénients.

MODÈLE É1 Moi, je préfère habiter la ville ; il y a beaucoup de bons restaurants et de cinémas.

É2 Il y a trop d'activité et trop de voitures en ville ; je préfère le calme à la campagne…

la ville : avantages = les restaurants, les cinémas,…

inconvénients = les voitures,…

la campagne : avantages = le calme,…

6-32 This can also be carried out as a whole-class activity, or students can be put into small groups as follows: advantages of the city, advantages of the country, etc. Circulate as groups prepare their lists and help out with ideas and vocabulary. Have groups report back, and summarize information orally and visually before students are polled to express their personal preference. As an additional follow-up, students can write about their personal preference.

6-33 La maison de vos rêves.
Imaginez que vous pouvez acheter une résidence secondaire. Décrivez-la d'après vos préférences, et comparez vos idées avec celles d'un/e partenaire.

1. Elle se trouve au bord de la mer ? à la montagne ? à la campagne ?
2. C'est une grande ou une petite maison ? simple ou élégante ?
3. Qu'est-ce que vous faites quand vous allez dans votre résidence secondaire ?

MODÈLE ➤ Ma résidence secondaire se trouve à la montagne. C'est un petit chalet, très simple mais confortable. Là-bas, il ne fait pas trop chaud en été, et il y a toujours de la neige en hiver. En été, donc, je peux faire des randonnées, et en hiver je peux faire du ski.

FORMES ET FONCTIONS

1. *Faire des suggestions avec l'imparfait*

- The imperfect (**l'imparfait**) is a tense that is used in a variety of ways. For example, it is used with **si** to make suggestions and to soften commands.

Si on **faisait** une promenade ?	*Shall we take a walk?*
Si tu **allais** à la pêche ?	*Why don't you go fishing?*
Si nous **allions** à la montagne ?	*How about going to the mountains?*

This section focuses on the formation of the *imparfait*. For that reason, we use a function of the *imparfait* unrelated to the expression of past events. You might point out that the main use of the *imparfait* is to express certain types of past events and that this function will be taught in the next section.

Show students how the rule for formation of the *imparfait* works for irregular verbs they have learned: *faire → nous faisons → il faisait, nous faisions,* etc. Point out that the singular and third-person plural forms are pronounced alike. In pronouncing these endings, French speakers vary between /e/, as in *thé,* and /ɛ/, as in *cette.*

- To form the **imparfait**, drop the **-ons** ending of the **nous** form of the present tense and add the **imparfait** endings. The only exception to this rule is the verb **être**, which has an irregular stem, **ét-**, as shown below.

L'IMPARFAIT					
INFINITIVE	jouer	partir	finir	descendre	être
NOUS FORM	jouons	partons	finissons	descendons	
IMPARFAIT STEM	**jou-**	**part-**	**finiss-**	**descend-**	**ét-**
je	jou**ais**	part**ais**	finiss**ais**	descend**ais**	ét**ais**
tu	jou**ais**	part**ais**	finiss**ais**	descend**ais**	ét**ais**
il elle on	jou**ait**	part**ait**	finiss**ait**	descend**ait**	ét**ait**
nous	jou**ions**	part**ions**	finiss**ions**	descend**ions**	ét**ions**
vous	jou**iez**	part**iez**	finiss**iez**	descend**iez**	ét**iez**
ils elles	jou**aient**	part**aient**	finiss**aient**	descend**aient**	ét**aient**

À vous la parole

Begin practice with a substitution drill: *Si on allait à la piscine ; nous, toi, vous,* etc.

6-34 Un week-end à la campagne. Transformez ces ordres en suggestions.

MODÈLE Jouons au golf !
➤ Si on jouait au golf ?

1. Faisons une randonnéel !
2. Travaille dans le jardin !
3. Descendez au bord du lac !
4. Organisons un pique-nique !
5. Faites une promenade dans la forêt !
6. Cherchons des tomates !
7. Fais du bricolage !
8. Allons à la pêche !
9. Faisons de la voile !

6-35 Pour une sortie. En groupes de trois personnes, organisez une petite sortie. Mettez-vous d'accord sur l'endroit et les distractions. Utilisez les verbes indiqués.

MODÈLES aller ; apporter ; faire

É1 Si on allait à la plage ? (ou chez Tracy ? etc.)

É2 Si tu apportais ta guitare ?

É3 Si on faisait un pique-nique ?

1. aller
2. apporter
3. acheter
4. jouer
5. faire
6. inviter

▲▲ 6-36 Projets pour le week-end. Avec un/e partenaire, faites des projets pour un week-end dans la nature. Décidez de la destination, du logement et des activités.

MODÈLE   É1 Si on allait à la plage ?
             É2 Oui, et si on faisait du camping ?
             É1 Bonne idée ! Si on faisait des promenades le matin
                  sur la plage ?, etc.

2. *L'imparfait: la description au passé*

● You have just learned to use the **imparfait** to make suggestions. You can also use this tense to describe situations and settings in the past.

Treat this topic on day two of the lesson, and first review forms using a substitution drill: *Si tu jouais au tennis ; nous, lui,* etc.

■ To indicate the time:

Il **était** une heure du matin.   *It was one o'clock in the morning.*
C'**était** en hiver.   *It was during the winter.*

■ To describe the weather:

Il **pleuvait** et il **faisait** froid. *It was raining and it was cold.*
Le ciel **était** gris.   *The sky was gray.*

■ To describe people and places:

C'**était** une belle maison.   *It was a nice house.*
La dame **avait** les cheveux roux.   *The woman had red hair.*
Elle **portait** un manteau noir.   *She was wearing a black coat.*

■ To express feelings or describe emotions:

Nous **avions** froid.   *We were cold.*
Ils **étaient** contents.   *They were happy.*

● Use the **imparfait** to express habitual actions in the past:

Tous les week-ends nous **faisions**   *Every weekend we would take*
   une randonnée dans les bois.   *(we took) a hike in the woods.*
Quand j'étais petit, on **passait** les   *When I was little, we used to spend*
   vacances chez mes grands-parents.   *vacations at my grandparents'.*

Here are some expressions often used with the **imparfait** to describe things that were done on a routine basis:

Remind students that *le* used before a day of the week or a word like *week-end* changes the meaning to "every Monday" or "every weekend," for example.

quelquefois	*sometimes*
souvent	*often*
d'habitude	*usually*
toujours	*always*
le lundi, le week-end	*every Monday, every weekend*
tous les jours, tous les soirs	*every day, every evening*
toutes les semaines	*every week*

À vous la parole

6-37 Une journée à la campagne. Complétez les phrases pour décrire une journée à la campagne chez les Santini.

MODÈLE il / faire beau
➤ Il faisait beau.

1. les oiseaux / chanter
2. le ciel / être bleu
3. les enfants / jouer dans le jardin
4. Mme Santini / préparer un pique-nique
5. M. Santini / travailler dans le jardin
6. les grands-parents / regarder les enfants
7. les enfants / jouer au foot

6-38 Test de mémoire. Regardez ces photos avec un/e partenaire et ensuite fermez votre manuel. Pouvez-vous vous rappeler tous les détails ? Pour chaque photo, indiquez :

1. quelle était la saison
2. quel temps il faisait
3. comment étaient les gens
4. quelles étaient leurs activités

6-38 Simplify by asking students questions: *C'était l'été ou l'hiver ? Il faisait beau ou il faisait mauvais ?* etc. Students may work in pairs or small groups, with partners checking for accuracy of the description. *Une station de ski* in France is depicted in the first photo and a Moroccan hillside overlooking the city of Fes in the second photo. You may also use your own photos or slides to cue responses, or students may describe a memorable day from a recent vacation.

👥 6-39 Votre enfance. Posez des questions à un/e camarade de classe pour savoir ce qu'il/elle faisait pendant son enfance.

MODÈLE   habiter ici

   É1   Est-ce que tu habitais ici ?

   É2   Non, j'habitais à Chicago avec mes parents.

1. habiter ici
2. avoir des animaux
3. aimer aller à l'école
4. faire du sport

5. jouer d'un instrument
6. aller souvent chez des amis
7. partir souvent en vacances
8. avoir une résidence secondaire

Lisons

6-40 Quand j'étais toute petite

A. Avant de lire. J.M.G. Le Clézio is a well-known and prolific French author. The excerpt you are about to read is from ***Printemps et autres saisons,*** a collection of short stories. Each one is set in a different season and tells the story of a particular woman. In this excerpt, Zinna, a young woman who has left her home in Morocco for the South of France, describes her childhood home in the **Mellah** (the Jewish quarter). Before you begin reading, take note of another essential character who figures prominently in the story: Zinna's elderly neighbor, **la tante Rachel**. Consider as you read why Rachel, whom Zinna never actually encounters in person, is very important to her narrative.

B. En lisant. As you read, answer the following questions.

1. The excerpt consists mainly of a quote: to whom is Zinna speaking? When and where is she telling her story?
2. Two houses are described in this passage; to whom do they belong? Describe each house: its size, the number of rooms, and any other physical features mentioned.
3. Describe the person who lives in the second house. Why is she an object of fascination for Zinna?

C. En regardant de plus près. Now think about the structure and larger meaning of this short text.

1. Early in the text, how does the narrator make it clear that Tomi (Gazelle) has often heard stories of Zinna's life in the Mellah?
2. Zinna's memory of the rooftop of her childhood home is vivid: describe the activities and the people involved.
3. Zinna's rooftop is contrasted with the balcony of the house of her neighbor, Rachel. What do we learn about Rachel from this description? What does Zinna imagine about Rachel's balcony, which she has never visited?

6-39 Have students work in pairs; as they report back what they have learned, ask follow-up questions. This exercise can lead into the reading in **Lisons.**

Avant de lire. *Characters mentioned include: Gazelle/Tomi ; Zinna ; le père de Zinna et son oncle Moché ; Khadija ; la (vieille) tante Rachel (une voisine). Have students guess why Tomi might have the nickname Gazelle.*

Stratégie

To understand a narrative, identify the main characters and the nature of their relationship with each other. Then as you read and reread the passage, focus on defining the significance of each character and how he or she figures in the story.

En lisant, Key: 1) Zinna to Gazelle/Tomi, on the beach, in the morning   2) Zinna's house—old, narrow, with one room downstairs, one room upstairs, and a ladder to the flat roof, where the laundry was done; Rachel's house—called "the blue house" because the door and upstairs windows were blue; a very high window opened out onto a round balcony   3) Rachel was called "Aunt Rachel," even though she was no one's aunt, as a sign of respect; it was said that she was rich, and that she had always refused to get married. Such a woman, independent-minded (that is, able to refuse a prearranged marriage) and well-off enough to be able to own a house without having to rely on a husband, would be a fascinating character in this society.

En regardant de plus près, Key: 1) Note the use of the *imparfait* and adverbs such as *toujours, généralement*   2) she describes the ladder used to climb to the roof, the washing she did, and having to push the fat Khadija up the ladder   3) we learn that Rachel never goes out on her balcony; Zinna imagines she could see all the surrounding countryside, the city, the river with its boats, all the way to the sea.

« Tu sais, Gazelle, quand j'étais toute petite, il n'y avait pas de plus beau quartier que le Mellah. »

Zinna commençait toujours ainsi. Elle s'asseyait sur la plage, et Tomi se mettait à côté d'elle. C'était généralement le matin...

« Alors, nous habitions une maison très vieille, étroite, juste une pièce en bas où couchait mon père avec mon oncle Moché, et moi j'étais dans la chambre du haut. Il y avait une échelle[1] pour grimper[2] sur le toit[3], là où était le lavoir[4]. C'était moi qui lavais le linge, quelquefois Khadija venait m'aider, elle était grosse, elle n'arrivait pas à grimper l'échelle, il fallait[5] la pousser. À côté de chez nous, il y avait la maison bleue. Elle n'était pas bleue, mais on l'appelait comme ça parce qu'elle avait une grande porte peinte en bleu, et les fenêtres à l'étage aussi étaient peintes en bleu. Il y avait surtout une fenêtre très haute, au premier, qui donnait sur un balcon rond. C'était la maison d'une vieille femme qu'on appelait la tante Rachel, mais elle n'était pas vraiment notre tante. On disait qu'elle était très riche, qu'elle n'avait jamais voulu se marier. Elle vivait[6] toute seule dans cette grande maison, avec ce balcon où les pigeons venaient se percher. Tous les jours, j'allais voir sa maison. De son balcon, je rêvais[7] qu'on pouvait voir tout le paysage, la ville, la rivière avec les barques qui traversaient, jusqu'à la mer. La vieille Rachel n'ouvrait jamais sa fenêtre, elle ne se mettait jamais au balcon pour regarder... »

5

10

15

20

25

[1]*ladder* [2]*climb* [3]*roof* [4]*washtub* [5]*it was necessary* [6]*lived* [7]*imagined*

Extrait de: J.M.G. Le Clézio « Zinna », *Printemps et autres saisons.* © Éditions GALLIMARD.

Après avoir lu. The contrast between the young Zinna and her mundane activity on the roof and the elderly Rachel, and what Zinna imagines she could see if she took the trouble to go out on her balcony, evokes the child's curiosity and desire to explore the world beyond her home.

D. Après avoir lu. Discuss the following questions with your classmates.

1. The contrast between Zinna's rooftop and Rachel's balcony is full of symbolism. What does it represent, in your opinion? What does it tell the reader about differences between Zinna and Rachel? Why are these differences significant?

2. Do you have a memory of a place closely associated with another person that stirred your imagination when you were younger?

Venez chez nous !
À la découverte de la France : les provinces

LE MYTHE DE L'HEXAGONE

Pour les Français, la France a la forme d'une figure géométrique : un hexagone. C'est aussi un hexagone équilibré, avec trois côtés bordés par des mers et trois côtés limités par d'autres pays[1].

Les frontières[2] de la France d'aujourd'hui ne sont pas des frontières naturelles. En fait, l'Hexagone est le résultat d'événements politiques qui ont réuni[3] peu à peu des peuples de langues et de cultures différentes. Au XIIe siècle, le royaume[4] de France s'est constitué[5] des régions de langue d'oïl au nord et celles[6] de langue d'oc au sud. Puis, d'autres régions ont été ajoutées[7] à ce nouvel ensemble[8] :

- la Bretagne en 1532
- le Pays Basque en 1620
- le Roussillon, la région autour de Perpignan, en 1659
- l'Alsace en 1681
- la Corse en 1768
- la Savoie et la région de Nice en 1860

[1]*other countries* [2]*borders* [3]*united* [4]*kingdom* [5]*was made up of* [6]*those* [7]*added* [8]*entity*

Additional activities to explore the **Venez chez nous !** topics are provided by:
- Student Activities Manual
- *Chez nous* video
- *Chez nous* Companion Website:
  http://www.prenhall.com/cheznous

To introduce this lesson and provide an overview of the diversity of the French regions, show the **Venez chez nous !** video montage (*À la découverte de la France : les provinces*). See whether students can identify various regions and/or specific sites. You might add slides and photos to enrich this presentation.

As you read this passage, have students look at the map in their textbook or display the map of France (IRCD, Ch. 6; IRCD, Maps). Have students identify the water borders and the borders with neighboring countries. Ask students to point out on the map the various regions mentioned. Have them compare the development of modern-day France with the development of the U.S., from the thirteen original colonies to the addition of the Louisiana Purchase, to the additions of Florida, Texas, California, Alaska, etc. You may wish to have students speculate on the origins of the various regional languages of France.

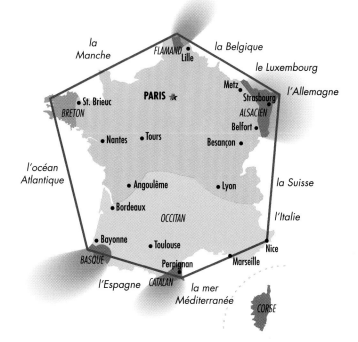

The regional languages of France include four Romance languages: *le catalan, le corse, l'occitan, le franco-provençal*; three Germanic languages: *le flamand, l'alsacien, le lorrain*; one Celtic language: *le breton*; and one language of unknown origin: *le basque*. The *loi Deixonne*, promulgated in 1951, first allowed the teaching of regional languages and, as a corollary, allowed *lycée* students to study a regional language for the *bac*. A 1974 amendment to the *loi Deixonne* expanded the definition of "regional languages." The teaching of regional languages received additional support with the *rapport Giordan* (1982), and the *loi Toubon* of 1994 is the most recent law allowing public-school instruction in the regional languages.

The U.S. Census identifies four regions: Midwest, South, Northeast, and West; students may identify others as well.

Les régions et les langues de France

Les habitants des régions françaises ont conservé une partie de leur culture à travers la musique, les fêtes et la cuisine régionales. La diversité culturelle se manifeste aussi par la langue. Dans ces régions, on entend encore parler les langues traditionnelles. Les communautés locales font un effort pour préserver ces langues, et on commence à enseigner les langues régionales à l'école. Voici quelques exemples de la langue de ces régions qui, tous, veulent dire : « Venez chez nous en…! »

- En Bretagne, le breton : **Deit genomb é Breizh !**
- En Alsace et en Lorraine, des dialectes allemands : **Komme zü uns ens Elsass !**
- En Corse, le corse : **Venite in Corsica !**
- Au Pays Basque, le basque : **Zatozte Euskal herrirat !**
- Dans tout le Midi, des dialectes occitans : **Venetz en Occitania !**

Et vous ?

1. Avec un/e partenaire, faites une liste des régions des États-Unis.
2. Quelles sortes de spécialités (la cuisine, la musique, les fêtes) est-ce qu'on trouve dans ces régions ?
3. D'après vous, est-ce qu'il existe des langues régionales aux États-Unis comme en France ? Expliquez.

le « Mai » ou la fête de Nice, sur la Côte d'Azur ; en niçois (une variété de l'occitan) : lu « Mai » o lu festin de Nissa

Combien de régions différentes est-ce que vous pouvez associer aux images sur ces timbres ?

Have students look at the stamps and see if they can identify the various regions illustrated on the stamps. The brown and white cow would be found in Normandy; the *cabines de bain* are from the beaches on the Atlantic coast; *le camembert* is from *Normandie* ; *le foie gras* is from *le Périgord* ; *la pétanque* is associated with *le Midi* ; and *la porcelaine* is associated with the city of Limoges in *le Limousin*.

Lisons

6-41 Dîner en chaussons ? Méfiez-vous !

A. Avant de lire. In this text, the linguist Henriette Walter explains how some words in French mean different things depending on the region of France in which they are used. Follow the progression of the passage by identifying the main idea of each paragraph; at the end, you should be able to articulate the essential point of Walter's discussion. Follow up by filling in the details with which Walters elaborates upon her main ideas.

B. En lisant. Trouvez la réponse (ou les réponses) à chaque question.

1. Quelle est l'idée principale du premier paragraphe ?
   a. Les Parisiens dînent beaucoup plus tard que les gens de province.
   b. Le fait qu'un mot a des sens différents dans les régions différentes peut avoir des conséquences pratiques.
   c. Les linguistes cherchent toujours à trouver le sens exact d'un mot.

2. Pour Henriette Walter, qui parle correctement — nous, ou les autres ?

3. Selon Henriette Walter, quelle est l'importance des expressions régionales ?
   a. elles permettent de deviner l'origine d'une personne.
   b. elles permettent de sauvegarder des différences culturelles.
   c. elles permettent de signaler que l'on est membre d'une communauté linguistique.

Stratégie

Identify the main idea of each paragraph as you read. This will help you to understand each paragraph's overall content and ultimately the progression and meaning of the passage as a whole.

En lisant, Key: 1) b 2) nous 3) a, c.

Dîner en chaussons ? Méfiez-vous° !

Mais, attention ! Si on vous invite à dîner, ou à souper, sans plus de précisions, vous ne pouvez être sûr de rien, car° si, à Paris, le *dîner* est le repas du soir, nombreuses sont les régions où c'est le repas de midi, celui° du soir étant le *souper*. Comme à Paris, le *souper* se prend beaucoup plus tard dans la nuit, généralement après le spectacle°, il pourrait y avoir des
5 rendez-vous manqués° !

    Enfin, si l'on me parle de *chaussons*, personnellement je comprendrai qu'il s'agit de ces « petites chaussettes tricotées° » que portent les bébés qui ne marchent pas encore », alors que pour la plupart des gens autour de moi, les *chaussons* sont des « pantoufles° de laine, au talon° recouvert ». Ces mêmes personnes, lorsqu'elles veulent parler de ce que j'appelle des *chaussons*
10 (de bébé), emploieront le terme de *bottons*. Et il me faut toujours faire un petit effort sur moi-même pour accepter l'usage, pour moi bizarre, de mes interlocuteurs°. Tant il est vrai qu'en matière de langue, ce sont toujours les autres qui semblent dévier° de la norme.

Les linguistes enquêtent°

L'emploi de mots comme… *dîner* ou *botton* peut évidemment être la source de petits malentendus°. Il peut aussi devenir un indice° permettant° à celui qui l'entend de deviner que
15 telle° personne est originaire de telle localité, ou encore, pour celui qui l'emploie, de l'utiliser comme un signe d'appartenance° à une même communauté linguistique.

Watch out!

parce que
the one
show
missed appointments

knitted slippers; heel

conversational partners to deviate investigate misunderstandings; indicator; allowing such and such belonging

Henriette WALTER. *Le français dans tous les sens.* © Éditions Robert LAFFONT.

C. En regardant de plus près. Maintenant examinez quelques caractéristiques du texte.

1. Complétez le schéma avec les sens différents pour les mots **dîner** et **souper** :

	À Paris	**Dans d'autres régions**
le dîner		
le souper		

2. Et aussi pour les mots **chausson** et **botton** :

	Pour Henriette Walter	**Pour la plupart de ses amis**
des chaussons		
des bottons	XXXXXXXXXX	

D. Après avoir lu. Discutez de ces questions avec vos camarades de classe.

1. En anglais aussi, est-ce qu'il y a des mots et des expressions qui ont des sens différents selon la région ? Est-ce que vous pouvez donner des exemples ?
2. Est-ce que vous employez des mots ou des expressions en anglais qui sont caractéristiques d'une région des États-Unis ? Donnez des exemples à un/e partenaire.

Observons

6-42 Visitons Seillans

A. Avant de regarder. Dans cette séquence vidéo, nous allons « visiter Seillans ». Seillans se trouve dans le Midi de la France, pas très loin de la Côte d'Azur. Regardez la photo de Seillans pour répondre à ces questions.

1. Qui est la personne qui va faire le guide dans la séquence vidéo, à votre avis ?
2. Seillans, c'est un centre urbain, une grande ville ou un petit village ?
3. À votre avis, quels aspects de Seillans est-ce que le guide va nous montrer ?

B. En regardant. Maintenant, regardez la séquence vidéo pour trouver la bonne réponse.

1. Seillans se trouve dans quelle région de la France ?
2. Seillans, c'est un village classé : pourquoi ?
3. À Seillans, vous allez remarquer (cochez les bonnes réponses) :

_____ des belles fontaines   _____ des églises romanes

_____ des villas magnifiques   _____ des collines boisées

_____ des petites places avec   _____ des paysages spectaculaires
           des arbres

4. Quels sont les produits locaux bien appréciés ?

_____ le vin   _____ les olives

_____ la lavande   _____ le coton

C. Après avoir regardé. D'après la description, est-ce que Seillans est un endroit que vous voudriez visiter ? Pourquoi ?

6-43 La ville de...

A. Avant d'écrire. Imaginez que vous préparez une brochure sur une ville de France. D'abord, choisissez une ville qui vous intéresse. Qu'est-ce que vous avez besoin de savoir pour préparer cette brochure ? Regardez la brochure sur Marseille à la page suivante pour avoir des idées et consultez des guides et des vidéos touristiques et des sites Internet pour pouvoir répondre aux questions suivantes :

1. Où se trouve cette ville en France ? (près de la mer ? à côté de Paris ?)
2. Quels sont les sites touristiques les plus intéressants dans cette ville ? Décrivez-les.
3. Quelles activités est-ce qu'on peut y pratiquer ? Est-ce qu'il y a des activités pour les personnes qui aiment le sport, les beaux-arts, l'histoire ?

B. En écrivant. Maintenant, en utilisant toutes ces informations, rédigez un texte (quatre petits paragraphes) qui décrit la ville. N'oubliez pas de donner un titre à votre brochure. Utilisez comme modèle la brochure pour Marseille. Pour élaborer votre projet, vous pouvez ajouter des images (photos, dessins, tableaux) de la ville.

C. Après avoir écrit. Présentez votre ville à vos camarades de classe et essayez de les persuader de la visiter.

Script for *Observons*

Monsieur le
maire de Seillans :   Oui, eh bien, nous sommes dans un vieux village provençal. Euh, Seillans fait partie des 148 plus beaux villages de France. Il a été sélectionné parce qu'il a un patrimoine très ancien, qui a gardé tout son caractère, son authenticité et euh beaucoup de charme. . . .
Ce village comprend aussi euh de nombreuses fontaines, des placettes ombragées. Euh, c'est un village typiquement provençal parce qu'il est perché, sur une colline. Et en cette saison, en automne, on a le plaisir de découvrir des paysages magnifiques. . . . C'est un village provençal aussi qui a son terroir, avec la culture de l'olivier, de la vigne... donc des produits locaux qui sont très appréciés.

Grand-père Roustan : C'est... C'est du vin. C'est du vin de Seillans. Château de Selves.

Avant d'écrire. As an introduction to the writing activity, treat the brochure as a reading. Have students look at the pictures on the cover to get some ideas about where the city is located and what kinds of activities can be done there. Then have them look at the various sub-sections of the brochure and summarize the information that can be gleaned from each part. Ask them what type of additional information they would want to include about the city they will be presenting. Refer students to the *Chez nous* Companion Website for links to cities and regions in France.

Après avoir écrit. As an alternative follow-up, divide the class into two groups: one group staffs "tourist booths" to promote their city; the other group circulates to gain information about each city. Then switch roles.

la nouvelle destination

MARSEILLE

Plan du
Centre

OFFICE DU TOURISME
ET DES CONGRÈS
www.marseille-tourisme.com

Marseille

Lieu d'habitat prédestiné depuis 28 000 ans, Marseille compte près d'un million d'habitants.

Paradis des plongeurs et des plaisanciers, les loisirs se pratiquent ici en pleine nature et toute l'année. Le bleu est sa couleur quotidienne.

À Découvrir, à Visiter

Les Monuments

Abbaye de Saint-Victor Bus 54, 55, 60, 61, 80 81 E5
   Fondée au Ve siècle par Jean Cassien sur la sépulture de Saint-Victor, martyr romain mort au IIIe siècle.

Château d'If (point de vue) Métro 1 Vieux Port + Bateau C6
   Ancienne forteresse construite sous François 1er en 1524... Le roman d'Alexandre Dumas, « le Comte de Monte Cristo » l'a rendu célèbre.

Les Musées

Musée des Beaux Arts Métro 2, Avenue Longchamp ; Bus 81 D3
Musée des Docks Romains Métro 1 Vieux Port D5
Musée d'Histoire de Marseille de Jardin des Vestiges Métro 1 Vieux Port D4

Les Plages

Le Parc Balnéaire du Prado
Métro 1 Castellane + bus 19
– **Plages du Roucas Blanc** (graviers, sable) : Pistes de vélo-cross, jeux d'enfants, jeu de boules, jeu de volley-ball, radeaux et plongeoirs, solarium
– **Plages du David** (galets) : Jeux de sable, 2 solariums
– **Plage des Véliplanchistes** : Réservée aux planches à voile

Parlons

6-44 Un voyage en France

6-44 Add variety to the **Parlons** activity by creating other "characters" or adding further specifications, for example, person A has a broken ankle, person B dislikes going to museums, etc. Have students present their dialogues and/or itineraries to the class.

Imaginez qu'avec deux de vos amis, vous décidez de faire un voyage de quinze jours en France cet été. Mais dans le groupe, il y a des personnalités très différentes :

a. Une personne est très sportive. Il/Elle adore assister à des matchs de tennis et de foot et il/elle aime bien faire de l'alpinisme, du canoë et du kayak.

b. Une personne se spécialise en histoire de l'art. Il/Elle veut visiter tous les musées possibles.

c. Une personne est très pantouflarde. Il/Elle veut faire le moins possible et surtout se détendre au maximum.

A. Avant de parler. Choisissez le rôle que vous allez jouer, et réfléchissez à vos projets préférés. Faites une petite liste des possibilités.

MODÈLE   Éb Il faut s'arrêter d'abord à Paris pour voir les musées et les monuments, par exemple, Le Louvre,…

B. En parlant. En groupes de trois, jouez les rôles. Essayez de persuader vos amis de visiter les sites qui vous intéressent et de faire les activités que vous préférez. Créez un itinéraire qui plaît à tout le monde.

MODÈLE   Éa On s'arrête d'abord à Paris où je peux assister au tournoi de tennis Roland-Garros.

Éb Oui, et quand tu es aux matchs, je visite les musées, par exemple,…

Éc Et moi, je peux m'asseoir à la terrasse d'un café pour regarder les gens.

Éa Et après trois jours, nous allons à…

C. Après avoir parlé. Partagez votre itinéraire avec les autres étudiants. Qui a l'itinéraire le plus intéressant ? Qui visite le plus grand nombre de villes ? Qui fait le plus de kilomètres ?

Le phare de Ploumanach, sur la côte de granit rose en Bretagne

Le château de Castelnaud, au-dessus de la Dordogne en Aquitaine

Vocabulaire

Leçon 1

pour décrire un immeuble	**to describe a building**
un ascenseur	elevator
un bâtiment	building
une cour	courtyard
des escaliers (m.)	staircase, stairs
un étage	floor (of a building)
garer la voiture	to park the car
le rez-de-chaussée	ground floor
le sous-sol	basement
un/e voisin/e	neighbor

pour situer un immeuble	**to situate a building**
un quartier (résidentiel)	(residential) neighborhood
une rue	street
situé/e	located, situated
tranquille	quiet, tranquil

pour parler d'un appartement	**to talk about an apartment**
un balcon	balcony
une chambre	bedroom
les charges (f.)	utilities
un cinq-pièces	3-bedroom apartment with living room and dining room
un couloir	hallway
une cuisine	kitchen
donner sur	to look onto or lead out to
une entrée	entrance, foyer
un/e locataire	renter
louer	to rent
le loyer	the rent
un/une propriétaire	homeowner; landlord/landlady
une salle à manger	dining room
une salle de bains	bathroom
un séjour, une salle de séjour	living room
un studio	studio apartment
une terrasse	terrace

des toilettes (f.), des W.-C. (m.)	toilet, water closet

verbes en -ir comme choisir	**verbs ending in -ir like choisir**
choisir	to choose
désobéir à	to disobey
finir	to finish
grandir	to grow taller, to grow up (for children)
grossir	to gain weight
maigrir	to lose weight
obéir à	to obey
pâlir	to become pale
punir	to punish
réfléchir à	to think
réussir à	to succeed/to pass
rougir	to blush

autres mots utiles	**other useful words**
chaque	each
maigre	thin, skinny
même	even
pâle	pale
propre	own

à quel étage ?		**on what floor?**
RdeCh	rez-de-chaussée	ground floor
1er	premier	first
2^e	deuxième	second
3^e	troisième	third
10^e	dixième	tenth
11^e	onzième	eleventh
12^e	douzième	twelfth
13^e	treizième	thirteenth
19^e	dix-neuvième	nineteenth
20^e	vingtième	twentieth
21^e	vingt et unième	twenty-first

Leçon 2

des meubles (m.)	**furniture**
une armoire	armoire, wardrobe
un canapé	couch

une cuisinière	stove		
un évier	sink		
un fauteuil	armchair		
un four	oven		
une lampe	lamp		
un lit	bed		
des placards (m.)	cupboards, kitchen cabinets		
un réfrigérateur	refrigerator		
des rideaux (m.)	curtains		
une table basse	coffee table		
un tapis	rug		

verbes de transfert — *verbs of transfer*

apporter	to bring
emprunter	to borrow
offrir (un cadeau)	to give (a gift)
prêter	to lend
remettre	to hand in/over

pour décrire un appartement ou un meuble — *to describe an apartment or a piece of furniture*

abîmé/e	worn, worn-out
agréable	pleasant
ancien/ne	old, antique
le centre-ville	downtown
chic	stylish
avec coin cuisine	with a kitchenette
confortable	comfortable (said of objects or places)
équipé/e	equipped
meublé/e	furnished
moderne	modern
un mur	wall
neuf/neuve	brand new
par terre	on the floor
pratique	practical
rénové/e	renovated
sous les toits	in the attic
sous	under
sur	on top of
le toit	roof

autres mots utiles — *other useful words*

des affaires (f.)	belongings, things
ranger	to put up, to put away
seulement	only
surtout	above all

verbes de communication — *verbs of communication*

demander	to ask
expliquer	to explain

Leçon 3

la vie à la campagne — *life in the country*

se détendre	to relax
une ferme	farm
un jardin	garden, yard
un potager	vegetable garden
une villa	house in a residential area, villa

la nature — *nature*

un arbre (fruitier)	(fruit) tree
un bateau (à voile)	(sail) boat
un bois	woods
un champ	field
une colline	hill
une forêt	forest
un lac	lake
une rivière	large stream or river (tributary)
une vallée	valley

quelques mots utiles — *some useful words*

au bord (du lac)	on the shore (of the lake)
un endroit	place
en effet	yes, indeed
formidable	great
il me semble	it seems to me
là(-bas)	there
s'occuper de	to take care of
posséder	to own

pour parler des activités habituelles dans le passé — *to talk about habituel activities in the past*

d'habitude	usually
le lundi	every Monday, on Mondays
le week-end	on weekends, every weekend

Quels sont les rapports entre les personnes ici ? Pour quelle occasion est-ce qu'elles se réunissent ?

Chapitre *7*

Les relations personnelles

Venez chez nous !
Les rituels

In this chapter:

- Describing and narrating past events
- Reporting what others say and write
- Expressing opinions
- Expressing emotions
- Understanding rites and rituals in the Francophone world

Leçon 1 *Les jeunes et la vie*

Additional practice activities for each **Points de départ** section are provided by:
- Student Activities Manual
- *Chez nous* Companion Website: **http://www.prenhall.com/cheznous**

POINTS DE DÉPART

Les jeunes parlent

TEXT AUDIO

Des jeunes se prononcent sur les racines et la famille :

Mes parents ont divorcé quand j'avais cinq ans, et j'ai ressenti l'absence de mon père. Heureusement, mon grand-père était là. Ancien professeur des écoles, il m'a appris à aimer les livres, en particulier les livres d'histoire. Ma mère était toujours très autoritaire, très exigeante — et moi, j'étais un enfant rebelle.
Pierre, 22 ans, étudiant en histoire

Je fais partie d'une famille assez « traditionnelle » : mon père travaille et ma mère, c'est une femme au foyer. J'ai des bons rapports avec mes parents. Ils m'ont donné une morale, une vision du monde, le goût du travail et une présence très sécurisante. Je suis bien dans ma peau.
Sarah, 18 ans, bachelière

Je suis franco-marocaine. J'ai commencé par refuser mes racines maghrébines, mais après j'ai compris que ces racines multiples (arabes, juives, françaises) sont une richesse fabuleuse. Par exemple, je ne suis pas vraiment pratiquante, mais je ne rate jamais le ramadan. Ce n'est pas une pratique imposée par ma famille, mais c'est une épreuve personnelle qui me permet de réfléchir, d'avancer dans la connaissance de ma personne.

Être français, ce n'est pas se couler dans le moule (*to pour oneself into the mold*) de la culture dominante. Tous avec nos racines, nous pouvons participer aux changements de la culture française et européenne.
Alima, 27 ans, jeune professionnelle

POUR PARLER DE LA FAMILLE

un père/une mère célibataire
un homme/une femme au foyer
un père/une mère absent/e
une famille monoparentale/recomposée/étendue
un beau-père, une belle-mère, un beau-frère, une belle-sœur,
   les demi-frères et sœurs
être autoritaire   exigeant/e   indulgent/e   rebelle   bien dans sa peau
avoir des bons rapports avec quelqu'un   avoir des racines multiculturelles

The quotes provide students with models for talking about their own experiences, interests and concerns. Display the quotes and read them aloud to the class, discussing as you go. Review the term *baccalauréat*, and relate it to *bachelière*. Point out that when *ancien* precedes the noun, it means "former." Also point out the expression *m'a appris à* and tell students that *apprendre* can be used to mean "to learn" and "to teach someone something" (*apprendre à quelqu'un à...*). Check students' comprehension of the following expressions by having them provide a paraphrase: *être autoritaire = dire aux autres ce qu'ils doivent faire ; être une femme au foyer = une femme qui ne travaille pas hors de la maison ; avoir des bons rapports avec quelqu'un = bien s'entendre avec quelqu'un ; avoir le goût du travail = être travailleur/travailleuse ; être bien dans sa peau = avoir confiance en soi.* Using Ex. 7-1, have students provide definitions/explanations in French for the vocabulary highlighted in the box. Incorporate information from **Vie et culture**. Ask students whether they can identify with the ideas expressed by any of the young people quoted here.

Vie et culture

Use this text in conjunction with the vocabulary presentation and ask students to define the various terms included here (see Ex. 7-1). Help students link *pacsé* to *un pacs* (*Pacte civile de solidarité*) which was presented in the *Venez chez nous* in Ch. 1. The main ideas of the text are expressed through the statistics: ask students to explain the meaning of each one. You might compare *la Sofres* to a national polling organization such as Gallup. Point out the verb *vivre* and remind students that it refers to personal and quality-of-life considerations (*Ils vivent ensemble*) while *habiter* refers to physical location (*J'habite Paris*). The full conjugation for *vivre* is provided in Appendix 4. The video clip *Une famille, style marocain* features a young Moroccan woman living in Nice who describes her family in France and in Morocco.

La famille à la carte

Qu'est-ce qu'une « famille » ? Avec ou sans enfants ? Deux parents, un seul, davantage[1] ? De quel sexe ? Nos idées sur la famille évoluent, et le vocabulaire le signale : on parle de familles monoparentales, de pères et de mères célibataires, de mères travailleuses et de pères absents, de familles recomposées, d'unions libres et de couples pacsés. En fait, le mariage « traditionnel », où la femme reste au foyer, est un phénomène devenu assez rare en France aujourd'hui : 80 % des Françaises de 25 à 49 ans travaillent. Et au lieu de[2] se marier, 17 % des couples en France choisissent de vivre ensemble en « union libre », c'est trois fois plus qu'il y a vingt ans. À votre avis, est-ce que le mariage « traditionnel » est aussi rare en Amérique du nord qu'en France ? Justifiez votre réponse.

Le langage des jeunes

C'est Jean-Paul Sartre qui a dit, « Il n'y a pas de sentiment plus communément partagé[3] que de vouloir être différent des autres ». C'est peut-être la devise[4] des jeunes, qui veulent se distinguer par leurs vêtements, leur musique et surtout par leur langage. Comment décrire le langage des jeunes Français ? La difficulté, c'est qu'il est toujours en train de changer. Voici quelques expressions courantes pour parler de ce qui est « bon » et de ce qui est « mauvais » :

bon : C'est génial, cool, top, super.

mauvais : C'est nul, pourri, naze.

Le **verlan** est un jeu langagier créé par des jeunes. En verlan, on forme des mots en inversant les syllabes, par exemple, **branché** (**à la mode**) devient **chébran**.

[1]plus   [2]instead of   [3]shared   [4]motto

Use the Sartre quote as a springboard for discussion of how young people strive to be different. In the examples provided, note the use of English borrowings. Students can provide similar examples from their native language. Point out that advertisers make great use of slang expressions in order to appeal to young people. Explain that the *verlan* term *les Beurs* refers to young people of Arab origin, born in France.

Est-ce que vous pouvez trouver l'équivalent en verlan des expressions suivantes ?

en français	en verlan
branché	tromé
laisse tomber (arrête)	chébran
pourri	Beur
Arabe	laisse béton
femme	ripou
métro	meuf

(branché → chébran indicated by arrow)

Et vous ?

Recently, rap and hip-hop music have been sources for new slang expressions in English; so have technological changes such as instant messaging.

1. Est-ce que les jeunes aux États-Unis ont un langage spécifique ? En quoi est-ce qu'il diffère de la langue ordinaire ?

2. En France, quelques expressions en verlan et d'autres mots argotiques sont passés dans la langue courante et sont utilisés par tout le monde. Par exemple, on dit un **boulot** (*expression familière*) pour un **travail**. Est-ce que vous pouvez trouver des exemples en anglais de ce même phénomène ?

According to the 2000 U.S. Census, the majority of households consist of married couples (52%). The number of unmarried couples increased substantially from the 1990 census (from 3.2 to 5.5 million), but still represents only about 5% of the total number of households surveyed.

À vous la parole

7-1 Définitions. Trouvez une définition pour chaque expression.

7-1 This exercise should be completed as the vocabulary is introduced.

MODÈLE   une mère célibataire

➤ C'est une mère qui n'a pas de partenaire.

1. une mère célibataire
2. un homme au foyer
3. la famille étendue
4. un père absent
5. une famille monoparentale
6. une famille recomposée
7. l'union libre

a. un couple qui vit ensemble sans être marié
b. un père qui n'habite pas avec ses enfants
c. une famille avec un seul parent
d. une famille avec des demi-frères ou sœurs
e. une mère qui n'a pas de partenaire
f. les parents, les grands-parents, les cousins…
g. un père qui reste à la maison et s'occupe de ses enfants

7-2 D'accord ou pas d'accord ? Est-ce que vous êtes d'accord avec les assertions suivantes ? Parlez-en avec un/e partenaire et expliquez votre réponse.

After completing Ex. 7-2, ask the class as a whole whether they agree or disagree with each statement.

For additional practice, use the following pair activity. To follow up, have students compare answers with the whole class.
Cause probable. Avec un/e partenaire, expliquez comment on est probablement arrivé à la situation décrite.
MODÈLE   Fatima n'est pas pratiquante.
É1   Peut-être qu'elle a refusé ses racines.
É2   Ou peut-être que ses parents n'ont pas imposé leurs pratiques religieuses.
1. Lucie est bien dans sa peau.
2. Laurent a été un enfant rebelle.
3. C'est sa mère qui a dû exercer l'autorité parentale.
4. Nathalie fait partie d'une famille recomposée.
5. Sandrine a le goût du travail.
6. Hervé fait partie d'une famille traditionnelle.
7. Hélène a ressenti l'absence de son père.

MODÈLE   Grandir dans une famille monoparentale, c'est une tragédie pour l'enfant.

É1   Si la famille étendue est là, ce n'est pas une tragédie.

É2   Voilà, et les amis peuvent aider la famille aussi. Donc, on n'est pas d'accord.

1. La famille exerce très peu d'influence sur les jeunes.
2. On apprécie toujours des parents autoritaires.
3. Les racines multiples, c'est une richesse.
4. Les jeunes veulent toujours se distinguer des parents.
5. Une femme au foyer, c'est mieux pour les enfants.
6. Être français, c'est s'assimiler à la culture dominante.
7. Le divorce n'a pas d'impact sur les enfants.

7-3 Et vous ? Avec un/e partenaire, complétez les phrases suivantes selon votre propre expérience.

MODÈLE   Mes parents m'ont appris…

É1   Mes parents m'ont appris à aimer la musique classique.

É2   Et moi, mon père m'a appris à apprécier la nature.

1. Mes parents m'ont appris…
2. J'étais un enfant…
3. Ma famille, c'est une famille…
4. J'ai des bons rapports avec…
5. Mon rêve (dream), c'est de…
6. Je suis bien dans ma peau parce que…

Stress the importance of a clear release of the final consonant in the third-person plural: *écrit* vs. *écrivent*; *lit* vs. *lisent*; *dit* vs. *disent*; point out the irregular form *dites*, and ask students what other verbs they know show this irregularity (*être/êtes* ; *faire/faites*).

FORMES ET FONCTIONS

1. *Les verbes de communication* écrire, lire *et* dire

- Here are three useful verbs of communication: **écrire**, *to write*; **lire**, *to read*; **dire**, *to say*, *to tell*.

SINGULIER		PLURIEL	
je/j'	écris	nous	écriv**ons**
	lis		lis**ons**
	dis		dis**ons**
tu	écris	vous	écriv**ez**
	lis		lis**ez**
	dis		**dites**
il	écrit	ils	écriv**ent**
elle }	lit		lis**ent**
on	dit	elles }	dis**ent**

IMPÉRATIF :	Écris !	Écrivez !	Écrivons !
	Lis !	Lisez !	Lisons !
	Dis !	**Dites** !	Disons !
PASSÉ COMPOSÉ :	il a **écrit**	il a **lu**	il a **dit**

- **Décrire**, *to describe*, is conjugated like **écrire**.

- All these verbs may take direct and indirect objects.

J'écris **une lettre à mes parents**.	*I'm writing a letter to my parents.*
Tu **leur** dis **bonjour** de ma part ?	*Will you say hello to them for me?*
Tu **lui** as écrit ?	*Did you write to him?*
Décris **ton cousin à Gabriel**.	*Describe your cousin to Gabriel.*
Vous écrivez **votre rapport** pour demain ?	*Are you writing your report for tomorrow?*
Elles disent toujours **la vérité**.	*They always tell the truth.*
Elle lit **ses poèmes à ses amis**, mais elle ne **les** lit pas **à ses parents**.	*She reads her poems to her friends, but she doesn't read them to her parents.*

À vous la parole

7-4 Étudiants étrangers.
Tout le monde est d'accord ! Comment est-ce que ces étudiants disent « oui » ? Choisissez un mot de la liste : **oui**, **da**, **ja**, **sì**, **sí**, **yes**

MODÈLE   Maria est espagnole.
>   ➤ Elle dit « sí ».

1. Peter et Helmut sont allemands.
2. Louis-Jean est haïtien.
3. Moi, je suis russe.
4. Isabel est mexicaine.
5. Michèle et moi, nous sommes belges.
6. Toi, tu es américaine.
7. Georges et toi, vous êtes suisses.
8. Alan, il est anglais.

Begin practice with a discrimination drill, singular vs. plural, for all three verbs. One person, or more? *Ils disent bonjour ; Elle lit le journal ; Il écrit une lettre ; Ils lisent beaucoup ; Elle ne dit pas grand-chose ; Elles écrivent bien ; Ils disent toujours « oui » ; Il lit des articles ; Elles lisent un magazine ;* etc. Follow with substitution drills: *Elle écrit une lettre ; nous —Nous écrivons une lettre,* etc.

7-4, Key: 1) *ja* 2) *oui* 3) *da* 4) *sí* 5) *oui* 6) *yes* 7) *ja, oui, si* 8) *yes*

7-5 Qu'est-ce qu'ils écrivent ?
Choisissez dans la liste ce qu'écrivent ces jeunes gens.

MODÈLE   Marc travaille pour le journal de l'université.
>   ➤ Il écrit des articles.

des articles	des critiques	des recettes (*recipes*)	des essais
des lettres	des poèmes	des programmes	

1. Anne et moi, nous étudions l'informatique.
2. Geoffrey et toi, vous êtes bons correspondants.
3. Je suis étudiant en littérature.
4. Laetitia aime faire la cuisine.
5. Jessica et Florian sont poètes.
6. Tu travailles pour un magazine.
7. Adrien va souvent au théâtre.

7-5 The verb *lire* does not have its own exercise here but you could expand on Ex. 7-5 by asking students what these people read (e.g., #1, *Nous écrivons des programmes et nous lisons des livres d'informatique*). The verb *lire* will be recycled in Ch. 11, L. 2 with the presentation of various reading materials.

7-6 Sondage.
Trouvez une personne qui…

MODÈLE   lit le journal tous les jours

>   É1 Est-ce que tu lis le journal tous les jours ?
>   É2 Oui, je lis le *New York Times*.
>   OU Non, je ne lis pas le journal, je regarde les infos à la télé.

1. lit le journal tous les jours
2. écrit à ses parents
3. dit toujours la vérité (*truth*)
4. écrit pour le journal de l'université
5. a lu au moins un roman (*novel*) cette année
6. va préparer un mémoire (*thesis*) ce semestre
7. veut nous dire quel est son âge
8. a déjà écrit une lettre dans une langue étrangère

7-6 Use as a mixing activity. Tell students to ask no more than two questions per person before moving on to another student. Limit time, and follow up by having students ask questions about the items they did not find. Synthesize the information gathered: how many people read a newspaper every day? How often do students write to their parents? What was the hardest category to get a positive response for?, etc.

2. Imparfait et passé composé : description et narration

Review the forms and uses of the *passé composé* and the *imparfait* before introducing this topic. This section contrasting the two tenses focuses on the functions of description and narration; the terms "background" and "foreground" can also be used. Have students study the examples in the second bulleted point to decide whether they involve description or narration; for visual impact, you might divide these examples into two columns.

Both the **passé composé** and the **imparfait** express past actions and states. They serve different functions in a narrative, however.

- The **passé composé** indicates that an event in the past has been completed. In a story or narrative, the **passé composé** is used to recount actions or events that move the story forward. In other words, the **passé composé** advances the plot; it answers the question, *What happened?*

Bruno **a terminé** ses études en juin.	*Bruno finished his studies in June.*
Il **a quitté** la fac.	*He left the university.*

- In contrast, the **imparfait** provides background information. It describes the setting or situation and answers the questions: *What were the circumstances? What was going on?*

Compare the following examples.

Il **était** fatigué.	*He was tired.*
Il **voulait** prendre des vacances.	*He wanted to take a vacation.*
Mais il n'**avait** pas d'argent.	*But he didn't have any money.*
Il **devait** trouver un emploi.	*He needed to find work.*
Alors il **a lu** les petites annonces.	*So he read the newspaper ads.*
Et il **a écrit** des lettres.	*And he wrote letters.*
Enfin, un jour, il **a eu** une réponse.	*Finally one day he got a response.*
Il **était** très heureux.	*He was very happy.*

You might point out that when the verbs listed here are used in the *passé composé*, they tend to have a distinctive meaning: *Elle a eu dix ans* = She turned ten (celebrated her tenth birthday). Also, point out that *faire* is generally used in the *imparfait* for weather expressions. In other expressions (*faire du sport, faire des courses*) it is frequently used in the *passé composé*.

- Use the **imparfait** to describe time, weather, ongoing actions, physical characteristics, psychological states and feelings, intentions, and thoughts. The following verbs, when used in the past, will more often appear in the **imparfait**.

avoir	Elle **avait** vingt ans en 2002.
devoir	Elle **devait** travailler comme serveuse.
être	Ils **étaient** contents de terminer leurs études.
faire	Il **faisait** froid. (*in weather expressions*)
penser	Je **pensais** qu'elle avait des bons rapports avec ses parents.
pouvoir	Ils ne **pouvaient** pas trouver d'emploi.
vouloir	Il ne **voulait** pas travailler dans un bureau.

À vous la parole

7-7 Des excuses. Pourquoi est-ce que ces gens ne sont pas venus en classe ? Expliquez la situation ou l'événement, selon le cas.

MODÈLE   Vanessa : elle / être malade
➤ Vanessa n'est pas venue parce qu'elle était malade.

David : il / tomber dans les escaliers
➤ David n'est pas venu parce qu'il est tombé dans les escaliers.

1. Ben : sa mère / téléphoner
2. Adrien : il / rater l'autobus
3. Marie : elle / dormir
4. Guillaume : son chien / manger ses devoirs
5. Annick : elle / préparer un examen
6. Grégory : il / travailler à la bibliothèque
7. Claire : elle / avoir un accident
8. Koffi : il / devoir terminer un rapport

7-7 Students have seen the past participle of *venir* in Ch. 5, L. 2. The full conjugation will be presented in Ch. 9, L. 2.
Key: 1) *lui a téléphoné* 2) *a raté* 3) *dormait* 4) *a mangé* 5) *préparait* 6) *travaillait* 7) *a eu* 8) *devait terminer.*
After completing Ex. 7-7, have students give you their own excuses for not coming to class, not doing their homework, etc.

7-8 Un accident de voiture. Racontez cette histoire au passé ; employez le passé composé ou l'imparfait, selon le cas.

MODÈLE   Il est huit heures du soir.
➤ Il était huit heures du soir.

1. Il fait très froid.
2. Il y a du verglas sur la route.
3. Je vais un peu vite (*fast*).
4. Soudain, une autre voiture passe devant moi.
5. J'essaie de m'arrêter, mais je ne peux pas.
6. Je heurte (*hit*) l'autre voiture.
7. Deux hommes sortent de cette voiture.
8. Ils ne sont pas contents.
9. Mais moi, je suis content parce que personne n'est blessé (*injured*).
10. Je téléphone à la police.
11. Ils arrivent tout de suite après.

7-8, Key: 1) *faisait* 2) *avait* 3) *allais* 4) *est passée* 5) *j'ai essayé, ne pouvais pas* 6) *j'ai heurté* 7) *sont sortis* 8) *n'étaient pas* 9) *j'étais, n'a été blessé* 10) *j'ai téléphoné* 11) *sont arrivés.*

7-9 Racontez une histoire. Racontez la journée d'Adrien d'après les dessins et en utilisant les mots-clés.

MODÈLE ➤ Hier, c'était samedi. Adrien s'est réveillé à huit heures, etc.

être samedi, se réveiller, faire beau, ne pas avoir cours

être à table, le téléphone/sonner, être Julie, vouloir jouer, dire oui

l'après-midi, faire chaud, jouer au tennis, tomber, être anxieuse

aller à l'hôpital, le médecin / dire / ne pas être sérieux

Maintenant, racontez votre journée d'hier à un/e partenaire.

7-10 Vérifier des alibis. Le gâteau d'anniversaire du professeur a été volé (*stolen*) entre midi et treize heures ! Avec un/e partenaire, préparez un alibi. Mettez-vous d'accord sur tous les détails. Attention ! Vos camarades de classe vont vous séparer et ensuite essayer de détruire votre alibi en vous posant des questions très détaillées !

MODÈLES É1 Où étiez-vous hier à midi ?
É2 Mon copain et moi, nous étions au gymnase.
É3 Qu'est-ce que vous faisiez ?
É2 Moi, je jouais au basket et lui aussi.

7-11 Je suis cadien

A. Avant de lire. The title of this poem, *Je suis cadien*, gives you essential information about the identity of the poet, Barry Ancelet (who takes the pen name Jean Arceneaux). He speaks **le français cadien**, and he is a descendent of French speakers who fled to Louisiana in the eighteenth century from the Canadian province of **Acadie** after refusing allegiance to the British crown. Since the poet has announced his Cajun French identity at the outset, are you surprised, looking at the first lines of his poem, to see that they are in English? Why do you think the poem is written in two languages, French and English? Can you put yourself in the poet's place, identifying with his feelings as a Louisiana schoolboy? What message do you think he will attempt to convey?

Voici le poète, Barry Ancelet. Pourquoi, à votre avis, est-ce qu'il est habillé ainsi ?

B. En lisant. Le poète exprime les pensées et les émotions d'un enfant cadien qui va à l'école publique en Louisiane. En lisant un extrait de ce poème, répondez aux questions suivantes.

1. Pourquoi est-ce que le poète répète la première phrase plusieurs fois ? À quelle punition pendant « leur temps de recess » est-ce qu'il fait référence ?
2. Le poète écrit, au vers 9, « Ça fait mal ; ça fait honte ». Quelle situation est-ce qu'il décrit ?
3. Dans les vers 25 à 42, on explique à l'enfant pourquoi il doit parler anglais. Est-ce que vous pouvez résumer les arguments ?
4. L'enfant n'est pas convaincu. Comment est-ce que les derniers vers (52 à 57) montrent cela ?

JE SUIS CADIEN (*extrait*)

I will not speak French on the school grounds.
I will not speak French on the school grounds.
I will not speak French…
I will not speak French…
I will not speak French…   5

bastards	Hé ! Ils sont pas bêtes, ces salauds.°
	Après mille fois, ça commence à pénétrer
anybody's head	Dans n'importe quel esprit.°
makes you ashamed	Ça fait mal ; ça fait honte.°
	Et on ne speak pas French on the school grounds 10
	Et ni anywhere else non plus.
	Jamais avec des étrangers.
You never know	On sait jamais° qui a l'autorité
damned	De faire écrire ces sacrées° lignes
	À n'importe quel âge. 15
	Surtout pas avec les enfants.
	Faut jamais que eux, ils passent leur temps de recess
	À écrire ces sacrées lignes.
	I will not speak French on the school grounds.
	I will not speak French on the school grounds. 20
They shouldn't have to	Faut pas qu'ils aient besoin° d'écrire ça
	Parce qu'il faut pas qu'ils parlent français du tout.
It shows; nothing but	Ça laisse voir° qu'on est rien que° des Cadiens.
	Don't mind us, we're just poor coonasses,
gotta hide it	Basse classe, faut cacher ça°. 25
	Faut dépasser ça.
	Faut parler en anglais.
	Faut regarder la télévision en anglais.
	Faut écouter la radio en anglais
	Comme de bons Américains. 30
	Why not just go ahead and learn English,
	Don't fight it, it's much easier anyway,
	No bilingual bills, no bilingual publicity.
	No danger of internal frontiers.
	Enseignez l'anglais aux enfants. 35
Take them all the way	Rendez-les tout le long°,
	Tout le long jusqu'aux discos,
	Jusqu'au Million Dollar Man.
anyway	On a pas réellement besoin de parler français quand même°.
	C'est les États-Unis ici. 40
	Land of the Free.
will always be	On restera toujours° rien que des poor coonasses.
	I will not speak French on the school grounds.
	I will not speak French on the school grounds.
that doesn't bother us	Coonass, non, non, ça gêne pas°. 45
	C'est juste un petit nom.
	Ça veut rien dire.
	C'est pour s'amuser, ça gêne pas.

On aime ça, c'est cute.

50 Ça nous fait pas fâchés°. *That doesn't make us mad.*

Ça nous fait rire°. *laugh*

Mais quand on doit rire, c'est en quelle langue qu'on rit ?

Et pour pleurer°, c'est en quelle langue qu'on pleure ? *cry*

Et pour crier ?

55 Et chanter ?

Et aimer ?

Et vivre ?

—Jean Arceneaux, de "Je suis Cadien," *Suite du loup*,
Éditions Perce-Neige, 1998.

C. En regardant de plus près.

Le poète permet au lecteur (*reader*) de s'identifier avec l'enfant cajun.

1. Pourquoi est-ce que le poème mélange (*mix*) l'anglais et le français ?
2. Dans le texte, on utilise un nom péjoratif : quelle est la réaction de l'enfant quand il entend ce nom ? Quelle est votre réaction quand vous le lisez ? Quelle réaction est-ce que le poète cherche, à votre avis ?
3. Le poème finit par une série de questions ; quel est l'effet de ces questions sur le lecteur ?

D. Après avoir lu.

Discutez de ces questions avec vos camarades de classe.

1. Est-ce que vous pouvez vous identifier avec le point de vue et les émotions exprimés dans ce poème ? Pourquoi ?
2. Est-ce que vous connaissez un peu l'histoire des immigrés en Amérique du Nord ? Est-ce que l'expérience de l'enfant cajun ressemble à l'expérience d'autres groupes d'immigrés, ou non ?

En regardant de plus près, Key: 1) it highlights the differing points of view of the Cajun and English speakers 2) he tries to laugh it off and pretend that it doesn't hurt him or make him angry; for the reader, it has a shock effect, which is likely the intent of the writer; other ethnically derogatory names could be substituted with the same effect 3) the poet conveys the idea that his language is inextricably linked to his identity and his way of life.

Après avoir lu. You might share your own cultural heritage with students, and ask: Does your family or your community recognize a particular cultural heritage? Do members make an effort to learn about and honor their cultural roots? In what ways do they do this?

Le quartier français à la Nouvelle Orléans.

Use the photographs to tell the story of important events in Sophie's life. Point out cultural information conveyed by the photos and captions: Catholic customs and holidays, the civil and religious wedding ceremonies. Include information contained in the **Vie et culture** notes. Encourage cross-cultural comparison by asking what major childhood events students' own family albums contain that are not pictured here. Some examples might include: first day of school, graduation, prom. Test comprehension by having students point to the event you describe; tell the date of Sophie's birthday and of their own birthday. Have students repeat key words.

Leçon 2 · Les grands événements de la vie

POINTS DE DÉPART

Les grands événements

TEXT AUDIO

La mère de Sophie regarde son album de photos.

Le 9 mai 1980, Sophie est née : elle était adorable !

Voilà Sophie à son baptême, avec sa marraine et son parrain.

Le jour de Noël 1982 ; Sophie avait 2 ans. Que de cadeaux !

C'était l'anniversaire de Sophie : 6 bougies sur le gâteau !

L'été 1995, Sophie a passé les grandes vacances à la plage avec son amie Virginie.

Le mariage de Sophie et Arnaud. La cérémonie civile a eu lieu à la mairie et ensuite la cérémonie religieuse, à l'église : la mariée était en blanc, le marié en smoking !

To treat the **Vie et culture**, create a chart to summarize the holidays, with the following columns for students to fill in: *Nom de la fête ; Date ; Activités spécifiques*. Let students add in American holidays (Halloween, Thanksgiving, and 4th of July, for example), then discuss similarities and differences. You may also wish to show the opening montage for **Venez chez nous !** (*Les rituels*), which features various national and religious holidays and rituals. See if students can match the various events they see on the video to the holidays and events mentioned here. Several active vocabulary words are introduced here. Be sure to point out:

Vie et culture

Les fêtes religieuses et officielles

Beaucoup de jours fériés en France sont des fêtes traditionnelles catholiques et la majorité des autres sont des fêtes nationales.

Noël est la plus grande fête de l'année. On décore le sapin (l'arbre de Noël) et l'on échange des cadeaux. Le soir du 24 décembre (pour certains c'est après la messe de minuit), on se réunit[1] pour un grand repas[2], le réveillon.

Le jour de l'An est précédé par le réveillon de la Saint-Sylvestre, la nuit du 31 décembre.

Le jour des Rois (l'Épiphanie) a lieu le 6 janvier. On partage un gâteau, la galette des rois, dans lequel on a caché la fève — un petit personnage en plastique ou en céramique. La personne qui trouve la fève dans sa part de galette est nommée le roi ou la reine[3] et porte une couronne en papier.

La Chandeleur, c'est le 2 février. Traditionnellement on mange des crêpes. Si vous faites sauter[4] une crêpe et si elle retombe dans la poêle[5], vous allez avoir de la chance toute l'année.

Pâques. Cette fête célèbre la résurrection du Christ. On offre aux enfants des œufs et des poules[6] en chocolat. Les enfants cherchent dans le jardin ou dans la maison les œufs cachés par leurs parents.

La fête du Travail. Le premier mai les ouvriers organisent des défilés et on offre un brin de muguet aux membres de sa famille.

[1]*gather together* [2]*meal* [3]*king or queen* [4]*flip* [5]*frying pan*
[6]*hens*

La fête nationale. Cette grande fête célèbre la prise de la Bastille et le début de la Révolution le 14 juillet 1789. Le soir, toutes les villes et les quartiers des grandes villes organisent un bal populaire et l'on tire un feu d'artifice. Le matin, les Parisiens peuvent assister au grand défilé militaire sur les Champs-Élysées, retransmis en direct à la télévision.

La Toussaint. Le 1er novembre, on honore les morts de la famille en mettant des fleurs, surtout des chrysanthèmes, sur leur tombe.

Et vous ?

1. Est-ce que vous célébrez certaines de ces fêtes dans votre région ? Est-ce que vos traditions sont différentes des traditions des Français ? Expliquez pourquoi.
2. Quelles fêtes nord-américaines n'ont pas d'équivalent en France ? Pourquoi ? À votre avis, est-ce que les fêtes nationales sont plus importantes chez vous que chez les Français ? Et les fêtes religieuses ?

jour férié, sapin, partager, galette, cacher, œuf en chocolat, brin de muguet, bal populaire, feu d'artifice, défilé, fleur. Students will need to recognize these words to complete the exercises and will find them useful to talk about holidays in general. Note that captions have not been provided for the photos here; encourage students to identify the holiday illustrated in each photo: *Pâques, le premier mai, la Chandeleur.*

You might suggest that students get more information about unfamiliar holidays that interest them by looking them up on the Internet and reporting to the class.

You might also put students into small groups to discuss a) their favorite holiday and how they celebrate it; b) the most significant holiday for North Americans, and why. Survey the class as a whole to find how many students described a birthday, family vacation, etc.

LEÇON 2 ◆ LES GRANDS ÉVÉNEMENTS DE LA VIE *deux cent soixante-dix-sept* **277**

LES VŒUX

Meilleurs vœux !	*Best wishes!*	Bonne année !	*Happy New Year!*
Félicitations !	*Congratulations!*	Bon voyage !	*Have a good trip!*
Bon/Joyeux anniversaire !	*Happy Birthday!*	Bonnes vacances !	*Have a good vacation!*
Joyeux Noël !	*Merry Christmas!*		

À vous la parole

7-12 Recycle forms of *dire* by suggesting a different subject for each item: *Vos amis ont eu un enfant ; vous. — Vous dites, « Félicitations ! »*

7-12 Qu'est-ce qu'on dit ? Qu'est-ce que vous dites dans les situations suivantes ?

MODÈLE   C'est l'anniversaire de votre mère.

➤ Je dis, « Bon anniversaire, maman ! »

1. Vos amis ont eu un enfant.
2. C'est le 25 décembre.
3. C'est la Saint-Sylvestre.
4. Vous assistez à un mariage.
5. Votre ami fête ses 20 ans.
6. Vos parents fêtent leurs 25 ans de mariage.
7. C'est le jour de l'An.
8. Vos cousins partent en voyage.

7-13 Since multiple responses are possible, you might have each group make a list and compare answers at the end. The video montage (*Les rituels*) for **Venez chez nous !** could accompany Ex. 7-13, since many of the items listed can be seen in the clip.

7-13 Jeu d'association. À quelle occasion est-ce que vous associez ces choses ou ces personnes ? Parlez-en avec un/e partenaire.

MODÈLE   un voyage

É1 Ce sont les grandes vacances.

É2 C'est un mariage.

1. un gâteau
2. des cadeaux
3. un document officiel
4. un grand dîner
5. un défilé militaire
6. des fleurs
7. la marraine
8. le maire (*mayor*)
9. le prêtre (*priest*), le pasteur, le rabbin, l'imam
10. un bébé

7-14 Tous les éléments. Quels sont les éléments importants pour une fête ? Avec un/e partenaire, décrivez une fête d'après les éléments suivants : **l'endroit, les gens importants, les vêtements/les accessoires, les activités**

MODÈLE   un anniversaire

É1 On peut fêter un anniversaire à la maison ou dans un restaurant, par exemple.

É2 Normalement, la famille et les amis sont présents. Il y a presque toujours un gâteau avec des bougies.

É1 Oui, on chante et on offre des cadeaux.

1. Noël
2. un mariage
3. un baptême
4. la fête nationale
5. les grandes vacances

Sons et lettres

La semi-voyelle /j/

When the letter **i** immediately precedes a vowel sound, it is pronounced /j/, as in the English word *yes*. It forms a single syllable with the following vowel. Compare:

le ma**ri** / le ma**rié**   étud**ie** / étud**iez**   boug**ie** / chang**iez**

Note that when **i** is preceded by a group of consonants and followed by a vowel sound, it is pronounced /i/ and forms a separate syllable. Compare:

le l**ien** / le cl**i**-ent   b**ien** / ou-bl**i**-er

The letter **y** is often pronounced /j/:

jo**y**eux   fo**y**er   L**y**on

Additional practice activities for each **Sons et lettres** section are provided by:
• Student Activities Manual
• Text Audio

Point out that in *étudie* and *bougie* the final *-e* is not pronounced and hence does not represent any sound. Remind students that the sequence *-ill* is often pronounced /j/ as well. This was presented in Ch. 6, L. 1.

Note the intervocalic glide in the second example: *client* /klijɑ̃/, *oublier* /ublije/.

Begin with a discrimination drill contrasting the first- and second-person plural of the present versus the corresponding forms of the imperfect. Have students raise their hand when they hear the imperfect (and therefore the glide /j/): *nous lisons, nous lisions, vous écrivez, vous écriviez, nous disions, nous disons, vous fêtez, vous fêtiez, nous célébrons, nous célébrions, nous jouions, nous jouons, vous chantez, vous chantiez.*

  You may also wish to add a drill in which students transform from the present to the imperfect: *vous écrivez —vous écriviez ; nous dansons, vous mangez, vous passez, nous faisons, nous allons, vous achetez, vous finissez, nous préférons.*

  Remind students that in *millier, million,* and *milliard, ll* represents /l/, not /j/. These are derivatives of *mille.*

À vous la parole

7-15 Imitation. Répétez ces mots ou expressions qui contiennent la semi-voyelle /j/ devant une voyelle orale.

mieux	le mariage	officiel	la mariée
l'union	traditionnelle	génial	monsieur
société	un million	vous chantiez	nous voulions

7-16 Contrastes. Comparez les deux mots ou expressions.

1. la vie / les vieux   le mari / le mariage
2. l'ami / le mieux   elle étudie / elle va étudier
3. le cri / crier   c'est pourri / c'est génial

7-17 Phrases. Maintenant lisez ces phrases.

1. La cérémonie officielle pour le mariage a lieu le 3 février.
2. Ces étudiantes étudiaient les sciences économiques à Lyon l'an dernier.
3. Dans la société actuelle, il y a des familles traditionnelles avec des femmes au foyer mais aussi des couples qui vivent en union libre.

FORMES ET FONCTIONS

1. L'imparfait et le passé composé : d'autres contrastes

Review uses of the *passé composé* and *imparfait* as presented in Ch. 6, L. 3 and Ch. 7, L. 1. First, have students brainstorm to list uses of each tense; use this summary as a point of departure for review practice before presenting the new information. A narrative such as that provided in Ex. 7-8 or 7-9, or workbook exercise SAM 7-6, would offer a good basis for review. This section focuses on adverbial cues to one-time versus habitual actions in the past and the use of the *imparfait* for ongoing actions as opposed to punctual actions. Review the various adverbial cues to repeated/habitual action, including use of the definite article with days of the week: *dimanche* (on Sunday) vs. *le dimanche* (on Sundays).

As you have seen, the choice of the **imparfait** or the **passé composé** to express the past often depends on the context and the speaker's view of the action or situation.

- Use the **passé composé** to express:

  - an action or state that occurred at a specific point in time:

    Elle est née **le jeudi 9 mai 1991**.   *She was born on Thursday, May 9, 1991.*

  - an action or state that occurred a specified number of times:

    Elle a visité le Canada **deux fois**.   *She visited Canada twice.*

- Use the **imparfait** to express:

  - enduring states in the past:

    Cécile était une enfant très sérieuse.   *Cécile was a very studious child.*

  - habitual actions in the past:

    D'habitude la famille allait au parc **le dimanche**.   *Usually the family would go to the park on Sundays.*

- Use the **imparfait** to express an ongoing action or state interrupted by another action, which is expressed by the **passé composé**.

  Sophie **regardait** la télé quand sa marraine **a téléphoné**.   *Sophie was watching TV when her godmother called.*

  Ils **quittaient** l'église quand il **a commencé** à pleuvoir.   *They were leaving the church when it started to rain.*

- Finally, some actions or states can be expressed either in the **passé composé** or the **imparfait**, depending on what the speaker means to say.

  Elle était malade pendant les vacances.   *She was sick during the vacation.* (emphasis on her state of being sick)

  Elle a été malade pendant les vacances.   *She got sick during the vacation.* (emphasis on the act of getting sick)

  Il avait peur.   *He was afraid.*

  Il a eu peur.   *He got scared/Something scared him.*

À vous la parole

7-18 Hier, ça n'allait pas ! Chloé a eu des problèmes hier. Les choses n'ont pas marché comme d'habitude. Expliquez !

MODÈLE arriver en avance
➤ D'habitude, elle arrivait en avance.
➤ Mais hier elle n'est pas arrivée en avance.

1. quitter la maison à 8 h
2. arriver la première
3. apporter son cahier
4. réviser sa leçon
5. finir ses devoirs
6. apporter ses livres
7. travailler à la bibliothèque
8. appeler ses amis

7-19 Qu'est-ce qu'ils faisaient ? Décrivez ce qui ces gens faisaient quand Solange est arrivée à la fête.

MODÈLE ➤ Quand Solange est arrivée, Marc travaillait dans sa chambre.

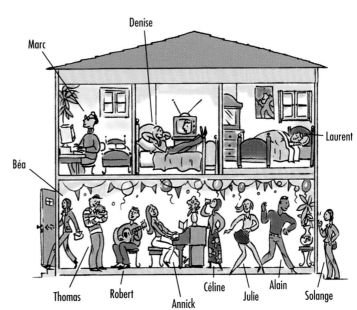

7-20 Mes quinze ans. Avec un/e partenaire, parlez de vos quinze ans. Comment étiez-vous ? Qu'est-ce que vous faisiez ? Qu'est-ce que vous avez fait ?

MODÈLES le caractère
É1 Moi, à quinze ans, j'étais très timide.
É2 Moi, à quinze ans, j'étais très indépendant et individualiste.

les voyages
É1 À quinze ans, je suis allée à Washington, D.C. visiter les monuments et les musées.
É2 Et moi, je suis allé en Floride avec ma famille.

1. le caractère
2. le physique
3. les amis
4. le sport
5. les voyages
6. les études
7. la musique
8. les projets d'avenir

2. L'adjectif démonstratif

This treatment allows for recycling of adjective placement and prenominal adjective forms, taught in Ch. 3, L. 1. Review those before presenting this new material. Point out to students that adjectives like *belle* follow the same pattern as the demonstrative, with two spoken and three written forms in the singular: *belle/bel/beau; cette/cet/ce.*

• The demonstrative adjective is used to point out specific people or things that are close at hand. The singular form corresponds to *this* or *that* in English, the plural, to *these* or *those*.

Tu aimes **les** fêtes ?	*Do you like holidays (in general) ?*
Tu aimes **cette** fête ?	*Do you like this holiday ?*

• Note the masculine singular form used before a noun beginning with a vowel sound. It is pronounced like the feminine form but has a different spelling.

Regarde **ce** gâteau !	*Look at this cake!*
Regarde **cet** œuf en chocolat !	*Look at that chocolate egg!*
Regarde **cette** cérémonie !	*Look at that ceremony!*

• Here are the forms of the demonstrative adjective.

	féminin	**masculin**	
		devant voyelle	*devant consonne*
singulier	**cette** fête	**cet** œuf	**ce** gâteau
pluriel	**ces** affiches	**ces** œufs	**ces** cadeaux

À vous la parole

Begin practice with a discrimination drill: *un homme, une femme ou impossible à dire ? Cette dentiste est sympa ; Ce comptable est sociable ; Ce secrétaire est efficace ; Cet agent de police est jeune ; Cette journaliste est dynamique ; Ce prof est doué ; Cet(te) architecte n'est pas réaliste ; Cette comptable est disciplinée.* Follow with a substitution drill: *Tu aimes cette fête ? gâteau , —Tu aimes ce gâteau ? ; bougies , cadeau , sapin , vacances , cérémonie , église ,* etc.

7-21, 7-22 These exercises can be cued with visuals if you have them available.

7-22 This allows students to practice dislocation, a very common and useful structure presented in Ch. 6, L. 1. It recycles information from the **Vie et culture** notes of this lesson and can be used in conjunction with that topic if you wish.

7-21 Regarde ça ! Imaginez que vous regardez des photos dans un album. Montrez les choses que vous remarquez à votre ami/e.

MODÈLE   un gros gâteau
> ➤ Regarde ce gros gâteau !

1. une belle église
2. des beaux feux d'artifice
3. des bougies
4. des œufs en chocolat
5. un pot de chrysanthèmes
6. des cadeaux magnifiques
7. un grand sapin
8. un beau brin de muguet

7-22 Qu'est-ce que vous offrez ? Imaginez que vous offrez un cadeau et identifiez l'occasion.

MODÈLE   un brin de muguet
> ➤ Ce brin de muguet, c'est pour la fête du Travail.

1. des chrysanthèmes
2. une poule en chocolat
3. des roses rouges
4. une carte de vœux
5. un gâteau au chocolat
6. une galette
7. des crêpes
8. un gros bouquet de fleurs

7-23 Qu'est-ce que c'est ? Proposez une définition ; vos camarades de classe doivent trouver la réponse.

MODÈLES É1 Ces fleurs sont pour les tombes le premier novembre.

É2 Ce sont des chrysanthèmes.

É3 Cette cérémonie a lieu dans une église, souvent avec un bébé.

É4 C'est un baptême.

Écoutons

7-24 Lise parle avec sa mère

A. Avant d'écouter. Dans cette conversation téléphonique, la mère de Lise lui donne des nouvelles (*news*) de la famille et de leurs connaissances. Avant d'écouter, pensez aux événements possibles que votre mère (ou un autre membre de votre famille) pourrait vous annoncer au téléphone.

B. En écoutant. Complétez le tableau suivant avec la personne mentionnée, la nouvelle et la réaction de Lise. La première nouvelle est donnée comme modèle.

personne mentionnée	nouvelle	réaction de Lise
her brother	*passed his exams*	*relief*

C. Après avoir écouté. Est-ce que les réactions de Lise vous ont surpris/e ? Pourquoi ? Est-ce que vous avez des conversations comme cela avec votre mère ou un autre membre de votre famille ? Comparez vos réponses avec vos camarades de classe.

You might ask students to write down some of the phrases *Lise* uses to react to her mother's news.

As a more extended follow-up, put students in pairs to plan and present a similar conversation. Suggest possible scenarios (a birth, a new car, a car accident, a new job, etc.) and provide a model:

Imaginez que vous téléphonez à un/e bon/ne ami/e pour annoncer une nouvelle. Avec un/e partenaire, créez un dialogue.

MODÈLE des fiançailles

É1 Allô, Claire ? C'est Christine. Écoute, David et moi, on va se marier !

É2 C'est vrai ? Félicitations ! Je suis très contente pour vous ! C'est pour quand, le mariage ?

É1 On n'a pas encore décidé ; peut-être pour le mois d'octobre…

7-23 You might have students work in pairs to create definitions with which to test their classmates. This could also be structured as a game with two teams.

Avant d'écouter. You might put students into pairs or small groups for this brainstorming activity.

Script for *Écoutons*

A : Allô, Maman ?

B : Bonjour, ma grande ! Ça va ?

A : Oui, pas mal, et toi ?

B : Oui, oui. Écoute, tu ne sais pas la nouvelle ?

A : Quoi ? Qu'est-ce qu'il y a ?

B : Ton frère, il vient d'avoir son bac !

A : Ouf ! Enfin ! Eh bien, il doit être content, non ?

B : Tu parles ! Mais, attends, nous avons eu une mauvaise nouvelle ce matin. Le voisin, M. Bertie, a eu un accident hier soir.

A : Ah non ! C'est pas vrai !

B : Si, si. Il est à l'hôpital, mais j'ai entendu dire qu'il va assez bien. Il n'y a pas eu d'autres blessés.

A : Heureusement. Dis-lui que je pense à lui quand tu vas le voir. Et sa fille Stéphanie, comment ça va, elle ?

B : Eh bien, ça y est ; elle a eu son bébé samedi dernier.

A : Ah bon !

B : Oui, c'est un petit garçon, il s'appelle Nicolas.

A : Nicolas ! Et ils vont bien tous les deux ?

B : Oui, oui, très bien. Ils sont rentrés chez eux mardi.

A : Ah, ben, ça, c'est bien.

B : Et en plus le mari de Stéphanie a trouvé un poste chez Darty.

A : Mais c'est super ! Qu'est-ce qu'il va faire là-bas ?

B : Il sera au bureau du personnel ; pour lui, c'est le poste idéal.

A : Ben, ils doivent être contents, eux.

B : N'est-ce pas ?

Leçon 3 Les émotions

Present the emotions using the dialogue along with its photo. Then use mime and description to present the list in the shaded box. Finally, use the illustrations of emotions (IRCD, Ch. 7) to model typical phrases; describe the situations by re-using the key vocabulary. Test comprehension by having students point to a picture of the attitude you describe or mime the emotion. Have students repeat key words and phrases: *Elle est heureuse ou elle est furieuse ?* etc.

POINTS DE DÉPART

Pour exprimer les sentiments et les émotions

`TEXT AUDIO`

MÉLANIE : Tu as l'air content, toi !

ANTOINE : En effet, je suis ravi. Écoute la bonne nouvelle : mon frère s'est fiancé. Il va se marier au mois de juin.

MÉLANIE : C'est super. Tu connais sa fiancée ?

ANTOINE : Oui, et on s'entend bien. Mais dis-moi, qu'est-ce que tu as, toi ? Tu n'as pas l'air heureuse. Tu te fais du souci ?

MÉLANIE : Eh bien, je suis assez inquiète ; je n'ai pas de nouvelles de ma sœur. Elle a eu un bébé le mois dernier et elle se dispute beaucoup avec son mari. Elle doit se reposer, mais c'est elle qui fait tout le travail.

ANTOINE : Calme-toi. Elle est probablement trop occupée pour t'appeler. Téléphone-lui.

LES SENTIMENTS

être heureux/-euse, content/e, ravi/e
être inquiet/inquiète, anxieux/-euse
être furieux/furieuse, fâché/e, en colère
être amoureux/-euse
être sensible
être triste, malheureux/-euse
être surpris/e
être embarrassé/e, gêné/e
être jaloux/-ouse

Qu'est-ce qu'on dit quand on perd son sang-froid ?

Vie et culture

Les Français s'expriment

Il y a beaucoup d'expressions fixes que les Français utilisent pour exprimer les émotions.
(L'accent et l'intonation sont très importants aussi !) Est-ce que vous pouvez marier les
expressions dans la colonne de droite aux émotions dans la colonne de gauche ?

1. la joie
2. la colère
3. l'indifférence
4. la tendresse
5. l'embarras
6. la surprise
7. la déception (*disappointment*)
8. l'inquiétude

a. Mon Dieu ! Oh, là, là !
b. Super ! Sensationnel ! Formidable ! Extra !
c. Excusez-moi ! Oh, pardon ! Je suis désolé/e !
d. Zut ! Mince ! Flûte !
e. Bof ! Ça m'est égal.
f. Ma chérie/mon chéri, mon cœur, ma puce
g. C'est pas vrai ! Pas possible ! Incroyable !
h. Espèce d'imbécile ! Crétin ! Quel idiot !

Et vous ?

Le mot juste. Qu'est-ce que vous dites dans
les situations suivantes ?

1. Vous avez laissé (*left*) vos devoirs dans la
   voiture.
2. Vous avez reçu une bonne note à un examen
   très difficile.
3. Vos amis vous demandent si vous préférez
   aller au cinéma ou regarder une vidéocassette ;
   vous n'avez pas d'opinion.

4. Vous regardez un enfant adorable, votre nièce
   ou votre neveu.
5. Votre colocataire a emprunté votre livre de
   français et l'a laissé à la bibliothèque.
6. Vous avez fait tomber un vase chez la grand-
   mère de votre ami.
7. Vous apprenez que votre ami/e a eu un
   accident de voiture.

Relate the exclamations in the **Vie et culture** to the emotions presented earlier. Provide formal and familiar forms where
appropriate. Have students repeat the phrases. Demonstrate the proper intonation patterns, including the *accent
d'insistance émotionnelle : Formidable ! Crétin !*, etc. Many terms of endearment are based on names for animals: *ma
puce, ma biche,* etc.
Key: 1) b 2) h 3) e 4) f 5) c 6) g 7) d 8) a

To expand on the **Et vous ?** exercise, have students work in pairs to make up their own situations and reactions. They
might create a short scene based on their scenario and then act it out in front of the class.

À vous la parole

7-25, 7-26 Students may work in pairs or groups. Have them come up with as many alternatives as possible, then compare notes with the class as a whole.

7-25 Lire les expressions du visage. Est-ce que vous et votre partenaire savez lire les émotions peintes sur le visage d'une personne ?

MODÈLE É1 Cette dame a l'air malheureuse ; peut-être qu'elle a appris une mauvaise nouvelle.

É2 Je pense qu'elle est anxieuse parce qu'elle n'a pas de nouvelles de son ami.

1. 2. 3. 4.

7-26 Des conseils. Quels conseils est-ce que vous pouvez donner aux personnes suivantes ?

MODÈLE Votre colocataire a des soucis.

➤ Ne t'en fais pas ! Ça va s'arranger.

1. Une amie est très anxieuse avant un examen.
2. Votre ami est furieux parce qu'il pense qu'on l'a insulté.
3. Un monsieur se fâche parce qu'il n'y a pas de place dans l'autobus.
4. Votre amie a tendance à être un peu jalouse.
5. Votre petit frère pleure parce qu'il ne trouve pas son DVD préféré.
6. Une femme est furieuse et elle crie très fort.
7. Vos copains sont anxieux avant un match de tennis.
8. Vos camarades s'inquiètent des notes qu'ils vont recevoir.

7-27 Les sentiments. Expliquez à votre partenaire dans quelle/s situation/s vous ressentez les sentiments suivants.

7-27 Nouns are for recognition only. Help students discover their meanings by associating them with the adjectives they know. For example, knowing *heureux* and *malheureux* helps to understand *le bonheur*. If students are curious, point out that *la déception* is related to *déçu/e*.

MODÈLE la tristesse

➤ Je suis triste quand mes parents se disputent.

1. le bonheur
2. la jalousie
3. l'inquiétude
4. l'anxiété
5. la colère
6. la surprise
7. la déception (*disappointment*)

For additional practice do a mixing activity where students need to interact with three other people in the class to find out how they are doing. Be sure to provide a model: *Ça va aujourd'hui ? — Pas vraiment. J'ai un examen important, et je suis un peu anxieux. — Ne t'en fais pas ! Tu vas réussir à cet examen.* Follow up by having students tell what they learned about the people they spoke to. As a variation, perhaps on another class day, have students tell each other what's new and react to the news: *Quoi de neuf ? — Eh bien, je vais bientôt me marier. Ah bon ? C'est formidable !* You might have students act out their conversations for the class as a whole.

Sons et lettres

TEXT AUDIO

Les semi-voyelles /w/ et /ɥ/

The semivowel /w/ is always followed by a vowel, and that vowel is very often /a/. To pronounce /w/, start from the word "tweet" in English: *tweet*/**toi**.

When followed by the sound /a/, the semivowel is usually spelled **oi**, as in **moi, trois**. It can also be spelled **ou**, as in **oui** or **jouer**. The spelling **oy** represents the sound /waj/, as in **employé** or **royal**. The semivowel /w/ also occurs in combination with the nasal vowel /ɛ̃/. In this case, it is spelled **oin**: **loin** or **moins**.

To pronounce the semivowel /ɥ/, as in **lui**, start from the /y/ of **du** but pronounce it together with the following vowel: **lu/lui**.

The sound /ɥ/ is frequently followed by the vowel /i/: **huit, je suis, la nuit, bruit, nuage, ennuyeux, s'essuyer**. It is always spelled with the letter **u** followed by another vowel.

When the combination *ou* occurs before a vowel, it may be pronounced as the semivowel /w/ or the corresponding vowel /u/: *louer* /lwe/ or /lue/. Most of these cases involve verb forms: *jouer, nous jouons, vous jouez*. However, it is preferable for students to pronounce forms like *un souhait* or *un jouet* with /w/. But note, as was the case for *i*, when *ou* occurs after consonant groups, the pronunciation of /u/ is obligatory. Compare: *louer* /lwe/ or /lue/ versus *trouer* /true/. However, the combination *oi* is pronounced /wa/ in this context: *trois*. The same principle applies to *u* before vowels: *nuage, tuer*.

À vous la parole

7-28 Contrastes. Comparez les paires de mots suivantes.

la **joi**e	**joy**eux	un m**oi**s	m**oin**s
le r**oi**	r**oy**al	la l**oi**	l**oin**
l'empl**oi**	empl**oy**er		

Maintenant, comparez les mots avec /w/ et /ɥ/.

| **ou**i | h**ui**t | Lo**ui**s | l**ui** |
| j**oin**t | j**ui**n | le s**oi**r | ess**ui**e |

The distinction between /w/ and /ɥ/ is a difficult one for American speakers partly due to the difficulty with the pairs /u/ and /y/. The exercises here are included on the text audio CD and can be used in class.

When treating the poem, point out the difference in the pronunciation of *oe* in *moelle, poème,* and *Noël.*

7-29 Poème. Lisez ce petit poème.

LE VER LUISANT

Ver l**ui**sant°, tu l**ui**s° à min**ui**t
Tu t'allumes sous les ét**oi**les°
Et quand tout dort, tu t'introd**ui**s°
Dans la lune° et ronge sa m**oe**lle°.

—Robert Desnos, *Chantefables et Chantefleurs.*
Librairie Grund, 1970.

glowworm; shine
stars
penetrate
moon; gnaw its marrow

FORMES ET FONCTIONS

1. Les verbes pronominaux idiomatiques

- Certain verbs change meaning when combined with a reflexive pronoun:

appeler	J'appelle mon chien.	*I'm calling my dog.*
s'appeler	Je **m'appelle** David.	*My name is David.*
entendre	J'entends un bruit.	*I hear a noise.*
s'entendre avec	Je **m'entends** bien avec eux.	*I get along well with them.*

- Here are some common idiomatic pronominal verbs:

s'amuser	Ils **se sont** bien **amusés**.	*They had a lot of fun.*
s'appeler	Je **m'appelle** Julie.	*My name is Julie.*
s'arranger	Ça va **s'arranger** !	*It will be all right!*
se calmer	**Calmez-vous**, voyons !	*Look here, calm down!*
se dépêcher	Il ne **se dépêchait** jamais.	*He never hurried.*
se détendre	Tu devrais **te détendre**.	*You should relax.*
se disputer	Ils **se disputent** tout le temps.	*They argue all the time.*
s'ennuyer	Je **m'ennuie** !	*I'm bored!*
s'entendre (avec)	Je **m'entends** bien avec lui.	*I get along well with him.*
se fâcher	Elle **se fâche** contre lui.	*She's getting angry at him.*
s'inquiéter	Ne **t'inquiète** pas !	*Don't worry!*
s'intéresser à	Tu **t'intéresses à** la musique ?	*Are you interested in music?*
s'occuper de	Tu **t'occupes de** lui ?	*Are you taking care of him?*
se passer	Qu'est-ce qui **se passe** ?	*What's happening?*
se promener	Elle **se promène** dans le parc.	*She takes a walk in the park.*
se rappeler	Je ne **me rappelle** pas.	*I don't remember.*
se reposer	On **se repose**.	*We're resting.*
se retrouver	On **se retrouve** ici ?	*Shall we meet here?*

- Many verbs can be used with a reflexive pronoun to show that the action is mutual, or reciprocal. In English we sometimes use the phrase *each other* to express this idea.

se téléphoner	Nous **nous** sommes téléphoné.	*We phoned each other.*
se rencontrer	On **s'est** rencontrés l'été dernier.	*We met last summer. (for the first time)*
s'embrasser	Ils **se** sont embrassés.	*They kissed.*
se fiancer	Ils **se** sont fiancés.	*They got engaged.*
se marier	Ils **se** sont mariés.	*They got married.*
se séparer	Ils **se** sont séparés.	*They separated.*

Before treating this topic, review reflexive pronominal verbs presented in Ch. 4, L. 1. Treat these verbs as new vocabulary. Remind students that several of these expressions were presented in the **Points de départ** for this lesson. Point out irregular forms: stem and spelling changes for *s'appeler/se rappeler, s'ennuyer, s'inquiéter, se promener*. Conjugations for these *-er* verbs with spelling changes are provided in Appendix 4.

Point out that there is no agreement of the past participle of *se téléphoner* because this verb takes an indirect object.

Begin practice with a discrimination drill: have students raise their hand when they hear a verb used pronominally: *Ils se reposent ; Il essuie la table ; Elle s'appelle Stéphanie ; J'entends un bruit ; Ils s'entendent bien ; Elle embrasse son fiancé ; Je m'ennuie ; On va se promener ; Vous passez chez moi demain ? ; Ils se séparent ?* etc. Follow up with a substitution drill to review forms: *Je m'amuse ; toi. —Tu t'amuses*, etc.

7-30 À la maternelle. Christophe se rappelle sa classe à l'école maternelle. Pour compléter ses descriptions, choisissez un verbe qui convient dans la liste ci-dessous.

MODÈLE   La maîtresse était toujours calme.
> Elle ne se fâchait jamais.

s'amuser	se dépêcher	s'ennuyer	s'entendre
se fâcher	s'occuper de	se rappeler	se reposer

1. Pendant la récréation les enfants jouaient ensemble.
2. À midi, on n'avait pas beucoup de temps pour aller à la cantine.
3. Une vieille femme préparait le déjeuner.
4. Après le déjeuner, tout le monde faisait la sieste.
5. Jacques et moi, nous étions des bons amis.
6. Je trouvais nos activités en classe très intéressantes.
7. Jacques n'oubliait jamais ses leçons.

7-31 Vary by suggesting that students present the love stories of famous couples of their choosing (e.g., Marc Antony and Cleopatra, Romeo and Juliette, Bill and Hillary Clinton, Jennifer Aniston and Brad Pitt, J-Lo and Ben Affleck) or even of friends and/or family members. Point out that not all verbs are used pronominally. Students may work in pairs or groups to complete this adaptation.

7-31 Histoire d'amour. Racontez cette histoire d'amour en vous servant des verbes indiqués.

MODÈLE   se rencontrer
> Ils se sont rencontrés au cinéma.

1. se parler de
2. tomber amoureux (*to fall in love*)
3. se fiancer
4. se marier

5. s'entendre bien
6. se disputer
7. se séparer
8. divorcer

7-32 Use as a mixing exercise; let students ask each other a maximum of two questions before moving on to someone else. After a few minutes, have students compare notes, asking questions about items they did not find. Take the opportunity to ask follow-up questions.

7-32 Trouvez une personne. Trouvez une personne qui…

MODÈLE   s'entend bien avec ses parents

   É1   Est-ce que tu t'entends bien avec tes parents ?
   É2   Non, je ne m'entends pas bien avec eux.
   OU   Oui, je m'entends bien avec eux.

1. s'entend bien avec ses parents
2. se rappelle son premier jour à l'école
3. s'amuse quelquefois au cours de français
4. s'occupe toujours du dîner le soir
5. ne se fâche jamais
6. s'est dépêchée ce matin
7. va se détendre ce week-end
8. se rappelle les heures de bureau du professeur

👥 7-33 Quand ? Avec un/e partenaire, expliquez quand cela vous arrive de…

MODÈLE vous fâcher

    É1 Quand est-ce que tu te fâches ?

    É2 Je me fâche quand ma sœur emprunte mes affaires.

1. vous fâcher
2. vous inquiéter
3. vous amuser
4. vous dépêcher

5. vous reposer
6. vous ennuyer
7. vous détendre

2. *Les verbes* connaître *et* savoir

The verbs **connaître** and **savoir** both mean *to know*, but they are used in somewhat different ways.

- **Connaître** means *to be acquainted with* or *to be familiar with* and usually refers to places and persons; **connaître** is always followed by a noun:

    Je **connais** bien sa famille.   *I know his/her family well.*

    Il ne **connaît** pas Abidjan.   *He is not familiar with Abidjan.*

    Vous **connaissez** ce poème ?   *Are you familiar with this poem?*

- When used in the **passé composé** with persons, **connaître** means *to have met*.

    J'**ai connu** mon copain l'été dernier.   *I met my boyfriend last summer.*

CONNAÎTRE *to know, to be familiar with*		
SINGULIER	PLURIEL	
je connai**s**	nous connaiss**ons**	
tu connai**s**	vous connaiss**ez**	
il } elle } connaî**t** on }	ils } elles } connaiss**ent**	

PASSÉ COMPOSÉ : **J'ai connu** Jamila l'été dernier.

Except for the use of the circumflex accent in the third-person singular, the present-tense forms of *connaître* are predictable, like regular -*ir*/-*iss*- verbs: beginning with the base *connaiss*-, the final consonant is lost in the singular forms. You might want to call attention to the use of the past participle as an adjective — *connu/e, inconnu/e* because of its frequent use.

- **Savoir** generally means *to know facts*, *information*, or *how to do something*. It can be used in five types of constructions:

    ■ Followed by an infinitive:

        Tu **sais** danser le tango ?   *Do you know how to dance the tango?*

        Ma mère ne **sait** pas se détendre.   *My mother doesn't know how to relax.*

    ■ Followed by a noun:

        Il **sait** sa leçon par cœur.   *He knows his lesson by heart.*

        Je ne **sais** pas tout.   *I don't know everything.*

        Nous **savons** la réponse.   *We know the answer.*

Note that in cases where the complement is a noun, native speaker usage is nuanced: one can say *Je connais le code de la route ; son adresse ; ses opinions.* But for things that are learned by rote memory, native speakers use *savoir: il sait mon numéro de téléphone ; elle sait sa leçon.*

- Followed by a sentence introduced by **que**:

Je **sais qu'**ils sont séparés.   *I know that they are separated.*

Elle **sait que** nous sommes fiancés.   *She knows that we're engaged.*

- Followed by a sentence introduced by a question word or **si** (*whether*).

Je ne **sais** pas **comment** sa copine s'appelle.   *I don't know his girlfriend's name.*

Tu **sais si** elle va venir ?   *Do you know if she's coming?*

- Used alone:

Qu'est-ce qu'elles **savent** ?   *What do they know?*

Je **sais**.   *I know.*

- When used to talk about the past, **savoir** in the **imparfait** means *knew*.

Elle **savait** que nous étions fatigués.   *She knew that we were tired.*

- When used in the **passé composé**, **savoir** means *to have learned* or *found out*.

J'**ai su** qu'elle était malade hier.   *I found out that she was sick yesterday.*

SAVOIR	*to know*		
SINGULIER		PLURIEL	
je	sais	nous	sav**ons**
tu	sais	vous	sav**ez**
il elle on	sai**t**	ils elles	sav**ent**

PASSÉ COMPOSÉ : **J'ai su** où il habitait.

À vous la parole

7-34 Les connaissances. Avec un/e partenaire, dites qui vous connaissez et qui vous ne connaissez pas.

MODÈLE   la famille de votre beau-frère/belle-sœur

➤ Je connais la sœur de mon beau-frère, mais je ne connais pas sa mère.

1. la famille de votre beau-frère/belle-sœur
2. la famille de votre colocataire
3. la famille de vos voisins
4. la famille de votre prof de français
5. la famille de votre meilleur/e ami/e
6. la famille de votre ami/e
7. la famille de votre femme/mari/fiancé/e

7-35 L'espion international. L'Interpol recherche Claude Martin, un grand espion. Est-ce que vous le connaissez ? Qu'est-ce que vous savez à son sujet ? Faites des phrases en employant **connaître** ou **savoir**.

MODÈLES où il travaille
➤ Je sais où il travaille.

la ville où il est né
➤ Je connais la ville où il est né.

1. M. Martin
2. qu'il parle portugais
3. les noms de ses camarades
4. sa femme
5. quand il est parti d'Italie
6. qu'il parle allemand
7. où M. Martin habite
8. pourquoi il est allé en Belgique
9. ses amis à Liège
10. quand il va repartir

7-35 Students may play the role of an Interpol inspector and question their classmates: *Est-ce que vous savez où il travaille ?* Students answer appropriately. Help students discover the meaning of *espion* through context and perhaps an example: *James Bond, c'est un espion.*

7-36 Trouvez une personne. Trouvez quelqu'un parmi vos camarades de classe qui sait/connaît… Comparez vos notes à la fin pour bien connaître vos camarades de classe !

MODÈLE jouer de la guitare
➤ Est-ce que tu sais jouer de la guitare ?

1. parler italien
2. une personne célèbre
3. le président de l'université
4. faire du ski
5. la ville de Washington, D.C.
6. la Belgique
7. jouer d'un instrument
8. le prénom du professeur
9. combien d'étudiants il y a à l'université

7-36 Use as a mixing exercise. Give students a limited amount of time to circulate, asking a maximum of two questions of each person before moving on to someone else. Follow up by having students ask about the items they did not find: *Qui sait jouer de la guitare ?* Ask additional questions to find out more information as appropriate.

Écrivons

7-37 Un souvenir marquant

Racontez votre souvenir le plus marquant.

As a prelude to writing, have students discuss their experience in class. As a variation, have students describe a person from their past, telling who the person was, what the person was like physically and in character, and why that person was memorable.

A. Avant d'écrire. Pensez à un souvenir très marquant. Pour vous aider à organiser vos pensées, réfléchissez aux questions suivantes.

Quelle était l'occasion ?	
C'est un souvenir heureux ou triste ?	
Qui était là ?	
Qu'est-ce que vous avez fait ?	
Quelles étaient vos émotions ?	

B. En écrivant. Maintenant, composez votre texte sous forme de paragraphe(s):

MODÈLE ➤ Mon souvenir le plus marquant, c'est un souvenir heureux. J'avais cinq ans, et j'étais fille unique. Un jour, mes parents m'ont dit qu'ils allaient à l'hôpital me chercher un petit frère ou une petite sœur. Ma grand-mère est venue à la maison pour rester avec moi. Deux jours après, quand j'ai entendu la voiture de mon père, j'ai crié, « Voici notre bébé ! Voici notre bébé ! ». C'était ma petite sœur. Et maintenant, c'est toujours ma meilleure amie.

You might have students share their story with classmates, either orally, or by distributing copies of stories (with the author's permission).

C. Après avoir écrit. Relisez votre texte :

1. Est-ce que vous avez employé le passé composé et l'imparfait dans des contextes appropriés ?
2. Est-ce que vous êtes satisfait/e de votre texte ?
3. Enfin, donnez un titre à votre texte, par exemple « L'arrivée de ma sœur ».

Venez chez nous !
Les rituels

Chaque culture exprime ses valeurs à travers ses rites et ses rituels. Voici quelques exemples de rituels du monde francophone.

Additional activities to explore the **Venez chez nous !** topics are provided by:
• Student Activities Manual
• *Chez nous* video
• *Chez nous* Companion Website: http://www.prenhall.com/cheznous

Une première communion en France

Use the video montage Les rituels to provide an overview of the lesson. Have students identify the various events they see and perhaps provide an appropriate reaction/expression of emotion : Félicitations ! etc.

Avant de regarder. You might work with students to develop this list and put the expressions on the board. See the Video Manual for activities that accompany the third speaker, a young woman who discusses her experiences with the rites of baptism and communion in the Catholic church.

7-38 Rites et traditions

A. Avant de regarder. Vous allez écouter des personnes qui parlent d'événements importants dans leur vie. Quels sont les événements les plus importants dans la vie d'une personne ? Préparez une liste avec vos camarades de classe.

MODÈLE ➤ la naissance (*birth*) d'un enfant, le baptême,…

B. En regardant. Pour chaque personne, répondez aux questions.

Marie-Julie

1. Marie-Julie explique qu'au Québec, lorsqu'elles se marient, les femmes doivent garder…
   a. leur nom de jeune fille
   b. le nom de leur mari
   c. les deux noms

Script for *Observons*

MARIE-JULIE : Je m'appelle Marie-Julie Kerharo, mais à toutes les fois où* je rentre au Québec, c'est Marie-Julie Lavoie parce qu'au Québec, les femmes doivent préserver leur nom de jeune fille tout le reste de leur vie. C'est une loi qui date des années 80, si je ne m'abuse pas, c'est 1986. Et depuis lors, les femmes n'ont pas le choix, elles doivent garder leur nom de jeune fille, même si elles sont mariées.

*In Standard French, *mais toutes les fois que*…

MONSIEUR LE MAIRE DE SEILLANS : Bonjour, j'ai le plaisir de vous accueillir dans la salle des mariages de la commune de Seillans. Je suis le maire et en cette qualité, je célèbre les mariages des habitants de la commune. C'est une cérémonie officielle, qui consiste à recueillir le consentement des mariés, en présence de deux ou quatre témoins.

BARBARA : Bonjour, bonjour Monsieur le maire.

M. LE MAIRE : Bonjour, Barbara.

BARBARA : Voilà, je m'appelle Barbara Roustan, je suis, euh, j'habite à Seillans. Il ne faut pas oublier aussi, je me suis mariée en 1988 dans cette salle de mariage. Et c'était un petit peu original parce que ma future belle-mère à l'époque était le maire de Seillans en 1988 et donc, elle était très émue à l'issue de ce mariage, de nous marier, et c'était magnifique, parce que c'était très familial et en même temps, c'était un mariage, voilà, un petit peu spécial.

2. C'est…
   a. une vieille coutume
   b. une loi récente
   c. une tradition dans certaines familles

Monsieur le maire de Seillans et Barbara

3. Pour lui, le mariage est un acte…
   a. de foi (*faith*).
   b. familial.
   c. officiel.
4. Les participants à la cérémonie sont : le maire, les mariés, et…
   a. leurs parents.
   b. leurs amis.
   c. leurs témoins (*witnesses*).
5. Pour Barbara, son mariage était un peu spécial parce que … était le maire.
   a. sa mère
   b. sa future belle-mère
   c. son futur mari

C. Après avoir regardé. Maintenant discutez des questions suivantes avec vos camarades de classe.

1. Est-ce que les femmes qui se marient chez vous peuvent choisir leur nom ? Quelles sont les traditions dans votre communauté ?
2. En quoi est-ce que les mariages chez vous sont semblables aux mariages en France ? En quoi est-ce qu'ils sont différents ?

Treat the text as a short reading; relate the information here to the photos provided.

Les rituels du mariage dans le monde francophone

Les rituels du mariage varient d'un pays[1] à l'autre. Comme vous le savez, en France on se marie d'abord à la mairie et après à l'église si les mariés le désirent. Les robes que les mariées portent en France et au Québec sont souvent blanches et ressemblent aux robes de mariée que vous avez sans doute vues[2] aux États-Unis. En Afrique francophone, les mariées de familles aisées[3] dans les grandes villes peuvent s'habiller de la même façon[4] ou elles peuvent se vêtir[5] de robes plus traditionnelles. Quelquefois, il y a même deux mariages : un mariage à l'européenne et un mariage traditionnel à l'africaine. Au Maroc, il y a un rituel précis pour la mariée : les femmes décorent les mains de la future mariée avec du henné pour la protéger du mal[6] et pour lui porter bonne chance[7] et lui donner de la fertilité.

[1]*country* [2]*seen* [3]riches [4]*the same way* [5]s'habiller [6]*protect from evil* [7]*luck*

Parlons

7-39 Le mariage

Au Maroc, on décore les mains de la mariée au henné.

Ce couple se marie à l'Hôtel de Ville de Paris.

A. Avant de parler. Examinez les photos de mariage dans le monde francophone et lisez les légendes (*captions*).

B. En parlant. Avec un/e partenaire, décrivez chaque image. Par exemple, qui sont ces personnes ? Qu'est-ce qu'elles font ? Qu'est-ce qu'elles portent ?

MODÈLE ➤ Sur cette photo, je pense que la femme se prépare pour aller à son mariage. Elle porte…

C. Après avoir parlé. À quel mariage est-ce que vous voudriez assister ? Qu'est-ce qui vous intéresse en particulier sur ces photos ? Comparez vos réactions à celles de vos camarades de classe.

Un mariage au Mali où la mariée et le marié arrivent sur le dos d'un dromadaire.

Stratégie

Draw on your personal experience to better understand and respond to the events and emotions expressed by a writer. For example, when you know the topic of a reading passage, think about it, before you read, in terms of your own life and your own memories and associations.

Have students describe their own experiences before reading the passage. Remind them that as they read, they should not expect to understand every word of the text, but instead should study the questions carefully and focus on finding the information specified.

En lisant, Key: 1) the first and second paragraphs correspond to the first part; the second part begins with — *Cours vite* 2) his mother, a bottle of magic water that will develop his intelligence; his father, a ram's horn filled with talismans to keep away evil spirits; 3) referring to Kankan as a holy city, believing in magic and evil spirits, using talismans; 4) Baba says good-bye to the elders of his village, and does so with a heavy heart; he says good-bye to his mother and father with tears and embraces. Neither parent will accompany him to the train station, because it would be too painful for all.

7-40 L'Enfant noir

A. Avant de lire. *L'Enfant noir*, published in 1954, was written by Camara Laye at the age of 25 while he was studying in Paris. This autobiographical novel recounts his experiences growing up in **la Haute-Guinée** in Sub-Saharan Africa. The following excerpt recounts an important "coming of age" experience: Baba, the main character, who is fifteen years old, is getting ready to leave home to live with his uncle and attend school in the distant city of Conakry. He is saying his good-byes, thinking about the implications of his departure, and experiencing a range of powerful emotions. Can you identify with Baba at this moment of transition? Have you had a similar experience—perhaps when you finished high school and went on to college? How did you feel about saying good-bye to friends and family and leaving behind a familiar setting? If you can draw on your own experience to help you understand the events and feelings evoked by Camara Laye, you will be better able to grasp and respond to them.

The writer mainly uses two past tenses to tell his story: the **imparfait** and the **passé simple**. The latter is a literary tense that has generally the same meaning as the **passé composé**. Here are some examples you will see in the text; find their equivalent:

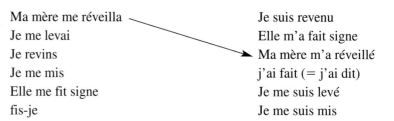

Ma mère me réveilla	Je suis revenu
Je me levai	Elle m'a fait signe
Je revins	Ma mère m'a réveillé
Je me mis	j'ai fait (= j'ai dit)
Elle me fit signe	Je me suis levé
fis-je	Je me suis mis

B. En lisant. Répondez à ces questions.

1. Ce passage peut être divisé en deux parties : (1) Le matin du départ et les cadeaux, et (2) Les adieux. Est-ce que vous pouvez identifier ces deux parties ?
2. Dans la première partie, les parents donnent à Baba ses cadeaux :

sa mère lui donne :	
pour :	
son père lui donne :	
pour :	

3. Dans cette partie, quels sont les éléments de la religion islamique et des traditions africaines que vous remarquez ?
4. Dans la deuxième partie, Baba doit faire ses adieux. À qui ? Quelle est sa réaction à chaque fois ?

Ma mère me réveilla à l'aube[1], et je me levai sans qu'elle dût insister. … Mes bagages étaient en tas[2] dans la case[3]. Soigneusement[4] calée[5] et placée en évidence, une bouteille[6] y était jointe.

—Qu'y a-t-il dans cette bouteille ? dis-je.

—Ne la casse[7] pas ! dit ma mère.

—J'y ferai attention[8].

—Fais-y grande attention ! Chaque matin, avant d'entrer en classe, tu prendras une petite gorgée[9] de cette bouteille.

—Est-ce l'eau[10] destinée à développer l'intelligence ? dis-je.

—Celle-là même ![11] Et il n'en peut exister de plus efficace[12] : elle vient de[13] Kankan !

J'avais déjà bu de cette eau : mon professeur m'en avait fait boire, quand j'avais passé mon certificat d'études. C'est une eau magique qui a nombre de pouvoirs et en particulier celui de développer le cerveau[14]. … Acheté dans la ville de Kankan, qui est une ville très musulmane et la plus sainte de nos villes, et manifestement acheté à haut prix[15], le breuvage[16] devait être particulièrement agissant[17]. Mon père, pour sa part, m'avait remis, la veille, une petite corne de bouc[18] renfermant des talismans ; et je devais porter continuellement sur moi cette corne qui me défendrait contre les mauvais esprits[19].

—Cours vite[20] faire tes adieux maintenant ! dit ma mère.

J'allais dire au revoir aux vieilles gens de notre concession[21] et des concessions voisines, et j'avais le cœur gros[22]. Ces hommes, ces femmes, je les connaissais depuis ma plus tendre enfance[23], depuis toujours je les avais vus à la place même où je les voyais, et aussi j'en avais vu disparaître[24] : ma grand-mère paternelle avait disparu ! Et reverrais-je[25] tous ceux auxquels je disais à présent adieu ? Frappé[26] de cette incertitude, ce fut comme si soudain je prenais congé[27] de mon passé même. Mais n'était-ce pas un peu cela ? Ne quittais-je pas ici toute une partie de mon passé ?

Quand je revins[28] près de ma mère et que je l'aperçus[29] en larmes[30] devant mes bagages, je me mis à pleurer à mon tour. Je me jetai dans ses bras[31] et je l'étreignis[32]. …

—Mère, ne pleure pas ! dis-je. Ne pleure pas !

Mais je n'arrivais pas moi-même à refréner[33] mes larmes et je la suppliai[34] de ne pas m'accompagner à la gare, car il me semblait qu'alors je ne pourrais jamais m'arracher[35] à ses bras. Elle me fit signe qu'elle y consentait. Nous nous étreignîmes une dernière fois, et je m'éloignai presque en courant[36]. …

Mon père m'avait rapidement rejoint et il m'avait pris la main[37], comme du temps où j'étais encore enfant. Je ralentis le pas[38] : j'étais sans courage, je sanglotais éperdument[39].

—Père ! fis-je.

—Je t'écoute, dit-il.

—Est-ce vrai que je pars ?

—Que ferais-tu d'autre ?[40] Tu sais bien que tu dois partir.

—Oui, dis-je.

Camara LAYE, *l'Enfant noir* © Éditions PLON

[1]*le lever du soleil* [2]*piled up* [3]*hut* [4]*Carefully* [5]*wedged* [6]*bottle* [7]*break* [8]*I'll be careful.* [9]*sip* [10]*water* [11]*Precisely !* [12]*effective* [13]*comes from* [14]*brain* [15]*at a high price* [16]*beverage* [17]*effective* [18]*ram's horn* [19]*spirits* [20]*Run quickly* [21]*property* [22]*a heavy heart* [23]*from my earliest childhood* [24]*I had seen some pass on* [25]*would I see again* [26]*struck* [27]*was leaving* [28]*came back* [29]*saw* [30]*in tears* [31]*arms* [32]*held her tightly* [33]*stop* [34]*begged* [35]*tear myself away* [36]*walked away hurriedly* [37]*took my hand* [38]*slowed my steps* [39]*was sobbing uncontrollably* [40]*What else would you do?*

C. En regardant de plus près. Dans ce passage Baba et sa famille expriment leurs émotions. Relevez les expressions qui servent à exprimer des émotions.

MODÈLE ➤ avoir le cœur gros,...

En regardant de plus près, Key: frappé de cette incertitude ; en larmes ; je me mis à pleurer ; Mère ne pleure pas ; j'étais sans courage ; je sanglotais

D. Après avoir lu. Enfin, discutez de ces questions avec vos camarades de classe.

1. Baba éprouve des fortes émotions quand il dit adieu à ses voisins et à sa famille. Est-ce que vous avez eu une expérience semblable ? Est-ce que Baba décrit une situation universelle, à votre avis, ou est-ce que ce récit reflète sa situation particulière en Haute-Guinée ?

2. Est-ce que vous avez eu une expérience qui a complètement changé votre vie ? Décrivez cela à un/e partenaire.

Les rites religieux et les fêtes populaires

Le ramadan

Le ramadan est un rituel pratiqué par les musulmans, les gens qui croient[1] en la religion islamique. Ils sont environ cinq millions en France, où l'islam est la deuxième religion après le catholicisme. Au Maghreb (au Maroc, en Algérie et en Tunisie), les musulmans sont en vaste majorité.

Le ramadan, le neuvième mois de l'année lunaire du calendrier islamique, est une période de jeûne[2]. Pendant ce mois, les musulmans ne peuvent ni manger, ni[3] boire[4] pendant la journée. Mais au coucher du soleil, les familles et les amis partagent des grands repas. Il y a aussi des fêtes foraines[5] où les gens s'amusent à la tombée de la nuit. À la fin du ramadan, il y a trois jours de fête qui s'appellent l'Aid-el-Fitr (qui veut dire **la fête de la rupture du jeûne**).

Voici le roi Arlequin, le roi du Carnaval

Le carême : Carnaval et Mardi gras

Les Chrétiens ont aussi un rituel de jeûne, la période du carême[6] (les quarante jours qui précèdent Pâques). Avant cette période assez stricte, il y a des fêtes importantes : à la Nouvelle-Orléans, par exemple, on fête le Mardi gras avec de la musique, de la danse et des déguisements[7]. En France, le Carnaval de Nice a lieu au mois de février avec ses Corsos de chars

Un défilé de Mardi gras à la Nouvelle-Orléans

décorés[8] et la célèbre Bataille de Fleurs[9] sur la Promenade des Anglais. Ces deux fêtes, à l'origine des fêtes religieuses, sont maintenant célébrées de façon[10] séculaire.

---

[1]*believe* [2]*fasting* [3]*neither, nor* [4]*to drink* [5]*traveling fairs* [6]*Lent* [7]*costumes, disguises* [8]*parade of decorated floats* [9]*battle of flowers*
[10]*in a way*

7-41 Une tradition importante

A. Avant d'écrire. Lisez les textes au sujet du rituel islamique, le ramadan, et les fêtes du Carnaval et de Mardi gras. Pensez maintenant aux rituels que vous pratiquez. Est-ce qu'il y a des rituels importants dans votre famille ? votre religion ? votre région ? votre université ? Choisissez un rituel avec des traditions que vous voulez décrire et faites une liste des éléments importants de ce rituel. Pensez à la dernière fois que vous avez participé à ce rituel, et indiquez un ou deux détails.

MODÈLE   La fête de *Homecoming*

Éléments importants	Détails
un match de football	*L'année dernière notre équipe a gagné contre l'université X.*
des chars décorés avec des fleurs	*Le char préparé par mes amis et moi était un désastre. Il y avait beaucoup de vent et toutes les fleurs en papier sont parties !*
un bal	*1. Je suis allé au bal avec Samantha, ma copine.* *2. Nous avons dansé jusqu'à une heure du matin.*

B. En écrivant. Maintenant, écrivez un paragraphe pour décrire la dernière fois que vous avez participé à ce rituel. N'oubliez pas de donner des détails et d'utiliser le passé composé et l'imparfait !

MODÈLE   La fête de *Homecoming*
> ➤ Une des traditions sur mon campus, c'est la fête de *Homecoming*. L'année dernière je me suis bien amusé avec mes amis. Notre équipe de football a bien joué pendant le match et elle a gagné ! Mais, le corso de chars pendant la mi-temps était un désastre pour mes amis et moi. Il faisait assez frais et il y avait beaucoup de vent. Les fleurs n'étaient pas bien fixées sur le char et elles ont commencé à partir. Le soir, il y avait un grand bal et j'ai dansé avec ma copine Samantha pendant des heures.

C. Après avoir écrit. Relisez votre texte pour vérifier surtout que vous avez bien utilisé le passé composé et l'imparfait pour exprimer les événements au passé. Échangez votre texte avec un/e camarade de classe pour comparer vos expériences.

Students will probably need help with vocabulary for this activity, as they are unlikely to know words specific to certain holidays and North American traditions. You might brainstorm with them or ask them to hand in a list of three or four words they will need. You could then prepare a master list for the use of the entire class, since many students will be asking for the same words. For this activity, it is important to emphasize to students that they need to stick with words and phrases that they know to tell their stories and not to make up new words. You might ask students to exchange first drafts with a classmate and have the classmate suggest places where more detail could be added to make the paragraph more interesting. After students get their drafts back and add more detail, have them exchange papers again with the same classmate for feedback before turning them in.

Vocabulaire

Leçon 1

pour parler de la famille	**to talk about the family**
un beau-frère	brother-in-law
une belle-sœur	sister-in-law
un demi-frère	half-brother
une demi-sœur	half-sister
divorcer	to divorce
une famille étendue	extended family
une famille monoparentale	single-parent family
une famille recomposée	blended family
une femme/ un homme au foyer	housewife/househusband
un père/ une mère célibataire	single father/mother
l'union libre (f.)	cohabitation

pour décrire une personne	**to describe a person**
absent/e	absent, missing
ancien/ne	former (placed before the noun)
autoritaire	authoritarian
avoir des bons rapports avec quelqu'un	to get along well with someone
avoir des racines (f.)	to have roots
juives	Jewish
maghrébines	North African
multiculturelles	multicultural
avoir une vision du monde	to have a world view
être bien dans sa peau	to have confidence in oneself
être pratiquant/e	to practice a faith
exigeant/e	strict, demanding
indulgent/e	indulgent, lenient
rebelle	rebellious
sécurisant/e	reassuring
traditionnel/le	traditional
travailleur/-euse	hard-working

pour parler des études et du travail	**to talk about studies and work**
apprendre à	to teach, to learn
avoir le goût du travail	to have a strong work ethic

verbes de communication	**verbs of communication**
décrire	to describe
dire	to say, to tell
écrire	to write
lire	to read

autres mots utiles	**other useful words**
comprendre (compris)	to understand (understood)
la connaissance	knowledge, understanding
une épreuve	test
faire partie de	to belong to
heureusement	fortunately
heureux/-euse	happy
permettre	to permit
rater	to miss
ressentir	to feel, be affected by
vivre	to live

Leçon 2

les grands événements de la vie	**major life events**
un anniversaire	birthday, anniversary
un baptême	baptism
une bougie	candle
un cadeau	gift
une cérémonie civile	civil ceremony
une fête religieuse	religious holiday
un gâteau	cake
les grandes vacances (f.)	summer vacation
un mariage	wedding
un/e marié/e	groom/bride
une marraine	godmother
un parrain	godfather

des vœux	wishes
un vœu	wish
Meilleurs vœux !	Best wishes!
Félicitations !	Congratulations!
Bon/Joyeux anniversaire !	Happy Birthday!
Joyeux Noël !	Merry Christmas!
Bonne année !	Happy New Year!
Bon voyage !	Have a good trip!
Bonnes vacances !	Have a good vacation!

pour parler des fêtes	to talk about holidays
avoir lieu	to take place
un bal populaire	a street dance
un brin de muguet	sprig of lily of the valley
cacher	hide
un défilé	parade
fêter	to celebrate
un feu d'artifice	fireworks
une fleur	flower
une galette	type of cake
un jour férié	public holiday
un œuf en chocolat	chocolate egg
partager	to share
un sapin	fir tree, Christmas tree

Leçon 3

les sentiments	feelings
avoir l'air (d'être) + adj.	to seem, to appear (to be) + adj.
Qu'est-ce que tu as ?	What's wrong?
amoureux/-euse	in love
anxieux/-euse	anxious
content/e	happy
embarrassé/e	embarrassed
en colère	angry
fâché/e	angry
furieux/-euse	furious
gêné/e	bothered, embarrassed
inquiet/inquiète	uneasy, anxious, worried
jaloux/-ouse	jealous
malheureux/-euse	unhappy
ravi/e	delighted
sensible	sensitive
surpris/e	surprised
triste	sad

pour exprimer les sentiments	to express feelings
crier	to yell
perdre son sang-froid	to lose one's composure
pleurer	to cry

quelques verbes pronominaux	some pronominal verbs
s'amuser	to have fun
s'appeler	to be named, called
s'arranger	to work out, to be all right
se calmer	to calm down
s'ennuyer	to become bored
s'entendre (avec)	to get along (with)
se fâcher (contre)	to get angry (at, with)
se faire du souci	to worry
Ne t'en fais pas !/ Ne vous en faites pas !	Don't worry!
s'inquiéter	to worry
se passer	to happen
se promener	to take a walk
se rappeler	to remember
se reposer	to rest
se téléphoner	to phone each another

dans la vie sentimentale	in one's emotional life
se disputer	to argue, to fight
s'embrasser	to kiss
se fiancer	to get engaged
se marier	to get married
se rencontrer	to meet (for the first time)
se séparer	to separate

autres verbes utiles	other useful verbs
connaître	to know, be familiar with
savoir	to know

quelques expressions utiles	some useful expressions
Ce n'est pas grave.	It's not serious.
fort (adv.)	loudly
une nouvelle	piece of news
si	whether, if
Voyons !	See here!

Qui va au marché ? Qu'est-ce qu'on achète ?
Qu'est-ce que vous voudriez acheter ?

 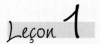
Venez chez nous !
Traditions gastronomiques

In this chapter:

- Ordering food and drink in a restaurant
- Describing meals and regional dishes
- Shopping for food
- Specifying quantities
- Recognizing the importance of cuisine and regional dishes in the Francophone world

Leçon 1 Qu'est-ce que vous prenez ?

POINTS DE DÉPART

Au café

TEXT AUDIO

Examine the photo and treat the dialogue first. Test students' comprehension: *On va au McDo, ou au café ?* etc. Explain key expressions using description, circumlocution and examples. Point out the growing popularity of fast-food restaurants in France—see the **Vie et culture** notes for more details. The café continues to play a part in the life of most French people as a place to socialize. Ask students whether they can think of a place that plays a similar role in their life.

ROMAIN : J'ai faim. On va au McDo ?

HÉLÈNE : Des hamburgers, des frites et du coca, quelle horreur ! Allons au café, c'est plus sympa.

(*au café*)

LE SERVEUR : Qu'est-ce que je vous sers ?

HÉLÈNE : J'ai très soif. Je voudrais seulement quelque chose à boire. Euh, une limonade, s'il vous plaît.

ROMAIN : Moi, j'ai faim. Je prends un croque-monsieur et une bière.

(*plus tard*)

ROMAIN : Monsieur !... L'addition, s'il vous plaît.

LE SERVEUR : J'arrive… Voilà.

HÉLÈNE : C'est combien ?

ROMAIN : Quatorze euros. On partage ?

HÉLÈNE : Sans problème.

Des boissons chaudes

un chocolat chaud

un café-crème

un thé au lait

Des boissons rafraîchissantes

une limonade

un Orangina

un coca

une cuillère

un jus d'orange

un citron pressé

du sucre

de l'eau minérale

des glaçons

Des boissons alcoolisées

du vin rouge

une bière

Des casse-croûte

un sandwich au jambon

une pizza

des crudités

des frites

un croque-monsieur

une salade

une glace

Present vocabulary using the visual of café fare (IRCD, Ch. 8): describe items in each semantic grouping to make meaning clear, for example: *un citron pressé, c'est du jus de citron avec de l'eau et du sucre.* Test comprehension (*Montrez le thé,* etc.), then have students repeat, using either/or questions: *C'est un café ou un chocolat chaud ?* Point out that the French generally drink less coffee than Americans, but prefer a stronger coffee. You might give students some of the more specific terms, *un déca, un crème,* either *un grand crème* or *un petit crème, un expresso, une noisette = un expresso avec un peu de lait ; un allongé = un expresso dilué avec de l'eau chaude, un café serré = un expresso très fort.* A customer may order *de l'eau minérale plate (Vittel, Évian) ou gazeuse (Perrier, Badoit). L'Orangina* and *la limonade* are also carbonated drinks. *Un croque-monsieur* is a grilled ham-and-cheese sandwich made with *pain de mie.* Most other sandwiches are made using *de la baguette.*

À vous la parole

8-1 Proposez des boissons. Proposez des boissons…

MODÈLE chaudes
➤ un café, un thé, un chocolat chaud

1. rafraîchissantes
2. gazeuses (*carbonated*)
3. alcoolisées
4. qui contiennent du jus de fruit
5. qui contiennent de la caféine
6. à prendre avec le dîner

8-1 Display the café items (IRCD, Ch. 8) as students complete the exercise.

8-2 Qu'est-ce que vous désirez ? Vous êtes au café. Dites ce que vous préférez d'après la situation donnée.

MODÈLE Vous êtes au McDo.

É1 Pour moi, un cheeseburger et un coca.

É2 Un hamburger avec des frites et une limonade.

1. Il fait très chaud.
2. Vous avez très froid.
3. Vous devez travailler très tard.
4. Il est 14 h et vous n'avez pas mangé.
5. C'est le matin.
6. Vous mangez une pizza et vous voulez boire quelque chose.
7. Vous avez très faim.
8. Vous avez très soif.

8-3 Au café. À tour de rôle, imaginez que vous êtes le serveur ou la serveuse. Vous prenez la commande de vos camarades qui sont les clients.

MODÈLE É1 Madame !

É2 Vous désirez ?

É1 Un café crème.

É2 Oui, et pour vous, mademoiselle ?

É3 Je voudrais un sandwich au jambon.

É2 C'est tout ?

É3 Non, une bière aussi, s'il vous plaît.

É2 Alors, pour monsieur, un café crème et pour mademoiselle un sandwich au jambon et une bière.

8-3 Use as a role-play activity. You may choose to act the part of the server. Use the photo from a café as a prompt, or bring in empty cups and bottles as props to enliven the activity.

Have students describe what they see in the photos; what would they most likely order? In 2004, there were close to 1000 McDonald's restaurants in France; in second place was Quick's, with about 330 restaurants. The number of traditional cafés has plummeted: from 200,000 in 1960 to fewer than 50,000 in 2003.

Vie et culture

La restauration à la chaîne

Les 86 chaînes de restauration en France aujourd'hui représentent 20 % des repas pris au restaurant. La plus importante est McDonald's, mais les Français mangent huit fois plus de sandwichs que de hamburgers. Ils achètent leurs sandwichs surtout dans des chaînes spécialisées (La Brioche Dorée, Au Bon Pain, Point Chaud) et pas forcément dans des cafés. Le nombre de cafés en France a beaucoup diminué, mais c'est encore un endroit agréable pour prendre un casse-croûte et discuter avec ses amis. Souvent, les cafés ont des terrasses où l'on aime prendre une boisson et regarder les gens passer.

Et vous ?

1. Est-ce qu'il y a beaucoup de cafés en Amérique du Nord ? Pourquoi, à votre avis ? Est-ce qu'il y a beaucoup de chaînes de restauration chez vous ?
2. Est-ce que vous allez habituellement au café pour retrouver vos amis ? Expliquez votre réponse.

Qu'est-ce que vous désirez ?

They have b[een] replaced to some degre[e] by fast food and speciali[zed] sandwich shops, as described he[re] in the cultur[e] note. See *Francoscopi[e]* *2003*, p. 21 for more information[.]

La Terrasse

1 CAFE CREME	3.40
1 CROISSANT	1.50

	HT 4.10	TVA 0.80	TTC 4.90
TVA 19.6%			

TOTAL	4.90

PRIX NETS SERVICE COMPRIS

Merci de votre visite, A Bientôt

Service compris

Regardez cette addition pour le café *La Terrasse*. Qu'est-ce qui a été commandé, et combien ça coûte (*cost*) ? Combien de taxes est-ce qu'on paie ? Quel est le total ? Est-ce que vous trouvez que c'est cher ?

Remarquez maintenant l'expression, « service compris ». Est-ce que vous pouvez deviner le sens de cette expression ? Dans les cafés, comme dans les restaurants en France, le service est toujours compris. C'est-à-dire que quand le serveur ou la serveuse vous apporte l'addition, il y a déjà un supplément inclus. Vous pouvez laisser un pourboire[1] en plus, mais ce n'est pas nécessaire.

[1]*tip*

Sons et lettres

La prononciation de la lettre *e*

You know that the letter **e** at the end of a word is usually not pronounced; it tells you that the consonant it follows is pronounced. Compare:

un anglais   vs.   une anglaise

However, final **e** may be pronounced in one-syllable words such as the pronouns **je** and **le**, the definite article **le**, the preposition **de** and the negative marker **ne**. Within a word, the letter **e** is pronounced in several different ways:

* Like the sound in **deux** [ø]

  ■ when followed by a single consonant letter:

  un se**mestre**   pre**mier**   une parte**naire**   vous pre**nez**

  ■ when followed by a consonant plus **r** or **l**:

  re**gretter**   un se**cret**   re**fléter**

* Like the sound in **mère** [ɛ]

  ■ in the final syllable of a word, when it is followed by one or more consonants:

  s**ert**   un archite**cte**   pre**nnent**

  ■ in a non-final syllable, when it is followed by two consonants (but see the exception below for double consonants):

  un se**rveur**   me**rcredi**   le re**staurant**   que**lque**

  ■ in a non-final syllable, when followed by an **x** (that letter represents the consonant groups **gz** or **ks**)

  un e**xemple**   e**xpliquer**   un e**xamen**

* Like the sound in **thé** [e] when it is followed by a double consonant:

  le de**ssert**   pre**ssé**   un e**ffort**

* Sometimes, in one syllable words like **je**, **te**, **le**, **de**, **ce**, etc., and in words like **samedi** and **omelette** the letter **e** is not pronounced; it is *elided*. For this reason a letter **e** pronounced with the vowel of **deux** is called an **unstable e**.

Compare the following two words. Look especially at the number of consonants before the unstable **e**:

ven**dre**di   sam**e**di

An unstable **e** is usually dropped within words when it comes after only one pronounced consonant. In **samedi**, it comes after a single consonant, /m/, so it is dropped. But in **vendredi**, it comes after two pronounced consonants /dr/, so it is retained.

This section anticipates the presentation of *prendre*, with its alternation between [ø] and [ɛ]: *prenons, prennent*. When the letter *e* is in non-final position, French speakers can produce a vowel ranging between [e] and [ɛ]. The *e instable* (*e muet, e caduc, schwa*, etc.) is pronounced variably: as zero (no sound) or a vowel ranging between /œ/ and /ø/. That vowel is often represented by the symbol [ə]. We propose that, when retained, unstable *e* should be pronounced as /ø/. This distinguishes it clearly from /a/ and /e/, as, for example in the pair *le livre* vs. *la livre* or *le chat* vs. *les chats*.

À vous la parole

Begin practice with a discrimination drill:
Levez le doigt quand vous entendez le son indiqué :
[ø] *comme dans peu en syllabe initiale : demander ; service ; depuis ; lever ; quelque ; devoir ; hier ; restaurant*
[ɛ] *comme dans mère en syllabe initiale : question ; derrière ; petit ; pressé ; descendre ; serveuse ; retour*

8-4 Comparez. Comparez la prononciation du **e** dans chaque colonne.

[ø] comme dans *deux*	[ɛ] comme dans *mère*
1. prenez	prennent
2. demain	hier
3. devoir	détester
4. petit	exemple
5. menu	restaurant
6. demande	accepte

8-5 If the question comes up, point out that unstable *e* is retained at the beginning of sentences (*Venez ! Je sors demain*) and in proper names like *Denise* and *Lefranc*. A full treatment of unstable **e** is provided in Ch. 11, L. 1 and L. 2.

8-5 Contrastes. Comparez la chute et le maintien du **e** instable. Répétez :

sam**e**di	vendredi
rar**e**ment	quelquefois
ach**e**tez	prenez
Mad**e**leine	Marguerite

8-6 Quel son ? Lisez les phrases suivantes en faisant attention à la lettre **e** prononcée comme la voyelle de **thé**, ou de **mère**, ou de **deux**. Faites tomber aussi les **e** instables. Les **e** instables qui ne tombent pas sont prononcés comme la voyelle de **deux**.

1. Vous prenez un dessert ?
2. Je vous sers quelque chose, mademoiselle ?
3. Dans ce restaurant, le service est excellent.
4. La serveuse a recommandé un citron pressé à Annette.
5. Appelez mercredi ou vendredi, jamais le samedi.
6. Elle explique la leçon à sa partenaire allemande.

Qu'est-ce que vous prenez ?

FORMES ET FONCTIONS

1. *Les verbes* prendre *et* boire

The verbs **prendre** and **boire** are irregular.

Additional practice activities for each **Formes et fonctions** section are provided by:
- Student Activities Manual
- *Chez nous* Companion Website:
  http://www.prenhall.com/cheznous

PRENDRE	*to take*		
SINGULIER		PLURIEL	
je	pre**nd**s	nous	prenons
tu	pre**nd**s	vous	prenez
il		ils	
elle }	prend	elles }	pre**nn**ent
on			

IMPÉRATIF : **Prends** un café ! **Prenez** du vin !
Prenons une pizza !

PASSÉ COMPOSÉ : J'ai **pris** un chocolat chaud.

BOIRE	*to drink*		
SINGULIER		PLURIEL	
je	**bo**is	nous	**bu**vons
tu	**bo**is	vous	**bu**vez
il		ils	
elle }	**bo**it	elles }	**boi**vent
on			

IMPÉRATIF : Ne **bois** pas ça ! **Buvez** de l'eau ! Ne
buvons pas trop !

PASSÉ COMPOSÉ : J'ai **bu** un café.

- The verb **prendre** is used with foods or beverages.

Je **prends** un citron pressé.	*I'm having lemonade.*
—Qu'est-ce que tu **as pris** ?	*—What did you have?*
—Un coca.	*—A Coke.*
On **prend** un sandwich au jambon et des frites.	*We're having a ham sandwich and fries.*

- **Prendre** also means *to take*.

On **prend** le bus ou un taxi ?	*Shall we take the bus or a taxi?*
Tu **prends** ton sac ?	*Are you taking your bag?*

- **Apprendre**, *to learn*, and **comprendre**, *to understand*, are formed like **prendre**.

Tu **apprends** l'italien ?	*You're learning Italian?*
Ils **comprennent** l'arabe.	*They understand Arabic.*

- **Boire** means *to drink*.

Qu'est-ce que tu **bois** ?	*What are you drinking?*
On **boit** du vin rouge.	*We're drinking red wine.*
Je n'**ai** pas **bu** de café.	*I didn't drink any coffee.*

These irregular verbs have three stems. Introduce the verbs inductively using questions and the vocabulary of the lesson; this might follow very naturally from the presentation and practice of the café fare. Ask students to tell how many different spoken forms they hear (four). Using the verb chart, start with the first-person plural and show how the vowel changes in the third-person plural: for *prendre*, /ø/ to /ɛ/; for *boire*, /y/ to /wa/. Like other verbs with four spoken forms, the consonant heard in the third-person plural is dropped in the singular forms. Point out to students that when *boire* is used without a complement, it is understood that one is talking about drinking alcohol. *Ils boivent* means "They drink (alcohol)" or "They are drinkers."

8-7 Quelle consommation ? Qu'est-ce que ces personnes prennent ou boivent ?

MODÈLE la dame âgée ?
> ➤ Elle prend un café crème.
> OU ➤ Elle boit un café crème.

1. et le jeune homme ?
2. et son amie ?

3. et les enfants ?

4. et le monsieur ?
5. et la petite fille ?

6. et les ouvriers ?

8-8 C'est logique. Posez une question logique pour savoir quelles langues ces personnes comprennent ou apprennent. Voici la liste des langues :
l'allemand, l'espagnol, le français, l'italien, le portugais, le russe

MODÈLES Bruno habite au Portugal.
> ➤ Alors il comprend le portugais ?

Je vais en Russie.
> ➤ Alors tu apprends le russe ?

1. Isabella habite en Italie.
2. J'habite en Russie.
3. Franz habite en Allemagne.
4. Nous habitons en France.
5. Mes cousins habitent en Espagne.

6. Guillaume et Pierre vont à Moscou.
7. Nous allons au Mexique.
8. Mélanie va en Allemagne.
9. Je vais au Portugal.
10. Nous allons au Québec.

8-9 Vos habitudes. Dites ce que vous prenez dans ces situations. Comparez votre réponse avec la réponse de votre partenaire.

MODÈLE le matin, avant d'aller en classe ?
> É1 Moi, je prends un café noir.
> É2 Et moi, un jus d'orange.

1. pendant la journée ?
2. quand vous n'avez pas le temps de manger ?
3. le soir, quand vous ne pouvez pas dormir ?

4. quand vous regardez la télé ?
5. quand vous êtes au cinéma ?
6. quand vous sortez avec des amis ?
7. quand vous avez très soif ?

2. L'article partitif

- Look at the following examples:

J'aime le café.	*I like coffee.*
Je n'aime pas le thé.	*I don't like tea.*
J'adore les croissants.	*I love croissants.*
Je déteste les bananes.	*I hate bananas.*

Nouns are of two types in French and in English. *Count nouns* refer to things that can be counted, for example, croissants. *Mass nouns* are things that normally are not counted, like coffee, tea, sugar, and water. Notice that, as in the examples above, count nouns can be made plural; mass nouns are normally used only in the singular. In all these examples, the definite article is used because the speaker is using the noun in a general sense, to express preferences.

- When you refer to a noun not previously specified, use the indefinite article if it is a count noun.

Il a mangé **un** sandwich.	*He ate a sandwich.*
Je prends **une** pizza.	*I'm having a pizza.*
Elle a acheté **des** oranges.	*She bought some oranges.*

Use the *partitive article* if it is a mass noun.

Tu veux **du** coca ?	*Do you want some Coke?*
Tu prends **de la** glace ?	*Do you want some ice cream?*
Je sers **de l'**eau minérale.	*I'm serving mineral water.*

- In the examples below, note the differences in meaning between the definite article, on the one hand, and the indefinite and partitive articles on the other. Here the definite article denotes a specific or presupposed item. The indefinite or partitive article denotes an unspecified item.

Definite article	**Indefinite or partitive article**
Il a pris **l'**orange.	Il a pris **une** orange.
He took the orange.	*He took an orange.* (***any** orange*)
(*the specific orange*)	
Vous voulez **les** sandwichs ?	Vous voulez **des** sandwichs ?
Do you want the sandwiches?	*Do you want sandwiches?*
(*these particular sandwiches*)	(*any sandwiches*)
Elle a mangé **le** pain.	Elle a mangé **du** pain.
She ate the bread.	*She ate some bread.*
(*this specific bread*)	

In both French and English we sometimes use the singular indefinite article with mass nouns: *Je voudrais une bière,* I'd like a beer. *Des* is the plural form of the indefinite article; there is no plural form of the partitive article. The partitive article is used with mass nouns and the indefinite article with count nouns. Both of these articles contrast with the definite article. Depending on the verb, the definite article carries the meaning of generic or of previously identified, specified or presupposed: *J'aime le vin* (generic), *Où est le vin ?* (presupposed), *Tu as acheté la pizza ?* (presupposed). The examples provided here, and the first exercises, emphasize these distinctions. Use the examples to illustrate these points as you explain.

- In negative sentences, both the indefinite and the partitive articles are replaced by **de/d'**:

Il prend **un** Orangina ?	—Non, non, il ne prend pas **d'**Orangina.
Je peux avoir **des** glaçons ?	—On n'a pas **de** glaçons, mademoiselle.
Vous servez **du** thé ?	—Non, nous ne servons pas **de** thé, monsieur.

À vous la parole

Begin practice with simple substitution drills. Begin by having students manipulate familiar forms: *Vous voulez du café ?* —*Oui, j'aime le café,* etc. This allows them to hear multiple examples of the partitive used in context. Remind students of the importance of the verb in determining the choice of article. Next have students use the new partitive forms: *Vous aimez le café ? —Oui, donnez-moi du café,* etc. Drill the negative forms as well: *Je ne prends pas de glace ; de l'eau minérale ; du thé,* etc.

For another simple exercise, put realia or pictures depicting types of food and drink in a bag. A student holding the bag answers questions from others about the contents: *Il y a du coca dans le sac ? —Oui, voilà le coca. Il y a des sandwichs ? —Non, il n'y a pas de sandwichs,* etc.

8-12 This contrasts the use of the non-definite (indefinite and partitive) articles to that of the definite article. As a follow-up, have students report back what their partner said.

Avant de lire. If you treated the earlier Prévert poem, **Familliale** in Ch. 4, L. 1, then you might use the following reading strategy for this new poem. Use your familiarity with a particular writer to predict the style and content of a new text. Ask students the following: Describe what you know about the way in which Prévert writes—is his language simple or complex? Does he tend to use description or narration? Will his subject likely be lighthearted or serious?

Stratégie

Use a poem's title to help you anticipate its focus and content. Consider as well that a title may have broader implications relating to the subjective as well as the literal meaning of a poem.

8-10 Ce n'est pas logique ! Corrigez ces phrases illogiques.

MODÈLE   Avec le café, je prends du vin blanc.
> Avec le café, je prends du lait.

1. Comme dessert, je prends une pizza.
2. Avec une pizza, je prends du café.
3. Quand j'ai très soif, je prends du vin.
4. Généralement, je prends de la bière avec des glaçons.
5. Quand il fait très chaud, on prend du chocolat chaud.
6. Dans un thé au lait, on met des frites.
7. Quand on veut manger quelque chose, on prend de la limonade.
8. Quand on veut boire quelque chose, on prend une pizza.

8-11 Au café. D'après les descriptions suivantes, imaginez ce que chaque personne prend au café.

MODÈLE   Vincent n'a jamais assez de temps pour manger le matin.
> Il prend seulement un café noir.

1. Mme Sauvert fait très attention de manger correctement.
2. Sophie voudrait un dessert.
3. Claire n'a pas très faim.
4. Rémi a très soif.
5. Antoine est végétarien.
6. Le petit Nicolas a très faim.
7. M. Berger mange souvent au fast-food.

8-12 Vos habitudes et préférences. Complétez chaque phrase et comparez votre réponse avec la réponse de votre partenaire.

MODÈLE   Le matin, je prends toujours…

É1 Le matin, je prends toujours du café.
É2 Je déteste le café. Moi, je prends toujours du thé.

1. Le matin, je prends toujours…
2. Quand je vais au McDo, je prends toujours…
3. Le week-end, je prends…
4. Quand j'ai très soif, j'aime…
5. Quand j'étudie très tard le soir, je prends souvent…
6. Ma boisson préférée, c'est…

Lisons

TEXT AUDIO

8-13 Déjeuner du matin

A. Avant de lire. The title of the poem that you are going to read is ***Déjeuner du matin***. What does it lead you to expect the poem will be about, at a literal and perhaps subjective level? How might a poem with this focus be organized?
As you read, consider the series of events that comprise the **déjeuner du matin**. Try to determine why the poet, Jacques Prévert, is focusing on this simple meal.

B. En lisant. Ce poème est une narration. Un personnage décrit une série d'incidents qui se passent pendant le déjeuner du matin. Pour comprendre son histoire, considérez les questions suivantes.

1. Il y a combien de personnages dans le poème ? Qui sont ces personnes, à votre avis ?
2. Qui raconte cette histoire, et comment ? N'oubliez pas que Prévert a commencé sa carrière en écrivant des scénarios pour le cinéma.
3. Résumez les activités. Par exemple, (a) le monsieur a bu une tasse de café, (b)…

C. En regardant de plus près.

Maintenant examinez les aspects suivants du poème.

1. Les personnages dans le poème n'ont pas de nom : ils sont simplement **il** et **je**. Qui sont ces personnages, à votre avis ?
2. Le poème décrit en général les actions du personnage masculin. Comment remarquez-vous la présence et les sentiments de l'autre personnage ?
3. Quel est le ton du poème : gai, triste ? Quelles techniques utilise Prévert pour communiquer cela ?

D. Après avoir lu. Maintenant que vous avez lu et discuté du poème :

1. Imaginez :
   a. ce qui s'est passé juste avant le début du poème
   b. ce qui se passe après la fin du poème
2. Le titre du poème est *Déjeuner du matin*. Est-ce que le petit-déjeuner est en réalité le sujet du poème ? Pourquoi, à votre avis, est-ce que Prévert a choisi ce titre ?

DÉJEUNER DU MATIN

Il a mis le café
Dans la tasse°
Il a mis le lait
Dans la tasse de café
Il a mis le sucre   5
Dans le café au lait
Avec la petite cuiller°
Il a tourné
Il a bu le café au lait
Et il a reposé la tasse   10
Sans me parler
Il a allumé
Une cigarette
Il a fait des ronds
Avec la fumée   15
Il a mis les cendres
Dans le cendrier
Sans me parler
Sans me regarder
Il s'est levé   20
Il a mis
Son chapeau sur sa tête
Il a mis
Son manteau de pluie
Parce qu'il pleuvait   25
Et il est parti
Sous la pluie
Sans une parole
Sans me regarder
Et moi j'ai pris   30
Ma tête dans ma main
Et j'ai pleuré.

     Jacques Prévert, *Paroles*.
     © Éditions Gallimard

cup

cuillère

Additional activities to develop the four skills are provided by:
- Student Activities Manual
- Text Audio
- *Chez nous* video
- *Chez nous* Companion Website:
  http://www.prenhall.com/cheznous

En lisant Mime the actions of the poem as students listen to the recording.

Have students guess the meaning of unfamiliar words based on their context: *tourné, allumé, des ronds, ma tête.* Point out related words: *les cendres/le cendrier, une parole/parlé.*

En regardant de plus près. Point out to students that the second character, *je*, appears very late in the poem. What effect does this have?

Après avoir lu. Point out to students the ambiguities in the poem, which allow for multiple interpretations by the reader. The reader must actively create some of the meaning of the poem.

As a more extended follow-up, ask students to recount one of their own daily activities using Prévert's style.

Leçon 2 À table !

POINTS DE DÉPART

Les repas

Present the vocabulary scene by scene, using the visuals for meals (IRCD, Ch. 8); you may want to treat this vocabulary over two days, for example, treating breakfast vocabulary on day one and the other meals on day two. Show on a map where the various families live. Describe each meal, model pronunciation, then test comprehension by having students point to the item you name. Have students repeat the new words: *C'est du beurre ou de la confiture ?* etc. As you move from one group to the next, review the most useful words already presented.

Teach the superordinate terms *une entrée, un plat principal, un dessert,* as well as *une viande* and *un légume.* These words appear in the **Vie et culture** notes and throughout the lesson and are helpful in organizing the various food words into categories for practice and review.

To review the food vocabulary, have students compete in teams to see how many items each team can list for a specific category. Send one member of each team to the board for each category, and give them a limited amount of time to write their lists. Sample categories: *les boissons rafraîchissantes ; les fruits ; les légumes ; les desserts.*

Point out cultural features: times for meals, size of meals, choices of snacks. *Une rôtie* is a type of toast; this is a Canadian expression. *Bacon* is pronounced /bakō/. Remind students that in Canada the meals are: *le déjeuner, le dîner, le souper.* In France also, many people refer to the evening meal as *le souper,* and soup is often served, as discussed in the reading, *Dîner en chaussons ? Méfiez-vous !* in the *Venez chez nous !* of Ch. 6. Small children often have an after-school snack, *le goûter,* around four o'clock, since dinner is typically served around eight o'clock. They may have *un pain au chocolat* (a chocolate croissant), or a portion of a *baguette* with a piece of chocolate inside (*du pain avec du chocolat*), *un fruit, un yaourt,* or *des tartines,* with juice or water to drink.

un bol de café au lait
un croissant
du lait
du sucre
du beurre
du pain
des céréales
des tartines
de la confiture

Les Sangala habitent à Bordeaux ; ils prennent le petit-déjeuner vers huit heures.

une tasse de café noir
du bacon
une tranche de pain grillé / une rôtie
un verre de jus d'orange
un œuf sur le plat
du poivre
du sel

Les Canadiens prennent souvent un petit-déjeuner copieux.

316 *trois cent seize* **CHAPITRE 8 ◆ DU MARCHÉ À LA TABLE**

des pommes de terre sautées

du poulet

une tarte aux pommes

une carafe d'eau

une bouteille de vin rouge

des haricots verts

du fromage

Les Dupuis habitent une ferme en Touraine ; ils déjeunent chez eux à midi et demi.

un yaourt

une pomme

une poire

des fruits

une banane

des biscuits

du pain avec du chocolat

Marie-Christelle, Jean-Pierre et Guillaume habitent en Belgique ; ils prennent le goûter vers quatre heures et demie.

une carafe d'eau

du fromage

des fruits

des asperges

du riz

du poisson

M. et Mme Haddad habitent en Algérie ; ils dînent vers huit heures.

Vie et culture

Use the restaurant menu to illustrate the categories described in the note and to provide additional examples of *entrées, plats principaux, desserts*.
Remind students that *une entrée* is a starter or appetizer and that *le plat principal* refers to the main course. Note the differences between the two menus offered, in terms of price and choice.

Le déjeuner

Pour les Français, le repas principal de la journée est le déjeuner. Quand c'est possible, les gens rentrent chez eux à midi pour manger en famille. Autrement, ils mangent dans un restaurant près de leur travail. En quoi consiste un déjeuner ordinaire ? Regardez ces menus trouvés à l'entrée d'un petit restaurant. D'abord, il y a une entrée ; indiquez une ou deux des entrées proposées. Ensuite, il y un plat principal (de la viande ou du poisson) servi avec un légume. Après, on peut choisir entre un fromage ou un dessert. À la fin du repas, on prend le café. Quel menu et quels plats est-ce que vous préférez et pourquoi ?

Le dîner

Le repas du soir, le dîner ou le souper, est moins copieux. Il commence souvent par une soupe. Ensuite on peut avoir une omelette, des pâtes, de la viande ou du poisson avec un légume. Pour finir, il y a un peu de fromage, un yaourt ou des fruits. Le dîner en famille commence assez tard, vers huit heures. Souvent on regarde le journal télévisé pendant le repas.

Et vous ?

1. Est-ce que vos habitudes sont semblables aux habitudes des Français, ou différentes ? Par exemple, quel est le repas principal de la journée chez vous ? Expliquez votre réponse.
2. Est-ce que vous dînez plus tôt ou plus tard que les Français le soir ? Pourquoi ? Est-ce que vous regardez la télé en même temps ?

Qui va déjeuner chez ses grands-parents ? À votre avis, est-ce que c'est un repas ordinaire ou un repas de fête ? En France, le grand repas de la semaine est le déjeuner du dimanche. Souvent on invite des membres de la famille ou des bons amis. Ces déjeuners sont très animés et très longs : ils peuvent durer entre deux et trois heures.

Point out that Saturday dinner is also a time when the French invite friends and family for a meal. Many French people enjoy entertaining in their homes for special occasions such as birthdays, baptisms, confirmations, etc., and the focus of the get-together is frequently an elaborate meal.

À vous la parole

8-14 Quel repas ? Selon la description, identifiez le repas.

MODÈLE   M. Maisonneuve prend des œufs sur le plat avec du jambon et des rôties.
> ➤ Il prend le petit-déjeuner.

1. Mme Lopez donne des pains au chocolat et du lait à ses enfants.
2. Mme Leroux prend seulement du café et un croissant.
3. Nicolas prend un yaourt et une pomme.
4. M. et Mme Poirier prennent des œufs avec des rôties.
5. Il est une heure ; les Schumann mangent du poisson avec du riz.
6. Nous sommes à Montréal, le soir. Mme Ladouceur sert de la soupe.
7. Avant de retourner au bureau, Marion et Gaëlle prennent un hamburger et des frites au McDo.
8. Il est huit heures du soir, et les Deleuze mangent du rosbif et des pommes de terre.

8-14 Personalize by having students describe one of their typical meals and let classmates guess which meal it is.

Alternative or review exercise:
Les bonnes combinaisons. Qu'est-ce qu'on prend avec la boisson ou l'aliment mentionné ? avec le café ? —du sucre ou du lait ; avec le thé ? avec le pain ? avec les œufs ? avec le poulet ? avec le poisson ? avec le fromage ? avec les hamburgers ?

C'est quel repas ? Qu'est-ce qu'ils prennent ?

8-15 Quels ingrédients ? Avec quoi est-ce qu'on fait les plats suivants ? Avec un/e partenaire, mettez-vous d'accord sur les ingrédients.

MODÈLE   une omelette ?

        É1   Avec quoi est-ce qu'on fait une omelette ?

        É2   On fait une omelette avec des œufs, du lait et du beurre.

        É1   Et aussi avec du jambon et du fromage.

1. un citron pressé ?
2. une omelette ?
3. un sandwich ?
4. une salade de fruits ?
5. une tartine ?
6. un croque-monsieur ?
7. un café au lait ?
8. un pain au chocolat ?

8-16 Follow up by comparing responses for each pair of students.

8-16 Vos préférences. Qu'est-ce que vous prenez d'habitude dans les situations suivantes ? Comparez vos habitudes avec celles d'un/e camarade de classe.

MODÈLE comme boisson, au petit-déjeuner ?

É1 D'habitude, je prends du café avec du sucre.

É2 Moi, je ne prends pas de boisson au petit-déjeuner.

1. comme boisson, au petit-déjeuner ?
2. à manger, au petit-déjeuner ?
3. à manger, au déjeuner ?
4. comme goûter, l'après-midi ?
5. quand vous voulez prendre une boisson, l'après-midi ?
6. comme boisson, au dîner ?
7. quand vous n'avez pas dîné, tard le soir ?
8. quand vous êtes très stressé/e ?
9. comme boisson, quand vous avez des invités ?

FORMES ET FONCTIONS

1. *Les expressions indéfinies et négatives*

The expressions *quelquefois* and *ne ... jamais* were presented in Ch. 4, L. 1; here they are treated more systematically along with other indefinite and negative expressions. Present using the examples, which provide a context for understanding meaning and usage.

• Look at the following examples:

—Tu manges **quelque chose** ?   —*Are you eating something?*

—Non, je **ne** mange **rien**.   —*No, I'm not eating anything.*

—Il y a **quelqu'un** à la porte ?   —*Is there someone at the door?*

—Non, il **n'**y a **personne**.   —*No, there's no one there.*

—Tu vas **quelquefois** au café ?   —*Do you go to the café sometimes?*

—Non, je **ne** vais **jamais** au café.   —*No, I never go to the café.*

As you can see in the examples above, the negative expressions are composed of two parts: **ne** … plus another element carrying the specific meaning.

• These negative expressions may also be used alone:

—Qu'est-ce que tu as ?   —**Rien**.

—Qui vient ce soir ?   —**Personne**.

—Tu es allé en Italie ?   —**Jamais**.

• **Rien** and **personne** may be used as the subject of a sentence; **ne** still precedes the verb:

Rien ne s'est passé hier.   *Nothing happened yesterday.*

Personne n'est venu.   *No one came.*

The following chart summarizes indefinite and negative expressions referring to time, things, and persons:

indéfini	négatif
quelquefois	ne … jamais
quelque chose	ne … rien
quelqu'un	ne … personne

- Note the placement of negative and indefinite expressions in the **passé composé** and **futur proche**:

Have students describe placement for *rien* and *personne* in the various tenses when they function as the subject.

—Tu **n'**as **rien** mangé ?   —Si, j'ai mangé **quelque chose.**

—Tu **n'**a **jamais** dîné ici ?   —Si, j'ai mangé ici **quelquefois.**

—Tu **n'**as vu **personne** ?   —Si, j'ai vu **quelqu'un.**

—Il **ne** va **rien** boire ?   —Si, il va boire **quelque chose.**

—Il **ne** va **jamais** nous accompagner ?   —Si, il va nous accompagner **quelquefois.**

—Il **ne** va inviter **personne** ?   —Si, il va inviter **quelqu'un.**

À vous la parole

8-17 Au négatif. Répondez avec une expression négative.

MODÈLE   Qu'est-ce que tu regardes ?
   ➤ Rien. Je ne regarde rien.

8-17 First complete the exercise by having students respond only with the negative expression. Then repeat the exercise, having students respond with a full sentence.

1. Qu'est-ce que tu écoutes ?
2. Qui nous invite à dîner ?
3. Quand est-ce qu'ils sont venus ?
4. Qu'est-ce qu'il y a dans ton verre ?
5. Qui est-ce que tu écoutes ?
6. Qu'est-ce que tu prends ?
7. Quand est-ce que tu vas au restaurant ?
8. Qui est-ce que tu invites ?

8-18 Une petite contradiction. Dites le contraire dans vos réponses !

MODÈLE   Est-ce qu'il y a quelqu'un au café ?
   ➤ Non, il n'y a personne.

   Vous ne travaillez jamais ?
   ➤ Si, je travaille quelquefois.

1. Il y a quelque chose sur la table ?
2. Est-ce qu'elle invite quelqu'un ?
3. Vous achetez quelque chose ?
4. Vous ne mangez rien ?
5. Personne n'a téléphoné ?
6. Il ne mange jamais au restaurant ?
7. Vous préparez quelquefois le dîner ?
8. Il y a quelqu'un à la porte ?

8-19 Des situations. Pour chaque situation, discutez avec un/e partenaire de ce que vous faites. Utilisez **ne … jamais**, **ne … personne**, **ne … rien** et leurs contraires **quelquefois**, **quelqu'un** et **quelque chose**.

MODÈLE   quand vous allez au café

    É1   Qu'est-ce que tu fais quand tu vas au café ?

    É2   Je ne prends jamais de café parce que je ne l'aime pas. Je prends quelquefois un thé ou un chocolat chaud. Et toi ?

    É1   Moi, je ne prends rien au café parce que c'est trop cher.

1. quand vous allez au café
2. quand vous allez au McDo
3. quand vous sortez avec des amis le week-end
4. quand vous partez en vacances en famille
5. quand vous avez beaucoup de travail à la fac
6. quand vous préparez un repas pour des amis
7. quand vous êtes en cours de français
8. quand vous n'avez pas beaucoup d'argent

2. *La modalité :* devoir, pouvoir *et* vouloir

• You saw in **Chapitre 3, Leçon 3** that the verbs **devoir**, **pouvoir**, and **vouloir** can be used to soften commands and make suggestions. Compare:

Attendez devant le café !	*Wait in front of the café!*
Vous **devez** attendre devant le café.	*You must wait in front of the café.*
Vous **pouvez** attendre devant le café.	*You can wait in front of the café.*
Vous **voulez** attendre devant le café ?	*Will you wait in front of the café?*

• The conditional forms make orders or suggestions sound even more polite. The conditional forms are generally equivalent to *should, could,* and *would like to*.

Vous **devriez** manger quelque chose.	*You should eat something.*
Ils **pourraient** nous accompagner au café.	*They could go with us to the café.*
Tu **voudrais** prendre un apéritif ?	*Would you like to have an apéritif?*

• Here are the conditional forms for **devoir**, **pouvoir**, and **vouloir**.

SINGULIER		PLURIEL	
je	dev**rais**	nous	dev**rions**
	pour**rais**		pour**rions**
	voud**rais**		voud**rions**
tu	dev**rais**	vous	dev**riez**
	pour**rais**		pour**riez**
	voud**rais**		voud**riez**
il	dev**rait**	ils	dev**raient**
elle	pour**rait**		pour**raient**
on	voud**rait**	elles	voud**raient**

À vous la parole

8-20 Au restaurant.
Le patron donne des instructions aux serveurs ; formulez des phrases plus polies.

MODÈLE   Pierre, prends la commande de cette dame !
> ➤ Pierre, tu pourrais prendre la commande de cette dame ?
OU ➤ Pierre, tu devrais prendre la commande de cette dame.

1. Jennifer, mets la table !
2. Sarah et Loïc, apportez ces plats à la cuisine !
3. Laurent et Olivier, prenez les commandes !
4. Nathalie, aide ce monsieur !
5. Grégory, apporte un plat chaud à cette dame !
6. David et Camille, mettez les salades ici !
7. Sarah et Camille, aidez Loïc !
8. Jennifer, va dans la cuisine !

8-21 Qu'est-ce qu'on devrait manger ?
Offrez une suggestion à chaque personne selon le cas.

MODÈLE   Stéphanie voudrait maigrir.
> ➤ Elle devrait manger une salade.
OU ➤ Elle pourrait prendre des crudités.

1. Mathieu n'aime pas la viande.
2. Nous adorons les fruits.
3. Jessica est végétarienne.
4. M. et Mme Dulac voudraient maigrir.
5. Je voudrais un petit dessert.
6. Nous n'aimons pas le fromage.
7. Jonathan et Ben vont courir dans un marathon.
8. Je vais au bord de la mer pour les vacances.

8-22 Bonnes résolutions.
Avec un/e partenaire, parlez de vos bonnes résolutions.

MODÈLE   boire de l'alcool

    É1 Est-ce que tu bois de l'alcool ?
    É2 Oui, mais je devrais boire moins. Et toi ?
    É1 Non, je ne bois pas.
    É2 C'est bien.

1. boire de l'alcool
2. faire régulièrement de l'exercice physique
3. manger des repas équilibrés
4. manger trop de desserts
5. dormir toujours assez
6. se détendre de temps en temps
7. regarder trop la télévision

Begin with a discrimination drill: *poli ou impoli ? ; Tu dois attendre ; Vous devriez manger ; Je veux un café ; Je voudrais un thé au citron ; Il devrait manger moins de sucre ; Vous devez vous coucher de bonne heure ; Nous voudrions prendre un dessert ; Elle veut manger un fruit ; Je voudrais du vin rouge ;* etc. Follow with a transformation drill, present tense to conditional: *Elle doit écouter — Elle devrait écouter,* etc.

8-20 This activity focuses on the *tu* and *vous* forms.

8-21 You might repeat the exercise, having students offer advice directly, using the *tu* or *vous* form.

8-22 Survey students afterwards to find out what the most popular resolutions are.

8-23 Un bon restaurant

This menu is from a moderately priced restaurant. Point out that in French restaurants, patrons can choose to order *un menu*, which offers a limited choice of items at a fixed price, or *à la carte*, which offers more choice but usually costs more as well. Treat the menu first as a reading, using cognates and context to discover the meaning of unfamiliar words and expressions. Tell students that, as in North America, restaurant dishes often have elaborate names that indicate ingredients or manner of preparation; students should not be concerned with understanding all the vocabulary. Instead, have students pick out basic vocabulary that helps them identify the main ingredient(s) of each dish.

A. Avant d'écouter. Regardez le menu du *Petit Villiers*. Dans ce restaurant, est-ce qu'on peut commander un menu, ou est-ce qu'il faut commander à la carte (c'est à dire, chaque plat séparément) ? Entre quelles catégories est-ce que les clients doivent choisir ?

Le Petit Villiers

75 AVENUE DE VILLIERS, 75017 PARIS – Tél. 01 48 88 96 59

Notre Chef, Laurent BEAUVALLET vous propose :

Notre Menu
16,00 €
Une entrée + un plat + un dessert

❧

Les Entrées

Médaillons de foie gras de canard
Soupe de poisson
Assiette de crudités
Tomates mozzarella à l'huile d'olive et basilic
Œuf mayonnaise
Suggestion du jour

❧

Les Plats

Viandes
Magret de canard au poivre vert, pommes sautées
Entrecôte grillée nature ou béarnaise
Suggestion du jour

Poissons
Dos de saumon nature ou béarnaise ou à l'huile d'olive parfumée d'origan
Truite meunière aux amandes, pommes vapeur
Filet de haddock au beurre fondu

❧

Les Desserts

Salade de fruits de saison
Crème brûlée à la cassonade
Mousse au chocolat noir
Crêpe à la marmelade de fruits et son coulis de framboises
Glaces ou sorbets (vanille, chocolat, café, cassis, poire)
Suggestion du jour

B. En écoutant. Maintenant écoutez le chef qui présente son restaurant sur un site Internet et complétez chaque phrase avec tous les éléments que vous entendez.

1. Laurent Beauvallet est…

   _____ le chef de cuisine.

   _____ le serveur.

   _____ le patron de l'établissement.

2. Le restaurant est…

   _____ ouvert du lundi au samedi.

   _____ fermé le lundi.

   _____ ouvert sept jours sur sept.

3. Le restaurant a…

   _____ une terrasse en été.

   _____ un menu pour enfants.

   _____ une salle avec une belle cheminée.

   _____ une petite salle pour les groupes de 20 personnes.

4. Le restaurant propose une cuisine…

   _____ exotique.

   _____ simple.

   _____ française.

   _____ à base de produits frais.

   _____ traditionnelle.

   _____ entièrement faite maison.

5. Écoutez de nouveau et regardez la carte ; cochez (√) les plats qui sont mentionnés.

C. Après avoir écouté. Est-ce que ce restaurant vous plaît ? Pourquoi ? Si vous alliez dans ce restaurant, qu'est-ce que vous voudriez prendre ?

Un bon restaurant niçois. Est-ce que vous aimeriez manger ici ? Pourquoi ?

Script for Écoutons

Bonjour, bienvenue au restaurant *Le Petit Villiers*. Je m'appelle Laurent Beauvallet. Je suis le chef de cuisine ainsi que le patron de l'établissement. Voilà maintenant plus de dix ans que nous sommes ouverts dans ce très beau quartier du 17e arrondissement. Nous sommes ouverts sept jours sur sept, midi et soir, durant toute l'année, et nous disposons d'une terrasse en été ainsi que d'une petite salle pouvant accueillir des groupes allant jusqu'à une vingtaine de personnes. Nous proposons une cuisine française de tradition entièrement faite maison. Nous avons un menu au prix de 16 euros comprenant une quinzaine d'entrées au choix, ainsi qu'une douzaine de plats et une quinzaine de desserts tels que médaillons de foie gras de canard, soupe de poisson, magret de canard au poivre vert, truite meunière aux amandes ainsi qu'en dessert crème brûlée à la cassonade, crêpe à la marmelade de fruits et son coulis de framboises. En sachant qu'il y a une entrée, un plat et un dessert qui changent chaque jour suivant la saison, le tout dans une ambiance décontractée. Au revoir et à très bientôt. [adapted from: www.paris.planresto.fr]

Après avoir écouté. You can follow up on this activity by putting students in groups to role play ordering food in a restaurant. Students can order from the menu provided in the book or if you have menus from other Francophone restaurants, you could bring them to class, perhaps copied so each student or group has one. A nice touch is to bring some round plastic trays and a few white towels to class for the students to use as props in their role-plays.

Leçon 3 *Faisons des courses*

POINTS DE DÉPART

Allons au supermarché

C'est samedi. Les Mathieu font les courses à Super U. Ils se trouvent au rayon fruits et légumes.

M. MATHIEU :	Qu'est-ce qui va bien avec le rôti de porc ? Des haricots ? J'aime ça, moi.
MME MATHIEU :	Il n'y a pas de haricots aujourd'hui.
M. MATHIEU :	Alors, des épinards ?
MME MATHIEU :	Les enfants les détestent. Les petit pois, c'est mieux.
M. MATHIEU :	Mais ils sont trop chers. Six euros le kilo !
MME MATHIEU :	C'est vrai, mais ils ont l'air délicieux et très frais.
M. MATHIEU :	Et pour le dessert, des fruits ?
MME MATHIEU :	Non, les fraises sont trop mûres, les pêches trop vertes et le reste trop cher.

À vous la parole

8-24 Quel rayon ? Nous sommes au supermarché. Où est-ce que vous entendez cela ? Choisissez vos réponses dans cette liste.

au rayon crémerie	au rayon boulangerie-pâtisserie
au rayon charcuterie	au rayon fruits et légumes
au rayon viandes et poissons	au rayon surgelés

MODÈLE Je voudrais une demi-douzaine de petits pains, s'il vous plaît.
> ➤ C'est au rayon boulangerie-pâtisserie.

1. Je mets les croissants dans un sac ?
2. Qu'est-ce que tu préfères, le pâté de campagne ou le jambon ?
3. Vous avez des sardines ?
4. Comme dessert, on prend de la glace ou un sorbet ?
5. Je vous recommande le brie, madame.
6. Il y a des côtelettes d'agneau et du poulet.
7. La pâtissière fait des gâteaux magnifiques !
8. Les melons sont beaux, mais ils sont chers.

Present the vocabulary using the grocery store image (IRCD, Ch. 8) and describing what one can find in each of the grocery store sections. Many of the products will be familiar to students, and some new items can be presented first for receptive control only. Test students' comprehension by having them point to an item you name; have them repeat, using either/or questions: *Ce sont des petits pois ou des champignons ?* etc. Then move on to the dialogue.

Let students listen to the dialogue, then ask questions to check comprehension. Have students role-play, using parts of the dialogue and varying the vocabulary: *Qu'est-ce qui va bien avec le poulet ?* — *Des petits pois ; Il n'y a pas de tomates.* — *Alors, des carottes.* Be sure to provide a clear model. Use the **Vie et culture** notes to talk about where people shop for food.

In conjunction with this section, you might wish to present the video clip *Pour faire une vinaigrette*, which includes key vocabulary and focuses on the ingredients needed and the process of preparing a simple recipe.

8-24 *Le rayon crémerie* has not been formally presented. Ask students what they think would be found in that section by focusing their attention on the word itself and the related word, *crème*. As a variation, bring in a net bag of food items and have students guess where you would have bought them. For items that you wish to make part of students' productive vocabulary, play "Kim's Game:" show students 8–10 articles which you then hide from view; they must write down a list of those articles.

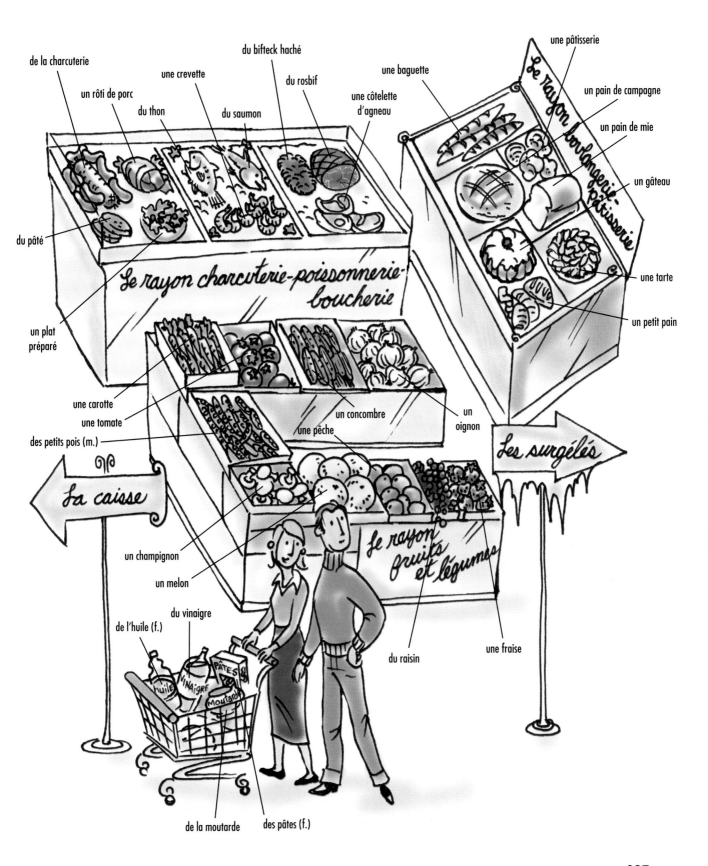

de la charcuterie

un rôti de porc

du thon

une crevette

du saumon

du bifteck haché

du rosbif

une côtelette d'agneau

du pâté

un plat préparé

Le rayon charcuterie-poissonnerie-boucherie

une baguette

une pâtisserie

un pain de campagne

un pain de mie

Le rayon boulangerie-pâtisserie

un gâteau

une tarte

un petit pain

une carotte

une tomate

des petits pois (m.)

un concombre

une pêche

un oignon

Les surgélés

La caisse

un champignon

un melon

Le rayon fruits et légumes

de l'huile (f.)

du vinaigre

du raisin

une fraise

de la moutarde

des pâtes (f.)

Vie et culture

Les petits commerçants et les grandes surfaces

Regardez ces photos de magasins d'alimentation[1]. Qu'est-ce que vous pouvez acheter dans chaque endroit ? Où est-ce que vous préférez faire les courses et pourquoi ?

Pour faire les courses, les Français ont beaucoup de choix. Ils peuvent aller chez les petits commerçants ou faire leurs courses une fois par semaine dans les grandes surfaces. Par exemple, le matin, beaucoup de Français achètent la baguette du petit-déjeuner chez le boulanger et les journaux[2] et les magazines chez le marchand de journaux. Pour les repas de fête, ils vont à la pâtisserie où ils achètent un gâteau ou des tartelettes. Autrement, comme les Américains, la majorité des Français

Une épicerie à Paris

vont faire les gros achats une ou deux fois par semaine dans les supermarchés ou les grandes surfaces comme Intermarché ou Super U. Dans les supermarchés on peut tout acheter en même temps au même endroit. Les grandes surfaces offrent aussi toutes sortes de nourriture. En plus, on y trouve des vêtements, des livres, des CD, des appareils électroniques (comme des télés, des magnétoscopes, etc.), et différentes choses pour la maison.

[1]food [2]newspapers

On trouve de tout dans une grande surface.

Le fromager vend une grande variété de fromages.

Use the photos to exploit the text and check for general comprehension: have students identify the various shops and summarize what items are generally purchased at each. Have them identify the main shopping options presented: neighborhood shops, supermarkets, and fresh markets. Ask them to describe differences between markets in France and those in other parts of the Francophone world. Help students see the relationship between words such as *le boulanger* (a person) and *la boulangerie* (a place) and *une tarte* and *des tartelettes* (small tarts). Help them derive from context the meaning of the expressions *faire leur marché, marché couvert, marché en plein air*. Follow up with the cross-cultural questions.

8-25 Des achats. Qu'est-ce que ces gens ont acheté ? Avec un/e partenaire, suggérez un ou deux produits.

MODÈLE   Pauline se trouve au rayon boucherie.

   É1 Elle achète un rôti.
   É2 Et aussi un poulet.

As you make cross-cultural comparisons, suggest to students some possible reasons for shopping where they do: *C'est plus facile, c'est moins cher*, etc.

Les marchés

Regardez ces photos de marchés en France et au Maroc. Qu'est-ce que vous pouvez acheter dans ces marchés ? Est-ce qu'il y a des marchés là où vous habitez ? Si oui, est-ce que vous allez quelquefois au marché pour faire des achats ? Quels sont les avantages d'acheter certains produits au marché ?

Pour acheter des fruits et des légumes frais, les Français aiment faire leur marché, surtout le samedi et le dimanche. Faire son marché, cela veut dire aller à un marché couvert ou en plein air. Il est vrai que les marchés sont moins pratiques que les supermarchés, en particulier en hiver ou quand il pleut. Alors pourquoi est-ce que les gens les préfèrent ? C'est parce que les produits sont plus

Un marché au Maroc

frais, et surtout parce que les marchés sont plus animés. On y trouve une grande variété de couleurs, d'odeurs et de bruits[3].

Il y a des marchés dans tous les pays[4] francophones. Aux Antilles et en Afrique ils sont encore plus vivants et intéressants qu'en Europe. La foule[5] est plus dense et les couleurs plus variées, les odeurs plus fortes, le langage plus expressif. Aller au marché est vraiment une bonne manière de connaître la culture des pays francophones.

[3]*noises*   [4]*countries*   [5]*crowd*

Un marché en plein air à Nîmes

1. Nicolas a trouvé un beau dessert.
2. M. Dumas va faire une salade.
3. Mme Ducastel est allée au rayon fruits et légumes pour acheter des fruits.
4. M. et Mme Camus choisissent entre le saumon et la truite.
5. Matthieu a seulement acheté des surgelés.
6. Gaëlle est allée au rayon crémerie.
7. Christophe est passé au rayon légumes.

Put students in pairs or small groups and have them plan a menu and the required shopping for a big dinner. Have students decide what they will serve: *comme entrée ? comme plat principal ? comme légume ? comme fromage ? comme boisson ? comme dessert ?* Be sure to model with a few students:

É1 On peut acheter du jambon et des crudités.

É2 Je déteste ça. Je préfère acheter des crevettes.

É1 C'est cher, mais d'accord. Et comme plat principal ? ...

Before completing this activity, review with students the meaning of *l'entrée* and *le plat principal*, both of which were presented in the **Vie et culture** notes in L. 2. Remind students to use vocabulary they have already learned to complete this exercise. As a follow-up, have each group describe their menu.

8-26 Vos goûts. Quelle est votre réaction si votre partenaire vous propose les aliments suivants ? Choisissez une des expressions suivantes pour répondre :

Super !	C'est délicieux !	J'aime ça.	Miam !
Oui, pourquoi pas ?	Je déteste ça.	Quelle horreur !	Beurk !

MODÈLE   les bananes trop mûres

　　　　É1 Tu aimes les bananes trop mûres ?

　　　　É2 Quelle horreur ! Je déteste ça !

1. les bananes trop mûres
2. les bananes vertes
3. le sel sur le melon
4. les fraises trop mûres
5. les spaghettis à la sauce tomate
6. le poulet à la moutarde avec beaucoup d'oignons
7. la soupe aux carottes
8. des fines tranches de concombre sur du pain
9. le saumon fumé (*smoked*)
10. le jambon cru (*cured ham*) avec du melon comme en Italie

Sons et lettres

TEXT AUDIO

Le *h* aspiré et le *h* muet

In French the letter **h** does not represent any sound. Most words beginning with **h** behave as if they began with a vowel, in other words *elision* and *liaison* are normally made. These words are said to contain **un h muet**.

Point out that most words written with *h* contain "mute h." Most dictionaries mark "aspirate h" words: the *Larousse* dictionaries use the asterisk, as do we; the *Robert* provides the phonetic transcription and uses the symbol ['].

l'hiver	l'histoire
les‿hommes	les‿habitudes
/z/	/z/
pas d'huile	s'habiller

Other words beginning with **h** behave as if they began with a consonant: there is neither *elision* nor *liaison*. These words contain **un h aspiré**. In the glossary at the end of this textbook and in the vocabulary lists in each chapter, these words are preceded by an asterisk (*).

un *hamburger	la *Hollande
les *haricots verts	les *hors-d'œuvre

Some words that begin with a vowel letter also behave as if they contain **un h aspiré**.

le nombre *un	le *onze novembre

À vous la parole

8-27 Contrastes. Comparez les deux mots ou expressions.

1. les *haricots verts   les hommes
2. la *Hollande   l'huile
3. un *hamburger   un hôpital
4. les *homards (*lobsters*) les huîtres (*oysters*)

8-28 Phrases. Répétez chaque phrase.

1. J'aime les *haricots verts avec de l'huile d'olive et du citron.
2. Comme fruits de mer, je préfère les huîtres, mais mon mari adore le *homard.
3. On a réservé une table le *onze avril à huit heures.
4. Dans cet hôtel, ils servent des asperges à la sauce *hollandaise.

FORMES ET FONCTIONS

1. *Les expressions de quantité*

- In **Chapitre 4**, **Leçon 1**, you learned that adverbs of quantity are followed by **de/d'** when used with nouns.

trop de	Il y a **trop de** sucre.	*There's too much sugar.*
beaucoup de	Elle a **beaucoup de** riz.	*She has lots of rice.*
assez de	Vous avez **assez d'**huile ?	*Do you have enough oil?*
peu de	J'ai très **peu de** café.	*I have very little coffee.*
ne … pas de	Tu n'as **pas de** sel ?	*Don't you have any salt?*

- Nouns of measure are used in the same way.

une tasse de	Prends **une tasse de** café.	*Have a cup of coffee.*
une boîte de	Donne-moi **une boîte de** sardines.	*Give me a can of sardines.*
	On va prendre **une boîte de** céréales ?	*Are we going to get a box of cereal?*
un kilo de	Achète **un kilo de** pommes.	*Buy a kilo of apples.*
un litre de	Il faut **un litre de** lait.	*We need a liter of milk.*

Review the expressions students already know with a communicative activity, perhaps one taken from Ch. 4, L. 1, before presenting the new material. Use the visual of quantities (IRCD, Ch. 8) to introduce these expressions; test comprehension by showing the image without labels and asking students to point to the item you describe.

Here are some useful expressions for specifying quantity.

une bouteille d'eau

une carafe de vin rouge

un bol de café

une assiette de crudités

un pot de moutarde

un verre de vin

une tasse de thé

un litre de coca

un morceau de brie

un paquet de riz

une tranche de pâté

un kilo de pommes de terre

un demi-kilo de tomates (500 g de tomates)

une douzaine d'œufs

Point out that *un bol* is generally reserved for coffee in the morning and/or cereal. Soup would be served in *une assiette creuse* especially in formal situations; at home, one might serve *un bol de soupe*. Have students tell: a) what items they would buy in the quantities specified: *une boîte ?* — *une boîte de sardines, une boîte de céréales,* etc.; b) how much of a product they would normally buy: *Des carottes ?* — *un kilo de carottes. Des sardines ?* — *une boîte de sardines. Des tomates ? du vin ? des œufs ? du riz ? du brie ? des pommes de terre ? des champignons ? de l'huile ? des crevettes ? des petits pois ?* Next, have students imagine they're making vegetable soup, and tell what they buy/don't buy: *Des pêches ? — Non, je n'achète pas de pêches. Des carottes ? des oignons ? des haricots verts ? des tomates ? des petits pois ? des asperges ? de la salade ? des champignons ? des pommes de terre ?*

À vous la parole

8-29 À table. Quelle quantité est-ce que vous prenez de ces aliments ?

MODÈLE   Vous prenez de l'eau ?
➤ Oui, donnez-moi un verre d'eau.

1. Vous prenez du jambon ?
2. Vous prenez du café au lait ?
3. Vous prenez du pain ?
4. Vous prenez des crudités ?

5. Vous prenez du vin ?
6. Vous prenez de la viande ?
7. Vous prenez du fromage ?
8. Vous prenez du thé ?

8-30 Un pot-au-feu. Qu'est-ce qu'il faut pour faire un pot-au-feu ? Regardez l'image du « pot-au-feu géant » préparé pour un festival d'été en Bretagne. Avec un/e partenaire, décidez de quelle quantité il faudrait pour préparer un pot-au-feu pour votre famille.

MODÈLE   É1 Pour un pot-au-feu géant, il
                    faut 260 kg de viande ! Et pour
                    ta famille ?

              É2 Pour ma famille, il faut
                    seulement un kilo de viande…

👥👥 **8-31 Préparation pour un repas.** Qu'est-ce qu'il faut acheter, et en quelles quantités ? Décidez avec votre partenaire.

MODÈLE   Marion va faire une omelette au jambon pour quatre personnes.

   É1   Elle doit acheter une douzaine d'œufs.
   É2   Et aussi quatre tranches de jambon.
   É1   Oui, c'est ça.

1. Cédric va inviter deux amis pour prendre le dessert.
2. Mme Salazar va faire un rôti de porc et des petits pois pour elle, son mari et leurs trois enfants.
3. Nous sommes en hiver. M. Bertrand voudrait préparer une salade de fruits.
4. Vanessa va servir du saumon à sept personnes. Quels légumes est-ce que vous lui suggérez ?
5. Audrey a invité ses parents, son fiancé et les parents de son fiancé à déjeuner dimanche. Qu'est-ce qu'elle pourrait servir comme entrée ?
6. M. Charpentier a des amis chez lui ; avec sa femme, ses deux enfants et lui, ça fait sept personnes. Il va chez le boulanger. Qu'est-ce qu'il devrait acheter ?
7. M. Papin a invité son chef de bureau et sa femme à dîner. Qu'est-ce que les Papin pourraient préparer comme plat principal ? Et comme dessert ?

2. *Le pronom partitif* en

• The pronoun **en** replaces nouns used with the partitive article or the plural indefinite article **des**:

Tu as **du beurre** ?   *Do you have butter?*
—Oui, j'**en** ai.   *—Yes, I have some.*

Vous avez acheté **de l'huile** ?   *Did you buy oil?*
—Oui, j'**en** ai acheté.   *—Yes, I bought some.*

Il n'y a pas **de sucre** ?   *There isn't any sugar?*
—Si, il y **en** a.   *—Yes, there is some.*

Qui veut **des fraises à la crème** ?   *Who wants strawberries with cream?*
—Jérémy **en** veut. Il aime bien ça.   *—Jeremy wants some. He likes that.*

• Like the direct-object pronouns, **en** is placed immediately before the conjugated verb of a sentence, unless there is an infinitive. In that case, it precedes the infinitive.

Qui a pris **du jus d'orange** ?   *Who drank orange juice?*
—Ce monsieur **en** a pris.   *—That man drank some.*
—Moi, je n'**en** ai pas pris.   *—Me, I didn't drink any.*

Tu vas acheter **des œufs** ?   *Are you going to buy eggs?*
—Non, je ne vais pas **en** acheter.   *—No, I'm not going to buy any.*
—Cyril, lui, il va **en** acheter.   *—Cyril, he's going to buy some.*

For a more personalized activity, put students into groups of three or four to plan a meal using the following activity. Have them write out their menu and grocery list. Give them five minutes to work, then let each group describe their meal.
Vous préparez un repas. Vous et vos amis, vous avez invité des gens à dîner. D'abord, décidez d'un menu. Ensuite, préparez une liste de choses à acheter. Enfin, distribuez les responsabilités : qui achète quoi, et où ?

MODÈLE É1 Comme entrée, on peut servir des crudités.
        É2 Oui, c'est bon et ce n'est pas cher. Ensuite, du rosbif ou du poulet ?
        É3 Moi, je préfère le poulet avec des haricots verts.
        É1 Donc, on va au rayon boucherie pour acheter un gros poulet de deux kilos.
        É2 Je vais au marché samedi matin pour acheter un kilo de haricots verts et…

Suggestions :
1. un dîner d'anniversaire
2. un pique-nique
3. un petit-déjeuner copieux
4. un repas pas cher
5. une autre idée ? précisez !

You may wish to point out that with *quelques* the noun is replaced by *en*, but *quelques-uns* or *quelques-unes* must be added: *Tu as quelques bouteilles de vin rouge ? —Oui, j'en ai quelques-unes.* No agreement of the past participle is made with *en*.

The object pronoun *en* is placed after the conjugated verb in affirmative commands and joined to it by a hyphen: *Donnez-en à Suzanne ! En* is placed before the conjugated verb in negative commands: *N'en donnez pas à Paul !* This point is treated in Ch. 12, L. 3.

- To replace nouns modified by an expression of quantity (including numbers), use **en**. The expression of quantity is placed at the end of the sentence.

Elle sert beaucoup **de glace** ?	*Does she serve a lot of ice cream?*
—Oui, elle **en** sert beaucoup.	*—Yes, she serves a lot (of it).*
Tu as pris **du vin rouge** ?	*Did you have some red wine?*
—Oui, j'**en** ai bu un verre.	*—Yes, I drank a glass (of it).*
Combien de **melons** est-ce que vous allez prendre ?	*How many melons are you going to take?*
—Nous allons **en** prendre trois.	*—We'll take three (of them).*

À vous la parole

8-32 This exercise simply requires students to demonstrate comprehension of pronoun usage. For additional practice: a) Show a picture of a market (for example, IRCD, Ch. 8) and ask students whether they can see certain items: *Il y a des carottes ? —Non, il n'y en a pas. / —Oui, il y en a.* b) Have students express their preferences as you point out various items: *Voici des carottes. —J'aime bien les carottes ; je vais en acheter un kilo. / —Je n'aime pas les carottes ; je ne vais pas en acheter.* For written practice that mixes the various tenses, see ex. SAM 8-23 in the Workbook.

8-32 Qu'est-ce qu'il a acheté ? David achète des provisions. D'après les indications, qu'est-ce qu'il a acheté ? Avec un/e partenaire, trouvez des possibilités.

MODÈLE Il en a acheté une douzaine.

> É1 Il a acheté une douzaine d'œufs.
> É2 Il a acheté une douzaine de citrons.

1. Il en a pris un pot.
2. Il en a acheté un morceau.
3. Il en a pris une douzaine.
4. Il en a acheté une bouteille.
5. Il en a pris deux paquets.
6. Il en a demandé deux.
7. Il en a pris beaucoup.
8. Il en a acheté un kilo.
9. Il en a demandé dix tranches.
10. Il en a acheté une boîte.

8-33 Elle en prend combien ? Voici la liste des provisions que Mme Serre achète pour sa famille. Quelles quantités est-ce qu'il lui faut ?

MODÈLE des carottes
> ➤ Elle en achète un kilo.

- carottes
- oignons
- petits pains
- pâtes
- moutarde
- vin
- eau minérale
- lait
- œufs
- saumon

8-34 Vous en avez combien ? Donnez une réponse logique et personnalisée, et comparez-la avec la réponse de votre partenaire. Ensuite, comparez vos réponses avec les autres étudiants dans votre cours.

MODÈLE des sœurs ?

> É1 J'en ai une.
> É2 Je n'en ai pas.

1. des sœurs ?
2. des frères ?
3. des amis ?
4. des problèmes ?
5. de l'argent ?
6. des devoirs ?
7. des responsabilités ?
8. des vacances ?

8-35 Vos habitudes alimentaires

A. Avant d'écrire. Réfléchissez à vos habitudes alimentaires. Dans une journée normale, combien de fois est-ce que vous mangez ? Quand ? Qu'est-ce que vous mangez ?

To complete the **Écrivons**, instruct students to actually keep track of what and when they eat during a 24-hour period.

1. Pour vous aider à organiser vos pensées, complétez ce tableau.

L'heure	Les aliments
MODÈLE *vers 9 h*	*un café (quelquefois un croissant)*
à midi	*un sandwich, de la soupe*

2. Ensuite, évaluez vos habitudes : Est-ce que vous mangez…

très mal ?   assez bien ?   très bien ?

B. En écrivant. Maintenant, décrivez et analysez vos habitudes.

1. Expliquez ce que vous mangez et à quel moment.
2. Faites une évaluation de vos habitudes alimentaires. Comment est-ce que vous mangez : très mal, mal, assez bien, bien ou très bien ?
3. Expliquez pourquoi vous avez ces habitudes alimentaires.

MODÈLE ➤ Normalement, je mange très mal. Le matin, je ne mange rien parce que j'ai un cours à huit heures et je dors jusqu'à sept heures et demie. Après mon premier cours, vers dix heures, je prends un café et parfois un croissant, et je vais à un autre cours. À midi, je vais au restaurant universitaire ; là-bas, je prends souvent…

C. Après avoir écrit.

1. Relisez votre paragraphe. Vérifiez que vous avez inclus toutes les informations nécessaires.
2. Relisez de nouveau votre paragraphe pour éliminer les fautes d'orthographe et les fautes de grammaire.
3. Échangez votre paragraphe avec quelqu'un dans votre classe. Est-ce qu'il/elle le comprend ? Faites les changements nécessaires.

Après avoir écrit. When they have completed the exercise, have students compare their eating habits: who eats best, and why?

Venez chez nous !
Traditions gastronomiques

Provide an overview of the lesson by showing the video montage *Traditions gastronomiques*; ask students whether they recognize specific regional dishes or can identify ingredients.

Activate students' background knowledge by asking them what words or ideas they associate with *la cuisine française*. Generate a list on the board. Have them do the same for American cuisine and compare the two lists. What stereotypes are revealed?

You may wish to identify the various dishes pictured and model pronunciation before students begin the exercise. In that case, students would be describing the dishes to each other and not matching the picture with the name.

Locate the various regions on a map and discuss why particular specialties might come from each region. For example, Marseille is a seaport city, hence the fish soup.

Parlons

8-36 Les plats régionaux

A. Avant de parler. La France a la réputation d'être le pays de la bonne table et des bons vins. C'est une réputation bien méritée. La cuisine française est très variée. Chaque région a ses plats particuliers qui dépendent de son climat, de ses produits et de ses traditions culturelles. Voici une liste de quelques spécialités régionales en France :

* la bouillabaisse marseillaise
* la choucroute alsacienne
* la quiche lorraine
* les crêpes bretonnes
* le coq au vin bourguignon
* la fondue savoyarde

Est-ce que vous connaissez déjà certains de ces plats ?

B. En parlant. Avec un/e partenaire, regardez ces images de spécialités et de plats régionaux. Décrivez chaque photo et essayez d'identifier le plat.

MODÈLE É1 Regarde cette image. C'est une soupe.

É2 Oui, une soupe de poisson. Il y a des morceaux de poissons.

É1 Oui, et aussi des tomates parce que le bouillon est rouge.

É2 C'est la bouillabaisse marseillaise ?

É1 C'est possible. Oui, c'est ça.

C. Après avoir parlé. Est-ce que vous et votre partenaire avez identifié tous les plats ? Comparez vos réponses aux réponses de vos camarades de classe.

L'origine des plats régionaux

Savez-vous que les plats régionaux les plus célèbres — la quiche lorraine, la choucroute alsacienne, la salade niçoise et la bouillabaisse — étaient à l'origine des plats de pauvres[1], c'est-à-dire, des plats qu'on faisait avec des produits assez ordinaires, donc pas chers, ou avec des restes[2] ? Prenons la bouillabaisse, par exemple. Au début, c'était un plat fait avec les poissons que les pêcheurs[3] ne pouvaient pas vendre. On faisait bouillir ces poissons, on ajoutait de la tomate et on servait cette soupe avec des tranches de pain. Aujourd'hui on fait la bouillabaisse avec des produits plus « nobles », donc plus chers : par exemple, on ajoute des fruits de mer[4] et on la sert avec des tranches de pain grillé.

[1]*poor people*   [2]*leftovers*   [3]*fishermen*   [4]*shell fish*

Et vous ?

1. Est-ce que vous connaissez certaines de ces spécialités françaises ? Quels plats est-ce que vous avez déjà goûtés ? Est-ce que vous les avez aimés ?
2. Est-ce qu'il y a des plats en Amérique du Nord considérés à l'origine comme des « plats de pauvres », faits avec des restes, mais qui sont devenus maintenant des spécialités régionales célèbres ?
3. Les spécialités régionales décrites ici sont basées sur des produits frais et des ingrédients de la région. Est-ce qu'il y a dans votre région des spécialités basées sur des produits locaux ? Est-ce qu'on peut trouver ces spécialités partout maintenant ou est-ce qu'elles se trouvent uniquement dans votre région ?

Have students skim the passage to glean the main idea: that the origin of many regional specialties is a common dish made of ingredients that are plentiful. The text includes a number of examples of the *imparfait* and can serve as a reminder of how this tense functions.

8-37 Voici les spécialités de chez nous

A. Avant de regarder. Est-ce que vous avez déjà dîné dans un restaurant marocain ? africain ? Si oui, quelles sont les spécialités que vous avez goûtées ? Regardez la photo — est-ce que vous reconnaissez certains de ces plats du Bénin ? Quels sont les ingrédients nécessaires pour préparer ces plats ?

Voici un buffet plein de spécialités du Bénin.

B. En regardant. Deux personnes vont décrire les spécialités de leur région. Trouvez toutes les bonnes réponses à chaque question.

1. Bienvenu décrit des spécialités du…
   a. Mali.
   b. Bénin.
   c. Cameroun.
2. D'abord, c'est de l'épinard avec…
   a. du poulet.
   b. du porc.
   c. des crevettes.
3. L'épinard est accompagné de pâte faite de…
   a. riz.
   b. maïs.
   c. plantain.
4. Le plantain, c'est une forme de…
   a. céréales.
   b. légume.
   c. banane.
5. Fadoua décrit une spécialité du…
   a. Maroc.
   b. Tchad.
   c. Midi de la France.

6. Pour préparer ce plat, il faut…
   a. un grand four.
   b. un couscoussier.
   c. une casserole.
7. Comme ingrédients, on peut mettre…
   a. de la viande.
   b. du poisson.
   c. des tomates.
   d. de la citrouille (_pumpkin_).
   e. des oignons.
   f. des navets (_turnips_).
   g. des concombres.
8. Pour servir, on met un bol avec du bouillon pour…
   a. boire.
   b. mélanger (_mix_) les ingrédients.
   c. mouiller (_moisten_) le plat.

C. Après avoir regardé. Est-ce que vous avez déjà goûté un de ces plats ? Est-ce que vous avez aimé ce plat ? Pourquoi ? Quel plat est-ce que vous voudriez essayer, et pourquoi ?

Lisons

8-38 Une recette louisianaise

A. Avant de lire. When you think of Louisiana, what types of food come to mind? Jambalaya? Gumbo? Crayfish étouffé? These typical dishes are made with local products, using traditional methods of preparation. Look at the recipe below and the photo that accompanies it: have you ever eaten pralines, another specialty of Louisiana? What will probably be among the main ingredients? Follow the text step-by-step, making sure you understand the procedures, the ingredients, and the quantities involved.

B. En lisant. Trouvez les réponses aux questions suivantes.

1. La recette est divisée en trois parties — quelles sont ces trois parties ?
2. Dressez une liste des ingrédients, par exemple : du sucre brun clair,…

Stratégie

Read a text such as a recipe intensively: make sure you understand each step as it is outlined before you proceed.

En lisant, **Key:** 1) a) a brief description including preparation time/difficulty; b) a list of ingredients; c) instructions for preparing the dish. 2) du sucre brun, du beurre, des œufs, du sel, de la farine, de la poudre à pâte, de la vanille, des pécans.

Pralines aux pacanes

Temps de préparation :
5 minutes

Temps de cuisson :
30 minutes

Difficulté : très facile

Traditionnellement, les pralines sont faites avec des noix de pécans ou pacanes qui poussent abondamment dans le Sud des États-Unis.

Mark Thomas/Getty Images, Inc. — Foodpix

Ingrédients pour 12 grandes pralines ou 48 morceaux

500 g de sucre brun clair
450 g de beurre fondu
2 œufs battus
1 pincée de sel

500 g de farine[1]
1 cuillerée à thé de poudre à pâte[2]
1 c. à thé de vanille
250 g de pécans

Préparation

1. dans un bol, mélanger le beurre, le sucre brun, les œufs battus et la vanille ;
2. dans un autre bol mélanger la farine, la poudre à pâte et le sel ;
3. incorporer le mélange de farine doucement au beurre-cassonade ;
4. incorporer les pacanes ;
5. déposer des cuillerées de ce mélange sur une plaque graissée et farinée ;
6. enfourner dans un four préchauffé à 160°C (325°F) pendant 30 min ;
7. laisser refroidir avant de servir.

[1] flour   [2] baking powder

Help students figure out the various cooking terms and ingredients they may not be familiar with. Note cooking terms of Louisiana French origin: *une cuillerée à thé,* literally, a teaspoonful, rather than *une cuillerée à café ; de la poudre à pâte* (baking powder), rather than *de la levure ; du sucre brun,* rather than *du sucre roux.* Note the variable spelling of *pécans/pacanes.*

Point out to students that directions in recipes (and in other contexts as well) are often written in infinitive form.

C. En regardant de plus près. Maintenant examinez quelques caractéristiques du texte.

1. Quand on prépare une recette, il est très important de bien mesurer les ingrédients. Quel est le sens exact des mots et des abréviations suivants ?
   a. g
   b. une pincée
   c. une cuillerée à thé
2. Les verbes suivants indiquent les méthodes de préparation. Quel est le sens de chaque verbe ?
   a. mélanger
   b. incorporer
   c. déposer
   d. enfourner
   e. laisser refroidir
3. Les adjectifs expliquent aussi la préparation ; quel est le sens des expressions suivantes ?
   a. du beurre **fondu**
   b. un œuf **battu**
   c. une plaque **graissée** et **farinée**

D. Après avoir lu. Discutez de ces questions avec vos camarades de classe.

1. Pourquoi, à votre avis, est-ce que c'est un bon exemple d'un plat louisianais ?
2. Est-ce que vous connaissez une autre recette qui ressemble à celle-ci ? Quelle est cette recette ?
3. Essayez cette recette, et apportez des pralines à votre professeur et à vos camarades de classe !

Un bon couscous. Est-ce que vous avez déjà mangé du couscous ? Où ?

écrivons

8-39 Les spécialités de chez vous

Gratin franc-comtois au fromage à raclette

Préparation
15 mn

Cuisson
15 mn

Ingrédients
(pour 4 personnes)
8 pommes de terre
1 oignon
250 g de fromage
à raclette
sel, poivre, ail
20 cl de vin blanc
sec du Jura

Conseil du Sommelier
Accompagner d'un vin blanc du Jura (le même que celui utilisé dans la recette)

Gratin franc-comtois au fromage à raclette

1 Couper les pommes de terre en rondelles puis les poêler dans du beurre 8 à 10 mn et les saler légèrement.

2 Émincer l'oignon, couper le fromage à raclette en lamelles.

3 Beurrer votre plat à gratin et le frotter à l'ail.

4 Dans ce plat, disposer les rondelles de pommes de terre, l'oignon, recouvrir de lamelles de raclette

Facultatif : arroser le tout de 20 cl de vin blanc sec du Jura

5 Poivrer et faire cuire au four thermostat 7/9 environ 15 mn.

Bon appétit !

Jean Perrin
Maître Fromager en Franche-Comté

Les vaches qui produisent le lait pour les fromages Jean PERRIN portent autour de leur cou des clarines, les cloches franc-comtoises traditionnelles.

A. Avant d'écrire. Vous allez préparer une petite brochure publicitaire pour décrire un aspect de la gastronomie de votre région.

1. D'abord, en petits groupes, faites une liste des plats et des boissons typiques de votre région.
2. Ensuite, chaque personne doit choisir un des plats ou une des boissons. Notez les ingrédients nécessaires pour préparer ce plat/cette boisson. Est-ce que cette spécialité est liée aux produits agricoles de votre région ?
3. Notez l'origine de ce plat/cette boisson. Est-ce que c'est une spécialité d'origine mexicaine ? italienne ? chinoise ?
4. Enfin, notez les traditions associées à ce plat/cette boisson. Est-ce qu'on mange ce plat pour une fête ? Avec qui est-ce qu'on le mange ? etc.

B. En écrivant. Maintenant rédigez un ou deux paragraphes qui décrivent cette spécialité. Regardez comme modèle la recette pour le **Gratin franc-comtois au fromage à raclette**. N'oubliez pas de donner un titre à votre brochure.

C. Après avoir écrit. Pour rendre votre brochure publicitaire plus intéressante :

1. Tapez votre description. N'oubliez pas de la relire pour vérifier que vous avez inclus toutes les informations nécessaires, et corrigez les fautes d'orthographe et de grammaire !
2. Trouvez une photo de votre spécialité pour illustrer votre description.
3. Trouvez (ou écrivez) une recette (en français) de votre spécialité.

To help students create a simple recipe for a regional specialty, provide conversion charts for measures and oven temperatures; see the IRM. Encourage them, however, to use the recipes they have seen as models.

Vocabulaire

Leçon 1

au café ou au restaurant	*in the cafe or in the restaurant*
l'addition (f.)	*bill*
avoir faim	*to be hungry*
avoir soif	*to be thirsty*
boire	*to drink*
prendre	*to have (to eat or drink)*

des boissons chaudes	*hot drinks*
un café (crème)	*coffee (with cream)*
un chocolat chaud	*hot chocolate*
un thé (au lait)	*tea (with milk)*

des boissons rafraîchissantes	*cold drinks*
un citron pressé	*lemonade*
un coca(-cola)	*cola*
de l'eau (minérale) (f.)	*water (mineral water)*
un jus d'orange	*orange juice*
une limonade	*lemon-lime soft drink*
un Orangina	*orange soda*
du sucre	*sugar*
des glaçons (m.)	*ice cubes*
une cuillère	*spoon*

des boissons alcoolisées	*alcoholic drinks*
une bière	*beer*
du vin (rouge, blanc, rosé)	*(red, white, rosé) wine*

des casse-croûte (m.)	*snacks*
un croque-monsieur	*grilled ham and cheese sandwich*
des crudités (f.)	*cut-up raw vegetables*
des frites (f.)	*French fries*
une glace	*ice cream*
un *hamburger	*hamburger*
une pizza	*pizza*
une salade verte	*green salad*
un sandwich (au jambon, au fromage)	*(ham, cheese) sandwich*

quelques expressions utiles	*some useful expressions*
commander	*to order*
comprendre	*to understand*
je voudrais…	*I would like…*
quelle horreur !	*how awful!*
sans probleme	*no problem*
Le service est compris ?	*Is the tip included?*

Leçon 2

les repas	*meals*
le petit-déjeuner	*breakfast*
le déjeuner	*lunch*
le goûter	*afternoon snack*
le dîner	*dinner*

au petit-déjeuner	*at breakfast*
prendre le petit-déjeuner	*to have breakfast*
le bacon	*bacon*
le beurre	*butter*
un café au lait	*coffee with milk*
des céréales (f.)	*cereal*
la confiture	*jam*
un croissant	*croissant*
un œuf (sur le plat/au plat)	*(fried) egg*
du pain	*bread*
un pain au chocolat	*chocolate croissant*
une rôtie	*piece of toast (Can.)*
une tartine	*slice of bread*
une tranche de pain grillé	*slice of toast*

au déjeuner	*at lunch*
un apéritif	*before-meal drink*
une entrée	*appetizer or starter*
un plat principal	*main dish*
un dessert	*dessert*

des aliments (m.)	*food*
une asperge	*asparagus*
un biscuit	*cookie*
le fromage	*cheese*
les *haricots verts (m.)	*green beans*
un légume	*vegetable*
des pâtes (f.)	*pasta*
le poisson	*fish*
une pomme de terre	*potato*
le poulet	*chicken*
le riz	*rice*

une soupe	soup	des plats préparés (m.)	prepared dishes
une tarte aux pommes	apple pie	un rôti (de porc)	(pork) roast
la viande	meat	le rayon fruits et légumes	produce aisle
un yaourt	yogurt	une fraise	strawberry

une soupe — soup
une tarte aux pommes — apple pie
la viande — meat
un yaourt — yogurt

des fruits (m.) — *fruits*

une banane — *banana*
une poire — *pear*
une pomme — *apple*

des épices (f.) — *spices*

le poivre — *pepper*
le sel — *salt*

d'autres mots utiles — *other useful words*

un bol (de café au lait) — *bowl (of coffee with hot milk)*
une bouteille — *bottle*
une carafe (d'eau) — *carafe (of water)*
une tasse — *cup*
un verre — *glass*
vers — *around, toward*

pour décrire — *to describe*

copieux — *copious, hearty*
grillé/e — *grilled, toasted*

quelques expressions indéfinies et négatives — *some indefinite and negative expressions*

quelque chose — *something*
quelqu'un — *someone*
ne … personne — *no one*
ne … rien — *nothing*

Leçon 3

les rayons du supermarché — *supermarket aisles*

le rayon boulangerie-pâtisserie — *bakery/pastry aisle*
   une baguette — *long, thin loaf*
   un pain de campagne — *round loaf of bread*
   un pain de mie — *loaf of sliced bread*
   une pâtisserie — *pastry*
   des petits pains (m.) — *rolls*
   une tarte — *pie*
le rayon boucherie — *meat counter*
   du bifteck haché — *ground beef*
   une côtelette d'agneau — *lamb chop*
   du rosbif — *roast beef*
le rayon charcuterie — *deli counter*
   du pâté — *pâté*

des plats préparés (m.) — *prepared dishes*
un rôti (de porc) — *(pork) roast*
le rayon fruits et légumes — *produce aisle*
   une fraise — *strawberry*
   une pêche — *peach*
   du raisin — *grapes*
   une carotte — *carrot*
   un champignon — *mushroom*
   un concombre — *cucumber*
   les épinards (m.) — *spinach*
   les *haricots (m.) — *beans*
   un melon — *cantaloupe*
   un oignon — *onion*
   les petits pois (m.) — *peas*
   une tomate — *tomato*
le rayon poissonnerie — *fish counter*
   une crevette — *shrimp*
   du saumon — *salmon*
   du thon — *tuna*
le rayon surgelés — *frozen foods*
   les surgelés (m.) — *frozen foods*

des condiments — *condiments*

l'huile (f.) — *oil*
la moutarde — *mustard*
le vinaigre — *vinegar*

pour décrire — *to describe*

avoir l'air (bon/mauvais) — *to appear/seem (good/bad)*
délicieux/-euse — *delicious*
frais/fraîche — *fresh*
mûr/e — *ripe*

pour faire les courses — *to shop for food*

un/e commerçant/e — *shopkeeper, merchant*
une épicerie — *small grocery*
une grande surface — *superstore*

des quantités (f.) — *quantities*

une assiette de (crudités) — *plate of (crudités)*
une boîte de (sardines) — *can of (sardines)*
une boîte de (céréales) — *box of (cereal)*
un demi-kilo de (tomates) — *half-kilo of (tomatoes)*
une douzaine d'(œufs) — *dozen (eggs)*
un kilo de (pommes) — *kilo of (apples)*
un litre de (lait) — *liter of (milk)*
un morceau de (fromage) — *piece of (cheese)*
un paquet de (riz) — *package of (rice)*
un pot de (moutarde) — *jar of (mustard)*
une tranche de (pâté) — *slice of (pâté)*

Voici un voyageur dans un train rapide en France. Est-ce que vous pensez que c'est une façon agréable de voyager ? Pourquoi ?

Chapitre 9

Voyageons !

Leçon 1 *Projets de voyage*

Leçon 2 *Destinations*

Leçon 3 *Faisons du tourisme !*

Venez chez nous !
Paris, ville lumière

In this chapter:

- Describing future plans
- Making travel plans
- Making arrangements for lodging
- Describing places and people
- Exploring French cities, especially Paris

Use the drawing of the taxi (IRCD, Ch. 9) as you describe the Mathieus' trip. Let students listen to the dialogue, then ask simple comprehension questions: *Comment est-ce que les Mathieu voyagent ? Quelle est leur destination ? Qu'est-ce que M. Mathieu emporte ? Qu'est-ce que Mme Mathieu a oublié ? Quelle est la solution proposée par M. Mathieu ?*

Leçon 1 *Projets de voyage*

You may want to introduce the expression *avoir besoin de* inductively before presenting this dialogue and the related vocabulary. Tell students to imagine that the class is taking a trip to Paris and that there are things you must bring because you need them. Start off with *Nous avons besoin de nos passeports* and ask students to provide other examples. You may also wish to review the conjugation of the verb *avoir* with students and remind students of a complementary expression they learned in Ch. 4, L. 3: *avoir envie de.*

POINTS DE DÉPART

Comment y aller ?

M. et Mme Mathieu partent en vacances au Cameroun. Ils prennent un taxi pour aller à la gare, et puis le train pour aller à l'aéroport pour prendre leur vol. Ils ont beaucoup de valises.

TEXT AUDIO

Additional practice activities for each **Points de départ** section are provided by:
• Student Activities Manual
• *Chez nous* Companion Website:
  http://www.prenhall.com/cheznous

MME MATHIEU : Tu as tout ? On n'a rien oublié ?

M. MATHIEU : Voyons. On a besoin de nos passeports et de nos billets. Tout est là. Non, je n'ai rien oublié. Et toi, tu n'as rien oublié ?

MME MATHIEU : Mais si ! J'ai laissé mon appareil photo sur la table dans la cuisine, zut !

M. MATHIEU : Ne t'en fais pas. J'ai mon nouvel appareil photo numérique ; je te le prête si tu veux.

MME MATHIEU : Merci, mon chéri, c'est très gentil.

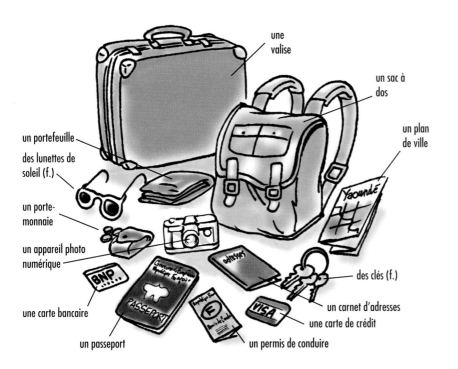

une valise

un sac à dos

un plan de ville

un portefeuille

des lunettes de soleil (f.)

un porte-monnaie

un appareil photo numérique

une carte bancaire

un passeport

des clés (f.)

un carnet d'adresses

une carte de crédit

un permis de conduire

Use the visual of the hand luggage (IRCD, Ch. 9) to present the vocabulary of travel items; provide a description for each item. Note that *un appareil photo numérique* is a digital camera and uses *une carte mémoire ;* *un appareil photo* requires *une pellicule.* You may wish to teach the vocabulary for both types of cameras. Tell students that they will also see *appareil numérique* for a digital camera. Test comprehension by having students 1) point to the items you name; 2) identify an item: *C'est un passeport ou un permis ?* Note that the French refer to their driver's license as « *le papier rose.* » You might also use objects to enliven this presentation. Then do Ex. 9-1.

LES MOYENS DE TRANSPORT

l'avion (m.)	le car	la moto	le train
le bateau	le métro	le RER	le vélo
le bus	la mobylette	le taxi	la voiture

When specifying a means of transportation, use…

- **prendre** plus the means of transportation preceded by an article or possessive:

Je prends **le** métro.	*I'm taking the subway.*
Ils prennent **un** taxi.	*They're taking a taxi.*
Elle prend **son** vélo.	*She's taking her bike.*

- verbs of travel such as **aller**, **partir**, or **voyager** followed by the preposition **en** or **à**, as specified below. In these cases, no article is used.

en avion, **en** bateau, **en** bus, **en** car, **en** métro, **en** RER, **en** taxi, **en** train, **en** voiture, **à** mobylette, **à** moto, **à** pied, **à** vélo

Nous partons **en** avion pour le Mali.	*We're leaving by plane for Mali.*
Moi, je vais au travail **en** métro, mais Christine va au travail **à** pied.	*I take the subway to work, but Christine goes to work on foot.*
Ils préfèrent voyager **en** train.	*They prefer to travel by train.*

À vous la parole

9-1 Qu'est-ce qu'il faut ? De quoi est-ce que les touristes ont besoin ?

MODÈLE   pour trouver les monuments dans une grande ville
➤ Ils ont besoin d'un plan de la ville.

1. pour payer l'hôtel ?
2. pour louer une voiture ?
3. pour ranger leur argent ?
4. pour prendre des photos ?
5. pour aller dans un pays étranger ?
6. pour rentrer dans leur chambre d'hôtel ?

9-2 Quel moyen de transport ? D'après les indications, quel/s moyen/s de transport est-ce que les personnes suivantes vont probablement utiliser ?

MODÈLE   Adeline habite près de Paris ; elle va faire des courses à Paris.
➤ Elle va prendre le RER pour aller à Paris, et ensuite le métro ou l'autobus pour faire ses courses.

1. Mme Duclair habite à Paris ; elle va rendre visite à sa grand-mère à Lyon.
2. Les Lefranc vont quitter la France pour passer des vacances aux Antilles.
3. La petite Hélène va à l'école primaire près de chez elle.
4. Robert habite une petite ville ; il va au centre-ville pour faire des courses.

5. M. Rolland doit traverser Paris pour aller au travail.
6. Maxime et Amélie vont faire un pique-nique à la campagne.
7. Mme Antonine voyage pour son travail : elle va à Lyon, à Rome et à Berlin.
8. Les Leclair vont visiter les îles grecques pendant les vacances.

Vie et culture

Show the brief video clip (*On prend le train*) and help students identify locations and activities pictured and mentioned in the voice-over. Make sure students understand the importance of the TGV and the Chunnel. Some of your students may have traveled by train in Europe and even via the Chunnel; ask them to share their impressions.

Voyager en train en France

Regardez la séquence vidéo, *On prend le train*. Qu'est-ce que vous remarquez ? Comment sont les trains français ? Pourquoi, à votre avis, est-ce que les Français, et les Européens en général, voyagent plus souvent en train que les Nord-Américains ?

En France, le système des trains est nationalisé. Tous les trains sont sous le contrôle de la Société nationale des chemins de fer français (la SNCF). Le TGV (Train à grande vitesse) est un des trains les plus rapides au monde. Par exemple, il parcourt[1] les 400 kilomètres qui séparent Lyon de Paris en seulement deux heures. Regardez la carte du réseau TGV : quelles sont les régions desservies par le train rapide ? Où est-ce que vous voudriez voyager en TGV ?

Depuis 1994, on peut traverser la Manche entre la France et l'Angleterre en train, en passant par le « Chunnel. » Ce tunnel est important parce qu'il relie le Royaume-Uni au continent européen. Ainsi, au départ de Lyon il faut seulement cinq heures pour arriver en Angleterre.

[1]*travels*

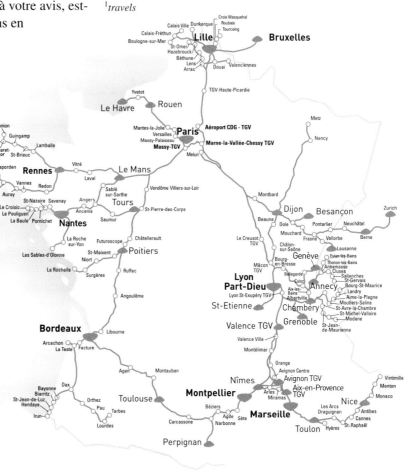

👥👥 9-3 Parlons des moyens de transport. Avec un/e partenaire, discutez de ces questions. Ensuite, comparez vos réponses et vos conclusions avec les conclusions de vos camarades de classe.

1. Comment est-ce que vous allez à vos cours ? Comment est-ce que vous faites vos courses ?
2. Est-ce qu'il y a un service de bus dans votre ville ? Un métro ? Comment est-ce que les habitants de votre ville vont au travail habituellement ?
3. Comment est-ce que vous rentrez chez vous pour les vacances ?
4. Est-ce que vous avez une voiture ? Si oui, quelle sorte de voiture : une voiture française, japonaise, américaine ?
5. Est-ce que le train passe par votre ville ? Où est-ce qu'on peut aller en train en partant de votre ville ?
6. Comment sont les trains américains comparés aux trains français ? Est-ce qu'il existe un TGV aux États-Unis ?
7. Pour voyager aux États-Unis, quel est votre moyen de transport préféré ? Pourquoi ?

Additional practice activities for each **Sons et lettres** section are provided by:
• Student Activities Manual
• Text Audio

Show that *liaison* implies *enchaînement* by inserting a pause after the first syllable and overarticulating the liaison consonant: *un gros␣homme* = /gro ɔm/, *ils␣ont* = /il zɔ̃/.

Sons et lettres

TEXT AUDIO

La liaison obligatoire

Recall that liaison consonants are pronounced only when the word that follows begins with a vowel. The pronunciation of these consonants is called **liaison**. Liaison is always accompanied by **enchaînement**: the liaison consonant is pronounced as part of the following word: **nous allons** /nu za lɔ̃/.

Liaison is not always made. In addition to occurring before a vowel, liaison depends on grammatical factors. Cases where liaison must always be made are called **liaisons obligatoires**. They are relatively limited. In this lesson and in Lesson 2 we list the cases of **liaisons obligatoires**.

Liaison /z/ is the most common liaison consonant because it indicates the plural. It is usually spelled **-s**, but in some cases it is spelled **-x**. Always pronounce liaison /z/:

• After the plural form of articles and adjectives that precede the noun:

les␣hôtels	des␣autos	ces␣étages
/z/	/z/	/z/
les␣anciennes␣églises	les grands␣immeubles	ces beaux␣avions
/z/ /z/	/z/	/z/

• After the singular adjectives **gros** and **mauvais**:

un gros␣homme	un mauvais␣hôtel
/z/	/z/

- After numerals:

trois‿heures   quatre-vingts‿ans   le six‿avril
/z/   /z/   /z/

- After the plural subject pronouns **nous**, **vous**, **ils**, **elles**:

nous‿habitons   vous‿utilisez   ils‿ont payé   elles‿adorent
/z/   /z/   /z/   /z/

- After the plural possessive adjectives **mes**, **tes**, **ses**, **vos**, **nos**, **leurs**:

mes‿amis   leurs‿enfants   nos‿itinéraires
/z/   /z/   /z/

- After one-syllable adverbs and prepositions (**pas**, **plus**, **très** ; **dans**, **sans**, **sous**) and the combination of the preposition **à** and **de** with the plural definite articles (**aux**, **des**):

très‿intéressant   dans‿un appartement   aux‿Antilles   sans‿argent
/z/   /z/   /z/   /z/

À vous la parole

9-4 Contrastes. Remplacez le premier nom par le second.

MODÈLE   un gros bateau / avion

       É1   Tu as dit un gros bateau ?
       É2   Non, un gros avion.

1. un mauvais quartier / endroit
2. deux trains / avions
3. les billets / appareil photos
4. des villes / îles
5. les belles Françaises / Américaines
6. les belles rues / avenues
7. ces beaux musées / hôtels
8. nous louons / achetons
9. ils partent / arrivent

9-5 Phrases. Répétez chaque phrase.

1. Vous allez aux Antilles ou en Afrique ?
2. Mes autres amis habitent aux États-Unis.
3. Cet avion part à trois heures et arrive à six heures.
4. C'est un mauvais endroit pour construire des grands immeubles.
5. En Italie il y a de très anciennes églises et de beaux hôtels.

Liaison obligatoire is relatively limited, so encourage students to memorize where it occurs. Use substitution drills to practice: 1) determiners and adjectives, singular to plural: l'homme > les hommes, une amie > des amies, cet enfant > ces enfants ; son ami > ses amis ; un petit appartement > des petits appartements ; la vieille église > les vieilles églises ; 2) the adjectives gros and mauvais, feminine to masculine: une grosse auto > un gros avion ; une mauvaise ouvrière > un mauvais ouvrier ; 3) numerals: deux immeubles [3] > trois immeubles ; six étages [10] > dix étages ; 4) pronouns, singular to plural: elle a les billets > elles ont les billets ; j'achète des lunettes > nous achetons des lunettes ; 5) prepositions, contrast aux and en with names of countries or regions: aux Antilles (Angleterre) > en Angleterre ; (États-Unis) > aux États-Unis.

9-5 Suggest that students first mark the liaisons obligatoires and then repeat.

FORMES ET FONCTIONS

1. *Le futur*

Additional practice activities for each **Formes et fonctions** section are provided by:
- Student Activities Manual
- *Chez nous* Companion Website: http://www.prenhall.com/cheznous

In view of its link with intentionality, it is more appropriate to refer to *le futur proche* as *le futur défini*, and to the so-called *futur simple* as *le futur indéfini*. We retain the traditional labels for the sake of convenience. The exercises stress the semantic and pragmatic distinctions between the two structures. Remind students that they can also express the notion of the future by using the present tense plus an adverbial expression: *Ils partent demain.*

Point out that typically the *futur* (*indéfini*) is used in weather forecasts, since weather is anything but fully predictable and certain: *Mardi sera marqué par une crête de haute pression qui apportera du soleil à l'ensemble des régions.*

- One may express future events in French using the **futur proche** or the **futur**. The two grammatical structures do not carry precisely the same meaning for French speakers. Compare:

  a. Ma tante **va avoir** un enfant.   *My aunt's going to have a baby.*

  b. Ils vont se marier et ils **auront** beaucoup d'enfants.   *They're going to get married, and they'll have lots of kids.*

In **a.** we assume that the aunt is expecting. In **b.** it is not certain that the couple to be married will have *any* children, let alone many.

- The difference between the **futur proche** and the **futur** is not primarily one of nearness or remoteness of the future event, but of its degree of certainty or definiteness. Compare:

  Je **ferai** la cuisine plus tard.   *I'll do the cooking later (perhaps).*

  Je **vais faire** la cuisine.   *I'm going to cook (right away).*

  L'été prochain je **vais aller** en Suisse.   *Next summer I'm going to Switzerland (definite).*

  Un jour, j'**irai** en Afrique.   *Someday I'll go to Africa (indefinite).*

- Use the **futur** to soften instructions and emphatic commands.

  Vous **traverserez** l'avenue et vous **tournerez** à gauche dans la rue Colbert.   *You cross the avenue and turn left at Colbert Street.*

  Tu **fermeras** la porte !   *Close the door!*

Note that the future stem is the same as the infinitive, except that: a) the final *-e* of *-re* verbs is dropped: *apprendre, j'apprendrai*; b) the *-e* of *-er* verbs is an unstable e and may or may not be pronounced, depending on the number of consonant sounds that follow or precede: *tu chanteras, tu parleras.*

- To form the future tense, add the future endings to the future stem. The future stem of regular verbs is the infinitive (for verbs ending in **-re**, remove the final **-e** from the infinitive).

LE FUTUR			
INFINITIVE ENDING:	**-er**	**-ir**	**-re**
FUTURE STEM:	**chanter-**	**partir-**	**vendr-**
je	chante**rai**	parti**rai**	vend**rai**
tu	chante**ras**	parti**ras**	vend**ras**
il elle on	chante**ra**	parti**ra**	vend**ra**
nous	chante**rons**	parti**rons**	vend**rons**
vous	chante**rez**	parti**rez**	vend**rez**
ils elles	chante**ront**	parti**ront**	vend**ront**

- The following verbs have irregular future stems:

acheter	j'**achèter**ai	devoir	je **devr**ai	pleuvoir	il **pleuvr**a
aller	j'**ir**ai	être	je **ser**ai	pouvoir	je **pourr**ai
appeler	j'**appeller**ai	faire	je **fer**ai	savoir	je **saur**ai
avoir	j'**aur**ai	préférer	je **préférer**ai		

À vous la parole

9-6 Préparatifs de voyage. La famille Meunier part en voyage. Mme Meunier donne des ordres très clairs à son mari Thomas et à ses enfants. Transformez les impératifs selon le modèle.

MODÈLE Thomas, achète les billets !
> ➤ Thomas, tu achèteras les billets !

1. Thomas, réserve une chambre !
2. Thomas, prépare la voiture !
3. Les enfants, faites vos valises !
4. Fred, range ta chambre !
5. Hélène, ferme les fenêtres !
6. Fred, mets ton beau pantalon !
7. Fred, prends cette valise !
8. Thomas, appelle un taxi !

9-7 Prévisions météo. Voici les prévisions météo pour le Canada et pour le monde entier. Quel temps est prévu pour les villes indiquées ?

MODÈLE à Ottawa
> ➤ Demain, il fera beau. La température sera de 18 degrés. Ce soir elle descendra jusqu'à 6 degrés.

1. à Québec
2. à Winnipeg
3. à Calgary
4. à Vancouver
5. à Paris
6. à Bruxelles
7. à Londres
8. à Honolulu

Au Pays		Demain	Le monde		Demain
Vancouver	Averses	14/8	Berlin	Ensoleillé	14/3
Victoria	Averses	13/8	Bruxelles	Ensoleillé	16/5
Edmonton	P/Nuageux	15/2	Buenos Aires	Nuageux	15/11
Calgary	P/Nuageux	19/3	Honolulu	P/Nuageux	29/23
Saskatoon	Ensoleillé	12/1	Lisbonne	Ensoleillé	27/14
Régina	P/Nuageux	11/2	Londres	P/Nuageux	19/8
Winnipeg	Nuageux	12/5	Los Angeles	Ensoleillé	23/12
Ottawa	Ensoleillé	18/6	New Delhi	P/Nuageux	34/23
Québec	Ensoleillé	18/5	New York	P/Nuageux	17/11
Moncton	Ensoleillé	17/6	Paris	Ensoleillé	19/6

Amener, (se) lever, and *(se) promener* show the same irregular future stem change as *acheter. Épeler* and *jeter* show the same stem change as *appeler.* In both cases, the pronunciation of the vowel [ɛ] is indicated by the *accent grave* or the double consonant. *Préférer*-type verbs (*préférer, espérer, répéter, suggérer*) are included here based on the 1990 Orthographic reform (règle 3a): "*On accentue sur le modèle de* **semer** *les futurs et conditionnels des verbes du type* **céder** : **je cèderai, je cèderais . . . .**" As with the *acheter*-type verbs, the *accent grave* here clearly indicates the pronunciation of [ɛ]. For formation of the conditional, see Ch. 11, L. 2.

Begin practice with discrimination drills: have students raise their hand when they hear a future event described: *Ils sont allés en Grèce l'été dernier ; Ils iront en Espagne l'été prochain ; Je prendrai l'avion pour aller en Belgique ; Nous voyageons souvent en train ; Elle attend le bus devant chez elle ; Tu partiras vraiment toute seule en Europe ? ; Vous avez oublié les billets ? ; Je n'oublierai pas mon appareil cette fois-ci ; Elles vont en ville en car tous les vendredis ; Elle achètera son billet la semaine prochaine.*

One person, or more than one? *Il sera en retard ; Ils feront le travail ; Elle prendra le bus ; Il louera une voiture ; Ils voyageront en première classe ; Elles feront le tour du monde en avion ; Elle prendra beaucoup de photos ; Ils rendront visite à des amis ; Elles achèteront des souvenirs à Paris.*

Practice with transformation drills to emphasize future stems: *Je suis (Je serai) ; Je regarde (Je regarderai) ; Je dors (Je dormirai),* etc. Continue with substitution drills for each regular verb group: *Je travaillerai beaucoup ; nous —Nous travaillerons beaucoup,* etc. *Il sortira ce week-end ; nous —Nous sortirons ce week-end,* etc. *Elle attendra à l'aéroport ; moi —J'attendrai à l'aéroport.*

9-6 For additional practice, have students imagine other situations in which an authority figure issues a lot of orders (i.e., teacher and student, employer and employee); students can work in pairs to create examples.

9-7 Before beginning the exercise, you may wish to review weather terms. This could be accomplished simply by asking students what the weather is like currently and what the forecast is for the coming weekend or days.

9-8 Pretend you are the fortune teller and act the role! Vary the exercise by having students take either the optimist's or the pessimist's point of view.

The verb *voir* is presented for productive control in Ch. 11, L. 1. Treat *je vois que* as a lexical expression here and point out *je vous vois* as well before students complete the exercise.

👥👥 **9-8 Boule de cristal.** Imaginez que vous allez chez une voyante. Voici ses prédictions. Avec un/e partenaire, tirez-en des conclusions. Voyons si vous avez compris la même chose.

MODÈLE Je vois que beaucoup d'argent passe entre vos mains.

> É1 Alors je serai très riche.
>
> É2 Alors je travaillerai dans une banque.

1. Je vois que vous voyagez beaucoup à cause du travail.
2. Je vois beaucoup d'enfants dans votre avenir.
3. Je vous vois devant une grande maison.
4. Je vous vois en compagnie d'une belle femme/d'un bel homme.
5. Je vois que vous avez beaucoup d'amis.
6. Je vois que vous êtes très célèbre.

👥👥 **9-9 Rêvons aux vacances.** Avec un/e partenaire, imaginez un voyage dans la ville ou l'endroit indiqué. Qu'est-ce que vous ferez ?

MODÈLE à Strasbourg

> É1 Nous nous promènerons dans la vieille ville. Nous visiterons la cathédrale.
>
> É2 Nous mangerons également une bonne choucroute.

1. en Touraine
2. à la Martinique
3. à La Nouvelle-Orléans
4. au Maroc
5. à Tahiti
6. au Québec
7. en Suisse
8. à Paris

9-9 You might have students suggest their own destinations. Be careful, however, that they suggest these place names to you first so that you can provide them with the correct preposition.

Use this pair activity for further practice:
L'an 2050. Parlez de vos prédictions pour l'an 2050 avec un/e partenaire.

MODÈLE travailler dans les usines
> É1 Personne ne travaillera dans les usines.
>
> É2 Tout le travail sera fait par des robots.

1. utiliser des ordinateurs
2. lire des livres
3. voyager en train
4. parler anglais
5. explorer la planète Mars
6. habiter sur la Lune ou dans l'espace
7. choisir une femme comme présidente

Help students discover the meaning of the words *lune* and *espace* through the cognates "lunar, space" and the context. See whether they can come up with additional examples of how things might be in 2050 using verbs they know.

To present, start with the examples and see whether students can derive the meaning and rules. Alternatively you can present this inductively by telling a story about your travels using *y* and asking students questions about whether they have been to the various places. For example: *L'été dernier, je suis allée en Angleterre avec ma famille. On y est allé en avion. D'abord on a visité Liverpool. Ma nièce y habite et fait ses études à l'Université de Liverpool. Est-ce que vous avez déjà visité l'Angleterre ? Comment est-ce que vous y êtes allé/e ? En avion ? Et Londres ? Vous y êtes allé/e aussi ? Comment ?* etc.

2. *Le pronom* y

• The pronoun **y** means *there*. It refers back to the name of a place, which can be introduced by a preposition such as **à**, **en**, **chez**, **devant**, or **à côté de**, for example.

—Tu es allé en Provence l'été dernier ?	—*You went to Provence last summer?*
—Oui, j'**y** suis allé avec mes parents.	—*Yes, I went there with my parents.*
—Tes cousins habitent au Canada ?	—*Your cousins live in Canada?*
—Non, ils n'**y** habitent plus.	—*No, they don't live there anymore.*
—Qui va aller chez Cécile ?	—*Who's going to Cécile's house?*
—Pas moi ; j'**y** suis allée hier.	—*Not me; I went there yesterday.*

• Like the other object pronouns, **y** is placed immediately before the conjugated verb, unless there is an infinitive. When there is an infinitive, the pronoun goes immediately in front of it.

Tu **y** vas ?	*Are you going there?*
Cet hôtel est abominable. Je ne peux plus **y** rester.	*This hotel is awful. I can't stay here any longer.*
Paris ? Oui, nous **y** sommes allés l'été dernier.	*Paris? Yes, we went there last summer.*

À vous la parole

👥👥 **9-10 C'est logique.** De quelle ville francophone est-ce qu'on parle probablement ? Il y a souvent plusieurs possibilités.

En Afrique : Dakar, Abidjan, Bamako

En Amérique du Nord : Québec, Montréal, La Nouvelle-Orléans

Les D.O.M. : Fort-de-France (Martinique), Pointe-à-Pitre (Guadeloupe), Cayenne (Guyane)

En Europe : Paris, Genève, Bruxelles, Nice

MODÈLE   On y va pour les sports d'hiver.
> ➤ À Genève.
> OU ➤ À Montréal.

1. On y trouve des belles plages.
2. Les gens y parlent créole.
3. On y parle anglais et français.
4. On y parle wolof et français.
5. On y parle flamand et français.
6. On y va pour le Carnaval.
7. Les Américains y vont pour parler français sans quitter l'Amérique du Nord.

9-11 Les voyageurs. En choisissant l'expression appropriée dans la colonne B, dites pourquoi les personnes suivantes visitent les endroits indiqués.

MODÈLE   Arnaud va aller à Paris.
> ➤ Il va y aller pour visiter la tour Eiffel.

A	**B**
1. Les Kerboul sont allés à La Nouvelle-Orléans.	acheter du bon vin
2. Les Dupuis vont aller dans les Alpes.	voir le Carnaval
3. Raymond veut aller à la Guadeloupe.	visiter les pyramides
4. Arnaud va aller à Paris.	visiter la tour Eiffel
5. Les Brunet sont allés sur la Côte d'Azur.	apprendre l'espagnol
6. Christiane voudrait aller au Mexique.	apprendre le créole
7. Les Santini vont en Égypte.	nager et se bronzer
8. M. Lescure va aller dans la région de Bordeaux.	faire du ski

To practice the placement of the pronoun *y*, complete quick substitution drills: *J'y suis allé/e ; nous — Nous y sommes allés*, etc. ; *Je vais y aller ; toi — Tu vas y aller*, etc.

9-10 This tests students' understanding of the use of the pronoun *y*; to simplify, have students answer with the location only. Answers include: 1) Dakar, Abidjan, Nice, Martinique, Guadeloupe   2) Fort-de-France, Pointe-à-Pitre, La Nouvelle-Orléans   3) Pointe-à-Pitre, Fort-de-France, La Nouvelle-Orléans   4) Dakar   5) Bruxelles   6) La Nouvelle-Orléans, Nice   7) Québec, Montréal, La Nouvelle-Orléans.

9-12 Have students add other places.

9-12 Vos habitudes. Demandez à votre partenaire s'il/si elle va aux endroits suivants pendant les vacances. Il/Elle doit vous donner une raison pour justifier sa réponse.

MODÈLE   dans des bons restaurants

       É1   Tu vas quelquefois dans des bons restaurants ?

       É2   Non, je n'y vais jamais.

       É1   Pourquoi ?

       É2   Parce qu'ils sont très chers et je n'ai pas assez d'argent pour y aller.

1. au théâtre
2. à des concerts de musique classique
3. à Disneyland Paris ou à Disney World
4. au musée
5. en Louisiane
6. en Europe
7. aux Antilles
8. dans un pays francophone autre que la France

Additional activities to develop the four skills are provided by:
- Student Activities Manual
- Text Audio
- *Chez nous* video
- *Chez nous* Companion Website:
  http://www.prenhall.com/cheznous

9-13 Votre attention, s'il vous plaît !

A. Avant d'écouter. Quand on voyage, on entend souvent des annonces à l'aéroport, à la gare, à la station de métro ou dans le métro. Quelle est la fonction de ces annonces ? Est-ce que vous pouvez donner quelques exemples ?

B. En écoutant. Écoutez ces annonces adressées aux voyageurs et complétez le tableau suivant.

1. La première fois que vous écoutez, dites où se trouvent les gens qui entendent l'annonce — **à l'aéroport**, à la gare, **à la station de métro**, **dans le métro** — et complétez la première colonne.
2. Ensuite, complétez la deuxième colonne. Déterminez si le message est adressé aux gens qui sont déjà dans l'avion ou le train, ou qui attendent un vol ou un train.
3. Dans la troisième colonne, indiquez ce que les gens qui entendent l'annonce doivent faire.
4. Enfin, notez dans la quatrième colonne, d'autres détails importants pour chaque annonce.

Script for *Écoutons*

1. Mesdames et messieurs, dans quelques instants, nous allons arriver en gare de Cannes. Cannes. Deux minutes d'arrêt.
2. Tous les passagers pour le vol Air France 342 à destination de Nouméa sont priés de se présenter à la porte 34 pour un départ immédiat.
3. Dans quelques instants, le train arrivera en gare. Éloignez-vous du bord du quai, s'il vous plaît.
4. Les passagers Dupont, Smith et Labonté sont priés de se présenter au comptoir Air France dans le Hall B.
5. Par mesure de sécurité (en accord avec la loi vigi-pirate) tout bagage suspect ou abandonné sera immédiatement détruit.
6. Terminus du train. Tous les passagers sont priés de descendre du train. Faites attention de ne rien oublier dans le train.

	Où	Pour qui ?	Action à prendre	Autres détails importants
1.	*la gare*	*dans le train*	*descendre*	*deux minutes d'arrêt*
2.				
3.			*s'éloigner du quai*	
4.				
5.			*faire attention*	
6.				

C. Après avoir écouté. Est-ce que vous avez déjà entendu des annonces de ce style ? Où ? Est-ce que vous les écoutez attentivement ? Pourquoi ?

On se dépêche pour prendre le train.

On attend le métro à Paris.

POINTS DE DÉPART

Où est-ce qu'on va ?

TEXT AUDIO

Je m'appelle David Diouf. Je suis du Sénégal et j'étudie à Paris. Ma langue maternelle, c'est le wolof, mais je parle aussi français. Je vais bientôt prendre l'avion pour aller à Dakar. Je vais passer les vacances chez moi cet été.

Je suis Denise Duclos. Je suis suisse. J'habite à Lausanne. Je parle allemand aussi bien que français. Je prends l'avion pour aller à Bruxelles pour une réunion de travail. Je vais rentrer en Suisse ce soir.

Mon nom, c'est Pierre Piron. Je suis belge et j'habite à Bruxelles. Je retourne au Mali où je vais reprendre mon travail pour Médecins sans Frontières.

Continents	Pays	Adjectif de nationalité
L'Afrique	l'Algérie	algérien/algérienne
	le Maroc	marocain/e
	le Sénégal	sénégalais/e
	la Côte-d'Ivoire	ivoirien/ivoirienne
	le Cameroun	camerounais/e
L'Asie	l'Inde	indien/indienne
	la Chine	chinois/e
	le Japon	japonais/e
	le Vietnam	vietnamien/vietnamienne
L'Océanie	l'Australie	australien/australienne
L'Amérique	le Canada	canadien/canadienne
... du Nord	les États-Unis	américain/e
	le Mexique	mexicain/e
... du Sud	la Colombie	colombien/colombienne
	l'Argentine	argentin/e
	le Brésil	brésilien/brésilienne
L'Europe	l'Allemagne	allemand/e
	l'Angleterre	anglais/e
	la Belgique	belge
	la Suisse	suisse
	la France	français/e
	l'Italie	italien/italienne
	l'Espagne	espagnol/e
	les Pays-Bas	néerlandais/e
	le Portugal	portugais/e

To practice continents, name a country and have students tell on which continent the country is found: *le Vietnam ? —le Vietnam est en Asie. le Sénégal ? —Le Sénégal est en Afrique, le Mexique ; les Pays-Bas ; le Brésil ; le Maroc ; la Chine ; l'Italie ; le Canada ; le Cameroun ; la Suisse ; l'Australie ; la Côte d'Ivoire*, etc. Here country names can be for recognition only.

Point out that whereas North Americans think of seven continents: *L'Afrique, l'Asie, l'Australie, l'Amérique du Nord, l'Amérique du Sud, l'Europe*, and *l'Antarctique*, the French divide the world into five continents: *l'Afrique, l'Asie, l'Amérique, l'Europe*, and *l'Océanie*.

Point out that the name of the inhabitants of a country is usually derived from the adjective of nationality, but it is written with a capital letter: *un Chinois, une Chinoise, les Ivoiriens*. The name of the language spoken in a country is often derived from the masculine form of the adjective of nationality: *les Portugais parlent portugais*. There are many exceptions to this general rule, however: *en Algérie, on parle arabe, berbère et français ; en Suisse, on parle allemand, français, italien, et romanche.*

À vous la parole

9-14 C'est quel pays ? Décidez quel pays on visite, d'après la description.

MODÈLE   On visite le palais de Buckingham et le *British Museum*.
   ➤ C'est l'Angleterre.

1. On s'assoit à la terrasse d'un café pour admirer la tour Eiffel.
2. On visite le Vatican.
3. Il y a des pyramides aztèques.
4. On peut visiter les souks (*les marchés*) de Marrakech.
5. On visite le château Frontenac à Québec.
6. Là-bas, il y a l'administration centrale de la Communauté Européenne.
7. C'est le seul pays d'Europe où l'on parle espagnol.

9-14 To include cities, give students two possibilities and let them choose the correct response: *Le palais de Buckingham, c'est à Londres ou à Bruxelles ?*
Key: 1) la France   2) l'Italie   3) le Mexique   4) le Maroc   5) le Canada   6) la Belgique   7) l'Espagne. Have students suggest additional items, perhaps using simple one-word associations: *les gondoles —l'Italie*, etc.

Vie et culture

Have copies of some of these guidebooks on hand for students to look at and compare; you might compare the description of the same site in all the books, or have students compare the design and information contained in each guide.

Les guides touristiques

Pour vraiment profiter d'un voyage, on peut se servir d'un guide touristique. Voici les guides français les plus connus :

Le Guide Michelin : Publiés par la compagnie Michelin, les guides rouges classent les hôtels et les restaurants selon[1] un système d'étoiles[2]. Les guides verts proposent des itinéraires et décrivent les sites touristiques.

Le Guide du routard : Ce guide est destiné aux touristes qui prennent la route et qui ont un budget limité pour le logement, les repas et les visites.

Le Guide Voir : Ce guide contient des photos magnifiques, des cartes et des illustrations, toutes en couleur.

Et vous ?

1. Quel guide préférez-vous ? Pourquoi ?
2. Est-ce que vous avez déjà utilisé des guides touristiques en Amérique du Nord ? Est-ce que ces guides sont semblables aux guides français ou différents ?

[1] *according to*   [2] *stars*

9-15, Key: 1) colombienne ; espagnol 2) belge ; français, flamand   3) suisse ; français, allemand, italien·   4) brésilien ; portugais   5) allemand ; allemand 6) italienne ; italien   7) chinoise ; chinois

9-15 Présentations. Selon l'endroit où chaque personne habite, indiquez sa nationalité et des langues possibles.

MODÈLE   Luc Auger habite à Québec.
➤ Il est canadien. Il parle français et probablement un peu anglais.

1. Maria Garcia est de Buenos Aires.
2. Sylvie Gerniers habite à Bruxelles.
3. Chantal Dupuis est de Genève.
4. Paolo Dos Santos habite à Rio de Janeiro.
5. Helmut Müller est de Berlin.
6. Maria Verdi habite à Milan.
7. Jin Lu est de Pékin.

9-16 Introduce by asking students if they have relatives or friends in other countries. Follow up by asking about trips students may have already made overseas.

As a culminating exercise, have students introduce themselves using the three examples in the **Points de départ** as models. Or, have them assume a new identity with a name indicative of the target language they choose and introduce themselves. Classmates can take notes and then be asked to recall the new identity of each student. This can become a fun game; you may want to give students a day to prepare.

9-16 Un voyage. Avec un/e partenaire, imaginez que vous partez visiter un pays lointain. Quel pays est-ce que vous choisirez ? Qu'est-ce que vous y ferez ?

MODÈLE   É1   Je visiterai la Suisse, parce que j'ai des cousins là-bas. Je ferai du ski dans les Alpes.

É2   Et moi, je visiterai l'Égypte. J'irai voir les pyramides.

Sons et lettres

TEXT AUDIO

La liaison avec *t*, *n* et *r*

After /z/, the next most common liaison consonant is /t/. It is usually spelled **-t**, but in some cases it is spelled **-d**. Pronounce liaison /t/:

- After the adjectives **petit** and **grand**, the form **cet**, and the numbers **huit**, **vingt**, **cent**:

  un peti**t** animal   un gran**d** immeuble   ce**t** hiver
  /t/   /t/   /t/
  il a hui**t** ans   ving**t** heures   cen**t** appartements
  /t/   /t/   /t/

- Liaison /t/ must also be pronounced in certain fixed phrases:

  Quel temps fai**t** -il ?   Quelle heure es**t** -il ?   Commen**t** allez-vous ?
  /t/   /t/   /t/

  Point out that these fixed expressions are instances of inverted questions.

- Although it is not obligatory, liaison is often made after the verb forms **ont**, **sont**, **vont**, and **font**. These are cases of optional liaison:

  ils son**t** ici   elles fon**t** un voyage   elles von**t** en Afrique
  /t/   /t/   /t/

  Except for the cases of the verbs pointed out here — ont, sont, font, and vont — beginning students should not be encouraged to make optional liaisons. Liaison should be avoided after other verb forms, for example: vous faites une excursion, elles prennent un TGV.

- Liaison /t/ is *never* pronounced after the word **et**:

  Pierre e**t** Alain   ving**t** e**t** un
                               /t/

Liaison /n/ occurs in the following cases:

- After **un** and the possessives **mon**, **ton**, **son**:

  u**n** hôtel   mo**n** église   to**n** auto   so**n** itinéraire
  /n/   /n/   /n/   /n/

- After the pronouns **on** and **en**, and the preposition **en**:

  o**n** y va   il e**n** a   e**n** octobre
  /n/   /n/   /n/

- After the adjectives **bon**, **certain**, **prochain**:

  un bo**n** avion   un certai**n** itinéraire   le prochai**n** arrêt
  /n/   /n/   /n/

  Point out the accompanying vowel change for bon (/bɔ̃/ to /bɔn/) and for certain and prochain (/ɛ̃/ to /ɛn/). Some speakers maintain the nasal vowel in the latter two adjectives.

Liaison /R/ occurs in **dernier** and **premier**:

  le premie**r** étage   le dernie**r** avion
  /R/   /R/

À vous la parole

9-17 Des beaux voyages. Refaites les phrases sur le modèle suivant en indiquant quel pays sera visité. Faites bien la liaison avec **on** et **en**.

MODÈLE Le Caire
➤ On ira en Égypte.

1. Londres   4. New Delhi   7. Rome
2. Madrid   5. Berlin   8. Buenos Aires
3. Alger   6. Sydney

9-18 Contrastes. Remplacez le premier nom par le second.

MODÈLE le prochain bateau / avion

É1 Tu as dit le prochain bateau ?

É2 Non, le prochain avion.

1. le dernier train / avion
2. le premier juin / août
3. le prochain taxi / arrêt
4. un certain voyage / itinéraire
5. un grand restaurant / hôtel
6. le petit bateau / avion
7. un mauvais magnétoscope / appareil photo
8. un gros monsieur / homme

FORMES ET FONCTIONS

1. *Les prépositions avec des noms de lieux*

Review the forms and uses of the prepositions *à* and *de* introduced in Ch. 2, L. 2 as you begin this presentation. Explain that a few city names contain the definite article, for example, *La Nouvelle-Orléans, Le Havre, La Haye, Le Mans,* and *Les Eyzies.* These will form the contractions *au* and *du* if they are masculine, and the contructions *aux* and *des* if they are plural. Point out the contrast *à Québec/au Québec* (the city vs. the province).

• You have learned to use the prepositions **à** (meaning *to, at,* or *in*) and **de** (meaning *from*) with the names of cities.

Elle arrive **à** Paris.   *She's arriving in Paris.*
Nous allons **à** Lille.   *We're going to Lille.*
Ils viennent **de** Québec.   *They're coming from Quebec City.*

• To express *to, at, in,* or *from* with the name of countries and continents, use the following prepositions in French:

	feminine country	masculine country beginning with a vowel	masculine country beginning with a consonant	plural country
to, at, in	**en** Suisse	**en** Haïti	**au** Maroc	**aux** Seychelles
from	**de** Belgique **d'**Afrique	**d'**Iran	**du** Canada	**des** États-Unis

• The names of all the continents are feminine. As a general rule, country names that end in **-e** are feminine, but you should note the following exceptions: **le Mexique, le Mozambique.** In general, names of countries that end in any letter other than **-e** are masculine: **le Canada, le Brésil, les États-Unis, les Pays-Bas.**

Ils habitent **en** Amérique latine.   *They live in Latin America.*
Nous sommes allés **en** Australie.   *We went to Australia.*
Salikoko a fait ses études **au** Canada. *Salikoko studied in Canada.*
Mon collègue va **aux** Pays-Bas.   *My colleague is going to the Netherlands.*

Je viens **du** Sénégal.   *I'm from Senegal.*

À vous la parole

9-19 Vos connaissances en géographie. Dites dans quel continent sont situés ces pays.

MODÈLE le Brésil
➤ C'est en Amérique.

1. le Mexique
2. Israël
3. le Nigéria
4. la Suisse
5. la République dominicaine
6. l'Afrique du Sud
7. la Chine
8. les États-Unis

Où est-ce que vous voudriez aller ?

9-20 Escales. Quelquefois il n'y a pas de vol direct entre deux villes. Dites dans quel pays les personnes suivantes doivent s'arrêter pour arriver à leur destination.

MODÈLE Mlle Schmidt : Berlin–Madrid–Lisbonne
➤ Elle doit s'arrêter en Espagne.

1. M. Ducret : Paris–Lisbonne–Abidjan
2. M. Thompson : Londres–Montréal–Chicago
3. Mme Smith : Londres–Paris–Barcelone
4. Mme Marconi : Marseille–Genève–Casablanca
5. Mlle Schmidt : Berlin–Londres–Québec
6. Mlle Bordes : Paris–New York–Mexico
7. M. Noyau : Marseille–Rome–Moscou

9-21 Vos origines. Beaucoup d'Américains ont des parents ou des grands-parents qui sont nés dans un pays étranger. Est-ce que certains membres de votre famille ou certains de vos camarades sont nés à l'étranger ?

MODÈLE É1 Tes parents ou tes grands-parents sont nés dans un pays étranger ?

É2 Oui, ma grand-mère. Elle est née en Chine. Et toi, où est-ce que tu es né ?

É1 Moi, je suis né aux États-Unis, en Californie…

Begin practice with simple substitution drills: *Je vais en France ; Canada ; Belgique ; Mexique ; Brésil ; Inde ; Suisse ; Pays-Bas ; Japon ; Côte d'Ivoire ; Italie ; Chine ; Portugal*, etc. *Je suis des États-Unis ; Pays-Bas ; France ; Portugal ; Sénégal ; Angleterre ; Colombie ; Maroc ; Espagne ; Australie ; Brésil ; Algérie ; Canada*, etc. Follow with an exercise where students match capitals and countries: *Dakar ? —Dakar est au Sénégal ; Tokyo ? (Japon) ; Paris ? (France) ; Lisbonne ? (Portugal) ; Bruxelles ? (Belgique) ; Ottawa ? (Canada) ; Rabat ? (Maroc) ; Yaoundé ? (Cameroun) ; Hanoï ? (Vietnam) ; Amsterdam ? (Pays-Bas) ; Canberra ? (Australie) ; Madrid ? (Espagne) ; Alger ? (Algérie) ; Pékin ? (Chine) ; Delhi ? (Inde) ; Bogota ? (Colombie) ; Buenos Aires ? (Argentine) ; Berne ? (Suisse) ; Brasilia ? (Brésil).*

9-19, Key: 1) en Amérique [Centrale] 2) en Asie 3) en Afrique 4) en Europe 5) en Amérique [du Nord] 6) en Afrique 7) en Asie 8) en Amérique [du Nord]

9-21 Students may need to use names of U.S. states. Here are the basic rules: use *en* for states whose name ends in -*e* (and are therefore feminine) and before masculine states beginning with a vowel: *en Floride, en Indiana*. For other masculine states, use *dans le: dans le Vermont*. Exceptions: *au Texas, dans le Maine.*

2. *Le verbe* venir

Present this verb inductively by providing many oral examples and asking questions that model the various forms: *Je viens de Chicago ; et vous, vous venez de Chicago aussi ? Et vos parents, ils viennent de...,* etc. Ask students to summarize forms and display the verb chart.

The main irregularity of this verb is the change from *ven-* /vən/ to *vienn-* /vjɛn/. The change to a nasal vowel in the singular forms is predictable from the loss of the final /n/ (it is analogous to the alternation *italienne/italien,* for example). The unstable *e* of *venons, venez,* and *venu* is usually dropped.

- The verb **venir** means *to come* or *to come from*:

VENIR *to come, to come from*		
SINGULIER		**PLURIEL**
je viens		nous ven**ons**
tu viens		vous ven**ez**
il }		ils }
elle } vien**t**		elles } vienn**ent**
on }		

IMPÉRATIF : **Viens ! Venez** ici ! **Venons** voir ces cartes !

PASSÉ COMPOSÉ : Je **suis venu/e** hier.

FUTUR : Je **viendr**ai demain.

- **Devenir** (*to become*), **revenir** (*to come back*), and **obtenir** (*to obtain*) are conjugated like **venir**:

Quand est-ce que tu **reviens** de Genève ?	*When are you coming back from Geneva?*
Mon frère est **devenu** très raisonnable.	*My brother has become very reasonable.*
—Qu'est-ce que vous **devenez** maintenant ?	*—What's new with you these days?*
—J'ai **obtenu** mon diplôme.	*—I got my degree.*

- To express an event that has just occurred, use **venir de** plus an infinitive.

Le train **vient de partir**.	*The train has just left.*
Nous **venons d'acheter** nos billets.	*We've just purchased our tickets.*

À vous la parole

Begin practice with a discrimination drill: one person or more than one? *Il vient demain ; Elles viennent d'Autriche ; Viens ici ! ; Ils viennent souvent ; Elle vient de partir ; Elles viennent la semaine prochaine ; Ils viennent avec moi ; Il vient seul ; Elles viennent de Paris ; Ils viennent ensemble ;* etc. Follow up with a simple substitution drill: *Je viens ce soir ; nous, lui,* etc.

9-22, Key: 1) l'Italie 2) l'Espagne, les pays d'Amérique du Sud, le Mexique 3) les États-Unis, l'Angleterre, l'Australie 4) la Suisse 5) l'Allemagne, la Suisse, l'Autriche 6) la Chine 7) la France, la Belgique, la Suisse, le Québec, les pays de l'Afrique francophone.

9-22 L'apprentissage des langues. Dites d'où ces personnes reviennent.

MODÈLE   Elles ont appris le portugais.
➤ Elles reviennent du Portugal ou du Brésil.

1. Elle a appris l'italien.
2. Il parle bien espagnol.
3. Nous avons appris l'anglais.
4. Je parle romanche.
5. Ils ont appris l'allemand.
6. Elles parlent chinois.
7. Il a appris le français.

9-23 Changement de caractère. Comment est-ce que ces gens changent ? Choisissez l'adjectif qui convient dans la liste :

adorable   désagréable   discipliné   égoïste   paresseux   sociable   timide

MODÈLE   Je rougis souvent.
➤ Je deviens timide.

1. Tu ne travailles pas beaucoup.
2. Roger écoute toujours ses parents.
3. Nous sommes furieux.
4. Mes chats sont gentils aujourd'hui.
5. Je ne donne rien aux autres.
6. Vous parlez à tout le monde.

9-24 Avant de venir en classe. Qu'est-ce que vous venez de faire, juste avant d'arriver en classe ? Expliquez-le à un/e partenaire.

MODÈLE   É1   Moi, je viens de déjeuner au resto U. Et toi ?
É2   Moi, je viens de travailler au labo de langues. Je viens de terminer mes devoirs.

Parlons

9-25 Un voyage

A. Avant de parler. Avec un/e camarade de classe, faites des projets de voyage dans un pays francophone (ou plusieurs pays francophones). Utilisez la carte du monde francophone que vous avez dans votre manuel et mettez-vous d'accord sur :

1. votre point de départ et votre destination (ou vos destinations)
2. l'intérêt touristique de cette région (ou de ces régions)
3. les choses que vous avez besoin d'emporter (*take along*)
4. la plus belle saison pour y aller
5. les moyens de transport que vous allez utiliser
6. le nombre de jours que vous allez passer dans chaque endroit

B. En parlant. Présentez vos projets à vos camarades de classe.

MODÈLE   ➤ Nous avons une semaine de vacances au mois de mars, et nous voulons aller à la Martinique. Nous allons prendre l'avion de New York à Fort-de-France…

C. Après avoir parlé. Est-ce que vos camarades de classe ont présenté des projets intéressants ? Quel/s voyage/s est-ce que vous avez préféré/s ? Quel voyage vous semble le plus exotique ? le plus compliqué ? le plus intéressant ?

Avant de parler. Put students into pairs or small groups to plan their description, then have them present their information to other members of the class. Suggest possible destinations, e.g., *le Québec, les Seychelles, le Maroc, la Guyane.* To make this activity more challenging, impose certain restrictions such as limits on means of travel (*vous avez le mal de mer et vous êtes claustrophobes*), amount of money to be spent (*vous êtes des étudiants pauvres*), or length of stay (*vous n'avez que deux jours de vacances*). This activity can be assigned as homework so that students have time to look up pertinent information on the region they select or are assigned to. The class can later vote on which presentation has been most convincing.

Leçon 3 *Faisons du tourisme !*

POINTS DE DÉPART

Le logement et les visites

La place Plumereau à Tours

You may wish to present this material over two days. If so, then treat the dialogue, directions and the **Vie et culture** note on lodgings on day 1, completing Ex. 9-26 and 9-27; treat historical and cultural sites on day 2, and complete Ex. 9-28.

To present, display the opening dialogue and let students listen to the exchange from the text audio. Ask simple questions to test comprehension. *Qui cherche un logement ? Pour combien de personnes ? Combien de temps est-ce que les Francard vont passer en Touraine ? Quel type de logement est-ce qu'on leur propose ? Où se trouve l'hôtel ?* Using the detail map of *Tours* (IRCD, Ch. 9), have students trace the route the Francard family will take to their hotel; have them find the *place Plumereau*, shown in the photo. Illustrate the meaning of each of the expressions in the shaded box, using the detail map.

Les Francard, une famille de touristes belges, viennent d'arriver à Tours. Ils rentrent dans l'Office de Tourisme pour chercher des renseignements et trouver un logement.

LA RÉCEPTIONNISTE : Bonjour, monsieur. Bonjour, madame.

M. FRANCARD : Bonjour, madame. Nous cherchons un logement pas trop cher pour trois nuits.

LA RÉCEPTIONNISTE : Oui, vous êtes combien ?

M. FRANCARD : Quatre personnes, donc nous aurons besoin de deux chambres.

LA RÉCEPTIONNISTE : Je peux vous proposer un petit hôtel deux étoiles en centre-ville. C'est 68 euros par chambre.

M. FRANCARD : Ça nous convient très bien.

LA RÉCEPTIONNISTE : Bon, alors, je vais faire une réservation sur Internet pour les deux chambres pour trois nuits.

...

LA RÉCEPTIONNISTE :	Bon, vous serez à l'Hôtel Château Fleuri ; ce n'est pas très loin d'ici.
M. FRANCARD :	L'hôtel se trouve où exactement ?
LA RÉCEPTIONNISTE :	Tenez, voici un plan du centre-ville. En sortant d'ici, vous allez prendre le boulevard. Ensuite vous tournez à droite dans la rue de Buffon. Continuez tout droit ; vous allez traverser la rue Émile Zola et ensuite prendre la rue de la Scellerie à gauche. L'hôtel se trouve au 7, rue de la Scellerie.
M. FRANCARD :	Merci, madame, et au revoir.
LA RÉCEPTIONNISTE :	Je vous en prie, monsieur, au revoir.

Tours, le centre-ville

Point out streets and squares named for well-known, writers (Voltaire, Émile Zola, Néricault Destouches); artists/composers (François Sicard, Bernard Palissy); statesmen (Jules Simon, Colbert, Jean Jaurès).

POUR INDIQUER LE CHEMIN

prendre la rue, l'avenue, le boulevard, la première/la deuxième à droite…

traverser la place…

tourner à droite/à gauche dans le boulevard…

continuer tout droit jusqu'à la rue…

Be sure to treat the **Vie et culture** before completing Ex. 9-26.

To expand the cultural content of the lesson, point out to students that the *Office de Tourisme* or *Syndicat d'Initiative* is an important resource for the French as well as for foreign travelers in France. You may want to display the home page of the Website for the *Fédération*

Vie et culture

Le logement

Si vous cherchez un logement pas cher en France, vous avez différents choix selon vos désirs et votre budget. Quels sont les avantages et les inconvénients de chaque option ? Quel type de logement est-ce que vous préférez et pourquoi ? Est-ce que vous avez les mêmes possibilités de logement dans votre pays ?

Nationale des Offices de Tourisme. As you show it, ask: Quels services sont proposés aux voyageurs ? Quels services vous semblent les plus importants pour un Français ? pour un Américain qui voyage en France ? and explain: Un Office de Tourisme existe dans beaucoup de lieux touristiques en France, donc c'est l'endroit où il faut aller pour commencer à planifier un séjour.

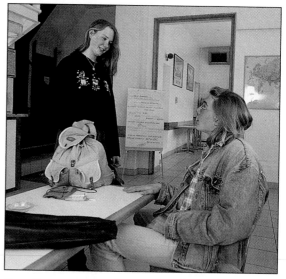

Si on est jeune, on peut rester dans une auberge de jeunesse.

You may wish to present historical and cultural sites on day 2 of the lesson. If so, this presentation can be enriched with slides, photos, or postcards of various locations in France. Use the drawing (IRCD, Ch. 9) to introduce the basic vocabulary: model pronunciation and describe each location. Test comprehension by having students point to the place you name. Have them repeat key terms by identifying: *C'est une cave ou une abbaye ?* etc.
Follow up with Ex. 9-28.

Des sites historiques et culturels

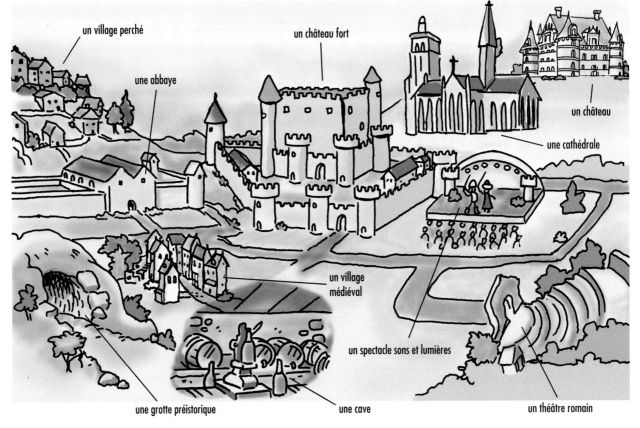

un village perché

une abbaye

un château fort

un château

une cathédrale

un village médiéval

un spectacle sons et lumières

une grotte préhistorique

une cave

un théâtre romain

Pendant l'été en France, les campings sont pleins de gens qui voyagent avec des caravanes, des camping-cars, ou simplement une tente.

Une autre possibilité est de rester chez l'habitant, dans un gîte rural à la campagne. C'est surtout une bonne option si on veut établir un contact avec les gens du pays.

À vous la parole

9-26 Où est-ce qu'ils vont loger ? D'après la description des touristes suivants, dites où ils vont probablement loger.

MODÈLE   Les Merten voudraient établir un contact avec les gens de la région.
➤ Ils vont loger dans un gîte rural.

1. Les Martini voudraient une chambre avec mini-bar, télévision et téléphone.
2. Christelle va passer trois jours à Bordeaux, mais c'est une étudiante et elle a un budget modeste.
3. Les Garcia voyagent avec leur caravane.
4. Max et ses copains veulent passer plusieurs semaines en Suisse sans dépenser (*spending*) trop d'argent.
5. Sébastien aime la nature ; il voyage avec son vélo et sa tente.
6. Les Smith aiment la campagne et ils voudraient pratiquer leur français.
7. Les Bénini voyagent en train et voudraient rester en ville.

9-27 Display the detail map of Tours (IRCD, Ch. 9) and have students take turns giving directions to their partner.
Key: 1) le musée des Beaux-Arts
2) la poste 3) la Basilique Saint-Martin
4) la place Plumereau 5) la préfecture
6) les Halles

To practice giving directions, put students in pairs and give each pair a slip of paper with a starting point and a destination. Using the detail map of Tours, they develop a set of directions, providing only the starting point and not the destination. Have each group exchange papers with another pair, who then try to follow the directions. See how many groups are successful. Suggested departure points/destinations: *de la gare à la cathédrale ; de la gare à l'Hôtel de ville ; de l'Hôtel de ville à la Faculté des lettres ; de la cathédrale à la poste ; de la place Plumereau à l'Hôtel de ville ; du musée des Beaux-Arts à la place Plumereau.*

9-27 Les bonnes indications. Imaginez que vous êtes devant la gare de Tours. Suivez les indications données et dites où est-ce que vous arrivez. Choisissez votre destination dans la liste suivante.

MODÈLE É1 Vous tournez à gauche dans le boulevard Heurteloup, ensuite à droite dans la rue Nationale et à droite dans la rue de la Scellerie. Vous arrivez au coin (*corner*) de cette rue et de la rue Voltaire.

   É2 C'est le Grand Théâtre ?

   É1 Oui, c'est ça.

la cathédrale	la Basilique Saint-Martin
le Grand Théâtre	les Halles
le musée des Beaux-Arts	la place Plumereau
la préfecture de police	la poste

1. Vous traversez le boulevard Heurteloup. Vous prenez la rue Bernard Palissy et vous continuez tout droit. À la place François Sicard, vous tournez à droite.
2. Vous tournez à gauche dans le boulevard Heurteloup et vous traversez la place Jean-Jaurès. C'est sur votre droite à côté du Palais de Justice.
3. Vous tournez à gauche dans le boulevard Heurteloup, vous traversez la rue Nationale et vous continuez tout droit. Vous prenez la deuxième rue à droite. Vous arrivez dans la rue Néricault Destouches. C'est là, en face de vous.
4. Le plus facile, c'est de suivre la rue Nationale jusqu'à la Loire et de prendre la rue des Tanneurs juste avant le quai de Pont-Neuf. Ensuite, vous tournez à gauche en face de la fac dans une petite rue piétonnière (*pedestrian street*).
5. Traversez le boulevard Heurteloup et prenez la rue de Buffon. Tournez à droite à la place de la Préfecture et continuez tout droit. C'est au coin de la rue Bernard Palissy sur votre droite.
6. Traversez le boulevard Heurteloup, prenez la rue de Buffon, tournez à gauche dans la rue de la Scellerie et continuez tout droit. Traversez la rue Nationale. Suivez la rue des Halles. C'est au bout (*at the end*) sur votre gauche.

9-28 To follow up, have the class compare answers to see which pair came up with the most exciting things to do.

9-28 À l'Office de Tourisme. Avec un/e partenaire, quelles visites est-ce que vous recommandez à ces touristes ?

MODÈLE Jérôme et Camille sont très sportifs et ils aiment les beaux paysages.

   É1 Ils peuvent faire du cyclotourisme.

   É2 Oui. Comme ça, ils se promèneront dans la nature et ils visiteront tous les petits villages.

La cité médiévale de Carcassonne

1. Les Martin sont fascinés par la préhistoire.
2. Sophie aime tout ce qui est spectacle.
3. Mme Francard s'intéresse aux arts décoratifs.
4. M. Francard aime surtout l'architecture de la Renaissance.
5. Pierre a étudié l'histoire des religions.
6. M. Dupin voudrait goûter les meilleurs vins de la région.
7. Audrey se passionne pour la peinture et la sculpture.
8. Vincent voudrait découvrir la France profonde.

FORMES ET FONCTIONS

1. *Les pronoms relatifs* où *et* qui

- Relative pronouns allow you to introduce a clause that provides additional information about a person, place or thing. When the relative pronoun **qui**, equivalent to the English *who* or *which/that*, is used to introduce this information, it is always followed by a verb.

Introduce the relative pronouns through examples. Meaning is fairly straightforward ; however, students will need to pay particular attention to the use of *où* with expressions of time, since English uses the relative "when." Ex. 9-29 treats this feature.

David est un guide **qui** a beaucoup de talent.	*David is a tour guide who is very talented.*
Rome est une ville **qui** est connue pour son architecture.	*Rome is a city that is known for its architecture.*

- **Où** can be used to introduce a place or a time; it is equivalent to the English *where* or *when*.

C'est une ville **où** il y a beaucoup de monuments historiques.	*It's a city where there are many historical monuments.*
L'automne en France, c'est la saison **où** il commence à faire froid.	*Autumn in France is the season when it starts to get cold.*

À vous la parole

9-29 En quelles saisons ? En quelles saisons est-ce qu'on peut faire les activités suivantes ?

MODÈLE   On va à la campagne chercher des pommes.
➤ L'automne est la saison où on va à la campagne chercher des pommes.

1. On peut faire un pique-nique à la montagne.
2. On peut faire du ski.
3. On va souvent au bord de la mer.
4. On fait des randonnées dans la forêt.
5. On commence à faire du jardinage.
6. On admire les fleurs à la campagne.
7. On va voir les matchs de football américain.
8. On a envie de voyager dans les pays chauds.

Besides these exercises, other simple exercises to practice use of relative pronouns include: a) recycling professions: *Un mécanicien ? — C'est un homme qui répare des voitures. Une serveuse ? — C'est une femme qui travaille dans un restaurant/sert des boissons. Un médecin ? Un professeur ? Un avocat ? Une comptable ? Un guide touristique ? Un/e réceptionniste à l'Office de Tourisme ? Un/e réceptionniste à l'hôtel ? Un agent de voyage ?* etc.; b) a guessing game—students describe a classmate and let others guess who they're describing: *C'est un étudiant qui joue de la guitare ; C'est une étudiante qui porte une jupe bleue ;* etc.

9-29 Before beginnning, you may wish to review the four seasons very quickly. As a variation, you might ask students to describe typical activities during each season of the year, or typical activities on a particular holiday: *Noël ? — C'est un jour où on offre des cadeaux,* etc.

9-30 As an alternative, you might also have students describe the town/city where your university is located, or another city of their choice.

9-30 Les grandes villes. Avec un/e partenaire, est-ce que vous pouvez décrire ces grandes villes ?

MODÈLE   New York

> É1   New York est une ville où il y a beaucoup de grands magasins.
>
> É2   New York est aussi une ville qui a beaucoup de théâtres et de cinémas.

1. San Francisco
2. Paris
3. La Nouvelle-Orléans
4. Los Angeles
5. Washington D.C.
6. Dakar
7. Québec
8. Genève

9-31 At the end, bring the class together as a group to compare responses.

9-31 Quelles sont vos préférences ? Pour le logement, les vacances, les gens ? Discutez de cela avec un/e partenaire.

MODÈLE   J'aime les hôtels…

> É1   J'aime les hôtels qui sont très modernes.
>
> É2   Moi, j'aime surtout les hôtels où il y a une piscine.

1. J'aime les hôtels…
2. Je préfère les villes…
3. Je n'aime pas les musées…
4. J'aime les vacances…
5. J'aime surtout visiter les endroits…
6. J'aime les gens…
7. Je n'aime pas beaucoup les gens…

2. Le pronom relatif que

Analyzing complex sentences as two independent clauses helps students understand the fact that relative pronouns have a double function: 1) linking two clauses; 2) replacing a co-referential noun.

- As you have learned, a relative pronoun allows you to introduce a clause that provides additional information about a person, place, or thing. The relative pronoun connects the clause that provides additional information to the main clause. In the example below, the clause that provides additional information, called the subordinate clause, is set off by brackets.

Le guide était bien informé. Le guide nous a fait visiter le château.

Le guide [**qui** nous a fait visiter le château] était bien informé.

The guide who gave us a tour of the château was well-informed.

In this example the relative pronoun that refers to the guide, **qui**, is the subject of the subordinate clause. As you have learned, **qui** is always followed by the verb phrase of the subordinate clause.

- **Que** is used when the relative pronoun is the direct object of the subordinate clause. Use **qu'** before words beginning with a vowel. The subject of the subordinate clause usually follows **que/qu'**.

With stylistic inversion, the subject may not follow directly: *Montréal est une ville qu'apprécient beaucoup les touristes.*

C'est une ville. J'aime beaucoup cette ville.

C'est une ville [**que** j'aime beaucoup].   *It's a city that I like a lot.*

Like **qui**, the relative pronoun **que/qu'** can refer either to a person or a thing.

Le guide **que** j'ai eu était très enthousiaste.   *The guide whom/that I had was very enthusiastic.*

Nous avons visité le musée **que** Mme Lerond a recommandé.   *We visited the museum (that) Mrs. Lerond recommended.*

Be careful! In English the words *whom* or *that* may be left out, but in French **que** must always be used.

- When you use the **passé composé**, the past participle agrees in number and gender with the preceding direct-object pronoun. In both examples below, **que/qu'** refers to a feminine plural noun, and the feminine plural form of the past participle is used.

Voilà les cartes postales **que** j'ai écrit**es**.   *Here are the postcards (that) I wrote.*

Vous connaissez les musiciennes **qu'**ils ont invit**ées** à jouer ?   *Do you know the musicians (that) they invited to play?*

Remind students that this is the case for any direct object that precedes the verb in the *passé composé*. In practice, however, many French speakers and writers do not make the agreement, so we consider this a minor point. This point was also addressed in Ch. 6, L. 1. The Workbook includes writing activities that focus on placement with the various tenses and rules of agreement.

À vous la parole

👤👤 **9-32 Vous connaissez ?** Est-ce que vous connaissez ces villes ou ces sites ? Parlez-en avec un/e partenaire.

MODÈLE   la statue de la Liberté

   É1 C'est un monument que je connais.

   É2 Moi aussi, c'est un monument que j'ai visité avec mes parents.

1. New York
2. la statue de la Liberté
3. Washington D.C.
4. le Smithsonian
5. Paris
6. la tour Eiffel
7. Londres
8. le *British Museum*

9-32 Before beginning, explain to students the meaning of the verb *connaître* in this specific context: that one has actually visited the place mentioned.

9-33 This includes all the relative pronouns introduced thus far; you might extend practice by asking students to provide additional examples of travel vocabulary to be defined.

9-33 Le mot juste.
Le voyageur a besoin d'un vocabulaire précis. Dans les définitions, on emploie souvent des propositions relatives. Est-ce que vous et votre partenaire pouvez définir les choses suivantes ?

MODÈLES un magnétoscope

É1 C'est un appareil qu'on utilise pour regarder une vidéocassette.

un théâtre

É2 C'est un endroit où on joue des pièces de théâtre.

un guide

É1 C'est une personne ou un livre qui explique l'histoire des monuments.

1. un appareil photo
2. un lecteur CD
3. un ordinateur portable
4. un musée
5. un office de tourisme
6. une agence de voyages
7. une réceptionniste
8. un agent de police

9-34 Souvenirs de voyage.
Quels sont vos souvenirs d'un voyage que vous avez fait ? Discutez de cela avec un/e partenaire.

MODÈLE le jour du départ

É1 C'était un jour que j'attendais avec beaucoup d'impatience.

É2 C'était un jour où il a fait très beau.

1. l'endroit visité
2. le logement
3. les activités
4. le dernier jour des vacances
5. le retour

Lisons

_____

Avant de lire. Camus is just one of many French writers who have traveled in and written about the United States. The list includes Alexis de Tocqueville, François-René de Chateaubriand, Michel Butor, Simone de Beauvoir, and Julien Green.

Stratégie
Use your knowledge of the historical context to better understand a personal narrative. What events that you are familiar with might color or shape the author's thinking and how? What might distinguish—in a particular era—the places he/she encounters and describes?

9-35 Voyage à New York

A. Avant de lire. This selection is an excerpt from ***Journaux de voyage*** by Albert Camus (1913–1960). Camus, who was born in Algeria and went to France in 1939, was the author of influential novels, among them ***L'étranger*** and ***La Peste***, as well as of plays and essays. He won the Nobel Prize for Literature in 1957. During his career, he also worked as a journalist. As a member of the French Resistance against the Nazis, he published the

Albert Camus, 1952

important clandestine newspaper ***Combat*** during the Second World War. It was as a journalist that he had occasion to travel to New York City in 1946.

1. What does the title of this collection, ***Journaux de voyage***, tell you about the type of text you are about to read? What types of information are you likely to find?

2. Now, think about the setting and date of the experience Camus relates. What historical events are likely still to dominate his frame of reference in 1946? What might seem striking about New York City to someone arriving from Europe at that date? And what comes to your own mind when you think of the city of New York in 1946? Compare your responses with those of a classmate.

B. En lisant. Trouvez les réponses aux questions suivantes.

1. Dans le premier paragraphe, quels mots et expressions expliquent…
   a. comment Camus a voyagé à New York ;
   b. le temps qu'il fait au moment de son arrivée ;
   c. comment il se sent à ce moment-là ?

2. Dans le deuxième paragraphe, Camus décrit New York, qu'il découvre pour la première fois. Comment est la ville ?

3. Dans le troisième paragraphe, Camus se prépare à débarquer. Pourquoi est-ce qu'il descend du bateau après tous les autres passagers ?

4. Dans le dernier paragraphe de cet extrait, il décrit ses premières impressions lorsqu'il se promène dans les rues de New York. Qu'est-ce qu'il remarque en particulier ?

C. En regardant de plus près. Maintenant, examinez quelques aspects de ce texte.

1. Dans le premier paragraphe, Camus mentionne « les gratte-ciel de Manhattan ». Vous connaissez déjà le mot « ciel ». Qu'est-ce que « les gratte-ciel » ?

2. Camus est allé à New York en 1946, juste après la Deuxième Guerre Mondiale. Dans le texte il fait allusion à cette période deux fois :
   a. Dans le troisième paragraphe, lorsqu'il est retenu au moment où il passe à l'immigration, il écrit, « Mystère, mais après cinq ans d'occupation ! » Qu'est-ce qu'il veut dire par cela ?
   b. Dans le dernier paragraphe, il écrit, « Je sors de cinq ans de nuit… ». Quel est le sens de ce commentaire ? Pensez au contexte historique.

En lisant, Key: 1. a) en bateau (autres mots-clefs : ancrons, débarquerons, mouettes) ; b) froid, gris, brume (à noter : la couleur du vent) ; c) tranquille. 2. l'ordre, la puissance, la force économique et l'inhumanité. 3. Il était retenu par le service de l'immigration. (Ses positions politiques sont à l'origine de ce soupçon.) 4. les gants des ramasseurs d'ordures, la circulation disciplinée, un manque de monnaie, les gens qui ont l'air de sortir d'un film, des lumières violentes, l'enseigne Camel.

En regardant de plus près, Key: 1. skyscrapers 2. a) After five years of occupation, one gets used to being detained without obvious reason; b) During the war, street lights were not turned on at night to avoid attracting the attention of bombers.

VOYAGE À NEW YORK

À 12 heures aujourd'hui, on aperçoit la terre. Depuis le matin, des mouettes[1] survolaient le bateau et semblaient suspendues, immobiles, au-dessus des ponts. Coney Island qui ressemble à la porte d'Orléans nous apparaît d'abord. « C'est Saint-Denis ou Gennevilliers, » dit L. C'est tout à fait vrai. Dans le froid,

5 avec le vent gris et le ciel plat, tout cela est assez cafardeux[2]. Nous ancrons dans la baie d'Hudson et ne débarquerons que demain matin. Au loin, les gratte-ciel de Manhattan sur un fond de brume[3]. J'ai le cœur tranquille et sec que je me sens devant les spectacles qui ne me touchent pas.

Lundi. Coucher très tard la veille. Lever très tôt. Nous remontons le port de New

10 York. Spectacle formidable malgré ou à cause de la brume. L'ordre, la puissance, la force économique est là. Le cœur tremble devant tant d'admirable inhumanité.

Je ne débarque qu'à 11 heures après de longues formalités où seul de tous les passagers je suis traité en suspect. L'officier d'immigration finit par s'excuser de m'avoir tant retenu. « J'y étais obligé, mais je ne puis vous dire pourquoi. »

15 Mystère, mais après cinq ans d'occupation ! ...

Fatigué. Ma grippe[4] revient. Et c'est les jambes flageolantes[5] que je reçois le premier coup de New York. Au premier regard, hideuse ville inhumaine. Mais je sais qu'on change d'avis. Ce sont des détails qui me frappent : que les ramasseurs d'ordures[6] portent des gants, que la circulation est disciplinée, sans intervention

20 d'agents aux carrefours[7], etc., que personne n'a jamais de monnaie dans ce pays et que tout le monde a l'air de sortir d'un film de série. Le soir, traversant Broadway en taxi, fatigué et fiévreux[8], je suis littéralement abasourdi[9] par la foire lumineuse. Je sors de cinq ans de nuit et cette orgie de lumières violentes me donne pour la première fois l'impression d'un nouveau continent (une

25 énorme enseigne[10] de 15 m pour les Camel : un G.I. bouche[11] grande ouverte laisse échapper d'énormes bouffées de *vraie* fumée. Le tout jaune et rouge.[)] Je me couche malade du cœur autant que du corps, mais sachant parfaitement que j'aurai changé d'avis[12] dans deux jours.

---

[1]oiseaux maritimes [2]déprimant [3]brouillard [4]flu [5]on shaky legs [6]garbage collectors
[7]intersections [8]feverish [9]stupéfait [10]billboard [11]mouth [12]I will have changed my mind

Albert CAMUS. *Journaux de voyage.* © Éditions GALLIMARD.

Après avoir lu, Key: 1. His first impression is negative (*hideuse ville inhumaine*), but he believes this impression will change (*j'aurai changé d'avis dans deux jours*).

You might also ask students: *Est-ce que vous avez déjà visité New York ? Si oui, comparez vos impressions avec celles de Camus. Si non, d'où vient l'image que vous avez de New York ?*

D. Après avoir lu. Discutez des questions suivantes avec vos camarades de classe.

1. Quelle première impression est-ce que Camus a de New York ? Est-ce qu'il pense que cette impression va durer, ou qu'elle va bientôt changer ?
2. Quel contraste est-ce que Camus remarque entre New York et les « cinq ans de nuit » qu'il a éprouvé (*experienced*) ? Est-ce que cette impression est positive ?
3. Imaginez un journaliste français qui arrive aujourd'hui à New York. Comparez ses impressions aux impressions de Camus en 1946 — quelles similarités et quelles différences est-ce qu'il pourrait y avoir ?

Venez chez nous !
Paris, ville lumière

Paris, comme vous le savez, est la capitale de la France. C'est aussi la ville la plus visitée du monde. C'est une belle ville remplie[1] d'histoire, de monuments intéressants, d'églises, de bons restaurants et de grands magasins et petites boutiques de spécialités. Il y en a pour tous les goûts. Paris est connue sous le nom de *Ville Lumière*. D'où cette désignation vient-elle ? C'est parce qu'à la fin du dix-neuvième siècle et au début du vingtième, Paris était le centre artistique et culturel du monde et

Notre-Dame de Paris

Additional activities to explore the **Venez chez nous !** topics are provided by:
- Student Activities Manual
- *Chez nous* video
- *Chez nous* Companion Website: **http://www.prenhall.com/cheznous**

la capitale de l'élégance, du luxe et des plaisirs. Beaucoup d'écrivains, de musiciens et d'artistes passaient au moins un an dans la *Ville Lumière* pour apprendre leur métier ou trouver de l'inspiration. Voilà pourquoi on appelle la fin du dix-neuvième siècle en France *la Belle Époque*.

La tour Eiffel et le Sacré-Coeur

[1]*full of*

Begin this lesson with a think-pair-share brainstorm activity. Ask each student to take out a piece of paper and write down the first three things that come to mind when you say "Paris." Then have students compare their list with that of a partner. Finally, make a list on the board with input from the whole class. As you write their responses on the board, group the answers together into categories, but without using titles (e.g., *les monuments, les musées, la cuisine, le shopping, l'histoire,* etc.). After you've finished, ask students to identify and label each group. You could also ask if any students have visited Paris and have them share their experiences and/or bring in any souvenirs they collected.

Use the video montage (*Paris, ville lumière*) to provide an overview of this lesson; see how many monuments students recognize. You might replay this montage after having treated the lesson; students should then recognize more landmarks. Treat the opening segment in the book by having students look for main ideas: what will they find in Paris? Why is Paris known as the "City of Light?" Students may also have heard of the "Gay Nineties," an expression used in the United States for this same period.

Observons

9-36 Two additional interviews are treated in the Video Manual.

9-36 Mes impressions de Paris

A. Avant de regarder. Est-ce que vous aimez visiter des grandes villes comme New York, Montréal ou Paris ? Est-ce que vous voudriez habiter une grande ville ? Pourquoi ? Même si vous n'avez jamais visité Paris, quelle idée est-ce que vous avez de cette ville célèbre ? Dans cette séquence, vous allez entendre deux Niçois qui décrivent leurs impressions de Paris.

FABIENNE : Alors je suis niçoise, mais je vais vous parler un petit peu de Paris. Nous, nous sommes dans le Sud de la France, Paris est beaucoup plus dans le Nord de la France. Nous avons entre les Niçois et les Parisiens toujours un petit conflit, qui ne se dit pas toujours, mais je suis mariée avec un Parisien, donc, j'ai dû faire mon deuil de cela. J'ai visité Paris un petit peu contrainte et forcée, et finalement cette ville m'a beaucoup plu, je… je dois le reconnaître. Peut-être pas la tour Eiffel, parce que c'est un monument qui m'a pas vraiment étonnée, peut-être à force de le voir en photo. Maintenant j'ai adoré vraiment toutes les activités, le shopping à Paris, chose que nous n'avons pas à Nice, peut-être. Nous avons à Nice le climat, à Paris ils ont toutes les activités. Et euh… j'aime bien les Parisiens, finalement.

EDOUARD : J'aime beaucoup Paris, c'est un lieu où je vais souvent et et où j'ai travaillé notamment. Et j'ai pu découvrir beaucoup d'endroits cet été, notamment la Bibliothèque François-Mitterrand, qui est un endroit très… très intéressant, je trouve. Mais il y a d'autres endroits, comme l'Opéra, qui est… bon, que tout le monde connaît et qui est… que je trouve magnifique. Euh, et sinon, euh bien, évidemment tous les grands monuments, comme la Concorde, la tour Eiffel. Et, euh… c'est un lieu où j'aime bien aller, euh… en vacances,… pour travailler…

B. En regardant. Trouvez la réponse (ou les réponses) à chaque question.

1. Fabienne dit qu'il y a toujours un petit conflit entre…
   a. les Français et les Américains.
   b. les Parisiens et les Niçois.
   c. les hommes et les femmes.

2. Pour elle, ce n'est pas un problème parce qu'elle…
   a. est mariée avec un Parisien.
   b. adore les Américains.
   c. est née à Paris.

3. À Paris, elle aime surtout…
   a. la tour Eiffel.
   b. le climat.
   c. le shopping.

4. Edouard est allé à Paris pour…
   a. voir sa famille.
   b. travailler.
   c. passer des vacances.

5. Il a découvert beaucoup de monuments, par exemple :

_____ l'Opéra de Paris   _____ l'arc de Triomphe   _____ la place de la Concorde

_____ le Louvre   _____ la tour Eiffel   _____ la Bibliothèque François-Mitterrand

C. Après avoir regardé. Maintenant discutez de ces questions avec vos camarades de classe.

1. Fabienne remarque qu'il y a un petit conflit entre les gens du Nord (les Parisiens) et les gens du Sud (les Niçois). Comment pourriez-vous expliquer ce conflit ? Est-ce qu'il existe des tensions ou de la concurrence (*competition*) entre les gens de régions différentes chez vous ? Si oui, pourquoi ?

2. Fabienne n'est pas très impressionnée quand elle voit la tour Eiffel pour la première fois. Pourquoi ? Est-ce que vous avez déjà eu cette expérience, de voir un monument ou une œuvre d'art célèbre pour la première fois et puis d'être déçu/e (*disappointed*) ?

3. Est-ce que les impressions de Fabienne et Edouard vous étonnent (*surprise*) ? Pourquoi ? Est-ce qu'elles diffèrent de vos propres impressions de Paris ?

Parlons

9-37 La visite d'un monument

Une façon agréable de voir les monuments de Paris est de prendre un bateau-mouche. Ces bateaux font des circuits touristiques avec des commentaires sur tous les monuments qui se trouvent au bord de la Seine. Regardez ce détail d'un plan de Paris et identifiez les monuments que vous reconnaissez.

If you have a collection of maps (e.g., from the department stores in Paris), you could bring them to class and have students work in groups to find the monuments on the *bateau-mouche* map and label them. You might also assign this as homework and have students go to the *Chez nous* Companion Website to find links to maps and tourist guides of Paris.

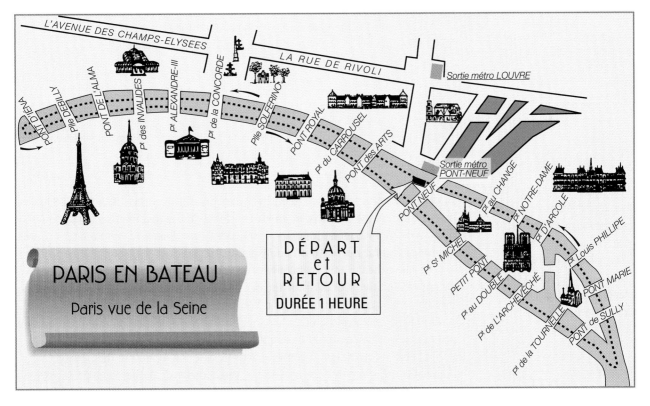

A. Avant de parler. Maintenant, c'est à vous de jouer le rôle d'un/e guide à bord d'un bateau-mouche à Paris. D'abord, choisissez un monument. Voici quelques possibilités :

1. l'Hôtel de Ville
2. la Conciergerie
3. les Jardins des Tuileries
4. le musée d'Orsay
5. l'obélisque de la Concorde
6. le Pont-Neuf
7. la tour Eiffel
8. Notre-Dame de Paris
9. les Invalides
10. le Louvre
11. le Grand Palais
12. l'Institut de France

Ensuite, préparez une description de votre monument ; considérez les questions suivantes :

1. Où se trouve ce monument ? Dans quel arrondissement ? Dans quelle rue ? À côté de quels autres sites importants ? Est-ce qu'il y a une station de métro à proximité ?

2. Quand est-ce que ce monument a été construit ? Par qui ? Pourquoi est-ce que ce monument est important aujourd'hui ?

Pour trouver des renseignements, consultez le site Web de *Chez nous* pour ce chapitre (choisissez *Web Resources* et cliquez sur *Textbook Web Links*), des encyclopédies et des guides touristiques.

B. En parlant. Présentez votre monument à vos camarades de classe. N'oubliez pas d'apporter des images (des photos, des affiches, etc.) de votre monument !

C. Après avoir parlé. Quelles sont les présentations les plus intéressantes ? Quels monuments est-ce que vous voudriez visiter maintenant ?

TEXT AUDIO

9-38 La Leçon

A. Avant de lire. For more than fifty years, in a little corner of the Latin Quarter near the Seine, the **Théâtre de la Huchette** has presented the two best-known plays written by Eugène Ionesco (1909–1994): *La cantatrice chauve* (*The Bald Soprano*) and *La Leçon* (both published in 1953).

In a tiny theater that seats only ninety people, millions have watched these two representative works of the theater of the absurd, a literary form which came into its own after the Second World War. The theater of the absurd rejects traditional dramatic structure, character portrayal, logic, and communication as it portrays a world seemingly turned upside down.

Although the exchange between a professor and a pupil in the passage below, from *La Leçon*, seems in many ways nonsensical, there is a progression in tone and character that hints at the violent event, a murder, that will be the play's dramatic climax. This progression also allows the playwright to make important comments about the nature of education and the relationship between professor and pupil. To grasp this progression and the related build-up in tension, focus as you read on the following aspects of the exchange:

1. There are comic elements at the beginning, but the tone gradually becomes more somber. How and why?

2. How does the nature of the professor's comments change over the course of this dialogue?

3. How do the nature of the pupil's responses and her demeanor gradually change as well?

Le Théâtre de la Huchette à Paris

L'intérieur du Théâtre de la Huchette. Est-ce que vous aimeriez voir une pièce dans cette salle ?

B. En lisant. Lisez le texte et ensuite répondez aux questions suivantes.

1. Identifiez quelques aspects comiques de cet extrait.

MODÈLE ➤ Le professeur est très surpris parce que l'élève sait combien font un et un ;…

2. Quelle est l'attitude de l'élève au début : est-ce qu'elle est timide ou est-ce qu'elle est sûre d'elle ? Comment est-ce que ses réponses évoluent pendant la leçon ? Pourquoi ?

3. Comment est le professeur au début : est-ce qu'il est poli et patient, par exemple ? Est-ce qu'il change d'attitude au cours de la leçon ? Comment et pourquoi ?

4. Comment est-ce que la relation entre le professeur et son élève a changé à la fin ?

LE PROFESSEUR :	Bon. Arithmétisons donc un peu.
L'ÉLÈVE :	Oui, très volontiers, Monsieur.
LE PROFESSEUR :	Cela ne vous ennuierait pas de me dire …
L'ÉLÈVE :	Du tout[1], Monsieur, allez-y.
LE PROFESSEUR :	Combien font un et un ?
L'ÉLÈVE :	Un et un font deux.

5

[1] *Not at all*

LE PROFESSEUR : *émerveillé² par le savoir de l'Élève :* Oh, mais c'est très bien. Vous me paraissez³ très avancée dans vos études. Vous aurez facilement votre doctorat total, Mademoiselle.

10   L'ÉLÈVE : Je suis bien contente. D'autant plus que⁴ c'est vous qui le dites.

LE PROFESSEUR : Poussons plus loin : combien font deux et un ?

L'ÉLÈVE : Trois.

LE PROFESSEUR : Trois et un ?

L'ÉLÈVE : Quatre.

15   LE PROFESSEUR : Quatre et un ?

L'ÉLÈVE : Cinq.

LE PROFESSEUR : Cinq et un ?

L'ÉLÈVE : Six.

LE PROFESSEUR : Six et un ?

20   L'ÉLÈVE : Sept.

LE PROFESSEUR : Sept et un ?

L'ÉLÈVE : Huit.

LE PROFESSEUR : Sept et un ?

L'ÉLÈVE : Huit… *bis.*

25   LE PROFESSEUR : Très bonne réponse. Sept et un ?

L'ÉLÈVE : Huit *ter.*

LE PROFESSEUR : Parfait. Excellent. Sept et un ?

L'ÉLÈVE : Huit *quater.* Et parfois neuf.

LE PROFESSEUR : Magnifique. Vous êtes magnifique. Vous êtes exquise. Je vous félicite
30   chaleureusement⁵, Mademoiselle. Ce n'est pas la peine⁶ de continuer. Pour l'addition, vous êtes magistrale. Voyons la soustraction. Dites-moi, seulement, si vous n'êtes pas épuisée⁷, combien font quatre moins trois ?

L'ÉLÈVE : Quatre moins trois ?… Quatre moins trois ?

LE PROFESSEUR : Oui. Je veux dire : retirez⁸ trois de quatre.

35   L'ÉLÈVE : Ça fait… sept ?

LE PROFESSEUR : Je m'excuse⁹ d'être obligé de vous contredire¹⁰. Quatre moins trois ne font pas sept. Vous confondez¹¹ : quatre plus trois font sept, quatre moins trois ne font pas sept… Il ne s'agit plus¹² d'additionner, il faut soustraire maintenant.

L'ÉLÈVE : *s'efforce de comprendre :* Oui… oui…

40   LE PROFESSEUR : Quatre moins trois font… Combien ?… Combien ?

L'ÉLÈVE : Quatre ?

LE PROFESSEUR : Non, Mademoiselle, ce n'est pas ça.

L'ÉLÈVE : Trois, alors.

LE PROFESSEUR : Non plus, Mademoiselle… Pardon, je dois le dire… Ça ne fait pas ça… mes
45   excuses.

L'ÉLÈVE : Quatre moins trois… Quatre moins trois… Quatre moins trois ?… Ça ne fait tout de même pas dix ?

---

²*amazed* ³*seem, appear* ⁴*all the more so because* ⁵*warmly* ⁶*There's no point* ⁷*exhausted* ⁸*take away* ⁹*I am sorry* ¹⁰*to contradict*
¹¹*confuse* ¹²*It's no longer a question*

LE PROFESSEUR : Oh, certainement pas, Mademoiselle. Mais il ne s'agit pas de deviner[13], il faut raisonner. Tâchons[14] de le déduire ensemble. Voulez-vous compter ?

L'ÉLÈVE : Oui, Monsieur. Un…, deux…, euh…   50

LE PROFESSEUR : Vous savez bien compter ? Jusqu'à combien savez-vous compter ?

L'ÉLÈVE : Je puis[15] compter… à l'infini.

LE PROFESSEUR : Cela n'est pas possible, Mademoiselle.

L'ÉLÈVE : Alors, mettons[16] jusqu'à seize.

LE PROFESSEUR : Cela suffit[17]. Il faut savoir se limiter[18]. Comptez donc, s'il vous plaît, je vous   55 en prie.

L'ÉLÈVE : Un…, deux…, et puis après deux, il y a trois… quatre…

LE PROFESSEUR : Arrêtez-vous, Mademoiselle. Quel nombre est plus grand ? Trois ou quatre ?

L'ÉLÈVE : Euh… trois ou quatre ? Quel est le plus grand ? Le plus grand de trois ou quatre ? Dans quel sens le plus grand ?   60

LE PROFESSEUR : Il y a des nombres plus petits et d'autres plus grands. Dans les nombres plus grands il y a plus d'unités que dans les petits…

L'ÉLÈVE : … Que dans les petits nombres ?

LE PROFESSEUR : À moins que[19] les petits aient[20] des unités plus petites. Si elles sont toutes petites, il se peut qu[21]'il y ait plus d'unités dans les petits nombres que dans les grands…   65 s'il s'agit d'autres unités…

L'ÉLÈVE : Dans ce cas, les petits nombres peuvent être plus grands que les grands nombres ?

LE PROFESSEUR : Laissons cela[22]. Ça nous mènerait beaucoup trop loin…

[13] *to guess*   [14] *Let's make an effort*   [15] peux   [16] *Let's say*   [17] *That's enough*   [18] *We have to know our limits*   [19] *Unless*   [20] ont   [21] *it may be that*   [22] *Let's drop it*

Extrait de: Eugène Ionesco, *La Leçon*. © Éditions Gallimard.

C. En regardant de plus près. Maintenant examinez quelques caractéristiques du texte.

1. Observez la rapidité du dialogue : à quel moment est-ce que les questions et les réponses se suivent très rapidement ? À quel moment est-ce que les réponses ralentissent (*slow down*) ? Qu'est-ce que cela signale ?

2. Étudiez les répliques (*lines*) du professeur et de l'élève séparément : qu'est-ce que cela révèle sur le développement de chaque personnage ?

D. Après avoir lu. Discutez des questions suivantes avec vos camarades de classe.

1. Dans cet extrait, il s'agit d'un dialogue absurde entre le professeur et l'élève. Est-ce que c'est, à votre avis, une critique du système éducatif ? Dans quel sens ?

2. Comment sont les relations entre les professeurs et les élèves, d'après Ionesco ?

3. À la fin de la pièce, il y a un meurtre ; qui va tuer qui, à votre avis ? Expliquez votre réponse.

En regardant de plus près, Key: 1) The dialogue finds its most rapid pace with the addition problems, then abruptly slows down when the subject turns to subtraction. This signals a change in the attitudes of the characters; it might also signal for the playwright a commentary on the nature of education, with its emphasis on rote learning. 2) Separating out the lines of the two characters and reading them this way can help students see more clearly the changes in their attitudes.

Après avoir lu, Key: 1) One interpretation is that the educational system encourages rote memorization to the extent that students are not able to improvise or create. 2) Ionesco may be trying to convey that the educational system gives the professor too much power over the student, even the power of "life and death." 3) In the play, it is the professor who kills the student, as he has the 40 other students who came before her that day. And as the play ends, yet another student rings the doorbell…

9-39 Des Américains à Paris

C'est Thomas Jefferson qui a dit : « *Every man has two countries, his own and France.* » Jefferson, comme tant d'autres Américains, était fasciné par la France et par la ville de Paris. Nommé Ambassadeur des États-Unis en France, il y est allé en 1784, succédant à Benjamin Franklin, et il y est resté cinq ans. Paris attirait non seulement des diplomates mais aussi des artistes, des ingénieurs, des écrivains et des chanteurs. À Paris, ils ont trouvé une certaine liberté, personnelle et artistique, qui manquait à leur vie américaine. Ils ont découvert aussi une autre façon de voir le monde, une autre ouverture culturelle.

Benjamin Franklin a été Ambassadeur des États-Unis en France de 1776 jusqu'en 1785.

Joséphine Baker, une vedette des Folies Bergères pendant les années vingt et trente.

Avant d'écrire This writing activity gives students the opportunity to practice presentational writing skills, consistent with Standard 1.3 in the National Standards for Foreign Language Learning. Students may work individually or with a partner to write brief biographies. Allow students a few days to prepare their biographies, and ask them to include a photo of the person. In addition to encyclopedias and the Internet, another useful resource is: Morton, Brian. *Americans in Paris: An Anecdotal Street Guide.* Ann Arbor, MI: The Olivia and Hill Press, 1984.

A. Avant d'écrire. Vous allez préparer une description de la vie parisienne d'un/e Américain/e. D'abord, choisissez une personne dans une des catégories indiquées. Ensuite, cherchez des renseignements sur son séjour (ou ses séjours) à Paris. Pour trouver des renseignements, consultez le site Web de ***Chez nous*** pour ce chapitre (choisissez *Web Resources* et cliquez sur *Textbook Web Links*), des encyclopédies et des biographies.

Diplomates	Ingénieurs/ Aventuriers	Écrivains
John Adams	Thomas Edison	e.e. cummings
Benjamin Franklin	Robert Fulton	Ernest Hemingway
Thomas Jefferson	Charles Lindbergh	Katherine Anne Porter
Franklin Roosevelt	Samuel Morse	Gertrude Stein
Woodrow Wilson	Orville & Wilbur Wright	Mark Twain

Musiciens	Danseurs/ Comédiens
Louis Armstrong	Fred Astaire
Aaron Copland	Joséphine Baker
Duke Ellington	P.T. Barnum
George Gershwin	Isadora Duncan
Cole Porter	Buster Keaton

B. En écrivant. Pour préparer votre description, répondez aux questions suivantes :

1. Quand et pourquoi est-ce que cet/te Américain/e est allé/e à Paris ?
2. Combien de temps est-ce qu'il/elle y est resté/e ? Pourquoi ?
3. Où est-ce qu'il/elle est allé/e ? (dans des cafés ? des bars ? des théâtres ?)
4. Comment est-ce que les Français ont réagi à la venue de cet/te Américain/e ?
5. Quelles ont été ses impressions de Paris ?

Rédigez deux paragraphes qui expliquent le séjour à Paris de cet/te Américain/e. Dans le premier paragraphe, donnez des détails sur son séjour (questions 1–3). Dans le deuxième paragraphe, parlez des réactions des Parisiens et de ses impressions de Paris (questions 4 et 5). Terminez votre texte avec une phrase qui résume l'importance du séjour parisien dans la vie de cette personne.

C. Après avoir écrit. Relisez votre texte pour vérifier si vous y avez mis toutes les informations nécessaires. Rajoutez des détails intéressants, corrigez les fautes, puis échangez votre texte avec des camarades de classe qui vont le lire. Ils vont vous dire s'ils ont compris votre texte, et ils vont vous proposer des changements, si nécessaire.

Après avoir écrit. Have students exchange descriptions for the purposes of peer editing. Then have them compare the experiences of their historical figures. Which people had similar experiences? Speculate on why this might be so.

Vocabulaire

TEXT AUDIO

Leçon 1

moyens de transport (m.)	means of transportation
à pied	on foot
un avion	plane
un bus	city bus
un car	excursion bus, intracity bus
un métro	subway
une mobylette	moped, motorscooter
une moto	motorcycle
le RER	commuter train between Paris and suburbs
un taxi	taxi
un train	train

pour faire un voyage	to take a trip
un aéroport	airport
un appareil photo	camera
un appareil (photo) numérique	digital camera
un carnet d'adresses	address book
une carte bancaire	debit card
une carte de crédit	credit card
une clé, une clef	key
un passeport	passport
un permis de conduire	driver's licence
un plan de ville	city map
un portefeuille	wallet
un porte-monnaie (inv.)	change purse
un sac à dos	backpack
une valise	suitcase
un vol	flight

autres expressions utiles	other useful expressions
avoir besoin de	to need
un billet	(train, plane) ticket
un ticket	(subway) ticket
oublier	to forget
tout	everything
Voyons…	Let's see . . .

Leçon 2

les continents (m.)	continents
l'Afrique (f.)	Africa
l'Amérique du Nord (f.)	North America
l'Amérique du Sud (f.)	South America
l'Asie (f.)	Asia
l'Europe (f.)	Europe
l'Océanie (f.)	Pacific

des pays (m.)	countries
une frontière	border
l'Algérie (f.)	Algeria
l'Allemagne (f.)	Germany
l'Angleterre (f.)	England
l'Argentine (f.)	Argentina
l'Australie (f.)	Australia
la Belgique	Belgium
le Brésil	Brazil
le Cameroun	Cameroon
le Canada	Canada
la Chine	China
la Colombie	Colombia
la Côte-d'Ivoire	Ivory Coast
l'Espagne (f.)	Spain
les États-Unis (m.)	the United States
la France	France
l'Inde (f.)	India
l'Italie (f.)	Italy
le Japon	Japan
le Maroc	Morocco
le Mexique	Mexico
les Pays-Bas (m.)	the Netherlands
le Portugal	Portugal
le Sénégal	Senegal
la Suisse	Switzerland
le Vietnam	Vietnam

des nationalités	nationalities
algérien/algérienne	Algerian
allemand/e	German
américain/e	American
anglais/e	English
argentin/e	Argentinian
australien/australienne	Australian
belge	Belgian
brésilien/brésilienne	Brasilian
camerounais/e	Cameroonian
canadien/canadienne	Canadian
chinois/e	Chinese
colombien/colombienne	Colombian
espagnol/e	Spanish
français/e	French
indien/indienne	Indian
italien/italienne	Italian
ivoirien/ivoirienne	Ivorian
japonais/e	Japanese
marocain/e	Moroccan
mexicain/e	Mexican
néerlandais/e	Dutch
portugais/e	Portuguese
sénégalais/e	Senegalese
suisse	Swiss
vietnamien/vietnamienne	Vietnamese

d'autres mots utiles	other useful words
une langue maternelle	native language
obtenir	to obtain
une réunion	meeting

Leçon 3

le logement	lodgings
loger (dans un hôtel)	to stay (in a hotel)
une étoile	one star
une auberge (de jeunesse)	inn, (youth) hostel

un camping	campground
un camping-car	R.V.
une caravane	trailer
un gîte (rural)	(rural) bed and breakfast
Cela vous convient ?	Does this suit you?
aller sur Internet	to go online

pour se renseigner	to get information
des renseignements (m.)	information
un guide	guide (tour guide or guide book)
un office de tourisme	tourism office

pour indiquer le chemin	to give directions
une avenue	an avenue
un boulevard	a boulevard
le chemin	the way
continuer (tout droit)	keep going (straight ahead)
tourner à (droite)	turn (right)
traverser	cross

des sites historiques et culturels (m.)	historical and cultural sites
une abbaye	abbey
une cathédrale	cathedral
une cave	wine cellar
un château	chateau
un château fort	fortress
une grotte préhistorique	prehistoric cave
un spectacle sons et lumières	sound and light historical production
un théâtre romain	Roman theater
un village médiéval	medieval village
un village perché	village perched on a hillside

Qu'est-ce qu'on fait dans ce parc à Paris ? Pourquoi ?

Chapitre 10

La santé et le bien-être

Leçon 1   *La santé*

Leçon 2   *Pour rester en forme*

Leçon 3   *Sauvons la Terre et la forêt*

Venez chez nous !
L'écologie

In this chapter:

- Discussing health and well-being
- Describing illnesses
- Giving advice
- Discussing environmental concerns
- Understanding ecological concerns in the Francophone world

Leçon 1 *La santé*

POINTS DE DÉPART

Le corps humain et les maladies

Additional practice activities for
each **Points de départ** section are
provided by:
- Student Activities Manual
- *Chez nous* Companion Website:
  http://www.prenhall.com/cheznous

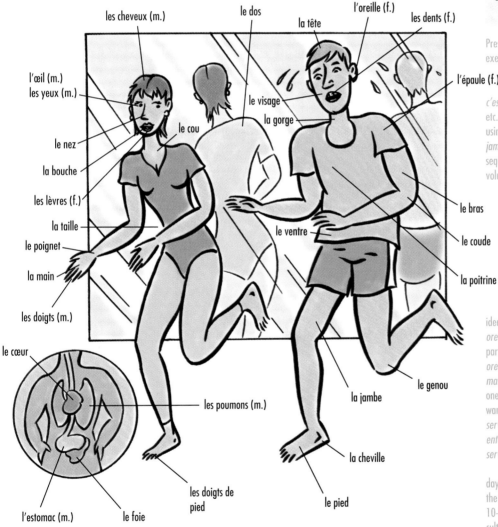

les cheveux (m.)
le dos
la tête
l'oreille (f.)
les dents (f.)
l'œil (m.)
les yeux (m.)
le visage
la gorge
l'épaule (f.)
le nez
le cou
la bouche
les lèvres (f.)
la taille
le ventre
le bras
le poignet
le coude
la main
la poitrine
les doigts (m.)
le cœur
le genou
les poumons (m.)
la jambe
la cheville
l'estomac (m.)
le foie
les doigts de pied
le pied

Present the parts of the body using the
exercising couple (IRCD, Ch. 10), naming
and describing the body parts: *Voici
les yeux ; vous avez deux yeux ;
c'est pour regarder. Au singulier, c'est un œil,*
etc. Or you might present this vocabulary
using TPR: *Touchez le bras, la main, la
jambe, les yeux,* etc. Follow the standard TPR
sequence, begining by having several
volunteers complete the action with you and
gradually have the volunteers
(and then the class as a whole)
respond to the commands without
the corresponding action on your
part. Test student comprehension
by playing "Simon says" (*Jacques
a dit...*). Using the unlabeled art
(IRCD, Ch. 10), have students
repeat the new vocabulary by
identifying parts of the body: *C'est une
oreille ou un œil ?*, then have them name
parts of the body that come in twos — *les
oreilles, les yeux, les bras, les jambes, les
mains*; then those for which they have only
one: *un cœur, une tête, un estomac.* You may
want to present the verbs of senses: *les yeux
servent à voir ; les oreilles servent à
entendre ; le nez sert à sentir ; les doigts
servent à toucher ; la langue sert à goûter.*
   To teach this vocabulary over two
days, begin on day 1 with parts of the body,
the expression *avoir mal*, and Ex. 10-1 and
10-2. On day 2, present the dialogue, the
cultural note, and *Maux et remèdes.*
Continue with Ex. 10-3 and 10-4.

Choose a "victim" from among the students, and use a toy hammer or bat to pretend you are inflicting pain on that person. Have students answer the question, *Où est-ce qu'il/elle a mal ?* You might focus on body parts not mentioned in the exercises. Follow up with Ex. 10-1 and 10-2.

VOUS AVEZ MAL ?

To indicate the location of body pains, use the expression **avoir mal à** plus the definite article and the body part. Remember that the preposition **à** contracts with the definite article **le, la, les**, in some cases:

J'ai mal à la tête.	*I have a headache.*
Il **a mal au** cœur.	*He's nauseated.*
Elle **a mal aux** pieds.	*Her feet hurt.*
J'ai mal partout.	*I hurt everywhere.*

Un malade imaginaire

TEXT AUDIO

Jacques Malveine est hypocondriaque. Il pense qu'il va mourir ce soir. Il appelle S.O.S. Médecins pour demander des conseils et un médecin vient tout de suite chez lui.

JACQUES : Je tousse, j'ai mal à la gorge, j'ai le nez qui coule, j'ai du mal à respirer. C'est une pneumonie, n'est-ce pas, docteur ?

LE MÉDECIN : Mais non, c'est un petit rhume. Vous n'avez même pas de fièvre !

JACQUES : Je dois rester longtemps au lit pour me soigner ? Je me sens très fatigué.

LE MÉDECIN : Pas du tout, au contraire, l'air frais vous fera du bien. Je vous donne quand même une ordonnance pour un médicament.

Use the art showing Jacques and his doctor to present the dialogue (IRCD, Ch. 10). Have students listen to the recording. See whether they can guess the meaning of *S.O.S. Médecins*, given the context. Test comprehension by demonstrating, asking simple questions or having students provide explanations: *Quels sont les symptômes de Jacques ? Toussez ! Quand vous avez le nez qui coule, vous avez besoin d'un thermomètre ou d'un Kleenex ?* Point out that temperature is measured in terms of the Celsius scale. The normal body temperature is 37°C; 40°C or 41°C indicate a high fever. You may wish to point out the humorous nature of Jacques' last name: *Malveine* means "bad luck" as *la veine* means good luck in familiar French. Of course, *veine* also refers to the veins in the body. Follow up by treating the cultural notes.

À vous la parole

10-1 J'ai mal ! Dites où ces personnes ont mal.

10-1 Use the image of the hikers (IRCD, Ch. 10) to complete the exercise.

MODÈLE Christiane
➤ Christiane, elle a mal au dos.

Thérèse   Denis   Mme Parizeau   M. Dubosc   Paul   Christiane

Vie et culture

Have students look at the newspaper excerpt and decide in what kind of paper they would find it and in what section. Discuss how this information would be useful to residents of the city and to visitors. For the various illnesses described in **À vous la parole**, have students indicate where they would go or whom they would call in each case. Note that a *sage-femme* is a midwife. Students may also be interested to learn that many cities often have numbers for *SOS Dentaire* for dental problems and *SOS Amitié*, a mental-health hotline. You may also wish to present a few words related to disabilities, such as *aveugle, non-voyant, sourd, malentendant,* and *fauteuil roulant.*

La médecine en France

Les Français ont un excellent système médical et l'on est toujours sûr de trouver un médecin et un pharmacien, même la nuit. Dans chaque ville, il y a un médecin et un pharmacien de garde[1] que l'on peut trouver en téléphonant à la police ou en regardant dans le journal. Lisez cet extrait d'un journal régional : Où se trouve la pharmacie de garde ? À qui est-ce qu'il faut téléphoner en cas d'urgence[2] ? Est-ce qu'il existe des services semblables là où vous habitez ?

[1]*on call*   [2]*emergency*

Une pharmacie de garde à Nice. Il est quelle heure maintenant ?

Infos Pratiques

Gardes

S.O.S. Médecins
(24/24 heures) : 08.20.58.20.20.

Médecins de garde
(24/24 heures) : 03.91.54.42.42

Médecins d'Urgences
(24/24 h) : 03.91.35.04.04

Sage-femme (de 22 heures à demain, 6 heures) Mme Mayella, 3, rue Vernier, tél. : 03.91.18.58.16

Ambulances : Alpha, tél. : 03.91.93.27.09 ; ABC, tél. : 03.91.88.18.08 ; Est, tél. : 03.91.54.55.46.

Pharmacies (de 19 heures, à demain, 8 heures) : La croix, 3, rue Voltaire ; Berger, 62, avenue Victor-Hugo.

10-2 Les excès. Dites où on peut avoir mal si on fait les choses suivantes.

10-2 Expand the exercise by having students suggest additional items.

MODÈLE   Si on mange trop de chocolat,…
➤ On a mal au ventre ou mal au cœur.

1. Si on passe trop de temps devant l'écran (*screen*) de l'ordinateur,…
2. Si on fait trop de jogging,…
3. Si on crie trop,…
4. Si on mange trop,…
5. Si on boit trop de vin,…
6. Si on écoute trop souvent de la musique trop forte,…
7. Si on a trop de problèmes,…
8. Si on est très fatigué,…

MAUX ET REMÈDES

Use the list to present illnesses and remedies; enrich the presentation by showing pictures or actual examples of the remedies listed.

Quand on a :
- de la fièvre, une grippe
- un rhume
- une forte toux
- une angine, une bronchite, une infection
- mal à l'estomac, mal au cœur

Quand on a :
- un coup de soleil

On peut prendre :
- de l'aspirine
- des gouttes pour le nez
- un sirop
- un antibiotique
- une tisane à la menthe

On peut mettre :
- une pommade

 **10-3 Diagnostics.** Faites un diagnostic pour chaque symptôme que votre partenaire vous donne.

MODÈLE   É1 J'ai mal à la gorge et j'ai 40° de fièvre.

   É2 Tu as sans doute une angine.

1. J'ai mal partout et un peu de fièvre.
2. J'ai 39° de fièvre.
3. J'ai le nez qui commence à couler.
4. J'ai envie de vomir.
5. Je tousse beaucoup et j'ai mal à la gorge.
6. J'ai une forte fièvre et j'ai du mal à respirer.
7. Mon dos est tout rouge et ça me fait mal. J'ai chaud.

10-4 Les malades imaginaires. Avec un groupe de camarades, imaginez que vous avez des petits problèmes de santé. Vous allez dire là où vous avez mal et quelle est la cause de vos douleurs (*discomfort*). Une personne de votre groupe va proposer des solutions.

MODÈLE   É1 J'ai mal à la tête. J'ai trop travaillé pour préparer ce cours.

   É2 Tu devrais prendre de l'aspirine et dormir plus.

   É3 Moi, je pense que j'ai un rhume. Je tousse, et j'ai le nez qui coule.

   É2 Alors, toi, tu devrais…

Sons et lettres

Les consonnes *s* et *z*

The letter **s** may represent either the sound /s/ or the sound /z/. A number of word pairs are distinguished by these two consonant sounds. In the middle of words, **-ss-** is pronounced as /s/ and **-s-** as /z/:

le dessert	*dessert*	le désert	*desert*
le coussin	*cushion*	le cousin	*cousin*
le poisson	*fish*	le poison	*poison*

At the beginning of words, the letter **s** is pronounced /s/; in liaison it is pronounced /z/. Compare:

   ils **s**ont / ils‿ont   vous **s**avez / vous‿avez

After a nasal vowel written with **n**, the letter **s** is pronounced /s/:

   conservation   penser   ensemble

Next to a consonant, **s** is pronounced /s/:

   rembourser   rester   l'estomac   respirer

But note the exception **Alsace**, where **s** is pronounced /z/.

The letter **c** is also pronounced /s/ before the letters **e** and **i** or when spelled with a cedilla.

   cent   **c**igarette   **ç**a   gar**ç**on

The letter **x** is pronounced:

- /s/ in: six   soixante   Bruxelles
- liaison /z/ in: six‿hommes   dix‿aspirines
- /gz/ in: l'examen   exagérer   exactement
- /ks/ in: le taxi   l'expérience   excellent

In France the -x of *Bruxelles* is usually pronounced /ks/. Make sure students understand that the -x of *six* is only pronounced /s/ when the word is pronounced alone or at the end of a phrase: — *Tu as combien de frères et de sœurs ? — J'en ai six ; — On est le combien aujourd'hui ? — Le six.* In liaison, the -x is pronounced /z/: *six‿hommes.*

À vous la parole

10-5 Contrastes. Prononcez chaque groupe de mots.

assez / le visage   ils passent / ils se taisent
les Écossaises / les Anglaises   passé / basé
tousser / une tisane   Alceste / l'Alsace
soixante / exacte   exotique / dix

Begin practice with a discrimination drill: are the two words or expressions the same or different? *le poisson/le poison ; le coussin/le coussin ; le dessert/le désert ; ils ont/ils sont ; le poison/le poison ; le cousin/le coussin ; ils ont/ils ont.* Students might also be amused by the following tongue twister: *Un chasseur sachant chasser sait chasser sans son chien.*

10-6 Proverbes. Répétez ces proverbes.

1. Poisson sans boisson, c'est poison.
2. Santé passe richesse.
3. Si jeunesse savait, si vieillesse pouvait.

FORMES ET FONCTIONS

1. *Les expressions de nécessité*

Additional practice activities for each **Formes et fonctions** section are provided by:
- **Student Activities Manual**
- *Chez nous* Companion Website: **http://www.prenhall.com/cheznous**

- You have learned to use a form of the verb **devoir** plus an infinitive to describe what one *must* or *should* do.

Pour maigrir, tu **dois suivre** un régime.   *To lose weight, you must go on a diet.*
Avec une si forte fièvre, elle **devrait se coucher**.   *With such a high fever, she should go to bed.*

- The following expressions that include the impersonal subject **il** can also be used with an infinitive to express obligation in a more general way:

il faut   *you have to/must*
il ne faut pas   *you must not*
il est nécessaire de   *it is necessary to*
il est important de   *it is important to*
il est utile de   *it is useful to*

This section allows students to gain familiarity with impersonal expressions before using them in complex sentences with the subjunctive, also taught in this lesson. In fact, use of the infinitive with these expressions is a good strategy for avoiding the more complex constructions using the subjunctive and is a tactic often employed by native speakers.

Il faut prendre des antibiotiques quand on a une infection.   *You have to take an antibiotic when you have an infection.*

Il ne faut pas aller à l'école avec de la fièvre.   *You mustn't go to school with a fever.*

En été, **il est important de porter** des lunettes de soleil.   *In summer, it's important to wear sunglasses.*

À vous la parole

10-7 S'habiller. Où est-ce qu'il faut mettre ces vêtements ?

MODÈLES un foulard ?

➤ Il faut le mettre autour (*around*) du cou.

un chapeau ?

➤ Il faut le mettre sur la tête.

1. des chaussettes ?
2. un pull-over ?
3. des gants ?
4. des chaussures ?

5. une cravate ?
6. une casquette ?
7. des bottes ?
8. une écharpe ?

10-8 Vary by having students answer the same questions for *une angine.*

10-8 Oui ou non ? Quand on a un gros rhume, est-ce qu'il faut faire les choses suivantes ?

MODÈLE rester au lit ?

➤ Non, il ne faut pas rester au lit. Il faut sortir et prendre l'air.

1. prendre de l'aspirine ?
2. appeler le médecin ?
3. prendre des gouttes pour le nez ?
4. prendre un antibiotique ?

5. bien manger ?
6. sortir avec ses amis ?
7. se coucher tôt ?

10-9 S.O.S. pharmaciens ! Avec un/e partenaire, à tour de rôle, imaginez que vous êtes pharmacien/ne et donnez des conseils pour chaque problème de santé.

MODÈLE É1 Je me sens toujours fatigué.

É2 Est-ce que vous dormez bien la nuit ?

É1 Pas toujours.

É2 Ah, il est important de dormir huit heures par nuit. Il faut aussi se coucher avant minuit.

1. J'ai mal à la gorge et j'ai le nez qui coule.
2. J'ai une forte fièvre et j'ai mal partout.
3. J'ai beaucoup de difficulté à maigrir.

4. J'ai une angine.
5. J'ai vraiment mal au cœur.
6. Je n'ai vraiment pas d'énergie.

2. *Le subjonctif des verbes réguliers*

Point out that complex sentences contain two clauses, each with its own inflected verb, connected by the conjunction *que.* Have students identify the main and the subordinate clauses of several types of complex sentences. Make it clear that the verb in the main clause is in the indicative; the verb in the subordinate clause in the subjunctive.

• You have learned to use the indicative mood to state facts and ask questions, the imperative to express commands, and the conditional (with **devoir**, **pouvoir**, and **vouloir**) to make suggestions. Whenever you express obligation, wishes, or emotions in complex sentences in French, you will need to use the *subjunctive* mood, **le subjonctif**. Compare the use of the present indicative and the present subjunctive; note that the subjunctive conveys a subjective, or personal, perspective rather than facts.

Nous **travaillons** plus qu'eux.	*We work harder than they do.*
Il est important que nous **travaillions** plus qu'eux.	*It is important that we work harder than they do.*

● All verbs take the same set of present subjunctive endings. These endings are added to the present stem, which is found by dropping the present indicative ending **-ent** from the **ils/elles** form.

Point out that the endings for singular and third-person plural forms of the present subjunctive are the same as the endings for the present indicative of *-er* verbs and that, for the *nous* and *vous* forms, the present subjunctive endings are the same as those of the imperfect.

LE SUBJONCTIF

INFINITIVE ENDING:	-er	-ir	-ir/-iss-	-re
ILS/ELLES FORM:	**donn**ent	**dorm**ent	**grossiss**ent	**descend**ent
Il faut que…				
je	donn**e**	dorm**e**	grossiss**e**	descend**e**
tu	donn**es**	dorm**es**	grossiss**es**	descend**es**
il elle on	donn**e**	dorm**e**	grossiss**e**	descend**e**
nous	donn**ions**	dorm**ions**	grossiss**ions**	descend**ions**
vous	donn**iez**	dorm**iez**	grossiss**iez**	descend**iez**
ils elles	donn**ent**	dorm**ent**	grossiss**ent**	descend**ent**

Contrast corresponding forms of the present indicative and the present subjunctive of the singular forms so that students clearly hear the final consonant present in the present subjunctive forms: *je dors/il faut que je dorme, tu sors/il vaut mieux que tu sortes.*

● The present subjunctive is used in complex sentences whose main clause contains a verb expressing necessity or obligation. The subordinate clause containing the present subjunctive form is always introduced by the conjunction **que**. Some of these expressions are:

il faut que	*you have to/must*
il ne faut pas que	*you must not*
il est nécessaire que	*it is necessary that*
il est important que	*it is important that*
il est utile que	*it is useful that*
il est urgent que	*it is urgent that*
il vaut/vaudrait mieux que	*it is/would be better (best) that*

Il faut que vous **arrêtiez** de fumer.	*You have to stop smoking.*
Il vaudrait mieux que nous **écoutions** le docteur.	*It would best if we listened to the doctor.*
Il est nécessaire qu'ils **se soignent** !	*They have to take care of themselves!*

When no specific subject is mentioned after these expressions, they are followed by an infinitive. Compare the following examples:

Il vaut mieux **attendre** le médecin.	*It's best to wait for the doctor.*
Il vaut mieux que vous **attendiez** le médecin.	*It's best that you wait for the doctor.*

À vous la parole

👥 10-10 C'est logique. Qu'est-ce qu'on dit dans chaque cas ? Travaillez avec un/e partenaire, et choisissez des verbes dans la liste suivante.

MODÈLE une mère à son enfant

    É1 Il faut que tu manges tes carottes !

    É2 Il ne faut pas que tu joues dans la rue !

arrêter	finir	jouer	manger	parler
payer	rendre	téléphoner	travailler	

1. un professeur à ses élèves
2. une étudiante à sa colocataire
3. un agent de police à un automobiliste
4. une sœur à son petit frère
5. un médecin à un patient
6. une jeune femme à son mari
7. une patronne (*boss*) à son employée

👥 10-11 Pour être en meilleure santé. Avec un/e partenaire, dites à ces gens ce qu'il faut faire.

MODÈLE Mes filles veulent sortir, mais elles ont de la fièvre.

    É1 Mais il ne faut pas qu'elles sortent.

    É2 Tu as raison (*You're right*), il vaut mieux qu'elles ne sortent pas.

1. Nous ne nous soignons pas assez.
2. Pierre ne maigrit pas.
3. Fatmah ne veut pas manger de légumes.
4. Nous ne consultons jamais le médecin.
5. Je ne consulte pas le dentiste.
6. Ma sœur continue à grossir.
7. Mon fils a mal aux yeux, mais il continue à lire tard le soir.

10-12 Obligations. Qu'est-ce que vous avez à faire ? Pour chaque verbe de la liste, précisez vos obligations en discutant avec un/e partenaire. Ensuite, comparez vos responsabilités avec celles de vos camarades de classe.

MODÈLE écrire

   É1 Il faut que j'écrive un essai pour mon cours de composition.

   É2 Et moi, il faut que j'écrive une lettre à ma mère.

1. écrire   **2.** travailler   **3.** rendre   **4.** finir   **5.** téléphoner   **6.** sortir

Lisons

TEXT AUDIO

10-13 Le Malade imaginaire

A. Avant de lire.
The following passage is an excerpt from a play by Molière, *Le Malade imaginaire*, written in 1673. "Molière" is the stage name of Jean-Baptiste Poquelin, born in 1622 to a bourgeois family in Paris. Molière's comedies still have broad appeal. An astute observer of behavior and language, he depicts widely recognizable types such as the miser, the hypocrite, and the arrogant nobleman. Conversely, Molière praises the good sense of the common man, often represented in his plays by the servant who outwits the foolish master. In this scene, the imaginary invalid Argan talks with his servant, Toinette, who has disguised herself as a doctor. Before reading the scene, answer these questions.

1. List a few differences that you might expect when reading a play as opposed to literary prose.
2. Given the title of the play, *Le Malade imaginaire*, and the fact that it is a comedy, what expectations do you have about the plot?

B. En lisant.
Examinez quelques aspects comiques de cet extrait en répondant aux questions suivantes.

1. Quelles sont les maladies préférées du « docteur » ?
2. Complétez le schéma avec les symptômes d'Argan et le diagnostic correspondant de Toinette. Pourquoi est-ce que cet échange est amusant ?

Les symptômes	Le diagnostic
des lassitudes par tous les membres	

3. Comment est-il possible qu'Argan ne reconnaisse pas sa servante Toinette ?

Stratégie

Use your familiarity with a particular literary genre to help you predict the content and structure of a text. What might you expect, for example, in reading a scene from a play as opposed to a prose passage? How can you adjust your own approach to the text accordingly?

Find out whether students are familiar with any of Molière's works; you might display photos or posters of stage productions. Go over the questions with students and help them generate ideas before tackling the text.

Additional activities to develop the four skills are provided by:
• Student Activities Manual
• Text Audio
• *Chez nous* video
• *Chez nous* Companion Website:
  http://www.prenhall.com/cheznous

En lisant, Key: 1) major illnesses like continued fevers, plagues, or cases of pleurisy   2) headaches, the lungs; clouded vision, the lungs; indigestion, the lungs; weakness in limbs, the lungs; colicky stomach pains, the lungs. This is amusing because there's one diagnosis for every problem!   3) Toinette is wearing a disguise, probably a long robe with hat and beard, and she is probably altering her voice; a photo is useful to convey this.

Scène X.— TOINETTE, en médecin ; ARGAN

TOINETTE : Vous ne trouverez pas mauvais, s'il vous plaît, la curiosité que j'ai eue de voir un illustre malade comme vous êtes ; et votre réputation qui s'étend[1] partout, peut excuser la liberté que j'ai prise.

ARGAN : Monsieur, je suis votre serviteur....

TOINETTE : Je suis médecin passager, qui vais de ville en ville, de province en province, de royaume en royaume, pour chercher d'illustres matières à ma capacité, pour trouver des malades dignes[2] de m'occuper.... Je veux des maladies d'importance, de bonnes fièvres continues..., de bonnes pestes[3],... de bonnes pleurésies[4], avec des inflammations de poitrine ; c'est là que je me plais[5], c'est là que je triomphe.... Donnez-moi votre pouls. Allons donc, que l'on batte comme il faut. Ah ! Je vous ferai bien aller comme vous devez. Ouais ! ce pouls-là fait l'impertinent[6] ; je vois bien que vous ne me connaissez pas encore. Qui est votre médecin ?

ARGAN : Monsieur Purgon.

TOINETTE : ... De quoi dit-il que vous êtes malade ?

ARGAN : Il dit que c'est du foie, et d'autres disent que c'est de la rate.

TOINETTE : Ce sont tous des ignorants. C'est du poumon que vous êtes malade.

ARGAN : Du poumon ?

TOINETTE : Oui. Que sentez-vous ?

ARGAN : Je sens de temps en temps des douleurs[7] de tête.

TOINETTE : Justement, le poumon.

ARGAN : Il me semble parfois que j'ai un voile[8] devant les yeux.

TOINETTE : Le poumon.

ARGAN : J'ai quelque fois des maux de cœur.

TOINETTE : Le poumon.

ARGAN : Je sens parfois des lassitudes par tous les membres.

TOINETTE : Le poumon.

ARGAN : Et quelquefois il me prend des douleurs dans le ventre, comme si c'était des coliques.

TOINETTE : Le poumon. Vous avez appétit à ce que vous mangez ?

ARGAN : Oui, Monsieur.

TOINETTE : Le poumon. Vous aimez à boire un peu de vin ?

ARGAN : Oui, Monsieur.

TOINETTE : Le poumon. Il vous prend un petit sommeil après le repas, et vous êtes bien aise de dormir ?

ARGAN : Oui, Monsieur.

TOINETTE : Le poumon, le poumon, vous dis-je.

---

[1]*reaches* [2]*worthy* [3]*plagues* [4]*lung diseases* [5]*j'aime* [6]*is acting impertinent* [7]*des maux* [8]*a curtain*

Extrait de : Molière, *Le Malade imaginaire*, Acte III, Scène X.

C. En regardant de plus près. Maintenant examinez les aspects suivants du texte.

En regardant de plus près, Key:
1) she will take Argan's pulse   2) *oui*   3) c

1. Toinette dit en bon médecin, **Donnez-moi votre pouls**. Qu'est-ce qu'elle va faire ensuite ? (Pensez à un mot en anglais qui ressemble au mot français, **pouls**.)

2. Ensuite, Toinette dit, **Ouais !** Cette prononciation correspond au mot...
   - **a.** où
   - **b.** oui
   - **c.** une

3. Argan ressent « des lassitudes par tous les membres ». Qu'est-ce que ça signifie, « les membres » ?
   - **a.** les yeux
   - **b.** les oreilles
   - **c.** les bras et les jambes

D. Après avoir lu. Discutez des questions suivantes avec vos camarades de classe.

To simplify, let students don costumes and mime the actions as the class listens to the recorded version of the scene. The costumes and actions should be amusing, bordering on slapstick.

1. À votre avis, quels remèdes est-ce que Toinette va suggérer pour le petit problème médical de son maître Argan ?

2. Molière a écrit beaucoup de pièces comiques au dix-septième siècle. Dans cette pièce, il se moque (*makes fun of*) des médecins de son époque. Pourquoi est-ce que nous trouvons aujourd'hui que c'est toujours amusant ?

3. Quelles techniques rendent ce dialogue comique, à votre avis ?

4. Imaginez comment les acteurs peuvent jouer cette scène. Avec un/e partenaire, jouez les rôles de Toinette et d'Argan vous-mêmes !

Argan discute de ses problèmes médicaux avec son frère. Toinette écoute attentivement.

Pour rester en forme

POINTS DE DÉPARTS

Santé physique et morale

POUR GARDER LA FORME

LES CONSEILS DU DOCTEUR LESPÉRANCE

Dans le journal *La Gazette du Matin*, le Dr Lespérance répond aux lettres des lecteurs qui veulent des conseils pour se remettre en bonne forme.

J'ai tendance à grossir et je voudrais commencer un régime pour maigrir. Est-ce que je devrais éliminer toutes les graisses de mon régime ? Est-ce que je pourrais supprimer complètement certains repas ?

Le Dr Lespérance : *Non, il faut surtout éviter de sauter un repas. Il vous faut faire des repas équilibrés, donc, prendre des graisses en quantité raisonnable. Consommez des produits laitiers équilibrés comme le fromage, surtout le fromage blanc et le yaourt. Surtout ne grignotez pas entre les repas ou en regardant la télévision.*

J'ai 58 ans. Depuis quelques années je ne fais plus de sport, et j'ai pris des kilos ; surtout au ventre. Je voudrais recommencer à faire du sport. Qu'est-ce que vous me conseillez ?

Le Dr Lespérance : *Je vous conseille un sport aérobic, le vélo, par exemple. Mais attention, en reprenant brutalement une activité sportive, vous risqueriez des blessures ou un accident cardiaque. Il vous faudrait consulter votre médecin et lui demander de vous faire un bilan médical. Après, commencez à faire de l'exercice progressivement, avec une période d'adaptation de plusieurs semaines. Commencez d'abord par la marche et la natation. La natation est excellente pour perdre du ventre. Essayez d'éliminer le tabac et buvez de l'alcool avec modération.*

J'ai souvent mal au dos mais j'aime les sports : le judo, le football et le tennis. On me dit d'abandonner ces sports. Qu'est-ce que vous en pensez ?

Le Dr Lespérance : *Je ne suis pas du tout d'accord avec ce conseil. Bien sûr, il faudrait éviter les sports de compétition ou les exercices physiques comme la gymnastique et la musculation. Vous pourriez essayer le vélo ou les randonnées et, en hiver, le ski. Ce sont d'excellents sports aerobic individuels qu'on pratique en plein air. Ils seront bons pour votre forme et votre moral.*

POUR RESTER EN PLEINE FORME

Il faut consulter le médecin de temps en temps
    manger des repas équilibrés
    faire du sport ou de l'exercice
    dormir huit heures par nuit
    se détendre de temps en temps

Il ne faut pas fumer
    boire trop d'alcool
    sauter des repas
    grignoter entre les repas
    suivre des régimes trop stricts

Vie et culture

Le stress

Regardez la séquence vidéo **On se stresse et on se détend**. Quelles sont les sources de stress mentionnées ? Quelles sont les méthodes employées par les gens que vous observez pour réduire le stress ? Est-ce que vous pensez que le stress se manifeste en Amérique du Nord de la même façon qu'en France ? Pourquoi ?

De plus en plus, les Français ressentent un sentiment de mal-être qui résulte sans doute du stress de la vie moderne : les conditions de travail,

As students watch the video clip, have them make two lists: one for the sources of stress presented and one for the ways in which people try to counteract these stresses. Ask them if what they see and hear is comparable to the situation in their own living environment. The health statistics cited were taken from Mermet, *Francoscopie 2003*, pp. 83-86.

l'anxiété face aux problèmes de la vie dans les grandes villes — la pollution, le bruit[1], le manque[2] de sécurité, la peur[3] du chômage[4], etc. Aujourd'hui 50 pour cent des Français disent qu'ils sont toujours fatigués et 20 pour cent ont du mal à dormir. En trente ans, le nombre de dépressions a été multiplié par six. Tous ces troubles se traduisent par une surconsommation de médicaments. Les Français sont toujours les plus gros consommateurs de médicaments en Europe.

[1]*noise*   [2]*lack*   [3]*fear*   [4]*unemployment*

À vous la parole

10-14 Des bons conseils. Avec un/e partenaire, donnez des conseils à chaque personne.

10-14 As an alternative, make this a whole-class brainstorming activity.

MODÈLE   J'ai pris trois kilos !

        É1 Il faut suivre un régime !

        É2 Il vaut mieux manger moins de graisses et de sucre !

        É1 Il est important de faire plus de sport !

1. Je voudrais faire du sport : j'aime la montagne.
2. Je voudrais faire un sport individuel.
3. Je voudrais faire de l'exercice, mais je n'aime pas le sport.
4. Je voudrais recommencer à faire du sport.
5. J'aimerais perdre quelques kilos.
6. Je voudrais perdre du ventre.
7. J'ai besoin de me détendre un peu, mais je n'aime pas les activités sportives ; je n'aime pas les activités en plein air non plus.

10-15 En pleine forme. Est-ce que vos camarades de classe sont en pleine forme ? Est-ce qu'ils ont des bonnes habitudes ? Renseignez-vous auprès de vos voisins.

MODÈLE   se sentir toujours bien

> É1   Tu te sens toujours bien ?
>
> É2   Non, j'ai souvent mal à la tête. Et toi ?
>
> É3   Moi, je suis en pleine forme ; je me sens toujours bien.

1. se sentir toujours bien
2. se détendre pendant le week-end
3. faire du sport
4. manger des repas équilibrés
5. dormir huit heures par nuit
6. boire beaucoup d'alcool
7. boire beaucoup de café ou de thé
8. être stressé/e
9. fumer

10-16 Pour combattre le stress.
Avec un/e partenaire, dressez une liste de choses qui sont sources de stress pour vous. Ensuite, établissez une autre liste de solutions pour combattre le stress. Comparez vos listes avec celles de vos camarades de classe. Qu'est-ce qui cause le stress chez les étudiants en général ? Quelles sont les solutions les plus efficaces pour combattre le stress, selon vous ?

Qu'est-ce qu'elles font pour combattre le stress ?

MODÈLE   les causes du stress

> É1   Pour moi, ce sont les examens qui causent du stress.
>
> É2   Et pour moi, c'est la famille et…

les solutions

> É1   Moi, pour réduire le stress, je fais du sport.
>
> É2   Et moi, j'écoute de la musique et…

With the introduction of many English words ending in -ing into the language (le jogging, le parking, le shopping, un smoking) some speakers also use the /ŋ/ of English smoking. Point out to students that even though these words may look like straight borrowings, the French word often has a different meaning from the corresponding English word: in some cases, this is due to the process of abbreviation, as for le parking (from parking lot); in other cases, French has created a new word based on an English model, as for le footing, (jogging), based on the model of le jogging from jogging. Point out the exceptional pronunciation of le shampooing /ɛ/; this earlier borrowing occurred before the introduction of /ŋ/ into the French sound system.

Sons et lettres

TEXT AUDIO

La consonne *gn*

The consonant /ɲ/, as in **campagne** or **soigne**, is pronounced with the tip of the tongue placed against the lower front teeth with the tongue body touching the hard palate. It is as if you were pronouncing /n/ and /j/ simultaneously. It is always spelled **gn**.

À vous la parole

10-17 Répétition. Répétez chaque mot.

le si**gne**	il ga**gne**	elle soi**gne**	ga**gne**r	l'Espa**gne**
les Espa**gn**oles	la monta**gne**	soi**gne**z	la bai**gn**oire	l'Allema**gne**

10-18 Phrases. Maintenant, répétez les phrases suivantes.

1. Il y a beaucoup de vignes magnifiques en Champagne et en Bourgogne.
2. Digne, Cagnes et Cannes sont en Provence.
3. Les Montaigne vont en Allemagne et en Espagne.
4. Ta nièce se soigne à Cannes ou à Cagnes ?
5. Diagnostic : votre fille a mal au poignet.

Begin practice with a discrimination drill: have students raise their hand when they hear you pronounce a word containing /ɲ/, for example: *montagne, monter, camper, campagne, soigne, Espagne, santé.*

Point out the exceptional pronunciation of *diagnostic* [djagnɔstik] which does not follow the general rule of *gn* = palatal nasal.

FORMES ET FONCTIONS

1. Le subjonctif des verbes irréguliers

- A small number of verbs have a special stem for the subjunctive.

faire	**fass-**	Il vaut mieux qu'elle **fass**e un régime.
pouvoir	**puiss-**	Il faut qu'il **puiss**e dormir.
savoir	**sach-**	Il est important qu'elles **sach**ent le nom du médecin.
pleuvoir	**pleuv-**	Il vaut mieux qu'il ne **pleuv**e pas le week-end.

- **Avoir** and **être** show many irregularities:

	avoir	*être*
j'	**aie**	**sois**
tu	**ai**es	**sois**
il / elle / on	**ait**	**soit**
nous	**ay**ons	**soy**ons
vous	**ay**ez	**soy**ez
ils / elles	**ai**ent	**soi**ent

DeVito (1997) reports that 78% of occurring subjunctives consist of regular *-er* verbs and the irregular verbs *avoir, être, faire,* and *pouvoir.* The percentage rises to 94% if the verbs *attendre, dire, finir, prendre,* and *venir* are added to the list. The more frequent irregulars are presented here; additional irregular verbs and *-er* verbs showing vowel changes are treated in L. 3.

Point out to students that a frequent use of *avoir* and *être* in the subjunctive is in commands: *Soyez raisonnable ! Aie de la patience !*

Begin practice by having students identify the irregular verb used in the examples you provide: *Il est important que je puisse consulter le pharmacien (pouvoir). Il est essentiel que tu sois raisonnable (être). Il faut que tu fasses un régime (faire). Il est nécessaire que tu saches son adresse (savoir). Il vaut mieux que tu aies des médicaments (avoir)*, etc. Continue with transformation drills, indicative to subjunctive: *Il fait beau. —Il faut qu'il fasse beau ; Il peut voir le médecin ; Il est raisonnable ; Il fait un régime ; Il peut se soigner*, etc. For Ex. 10-19, encourage students to provide suggestions using the verbs: *avoir, être, faire, pouvoir*, and *savoir*.

10-20 This contrasts the infinitival construction with the subjunctive. To vary, have students offer advice to a friend: *Il faut que tu aies du temps libre.*

10-19 Prendre des bonnes habitudes. Expliquez comment Thomas doit changer certaines de ses habitudes pour améliorer sa santé.

MODÈLE   Il n'est pas raisonnable.
   ➤ Il faut qu'il soit raisonnable.

1. Il ne fait pas de repas équilibrés.
2. Il ne dort pas assez.
3. Il ne fait pas de sport.
4. Il ne sait pas quel est son taux (*level*) de cholestérol.
5. Il n'a pas de vacances.
6. Il ne sait pas se détendre.
7. Il n'est pas très énergique.
8. Il ne fait pas attention à sa santé.

10-20 Pour combattre le stress. Imaginez que vous conseillez une personne qui voudrait combattre le stress. Regardez le modèle et donnez vos conseils d'une manière plus personnelle.

MODÈLE   Il faut avoir du temps libre.
   ➤ Il faut que vous ayez du temps libre.

1. Il faut avoir des loisirs.
2. Il faut être plus relax.
3. Il est utile de faire du yoga.
4. Il est important de savoir comment se détendre.
5. Il vaut mieux être patient/e.
6. Il est important d'avoir des amis.
7. Il vaut mieux faire du sport aussi.
8. Il faut pouvoir dormir sept ou huit heures par nuit.

10-21 Divide the class into groups of three or four students and give each one a scenario. Groups could then present their advice to the class, who could guess what their problem was.

10-21 Solutions. Comment est-ce qu'on pourrait résoudre les problèmes suivants ? Discutez des solutions possibles avec des camarades.

MODÈLE   É1 Je ne réussis pas dans mes études ; j'ai toujours de très mauvaises notes.
   É2 Il faut que tu fasses plus d'efforts, et que tu en parles avec tes profs.
   É3 Oui, et il est important que tu sois toujours en classe et que tu lises les textes.

1. Je ne réussis pas dans mes études ; j'ai toujours de très mauvaises notes.
2. J'ai de très mauvaises relations avec mes parents.
3. Je ne me sens pas bien ; je suis toujours fatigué/e.
4. Je suis très stressé/e par tous mes problèmes.
5. J'ai besoin de maigrir, mais j'ai beaucoup de difficulté à le faire.

2. Le subjonctif avec les expressions de volonté

- When the main verb of a sentence expresses a desire or wish, the verb of the following clause is usually in the subjunctive.

> Elles veulent qu'il **parte**. *They want him to leave.*
>
> Je préfère qu'il **attende** jusqu'à demain. *I prefer that he wait until tomorrow.*

Here are some verbs used to express desires or wishes that are followed by the subjunctive:

aimer	*to like*	exiger	*to require, demand*
aimer mieux, préférer	*to prefer*	souhaiter	*to hope, wish*
demander	*to request*	vouloir	*to want*
désirer	*to desire, want*		

Point out that the equivalent English sentence may be in the subjunctive (*that he wait*), but is most often an infinitive construction (*to leave*).

Espérer, which will be presented in Ch. 12, L. 1, is an exception and is followed by the future tense: *J'espère qu'il viendra demain.*

- When the subject is the same for both parts of the sentence, use an infinitive construction instead of the subjunctive. Compare the following examples:

> Il voudrait **rester** ici. *He'd like to stay here.*
>
> Il voudrait **que ses enfants restent** ici. *He'd like his children to stay here.*
>
> Elle souhaite **avoir** des enfants. *She hopes to have children.*
>
> Elle souhaite **que vous ayez** des enfants. *She hopes you will have children.*

À vous la parole

10-22 Devant le petit écran. M. Lemoël a eu une journée très stressante. Il est rentré tard et il voudrait se détendre. Dites ce qu'il va probablement répondre à sa femme.

10-22 This practices the use of the infinitive when the subject is the same in both clauses.

MODÈLE Chéri, qu'est-ce que tu veux qu'on fasse ? On pourrait sortir ce soir ou rester à la maison.
> ➤ Je voudrais rester à la maison.
OU ➤ Je voudrais qu'on sorte.

1. Chéri, qu'est-ce que tu veux qu'on fasse ? On pourrait inviter des amis ou rester seuls à la maison.
2. Et qu'est-ce qu'on fait pour le dîner ? On le prépare ensemble ou on commande une pizza ?
3. Et après, tu veux lire ton magazine ou tu veux regarder la télé avec moi ?
4. Chéri, il y a un match de foot et un film à la télé. Qu'est-ce que tu préfères regarder ?
5. On attend le film français de 22 heures ou on regarde le film américain qui passe maintenant ?
6. Tu as soif ? Tu veux prendre un thé ou un jus de fruit ?

10-23 Il faut suivre les conseils du médecin.

Des amis viennent demander à Pierre s'il peut faire les choses suivantes. Mais son médecin lui a donné des conseils très précis. Jouez le rôle de Pierre.

MODÈLES Tu vas faire du sport ?

➤ Oui, le médecin veut que je fasse du sport.

Tu vas sauter des repas ?

➤ Non, le médecin ne veut pas que je saute des repas.

1. Tu vas fumer une cigarette ?
2. Tu vas faire attention à ta santé ?
3. Tu vas sortir en boîte (*club*) ?
4. Tu vas faire un régime ?
5. Tu vas manger du bifteck ?
6. Tu vas faire la fête toute la nuit ?
7. Tu vas être raisonnable ?

10-24 Harmonie ou conflit.

Parlez-en avec un/e partenaire : pour chaque catégorie, dites si vous et vos parents partagez les mêmes souhaits, désirs, etc.

MODÈLE votre future profession : votre souhait

É1 Je souhaite être actrice. Mes parents souhaitent que je sois médecin.

É2 Mes parents souhaitent que je sois avocat, et moi aussi, je souhaite être avocat.

1. vos études : votre souhait
2. vos projets pour l'été prochain : votre préférence
3. votre prochaine voiture : votre désir
4. votre futur/e mari ou femme : votre préférence
5. vos futurs enfants : votre souhait
6. votre lieu de résidence éventuel : votre désir

TEXT AUDIO

10-25 Au cabinet du Dr Gabriel

A. Avant d'écouter. Vous allez entendre deux conversations entre le Dr Marie Gabriel et ses patients. Avant d'écouter, pensez à la dernière fois que vous êtes allé/e chez le médecin. Quelles questions est-ce que le médecin vous a posées ? Quels étaient vos symptômes ? Quels conseils ou médicaments est-ce que le médecin vous a donnés ? Dressez une liste de deux ou trois questions que le Dr Gabriel pourrait poser à ses patients.

B. En écoutant. Trouvez la réponse à chaque question en écoutant les consultations.

1. D'abord le médecin parle à Christine, qui ne se sent pas bien.
   a. Quels symptômes est-ce qu'elle mentionne ?
   b. Quelle maladie est-ce qu'elle pense avoir ?
   c. Quels conseils est-ce que le médecin lui donne ?
2. Ensuite, le Dr Gabriel parle avec M. Albertini.
   a. Depuis combien de temps est-ce que M. Albertini essaie d'arrêter de fumer ?
   b. Quel est son problème ?
   c. Quelle/s suggestion/s est-ce que le docteur lui donne ?

C. Après avoir écouté. Discutez de ces questions avec vos camarades de classe.

1. Est-ce que vous avez déjà souffert de la mononucléose ou est-ce que vous connaissez quelqu'un qui l'a eue ? Combien de temps est-ce qu'il a fallu pour retrouver la forme ?
2. Est-ce que vous fumez ou est-ce que vous avez des amis ou des membres de votre famille qui fument ? Est-ce qu'ils ont envie d'arrêter ? Est-ce qu'ils ont déjà essayé d'arrêter ? Est-ce que vous êtes d'accord avec les conseils du Dr Gabriel ? Pourquoi ?

espace **sans** tabac

Leçon 3 — *Sauvons la Terre et la forêt*

« La Smart » est une voiture très écolo ! Est-ce que vous aimeriez en avoir une ?

POINTS DE DÉPART

Pour protéger l'environnement

TEXT AUDIO

Trois amis — Céline, Sébastien et Léa — sont assis à la terrasse d'un café. Ils prennent un verre et parlent des problèmes écologiques dans leur ville.

CÉLINE : L'air devient vraiment pollué ici ! Regarde, on dirait du brouillard mais c'est de la pollution ! Avec tous ces gaz toxiques, on ne pourra bientôt plus respirer !

SÉBASTIEN : C'est vrai. Si on ne change pas notre manière de vivre, nous allons contaminer toute la Terre.

CÉLINE : Et si on continue à polluer les fleuves et les rivières sans essayer de les nettoyer, il n'y aura plus d'eau potable.

LÉA : C'est pas grave. On pourra toujours boire de l'eau minérale.

CÉLINE : Toi, tu n'es jamais sérieuse !

LÉA : Si, mais, moi, je suis optimiste. Avec les nouvelles technologies, on trouvera bien des solutions à tous ces problèmes.

SÉBASTIEN : Oui, on quittera la Terre pour aller habiter sur la Lune !

LES POLLUTIONS	SONT CAUSÉES PAR...
la pollution atmosphérique	• les gaz d'échappement (qui viennent des voitures)
	• les gaz toxiques
la pollution de l'eau et du sol	• les déchets industriels (les produits chimiques)
	• les déchets domestiques (les ordures)
la pollution sonore	• le bruit des moteurs
	• les stéréos mises à fond

Vie et culture

La pollution sonore

« Ce qui[1] est bien ne fait pas de bruit et ce qui fait du bruit ne fait pas du bien. » C'est le slogan des victimes de la pollution sonore. Les Français se plaignent[2] plus du bruit que de toute autre nuisance. Quelles sont les causes principales du bruit ? — les voitures et les motos, les avions, les sirènes des ambulances et des voitures de police et les alarmes des appartements et des voitures. D'après la loi française de 1992, l'intensité du bruit ne doit pas dépasser 85 décibels dans les usines et les autres lieux de travail, mais on sait que dans les concerts de rock, par exemple, le son atteint[3] souvent plus de 100 décibels !

On fait du canoë près du Pont du Gard (à coté de Nîmes).

Et vous ?

1. De quelle forme de pollution est-ce que les Américains se plaignent le plus ? Pourquoi, à votre avis ?
2. Quand est-ce que vous vous plaignez du bruit ? Quelles sont les conséquences d'être exposé à trop de bruit ?

L'écotourisme

Les Français sont de plus en plus nombreux à faire du tourisme vert. Dans les régions rurales en France les agriculteurs ouvrent des gîtes pour accueillir[4] un petit nombre de touristes. Les habitants des villes peuvent y découvrir les charmes de la vie rurale, la cuisine régionale, les coutumes et l'histoire locale. Des organisations locales organisent aussi des visites guidées et des promenades dans des sites historiques et touristiques.

À l'étranger, les Français ont la possibilité de faire le même type d'écotourisme. À Madagascar et à la Guadeloupe par exemple, l'office de tourisme propose toutes sortes de randonnées pour découvrir la faune et la flore[5] locales. La devise[6] du tourisme vert, c'est « Ne prenez que des photos ; ne laissez que des traces de pas[7]. »

Un autre aspect du tourisme vert, ce sont les chantiers[8] pour les jeunes à partir de 14 ans. Il y a des chantiers archéologiques, d'autres où les jeunes replantent des arbres ou nettoient des forêts pour les protéger des incendies[9], d'autres enfin où ils nettoient des rivières pour les sauvegarder. En somme, avec l'écotourisme, les gens des villes reprennent contact avec la nature et apprennent l'importance de préserver notre Terre.

Pourquoi, à votre avis, est-ce que le tourisme vert est très développé en France ? Où est-ce qu'on trouve des possibilités d'écotourisme en Amérique du Nord ?

[1] that which [2] complain [3] reaches [4] welcome [5] animal/plant species [6] motto [7] footprints [8] work camps [9] fires

10-26 This exercise uses realia both to present new vocabulary and to work with it in context. Before beginning, go over the poster with the students and have them identify cognates and near-cognates: *économiser, non biodégradable, huile usée, recyclage, recycler, sac en plastique, sauver, transport en commun.* Illustrate other vocabulary with pictures, drawings or realia (bring in examples of *un panier, un emballage en plastique, une boîte de conserve, une bouteille en verre, une poubelle*). Have students figure out the meaning of words like *éteindre, gaspiller, laisser les lumières allumées, trier,* and *verser* through context. Have students describe additional sources of pollution. As you work with the text, ask students to evaluate the suggestions: are they all relevant in North America, as in France? Do any seem inappropriate?

À vous la parole

👥 **10-26 Contre chaque nuisance, il y a des solutions !** Pour chaque problème indiqué, trouvez une solution sur le poster suivant en travaillant avec un/e partenaire. Attention ! Quelquefois il y a plus d'une solution.

MODÈLE   É1 Il y a beaucoup de destructions d'arbres et de forêts.

             É2 Utilisez du papier recyclé !

1. Il y a beaucoup de destructions d'arbres et de forêts.
2. Il y a trop de sacs en plastique et d'emballages non biodégradables.
3. Nous gaspillons l'électricité.
4. Nous utilisons trop d'eau. Bientôt il n'y aura plus d'eau potable.
5. L'air devient vraiment pollué. Avec tous ces gaz toxiques, on ne pourra bientôt plus respirer.
6. Il y a trop de déchets dans la décharge municipale (*garbage dump*).
7. L'eau devient très polluée à cause des huiles usées.

POUR LA PROTECTION DE L'ENVIRONNEMENT

- Utilisez du papier recyclé ! Ce sont des arbres et des forêts sauvés de la destruction.
- Faites vos courses avec des paniers ; les commerçants n'auront plus besoin de sacs en plastique ou d'emballages non biodégradables.
- Ne gaspillez pas l'eau ! Prenez une douche au lieu d'un bain ; c'est 20 litres d'eau et de l'énergie économisées.
- Triez les déchets domestiques ; mettez les ordures, les boîtes de conserve usées, le papier, les bouteilles en verre dans de différentes poubelles ; cela permet le recyclage.
- Ne versez pas les huiles de cuisine ou de moteur usées dans l'évier ; elles empêchent l'oxygénation de l'eau. Mettez-les dans un récipient et apportez-les au centre de recyclage de votre quartier.
- Utilisez les transports en commun.
- Ne laissez pas les lumières allumées ; éteignez-les en sortant de la salle.

10-27 As a follow-up, see which group generated the most answers for each item.

👥 **10-27 Changeons le comportement des gens.** Avec un/e partenaire, suggérez des alternatives moins polluantes. Voici quelques verbes utiles : **économiser, gaspiller, recycler, trier, utiliser**.

MODÈLE   Je prends ma voiture pour aller en ville.

             É1 Mais non ! Il faut prendre les transports en commun !

             É2 Ou bien, il faut y aller à vélo.

1. Je prends ma moto pour aller à la bibliothèque.
2. Je vais prendre un bon bain très chaud.
3. J'ai besoin d'un nouveau cahier et de papier pour mes cours.
4. Jetons l'huile usée du moteur dans l'évier.
5. Mettons ces vieilles boîtes, ces bouteilles et ces magazines dans la poubelle.
6. Donnons des sacs en plastique à nos clients.

👥 **10-28 Les soucis écologiques chez vous.** Quelles sont les problèmes liés à l'environnement chez vous et qu'est-ce qu'on fait pour les réduire ? Parlez-en avec un/e partenaire.

MODÈLE   la pollution sonore

> É1 Dans la résidence où j'habite tous mes voisins mettent leur chaîne stéréo trop fort. Alors, je ne peux pas travailler dans ma chambre. Je dois aller à la bibliothèque. Pendant la nuit, il y a des motos qui passent dans la rue ; ça me réveille.

> É2 Dans ma résidence, on n'a pas le droit de mettre la musique trop fort après dix heures du soir.

1. la pollution sonore
2. la pollution atmosphérique
3. la pollution des lacs et des rivières
4. le gaspillage d'énergie
5. les déchets non biodégradables

As an additional or review exercise, have students work with a partner to determine the advantages of each of the following measures: *faire du compost ; remplacer les autobus par des tramways ; interdire les voitures individuelles en ville ; faire du jardinage ; ouvrir des gîtes ruraux ; se promener dans la forêt en vélo ; planter des arbres ; nettoyer les forêts ; nettoyer les rivières*

MODÈLE   faire du compost

> É1 On peut utiliser certains déchets domestiques dans le jardin.

> É2 Oui, comme ça, on peut améliorer la qualité de la terre.

👥👥 **10-29 Posters et slogans.** Imaginez que vous préparez un poster ou un slogan pour une manifestation écologique. Les posters et les slogans prennent souvent la forme d'une phrase impérative ou alors ils contiennent les expressions **À bas**… (*Down with*…), **Plus de**… (*No more*…), **Vive**… Organisez-vous en groupes de trois ou quatre et trouvez des slogans intéressants pour protester contre les activités polluantes et pour encourager les mesures écologiques.

MODÈLES   l'utilisation de voitures pour aller en cour
> ➤ Plus de voitures dans le centre du campus !
> ➤ À bas les voitures sur le campus !
> ➤ En ville, à vélo !

l'utilisation des transports en commun
> ➤ Vive le tramway et le métro !
> ➤ Oui au covoiturage !
> ➤ En bus, plus on est de fous, plus on vit !

1. la construction de centrales nucléaires
2. la réduction du bruit dans les résidences universitaires
3. le développement du tourisme vert
4. le gaspillage de papier
5. les randonnées en vélo
6. le remplacement des autobus par des tramways
7. les vacances d'été dans un chantier de jeunesse

10-29 Demonstrate the rhythmic chanting typical of slogans:

À bas les grosses voitures !
• • • • • • •

where each bullet represents a syllable and the double bullet the final stressed syllable. Treat this exercise as a contest. The group that comes up with the best slogan for each item might be given some prize or recognition. You might ask students to create posters and post them on campus or on a Web site. Go over the models and check to see that students understand that *le covoiturage* means "carpooling." The last example is word play based on the proverb, *Plus on est de fous, plus on rit !* (in English, "The more, the merrier.")

FORMES ET FONCTIONS

1. Le subjonctif avec les expressions d'émotion

Many of these expressions were introduced in Ch. 7, L3. You may wish to review them with an activity from that lesson before presenting their use in the subjunctive. Before treating this use of the subjunctive, have students summarize forms and uses of the subjunctive. Provide examples as in the text and have students analyse. Let students create additional examples using the expressions in the list.

- Use the subjunctive in the second clause when the main clause expresses any emotion: anger, fear, joy, sadness, etc.

Je regrette que vous **partiez**.	*I'm sorry (that) you're leaving.*
Elle est contente que tu **sois** là.	*She's happy (that) you're here.*

- Here are some verbs and expressions that convey emotion and are followed by the subjunctive:

être content/e, enchanté/e, heureux/ heureuse, ravi/e	*to be happy, pleased*
être déçu/e	*to be disappointed*
être étonné/e, surpris/e	*to be surprised*
Il est/C'est étonnant que…	*It is surprising that…*
regretter, être désolé/e, triste	*to be sorry, sad*
Il est/C'est malheureux, dommage que…	*It's unfortunate, too bad that…*
être fâché/e, furieux/furieuse	*to be angry, furious*
avoir peur	*to be afraid*
être inquiet/inquiète	*to be worried*

- When the subject of the main clause and the subordinate clause is the same, **de** plus an infinitive is used after these expressions.

Je regrette **de partir**.	*I'm sorry to leave.*
Elle a peur **de ne pas réussir**.	*She's afraid of not succeeding.*
Nous sommes surpris **de vous voir**.	*We're surprised to see you.*

À vous la parole

10-30 Display the list of expressions of emotion requiring the subjunctive to provide students with ideas for the exercise. To expand, have students suggest solutions, using expressions of obligation or necessity: *Il ne faut pas que les gens jettent des papiers partout ; il faut mettre sur le campus ou en ville des boîtes pour recycler*, etc.

10-30 La pollution chez nous. La pollution existe sur votre campus ; quelle est votre réaction face à ce problème et aux solutions envisageables ?

MODÈLE   Les gens jettent des papiers partout.
➤ Je suis surprise que les gens jettent des papiers partout.

1. Dans les résidences, on ne fait pas de recyclage.
2. Mes amis prennent la voiture pour aller en ville.
3. Certaines personnes ne prennent pas leurs responsabilités.
4. Tu choisis le vélo et pas la voiture.
5. Le président de l'université peut faire un règlement.
6. Les messages publicitaires contre la pollution ne sont pas utiles.
7. Les gens sont d'accord pour modifier leurs actions.

10-31 Votre réaction. Exprimez votre réaction face à ces situations.

MODÈLES Vous trouvez des déchets par terre.
➤ Je suis furieux de trouver des déchets par terre.

Vos voisins ne font pas de recyclage.
➤ Je suis déçue qu'ils ne fassent pas de recyclage.

1. Vous faites du recyclage.
2. Il y a beaucoup de bruit dans votre quartier.
3. En ville, vous pouvez prendre le bus.
4. Vos parents font de l'écotourisme.
5. Vos amis sont toujours en voiture.
6. Votre ami/e gaspille de l'eau.
8. Votre voisin/e est très écologiste.

10-31 To expand, elicit multiple reactions to each statement. For the model sentences, have students identify which was spoken by a man and which by a woman.

10-32 Le plus grand problème. Quel est, pour vous, le plus grand problème en ce qui concerne l'environnement dans les domaines suivants ? Comparez votre opinion avec celle de vos camarades de classe.

10-32 Follow up by having groups report back to the class as a whole.

MODÈLE la pollution en général

É1 Je pense que le plus gros problème, ce sont les déchets. On jette beaucoup de choses. Il faut que tout le monde (*everyone*) fasse du recyclage.

É2 Je suis d'accord. Mais j'ai peur que les gens ne soient pas d'accord pour changer leurs habitudes. Le gouvernement doit aussi travailler à nettoyer l'eau et le sol.

1. la pollution en général
2. la pollution de l'eau
3. la pollution sonore
4. la préservation des ressources naturelles
5. la surpopulation

Trop de déchets ? Il vaudrait mieux recycler.

2. D'autres verbes irréguliers au subjonctif

● A few verbs have two stems in the subjunctive: one for the singular forms and the third-person plural, the other for the **nous** and **vous** forms. The second stem comes from the **nous** form of the present indicative. The regular subjunctive endings are used in all cases.

	present indicative	present subjunctive
boire	ils **boiv**ent	que je **boiv**e
	nous **buv**ons	que nous **buv**ions
devoir	ils **doiv**ent	que je **doiv**e
	nous **dev**ons	que nous **dev**ions
prendre	ils **prenn**ent	que je **prenn**e
	nous **pren**ons	que nous **pren**ions
venir	ils **vienn**ent	que je **vienn**e
	nous **ven**ons	que nous **ven**ions

Il faut que tu **boives** de l'eau.   *You must drink some water.*
Il faut que vous **buviez** moins de café.   *You must drink less coffee.*

● **Aller** and **vouloir** also have two stems for the subjunctive, one of which is irregular.

		present subjunctive
aller	**aill-**	que **j'aill**e
	nous **all**ons	que nous **all**ions
vouloir	**veuill-**	que je **veuill**e
	nous **voul**ons	que nous **voul**ions

Il faut que tu **ailles** chez le médecin.   *You must go to the doctor.*
Elle est contente que vous **alliez** bien.   *She's happy you are doing well.*

● Verbs in **-er** that have two stems in the present indicative show the same pattern in the subjunctive. As is the case for all **-er** verbs, only the **nous** and **vous** forms of the subjunctive are different from the indicative forms.

	present indicative	present subjunctive
préférer	nous **préfér**ons	que nous **préfér**ions
	ils **préfèr**ent	qu'ils **préfèr**ent
acheter	nous **achet**ons	que nous **achet**ions
	ils **achèt**ent	qu'ils **achèt**ent
appeler	nous **appel**ons	que nous **appel**ions
	ils **appell**ent	qu'ils **appell**ent
nettoyer	nous **nettoy**ons	que nous **nettoy**ions
	ils **nettoi**ent	qu'ils **nettoi**ent

Il faut que nous **achetions** du papier recyclé.	*We have to buy recycled paper.*
Il vaut mieux qu'ils **appellent** le médecin.	*It's best they call the doctor.*
Il faudrait que vous **nettoyiez** cette rivière polluée.	*You should clean up this polluted river.*

À vous la parole

10-33 C'est important ! Pour réduire la pollution, qu'est-ce qu'il est important de faire ?

MODÈLE les jeunes / nettoyer les rivières
➤ Il est essentiel que les jeunes nettoient les rivières.

1. les familles / prendre des douches et pas de bains
2. la ville / pouvoir établir un programme de recyclage
3. nous / aller apporter les déchets à la décharge municipale
4. vous / acheter des produits recyclables
5. les étudiants / prendre les transports en commun
6. nous / réduire le nombre de déchets
7. tu / devenir plus écologique
8. nous / aller régulièrement au centre de recyclage

10-34 Nos préférences. Avec un/e partenaire, décidez si vos préférences sont les mêmes que les préférences de votre professeur. Comparez vos réponses avec les réponses de vos camarades de classe.

MODÈLE essayer de toujours parler en français en classe

É1 Je n'aime pas essayer de toujours parler en français.
É2 Moi ça va. Et le prof préfère que nous essayions de toujours parler en français.

1. faire les devoirs
2. acheter un bon dictionnaire
3. prendre des notes
4. aller au labo de langues
5. venir en classe tous les jours
6. essayer de faire des crêpes
7. aller voir des films français

10-33 This exercise practices the subjunctive in the context of expressions of necessity. You might provide a list of expressions for students to choose from as they complete the exercise. Students have seen the verb *réduire* in L. 2 of this chapter. You may present the full conjugation or just help students with the form *que nous réduisions*. The full conjugation can be found in Appendix 4.

10-34 This allows students to practice the use of the infinitive as well as the subjunctive in appropriate contexts with expressions of preference. Provide a list of expressions for students to choose from.

10-35 Que d'émotions ! Avec un/e partenaire, réagissez à ce que dit votre professeur. Comparez votre réaction avec la réaction de vos camarades de classe.

MODÈLES   Il n'y a pas de devoirs ce soir.

  É1   Je suis surpris qu'il n'y ait pas de devoirs.

  É2   Je suis contente qu'il n'y ait pas de devoirs.

  Vous aurez un examen vendredi.

  É1   Je suis triste d'avoir un examen vendredi.

  É2   Moi aussi !

1. Il n'y aura pas cours demain.
2. Tout le monde ira au restaurant ensemble ce week-end.
3. Je vous achèterai un souvenir en France cet été.
4. Vous n'aurez pas d'examen final.
5. Les résultats du dernier examen sont excellents.
6. Vous faites beaucoup de progrès en français.

10-36 Le mot caché

Est-ce que vous avez déjà participé à un débat ? Il faut donner des arguments pour ou contre une affirmation. Dans cet exercice, vous allez participer à un débat, tout en essayant de cacher un mot inattendu (*unexpected*).

A. Avant de jouer. Le professeur divise la classe en deux équipes et il/elle propose une assertion.

MODÈLE   Il faut interdire (*forbid*) l'utilisation des voitures sur le campus.

Le professeur indique à chaque équipe si elle doit être d'accord ou en désaccord avec l'assertion. Ensuite, chaque équipe tire au sort (*draws at random*) un des mots inattendus préparés par le professeur.

MODÈLE   Vous tirez le mot « poisson ».

Avec votre équipe, préparez vos arguments en essayant de placer votre mot une ou deux fois dans le débat dans un contexte plausible.

B. En jouant. Après cinq minutes de préparation, les membres de chaque équipe donnent leurs arguments.

MODÈLE   ➤ …Par exemple, moi, j'habite en ville, et tous les jours je respire les gaz d'échappement des voitures. Il y a une mauvaise odeur, comme du vieux poisson !…

C. Après avoir joué. Après avoir entendu tous les arguments, chaque équipe essaie de découvrir le mot caché de l'équipe adverse. L'équipe qui découvre le mot caché reçoit un point ; l'équipe qui réussit à cacher son mot reçoit un point ; l'équipe qui ne réussit pas à placer son mot pendant le débat perd un point.

Venez chez nous !
L'écologie

Décrivez ce poster. Qui est-ce qui l'a préparé ? Pourquoi ?

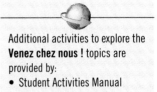

Additional activities to explore the **Venez chez nous !** topics are provided by:
- Student Activities Manual
- *Chez nous* video
- *Chez nous* Companion Website: **http://www.prenhall.com/cheznous**

Use the video montage (*L'écologie*) to provide an overview for this lesson; have students describe the forms of pollution and the remedies they see.

Dans le monde entier des gens font des efforts pour protéger l'environnement, pour empêcher[1] la destruction des forêts, des rivières et des prairies, et pour conserver nos ressources naturelles. En France, des initiatives sont prises pour réduire la pollution et éliminer le gaspillage des ressources énergétiques. La ville de Strasbourg, par exemple, a introduit des tramways qui marchent à l'électricité, donc qui ne polluent pas. En Afrique, au Sénégal et en Côte d'Ivoire, il y a de nombreux parcs naturels pour la protection des animaux sauvages. Ces parcs servent aussi de centres de recherche pour l'histoire naturelle et la conservation de la nature. Voici donc des exemples, dans le monde francophone, de questionnements et de réponses face aux problèmes écologiques actuels.

[1]*to prevent*

Observons

10-37 L'environnement et nous

A. Avant de regarder.
Vous allez entendre deux personnes parler de l'environnement.

1. Fabienne travaille dans une grande ville, mais elle habite à la campagne. Pourquoi, à votre avis, est-ce qu'elle a pris cette décision ?
2. Jean-Claude est de Madagascar. Il trouve que c'est dommage que les habitants de cette île détruisent le paysage. Pourquoi est-ce qu'ils font cela, à votre avis ?
3. Maintenant écoutez et regardez pour trouver les réponses.

B. En regardant.
Entourez les réponses correctes. Il peut y avoir une ou plusieurs réponses possibles pour chaque question.

1. Fabienne dit…
   a. qu'elle a trouvé la bonne solution contre la pollution.
   b. qu'elle n'a pas de leçon à donner.
   c. que c'est le gouvernement qui devrait s'occuper du problème.
2. Elle habite à la campagne parce qu'elle…
   a. adore la nature.
   b. déteste la ville.
   c. a des animaux.
3. Elle trouve qu'en ville, il y a trop de…
   a. circulation.
   b. gens.
   c. bruit.
4. Le seul inconvénient d'habiter la campagne, c'est…
   a. le manque d'activités.
   b. la distance.
   c. la solitude.
5. Jean-Claude est né à Madagascar. Il dit que c'est…
   a. une grande ville.
   b. une île magnifique.
   c. une région montagneuse.
6. Selon lui, il faut surtout protéger…
   a. l'eau des rivières.
   b. la terre.
   c. les plantes et les animaux.
7. Les habitants détruisent leur environnement pour avoir…
   a. de l'argent.
   b. des maisons.
   c. des usines.

C. Après avoir regardé. Est-ce que les problèmes mentionnés par Fabienne et Jean-Claude sont les mêmes problèmes écologiques que chez vous ? Dans quelles autres régions du monde est-ce que ces problèmes existent ? Quelles sont les solutions possibles à ces problèmes ?

Parlons

10-38 Les problèmes écologiques et leurs solutions

A. Avant de parler. Dans la Leçon 3 et dans ce *Venez chez nous !*, il y a quelques photos de problèmes écologiques et/ou de leurs solutions possibles. En groupes de deux ou trois, choisissez une de ces photos ou trouvez une autre photo qui illustre un problème écologique ou une solution dans le monde francophone.

B. En parlant. Identifiez et décrivez le/s problème/s représenté/s sur votre image. Ensuite proposez quelques solutions possibles. Enfin, considérez d'une façon critique vos solutions : ont-elles une portée (*reach*) universelle ou sont-elles plutôt limitées à une certaine région ou à un certain pays ? Expliquez pourquoi.

MODÈLE ➤ Cette photo montre une réserve naturelle à Madagascar. Ces réserves offrent une solution au problème de la déforestation. À Madagascar, on perd une partie des forêts tous les ans. Cette destruction cause des problèmes d'érosion mais aussi la disparition de plusieurs types d'animaux et de fleurs. Le gouvernement et des organismes internationaux ont créé un certain nombre de réserves naturelles qui sont protégées. Ces réserves sont importantes pour sauvegarder les plantes et les animaux locaux. Nous pensons que c'est une bonne solution qui peut s'appliquer à d'autres pays. Mais, dans certains pays où il n'y a pas assez de terre pour toute la population, cette solution peut être difficile.

Students can go to the *Chez nous* Companion Website for this chapter for links to Francophone sites dealing with ecological problems and solutions. You might also suggest that students consult magazines or publications such as *National Geographic, Sierra Magazine, Natural History, Smithsonian* in English or *Géo, Terre Sauvage, Science et Nature, Mer & Océan,* or the French version of *National Geographic* for pictures.

Avant de parler. You may wish to develop this **Parlons** activity into a more formal oral presentation project, either in small groups or as individuals. This topic lends itself easily to research on the Web (consult the *Chez nous* Companion Website for this chapter for specific suggestions and links) and would be ideal as the subject of an *exposé oral.*

Une réserve naturelle à Madagascar

La déforestation à Madagascar

C. Après avoir parlé. Maintenant, partagez votre image et vos solutions avec vos camarades de classe. Quel groupe a le problème le plus difficile à résoudre ? Quel groupe a trouvé la meilleure solution à son problème ?

Lisons

10-39 L'arbre nourricier

Stratégie

Use your familiarity with the folktale genre to understand the style and purpose of folktales from another culture. For example, do you know any tales in your own language in which animals are the main characters? How are the animals presented and what role do they have?

Avant de lire. Lead students to draw the parallel between the purpose and literary style of this African folktale and the fables of Aesop (*Esope* in French) and La Fontaine. Ask them to provide examples: *The Tortoise and the Hare, The Fox and the Crow,* etc. Students may also be familiar with the *Uncle Remus Stories,* which have animal characters, including a rabbit who regularly outwits a fox and a bear. See whether students can re-tell the story of the goose that laid the golden eggs, since its moral is similar to that of the tale recounted here.

A. Avant de lire. The animals in a folktale are often personified and made to speak to humans or among themselves. Reminiscent of the story of the goose that laid golden eggs, *L'arbre nourricier* features two widely known characters from African and Caribbean folklore, the hare and the hyena. The hyena is slow-witted and gluttonous; the hare embodies cleverness. The hyena's gluttony makes him vulnerable to the hare's trickery, which leads to his demise. Do these characters remind you of characters in folktales that you have heard or read? Why might talking animals be featured in a folktale?

This adaptation of a folktale collected from the Soninke people in Senegal conveys the need to protect trees in the arid Sahel region, between the Sahara Desert and the equatorial forests of Africa. It opens when the storyteller says **Xay** (pronounced *Hi*), the traditional formula with which Soninke folktales begin. The audience responds in kind and the storyteller can proceed.

B. En lisant. Cherchez les réponses aux questions suivantes.

1. Dans la première partie du conte :
   a. Oncle Hyène et Oncle Lièvre vont chercher de la nourriture pour leurs familles : qu'est-ce qu'ils trouvent ?
   b. De quelles parties de l'arbre est-ce qu'Oncle Lièvre goûte ?
   c. Quelle est l'importance du mot magique « dunwari » ?

2. Dans la deuxième partie du conte :
   a. Qu'est-ce qu'Oncle Hyène doit dire quand il arrive sous l'arbre ?
   b. Qu'est-ce qu'Oncle Hyène décide de faire avec l'arbre ?

3. Dans la troisième partie du conte :
   a. Pourquoi est-ce qu'Oncle Hyène appelle sa famille et puis la moitié du village ?
   b. Comment est-ce qu'Oncle Hyène meurt ?
   c. Qu'est-ce qui se passe avec l'arbre ?

C. En regardant de plus près. Maintenant, examinez les aspects suivants du texte.

1. En étudiant le contexte, expliquez le sens des expressions suivantes :
   a. il a mangé à sa faim
   b. mettre un coussinet sur sa tête
   c. cet arbre merveilleux

2. Vous connaissez sans doute le premier mot dans chaque paire de mots apparentés ci-dessous. Quel est le sens du deuxième mot dans chaque cas ?
   a. porter / un porteur
   b. appeler / un appel
   c. parler / la parole

D. Après avoir lu. Discutez des questions suivantes avec vos camarades de classe.

1. Un conte, c'est surtout un texte oral ; il faut l'écouter. Quelles caractéristiques d'un texte oral est-ce que vous remarquez dans ce conte ?
2. Quel est le rôle des animaux dans ce conte ? Pourquoi, à votre avis, est-ce que le narrateur a choisi ces animaux comme personnages principaux ?
3. Quelle est la morale du conte ?
4. Comparez le message écologique donné dans ce conte avec celui de la liste de recommandations que vous trouvez à la page 408. Quel message est le plus efficace ? Pourquoi, à votre avis ?

❖ ❈ L'arbre nourricier ❖

Dites-moi « xay » !

–Xay !

Il y avait la famine au village. Oncle Hyène et Oncle Lièvre ont décidé d'aller chercher de la nourriture pour leurs familles. Oncle Hyène est parti mais n'a rien trouvé. Oncle Lièvre s'est mis aussi en route[1]. Après avoir marché longtemps il a rencontré un arbre. Il s'est arrêté sous son ombre[2] et a dit :

–Arbre, que ton ombre est fraîche !

–Tu as goûté mon ombre mais tu n'as pas goûté mes feuilles[3].

Alors Lièvre a pris plusieurs feuilles et les a goûtées.

–Arbre, que tes feuilles sont bonnes !

–Tu as goûté mes feuilles mais tu n'as pas encore goûté mon écorce[4].

Lièvre a pris un bout d'écorce et l'a mis dans sa bouche. Il a dit :

–Arbre, que ton écorce est bonne !

–Tu as goûté mon écorce mais tu n'as pas goûté ce qu'il y a dans mon ventre.

–Comment faire pour en avoir ?

–Si tu dis « dunwari », je m'ouvrirai.

Lièvre a dit « dunwari » et l'arbre s'est ouvert. Il y est entré et a mangé à sa faim. Quand il avait assez mangé, il a pris de la nourriture pour sa famille.

De retour au village, Oncle Lièvre a dit à Oncle Hyène qu'il avait rencontré un arbre, qu'il avait mangé à sa faim et qu'il avait rapporté de la nourriture à sa famille. Oncle Hyène lui a dit :

–Montre-moi où tu as trouvé cet arbre merveilleux. J'irai à mon tour demain matin. Quand j'aurai mangé à ma faim, je rapporterai de la nourriture à ma famille.

–D'accord, lui a répondu Lièvre, demain matin je te montrerai cet arbre.

Il se sont mis en route le lendemain[5], et Lièvre a indiqué le chemin à Hyène :

–Tu marcheras, marcheras jusqu'à cet arbre là-bas. Tu t'arrêteras dessous et tu diras « que ton ombre est bonne ! »

Hyène est allé jusqu'à l'arbre, et il lui a dit :

–Arbre, que ton ombre est bonne !

–Tu as goûté mon ombre mais tu n'as pas goûté mes feuilles.

Hyène a pris plusieurs feuilles et les a goûtées.

–Arbre, que tes feuilles sont bonnes !

–Tu as goûté mes feuilles mais tu n'as pas goûté mon écorce.

Hyène a pris un bout d'écorce et l'a mis dans sa bouche. Il a dit :

–Que ton écorce est bonne !

–Tu as goûté mon écorce mais tu n'as pas goûté ce qu'il y a dans mon ventre.

–Comment faire pour en avoir ?

–Si tu dis « dunwari », je m'ouvrirai.

Hyène a dit « dunwari » et l'arbre s'est ouvert. Il y est entré et a mangé à sa faim. Quand il avait assez mangé, il a pris de la nourriture pour sa famille.

Oncle Hyène s'est dit alors : « Ah ! Si j'avais quelqu'un pour m'aider je rapporterais cet arbre au village. » L'arbre lui a répondu :

–Tu n'as pas besoin de porteurs, je peux t'aider moi-même. Mets ton coussinet[6] sur la tête.

Hyène a mis son coussinet sur la tête, puis a porté l'arbre sur sa tête, et l'a emporté au village. Arrivé là, il a appelé :

–Venez vite ! J'ai rapporté quelque chose de la forêt ! Venez m'aider à déposer ce lourd fardeau[7] !

Sa femme et ses enfants sont venus mais n'ont pas réussi à déposer l'arbre.

–Eh bien ! Appelez la moitié du village !

La moitié du village est venue mais sans résultat.

–Alors, appelez tout le village !

Le village entier est venu mais sans succès.

Écrasé sous le poids[8] de l'arbre, Hyène est mort. Alors l'arbre est parti et est retourné à sa place dans la forêt. Je remets le conte là où je l'ai trouvé.

---

[1]*est parti* [2]*shade* [3]*leaves* [3]*bark* [5]*le jour suivant* [6]*small cushion* [7]*burden* [8]*weight*

Écrivons

10-40 Une brochure

A. Avant d'écrire. Le gouvernement québécois publie souvent des brochures qui contiennent des conseils pour préserver l'environnement. Imaginez que vous faites partie d'une équipe qui doit préparer une de ces brochures. Voici quelques sujets possibles :

1. la lutte (*fight*) contre le bruit
2. l'utilisation des transports en commun
3. le tri et le recyclage des déchets
4. la conservation des ressources énergétiques
5. la conservation des forêts

D'abord, choisissez votre sujet puis notez deux ou trois aspects du problème et deux ou trois solutions possibles.

B. En écrivant. Maintenant, rédigez un texte qui décrit le problème et les solutions. N'oubliez pas que dans les brochures de ce type, on utilise souvent des statistiques, des impératifs et des slogans. N'oubliez pas non plus de trouver un titre pour votre brochure.

En écrivant. Students can work on this writing project with a partner or in small groups. Encourage them to think up creative solutions to the problems they identify. In **Avant d'écrire**, help students figure out the meaning of *le tri* based on the verb *trier*.

MODÈLE

Réduire pour un Québec plus propre !

Savez-vous que les Québécois produisent assez de déchets pour remplir 5 millions de sacs poubelles chaque jour ?

Il faut réduire nos déchets !

Pensez à recycler le papier, le plastique, le verre, le carton et les boîtes de conserve !

Recyclons ensemble pour une meilleure qualité de vie au Québec !

C. Après avoir écrit. Améliorez votre brochure en rajoutant des images. Imprimez-la et distribuez-la à vos camarades de classe. Qui a la brochure qui explique le mieux le/s problème/s ? Qui propose les solutions les plus innovatrices ? les mieux adaptées au problème ?

Vocabulaire

Leçon 1

le corps humain	*the human body*
la bouche	*mouth*
le bras	*arm*
les cheveux (m.)	*hair*
la cheville	*ankle*
le cœur	*heart*
le cou	*neck*
le coude	*elbow*
les doigts (m.)	*fingers*
les doigts de pied (m.)	*toes*
le dos	*back*
l'épaule (f.)	*shoulder*
l'estomac (m.)	*stomach*
le foie	*liver*
le genou	*knee*
la gorge	*throat*
la jambe	*leg*
les lèvres (f.)	*lips*
le nez	*nose*
l'œil (m.) (les yeux)	*eye (eyes)*
l'oreille (f.)	*ear*
le pied	*foot*
le poignet	*wrist*
la poitrine	*chest*
les poumons (m.)	*lungs*
la taille	*waist*
la tête	*head*
le visage	*face*
le ventre	*belly, abdomen*

des maladies (f.) et des symptômes (m.)	*sicknesses and symptoms*
une angine	*strep throat, tonsillitis*
avoir du mal à (respirer)	*to have difficulty (breathing)*
avoir mal à (la tête)	*to hurt (to have a headache)*
avoir mal partout	*to hurt everywhere*

une bronchite	*bronchitis*
un coup de soleil	*sunburn*
de la fièvre	*fever*
la grippe	*flu*
une infection	*infection*
un mal (des maux)	*pain/s, ache/s*
le mal au cœur	*nausea*
un/une malade	*sick person*
le nez qui coule	*runny nose*
une pneumonie	*pneumonia*
un rhume	*cold*
se sentir (fatigué/e)	*to feel (tired)*
tousser	*to cough*
une toux	*cough*

pour se soigner	*to take care of oneself*
un antibiotique	*antibiotic*
une aspirine	*aspirin*
demander des conseils (m.)	*ask for advice*
un diagnostic	*diagnosis*
des gouttes (f.) pour le nez/les yeux	*nose/eye drops*
longtemps	*a long time*
un médicament	*medicine, drug*
une ordonnance	*prescription*
une pommade	*ointment, salve*
un remède	*remedy*
un sirop	*cough syrup*
une tisane (à la menthe)	*(mint) herbal tea*
tout de suite	*right away, immediately*

expressions de nécessité	*expressions of necessity*
Il est important que	*It is important that*
Il est nécessaire que	*It is necessary that*
Il est urgent que	*It is urgent that*
Il est utile que	*It is useful that*
Il faut que/Il ne faut pas que	*You must/must not*
Il vaut/vaudrait mieux que	*It is/would be better (best) that*

Leçon 2

pour rester en pleine forme	*to stay in good shape*
recommencer à (faire de l'exercice)	*to start (exercising) again*
consulter le médecin	*to see a doctor*
(faire/suivre) un régime	*(to be on a) diet*
un repas équilibré	*well-balanced meal*
réduire le stress	*reduce stress*

choses à éviter pour rester en forme	*things to avoid to stay in shape*
l'alcool (m.)	*alcohol*
fumer	*to smoke*
la graisse	*fat, grease*
grignoter	*to snack*
sauter (un repas)	*to skip (a meal)*

quelques verbes de volonté qui exigent le subjonctif	*some verbs of volition that require the subjunctive*
aimer (mieux)	*to like (prefer)*
désirer	*to desire, to want*
exiger	*to require, to demand*
souhaiter	*to hope, to wish*

autres expressions utiles	*other useful expressions*
être d'accord	*to agree*
de temps en temps	*from time to time*

Leçon 3

bon pour l'environnement	*good for the environment*
économiser	*to save, economize*
essayer	*to try*
éteindre (les lumières)	*to turn off (the lights)*
nettoyer	*to clean*
un panier	*a basket*
préserver	*to preserve*
protéger	*to protect*
le recyclage	*recycling*
recycler	*to recycle*
respirer	*to breathe*
sauver, sauvegarder	*to protect*
les transports en commun (m.)	*public transportation*
trier	*to sort*
utiliser	*to use*

mauvais pour l'environnement	*bad for the environment*
un bruit	*sound, noise*
contaminer	*to contaminate*
la décharge municipale	*garbage dump, landfill*
les déchets (m.) domestiques/industriels	*household/industrial waste, refuse*
gaspiller	*to waste*
un gaz	*gas*
les gaz d'échappement (m.)	*exhaust fumes*
l'huile usée (f.)	*waste (used) oil*
laisser les lumières allumées	*to leave the lights on*
mettre la musique à fond	*to turn the music up loud*
non biodégradable	*nonbiodegradable*
une nuisance	*harmful thing*
les ordures (f.)	*trash, waste*
polluer	*to pollute*
la pollution (atmosphérique/sonore)	*(air/noise) pollution*
un produit chimique	*chemical product*
un sac en plastique	*plastic sack/bag*
toxique	*toxic*
verser	*to pour*

des choses menacées par la pollution	*things threatened by pollution*
l'air (m.)	*air*
l'eau potable (f.)	*drinking water*
l'environnement (m.)	*environment*
un fleuve	*river*
le sol	*ground, earth*
la terre (la Terre)	*earth (the Earth)*

autres mots utiles	*other useful words*
un emballage	*packaging*
la lune (la Lune)	*moon (the Moon)*
un moteur	*engine*
une poubelle	*trash can*

quelques expressions d'émotion qui exigent le subjonctif	*some expressions of emotion that require the subjunctive*
avoir peur que	*to be afraid*
être déçu/e que	*to be disappointed*
Il est/C'est dommage que	*It's too bad, a shame*
être étonné/e que	*to be surprised*
Il est/C'est étonnant que	*It's surprising*

Une réalisatrice tourne un film à Paris

Chapitre 11

Quoi de neuf ?
cinéma et médias

In this chapter:

- Expressing opinions about the media
- Expressing cause and effect
- Ordering events
- Describing and narrating events in the past
- Discovering the media in the French speaking world

Venez chez nous !
Le cinéma

Le grand et le petit écran

As you begin this lesson, ask students what they know about Francophone TV, film, the press, and literature. Suggest that students visit the library to see what periodicals are available in French and the library or video store for names of directors and stars of Francophone films. Have them check the *Chez nous* Companion Website for links to French periodicals and news media online.

Additional practice activities for each **Points de départ** section are provided by:
- Student Activities Manual
- *Chez nous* Companion Website: **http://www.prenhall.com/cheznous**

POINTS DE DÉPART

Qu'est-ce qu'il y a à la télé ?

TEXT AUDIO

You may wish to teach this vocabulary over two days; if so, then present television vocabulary and complete Ex. 11-1 through 11-3 on day 1; continue with film vocabulary and the remaining exercises on day 2.

Mercredi 14 avril

TF1	FRANCE 2	FRANCE 3	CANAL+
20.55 **Combien ça coûte ?** *Show business is business.* Magazine. Présentation : Jean-Pierre Pernaut. Invités : Jean-Marie Bigard. 140 mn.	**21.00** **Faites le 15** Téléfilm d'Etienne Dhaene (France, 2003). 105 mn. Inédit. Avec Jean-Yves Berteloot, Pascale Rocard, Nadia Barentin.	**20.55** **Des racines et des ailes** *Spécial Lille, capitale européenne 2004.* Magazine. Présentation : Patrick de Carolis. 115 mn.	**21.00** **Laisse tes mains sur mes hanches** Comédie romantique de Chantal Lauby (France, 2003). 105 mn. Inédit. Avec Chantal Lauby, Rossy de Palma.
23.15 **Fear factor** *Jeu.* Présentation : Denis Brogniart. 60 mn. Comme chaque semaine, des candidats vont devoir affronter leurs peurs les plus intimes.	**22.45** **Ça se discute** *Le chagrin d'amour peut-il rendre fou ?* Magazine. Présentation : Jean-Luc Delarue. 125 mn.	**23.25** **Régionales** Magazine. 55 mn. Une sélection de documentaires et de magazines de votre Région.	**22.45** **Tai-Chi Master** Film d'action de Yuen Woo-ping (Hongkong, 1993). 90 mn. Inédit. Avec Jet Li, Michelle Yeoh, Chin Siu-hou.

CHRISTELLE : Qu'est-ce qu'il y a à la télé ce soir ?

THOMAS : Attends, je vais regarder dans Télérama. … Bon, sur TF1, il y a un magazine et un jeu. Sur France 2, il y a un téléfilm français qui n'a pas l'air très intéressant. Sur France 3, il y a un magazine sur Lille et des documentaires régionaux.

CHRISTELLE : Bof ! Il y a beaucoup de magazines. Ça ne m'intéresse pas trop. Il n'y a pas de films ce soir ?

THOMAS : Si, sur Canal+ il y a une comédie romantique à 9 heures et ensuite un film d'action chinois à 10 h 45. Qu'est-ce que tu préfères ?

CHRISTELLE : Tu rigoles ? Tu sais bien que je n'aime pas les films d'action.

THOMAS : D'accord. Allons pour la comédie romantique. Tu peux allumer la télé ?

CHRISTELLE : Mais, c'est toi qui as la télécommande !

THOMAS : Ah bon ? Ah, la voilà !

CHRISTELLE : Arrête de zapper ! Mets Canal+ !

THOMAS : Allez, c'est bon.

Treat the TV listings first as a reading. As an overview, have students describe TV listings and programming in general: typical format, types of programs shown at particular times of the day, etc. Note: the use of the 24-hour clock; that programs do not always begin on the hour or half-hour; general programming tendencies. Selected listings are provided. You can easily obtain current TV listings on the Web; consult the *Chez nous* Companion Website for helpful links. You may want to display a current listing as you present this vocabulary.

Show the dialogue as students listen. Have students match information in the dialogue to information in the listings provided. Use the dialogue as a model, for the role-play activity in Ex. 11-2. Point out the expressions *Bof !* and *Tu rigoles ?* and help students figure out their meaning. A less familiar way of saying *Tu rigoles ?* would be *Tu plaisantes ?*

DES GENRES D'ÉMISSIONS

un dessin animé

un divertissement

un documentaire

une émission sportive

un feuilleton

un film

un jeu télévisé

le journal télévisé (le JT), les informations (les infos)

un magazine

une émission de musique

une émission de télé-achat

une émission de télé-réalité

un reportage

une série

Gérard Depardieu et Christian Clavier jouent dans le film comique *Astérix et Obélix : Mission Cléopâtre*, basé sur la célèbre bande dessinée.

Merzak Allouache est le metteur en scène du *Journal de Yasmine*, tourné en Algérie.

DES GENRES DE FILMS

un film d'aventures	raconte les aventures d'un personnage courageux
un film de science-fiction	raconte des événements futuristes et imaginaires
un film d'espionnage	est plein de suspense, avec des agents secrets qui partent en mission
un film policier	raconte un crime et l'enquête (*investigation*) pour retrouver le criminel
un film historique	raconte des événements historiques ou la vie d'un personnage historique
un film d'horreur	doit faire peur aux gens ; il y a des monstres, des fantômes, des vampires, ou bien des psychopathes
une comédie musicale	raconte une histoire dansée et chantée
une comédie	raconte les mésaventures amusantes des gens
un documentaire	est un reportage sur la société, l'histoire, la nature, la science, la religion, etc.
un drame psychologique	examine les relations entre les gens
un western	est un film d'aventures avec des cow-boys dans le Far West
un dessin animé	est fait surtout pour les enfants ; il met en vedette, par exemple, des animaux qui parlent

Present the various types of films using the photos and descriptions. Have students help you elaborate on descriptions provided. Begin practice with a recognition exercise: *Donnez-moi un exemple d'un film d'aventures.* Begin student production with a simple repetition drill: *« James Bond » est-ce que c'est un film d'aventures ou un film d'espionnage ?* Also, for each film listed in the *magazine télé*, have students identify: type of film, country of origin, director, principal actors, and length of film.

Find out whether students know famous actors, actresses, and directors: *Nicole Kidman ? — C'est une actrice australienne. Elle est très belle et elle joue souvent dans des drames psychologiques.* Other possibilities: Halle Berry, Audrey Tautou, Akira Kurasowa, Isabelle Adjani, Sean Penn, Jean-Luc Godard, Gwyneth Paltrow. Have students suggest others.

À vous la parole

👥 11-1 Quel genre d'émission ? Imaginez que vous lisez un magazine télé. Selon ces descriptions partielles déterminez avec un/e partenaire le genre de chaque émission.

MODÈLE   dernier épisode

   É1   C'est peut-être une série.

   É2   S'il y a des épisodes, c'est probablement un feuilleton.

1. avec notre invitée, la chanteuse…
2. l'astrologie face à la science
3. le journal de la semaine
4. à gagner cette semaine : un voyage à Tahiti
5. série américaine
6. matchs finals de la Ligue des champions
7. des recettes : ris de veau, fumet aux vieux cèpes, galettes de pommes de terre
8. l'île aux enfants

11-1 To vary the exercise or use as review, see *Francoscopie 2003*; its section called *Rétroscopie*, pp. 20–22, gives names of popular television programs over the past 20 years. This exercise requires students to use contextual clues to identify program types. **Key:** 1) une émission de musique 2) un documentaire 3) le journal télévisé 4) un jeu télévisé 5) une série 6) une émission sportive 7) une émission de cuisine 8) une émission pour enfants/un dessin animé. Additionally, have students tell what kind of program they associate with specific people: *Jacques Cousteau ? — un documentaire* ; *Diane Sawyer ?* etc. Ask students to generate examples on their own.

TF1

14.45 Ma vie de star. Téléfilm de Steven Robman. (2/2). (2000). **16.20** Le protecteur. La peur du scandale. ♥**17.10** 🔲 Dawson. La belle et le bête. **18.00** Le bigdil. **19.00** La Ferme Célébrités. ■ **20.00** Journal.

Le choix de Téléobs

♥♥ **20.35 Football**
Ligue des champions. Finale. Monaco (Fra)/FC Porto (Por). A l'Arena Aufschalke de Gelsenkirchen (Allemagne) EN DIRECT.

22h55

♥♥ **Columbo**
Téléfilm policier américain.
Avec Peter Falk (Columbo). 1 h 30. 🔲

FRANCE 2

♥**14.50 Tennis.** Tournoi du Grand Chelem. Internationaux de France. 3e jour. A Roland-Garros, à Paris. EN DIRECT. ♥**18.50 On a tout essayé.** ■ **20.00** 🔲 Journal. **20.50** Tirage du Loto.

21h00

♥ **L'instit : Aurélie**
Téléfilm dramatique franco-belge de Roger Kahane. (2001). 1 h 30.

22h40

♥ **Ça se discute**
Magazine de sociétés. Présenté par Jean-Luc Delarue. Hyperactivité, anxiété, autisme : comment grandit-on avec un trouble du comportement ?

FRANCE 3

15.00 🔲 Questions au gouvernement. **16.05** TO3. ♥**17.35** 🔲 **C'est pas sorcier.** Les mammouths : la parole est à la défense. **18.05** Questions pour un champion. **18.40** 19/20. **20.00** Météo. **20.05** Le fabuleux destin de... ♥**20.35 Le journal de Roland-Garros.**

Le choix de Téléobs

♥♥ **20.55 Des racines et des ailes**
Magazine de reportages.
Présenté par Patrick de Carolis.
Depuis le musée gallo-romain de Périgueux. 🔲

■ **23.10 Soir 3**

23h35

♥♥ **Légende**
Documentaire. Réalisé par Emmanuelle Daude. Bourvil par Philippe Labro. 🔲

CANAL+

14.00 L'affaire Van Aken. Téléfilm. (2003). **15.30** Le journal des sorties. **15.40** Disparition. ♥**17.10** Boomtown. 🔲 **18.40** Merci pour l'info. 🔲 **19.55** Les Guignols. ♥ **20.05** 20h10 pétantes.

21h00

♥ **Toutes les filles sont folles**
Comédie sentimentale française de Pascale Pouzadoux. (2003). 1 h 25.

22h20

♥ **Le cœur des hommes**
Comédie de mœurs française de Marc Esposito. (2003). 1 h. 🔲

France 5/Arte

15.45 Planète insolite. ♥**16.40 Les petits bouddhas et les tigres. 17.35** Si vous étiez... **17.50** C dans l'air. ♥**19.00** La course ou la vie. **19.45** Arte info. **20.00** Le journal de la culture. ♥**20.15** Eurovision backstage.

20h40

♥♥ **Les mercredis de l'Histoire - Citizen Berlusconi.** Documentaire. Réalisé par Susan Gray en 2003.

21.40 ARTE reportage. ♥**22.30 Le dessous des cartes.** Zimbabwe (1) : Une histoire coloniale. Mines d'or, royaumes zoulous, colonisation anglaise, ségrégation raciale. « Le Dessous des cartes » analyse la formation du Zimbabwe, Etat enclavé.

Le choix de TéléObs

♥♥♥ **22.45** Amours chiennes (Amores perros) Drame mexicain d'Alejandro González Iñárritu. (2000). VO. 2 h 33.

M6

17.25 Le meilleur du ridicule. **17.55** Les Colocataires. ♥**18.50 Charmed.** Le diable au corps. ■ **19.50** Six'/Météo. **20.05** Une nounou d'enfer. L'amour est aveugle. **20.40** Les Colocataires/Décrochages info.

20h50

Les Colocataires
Présenté par Fred Courtadon. Télérealité.

23h15

Le gigolo
Téléfilm de suspense allemand de Michael Rowitz. (1998). 1 h 31.

11-2 As a variation, give students a specific time and have them choose a program from the listings. Consult the *Chez nous* Companion Website for links to sites with program guides.

👥 11-2 Les émissions d'aujourd'hui. Qu'est-ce qu'on peut regarder aujourd'hui? Avec un/e partenaire, jouez les rôles de deux amis. Consultez le magazine télé et discutez de vos choix.

MODÈLE É1 J'ai envie de regarder un match.
É2 Si on regardait le match de foot sur TF1 ?

1. J'aime bien les films étrangers.
2. J'adore les séries américaines.
3. Il n'y a pas de magazine sur France 2 ce soir ?
4. Pourquoi pas un film ce soir ?
5. J'ai envie de regarder quelque chose de différent.
6. J'ai mal à la tête, alors rien de sérieux pour moi ce soir !
7. Il y a un documentaire ce soir ?
8. J'aime bien les émissions de télé-réalité.

Vie et culture

La télévision en France

Regardez les extraits du magazine télé. À quelle heure est-ce que les principales chaînes passent le journal télévisé, et ensuite les émissions les plus populaires ? Quels genres d'émissions est-ce qu'on peut voir à la télé pendant la soirée ? Est-ce que ce sont les mêmes genres d'émissions que les émissions que vous voyez chez vous ?

Les Français regardent en moyenne trois heures et 19 minutes de télévision par jour. Les chaînes que les Français regardent le plus sont les chaînes publiques comme France 2 et France 3, mais beaucoup de Français regardent aussi des chaînes privées comme TF1 et Canal+ ou bien ils s'abonnent[1] aux chaînes diffusées par câble ou par satellite.

L'influence de la télé américaine est très répandue[2] en France. On y trouve un grand nombre de films et séries américains doublés[3] en français. Est-ce que vous pouvez en trouver des exemples dans l'extrait du programme que vous avez ici ? Avec le câble et le satellite, les Français peuvent regarder des émissions internationales diffusées en version originale quelquefois avec des sous-titres — des chaînes en anglais comme CNN aussi bien que des chaînes allemandes, espagnoles et italiennes, par exemple.

[1] *subscribe* [2] *widespread* [3] *dubbed*

Discuss the availability (or unavailability) of international programming and have students find out the possibilities for watching French-speaking TV in your area. Is TV5 available by satellite, for example? Compare typical times when TV news, films, game shows, etc., are aired. The information provided here is based on *Francoscopie 2003*, pp. 417–427. Have students compare TV programming and viewing habits in France and North America. A 2003 study by Eurodata TV Worldwide shows that the global average daily viewing time is now three hours and 39 minutes. The study was based on statistics from 72 countries or regions. North Americans watched on average four hours and 21 minutes per day. Students can access French TV magazines through links on the *Chez nous* Companion Website. As a follow-up activity, have students examine TV listings in detail to see what types of American films and programs are popular in France. What image does this convey of the United States?

11-3 Émissions préférées. Quelles sont vos émissions préférées ? Classez ces émissions par ordre de préférence et parlez-en avec un/e camarade de classe. Ensuite, comparez vos listes avec les listes des autres membres de la classe.

11-3 Summarize results for the class as a whole.

MODÈLE moi

1. émissions sportives
2. films
3. séries

mon partenaire

1. émissions de musique
2. informations
3. films

É1   J'aime surtout les émissions sportives — le basket-ball et le football américain. Mais je regarde aussi des films et quelquefois des séries. Et toi ?

É2   J'aime les émissions de musique, surtout les concerts, mais il y a très peu de musique classique sur les chaînes privées. Je regarde les infos tous les soirs, et quelquefois un film le week-end.

11-4 Caractéristiques des films. Pour être jugé bon, un film doit posséder certaines caractéristiques. Quelles sont ces caractéristiques ?

MODÈLE un drame psychologique

    É1 Un bon drame psychologique doit être triste.

    É2 Dans un bon drame psychologique, on trouve un problème social.

1. un film de science-fiction
2. un western
3. un film d'espionnage
4. un film d'horreur
5. un film d'aventures
6. une comédie musicale
7. une comédie
8. un film historique

11-5 Ça dépend des jours. Quelquefois on préfère un type de films, d'autres fois on préfère un autre type. Quel type de films est-ce que vous et votre partenaire préférez voir dans les situations suivantes ?

MODÈLE quand vous êtes triste ?

    É1 Moi, je préfère les drames psychologiques.

    É2 Moi non ; j'aime plutôt les comédies.

1. quand vous êtes heureux/heureuse ?
2. quand vous avez un problème que vous voulez oublier ?
3. quand vous venez de passer un examen ?
4. quand vous êtes avec votre petit frère ou un autre petit garçon ?
5. quand vous êtes avec votre petite sœur ou une autre petite fille ?
6. quand vous êtes avec vos parents ?
7. quand vous êtes avec votre copain/copine ?

Sons et lettres

TEXT AUDIO

Le *e* instable et les groupes de consonnes

In Chapter 8 you learned that, generally speaking, an unstable **e** is dropped within words when it occurs after only one pronounced consonant (**un feuilleton**) but that it is retained when it occurs after two pronounced consonants (**le gouvernement**). This general rule also applies across words in phrases. Compare:

dans ce film	avec ce film
Essaie de zapper !	Arrête de zapper !
On peut regarder.	Elles peuvent regarder.
C'est le journal télévisé.	On préfère le journal télévisé.
beaucoup de chaînes	quelques chaînes

Within words, unstable **e** is retained when it occurs after a group of consonants ending in /r/ or /l/. Compare:

nous montͬerons	nous montrerons
facilͤment	simplement

Unstable **e** occurs in many one-syllable grammatical words: the pronouns **je**, **te**, **me**, **se**, **le**; the negative particle **ne**; the determiners **le**, **ce**; the preposition **de**; the conjunction **que**. In these words, the unstable **e** is usually retained when it occurs at the beginning of a phrase. Compare:

je peux	Mais jͤ peux sortir.
Ne fais rien.	On nͤ fait rien.
ce documentaire	C'est cͤ documentaire.
Me téléphonͤras-tu ?	On mͤ téléphonͤra.

This principle applies to combinations of two one-syllable words. Note that when two unstable **e**'s occur in succession, one of them is generally deleted.

Je nͤ sais pas.
De nͤ pas lͤ faire est triste.
Ne lͤ regarde pas.
On nͤ **le** veut pas.
Essaie de lͤ faire.

We present a simpler version of what is referred to as *la loi des trois consonnes* that takes into account only the number of consonants preceding unstable *e*. Even the *loi des trois consonnes* is an approximation: an important factor is the nature of the consonants involved. For example, compare: *nous montrerons*, where unstable *e* is always retained, to *nous regardͤrons*, where it may be deleted even though this results in three consonants coming together. To train students to be aware of the "two-consonant" principle, it would be useful to review the contrastive examples and have students count the number of consonants that precede the unstable *e*.

À vous la parole

11-6 Comptons les consonnes ! Indiquez les **e** instables qui devraient être prononcés.

MODÈLES ➤ nous dͤvons   nous montrerons

1. le petit écran
2. une vedette
3. le festival de Cannes
4. une série de films
5. l'autre chaîne
6. Arrête de parler.
7. J'aime ce magazine.
8. Tu ne regardes pas ?
9. Pas de musique.

11-6 After checking answers, have students produce the phrases with the correct deletion and retention of unstable *e*'s.

Key:
1. le pͤtit écran
2. unͤ vedette
3. le festival dͤ Cannes
4. unͤ série dͤ films
5. l'autre chaîne
6. Arrête de parler.
7. J'aime cͤ magazine.
8. Tu nͤ regardes pas ?
9. pas dͤ musique

11-7 Choix d'émissions. Lisez le dialogue suivant phrase par phrase en ne prononçant que les **e** instables indiqués.

—Arrête de zapper ! Qu'est-ce que tu m'énerves !

—Je ne trouve rien d'intéressant. Qu'est-ce que tu veux qu'on regarde ?

—Regardons dans le magazine télé. Tiens, je vois qu'on passe le célèbre film *Au revoir, les enfants*.

—Je l'ai déjà vu, ce film. Je ne l'ai pas trouvé si bon que ça.

—Alors ne le regarde pas. Va dans ta chambre écouter de la musique.

11-7 Before reading the dialogue out loud, have students cross out the unstable *e*'s that will not be retained.

Additional practice activities for each **Formes et fonctions** section are provided by:
- Student Activities Manual
- *Chez nous* Companion Website: http://www.prenhall.com/cheznous

Point out that these verbs have three spoken forms. The third-person singular and plural forms sound alike: *il croit/ils croient; elle voit/elles voient.* The *nous* and *vous* forms contain the sound /j/, as in English "yes." In the spelling, the sound /j/ in the *nous* and *vous* forms is reflected by the letter *y: croyons, voyez.* Also point out that only *voyons* occurs as an imperative form of *voir.* It is used idiomatically, as a sort of filler: *Voyons, qu'est-ce qui ne va pas ? Du silence, voyons !*

FORMES ET FONCTIONS

1. *Les verbes* croire *et* voir

- Here are the forms of the verb **croire** and of the verb **voir**, which is conjugated like **croire**.

	CROIRE *to believe*	**VOIR** *to see*
SINGULIER		
je	crois	vois
tu	crois	vois
il elle on	croit	voit
PLURIEL		
nous	croy**ons**	voy**ons**
vous	croy**ez**	voy**ez**
ils elles	croi**ent**	voi**ent**

IMPÉRATIF : **Crois**-moi !   **Croyez**-nous !   **Croyons** aux jeunes !   **Voyons** !

PASSÉ COMPOSÉ : J'ai **cru** ce qu'il disait.   J'ai **vu** cette émission.

FUTURE : Je le **croir**ai quand je le **verr**ai.

- Use the verb **croire**:

  - to indicate that you believe someone or something:

    Je **crois** Jean.   *I believe John.*
    L'histoire de cette actrice ?   *This actress' story? We believe it.*
     Nous la **croyons**.

  - to indicate that you believe in something or someone. In this case, use **croire** along with the preposition **à**.

    Nous **croyons à** l'avenir du cinéma. *We believe in the future of film.*
    Ils **croient au** Père Noël.   *They believe in Santa Claus.*

  - Note, however, the following special expression.

    Nous **croyons en** Dieu.   *We believe in God.*

- Here are some common expressions using **croire**:

  Je crois. / Je crois que oui.   *I think so.*
  Je ne crois pas. / Je crois que non.   *I don't think so.*

À vous la parole

11-8 Les croyances.
À quoi croient ces personnes ? Pour chaque phrase, choisissez dans la liste suivante la réponse qui convient.

MODÈLE   Mme Martin achète des billets de LOTO chaque semaine.
➤ Elle croit à la chance.

Réponses possibles :

l'amour	la chance	la médecine
l'argent	Dieu	le Père Noël
l'avenir	la discipline	le plaisir

1. Je voudrais avoir beaucoup d'enfants.
2. Anne a six ans, son frère a quatre ans.
3. Geoffrey est un jeune homme sentimental.
4. Vous travaillez vingt-quatre heures sur vingt-quatre.
5. M. Leblanc va à l'église toutes les semaines.
6. Nous sortons jusqu'à trois heures du matin tous les soirs.
7. M. Gervais a trois enfants et il est très autoritaire.
8. Quand il ne se sent pas bien, il va tout de suite voir le médecin.

👥 11-9 Allons au cinéma.
Avec un/e partenaire, imaginez ce que les gens voient habituellement quand ils vont au cinéma.

MODÈLE   Maryse adore la musique et la danse.

É1   Habituellement, elle va voir une comédie musicale.

É2   Ou peut-être un documentaire sur le théâtre.

1. Les Keller vont au cinéma pour se détendre.
2. Jean-Pierre aime le suspense.
3. Rémi et ses parents préfèrent les films de Disney.
4. Nous aimons les films où il y a des extraterrestres.
5. Je suis passionné par l'histoire.
6. Christiane aime les films qui décrivent une rencontre sentimentale.
7. Vous aimez que les films vous fassent peur.
8. Et toi ?

Practice *croire* first using a substitution drill: *Je crois au Père Noël ; vous. — Vous croyez au Père Noël*, etc.

11-8 Make sure students understand all the possible responses before beginning. Help them figure out the meaning of *avenir* from *à plus venir*.

11-9 Finish by asking students what types of films they usually go to see.

11-10 Begin practice of *voir* with a substitution drill : *Je vois un éléphant ; toi ?*, etc. Finish by asking students what types of film they usually go to see.

11-10 Que de choses à voir ! Expliquez ce que chaque personne voit — attention au temps du verbe !

MODÈLES Nous avons visité Paris.
➤ Nous avons vu la tour Eiffel.

Les Davy allaient souvent au zoo.
➤ Ils voyaient des lions, des tigres et des éléphants.

1. J'irai à Nice pour les vacances.
2. Vous êtes allés au Québec ?
3. Ils vont visiter Los Angeles.
4. Tu visites la ville de Tours ?
5. Elles sont allées à Paris cet été.
6. Nous irons à New York le mois prochain.
7. Ma copine va aller en centre-ville.

11-11 Qu'est-ce que vous voyez ? Choisissez une destination, imaginez que vous partez et préparez une petite description : qu'est-ce que vous voyez de votre chambre d'hôtel ? Ensuite, présentez votre description à vos camarades de classe ; ils vont essayer de trouver votre destination.

MODÈLE É1 Je vois beaucoup de personnes qui portent des maillots de bain. Il fait très chaud. Je vois le drapeau (*flag*) français et le drapeau européen. Je vois des gens qui mangent de la glace et qui se promènent.

É2 Je vois une immense plage. Je vois beaucoup de personnes très riches et quelques personnes célèbres.

É3 Je crois que vous êtes dans le Sud de la France.

É1 Oui, mais où ?

É3 Je crois que vous êtes à St-Tropez.

É2 Oui, c'est ça.

2. *La conjonction* que

You might point out that the verb *voir* can also be used with the conjunction *que*: *Je vois qu'ils sont déjà partis.*

You may wish explain to students that, in written French, these expressions used in the negative take the subjunctive; however, this is not obligatory in spoken French: *Je ne pense pas que c'est un bon acteur. / Je ne pense pas que ce soit un bon acteur.*

• To express an opinion, use a verb such as **croire**, **penser**, and **trouver** plus the conjunction **que**. Notice that the conjunction is not always expressed in English but must be present in French.

Ils **pensent que** Spielberg est un grand metteur en scène.
They think (that) Spielberg is a great director.

Je **crois qu'**ils ont raison.
I think (that) they are right.

Elle **trouve que** c'est un bon film.
She thinks (that) it's a good film.

- Use the verb **dire** plus the conjunction **que** to report what someone says.

Elle a dit **que** ce film est excellent.	*She said (that) this film is excellent.*
Il dit **que** cet acteur va gagner un prix.	*He says this actor is going to win an award.*

À vous la parole

👥 11-12 C'est mon avis. Avec un/e partenaire, donnez votre opinion sur les sujets suivants. Ensuite, comparez vos idées avec les idées des autres étudiants de votre classe.

MODÈLE le plus grand metteur en scène

    É1 Je pense que Peter Jackson est le plus grand metteur en scène.

    É2 Je ne pense pas. Je crois que c'est Quentin Tarantino.

1. le plus grand metteur en scène
2. le plus beau film
3. la plus grande actrice
4. l'acteur le plus amusant
5. le film le plus connu

👥 11-13 Les opinions sur la télé. Quelle est votre opinion, et l'opinion de votre partenaire ? Comparez vos idées avec les idées de vos camarades de classe.

MODÈLE La télé peut informer les gens.

    É1 Oui, je crois que la télé peut informer les gens.

    É2 Je suis tout à fait d'accord, je crois qu'il est utile de regarder le journal télévisé, par exemple.

    (*aux autres*) Nous croyons que la télé peut informer les gens. Par exemple,…

1. La télé peut informer les gens.
2. Les acteurs ont une responsabilité vis-à-vis de leur public.
3. Les séries américaines donnent une fausse (*false*) image de la vie aux États-Unis.
4. La télé banalise la violence.
5. La télé peut être très instructive pour les enfants.
6. La puce « V » (*the V chip*) est absolument nécessaire.

Lisons

Stratégie

To grasp to the fullest a personal narrative that is closely associated with a historical period, draw on your knowledge of relevant events and related historical references. When these have shaped a person's experience, you will be able to understand the text only if you understand the historical framework and think about its implications even for everyday activities.

Additional activities to develop the four skills are provided by:
- Student Activities Manual
- Text Audio
- *Chez nous* video
- *Chez nous* Companion Website: http://www.prenhall.com/cheznous

11-14 Mon premier souvenir de cinéma

François Truffaut parle avec des jeunes acteurs qui jouent dans son film *L'Argent de poche.*

A. Avant de lire. In this passage the famous French filmmaker François Truffaut (1932–1984) recalls the first time he saw a movie as a young boy. This took place in 1939, when Truffaut was only seven years old; he relates the experience—and subsequent visits to the cinema—in extensive detail that is directly related to the situation of France at that time. What major world event would have colored his evening and that of everyone else in the movie theater? To understand the text, it is essential that you understand references to the following historical events: **la fin de la guerre, l'Armistice, l'Occupation.** Be alert also to Truffaut's evocation of the complex implications of these events even within such an everyday context as going to see a movie.

B. En lisant. Cherchez les réponses aux questions suivantes.

1. Dans la première partie du texte, trouvez…
   a. le nom du théâtre où François Truffaut a vu son premier film.
   b. le titre du film.
   c. le nom de l'actrice principale, de l'acteur principal.
   d. le genre du film et son sujet.
   e. le nom du metteur en scène.
2. Truffaut pense que c'était une expérience assez exceptionnelle — pourquoi ?
3. Pendant l'Occupation, quelle est l'importance du cinéma pour les Parisiens, selon Truffaut ? Quelle est l'ironie de cette situation ?
4. Pour le jeune François Truffaut, quelle est la pire chose qui pourrait arriver pendant le film ?

Mon premier souvenir de cinéma remonte à 1939, quelques mois avant la fin de la guerre. Cela se passait à la Gaieté Rochechouart, un très grand cinéma en face du square d'Anvers. On y jouait *Paradis perdu* avec Micheline Presle, d'une beauté et d'une douceur extraordinaires, et
5 Fernand Gravey. La salle était pleine de permissionnaires en uniformes accompagnés de leur jeune femme ou de leur maîtresse. On sait peut-être que ce superbe mélodrame d'Abel Gance se déroule[1] de 1914 jusqu'en 1935, et qu'une large section du film est consacrée[2] à la guerre, aux tranchées[3], aux usines de munitions où travaillaient les femmes, etc.
10 La coïncidence entre la situation des personnages du film et celle des spectateurs était telle que[4] la salle entière pleurait, des centaines de mouchoirs[5] trouaient de points blancs[6] l'obscurité du cinéma, je ne devais plus jamais par la suite ressentir une telle unanimité émotionnelle devant la projection d'un film. Il est bien connu que les périodes de guerre ou
15 simplement de pénurie[7] et de dénuement[8] sont favorables à la fréquentation des salles de cinéma. Après l'Armistice, quand les Allemands occupèrent le pays, le cinéma devint un refuge pour tous et pas seulement au sens figuré ; il cessa de l'être à un certain moment, quand on procéda à des vérifications d'identité à la sortie des salles pour repérer[9] les jeunes gens
20 en âge de rejoindre les travailleurs français en Allemagne. Comme ce n'était pas encore mon problème, ma seule angoisse en regardant le film était que la projection soit interrompue par une alerte : dans ce cas, il fallait quitter la salle en prenant un ticket de sortie et attendre dans la cave du cinéma la fin de l'alerte.

[1]*takes place* [2]*dedicated* [3]*trenches* [4]*such that* [5]*handkerchiefs* [6]*dotted* [7]*poverty* [8]*destitution* [9]*to spot*

François Truffaut, *Préface*, « *Le cinéma de l'occupation* » d'André Bazin.

C. En regardant de plus près. Maintenant examinez les aspects suivants du texte.

1. Truffaut écrit que le théâtre était plein de « permissionnaires en uniformes ». Dans cette expression, vous voyez le mot « permission ». D'après ce mot et le contexte, quel est le sens du mot « permissionaires » ?

2. Truffaut utilise **le passé simple** pour parler de certains événements historiques. Est-ce que vous pouvez donner la forme correspondante au **passé composé** ?

   a. les Allemands **occupèrent**.
   b. le cinéma **devint**.
   c. il **cessa**.
   d. on **procéda**.
   e. je **pris**.

D. Après avoir lu. Discutez des questions suivantes avec vos camarades de classe.

1. Selon Truffaut, à quels moments est-ce que les gens vont au cinéma ? Est-ce que vous partagez son avis ?

2. Est-ce que vous pensez que cette première expérience au cinéma a été très importante pour Truffaut ? Pourquoi ?

Leçon 2 *On s'informe*

POINTS DE DÉPART

La lecture et vous TEXT AUDIO

To introduce the new vocabulary, have students complete the *questionnaire*. To check comprehension, total the responses for the group. Have students repeat key words and phrases.

Quelles sont vos habitudes de lecture ? Complétez le questionnaire pour en savoir plus ! D'après vos résultats, est-ce que vous êtes un lecteur sérieux, un lecteur occasionnel ou un lecteur pragmatique ? Comparez vos réponses aux réponses de vos camarades de classe.

Une librairie parisienne

Indiquez vos trois types de lecture préférés :

- ☐ les journaux (nationaux, régionaux, spécialisés—sport, économie)
- ☐ les magazines (d'information, de télévision, féminins ou familiaux)
- ☐ les romans (d'amour, historiques, policiers, de science-fiction)
- ☐ les livres de loisirs (de cuisine, de sport, de bricolage, de jardinage)
- ☐ les livres d'art (sur la peinture, l'architecture, le cinéma)
- ☐ les livres d'histoire ou les biographies
- ☐ les livres sur la science ou la technologie (la santé, l'informatique)
- ☐ les poésies
- ☐ les bandes dessinées (les BD)
- ☐ les ouvrages de référence (le dictionnaire, l'atlas, l'encyclopédie)

Comment choisissez-vous un livre ?

- ☐ les recommandations des critiques dans la presse ou à la télévision
- ☐ les recommandations d'amis
- ☐ la réputation de l'auteur
- ☐ la publicité

Comment obtenez-vous les livres ?

- ☐ vous les empruntez à une bibliothèque
- ☐ vous les empruntez à des amis
- ☐ vous les achetez dans une librairie
- ☐ vous êtes abonné/e à un club lecture

Pourquoi lisez-vous ?

- ☐ pour vous détendre
- ☐ pour vous instruire
- ☐ pour vous distraire

Quand lisez-vous ?

- ☐ en vacances
- ☐ en voyage ou dans les transports publics
- ☐ à la bibliothèque
- ☐ chez vous
- ☐ en écoutant de la musique
- ☐ au lit pour vous endormir

À vous la parole

11-15 Un livre ou un magazine pour tout le monde. Quel type de livre ou de magazine est-ce qu'on pourrait offrir à chaque personne décrite ici ?

MODÈLE un enfant
> On pourrait lui offrir une histoire d'enfants ou une bande dessinée.

1. un étudiant qui prépare son diplôme en journalisme
2. quelqu'un qui n'a pas souvent l'occasion d'aller au musée
3. quelqu'un qui aime bricoler
4. quelqu'un qui apprend l'anglais
5. quelqu'un qui regarde souvent la télévision
6. quelqu'un qui s'intéresse à l'histoire
7. quelqu'un qui adore la science-fiction
8. quelqu'un qui fait beaucoup de sport

Vie et culture

La presse française

Further activities for use with this clip can be found in the Video Manual. To check students' comprehension of the cultural notes, use a recognition exercise: *Donnez-moi un exemple d'un magazine américain à caractère familial.* — *La Sélection du Reader's Digest.* Point out that the French tend to buy newspapers and magazines at *un tabac* or *un kiosque.* In contrast, Americans tend to receive home delivery of newspapers and to subscribe or buy magazines at the supermarket.

Regardez la séquence vidéo, *Je lis la presse,* où Pauline montre et décrit ses journaux et magazines préférés. D'après sa description, qu'est-ce qu'un quotidien ? un hebdomadaire ? un mensuel ?

Pauline achète *Le Monde,* mais elle est abonnée au quotidien *Libération.* Comment est-ce qu'elle décrit son magazine préféré, *Le Nouvel Observateur* ? Quel autre hebdomadaire est-ce qu'elle achète, et pourquoi ? Pauline a acheté un mensuel, *Géo* ; pourquoi ?

Voici la liste des dix hebdomadaires les plus lus en France pour la période allant de juillet 2003 à juin 2004. Pour chaque magazine, identifiez son genre : par exemple, est-ce que c'est un magazine féminin ? un magazine télé ? Qu'est-ce que vous pouvez déduire des priorités ou des goûts des gens qui les achètent ?

Le Top Ten des hebdomadaires les plus lus

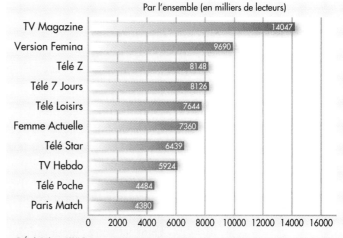

Par l'ensemble (en milliers de lecteurs)

Magazine	Lecteurs
TV Magazine	14047
Version Femina	9690
Télé Z	8148
Télé 7 Jours	8126
Télé Loisirs	7644
Femme Actuelle	7360
Télé Star	6439
TV Hebdo	5924
Télé Poche	4484
Paris Match	4380

© Étude Audience AEPM France.

Quels journaux et magazines est-ce que vous reconnaissez dans ce kiosque qui se trouve à Marrakech au Maroc ?

The chart indicates the number of readers in thousands (as indicated in the legend) as determined by a survey carried out by AEPM (*Audiences, études sur la presse magazine*). More information can be obtained from their website (see the *Chez nous* Companion Website for links). *Francoscopie 2003* also presents interesting information on the French press on pages 440–445. The French spend half their leisure time in front of the TV, hence the large number of TV magazines. Ask students to identify the most popular magazines in the U.S. Various sources cite: 1. NRTA/AARP Bulletin 2. Modern Maturity 3. Readers' Digest 4. TV Guide 5. National Geographic 6. Better Homes and Gardens 7. Family Circle 8. Good Housekeeping 9. Ladies' Home Journal 10. Women's Day

11-16 *Télérama* includes a guide to TV programming, reviews of current films, and book reviews. It is popular with well-educated readers and is purchased even by people who have no television. As a follow-up to this exercise, ask students 1) which of the books and magazines listed they would choose for themselves, and why; 2) what type of book or magazine they would buy for a friend or family member. Have students role play a situation in which they ask a bookseller's advice.

11-17 This can be carried out in pairs, in small groups, or as a whole-class exercise; summarize results at the end of group discussion.

11-16 D'après le titre. D'après le titre, c'est quel genre de livre, de journal ou de magazine ?

MODÈLE *La Maison de Marie-Claire*
➤ C'est probablement un magazine féminin.

1. *Télérama*
2. *InfoMatin*
3. *Elle*
4. *La Semaine du Foot*
5. *Les Années 80*
6. *Lucky Luke dans le Far Ouest*
7. *Le Guide Pratique du Droit*
8. *Cuisine Minceur*

11-17 Et vous ? Quelles sont vos habitudes ? Comparez-les avec les habitudes d'un/e camarade de classe.

1. Qu'est-ce que vous lisez tous les jours ? — le journal, des magazines ? quels journaux ou magazines ?
2. Quels ouvrages de référence est-ce que vous avez chez vous ?
3. Qu'est-ce que vous lisez pour vos cours ?
4. Qu'est-ce que vous lisez pour vous informer ? pour vous détendre ?
5. Qu'est-ce que vous lisez quand vous êtes en vacances ?
6. Quel est le dernier livre que vous avez lu ? Est-ce que vous êtes en train de lire un livre maintenant ?
7. Quel est votre auteur préféré ?

Sons et lettres

TEXT AUDIO

Le *e* instable et les groupes consonne + /j/

Treat this topic after presenting the conditional in this lesson or in conjunction with that presentation.

Unstable **e** is pronounced when it occurs before groups consisting of a consonant plus the semivowel /j/. Compare the corresponding present indicative versus imperfect or present subjunctive **nous** and **vous** forms:

nous app**e**lons	nous app**e**lions
vous d**e**vez	vous d**e**viez
vous ach**e**tez	il faut que vous ach**e**tiez
nous j**e**tons	il est nécessaire que nous j**e**tions

These groups also occur in the conditional **nous** and **vous** forms. Compare the corresponding future and conditional forms:

nous zapp**e**rons	nous zapp**e**rions
vous trouv**e**rez	vous trouv**e**riez

Recall that **i** is pronounced as the vowel /i/ rather than the semivowel /j/ after consonant groups ending with /r/ or /l/, for example: **le cl**i**ent, cr**i**er.** Such combinations occur especially in the **nous** and **vous** forms of the conditional of **-re** verbs. Compare:

vous prendrez	vous prendriez
nous nous détendrons	nous nous détendrions

À vous la parole

11-18 Changements de temps. Mettez le verbe à la forme correspondante du temps indiqué.

1. à l'imparfait

MODÈLE   vous jetez
➤ vous jetiez

nous amenons   vous devez   nous appelons
vous achetez   nous épelons

2. au futur

MODÈLE   il est
➤ il sera

elles font   je montre   elle regarde   ils doivent

3. au conditionnel

MODÈLE   nous vendrons
➤ nous vendrions

nous regarderons   vous descendrez   vous ferez
nous prendrons   vous réparerez

11-19- Comptine. Lisez à voix haute cette comptine.

11-19 *Une pomme reinette* is a variety of apple; *une pomme d'api* is a type of apple, red on one side, that no longer exists.

> Pomme de reinette et Pomme d'api.
> D'api d'api rouge,
> Pomme de reinette et Pomme d'api
> D'api d'api gris.
>
> C'est à la halle°   marché
> Que je m'installe
> C'est à Paris que je vends mes fruits.
> Pomme de reinette et pomme d'api
> D'api d'api gris.

FORMES ET FONCTIONS

1. Le conditionnel

• You have used the conditionnel forms of **devoir**, **pouvoir**, and **vouloir** to express obligation, to soften commands, and to make suggestions.

Tu **pourrais** lire un roman.   *You could read a novel.*
On **devrait** acheter le journal.   *We should buy the newspaper.*

Use an activity from Ch. 8, L. 2 to review the forms and use of these verbs in the conditional before going on to the new information. Use examples as in the text to introduce additional uses of the conditional.

- Here are some additional uses of the conditional:
  - to express events or situations that are hypothetical or conjectural:

J'**aimerais** acheter un bon dictionnaire, mais c'est cher.	*I'd like to buy a good dictionary, but it's expensive.*
Tu **vendrais** vraiment ce livre ?	*Would you really sell this book?*
Nous **voudrions** être riches !	*We would like to be rich!*

  - to express future events or situations in relation to the past. Compare the uses of the future with the present and the conditional with the **passé composé** in the following pair of sentences:

Future event with relation to the present:

Il **dit** qu'il ne **jettera** plus ses journaux.	*He says that he won't throw away his newspapers anymore.*

Future event with relation to the past:

Il **a dit** qu'il ne **jetterait** plus ses journaux.	*He said that he wouldn't throw away his newspapers anymore.*

- The conditional is formed by adding the imperfect endings to the future stem.

SINGULIER		PLURIEL	
je	donner**ais**	nous	donner**ions**
tu	donner**ais**	vous	donner**iez**
il elle on	donner**ait**	ils elles	donner**aient**

Here are the conditional forms of the main verb groups. Verbs that have an irregular future stem use that same stem in the conditional: **j'irais**, **j'aurais**, **je serais**, etc.

verb group	infinitive	conditional
-er	parler	je **parlerais**
-ir	partir	je **partirais**
-re	vendre	je **vendrais**

Verbs with spelling changes in the present tense show those spelling changes in the conditional as well.

verb group	infinitive	conditional
-yer	nettoyer	je **nettoierais**
-er (with spelling change)	jeter	je **jetterais**
	se lever	je me **lèverais**
	préférer	je **préfèrerais**

À vous la parole

11-20 Vous aussi ? Avec plus d'argent, qu'est-ce que vous feriez ? Êtes-vous d'accord avec ces gens ?

MODÈLE   Je m'achèterais une nouvelle voiture.

       ➤ Moi aussi, je m'achèterais une nouvelle voiture.

   OU   ➤ Moi non, je m'achèterais un grand bateau.

1. Je voyagerais tout le temps.
2. Je ne travaillerais plus.
3. Je partagerais l'argent avec ma famille.
4. Je prêterais de l'argent à mes amis.
5. Je m'achèterais un château en France.
6. J'irais dîner dans les meilleurs restaurants.
7. Je me construirais une grande piscine.

11-21 Des bons conseils. Quel conseil est-ce que vous et votre partenaire donneriez à ces personnes ?

MODÈLE   Je ne suis pas très bien informé.

       É1 À ta place, je regarderais les infos le soir.

       É2 Tu devrais lire le journal plus souvent.

1. Ma fille regarde trop la télé.
2. J'ai envie de me détendre ce soir.
3. Nous partons bientôt en vacances.
4. Dans ma famille, on se dispute toujours pour choisir une émission de télé.
5. J'ai envie de lire un bon livre ce week-end.
6. J'ai du mal à choisir un candidat au moment des élections.
7. Je n'aime pas la violence.

11-22 Vous avez le pouvoir ! Avec un/e partenaire, imaginez que vous êtes dans les situations suivantes. Qu'est-ce que vous feriez ? Ensuite, comparez vos idées avec celles de vos camarades de classe.

MODÈLE   Vous êtes le professeur de votre cours de français.

       É1 Je donnerais moins de devoirs.

       É2 Je ne permettrais pas aux étudiants de parler anglais.

1. Vous êtes le professeur de votre cours de français.
2. Vous êtes le président/la présidente de votre université.
3. Vous êtes un journaliste célèbre.
4. Vous êtes un écrivain connu.
5. Vous êtes le directeur d'une grande chaîne de télévision.
6. Vous êtes le maire (*mayor*) de votre ville.
7. Vous êtes le président/la présidente des États-Unis.

Begin practice with a discrimination drill, having students raise their hand when they recognize the conditional: *rêve ou réalité ? Je vais acheter une nouvelle voiture (réalité). J'achèterais aussi une nouvelle maison (rêve). Nous allons en Suisse (réalité). Vous iriez en Belgique ? (rêve). Elle ferait le tour du monde (rêve). Tu travailles beaucoup (réalité). Vous travailleriez avec Brad Pitt (rêve). Nous irions au festival de Cannes (rêve). Nous regarderons le festival à la télé (réalité),* etc. Follow with a simple substitution drill to practice endings: *Je parlerais français ; nous. —Nous parlerions français,* etc. Review irregular stems: *Je suis riche. —Je serais riche ; J'ai une grande maison. —J'aurais une grande maison,* etc.

11-20 Have several students reply for each item, elaborate on their answers, or suggest other possibilities.

11-21 Follow up by comparing responses for each item.

11-22 Have students name other important positions and ask their classmates to say what they would do if they occupied those positions.

2. L'ordre des événements

These expressions provide students with a means of ordering events that will allow them to avoid multiple tensed clauses. To present, provide multiple examples such as those found in the text and have students order the events: 2, 1 or 1, 2.

• To order events in time, you can use the expression **avant de** plus an infinitive. This expression can be used whether the time frame is past, present, or future.

Avant d'aller au travail, j'ai regardé les infos.
Before going to work, I watched the news.

Avant de me coucher, je lis un peu.
Before going to bed, I read a little.

Le ministre va y réfléchir **avant de répondre** aux journalistes.
The minister will think about it before responding to the journalists.

• The expression **après avoir/après être** plus the past participle can be used in a similar way to order events. Choose **avoir** or **être** based on how the particular verb is conjugated in the **passé composé**.

Après avoir entendu la nouvelle, j'ai téléphoné à ma sœur.
After hearing the news, I called my sister.

Le soir, je lis le journal **après avoir regardé** les infos.
In the evening, I read the paper after watching the news.

Après s'être installé, l'ambassadeur se réunira avec son personnel.
After getting settled in, the ambassador will meet with his staff.

À vous la parole

11-23 Vos activités. Avec un/e partenaire, parlez de vos activités passées, actuelles et futures.

11-23 To prepare the exercise, you might first ask students to identify the time frame for each item (past/present/future); then put them to work in pairs.

MODÈLE Avant de venir en classe aujourd'hui,…

   É1 Avant de venir en classe aujourd'hui, j'ai travaillé à la BU.

   É2 Et moi, avant de venir en classe, j'ai déjeuné au resto U.

1. Avant de venir en classe aujourd'hui,…
2. Après avoir fait les devoirs hier soir,…
3. Avant de me coucher, normalement…
4. Avant de sortir avec mes amis le week-end,…
5. Après avoir passé mes examens ce semestre,…
6. Après avoir terminé mes études,…
7. Avant de prendre ma retraite (*to retire*),…

11-24 Une journée typique. Expliquez quel est l'ordre logique des événements, à votre avis.

MODÈLES manger, se brosser les dents
➤ Après avoir mangé, je me brosse les dents.

se brosser les dents, boire mon café
➤ Avant de me brosser les dents, je bois mon café.

1. s'habiller, prendre une douche
2. mettre un manteau, sortir
3. arriver au bureau, acheter le journal
4. travailler un peu, déjeuner
5. quitter le bureau, téléphoner au chef de section
6. quitter le bureau, aller au supermarché
7. manger, faire la cuisine
8. regarder la télé, se coucher

11-25 Dernières nouvelles. Imaginez le reportage d'un journaliste, qui doit utiliser un style plus sophistiqué.

MODÈLE Le président a parlé avec le ministre. Ensuite, il a donné une conférence de presse.
➤ Après avoir parlé avec le ministre, le président a donné une conférence de presse.
OU ➤ Avant de donner une conférence de presse, le président a parlé avec le ministre.

1. Le ministre a parlé devant le Sénat, mais d'abord il a lu la proposition.
2. L'ambassadeur a annoncé la nouvelle, mais d'abord il a téléphoné au président.
3. Le sénateur se réunira (*will meet*) avec son personnel et ensuite il annoncera son plan économique.
4. Le ministre annoncera sa réforme éducative, mais d'abord il va prévenir (*to inform*) la presse.
5. Le journaliste a interviewé le président et ensuite il a écrit son article.

11-26 Narration. Expliquez à votre partenaire ce que vous avez fait hier, et ce que vous allez faire demain. Utilisez les expressions de la liste.

d'abord	avant de + infinitif	après avoir	} + participe passé
ensuite	enfin	après être	

MODÈLE ➤ Hier, c'était dimanche. Je me suis levé très tard. D'abord, j'ai pris mon petit-déjeuner. Après avoir mangé, je me suis douché. Avant de sortir, j'ai lu le journal…

Script for *Écoutons*

MALE VOICE 1 : Vous écoutez France Inter. Il est 8 h 30. [Music.] 8 h 30. L'heure de la revue de presse d'Éric Richard. Bonjour Éric.

MALE VOICE 2 : Bonjour. Comme vous le savez tous, c'est le moment des élections européennes et tous les journaux en parlent. Ce matin, à la une du *Figaro*, il y a un long article qui présente les candidats et leurs positions. Dans *Libération*, il y a un sondage qui indique que 32 % des Français ne connaissent pas les candidats et ne s'intéressent pas particulièrement à ces élections. À ce propos, vous trouverez dans *la Nouvelle République* un éditorial qui dit que la classe politique française ne semble pas très préoccupée par l'avenir de l'Union Européenne. Histoire à suivre en tout cas. Les élections sont dans deux semaines.

Tournons-nous vers le sport. Le journal *la Montagne* écrit ce matin en première page que le Paris St-Germain a gagné la coupe de France de football. Malheureusement, le match n'a pas été très intéressant avec un seul but. Comme le dit le journal *l'Équipe* : « Hier soir au stade de France, on s'est un peu ennuyé. Un match sans panache. »

Cette semaine, l'hebdomadaire *le Point* se tourne vers la Bretagne avec un reportage sur les charmes de cette région et ses efforts pour protéger son patrimoine avec la création de réserves naturelles régionales.

Dans le mensuel *Première*, tout un dossier consacré aux festivals de cinéma. C'est fini pour cette année le festival de Cannes, mais pour les amateurs de l'Amérique, le festival du cinéma américain de Deauville arrive dans quelques mois.

Allez bonne journée et bonne lecture à tous.

En écoutant, Key: 1) la politique, le sport, l'environnement, le cinéma ; 2) *Libération*, la Nouvelle République ; la Montagne, l'Équipe ; le Point ; Première ; 3) Answers include : Il y a des élections européennes dans deux semaines. Les Français ne s'intéressent pas beaucoup à ces élections ; L'équipe du Paris St-Germain a gagné la Coupe de France. Le match n'a pas été très intéressant ; La région de La Bretagne a créé des réserves naturelles ; Le festival de Cannes est fini ; Il y aura un festival du cinéma américain à Deauville.

 Écoutons

TEXT AUDIO

11-27 Revue de presse

A. Avant d'écouter. En France, vous pouvez entendre régulièrement à la radio ou même à la télévision le matin, une revue de presse. Dans ces émissions, un journaliste résume et commente des articles récents qu'il a sélectionnés. Dans cette revue de presse, vous allez entendre un journaliste qui parle de quatre thèmes différents : **le sport**, **la politique**, **les régions** et **la culture**. Avec un/e partenaire, pensez aux mots-clés que le journaliste pourrait employer pour parler de chaque thème. Par exemple, pour le thème **de la politique**, on pourrait entendre des mots comme **élections**, **président**, **parti politique**. Quand vous écoutez cette revue de presse, utilisez les mots-clés que vous avez identifiés pour vous aider à comprendre.

B. En écoutant. Complétez le tableau en écoutant la revue de presse.

1. Pendant la première écoute, indiquez dans la première colonne, le thème (**sport**, **politique**, **région**, **culture**) pour chaque partie.
2. Écoutez de nouveau et entourez les magazines ou journaux mentionnés dans chaque partie. Il peut y avoir plusieurs sources pour chaque thème. (Attention : pour le premier thème, seulement un des journaux mentionnés a été sélectionné comme modèle. C'est à vous de trouver les autres).
3. Écoutez une dernière fois et complétez la troisième colonne avec un fait intéressant que vous avez appris pour chaque thème.

Thème	Source(s)		Un fait intéressant
1. *la politique*	(le Figaro) Libération le Monde	le Parisien la Nouvelle République	*Les élections européennes sont dans deux semaines.*
2.	la Montagne les Echos	la Voix du Nord l'Équipe	
3.	l'Express le Nouvel Observateur	le Point	Students can listen to a *revue de presse* on the Internet; see the *Chez nous* Companion Website for links. You may wish to use the daily version of *la revue de presse* from the morning
4.	Géo Prima	Première Marie-Claire	show *Télématin*. It can be downloaded from the Web. Although the French would be too complicated for students to follow without help, this *revue* has the advantage of showing

headlines and articles as they are mentioned.

C. Après avoir écouté. Maintenant, répondez aux questions suivantes avec vos camarades de classe.

1. Après avoir écouté cette revue de presse, est-ce que vous avez envie de lire un de ces articles ? Quel(s) article(s) vous intéresse(nt) particulièrement ? Pourquoi ?
2. Est-ce que vous aimeriez écouter une revue de presse chez vous ? Pourquoi ?

Leçon 3 Êtes-vous branché informatique ?

POINTS DE DÉPART

Les autoroutes de l'information

Comment est-ce que vous vous servez de l'ordinateur ? C'est indispensable pour les études, le travail et les loisirs !

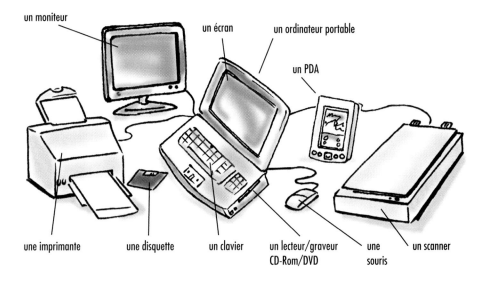

un moniteur · un écran · un ordinateur portable · un PDA · une imprimante · une disquette · un clavier · un lecteur/graveur CD-Rom/DVD · une souris · un scanner

• Pour écrire : il y a des logiciels de traitement de texte : Word, par exemple. N'oubliez pas de sauvegarder votre fichier sur une disquette ou un CD, pour éviter de perdre votre travail !

• Pour apprendre : l'ordinateur rend possible un enseignement multimédia et interactif. Chaque étudiant travaille à son propre rythme.

• Pour communiquer : beaucoup de gens font du télétravail, grâce au courrier électronique sur Internet. Tout le monde a son adresse électronique. On peut envoyer un courriel avec une pièce jointe — un document, une photo, etc. Des réseaux comme Internet permettent de communiquer dans le monde entier et donnent accès à des moteurs de recherche et des bases de données que l'on peut utiliser pour la recherche, les affaires et l'éducation. Il existe bien des campus virtuels et des télécours en ligne !

• Pour jouer : même les enfants se servent de l'ordinateur pour dessiner, pour faire de la musique, pour jouer tout simplement. Il ne vous manque jamais de partenaire !

À vous la parole

11-28 As an alternative or review exercise, you might have students work in pairs to create their own definitions with which to test classmates.

11-28 Définitions. Trouvez le mot qui correspond à chaque définition.

MODÈLE C'est l'appareil qu'on utilise pour imprimer un texte.
➤ C'est l'imprimante.

1. C'est un logiciel utilisé pour écrire des textes.
2. C'est un ordinateur qu'on peut facilement transporter.
3. C'est sur cette partie de l'ordinateur qu'on tape (*types*).
4. C'est un message qu'on reçoit par Internet.
5. C'est ce qu'on regarde lorsqu'on utilise l'ordinateur.
6. On l'utilise pour sauvegarder un fichier.
7. C'est un terme général pour les programmes.
8. Cela permet un enseignement visuel et interactif.
9. Cela permet de reproduire une photo ou un texte.

11-29 This allows recycling of vocabulary for other technological devices. Have students work in pairs, then compare responses for the class as a whole.

11-29 Vous êtes technophile ? Vous êtes technophile ou technophobe ? Combien de ces appareils est-ce que vous savez utiliser ? Comment est-ce que vous les utilisez ? Comparez vos réponses avec les réponses d'un/e partenaire.

MODÈLE un magnétoscope

É1 Mes parents ont un magnétoscope chez eux. Je l'utilise pour regarder des films sur vidéocassettes, mais malheureusement je ne sais pas comment le programmer.

É2 J'ai un magnétoscope, mais je ne l'utilise pas beaucoup. J'utilise plus le lecteur DVD.

1. un fax
2. un logiciel de traitement de texte
3. le courrier électronique
4. un moteur de recherche
5. un magnétoscope
6. un lecteur DVD
7. un répondeur automatique
8. un scanner
9. un appareil photo numérique
10. un graveur CD

11-30 Follow up with the class as a whole to find out students' most frequent uses of the computer.

11-30 L'ordinateur et vous. Trouvez un/e partenaire et posez-lui les questions suivantes.

1. Est-ce que tu as un ordinateur chez toi ? à la résidence ?
2. Avec qui est-ce que tu échanges des courriels ?
3. Est-ce que tu utilises la messagerie instantanée ? avec qui ? quand ?
4. Est-ce que tu envoies régulièrement des pièces jointes ?
5. Combien de temps par semaine est-ce que tu passes en ligne ?
6. Combien d'heures par jour est-ce que tu te sers d'un ordinateur ?
7. Est-ce que tu participes aux forums de discussion ?
8. Quel logiciel de traitement de texte est-ce que tu préfères ? Pourquoi ?

Vie et culture

Le Minitel et l'Internet

Le Minitel, développé en France au début des années 80, était la première autoroute télématique francophone et un prédécesseur de l'Internet. Aujourd'hui encore, il existe plus de six millions de Minitels en France et l'on peut accéder à ses bases de données depuis l'Internet, à condition d'être abonné au Minitel. Avec le Minitel, on peut trouver des renseignements, faire ses comptes[1], réserver et acheter.

Grâce à un réseau international bien plus développé, l'Internet tend à remplacer le Minitel de nos jours. En fait, le français est la deuxième langue de l'Internet après l'anglais. Les

minitel.com
gagnez du temps en un rien de temps

francophones et les francophiles peuvent surfer sur Internet en se servant de moteurs de recherche comme Google France, Yahoo ! France ou Altavista France.

Depuis bientôt trente ans, avec le Minitel, les Français ont l'habitude de faire des réservations, payer les factures[2], vérifier les numéros de téléphone et les séances de cinéma et même s'inscrire dans les cours à la fac. Est-ce que vous utilisez l'Internet pour les mêmes fonctions ? Pourquoi ?

[1] to manage one's accounts   [2] bills

Voici l'écran d'un Minitel. Quel numéro est-ce qu'on recherche ?

The French government preferred to invest in the development of the Minitel in the 1980s, because the future of the Internet was less certain. You might point out that in early 2004, only 42% of French homes had a personal computer; the percentage in the U.S. at the same time was 80%.

FORMES ET FONCTIONS

1. Les phrases avec si...

The conjunction **si** is used in a clause that expresses a condition. It is often accompanied by another clause that expresses the result.

Point out that the clauses may be ordered in either way, as in the examples provided.

- Use **si** plus the present tense to express a condition that, if fulfilled, will result in a certain action (stated in the present or future).

Si je **trouve** ce nouveau roman, je l'**achète**/je l'**achèterai**.	*If I find this new novel, I'm buying it/I will buy it.*
Elle nous **accompagne/accompagnera** au cinéma **si** elle **a** le temps.	*She is going/will go with us to the movies if she has the time.*

- Use **si** plus the imperfect if the situation is hypothetical; the result clause will then be in the conditional.

Si j'**avais** assez d'argent, je m'**achèterais** un nouvel ordinateur portable.	*If I had enough money, I would buy myself a new laptop.*
Ils **pourraient** répondre plus rapidement **s'**il leur **envoyait** un courriel.	*They could respond more quickly if he sent them an e-mail.*

À vous la parole

11-31 and 11-32 To vary or provide review, change the tense/mode: *Si tu achetais un portable,...* ; *Si tu deviens journaliste, tu écriras...* etc.

11-31 Sur l'autoroute de l'information. David explique à son amie Céline comment démarrer sur l'autoroute de l'information. Terminez chaque phrase d'une façon logique.

MODÈLE Si tu achètes un ordinateur portable,...
> ➤ Si tu achètes un ordinateur portable, tu pourras apporter ton ordinateur en classe.

1. Si tu as besoin d'écrire un texte,...
2. Si tu ouvres un nouveau fichier,...
3. Si tu veux écouter de la musique,...
4. Si tu cherches un numéro de téléphone,...
5. Si tu veux avoir les dernières nouvelles,...
6. Si tu as le temps de jouer,...
7. Si tu veux regarder un film sur ordinateur,...

11-32 Choix de profession. Quelques jeunes gens ne peuvent pas décider quelle profession choisir. Qu'est-ce qu'ils feraient s'ils choisissaient une profession dans les arts ou dans les médias ?

11-32 Have students suggest other professions and answers.

MODÈLE   journaliste
➤ Si vous étiez journaliste, vous pourriez écrire des articles pour un journal ou un magazine.

1. présentateur à la télé
2. acteur/actrice
3. metteur en scène
4. chanteur/chanteuse

5. photographe
6. musicien/ne
7. chef d'orchestre
8. écrivain

11-33 Des rêves et des projets. Qu'est-ce que vous ferez ou feriez dans les situations suivantes ? Avec un/e partenaire, parlez de vos projets et de vos rêves (*dreams*).

Recycle food vocabulary with the following type of exercise:

Quels plats ?

MODÈLE   des œufs et des champignons
➤ Si j'avais des œufs et des champignons, je ferais une omelette.

MODÈLE   être une actrice/un acteur célèbre
É1   Si tu étais une actrice célèbre, qu'est-ce que tu ferais?
É2   Je serais très riche et j'habiterais à Beverly Hills.

1. avoir ton diplôme demain
2. être millionnaire
3. trouver un emploi aujourd'hui
4. aller en vacances
5. être en France
6. être le président/la présidente des États-Unis
7. avoir 50 ans

2. *Les expressions* depuis *et* il y a … que

Depuis and **il y a … que** are used with an expression of time and the present tense to indicate that an event that began in the past is still going on in the present.

- **Depuis** is used with an expression of time to indicate how long an event has been going on. To ask how long something has been going on, use **depuis combien de temps ?**

Point out that *Depuis combien de temps ?* is the preferred question to use when asking about duration of an event or activity, and *Depuis quand ?* is used when the speaker wants to know specifically when the event began. In actual conversation, however, a person may respond by specifying either the beginning or the duration of the event. The use of *depuis* with an expression referring to *heure(s)* is ambiguous and may refer to a period of time or a specific point in time: *Je t'attends depuis une heure.* (I've been waiting for you for an hour/since one o'clock.)

—**Depuis combien de temps** est-ce que tu écris des poèmes ?

—*How long have you been writing poems?*

—J'écris des poèmes **depuis** trois ans.

—*I've been writing poems for three years.*

- **Depuis** can also be used to indicate specifically when an event began. Use **depuis quand ?** to ask when an event started.

—**Depuis quand** est-ce que tu travailles ici ?

—*Since when have you been working here?*

—Je travaille ici **depuis** 2002.

—*I've been working here since 2002.*

- To emphasize the length of time that something has been going on, use **il y a**, plus a time expression, plus **que**.

Il y a combien de temps que tu as cet ordinateur ?

How long have you had this computer?

Il y a trente minutes que je suis en ligne.

*I've been online for **thirty minutes**.*

À vous la parole

11-34 Ça fait longtemps ! Mettez l'accent sur la durée en utilisant **il y a … que**.

MODÈLE   Julie est à la fac depuis trois ans.

➤ Il y a trois ans que Julie est à la fac.

1. Elle étudie l'informatique depuis deux ans.
2. Elle travaille à la B.U. depuis trois heures.
3. Elle a son nouvel ordinateur depuis dix semaines.
4. Elle prépare un site Web depuis un mois.
5. Elle utilise un appareil photo numérique depuis quelques semaines.
6. Elle cherche une imprimante depuis quinze jours.

11-35 La biographie d'un journaliste. Avec un/e partenaire, parlez de la carrière de David en précisant depuis quand ou depuis combien de temps il fait les choses suivantes.

MODÈLE   1990 David devient photographe.

É1 Depuis quand est-ce que David est photographe ?

É2 Il est photographe depuis 1990.

OU

É1 Depuis combien de temps est-ce que David est photographe ?

É2 Il est photographe depuis [quinze ans].

1990   David devient photographe.
1992   David étudie l'anglais.
1994   David travaille pour un magazine.
1996   David voyage pour le travail.
1997   David gagne des prix pour ses reportages.
2000   David a son bureau à Londres.
2002   David visite les États-Unis tous les ans.
2004   David est chef de bureau.

👥 11-36 Et vous ? Posez des questions à un/e partenaire pour savoir s'il/si elle fait les choses suivantes, et si oui, depuis combien de temps.

11-36 Follow up by having students tell something they learned about their partner.

MODÈLE   pratiquer un sport

        É1 Est-ce que tu pratiques un sport ?

        É2 Oui, je joue au basket.

        É1 Depuis combien de temps est-ce que tu joues au basket ?

        É2 Depuis sept ans.

1. pratiquer un sport
2. jouer d'un instrument
3. lire le journal
4. habiter la résidence ou un appartement
5. travailler
6. avoir une connexion Internet
7. avoir un scanner
8. être fiancé/e ou marié/e

Écrivons

11-37 Participer à un forum de discussion sur Internet

A. Avant d'écrire. Imaginez que vous allez participer à un forum de discussion (*un fordit*) au sujet de l'importance des médias dans la vie des étudiants.

1. D'abord, dressez une liste de questions que vous voudriez poser aux autres membres du forum. Quels aspects de ce sujet vous intéressent ?
2. Les cinq opinions suivantes viennent de ce forum. Lisez-les et choisissez-en une à laquelle vous voudriez répondre.

If you belong to a forum, you might let students have a look at postings; be aware, however, that typically you will find many slang expressions and grammatical errors typical of spontaneous speech and writing.

```
La jeune génération, trop orientée vers le visuel, ne
    possède plus la capacité de lire. —Robert

Les médias ont trop de pouvoir parce qu'ils
    déterminent quelles informations nous allons lire et
    voir. —Une amie

Les étudiants d'aujourd'hui restent mal informés, malgré
    (in spite of) une véritable explosion des médias.
    —Vanessa

Si notre société devient de plus en plus violente, c'est
    parce que les médias nous y habituent. —Céline

Les nouvelles universités, entièrement « en ligne »,
    nous préparent mieux pour le monde du travail que les
    universités plus traditionnelles. —Benoît
```

B. En écrivant. Maintenant, composez une réponse à une de ces personnes. Êtes-vous d'accord ou pas avec l'opinion exprimée ?

Pour exprimer votre opinion	Pour réagir aux opinions des autres
Je pense/Je crois/Je trouve que…	Je (ne) suis (pas) (tout à fait) d'accord…
À mon avis,…	Au contraire…
Pour moi,…	D'un autre côté,…

MODÈLES ➤ Je ne suis pas tout à fait d'accord avec Vanessa. Je trouve que certains jeunes gens aujourd'hui sont très bien informés. Tous mes amis lisent au moins un journal par jour, et nous discutons ensemble des événements politiques. Je sais que ce n'est pas toujours le cas, mais,…

➤ Je suis tout à fait d'accord avec Céline pour dire que la télévision banalise la violence, et que les gens s'habituent de plus en plus à accepter la violence dans la vie de tous les jours. On voit de la violence non seulement pendant le journal télévisé, mais aussi dans tous les feuilletons et séries les plus populaires. Même les émissions pour enfants…

C. Après avoir écrit.

You might also set up a forum among different sections of the same course or between a more advanced class and this class.

1. Créez un mini-forum dans votre classe et échangez vos opinions. Est-ce que vous partagez les mêmes opinions sur les différents sujets ?
2. Visitez un forum français pour découvrir d'autres sujets de discussion.

Ces étudiants travaillent à la terrasse d'un café avec un ordinateur portable.

Venez chez nous !
Le cinéma

Les Français ont joué un grand rôle dans le développement du cinéma. C'est en 1895 à Lyon que les frères Lumière inventent le cinématographe, une machine qui permet de produire les premiers films. Deux ans après, le premier studio cinématographique est construit à Montreuil, près de Paris. Depuis, le film français est devenu un véhicule important de la culture francophone.

Additional activities to explore the **Venez chez nous !** topics are provided by:
- Student Activities Manual
- *Chez nous* video
- *Chez nous* Companion Website: http://www.prenhall.com/cheznous

Louis et Auguste Lumière ont présenté le premier film de l'histoire du cinéma en 1895 : *la Sortie des usines Lumière.*

Voyage dans la Lune, tourné en 1902 par Georges Méliès, est le premier film de science-fiction.

Introduce this lesson by asking students what they know about the early film industry. How many have heard of *les frères Lumière*? You might show one or more of the Lumière brothers' first films, which are very short but include some interesting features, such as traveling shots and dissolves. Another interesting early film to show is Méliès' *Voyage dans la Lune*, which includes many special effects (Méliès was first and foremost a magician).

Observons

11-38 Réflexions sur le cinéma

A. Avant de regarder. Si vous habitiez les environs de Cannes, qu'est-ce que vous pourriez faire au moment du festival international du film ? Faites une liste d'activités possibles. Vous allez entendre une Niçoise qui décrit sa propre expérience, puis un étudiant à l'Université de Nice qui décrit ses préférences cinématographiques.

Avant de regarder. Help students generate a list of things they could see and do during the festival.

This activity makes use of the first two interviews in the **Observons** clip; two additional interviews are treated in the Video Manual.

FABIENNE : Vous savez que sur la Côte d'Azur nous avons Cannes, qui est pas très loin de Nice. Vous avez un tas de célébrités, de toutes nationalités qui euh viennent pour la promotion de leurs films. Je suis um très souvent aussi sur la ville de Cannes, donc j'aperçois souvent le festival de Cannes et j'ai eu l'occasion de côtoyer quelques petites célébrités — un petit coucou, comme ça de de quelques minutes. Voilà.

ÉDOUARD : Donc j'aime beaucoup le cinéma. Euh, j'y vais autant que je peux, ce qui est pas beaucoup, en tant que… parce que je suis étudiant. Euh mais dès que je peux, par contre, je loue un un DVD et je regarde ça avec des amis. Les derniers films que j'ai vus, c'est *Harry, un ami qui vous veut du bien*, euh un film français. Ou sinon, *L'auberge espagnole*. Je vous conseille de le voir, d'ailleurs. Euh sinon, ben, les grands classiques, comme euh *Le Seigneur des anneaux*, ou *Matrix*. Et euh, j'espère bientôt en voir un autre, ce soir peut-être.

B. En regardant. Trouvez toutes les bonnes réponses possibles à chaque question.

1. Selon Fabienne, des célébrités viennent à Cannes…
   a. de tous les pays.
   b. à tous les moments.
   c. pour les vacances.
   d. pour la promotion de leurs films.

2. Fabienne … à Cannes au moment du festival.
   a. ne va jamais
   b. est souvent
   c. va tous les ans

3. Elle a eu l'occasion … quelques célébrités.
   a. de voir
   b. de dîner avec
   c. d'interviewer

4. Édouard va au cinéma…
   a. aussi souvent que possible.
   b. très souvent.
   c. tous les soirs.

5. Le dernier film qu'il a vu, c'était un film…
   a. américain.
   b. espagnol.
   c. français.

6. Pour lui, un grand classique du cinéma, c'est…
   a. *Harry, un ami qui vous veut du bien.*
   b. *L'auberge espagnole.*
   c. *Le Seigneur des anneaux.*
   d. *Matrix.*

Après avoir regardé. As a follow-up, have the class create a list of classic films, then develop a description in French for each of them. See the *Chez nous* Companion Website for links to French cinema sites.

C. Après avoir regardé. Maintenant discutez des questions suivantes avec vos camarades de classe.

1. Est-ce qu'il est possible pour les gens chez vous de côtoyer (*to get close to*) des célébrités comme le fait Fabienne à Cannes ? Pourquoi est-ce que les gens aiment cela, à votre avis ?

2. Est-ce que vous êtes d'accord avec Édouard quand il nomme des « grands classiques » ? Quels sont les grands classiques pour vous ?

Les festivals internationaux de films

Il y a de nombreux festivals de films chaque année. Un des plus connus est en France, à Cannes. Tous les ans, pendant quinze jours au mois de mai, la charmante ville touristique de Cannes devient la capitale cinématographique du monde. Le Festival International du Film est surtout un congrès professionnel : producteurs, metteurs en scène et vedettes y viennent pour se rencontrer, pour échanger des idées, pour essayer de vendre leurs nouveaux films et pour distribuer des « Palmes » pour les meilleurs films de l'année.

Pour savoir quels sont les meilleurs films canadiens, vous pouvez regarder Le Gala des Jutra. C'est le festival cinématographique qui a lieu chaque année au mois de mars au Québec. Et pour savoir ce qui se passe dans le cinéma africain, il faut aller au mois de février à Ouagadougou, au Burkina Faso. C'est là que vous trouverez le FESPACO, le Festival Panafricain du Cinéma et de la Télévision de Ouagadougou, un des festivals le plus grand et le plus important sur le continent d'Afrique. Ce grand festival a lieu tous les deux ans avec l'objectif de favoriser la diffusion de toutes les œuvres du cinéma africain ainsi que de contribuer au développement et à la sauvegarde du cinéma africain.

Le logo du FESPACO

Show the video montage *Le cinéma* to preview discussion of the Cannes film festival. Once students have read and discussed the text, see whether they can narrate the various events shown in the montage. Ask students if they enjoy watching the Oscars and if so, why, and whether they are familiar with any other film festivals. See the *Chez nous* Companion Website for links to francophone film festivals.

Le Palais des Festivals à Cannes

Denys Arcand, le réalisateur québécois, a remporté plusieurs Jura en 2004 pour son film *les Invasions barbares.*

Stratégie

Considering the type of text you are reading and its conventions can help you to approach it knowledgeably. For example, your expectations about style and content can alert you as to what you should be watching for when you read reviews of a book or film.

11-39 Critiques d'un film canadien

Regardez cette photo du film franco-canadien *Les Invasions barbares*. Qu'est-ce qui se passe dans le film, à votre avis ?

Avant de lire. Complete this activity in class. Make a list of the expectations students have about what they are about to read, then see how this list compares with the information asked for in **En lisant.** Elements frequently found in movie reviews include title, name of director/producer, names of lead actors, a brief summary, a comparison of the film with other similar films, and a statement of the author's opinion of the film.

From the photo and the caption, students can glean: the title of the film, the relationship between two of the main characters, and the situation portrayed in the film.

Point out the distinction between *la critique* (review) and *le critique* (reviewer). In the third review, help students make sense of the third sentence (beginning with *Dépité de…*) by separating out the various elements and deciding to which character (the son or the father) each pronoun refers.

A. Avant de lire. Multiple Web sites exist today where moviegoers can post their opinion of recent films. Here we have three reviews of the French Canadian film *Les Invasions barbares*. Before you read them, think about the types of information you would expect to find in a film review. For example, in each review there will almost certainly be references to the plot and characters, which you can watch for, as well as an evaluation of the film. What other conventions are the reviews all likely to reflect? How, on the other hand, are the reviews likely to be different?

B. En lisant. Cherchez les réponses aux questions suivantes.

1. En général, est-ce que les critiques de ce film sont positives ou négatives ? Qu'est-ce qui a influencé votre réponse ?
2. Trouvez un extrait dans une des critiques qui résume le scénario du film.
3. Identifiez les personnages principaux et les acteurs principaux.

4. Qui est le metteur en scène du film ? Comment est-ce que vous le savez ?

5. Pour les personnes qui écrivent les deux premières critiques, quels sont les points forts du film ? Par exemple, elles trouvent que les acteurs jouent bien.

6. Pour le troisième critique, quels sont les points faibles du film ?

Accueil > Films > Critiques du film *Les Invasions barbares*

Par Christine K.   note 9/9

Un film magnifique à voir absolument !
De l'émotion, de l'humour, de l'amitié, beaucoup d'amour et des acteurs merveilleux... et ce petit accent canadien qui nous enchante !

Beaucoup de thèmes sont abordés[1] dans ce film : la mort, la peur de vieillir, la solitude, l'amitié, l'amour, les enfants...   5

Par Fred   note 9/9

Ce film m'a bouleversé[2] par la force des sentiments qu'expriment ces merveilleux acteurs. L'histoire est simple, pourtant si[3] commune. Un homme au bout du chemin[4] de la vie, entouré de ses amis et de sa famille, revient sur son passé et en mesure les erreurs et par là même[5] se rapproche de[6] son fils, de son ex et de lui-même surtout. Tout cela est raconté avec énormément d'humour et d'amour. Plusieurs vies se croisent[7], alors qu'elles

5

n'auraient jamais dû[8]. La mort rapproche[9] les êtres, l'amour les sépare, mais l'amitié reste toujours. C'est ce que je retiens[10] de ce film. Rarement un film ne m'a autant[11] remué les tripes[12], depuis *Midnight Express* peut-être. Je retourne le voir cette semaine.   10

Merci M. Arcand.

Extrait du site Cine Kritik, courtesy of Matthieu Granacher.

« Les Invasions barbares », 2003,

de : **Denys Arcand**   ★★★☆☆☆

Rémy (Rémy Girard), le mari de Louise (Dorothée Berryman) est très gravement malade. Leur fils Sébastien (Stéphane Rousseau)... est appelé en urgence. Il arrive avec sa compagne Gaëlle (Marina Hands). Dépité[13] de voir son père, avec lequel il n'entretenait[14] pratiquement aucun lien[15], mal soigné dans un hôpital canadien, il lui fait spécialement installer une chambre et contacte ses anciens amis, Diane (Louise Portal), Dominique (Dominique Michel), Claude (Yves Jacques). Pour éviter que son père ne souffre trop, il décide de trouver un moyen d'acquérir[16] de l'héroïne et, pour ce faire[17], rencontre la fille de Diane, Nathalie (Marie-Josée Croze), qui se drogue...

5

10

... [Dans ce film,] on assiste à une vague histoire de réconciliation père-fils, assez peu convaincante... ; à l'angoisse d'un homme qui a joui[18] totalement de la vie en égoïste parfait, et se retrouve confronté au grand

15

départ, avec la désolante impression d'une vacuité[19] de son existence ; mais toute cette valse[20] autour du mourant[21]... laisse relativement indifférent[22]... On découvre, par ci par là, quelques éclairs de tendresse, mais l'impression... que tout cela est préfabriqué, calibré, demeure[23]... présente.   20

Que ce film ait eu le prix du scénario[24] à Cannes et que le prix d'interprétation[25] ait été attribué à Marie-Josée Croze, laisse quand même rêveur[26] ! ... Quant[27] au scénario, j'avoue[28] être encore plus étonné ! Qu'y a-t-il de si remarquable dans cette réunion pré-mortuaire alternant scènes hospitalières et réunions amicales... ? Pour moi, il y a là un mystère, pour le moment insoluble !...   30

Au final, une assez grosse déception.

Bernard Sellier

Extrait de la critique du film « Les Invasions barbares », parue sur le site Web « Spirale d'Amour » : http://giridhar.free.fr

---

[1] *tackled*   [2] *bowled over*   [3] *and yet so*   [4] *at the end of the road*   [5] *in doing so*   [6] *draws closer to*   [7] *cross*   [8] *might never have done so*   [9] *brings closer*   [10] *retain*
[11] *so much*   [12] *moved*   [13] *vexed*   [14] *maintained*   [15] *no ties*   [16] *acquire*   [17] *in doing so*   [18] *enjoyed*   [19] *emptiness*   [20] *dance*   [21] *dying man*   [22] *leaves one cold*
[23] *remains*   [24] *screenplay*   [25] *best supporting actress*   [26] *leaves one wondering*   [27] *as for*   [28] *confess*

C. En regardant de plus près. Maintenant examinez les aspects suivants de ces critiques.

1. Quels sont les éléments communs à ces trois critiques ?
2. Chaque personne organise sa critique d'une manière personnelle. Par exemple, la première personne a) donne son évaluation ; b) donne une liste des points forts du film ; c) énumère les thèmes du film. Comment est-ce que les autres critiques sont organisées ?
3. Dans chaque critique, trouvez une phrase ou une expression qui résume l'opinion de la personne qui l'a écrite.

D. Après avoir lu. Discutez des questions suivantes avec vos camarades de classe.

1. Est-ce que vous pouvez résumer l'opinion de chaque critique ? Quelle critique vous semble la plus convaincante et pourquoi ?
2. D'après ce que vous avez lu, quelle impression est-ce que vous avez de ce film ? Est-ce que vous voudriez le voir ? Pourquoi ? Est-ce que vous avez déjà vu un film semblable ? Si oui, décrivez-le.

11-40 La critique d'un film

A. Avant d'écrire. Pensez aux critiques de films que vous avez déjà lues. Quels sont les éléments importants d'une bonne critique ?

B. En écrivant. Choisissez un film que vous avez vu récemment et écrivez une petite critique.

1. D'abord, notez le nom du metteur en scène et des acteurs principaux. Quels rôles est-ce qu'ils jouent ?
2. Ensuite, faites un résumé assez bref de l'intrigue puis écrivez quelques phrases qui donnent plus de précisions sur l'histoire. Utilisez le vocabulaire que vous connaissez.
3. Enfin, n'oubliez pas de donner votre opinion sur ce film.

C. Après avoir écrit. Échangez votre critique avec un/e camarade de classe ou lisez votre critique pour vos camarades de classe. Ne donnez pas le titre du film. Les autres vont essayer de deviner de quel film il s'agit.

11-41 Un questionnaire sur le cinéma

A. Avant de parler. Ce questionnaire a pour objectif de sonder les opinions des Français à propos du cinéma. Quelles sont les questions posées ? Comment est-ce que vous interprétez les réponses ?

LES FRANÇAIS FONT LEUR CINÉMA

QUESTION : Voici un certain nombre d'opinions que l'on entend aujourd'hui à propos du cinéma. Vous-même, dites-moi pour chacune d'entre elles, si vous la partagez tout à fait, assez, peu ou pas du tout ?

A) La présence de vedettes au générique d'un film ne garantit pas le succès de ce film :

	%
- Tout à fait	46
- Assez	29
- Peu	12
- Pas du tout	8
- NSP*	5

B) Le fait que la télévision diffuse un grand nombre de films donne moins envie d'aller au cinéma :

- Tout à fait	42
- Assez	26
- Peu	13
- Pas du tout	16
- NSP	3

C) Un bon film n'a pas forcément de succès :

- Tout à fait	40
- Assez	31
- Peu	14
- Pas du tout	7
- NSP	8

D) Il y a moins de bons films qu'avant :

- Tout à fait	28
- Assez	20
- Peu	22
- Pas du tout	19
- NSP	11

QUESTION : Parmi les choses suivantes, qu'est-ce qui vous donne le plus envie d'aller voir un film ?

	1er choix %	2e choix %	Total %
- Les acteurs	25	24	49
- Le metteur en scène	5	6	11
- Le sujet	37	20	57
- Les critiques	5	8	13
- Le bouche-à-oreille	9	10	19
- Les extraits à la télévision ou les bandes-annonces dans les salles	8	13	21
- Les récompenses qu'il a pu obtenir (Palme à Cannes, Oscar, César...)	3	5	8
- L'affiche	1	2	3
- NSP	7	11	18

QUESTION : Généralement, préférez-vous... ?

- Les films français	49
- Les films américains	17
- Les films étrangers autres qu'américains	4
- Pas de préférence (spontanée)	28
- NSP	2

* Ne se prononcent pas

B. En parlant. Discutez de ces mêmes questions avec un/e partenaire pour découvrir vos opinions.

MODÈLE É1 Est-ce que tu penses que la présence d'une vedette garantit le succès d'un film ?

É2 Pas du tout. Il y a des bons acteurs qui ont fait des mauvais films qui n'ont pas eu de succès...

C. Après avoir parlé. Avec votre professeur et les autres étudiants, partagez vos réponses et établissez un schéma pour comparer vos réponses aux réponses des Français. Est-ce que vous voyez beaucoup de similarités ou beaucoup de différences ?

Bring the group together at the end to compare responses. Create a similar chart for the class results, and ask for a show of hands for each question. You can record raw numbers or have students help you calculate percentages.

Vocabulaire

Leçon 1

des genres d'émissions	kinds of programs
un dessin animé	cartoon, animated film
un divertissement	variety show
un documentaire	documentary
une émission sportive	sports event
un feuilleton	soap opera
un jeu télévisé	game show
le journal télévisé (le JT)	news broadcast
les informations (les infos)	news
un magazine	news magazine
une émission de musique	music program
une émission de télé-achat	infomercial
une émission de télé-réalité	reality show
un reportage	special report
une série	series

pour regarder la télévision	to watch TV
allumer	to turn on (an appliance)
une chaîne	TV station
un écran	screen
un magazine télé	listing of TV programs
une télécommande	remote control
zapper	to channel-surf

des genres de films	types of films
une comédie	comedy
une comédie musicale	musical
un drame psychologique	psychological drama
un film d'aventures	adventure film
un film d'espionnage	spy film
un film historique	historical movie
un film d'horreur	horror movie
un film policier	detective/police movie
un film de science-fiction	science fiction movie
un western	western

pour parler des films	to talk about films
célèbre	famous
doublé/e	dubbed
doubler	to dub
un metteur en scène	film or stage director
le personnage (principal)	(main) character
plein de	full of
des sous-titres (m.)	subtitles
tourner (un film)	to shoot (a film)
une vedette	a movie star
en version originale (en v.o.)	in the original language

quelques verbes	some verbs
croire	to believe
Je crois/Je crois que oui	I think so
Je ne crois pas/ Je crois que non	I don't think so
raconter	to tell
voir	to see

Leçon 2

à lire	to read
un atlas	atlas
une bande dessinée (une BD)	comics, comic book
une biographie	biography
une encyclopédie	encyclopedia
un hebdomadaire	weekly (publication)
un journal (des journaux)	newspaper(s)
un livre d'art	art book
un livre de cuisine	cookbook
un livre d'histoire	history book
un livre de loisirs	book on leisure time or hobbies
un magazine	magazine
un mensuel	monthly (publication)
un ouvrage de référence	reference book
la poésie	poetry

la presse	the press
une publicité (une pub)	advertisement
un quotidien	daily (publication)
un roman	novel

pour choisir un livre — to choose a book

un auteur	author
une recommandation	recommendation

où obtenir un livre/ un magazine — where to get a book/ a magazine

s'abonner (à)	to subscribe (to)
un kiosque	newsstand

pour situer l'action dans le temps — to order events in time

avant de + inf. …	before . . .
après avoir/être + part. passé …	after having . . .

quelques mots utiles — some useful words

se distraire	to amuse oneself
s'informer	to get information
s'instruire	to educate oneself, to improve one's mind

Leçon 3

un ordinateur (un ordi)	computer
un clavier	keyboard
une disquette	diskette
un graveur CD	CD burner
une imprimante	printer
un lecteur CD-ROM, DVD	CD-ROM drive, DVD drive
un moniteur	monitor
un ordinateur portable	laptop
un PDA	PDA
un scanner	scanner
une souris	mouse

pour travailler à l'ordinateur — to work at the computer

une base de données	database
un courriel	e-mail message

le courrier électronique	e-mail
en ligne	online
envoyer	to send
un fichier	computer file
imprimer	to print
un logiciel	software program
un moteur de recherche	search engine
une pièce jointe	attachment
la recherche	research
un réseau	network
sauvegarder (un fichier)	to save (a file)
le traitement de texte	word processing, editing

pour exprimer la durée — to express duration

depuis combien de temps ?	for how long?
depuis quand ?	since when?
il y a… que	it's been . . . , for . . .

autres mots utiles — other useful words

les affaires (f.)	business
l'enseignement (m.)	instruction, teaching
éviter	to avoid
grâce à	thanks to
manquer	to miss, to be lacking
se servir de (quelque chose)	to use (something)
tout le monde	everyone

pour exprimer une opinion — to express an opinion

Je pense / Je crois / Je trouve que…	I think / I believe / I find that . . .
À mon avis,…	In my opinion, . . .
Pour moi,…	For me, . . .

pour réagir à une opinion — to react to an opinion

Je suis (tout à fait) d'accord…	I agree (completely)
Je ne suis pas (tout à fait) d'accord…	I do not (completely) agree
Au contraire,…	To the contrary, . . .
D'un autre côté,…	On the other hand, . . .

Cette représentation de l'opéra d'*Aïda* a lieu dans un théâtre romain en Provence. Est-ce que vous pouvez trouver l'orchestre ? les acteurs principaux ? le chœur ?

Chapitre 12 *Les beaux-arts*

Leçon 1 *Fêtons la musique !*

Leçon 2 *L'art et ses formes d'expression*

Leçon 3 *Allons voir un spectacle !*

Venez chez nous !
Modes d'expression artistique

In this chapter:
- Talking about the arts
- Narrating in the past, present, and future
- Expressing cause and effect
- Discussing the arts in the French speaking world

Leçon 1   *Fêtons la musique !*

POINTS DE DÉPART

Tu es musicien ?

TEXT AUDIO

Additional practice activities for each **Points de départ** section are provided by:
- Student Activities Manual
- *Chez nous* Companion Website: http://www.prenhall.com/cheznous

Begin the lesson by reviewing music vocabulary from Ch. 2, L. 2, reminding students to use *jouer de* with a musical instrument. Have them listen to the dialogue as they look at the text. Ask simple questions to test comprehension: *De quel instrument est-ce que Claire joue ? Et Ben ?* etc. Point out useful conversational expressions such as *Bof, C'est entendu, Tu plaisantes !* The children's book *Sophie la vache musicienne*, written by Geoffroy de Pennart (Kaléidoscope, 1999), can be used as a complement to this lesson. Written mostly in the present tense, the text is quite accessible.

Claire arrive au café avec son violon.

BEN :   Tiens, je ne savais pas que tu étais musicienne !

CLAIRE :   Bof, pas vraiment. Je joue pour le plaisir.

BEN :   Tu fais partie d'un orchestre ?

CLAIRE :   Non, je joue quelquefois avec des copains, c'est tout.

BEN :   De la musique classique ?

CLAIRE :   Non, c'est surtout de la musique traditionnelle ou folklorique.

BEN :   Ah, c'est intéressant ! Tu me diras quand tu feras un concert ?

CLAIRE :   C'est entendu. Mais est-ce que ça t'intéresserait de jouer avec nous ?

BEN :   Tu plaisantes ! Avec mon saxophone ?

CLAIRE :   Et pourquoi pas ?

Display the musicians and their instruments (IRCD, Ch. 12) and describe each group. Test comprehension by having students point to the instrument you name; find out if students in the class, or anyone in their family, play any of the instruments pictured. Note that in France, *une flûte* is a recorder; the expression used for a flute is *une flûte traversière*.

Quelques instruments

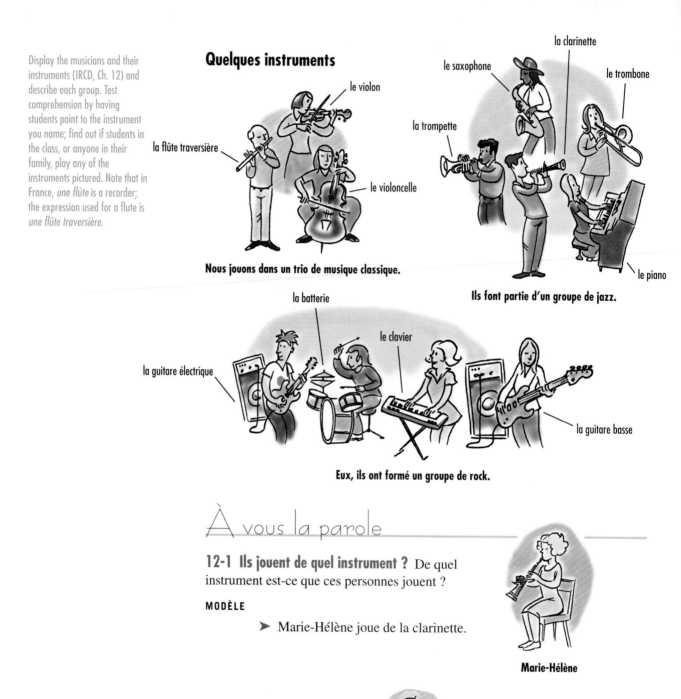

le violon

la flûte traversière

le violoncelle

Nous jouons dans un trio de musique classique.

la clarinette

le saxophone

le trombone

la trompette

le piano

Ils font partie d'un groupe de jazz.

la batterie

le clavier

la guitare électrique

la guitare basse

Eux, ils ont formé un groupe de rock.

À vous la parole

12-1 Ils jouent de quel instrument ? De quel instrument est-ce que ces personnes jouent ?

MODÈLE

➤ Marie-Hélène joue de la clarinette.

Marie-Hélène

1. **Claire et moi**　　2. **Thomas**　　3. **Sylvie et toi**

4. Adrien

5. Fred

6. Vanessa et David

La Fête de la Musique always occurs on the summer solstice, the longest day of the year. Consult the *Chez nous* Companion Website for links to sites with more information. You may wish to play the video clip *J'aime beaucoup le jazz*, in which the speaker discusses her music preferences and a concert she attended. Have students pick out the details she uses to describe the singer's style.

Vie et culture

La Fête de la Musique

Regardez cette affiche pour la Fête de la Musique en France. Où est-ce que cette fête se déroule[1] ?

Quelle est la date de la fête ? Pourquoi, à votre avis, est-ce que l'on a choisi cette date ?

En 1982, Maurice Fleuret, ancien Directeur de la musique et de la danse au Ministère de la Culture, a remarqué que cinq millions de Français, y compris[2] un jeune sur deux[3], jouaient d'un instrument. Son rêve[4], c'était de créer un jour où tous les Français pourraient fêter la musique ensemble — non seulement dans les salles de spectacle, mais aussi chez eux, dans les cafés et dans la rue. Alors en 1982, la première Fête de la Musique a eu lieu en France. Pendant toute la journée et toute la soirée, vous pouvez voir des musiciens amateurs et professionnels qui jouent de la musique dans les parcs et les cafés, dans la rue ou chez des gens. Est-ce que vous aimeriez participer à la Fête de la Musique ? Pourquoi ?

[1] *take place*   [2] *including*   [3] *one out of two young people*   [4] *dream*

12-2 Before completing this exercise, ask students to look up the musicians they do not know; alternatively, complete this as a group activity. 1) Placido Domingo is a Spanish opera singer; 2) Eric Clapton is a British singer and guitarist; 3) Yo Yo Ma is a Chinese-American cello player; 4) Elton John is a British singer and piano player; 5) Josh Groban is an American singer; 6) Céline Dion is a Canadian singer; 7) Bill Clinton, American president, is known for playing the saxophone; 8) Louis Armstrong was an American jazz musician who played the cornet and the trumpet; 9) Sting is a British singer who also plays the guitar, the piano, the harmonica, and the saxophone.

12-3 Follow up by having each group tell which concert they would most like to attend.

👥👥 **12-2 Des musiciens célèbres.** Avec un/e partenaire, identifiez ces musiciens célèbres.

MODÈLE   Ella Fitzgerald

      É1   C'était une chanteuse américaine.

      É2   Oui, elle chantait du jazz.

1. Placido Domingo
2. Eric Clapton
3. Yo Yo Ma
4. Elton John
5. Josh Groban
6. Céline Dion
7. Bill Clinton
8. Louis Armstrong
9. Sting

👥👥 **12-3 Choisir un concert.** Regardez cet extrait de journal pour choisir un concert avec votre partenaire, selon la situation décrite.

MUSIQUE

Les midis du Louvre Georges Blanchard, violon, Raoul Galan, piano. Œuvres de Grieg, Saint-Saëns, Mozart. 12 h 30. Auditorium du Louvre. Pl : 10 et 15 €.

Orchestre de Paris Dir : Sir Georg Solti. Chœur de l'Orchestre de Paris. Dir : Arthur Oldham, Jeanne Beltran, soprano, Kevin Long, ténor, René Papon, basse. Dans « les Saisons » de Haydn. 20 h. Salle Pleyel. Pl : 25 à 100 €.

Le piano romantique Concert-lecture. Laurent Duvalier, piano. Œuvres de Chopin. Maison de la Radio. 19 h 30. Entrée libre.

Concert de guitare Antoine Tessier, Luis Aragon. Du classique au populaire… de l'Amérique du Nord aux Latinos. 20 h 30. Petit Théâtre de Montmartre. Pl : 12 et 20 €.

MODÈLE   Vous voulez écouter de la musique pendant l'heure du déjeuner.

      É1   Est-ce que nous pouvons assister à un concert pendant l'heure du déjeuner ?

      É2   Oui, au Louvre il y a un concert de musique classique à 12 h 30.

1. Vous voudriez assister à un concert avec plusieurs styles de musique.
2. Vous aimeriez entendre un grand orchestre.
3. Vous aimez les concerts de piano et surtout la musique classique.
4. Vous adorez écouter des gens qui chantent.
5. Vous préférez la guitare classique.
6. Vous aimez la musique, mais vous n'avez pas beaucoup d'argent.

FORMES ET FONCTIONS

Vue d'ensemble : les verbes suivis de l'infinitif

Many verbs in French can be followed by an infinitive. Some are followed directly by an infinitive, and some require a preposition before the infinitive.

- As you have learned, the **futur proche** is one case where the verb **aller** is directly followed by an infinitive.

    Elle **va chanter** avec sa chorale
    mercredi prochain.

    *She is going to sing with her
    chorus next Wednesday.*

- Verbs expressing likes and dislikes, including **adorer**, **aimer**, **désirer**, **détester**, and **préférer**, are also directly followed by the infinitive.

    J'**aime** bien **écouter** de la musique
    classique, mais mon copain
    préfère écouter du jazz.

    *I like listening to classical music
    but my boyfriend prefers
    listening to jazz.*

- The verbs **devoir**, **pouvoir**, and **vouloir** are directly followed by an infinitive.

    —Tu **veux venir** avec nous à
    un concert ce soir ?

    —*Do you want to come with us
    to a concert tonight?*

    —Malheureusement, je ne **peux**
    pas **venir**. Je **dois travailler** ce soir.

    —*Unfortunately, I can't come.
    I have to work tonight.*

- Other verbs directly followed by the infinitive are: **espérer**, **falloir** (**il faut**), and **savoir**.

    —Vous **savez jouer** du violon ?

    —*Do you know how to play
    the violin?*

    —Non, mais **j'espère apprendre**
    bientôt.

    —*No, but I hope to learn soon.*

- Many other verbs require a preposition, either **à** or **de**, before the infinitive. The particular preposition required for each verb must be memorized. Here are some of the most frequently used verbs.

These verbs, among others, require **à** before an infinitive:

aider à	*to help*	Il m'**aide à chanter** mieux.
apprendre à	*to learn*	J'**apprends à jouer** du piano.
commencer à	*to begin*	Elle **a commencé à jouer** de la flûte traversière quand elle avait neuf ans.
continuer à	*to continue*	Nous **continuons à apprécier** le jazz.
inviter à	*to invite*	Je t'**invite à aller** à un concert avec moi.
réussir à	*to succeed*	Vous **avez réussi à jouer** du piano.

Additional practice activities for each **Formes et fonctions** section are provided by:
- Student Activities Manual
- *Chez nous* Companion Website: http://www.prenhall.com/cheznous

Ch. 12 has only one **Formes et fonctions** per lesson: these synthesize major topics and introduce more sophisticated structures. Three additional topics are treated in the Appendices: *le plus-que-parfait, le futur antérieur,* and *le passé du conditionnel.* You may wish to introduce these if you are using *Chez nous* over three semesters or have a more advanced class. Explanations and exercises integrate thematically with Ch. 12. We suggest using *le plus-que-parfait* (Appendix 1) as **Formes et fonctions 1** in L. 2; *le futur antérieur* (Appendix 2) as a third grammar topic in L. 2; and *le passé du conditionnel* (Appendix 3) as the first grammar topic in L. 3.

This material combines review (of modal verbs, verbs of preference followed by an infinitive, and the *futur proche*) with new information about prepositions following certain verbs when used with an infinitive.

Additional verbs which take *à* before an infinitive include: *s'amuser à, avoir du mal à, chercher à.* Note that *continuer* can be followed by either *à* or *de: continuer à parler, continuer de parler.*

Additional verbs which take *de* before an infinitive include: *avoir besoin de, avoir envie de, avoir peur de, conseiller de, demander de, se dépêcher de.*

These verbs, among others, require **de** before an infinitive:

accepter de	*to agree*	Il **a accepté de jouer** avec nous.
arrêter de	*to stop*	J'**ai arrêté de jouer** du piano il y a longtemps.
décider de	*to decide*	Ils **ont décidé de former** un orchestre ensemble.
essayer de	*to try*	Je vais **essayer de chanter** plus.
finir de	*to finish*	Elle **finit de suivre** des cours lundi.
oublier de	*to forget*	J'**ai oublié d'apporter** ma clarinette à la répétition (*rehearsal*).
refuser de	*to refuse*	La diva **refuse de chanter** cette aria.
rêver de	*to dream of*	Elle **rêve d'être** musicienne professionnelle.

Note that **venir** can also be followed by **de** but that this expression has a special meaning: to have just done something.

Je **viens d'apprendre** cette chanson.   *I've just learned that song.*

À vous la parole

12-4 To simplify, provide verbs as cues: 1) faire, réviser   2) suivre, aimer 3) venir, aller, assister   4) danser, faire 5) écouter, faire, jouer   6) jouer, apprendre   7) chanter, jouer 8) écouter, jouer

12-4 Des détails. Pour chaque phrase, ajoutez un verbe logique pour donner plus de détails.

MODÈLE   Adrien apprend la flûte à l'école.
➤ Adrien apprend à jouer de la flûte à l'école.

1. Elle finit ses devoirs pour le prof de piano.
2. Je continue mes leçons de chant.
3. Tu as oublié le concert hier soir ?
4. Delphine arrête la danse.
5. Nous adorons le jazz.
6. J'essaie le saxophone.
7. Vous commencez avec ce groupe folklorique ?
8. Tu préfères quel type de musique ?

12-5 This type of exercise is familiar, but the qualities students are looking for are more complex. Encourage students to engage in longer conversations with fewer students to discover the hidden musical talents and desires among class members.

12-5 Les talents et les projets musicaux. Identifiez qui dans votre classe a des talents et des projets musicaux. Posez des questions à vos camarades de classe pour découvrir qui fait quoi. N'oubliez pas d'inclure le professeur !

MODÈLE   savoir jouer d'un instrument

É1 Est-ce que tu sais jouer d'un instrument ?
É2 Non, je ne sais pas jouer d'un instrument.
OU Oui, je sais jouer un peu de piano, mais j'aimerais apprendre à jouer du saxophone.

1. savoir jouer d'un instrument
2. aimer chanter
3. commencer récemment à jouer d'un instrument
4. vouloir faire partie d'un groupe musical
5. rêver d'être chanteur/euse de rock (de rap, de jazz, d'opéra)
6. refuser d'écouter du rap
7. réussir à chanter de l'opéra
8. essayer de jouer d'un instrument

 12-6 Pendant les vacances. C'est bientôt les vacances. Avec un/e partenaire, discutez de vos projets.

12-6 Compare answers and decide who has the most ambitious vacation plans, the most realistic, the funniest, the most original.

MODÈLE   Pendant les vacances, je refuse…

>   É1 Pendant les vacances, je refuse de me lever tôt. Et toi ?
>   É2 Et moi, je refuse de travailler. Je voudrais me reposer à la plage.

1. Pendant les vacances, j'ai accepté…
2. Je vais certainement…
3. Mais, j'ai aussi décidé…
4. J'aimerais apprendre…
5. Si j'avais le temps, je voudrais…
6. Je pourrais toujours…
7. En fait, je rêve…
8. Finalement, je sais que je vais réussir…

Écoutons

TEXT AUDIO

12-7 À la claire fontaine

A. Avant d'écouter. Est-ce que vous connaissez des chansons traditionnelles en anglais — *Auld lang syne*, ou *Greensleeves*, par exemple ? Est-ce que vous connaissez aussi des chansons traditionnelles françaises ? Si oui, quelles chansons ? Quels sont souvent les sujets ou les thèmes des chansons traditionnelles ?

Daniel le Mée qui chante « À la claire fontaine »

Dans cette chanson, *À la claire fontaine*, il s'agit d'une personne — Pierre ; d'une fleur — la rose ; et d'un oiseau — le rossignol (*nightingale*). Souvent, dans les chansons

Additional activities to develop the four skills are provided by:
• Student Activities Manual
• Text Audio
• *Chez nous* video
• *Chez nous* Companion Website: http://www.prenhall.com/cheznous

American students are most likely to be familiar with French traditional songs such as *Frère Jacques* and *Alouette*.

À la claire fontaine / M'en allant promener / J'ai trouvé l'eau si claire / Que je m'y suis baignée

Il y a longtemps que je t'aime / Jamais je ne t'oublierai

J'ai trouvé l'eau si claire / Que je m'y suis baignée / À la feuille d'un chêne / Je me suis essuyée

Il y a longtemps que je t'aime / Jamais je ne t'oublierai

À la feuille d'un chêne / Je me suis essuyée / Sur la plus haute branche / Le rossignol chantait

Il y a longtemps que je t'aime / Jamais je ne t'oublierai

Sur la plus haute branche / Le rossignol chantait / Chante, rossignol, chante / Toi qui as le cœur gai

Il y a longtemps que je t'aime / Jamais je ne t'oublierai

Chante, rossignol, chante / Toi qui as le cœur gai / Tu as le cœur à rire / Moi je l'ai à pleurer

Il y a longtemps que je t'aime / Jamais je ne t'oublierai

Tu as le cœur à rire / Moi je l'ai à pleurer / C'est de mon ami Pierre / Qui ne veut plus m'aimer

Il y a longtemps que je t'aime / Jamais je ne t'oublierai

C'est de mon ami Pierre / Qui ne veut plus m'aimer / Pour un bouton de rose / Que tantôt j'ai donné

Il y a longtemps que je t'aime / Jamais je ne t'oublierai

Pour un bouton de rose / Que tantôt j'ai donné / Je voudrais que la rose / Fût encore au rosier

Il y a longtemps que je t'aime / Jamais je ne t'oublierai

Je voudrais que la rose / Fût encore au rosier / Et que mon ami Pierre / Fût encore à m'aimer

Il y a longtemps que je t'aime / Jamais je ne t'oublierai

In the song, the last two lines of each verse are repeated as the first two lines of the following verse. This establishes a rhythm and aids in remembering and continuing the song and its story.

The *Chez nous* Companion Website provides links to sites with the words and music to many traditional French songs. You might have students listen to some of these in class or research the topic further outside of class.

traditionnelles, il y a beaucoup de répétitions, et c'est le cas pour cette chanson. Il y a un refrain, mais d'autres vers (*lines*) se répètent aussi. Ces répétitions vont vous aider à comprendre la chanson.

B. En écoutant. Trouvez les réponses aux questions suivantes.

1. Identifiez les instruments que vous entendez.

2. Identifiez la voix que vous entendez : est-ce que c'est une voix…
   a. de baryton   b. de ténor   c. de basse ?

3. Quels sont les thèmes de la chanson ?
   a. l'amour   b. la nature   c. le regret

4. Dans cette chanson, il y a plusieurs couplets et un refrain ; quel est le refrain ?

5. Dans cette chanson, il y a beaucoup de répétition. Quels sont les vers (*lines*) répétés ? Pourquoi, à votre avis ?

C. Après avoir écouté. Est-ce que cette chanson vous plaît ? Pourquoi ? Les chansons traditionnelles sont très populaires parmi les Français. On les chante pour les fêtes et surtout aux mariages. À quels moments est-ce qu'on chante des chansons traditionnelles (ou d'autres chansons) chez vous ?

La Fontaine des quatre dauphins à Aix-en-Provence, sculptée par Jean-Claude Rambot en 1667

Leçon 2 L'art et ses formes d'expression

POINTS DE DÉPART

Les artistes et leurs œuvres d'art

Les artistes au travail

Begin by presenting artists using the line art (IRCD, Ch. 12) and asking questions such as *Qui peint ? Qui sculpte ? Qui fait/prend une photo ?* The noun *peintre* is only used in the masculine form, *photographe* can be both masculine and feminine, and *sculpteur* has a distinct feminine form: *une sculptrice* or *une femme sculpteur*. You may wish to present the corresponding verbs: *peindre, sculpter, dessiner, photographier* or *faire/prendre une photo*. Begin practice of *peindre* with a discrimination drill: *une personne ou plus ? Elle peint un tableau. Elles peignent un portrait. Ils peignent souvent le week-end. Il peint beaucoup. Elle peint bien. Elles peignent comme des vraies artistes.* Follow up with a substitution drill: *Pablo peint un tableau ; toi ? — Tu peins un tableau*, etc. Continue by presenting artistic styles using the images in the textbook or other reproductions of them you may have. Discuss students' preferences and their knowledge of works of art and artists.

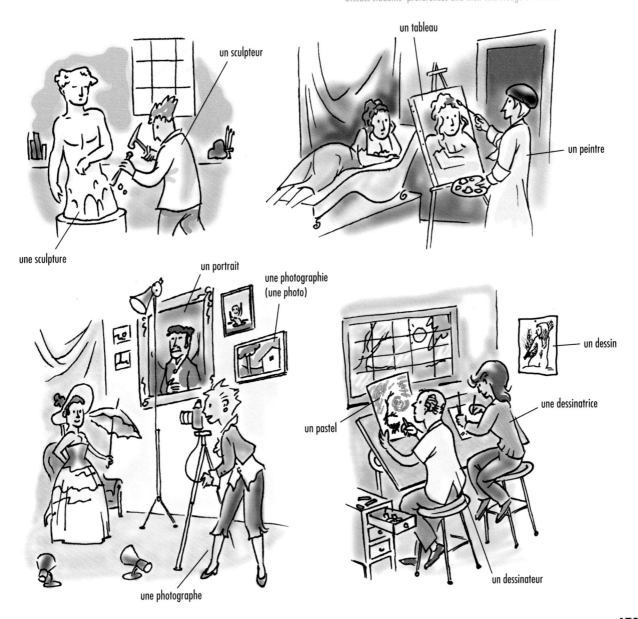

Jean-Baptiste Siméon Chardin a peint cette nature morte. Cette composition représente des objets de cuisine. C'est un tableau de style réaliste avec des couleurs assez sombres.

Jean-Baptiste Siméon Chardin (1699–1779), « Menu de gras et ustensile de cuisine », Louvre. Paris, France. Bridgeman Art Library.

Henri Rousseau a peint ce tableau dans le style primitif. Le sujet de ce tableau est une femme qui se promène dans une forêt exotique avec des fleurs et des arbres immenses. Les couleurs sont très vives.

Henri J.F. Rousseau (1844–1910) « Femme se promenant dans une forêt fantastique » 1905. Oil on canvas/The Barnes Foundation, Merion, Pennsylvania, USA/The Bridgeman Art Library.

Ce tableau abstrait et cubiste de Fernand Léger s'intitule *Éléments mécaniques*. C'est un bon exemple d'art moderne avec ses formes géométriques qui se répètent.

« Éléments mécaniques » 1918–23 (Oil on canvas) by Fernand Leger (1881–1955). Kunstmuseum, Basle, Switzerland/Peter Willi/Bridgeman Art Library.

Claude Monet a peint ce paysage d'hiver. Regardez l'utilisation de la lumière et surtout ses reflets sur la neige. Monet a été le grand maître des impressionnistes.

Claude Monet (1840–1926), « La pie, Effet de neige », Musée d'Orsay. Paris.

Note that the verb **peindre** is irregular:

—Qu'est-ce que vous **peignez** en ce moment?

—Je **peins** une nature morte avec des belles fleurs.

PEINDRE	*to paint*		
je	peins	nous	peign**ons**
tu	peins	vous	peign**ez**
il	} peint	ils	} peign**ent**
elle		elles	
on			

PASSÉ COMPOSÉ : Renoir **a peint** beaucoup de portraits.

Vie et culture

Les musées à Paris

Testez votre connaissance des musées à Paris : Quel est le plus grand musée du monde qui s'y trouve ? Quel musée d'art parisien était autrefois[1] une gare ? Dans quel musée est-ce que vous pouvez voir des sculptures dans un beau jardin ? Dans quel musée est-ce que vous pouvez admirer les tableaux *les Nymphéas* de Monet ? Des musées, il y en a pour tous les goûts à Paris. Par exemple :

Le Centre Pompidou	l'art moderne et l'art contemporain
Le musée de Cluny	l'art médiéval et les tapisseries de *la Dame à la Licorne*[2]
Le musée d'Orsay	les impressionnistes et les postimpressionnistes
Le musée des Arts décoratifs	les meubles, les céramiques, les tapisseries, les textiles
L'Orangerie	les impressionnistes et surtout *les Nymphéas* de Monet

Students can complete a virtual visit of many of these museums. Visit the *Chez nous* Companion Website for links. For cross-cultural comparison, ask students to list museums in their city and/or region, or to make a list of museums they have visited and have enjoyed. Have students compare answers.

Le musée du Louvre et sa pyramide

Le musée Picasso	des œuvres des maîtres modernes, surtout Picasso
Le musée Rodin	une collection de sculptures de l'artiste exposées dans le jardin et la maison

Trouvez des renseignements sur un des musées mentionnés sur l'Internet et parlez-en avec vos camarades de classe. Pourquoi est-ce que vous aimeriez visiter ce musée ?

[1]*formerly*   [2]*unicorn*

12-8 As a follow-up, ask students what type of art they prefer and which works of art they would like to have in their room or apartment. You could also have students discuss these questions in pairs.

12-8 Qu'est-ce que c'est ? Identifiez ces œuvres d'art.

MODÈLE

➤ C'est une nature morte.

1.

2.

3.

4.

5.

6.

7.

8.

12-9 Artistes célèbres.

Avec un/e partenaire, choisissez deux artistes qui vous intéressent dans la liste suivante. Faites quelques recherches et présentez-les devant la classe. Parlez du style de chaque artiste et de ses œuvres d'art. Si possible, montrez une photo d'une de ses œuvres à vos camarades de classe.

Vincent Van Gogh *Autoportrait*, 1889, musée d'Orsay, Paris.

MODÈLE

É1 Nous avons choisi Claude Monet et Vincent Van Gogh.

É2 Van Gogh était un peintre néerlandais de style postimpressionniste. Il a peint surtout des paysages et des portraits. Il a aussi fait trente-cinq autoportraits. Voici un autoportrait qu'il a peint vers la fin de sa vie.

É1 Et moi, je vais parler de Claude Monet qui…

1. Marc Chagall
2. Eugène Delacroix
3. Mary Cassatt
4. Pablo Picasso
5. Berthe Morisot
6. Camille Claudel
7. Auguste Rodin
8. Georges Braque
9. Robert Doisneau
10. Henri Matisse
11. Auguste Renoir
12. Claude Lorrain

12-10 Une œuvre d'art que vous aimez.

Apportez en classe une œuvre d'art ou une reproduction d'œuvre d'art. Présentez-la à vos camarades de classe. N'oubliez pas de parler de l'artiste, du type d'art et de dire pourquoi vous l'aimez.

MODÈLE

➤ Voici une œuvre d'Henri Matisse. C'est un collage qui s'appelle *Les bêtes de la mer*. C'est assez abstrait et très coloré. J'aime la technique de Matisse et le sujet de ce collage. Les couleurs sont très vives et très intenses. Il y a beaucoup d'énergie exprimée dans ce collage.

les bêtes de la mer…
H. matisse 50

FORMES ET FONCTIONS

Vue d'ensemble : l'emploi des temps verbaux

For each example, have students identify the time reference: present, present progressive, past, or future.

● The present indicative is the most versatile tense in French. As you know, it is used to express habitual actions or states and ongoing actions or events. When used with an appropriate time expression, the present can also be used to recount past events and describe future ones:

Il **parle** français couramment.	*He speaks French fluently.*
Elle **peint** une nature morte pour l'anniversaire de sa mère.	*She is painting a still life for her mother's birthday.*
En 1874, Monet, Degas, Renoir et d'autres artistes **exposent** leurs tableaux. C'**est** le début de l'impressionnisme.	*In 1874, Monet, Degas, Renoir and other artists exhibited their paintings. It was the beginning of Impressionism.*
Nous **allons** au musée **demain**.	*We're going to the museum tomorrow.*

● To talk about two events that occur at the same time, use the conjunctions **pendant que** (*while*) or **quand** (*when*).

■ To describe ongoing or habitual actions, both verbs are in the present:

Il lit le programme **pendant que** j'achète les billets.	*He's reading the program while I'm buying the tickets.*
Quand je suis à Paris, je vais toujours au théâtre.	*When I'm in Paris, I always go to the theater.*

Point out the use of the future tense in both clauses, which is unlike English usage. Note that *pendant que* can be followed by the present tense: *Pendant que tu lis/liras le programme, j'irai acheter les billets.* To express a sequence of events in the future, the *futur antérieur* refers to an event that will have happened before the event indicated by the *futur simple*: *Quand elle sera partie, je te téléphonerai.* The *futur antérieur* is presented, along with practice activities in Appendix 2; you may wish to treat it at the end of this lesson.

■ To talk about future events that will occur at the same time, French uses the future tense after the conjunction **quand**. Note that English uses the present tense in this case.

Nous irons voir l'exposition **quand** nous **serons** à Nice.	*We'll go see the exhibition when we are in Nice.*
Quand on **ira** au musée, n'apporte pas ton baladeur.	*When we go to the museum, don't bring your Walkman.*

Point out that although both verbs express past events, it is not necessary that both be in the same past tense (i.e., one verb may be in the *passé composé* and the other in the *imparfait*).

■ When talking about simultaneous events in the past, use a past tense for both verbs:

Nous avons vu une pièce intéressante **quand** j'étais à Paris.	*We saw an interesting play when I was in Paris.*
Pendant qu'elle parlait, je regardais les tableaux.	*While she was talking, I was looking at the paintings.*

À vous la parole

12-11 D'une pierre deux coups.
On est tous pressés. Pour gagner du temps, suggérez des activités que ces personnes peuvent faire pendant qu'elles font autre chose.

MODÈLE Pendant qu'elle lit le journal, ma mère…
➤ boit son café.

1. Pendant qu'elle regarde la télé, ma sœur…
2. Quand je fais du sport…
3. Pendant que mon professeur déjeune…
4. Quand je parle au téléphone…
5. Pendant que je vérifie mon courrier électronique…
6. Quand mes parents sont dans la voiture, ils…
7. Pendant que mon colocataire fait ses devoirs…
8. Quand je suis dans l'avion ou dans le train…
9. Pendant qu'il prend sa douche, mon frère…

12-12 Les vacances du passé.
Complétez les phrases pour parler de vos vacances dans le passé. Comparez vos souvenirs avec un/e partenaire.

MODÈLE Quand j'étais petit/e,…

É1 Quand j'étais petit/e, nous passions toujours l'été dans le Maine.

É2 Tu avais de la chance. Moi, je devais rester chez moi et souvent je suivais des cours d'été.

1. Quand j'étais petit/e,…
2. Quand j'allais au lycée,…
3. Quand les vacances arrivaient,…
4. Pendant que je m'amusais,…
5. Pendant que mes parents travaillaient,…
6. Quand il faisait plus chaud,…
7. Quand les vacances ont terminé,…

12-13 Des projets.
Qu'est-ce que vous ferez dans les situations suivantes ? Avec un/e partenaire, parlez de vos projets.

MODÈLE quand tu seras en vacances ?

É1 Qu'est-ce que tu feras quand tu seras en vacances ?

É2 J'irai en Californie pour travailler. Et toi ?

É1 Pas moi, je resterai chez mes parents.

1. quand tu seras en vacances ?
2. quand tu auras ton diplôme ?
3. quand tu auras un emploi ?
4. quand tu seras riche ?
5. quand tu auras 50 ans ?

Each of these exercises focuses on a particular time frame. Begin with an exercise including multiple tenses and ask students to identify the time frame: *Quand tu sortiras, je te donnerai un parapluie : futur ; Je bois du café pendant que je fais mes devoirs : présent ; En 2004, le Président Reagan meurt à l'âge de 93 ans : présent employé pour parler du passé ; Demain, ils partent en vacances : présent employé pour parler du futur ; Quand elle était petite, elle jouait de la clarinette : passé ; Je te téléphonerai quand je saurai quelque chose de plus : futur.* Alternatively, you could produce only the first part of the sentence and ask students to complete it in an appropriate manner.

12-11 As an alternative, put students in groups, asking them to generate numerous possibilities for each "multi-tasking" situation. Make this into a game by giving one point for each realistic situation suggested. The group with the most suggestions, and hence the most points, wins.

12-12 Review the formation of the *imparfait* before completing this exercise. Remind students that sentences may include both the *passé composé* and the *imparfait*.

12-13 Review the formation of the *futur simple* before completing this exercise.

Parlons

12-14 This oral presentation is most effective if accompanied by visuals, perhaps using a poster or presentational software. Encourage students to think about how they can best organize the information verbally and visually to make it appealing. If you decide to grade this activity, give points for the visual as well as the oral aspects of the presentation: visual appeal, organization, clarity, completeness, and comprehensibility (i.e., were classmates able to follow the presentation?). Encourage listeners to ask questions and provide feedback. See the *Chez nous* Companion Website for links to additional Francophone art museums.

12-14 Visites de musées

Avec un/e partenaire, présentez un musée d'art francophone à vos camarades de classe. Choisissez un musée de la liste ci-dessous, ou trouvez un autre musée qui vous intéresse particulièrement :

en Afrique :

> le musée Manéga [au Burkina Faso]
> le musée national du Mali
> le musée d'art africain de Dakar [au Sénégal]

au Canada :

> le musée d'art contemporain de Montréal
> le musée d'art de Joliette

en Europe :

> le musée d'art moderne et d'art contemporain de Liège [en Belgique]
> le musée de l'art Wallon [en Belgique]
> le musée d'art et d'histoire de Genève [en Suisse]
> le musée d'art et d'histoire de Neuchâtel [en Suisse]
> le musée d'art moderne Lille Mètropole [en France]
> le musée Chagall à Nice [en France]
> la Fondation Maeght [en France]

A. Avant de parler. Pour préparer un exposé ou un poster, cherchez des renseignements dans les catégories suivantes :

● Description générale :

MODÈLE ➤ Le musée national des beaux-arts du Québec contient plus de 20 000 œuvres qui viennent du Québec.

● Informations pratiques : l'adresse du musée, les jours et les heures d'ouverture, les tarifs

MODÈLE ➤ Le musée se trouve dans le Parc des Champs-de-Bataille dans la ville de Québec. Il est ouvert de 10 h à 18 h tous les jours de la semaine en été et jusqu'à 21 h le mercredi. C'est 10 $ pour les adultes, 5 $ pour les étudiants et 3 $ pour les enfants de 12 à 16 ans.

- Les collections

MODÈLE ➤ Il y a des collections d'art ancien, d'art moderne et d'art contemporain.

- Une ou deux œuvres d'art que vous allez présenter avec plus de détail

MODÈLE ➤ Nous avons choisi une sculpture et un paysage. La sculpture s'appelle *Soupir du Lac*. Louis-Philippe Hébert l'a sculptée en 1902. C'est la sculpture d'un Amérindien…

- Votre commentaire personnel

MODÈLE ➤ Nous pensons que ce musée serait intéressant à visiter. On peut y voir des œuvres d'artistes qui ne sont pas très connus en dehors (*outside of*) du Canada.

B. En parlant. Avec votre partenaire, faites votre exposé ou présentez votre poster à vos camarades de classe.

C. Après avoir parlé. Considérez les questions suivantes avec vos camarades.

1. Quels étaient les musées les plus intéressants ?
2. Quels musées est-ce que vous aimeriez visiter ? Pourquoi ?

Leçon 3 *Allons voir un spectacle !*

In conjunction with this **Points de départ**, you may wish to show the video segment *Le théâtre et l'opéra*, in which Christian, pictured below, describes visits to the theater and the opera in Nice. Point out that the verb *s'abonner*, which students learned in Ch. 11, L. 2, is equivalent to having "season tickets" to the theatre.

POINTS DE DÉPART

Le spectacle

TEXT AUDIO

Pour voir un ballet ou un opéra, vous pouvez aller au palais Garnier à Paris. Le palais Garnier est un chef-d'œuvre de l'architecture théâtrale du XIXe siècle. Dans la salle de spectacle, le plafond (*ceiling*) a été peint par Marc Chagall en 1964.

Christian et sa femme vont souvent au Théâtre National de Nice pour voir des spectacles. Ils y sont abonnés. Ce théâtre est assez moderne ; il a été construit en 1989.

Have students listen to the dialogue as they look at the text. Have students list activities Rémi and Sophie are considering: which would they like to do, and which have they decided not to do? Ask students to pick out expressions used to express the idea that one isn't interested in doing something or is hesitating: *pas si vite, je ne suis pas un fanatique de danse, ça (ne) me dit rien, ça risque d'être assez cher*; and expressions used to indicate this might be a possibility: *un spectacle plutôt, pourquoi pas, j'aimerais bien voir ça, ça ne fait rien, ça vaut le coup, après tout, on va se faire un petit plaisir*. Point out the structure *Ça fait longtemps que* and mention that it is a version of *il y a … que*, which students learned in Ch. 11, L. 3.

Rémi et Sophie planifient leur week-end.

SOPHIE : Alors, qu'est-ce qu'on fait samedi soir ?

RÉMI : Je ne sais pas. Tu as acheté *Pariscope* ?

SOPHIE : Bien sûr, mais… il y a beaucoup de choix. Qu'est-ce que tu veux faire ? voir un film ? aller à un concert ? aller au musée ?

RÉMI : Un spectacle plutôt, pourquoi pas une pièce de théâtre ?

SOPHIE : Ou un opéra… ou même un ballet ! Ça fait longtemps qu'on n'est pas allé voir un spectacle de danse.

RÉMI : Eh, pas si vite ! Tu sais bien que je ne suis pas un fanatique de danse. Regarde les pièces qui passent en ce moment.

SOPHIE : Eh bien, il y a les classiques à la Comédie-Française : *Dom Juan* de Molière et *Ruy Blas* de Victor Hugo.

RÉMI : Bof. Ça me dit rien.

SOPHIE : Tiens, à l'Opéra Bastille, il y a *La flûte enchantée* de Mozart ; j'aimerais bien voir ça !

RÉMI : Ah oui, moi aussi. Tu crois qu'il y aura encore des places ?

SOPHIE : Je vais téléphoner pour voir s'il en reste. Mais ça risque d'être assez cher.

RÉMI : Ça ne fait rien. Pour un bon opéra, ça vaut le coup. Après tout, c'est bientôt ton anniversaire. On va se faire un petit plaisir.

Vie et culture

Pariscope

Pariscope, c'est un périodique indispensable pour planifier une visite à Paris. Il sort tous les mercredis. Son nom est un jeu de mots qui combine « Paris » et « périscope ». Regardez le sommaire : quels renseignements est-ce que vous y trouverez ? Qu'est-ce que vous pourriez faire à Paris ? Qu'est-ce que vous choisiriez de faire ? Est-ce qu'il y a un magazine semblable pour votre ville ou votre région ? Qu'est-ce que vous faites pour trouver des idées, des renseignements, quand vous voulez sortir ?

You may wish to treat the sommaire *from* Pariscope *as a reading before addressing the questions in the* Vie et Culture. *Have students identify the time period and list the various types of activities covered in this publication: theater, music, cinema, etc.. If you have a copy of an old* Pariscope, *bring it to class to show students. You may wish to replay the video clip* Je lis la presse *from Ch. 11, especially the last section where the speaker shows and describes* Pariscope.

sommaire
mercredi 9 au mardi 15 juin 2004

12-15 Students may complete this activity in pairs. Give them time to scan the listings and decide on a few possibilities for each category.

12-15 Sorties. Regardez les pages *à venir* de *Pariscope* et suggérez une ou deux possibilités de sorties dans les catégories suivantes :

MODÈLE cinéma

➤ On pourrait voir *Ladykillers*. C'est en v.o. à UGC Ciné Cité Les Halles.

1. cinéma
2. théâtre
3. concerts
4. spectacles de danse
5. opéra
6. expositions

à venir

Pour faciliter vos sorties, une sélection des prochains spectacles et événements

4

Jacques Weber
« *Seul en scène* »
À partir du 22 juin
Gaîté-Montparnasse
01.43.22.16.18

Oncle Vania
D'Anton Tchekhov, Mise en scène Yves Beaunesne. Avec Roland Bertin. Du 10 juin au 24 juillet. Théâtre national de la Colline. 01.44.62.52.52

Réservez dès maintenant
Vos places de concerts

Patti Smith. Les 7 et 8 juillet. Le Bataclan
Lionel Richie. Le 30 septembre. Zénith
Yannick Noah. Le 2 octobre. Bercy (Palais Omnisports de Paris)
Michel Sardou. Du 6 octobre au 13 novembre. Olympia

Pour réserver…

08.92.68.33.68 ou www.ticketnet.fr ou www.francebillet.com et dans tous les points de ventes habituels.

Ladykillers
2004. 1 h 45. Comédie américaine en couleur de Joel et Ethan Coen avec Tom Hanks, Irma P. Hall, Marlon Wayans, J.K. Simmins, TziMa, Ryan Hurst.
*UGC Ciné Cité Les Halles 2 v.o. * MK2 Odéon 32 v.o.
*UGC Odéon 40 v.o. *UGC Montparnasse 39 v.f. *UGC Lyon-Bastille v.f.

Mother India
1960. 2 h 50. Drame indien en couleur de Mehboob Khan avec Nargis, Rajendra Kumar, Sunil Dutt, Raaj Kumar.
*Racine Odéon 34 v.o. *Publicis cinémas 50 v.o.
*L'Archipel Paris Ciné 67 v.o.

Poids léger
2004. 1 h 30. Comedie dramatique française en couleurs de Jean-Pierre Améris avec Nicolas Duvauchelle, Bernard Campan, Sophie Quinton, Maï Anh Lé.
UGC Ciné Cité Les Halles 2 * MK2 Odéon 32 *UGC Rotonde Montparnasse 41 *UGC Normandie 54*
Gaumont Opéra Français 58 * MK2 Bibliothèque 80

arts

Sun City de Peter Granser
photo
Galerie
Kamel Mennour
60, rue Mazarine (6e)

Montagnes célestes
monts et merveilles
peinture
Galeries Nationales
du Grand Palais
Jusqu'au 28 juillet

musique

Marc Berthoumieux
jazz
le 9 et 10 juillet
Sunset

Compagnie Instante Flamenco
« Barrio Flamenco »
danse
Jusqu'au 27 juin
Trianon

« Opéras en plein air »
« La Bohème »
musique
À partir du 18 juin
Parc de Sceaux

5

"Le choix de Pariscope"

👥 **12-16 Qu'est-ce qu'on fait ?** Avec un/e partenaire, proposez quelques sorties pour ce week-end.

MODÈLE É1 Qu'est-ce qu'on fait ce week-end ?

É2 Pourquoi pas aller au cinéma ? Il y a un nouveau film avec Nicole Kidman que j'aimerais voir.

É1 Non, ça me dit rien. Je n'aime pas cette actrice. Un concert plutôt ?

É2 Peut-être, mais…

12-16 Have several groups perform their dialogue in front of the class. To vary the activity, specify the number of activities that students must suggest before agreeing on one. You might also have students work with one partner for a specified length of time and then switch partners to determine with whom they have more compatible interests.

👥 **12-17 Les sorties.** Avec un/e partenaire discutez de vos préférences culturelles.

MODÈLE Est-ce que vous préférez le théâtre, le cinéma, la danse ou l'opéra ?

É1 J'adore l'opéra. Je sais que c'est un peu curieux parce que beaucoup d'étudiants n'aiment pas l'opéra. Mais moi, j'adore ça.

É2 Pas moi. J'aime plutôt la danse. Je fais du ballet depuis 12 ans et j'aime bien aller à des spectacles de danse.

É1 Tu y vas beaucoup ? Moi, je ne vais pas très souvent à l'opéra parce que c'est cher.

É2 Je vais assez souvent à des spectacles de danse sur le campus. Tu sais, ce n'est pas très cher et ça vaut vraiment le coup…

1. Est-ce que vous préférez le théâtre, le cinéma, la danse ou l'opéra ?

2. Est-ce que vous assistez régulièrement à des spectacles ? Combien de fois par semaine, par mois ou par an ? Avec qui est-ce que vous y allez ?

3. Combien d'argent est-ce que vous consacrez (*devote*) aux sorties culturelles par semaine ou par mois ?

4. Est-ce qu'il y a des spectacles sur votre campus qui ne sont pas très chers pour les étudiants ? Est-ce que vous y allez ? Pourquoi ?

5. Est-ce que vos habitudes culturelles sont différentes des habitudes de vos parents ? Est-ce qu'ils sont abonnés à un théâtre ou à un opéra par exemple ? Et vous ?

6. Est-ce que vous avez les mêmes préférences pour les spectacles de musique et de danse, les pièces de théâtre et les films que vos parents ou que vos amis ?

Une jeune actrice sur scène

FORMES ET FONCTIONS

Vue d'ensemble : les combinaisons de pronoms compléments d'objet

This feature is presented for recognition and limited productive control of the most frequent combinations, based on DeVito's (1997) extensive corpus of conversational French. Provide a general review of pronoun forms and placement before introducing the new material.

You have learned about direct- and indirect-object pronouns, **le**, **la**, **les**, **lui**, **leur**, **me**, **te**, **nous**, **vous**, the reflexive pronoun **se**, the partitive pronoun **en**, and the locative pronoun **y**. As you know, these pronouns are used to avoid repetition and are generally placed before the conjugated verb. There are some special rules to learn when you use two pronouns in the same sentence.

- Certain pronoun combinations are quite common in French:

  - The expression **il y en a**:

    —Il y a des places qui restent
    à 25 euros ?

    —Oui, **il y en a** quelques-unes,
    mais il faut vous dépêcher.

    —Are there any seats left for
    25 euros?

    —There are a few (of them) left,
    but you must hurry.

- Combinations involving a person and a thing (or things):

Tu **me le** prêtes ?	*Will you lend it to me?*
Je **te** l'offre.	*I'm giving it to you.*
Il **me** l'a déjà dit.	*He already told me.*
Tu pourrais **me** l'appporter ?	*Could you bring it to me?*
Ne **leur en** donne pas !	*Don't give them any!*

- When two object pronouns (*direct*, *indirect*, *reflexive*) occur together, their order is as follows:

subject	me te se nous vous	le/l' la les	lui leur	y	en	**verb**

Make it clear to students that statements such as *Voilà mon billet ; apporte-le-moi !* and *Donnez-nous-en !* would be considered impolite in many contexts. It is better for students to avoid these constructions and use the modal verbs they have learned: *Tu pourrais me l'apporter ?* Point out the use of the hyphen to connect pronouns to the verb in written affirmative commands and the elision of *moi* and *toi* before en. For the first-person singular imperative, native speakers will use both *Donne-le-moi !* and *Donne-moi-le !*

- In affirmative commands, the order is somewhat different:

Voilà mon billet ; apporte-**le-moi** !	*There's my ticket; bring it to me!*
Donnez-**nous-en** !	*Give us some!*
Voilà du café ; sers-**t'en** !	*Here's coffee; help yourself!*

verb	le la les	moi/m' toi/t' lui nous vous leur	y	en

À vous la parole

12-18 À un concert. Vous écoutez des gens qui parlent pendant l'entracte (*intermission*) d'un concert de musique classique. Avec un/e partenaire, imaginez de quoi ils parlent probablement.

MODÈLE Il y en a beaucoup.

   É1 Il y a beaucoup de musiciens.

   É2 Il y a beaucoup de violons.

1. Tenez, je vous le donne.
2. Non, il n'y en a pas.
3. Vous m'en donnez deux, s'il vous plaît ?
4. Est-ce que vous le lui avez donné ?
5. Passez-les-moi, s'il vous plaît.
6. Pas de problème ; il y en a pour tout le monde.

12-18 This exercise focuses on the comprehension of pronoun combinations. Before completing, brainstorm with students about what people do during intermission of a show and what they might talk about.

12-19 Il y en a combien ? Avec un/e partenaire, trouvez la bonne réponse.

MODÈLES musiciens dans un trio

   É1 Il y a combien de musiciens dans un trio ?

   É2 Il y en a trois.

   francophones au Québec

   É1 Il y a combien de francophones au Québec ?

   É2 Il y en a environ six millions.

1. musiciens dans un quartette
2. flûtes traversières dans un orchestre
3. semaines dans un semestre/trimestre
4. examens pour le cours de français
5. étudiants dans le cours de français
6. ordinateurs dans le labo de langues
7. étudiants à l'université
8. personnes dans votre ville

12-19 Vary by reversing question and response: for example, a student might say: *il y en a vingt* and a classmate might guess *ordinateurs au labo* or *étudiants dans la classe.* As another variation, have students tell how many numbers are found in: telephone numbers, social security numbers, dates, etc.; tell how many of certain items there are in their rooms — windows, electronic devices, magazines, etc.

12-20 Qui en prend ? Après le concert, il y a une réception pour les musiciens et leurs invités. On arrose (*toast*) l'événement avec du champagne. À qui est-ce qu'on en sert ?

MODÈLE au chef d'orchestre ?
   ➤ Oui, on lui en sert.

1. à sa mère ?
2. à son fils de sept ans ?
3. au pianiste ?
4. à ses amis ?
5. à sa femme ?
6. à sa petite fille ?
7. aux membres de l'orchestre ?

12-21 Donnant donnant. Est-ce que vous faites les choses suivantes pour votre colocataire ou votre meilleur/e ami/e et est-ce qu'il ou elle les fait pour vous ?

MODÈLES prêter l'ordinateur

É1 Tu lui prêtes ton ordinateur ?

É2 Non, je ne le lui prête jamais.

É1 Et il te prête son ordinateur ?

É2 Non, il ne me le prête jamais.

1. prêter l'ordinateur
2. prêter le dictionnaire de français
3. prêter des vêtements
4. prêter des livres
5. emprunter des CD
6. envoyer une carte d'anniversaire
7. s'offrir des cadeaux
8. demander des conseils

Lisons

Stratégie

When you approach a song or poem, consider the importance of repetition—of a word or image, as well as of a line or refrain. What is the immediate effect of such repetition? How does it enhance the overall thematic impact?

Ask students if they know the story of Carmen or have seen a production of the opera. You may wish to play the music as you treat the text in class. The aria L'amour est un oiseau rebelle is also known as the Habanera. The prelude to Act I is a well-known piece of music that would also give the students the flavor of the opera (it has been widely used in commercials).

12-22 Carmen

A. Avant de lire. You are going to read an excerpt from the libretto of the opera *Carmen*, written by Henri Meilhac and Ludovic Halévy and based on a short story by Prosper Mérimée, a nineteenth-century writer. Music for the opera was composed by Georges Bizet. *Carmen* is the story of a high-spirited gypsy who loves freely. The opera was at first poorly received because it shocked the morals of the Parisian bourgeoisie. Bizet died three months to the day after the opera opened on June 3, 1875, at the

Voici des personnages d'une représentation de Carmen en 1996. Est-ce que vous pouvez identifier Carmen ?

age of 37, and so did not live to see the enormous success of *Carmen*, which has become one of the most popular operas in the world.

The scenes you will read are from the first act and include the famous aria, *L'amour est un oiseau rebelle*, or *Havanaise*. They introduce the central characters: Carmen, a beautiful young woman who works in a cigar factory, and don José, the soldier who will become her lover. The opera ends tragically when a desperate don José finds no other solution but to kill Carmen, who no longer loves him.

Before you even read the text, you can identify lines that are repeated and notice by whom they are sung or spoken. Then, as you read, consider how these repetitions hold the story together and advance the action. Focusing on these repeated lines will help you to have an easier time understanding what is going on and also appreciating the passage as a whole.

B. En lisant. Répondez aux questions suivantes.

1. Quelle est la question que les jeunes gens posent à Carmen ? Quelle est sa réponse ?
2. Quel est le message dans la première strophe de la *Havanaise ?*
   « L'amour est un oiseau rebelle / que nul ne peut apprivoiser, / et c'est bien en vain qu'on l'appelle, / s'il lui convient de refuser ! »
3. Les paroles de Carmen : « Si tu ne m'aimes pas, / si tu ne m'aimes pas, je t'aime ! / Mais si je t'aime, / si je t'aime, prends garde à toi ! » évoquent l'intrigue centrale de l'opéra. Regardez les deux premiers vers : « Si tu ne m'aimes pas, je t'aime ! » Quelle action de Carmen illustre ces paroles ?
4. Comment est-ce que Carmen déclare son amour pour don José ?
5. Quelle est la première réaction de don José ?

En lisant, Key: 1) Les gens demandent si elle va les aimer et quand. Elle dit que peut-être, mais certainement pas aujourd'hui. 2) Le message c'est que l'amour n'est pas quelque chose qu'on peut prévoir. On ne peut pas forcer l'amour. 3) Quand Carmen choisit don José parce qu'il ne s'intéresse pas à elle. 4) Elle lui jette une fleur. 5) Il pense que c'est curieux parce qu'il ne l'a pas appelée. Il est certainement troublé aussi et il dit que Carmen doit être une sorcière.

Scène V

Les mêmes, Carmen

Les soldats *(B)*
Mais nous ne voyons pas la Carmencita[1] !

[Entrée de Carmen]

Jeunes gens *(T)*
La voilà !

Soldats *(B)*
La voilà !

Chœur *(SATB)*
La voilà
voilà la Carmencita !

Entre Carmen. Absolument le costume et l'entrée indiqués par Mérimée. Elle a un bouquet de cassie[2] à son corsage[3] et une fleur de cassie dans le coin de la bouche. Trois ou quatre jeunes gens entrent avec Carmen. Ils la suivent, l'entourent, lui parlent. Elle minaude[4] et caquette[5] avec eux. Don José lève la tête. Il regarde Carmen, puis se remet à travailler à son épinglette[6].

Les jeunes gens *(T) entrés avec Carmen*
Carmen ! sur tes pas nous nous pressons tous !

The libretto is reproduced here in its original form. Explain that words in italics are stage directions, and letters in parentheses refer to the various voice parts: bass, tenor, alto, soprano.

5

[1] la petite Carmen; *term of endearment*   [2] *tropical flower*   [3] *blouse*   [4] *flirts*   [5] *gossips*   [6] *long pin used to clean a rifle*

Carmen ! sois gentille, au moins réponds-nous,
et dis-nous quel jour tu nous aimeras !
Carmen, dis-nous quel jour tu nous aimeras !

Carmen *les regardant [gaîment]*
10   Quand je vous aimerai ? Ma foi[7], je ne sais pas…
Peut-être jamais !… peut-être demain !…
[résolument]
Mais pas aujourd'hui… c'est certain.

Havanaise
L'amour est un oiseau rebelle
que nul[8] ne peut apprivoiser[9],
15   et c'est bien en vain qu'on l'appelle,
s'il lui convient[10] de refuser !
Rien n'y fait, menace ou prière[11],
l'un parle bien, l'autre se tait[12] ;
et c'est l'autre que je préfère,
20   il n'a rien dit, mais il me plaît.

Chœur des cigarières[13] et jeunes gens *(SATT)*
L'amour est un oiseau rebelle
que nul ne peut apprivoiser,
et c'est bien en vain qu'on l'appelle,
s'il lui convient de refuser !

Carmen
25   L'amour ! l'amour ! l'amour ! l'amour !

Carmen
L'amour est enfant de Bohême,
il n'a jamais, jamais connu de loi,
si tu ne m'aimes pas, je t'aime,
si je t'aime, prends garde à toi !

Chœur (cigarières, jeunes gens et soldats) *(SATB)*
30   Prends garde à toi !

Carmen
Si tu ne m'aimes pas,
si tu ne m'aimes pas, je t'aime !

Chœur *(SATB)*
Prends garde à toi !

Carmen
Mais si je t'aime,
35   si je t'aime, prends garde à toi !

…

---

[7]*indeed*   [8]*personne*   [9]*tame*   [10]*suits one*   [11]*prayer*   [12]*is quiet*   [13]*women who work in the cigar factory*

Scène

Les jeunes gens *(T)*
Carmen ! sur tes pas nous nous pressons tous !
Carmen ! sois gentille, au moins réponds-nous !
réponds-nous, ô Carmen !
sois gentille, au moins réponds-nous !

Moment de silence. Les jeunes gens entourent Carmen, celle-ci les regarde l'un après l'autre, sort du cercle qu'ils forment autour d'elle et s'en va droit à don José, qui est toujours occupé de son épinglette.

Mélodrame

Carmen
Eh ! compère[14], qu'est-ce que tu fais là ?...   40

José
Je fais une chaîne du fil de laiton[15], une chaîne pour attacher mon épinglette.

Carmen *riant*
Ton épinglette, vraiment ! Ton épinglette... épinglier[16] de mon âme[17]...

Elle arrache de son corsage la fleur de cassie et la lance à don José. Il se lève brusquement. La fleur de cassie est tombée à ses pieds. Éclat de rire général ; la cloche de la manufacture sonne une deuxième fois. Sortie des ouvrières et des jeunes gens sur la reprise de :

Cigarières *(SA) [riant entre elles]*
L'amour est enfant de Bohême,
il n'a jamais, jamais connu de loi,
si tu ne m'aimes pas, je t'aime,   45
si je t'aime, prends garde à toi !

Carmen sort la première en courant[18] et elle entre dans la manufacture. Les jeunes gens sortent à droite et à gauche. Le lieutenant qui, pendant cette scène, bavardait[19] avec deux ou trois ouvrières, les quitte et rentre dans le poste après que les soldats y sont rentrés. Don José reste seul.

Scène VI

José

Dialogue

José
Qu'est-ce que cela veut dire, ces façons[20]-là ?... Quelle effronterie[21] !...
en souriant

---

[14]ami   [15]*bronze wire*   [16]*person who makes or sells pins*   [17]*soul*   [18]*running*   [19]parlait   [20]manières
[21]*impudence*

Tout ça parce que je ne faisais pas attention à elle !... Alors, suivant l'usage des femmes et des chats qui ne viennent pas quand on les appelle et qui viennent quand on ne les appelle pas, elle est venue...
Il regarde la fleur de cassie qui est par terre à ses pieds. Il la ramasse.
Avec quelle adresse elle me l'a lancée, cette fleur... là, juste entre les deux yeux[22]... ça m'a fait l'effet d'une balle[22] qui m'arrivait...
il respire le parfum de la fleur,
Comme c'est fort !... certainement s'il y a des sorcières[23], cette fille-là en est une.

50

[22]*a bullet*   [23]*witches*

En regardant de plus près. Explain that *l'un* and *l'autre* in the lines: « *l'un parle bien, l'autre se tait / et c'est l'autre que je préfère* » refer to different potential suitors for Carmen. You could also point out the *jeu de mots* in Carmen's statement: « *Ton épinglette, vraiment ! Ton épinglette... épinglier de mon âme...* » **Key:** 1) **La** c'est Carmen ou la Carmencita 2) un oiseau rebelle est libre et n'obéit pas à l'autorité, c'est vrai pour l'amour parce qu'on ne peut pas le forcer ; la répétition est appropriée pour une chanson et souligne un élément central de l'opéra : les sentiments amoureux de Carmen 3) Carmen est bohème et donc cette image est appropriée parce qu'elle décrit Carmen et exprime le fait qu'on ne peut pas contrôler l'amour   4) Carmen est venue vers don José sans qu'il l'appelle. Elle est donc comme un chat qui n'obéit pas à son maître mais qui fait ce qu'il a envie de faire. On dit souvent aussi que les chats ne viennent pas quand on les appelle et qu'ils vont surtout vers les gens qui n'aiment pas les chats   5) Don José compare la fleur à une balle de fusil qu'il reçoit entre les deux yeux. Cette image est très appropriée parce que don José est soldat et que le fusil est son instrument de combat. Notez que cette comparaison est très forte : c'est l'image de l'amour qui tue. La fleur qui est normalement associée à la fraîcheur, l'innocence, la légèreté, etc., est comparée à une balle qui donne la mort. Avec cette image, le thème de l'amour est associé, dès cette scène, à celui de la mort, ce qui annonce la fin tragique de la relation entre Carmen et don José : il va la tuer.

C. En regardant de plus près. Maintenant, examinez les aspects suivants du texte.

1. Dans la phrase **La voilà** à la ligne 2, qu'est-ce que **la** signifie ?
2. Carmen chante **L'amour est un oiseau rebelle** pour la première fois à la ligne 13. Qu'est-ce que cette image suggère pour vous ? À votre avis, pourquoi est-ce que cette image est répétée plusieurs fois ? Quel est l'effet de cette répétition ?
3. Dans la même chanson, Carmen proclame : **L'amour est enfant de Bohème** pour la première fois à la ligne 26. Réfléchissez à cette image. Qu'est-ce qu'elle veut dire ? Ce vers est répété dans cet extrait. À quel moment ? Pourquoi ?
4. Quand il reçoit la fleur de la part de Carmen, don José compare les actes de Carmen aux actes d'un chat. Quelle comparaison est-ce qu'il fait ? À votre avis, est-ce qu'il a raison de faire cette comparaison ? Pourquoi ?
5. Don José utilise une autre métaphore pour décrire la sensation qu'il éprouve après avoir reçu la fleur de Carmen. Quelle est cette métaphore ? Est-ce que c'est approprié ? Pourquoi ?

D. Après avoir lu. Discutez des questions suivantes avec vos camarades de classe.

1. Qu'est-ce que vous pensez de Carmen et de don José ? Qui semble le plus sympathique dans ce premier acte ? Pourquoi ?
2. Est-ce que vous avez déjà vu une représentation de l'opéra *Carmen* ? Si oui, partagez vos impressions avec vos camarades de classe. Sinon, est-ce que cet extrait vous donne envie de le voir ? Pourquoi ?

To expand on this activity, have students watch a video performance of the opera outside of class and write a critique of the performance. If *Carmen* happens to be playing in your area, you may consider having students attend the performance and write about or discuss it afterwards.

Venez chez nous !
Modes d'expression artistique

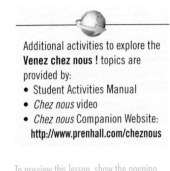

Additional activities to explore the **Venez chez nous !** topics are provided by:
- Student Activities Manual
- *Chez nous* video
- *Chez nous* Companion Website: http://www.prenhall.com/cheznous

To preview this lesson, show the opening montage for *Modes d'expression artistique*. Have students identify the various types of art and music they see expressed in the montage. Help students understand the meaning of the words *artisan* and *artisanat* through the **Observons** activity and the discussion of *artisanat* that follows.

Un artiste dessine devant une sculpture au Louvre.

Partout dans le monde, les gens s'expriment à travers l'art. Dans le monde francophone, on trouve une grande variété de modes d'expression artistique : des grands maîtres de l'impressionnisme français aux masques et sculptures africains en passant par l'art de style primitif haïtien. Côté musique, on trouve le zydeco en Louisiane, l'Afropop à Madagascar ou en Guinée ainsi que des grands compositeurs comme Bizet, Debussy et Ravel et les rappeurs de nos jours. Il y a également des nombreux artisans, c'est-à-dire des personnes qui créent des œuvres à la main que l'on peut acheter partout dans le monde francophone.

Observons

12-23 L'art et l'artisanat

Script for *Observons*
Note that the elements in brackets reflect standard usage and have been added to the written transcripts. They were not pronounced by the speaker(s) in question.

Bonjour, je m'appelle Sylviane Leibovitz. Je suis euh artisan ou artiste sérigraphe. Je suis une des dernières sérigraphes manuelles qui existent en France. Euh la sérigraphie se fait maintenant avec des appareils très sophistiqués. Euh moi, je travaille encore presque comme travaillaient les Chinois il y a trois mille ans avec des produits un peu plus modernes mais le principe est le même. Euh, tout ce que vous voyez dans ce magasin euh a été produit à l'atelier, là, à côté. Je travaille euh aussi en fonction des de ce qu'on me demande les les clients c'est-à-dire [que] je peux faire des choses tout à fait personnalisées euh dans le style de de ce qu'on me demande avec des motifs, des motifs tirés du folklore, ou de la nature ou des animaux ou bien enfin, tu sais, il y a des inspirations très très diverses… mais toujours en adaptant euh au goût de de la clientèle.

A. Avant de regarder. Est-ce que vous connaissez des artistes ou des artisans ? De quelles sortes ? Où est-ce qu'ils vendent leurs créations ? Écoutez Sylviane, une artiste sérigraphe à Seillans, qui nous montre son art, son atelier et son magasin à côté.

B. En regardant. Entourez toutes les réponses possibles.

1. Sylviane dit qu'elle est…
   a. une sérigraphe parmi (*among*) beaucoup d'autres en France.
   b. une des dernières sérigraphes manuelles en France.
   c. la meilleure artiste sérigraphe en France.

2. La sérigraphie moderne se fait…
   a. à la main.
   b. dans les usines.
   c. avec des machines sophistiquées.

3. Sylviane travaille comme…
   a. les Chinois il y a 3000 ans.
   b. les artisans du Moyen Âge.
   c. ses parents il y a 30 ans.

4. Elle réalise ses créations…
   a. chez elle dans une petite pièce.
   b. chez des amis qui ont un bon atelier.
   c. dans un atelier à côté de son magasin.

5. Elle peut faire des choses…
   a. personnalisées.
   b. dans le style demandé par ses clients.
   c. très sophistiquées.

6. Pour ses motifs, elle s'inspire…
   a. des fruits et légumes.
   b. du folklore.
   c. de la nature.
   d. des enfants.
   e. des animaux.

C. Après avoir regardé. Maintenant discutez des questions suivantes avec vos camarades de classe.

1. Est-ce que vous connaissiez la sérigraphie ? Qu'est-ce que vous pensez des objets que vous avez vus dans la vidéo ? Est-ce que vous aimeriez avoir un tee-shirt ou un foulard décoré selon la technique de la sérigraphie?
2. Sylviane dit qu'elle est « **artisan ou artiste sérigraphe** ». Quelle est la différence à votre avis ? Est-ce que vous pensez qu'elle est artiste ou plutôt artisan ? Pourquoi ?

Après avoir regardé. The definition of an artisan, according to the *Petit Robert*, is *Personne qui exerce un métier manuel pour son propre compte, aidée souvent de sa famille, de compagnons, apprentis*, etc. In France, the term is also used to describe the production of food in expressions such as *du pain artisanal, du chocolat artisanal*, and so forth. Question 2 leads into the discussion of art and *artisanat* below. Ask students their opinion as to whether a jewelry maker or a watch repair person, for example, is an artisan or an artist and why they think so.

Looking at the pictures, continue the discussion about the differences between *l'art* and *l'artisanat*. Is one more valued than the other? Is one more practical? Is there a cultural dimension to what is termed art? Use this as a springboard to discuss African art in particular and as an introduction to the **Lisons** that follows.

L'artisanat

Les artisans peuvent avoir un métier très créatif. En France comme dans d'autres pays francophones, les artisans travaillent à leur compte[1] et gagnent leur vie avec la vente des œuvres qu'ils ont créées. Dans certains cas, il peut être assez difficile de déterminer s'il s'agit d'art[2] ou d'artisanat, parce qu'après tout, le mot « artisan » contient bien le mot « art ». Par exemple, est-ce que les masques africains sont considérés comme de l'artisanat ou comme des œuvres d'art, ou comme les deux à la fois[3] ? Il est certain que ces masques ont inspiré des artistes modernes comme Pablo Picasso et Henri Matisse. Ils font partie aussi des grandes collections d'art dans certains musées du monde et dans des collections privées.

[1] *are self-employed* [2] *if it's about* [3] *at the same time*

Au Bénin, on peut trouver des belles tapisseries comme ce « Lion dans la forêt ».

Cet artisan haïtien vend ses tableaux aux amateurs (*aficionados*) d'art folklorique

Stratégie

Use what you know about the famous people, historical events, and general subject matter of an expository text to better understand the content. If you are not familiar with some of the people or events mentioned, consider doing preliminary research to familiarize yourself with them before you tackle the text.

12-24 You might have students look at the pictures and discuss similarities between the African masks and Picasso's paintings. Alternatively, have students read the text first, then look at and discuss the pictures. In 2002–2003, an exhibition on Picasso and Matisse was presented in London, Paris, and New York. A comprehensive Web site from this exhibition details the mutual influences of these artists. One section deals with how both Matisse and Picasso were inspired by African art and includes links to photographs of their work. See the *Chez nous* Companion Website for links.

Avant de lire. The text mentions the fifteenth and twentieth centuries. When Africa was first discovered by the West, its art was considered mainly a curiosity or the crude expression of an "inferior" people. In the twentieth century, modern artists such as Matisse and Picasso appreciated African art on its own terms and found inspiration in it to break with the canons of traditional art. The artists mentioned are Matisse, Picasso, Gauguin, and Vlaminck (an artist of Flemish origins born in Paris in 1876, contemporary to Matisse and Picasso). These artists can all be classified as representative of *l'art moderne*. *Cubisme* is the artistic movement mentioned in the text. The first cubist work is *Les demoiselles d'Avignon* by Picasso, shown in the textbook. The connection to African art is quite explicit in this painting.

En lisant, Key: 1) les navigateurs portugais au xvᵉ siècle   2) la puissance, l'abstraction, la richesse, la variété, la vitalité, les valeurs humanistes   3) pendant « les années folles »   4) dans des musées et des galeries d'art.

12-24 La découverte de l'art africain

Des masques africains

En 1907, Pablo Picasso lance un nouveau style, le cubisme, avec ce tableau, *Les demoiselles d'Avignon*. Regardez le visage de ces femmes. Quelle est la ressemblance avec les masques africains ?

Pablo Picasso, « Les demoiselles d'Avignon ». 1907. Art Resource. NY.

A. Avant de lire. This passage mentions several famous artists, artistic movements, and historical periods. Before reading, scan the text in order to identify the two centuries indicated by Roman numerals. How was exposure of the West to African culture changing during those centuries? Now, locate the names of four artists. Do you know these artists? What type of art are they associated with? Finally, look for the name of a specific artistic movement mentioned in the passage. What do you know about this type of art? Do you know any artists associated with this movement? Use this background information to help you understand the text as you read it more closely.

B. En lisant. Répondez aux questions suivantes.

1. D'après le texte, qui a découvert l'art africain et quand ?
2. Au vingtième siècle, plusieurs artistes ont reconnu les qualités de l'art africain. D'après le texte, quelles sont ces qualités ?
3. D'après le texte, quand est-ce que les grandes collections privées ont commencé ?
4. Où est-ce qu'on peut voir de l'art africain de nos jours ?

La découverte de l'art africain

À partir du XVe siècle les navigateurs portugais explorent l'Afrique et l'Europe et découvrent peu à peu l'art africain…

La véritable rencontre de l'art africain et de l'Europe se fait au XXe siècle.

Il y est décelé[1] une nouvelle écriture qui va répondre pour certains artistes comme Matisse, Picasso, Gauguin, Vlaminck, à leur préoccupation[2] et marquer le point de départ de la rupture avec les normes académiques. Ces artistes occidentaux sont les premiers à reconnaître autant de valeurs humanistes chez les artistes africains. Ils admirent la puissante abstraction de cette expression, la richesse, la variété, la vitalité qui rayonnent[3] dans cet art. Ils y trouvent une nouvelle source d'inspiration et même un style nouveau, le Cubisme, art abstrait qui casse le carcan[4] des lois imposées aux artistes depuis la Renaissance. 5 10

Enfin, les objets d'art africain vont être regardés comme des œuvres d'art. Il n'était plus[5] question de beauté, de laideur, mais bien d'une émotion directe, d'une manifestation spontanée. 15

L'engouement[6] pour l'art africain caractérise « les années folles ». C'est aussi bien sûr le temps des grandes collections privées.

De nos jours, des centaines d'expositions d'art africain sont organisées chaque année dans le monde. Des musées, des galeries d'art et des collectionneurs privés s'arrachent[7] ces œuvres dans les grandes ventes aux enchères[8] internationales et atteignent[9] des prix records. 20

[1] remarqué [2] concerns [3] shine forth [4] yoke [5] no longer [6] l'enthousiasme [7] grab up [8] auctions [9] reach

Source: Babette Gazeau, http://www.danse-africaine.net

C. En regardant de plus près. Maintenant, examinez les aspects suivants du texte.

1. Regardez l'expression **une nouvelle écriture** à la ligne 4. Vous savez que le mot **écriture** a un rapport avec le verbe **écrire**. Normalement, ce mot veut dire « les signes graphiques qu'on utilise pour écrire ». Mais ici ce mot a une autre signification. Quelle est la signification du mot **écriture** dans ce texte ?

2. Regardez le verbe **reconnaître** à la ligne 7. Vous remarquez sans doute le verbe **connaître** dans ce verbe. Si vous considérez en plus le contexte, qu'est-ce que ce verbe veut dire ?

3. À la ligne 14, on parle de **beauté** et de **laideur**. Ces deux noms sont dérivés d'adjectifs qui décrivent l'apparence physique. Quel est l'adjectif qui correspond à **beauté** ? Si vous savez que **laid** est un synonyme de l'adjectif **moche**, quelle est la signification de **laideur** ?

4. Regardez le mot **centaines** à la ligne 18. Quel chiffre est-ce que vous remarquez dans ce mot ? D'après cela, que veut dire la phrase : **des centaines d'expositions** ?

En regardant de plus près, Key: 1) It is used here in an abstract sense, to talk about the system artists will use in creating their art 2) to recognize 3) *beau, belle ; laid* : ugly, ugliness 4) *cent* : one hundred, hundreds.

D. Après avoir lu. Discutez des questions suivantes avec vos camarades de classe.

1. Est-ce que vous avez déjà vu des expositions d'art africain dans un musée ou dans une galerie ? Qu'est-ce que vous pensez des œuvres d'art que vous avez vues ?

2. À votre avis, est-ce que les civilisations africaines ont eu une influence sur d'autres mouvements artistiques en Occident ? Dans quels domaines ? Est-ce que cette influence est toujours reconnue ? Pourquoi, à votre avis ?

12-25 Have students exchange drafts and encourage them to revise based on peer feedback. You might collect the final version and create an "art catalogue" for the class. Alternatively, you might post the best compositions, accompanied by illustrations, on a class or school website.

12-25 L'art chez moi

A. Avant d'écrire. Pensez aux œuvres d'art et à leurs reproductions qu'il y a dans votre chambre, dans votre appartement ou chez vos parents et faites-en une petite liste. Est-ce que vous pouvez identifier un style ou des préférences pour un certain type d'art ou pour un certain artiste ? Quel est l'œuvre d'art que vous préférez ? C'est un tableau, une sculpture, un dessin, une photo ou… ? Pourquoi est-ce que vous aimez cette œuvre en particulier ?

B. En écrivant. Rédigez un texte de trois ou quatre paragraphes qui décrivent le(s) type(s) d'art et votre œuvre préférée chez vous.

1. Pour commencer, complétez ce tableau qui va vous aider à organiser votre texte.

Introduction Dites où se trouvent ces œuvres d'art et décrivez-les brièvement. **MODÈLE** ➤ l'art africain chez mes parents : des masques, des sculptures, des batiks, des tableaux	VOUS :
Paragraphe 2 Faites une description générale des différentes œuvres d'art. **MODÈLE** ➤ des masques accrochés (*hung*) aux murs : sculptés dans du bois, visages expressifs ; petites sculptures en bois : des femmes et des animaux ; des batiks et…	VOUS :

Paragraphe 3 Décrivez votre œuvre d'art préférée. **MODÈLE** ➤ le grand batik au-dessus (*above*) de la cheminée : une scène de village, beaucoup de couleurs très vives, des tons jaunes et orange	VOUS :
Paragraphe 4 Dites pourquoi vous aimez cette œuvre et expliquez son importance pour vous. **MODÈLE** ➤ le souvenir du village de ma grand-mère au Ghana	VOUS :

2. Maintenant, utilisez vos notes pour rédiger votre texte. Si vous voulez, vous pouvez accompagner votre texte d'une image ou d'une photo de votre œuvre préférée.

MODÈLE ➤ J'aime bien l'art africain. Mon père vient du Ghana et donc nous avons chez nous beaucoup d'œuvres d'art qui viennent de son pays. Il y a des masques, des sculptures, des batiks et des tableaux.

Nous avons des masques accrochés aux murs. Ils sont sculptés dans du bois et ils ont des visages très expressifs. Nous avons aussi beaucoup de petites sculptures en bois qui représentent des femmes et des animaux. J'aime bien la sculpture d'une femme avec un enfant à ses pieds. C'est très joli. Il y a aussi des batiks et…

J'aime surtout un grand batik que nous avons accroché au-dessus de la cheminée. C'est une scène de village avec des petites maisons, des baobabs, des femmes qui préparent à manger, des enfants qui jouent, des hommes qui travaillent dans les champs. Il y a beaucoup de couleurs très vives surtout dans des tons jaunes et orange. Je peux contempler ce batik pendant des heures.

Ce batik me rappelle le village de ma grand-mère au Ghana et quand je le regarde, je pense à elle…

C. Après avoir écrit. Relisez votre texte pour vérifier si vous y avez mis toutes les informations nécessaires. Rajoutez des détails intéressants et corrigez les fautes. Donnez un titre à votre texte et si vous avez une photo ou un dessin, écrivez une légende (*caption*). Ensuite, échangez votre texte avec vos camarades de classe. Est-ce que vous avez les mêmes goûts artistiques ou est-ce vos goûts sont différents ?

Play samples of Cajun and Zydeco music and have students identify the instruments they hear. To illustrate Cajun music, play songs performed by the great Cajun fiddler Dewey Balfa and various groups made up of his family members—the *Balfa Brothers* and *Balfa Toujours*. Zydeco musicians include the "king of Zydeco" Clifton Chénier, Beau Jocque, John Delafosse, or Buckwheat Zydeco. The popular group *BeauSoleil* plays Cajun and Zydeco music. See the *Chez nous* Companion Website for links to Web sites devoted to both types of music.

Les musiques cadienne et zydeco en Louisiane

Laissez les bons temps rouler !

BeauSoleil, un groupe de musiciens cadiens, en concert à New York. Michael Doucet joue du violon, Jimmy Breaux joue de l'accordéon et David Doucet joue de la guitare.

Les musiques cadienne et zydeco sont très populaires aux États-Unis comme en Europe pour danser et faire la fête. Mais il faut être en Louisiane pour aller à une soirée « fais dodo » où l'on peut manger les spécialités locales, écouter de la bonne musique, danser et s'amuser. Quelle est la différence entre ces deux musiques louisianaises ?

La musique cadienne est la musique des descendants d'Acadiens. Les Acadiens ont quitté le Canada et sont arrivés en Louisiane au dix-huitième siècle. Ils ont été chassés de leur région, l'Acadie (aujourd'hui le Nouveau-Brunswick et la Nouvelle-Écosse), parce qu'ils refusaient de se soumettre à l'autorité du gouvernement britannique. Cette musique a été influencée par la valse, la mazurka et la polka qui venaient d'Europe, et par la musique folklorique, country et swing d'Amérique du Nord. Les deux instruments essentiels sont le violon et l'accordéon. On y entend aussi souvent le triangle ou ti-fer (petit fer).

La musique zydeco, au rythme syncopé, a été créée par des Louisianais d'origine africaine. Ses influences sont plutôt le blues, le jazz et le rock. Au lieu du violon, c'est la guitare qui est l'instrument de base du zydeco à côté de l'accordéon. On y trouve aussi des guitares et des contrebasses électriques et même de la batterie.

Parlons

12-26 As a model, show the video clip *J'aime beaucoup le jazz.* Have students note expressions used by the speaker to describe this music and a particular musician, and have them note how she incorporates a musical selection into her description. See the IRM for suggestions on assessing an oral presentation. Encourage students to practice before making their presentation. Bring a CD player to class to allow them to share their musical sample. For a particularly large class, you may have students complete this assignment in pairs.

12-26 La musique que je préfère

Quel type de musique est-ce que vous préférez ? le jazz ? la musique pop ? le rock ? le rap ? la musique punk ? Qui est votre musicien/ne préféré/e ? Préparez un exposé sur la musique que vous aimez et présentez-le à votre classe.

A. Avant de parler. Pour faire un bon exposé oral, il faut se préparer à l'avance :

1. D'abord, pensez à la musique et/ou au musicien/à la musicienne que vous voudriez présenter.

2. Ensuite, pensez aux choses que vous aimeriez dire : par exemple, vous pourriez décrire le style de musique, parler un peu de son histoire et donner ses caractéristiques. Si vous présentez un/e musicien/ne ou un groupe, vous pourriez mentionner quelques aspects de sa biographie, parler de sa musique et dire pourquoi vous l'appréciez.

3. Il est important que vos camarades de classe puissent comprendre votre exposé, donc ne cherchez pas de mots compliqués dans le dictionnaire. Essayez plutôt d'utiliser des mots que vous connaissez et d'accompagner votre exposé avec des supports visuels.

4. Pour rendre votre présentation plus intéressante, pensez aussi à apporter quelques extraits que vous pouvez faire écouter aux autres.

B. En parlant. Présentez votre exposé à vos camarades.

MODÈLE ➤ D'habitude, je préfère le rock, mais la semaine dernière, je suis allée à un concert de *BeauSoleil* avec mes parents et j'ai décidé de faire mon exposé sur ce groupe cadien. Le musicien principal du groupe s'appelle Michael Doucet, il joue du violon et chante. Son frère, David Doucet, fait partie du groupe aussi. Lui, il joue de la guitare. Bien sûr, il y a un accordéon dans ce groupe ; c'est Jimmy Breaux, le petit-fils d'un célèbre joueur d'accordéon cadien, qui joue de l'accordéon pour *BeauSoleil*. Les autres musiciens du groupe jouent de la batterie, de la guitare électrique et aussi du violon.

Les musiciens de *BeauSoleil* jouent ensemble depuis 30 ans. Ils font de la musique traditionnelle et composent aussi des nouvelles chansons…

Le concert était super. Il y avait beaucoup d'énergie et d'enthousiasme. En fait, Michael Doucet a encouragé tout le monde à danser…

Voici un extrait d'une de leurs dernières chansons…

C. Après avoir parlé. Quelles présentations ont été particulièrement intéressantes ? Pourquoi ? Est-ce que vous aimeriez en savoir plus sur un style de musique ou sur un/e musicien/ne en particulier ?

Vocabulaire

TEXT AUDIO

Leçon 1

la musique	music
… classique	classical music
folklorique	folk music
traditionnelle	traditional music
un chœur	chorus
un opéra	opera
un orchestre	orchestra
une représentation	production
un trio	trio

quelques instruments (m.)	some instruments
la clarinette	clarinet
le clavier	keyboards
la flûte traversière	flute
la guitare basse	bass guitar
la guitare électrique	electric guitar
le trombone	trombone
la trompette	trumpet
le violon	violin
le violoncelle	cello

quelques verbes suivis de à ou de devant l'infinitif	verbs followed by à or de before an infinitive
accepter de	to accept
aider à	to help
arrêter de	to stop
continuer à	to continue
décider de	to decide
essayer de	to try
refuser de	to refuse
rêver de	to dream of

d'autres mots utiles	other useful words
C'est entendu	It's understood; OK
espérer	to hope

Leçon 2

les artistes et leur art	artists and their art
un dessin	sketch/drawing
un dessinateur/ une dessinatrice	draftsman/woman
un maître	master
une nature morte	still life
une œuvre d'art	work of art
un pastel	pastel
un paysage	landscape
peindre	to paint
un/e photographe	photographer
une photo(graphie)	photo(graph)
un portrait	portrait
un sculpteur	sculptor
un tableau	painting
une tapisserie	tapestry

pour parler d'art	to talk about art
la composition	composition
une couleur	color
sombre	somber, dark
vive	bright, vivid
l'utilisation de la lumière	use of light
s'intituler	to be titled
un reflet	reflection
le style	style
abstrait	abstract
cubiste	cubist
impressionniste	Impressionist
primitif	primitive
le sujet	subject

pour situer l'action dans le temps	to situate events in time
pendant que	while

Leçon 3

quelques expressions pour se décider	expressions used in deciding
après tout	after all
ça (ne) me dit rien	I'm not interested in that
ça (ne) fait rien	that doesn't matter
ça vaut le coup	it's worth it (fam.)
un choix	choice
être fanatique de	to be a fan of

pas si vite	not so fast
planifier	to plan
plutôt	rather
pourquoi pas ?	why not?
risquer de…	to run the risk of…
se faire un petit plaisir	to treat oneself

quelques expressions utiles	useful expressions
un chef-d'œuvre, des chefs-d'œuvre	masterpiece(s)
un spectacle	show

Appendices

Appendice 1 *Le plus-que-parfait*

- Use the **plus-que-parfait** to order events in the past or to describe an event in the past that occurred before another past event (even an implied event).

J'ai appris que l'exposition sur Renoir **avait** déjà **finie**.

I learned that the Renoir exhibit had already finished.

Quand on est arrivé, le spectacle **avait** déjà **commencé**.

When we arrived, the show had already begun.

Nous ne **nous étions** jamais **rencontrés**.

We had never met.

- To form the plus-que-parfait, use the imperfect of **avoir** or **être** and the past participle.

Point out to students that the final s on *partis* in the form *on était partis* reflects the fact that *on* is used here as the equivalent of *nous*. In actual fact, this usage is variable. Grammatical agreement can be made with *on* as either a singular or plural subject, even though the subject is semantically plural when used as the equivalent of *nous*.

j'**avais** joué	j'**étais** parti/e
tu **avais** joué	tu **étais** parti/e
il ⎫	il **était** parti
elle ⎬ **avait** joué	elle **était** partie
on ⎭	on **était** partis
nous **avions** joué	nous **étions** parti/e/s
vous **aviez** joué	vous **étiez** parti/e/s
ils ⎫	ils **étaient** partis
elles ⎬ **avaient** joué	elles **étaient** parties

- Use the **plus-que-parfait** to report what someone said they did in the past.

Elle dit : « Je lis le programme. »

Elle a dit qu'elle lisait le programme.

Elle dit : « J'ai lu le programme. »

Elle a dit qu'elle **avait lu** le programme.

A1-1, A1-2 These exercises test students' comprehension of the *plus-que-parfait*. To begin productive practice, use substitution drills: *J'avais déjà téléphoné ; lui — Il avait déjà téléphoné*, etc. *J'étais déjà partie ; nous — Nous étions déjà partis*, etc. Continue with meaningful practice — for example, having students describe things they had done before a particular time: *À huit heures… — je m'étais déjà levé*, etc. or *Quand mon colocataire est rentré… — j'avais déjà mangé ; j'avais terminé mes devoirs ; j'avais déjà fait la cuisine*, etc.

À vous la parole

A1-1 Histoire d'amour. Voici quelques moments dans la vie de Camille Claudel et d'Auguste Rodin, deux sculpteurs français qui étaient ensemble pendant dix ans. Ils se sont séparés définitivement en 1898. Est-ce que les actions suivantes se sont passées avant ou après cette rupture ?

MODÈLE Camille Claudel était allée à Paris pour sculpter.
➤ avant la rupture

1. Ils s'étaient souvent disputés.
2. Ils s'étaient rencontrés à Paris.
3. Elle a sculpté *la Vague*.
4. Elle avait commencé à travailler dans l'atelier (*studio*) de Rodin.
5. Ils étaient tombés amoureux.
6. Camille Claudel avait beaucoup influencé l'œuvre de Rodin.
7. Auguste Rodin est retourné à sa maîtresse Rose Beuret.
8. Camille Claudel est morte à l'âge de 79 ans.

A1-1 This simple discrimination drill is designed to help students learn to recognize the *plus-que-parfait* and its functional usage. To follow up, have students construct a narrative about the lives of these two sculptors and reorder the sentences logically. *Camille Claude était allée à Paris. Ils s'étaient rencontrés...* For further productive practice, put students in small groups and have them present the romantic histories of famous couples (e.g., Romeo and Juliette, Princess Di and Prince Charles) or of friends or family members.

A1-2 Une sortie.
Un après-midi, Pierre et Nathalie sont sortis ensemble. Pour chaque phrase, indiquez l'ordre des événements.

MODÈLE   Ils étaient arrivés au café quand Nathalie a suggéré d'aller voir une exposition.

1. Ils sont arrivés au café.   2. Nathalie a suggéré d'aller voir une exposition.

1. Ils avaient fini de boire leur café quand ils ont décidé d'aller au musée.
2. Avant de choisir une exposition, ils avaient acheté *Pariscope*.
3. Quand ils sont entrés dans le musée, la visite guidée avait déjà commencé.
4. Pierre avait déjà vu l'exposition, mais il n'a rien dit.
5. Après avoir vu l'exposition, ils sont allés chez Nathalie.
6. Ils avaient parlé de l'exposition avant de manger.
7. Pierre avait rangé la cuisine un peu avant de partir.

A1-3 Explications.
Complétez ces phrases avec un verbe au **plus-que-parfait** choisi de la liste suivante pour mieux expliquer la situation.

| acheter | étudier | lire | répéter |
| commencer | jouer | manger | terminer |

MODÈLE   Le groupe s'est arrêté de chanter plus tôt que prévu parce qu'il … à pleuvoir.
➤ avait déjà commencé

1. Nous sommes arrivés tellement en retard que le concert…
2. Quand le nouveau metteur en scène est finalement arrivé, les acteurs … pendant trois semaines.
3. C'est dommage mais quand il a téléphoné pour m'inviter au restaurant, j'…
4. J'ai perdu le *Pariscope* que mon copain…
5. Quand nous avons vu cet opéra, nous … le livret (*libretto*).
6. Quand elle est allée au Louvre, elle … l'histoire de l'art.
7. Il ne savait pas que ce groupe … ta chanson préférée.

For further practice with the *plus-que-parfait*, ask students to transform the following direct statements into indirect statements. *Laure a dit : « J'ai rencontré mes amis au concert hier soir. » —Laure a dit qu'elle avait rencontré ses amis au concert hier soir ; Kevin nous a dit : « Je n'ai pas pu inviter mes parents au spectacle. » Manon a dit : « Romain et moi n'avons pas aimé le concert. » Pauline a dit : « J'ai adoré ce concert de jazz. » Hugo a écrit : « La mise en scène de l'opéra a été magnifique. » Gregory nous a dit : « Mes parents sont venus pour l'exposition. » Aurore a écrit : « J'ai obtenu le rôle principal dans la pièce de ce semestre. »*

Appendice 2 *Le futur antérieur*

This point was introduced in Ch. 12, L. 2. It is important to remind students that these types of sentences contain two future tenses in French; either the *futur simple* when the events are simultaneous, or the *futur antérieur* and the *futur simple* when one action in the future precedes the other. This usage is quite different from English and bears stressing.

- Remember that when two future events are simultaneous, the future tense is used in both clauses.

Dès que j'**aurai** vingt-et-un ans, j'**irai** au nouveau club.	*As soon as I'm twenty-one, I'll go to the new club.*

- When one future event will have been completed before a second future event occurs, use the **futur antérieur** to convey the order of these events. Use the **futur antérieur** in a clause introduced by an expression such as **aussitôt que**, **dès que**, **quand**, or **lorsque** to express the earlier event.

Quand Rachid **aura terminé** cette sculpture, il la montrera à sa femme.	*When Rachid has finished this sculpture, he'll show it to his wife.*
Nous irons voir l'exposition **aussitôt qu'**il **aura terminé** ses devoirs.	*We will go to see the exhibit as soon as he has finished his homework.*
Dès que nous **aurons dîné**, nous sortirons.	*As soon as we have eaten, we will go out.*

- The **futur antérieur** may also be used with a temporal expression to indicate that an action will have been finished at that moment.

En l'an 2050 on **aura** tout **vu**.	*In the year 2050, we will have seen it all.*
J'espère que la pièce **aura fini avant dix heures et demie**.	*I hope that the play will have ended by 10:30.*

- To form the **futur antérieur**, use the future tense of **avoir** or **être** plus the past participle.

Point out to students that the final *s* on *partis* in the form *on sera partis* reflects the fact that *on* is used here as the equivalent of *nous*. In actual fact, this usage is variable.

Grammatical agreement can be made with *on* as either a singular or plural subject, even though the subject is semantically plural when used as the equivalent of *nous*.

j'**aurai** joué	je **serai** parti/e
tu **auras** joué	tu **seras** parti/e
il	il **sera** parti
elle ⎫ **aura** joué	elle **sera** partie
on ⎭	on **sera** partis
nous **aurons** joué	nous **serons** parti/e/s
vous **aurez** joué	vous **serez** parti/e/s
ils ⎫ **auront** joué	ils **seront** partis
elles ⎭	elles **seront** parties

À vous la parole

A2-1 Des projets. Qu'est-ce que vous ferez dans les situations suivantes ? Avec un/e partenaire, parlez de vos projets.

Begin practice with a simple substitution drill. Have students change short sentences from the *futur simple* to the *futur antérieur*. *Il rentrera. — Il sera rentré ; On viendra. — On sera venus ;* etc.

MODÈLE   Dès que j'aurai terminé mes devoirs ce soir,…

      É1   Dès que j'aurai terminé mes devoirs ce soir, je regarderai un peu la télé. J'adore Jay Leno.

      É2   Pas moi. Je préfère dormir. Dès que j'aurai terminé mes devoirs, je me coucherai.

1. Aussitôt que je me serai réveillé/e demain matin, je…
2. Dès que le week-end sera arrivé, je…
3. Lorsque j'aurai fini avec les examens finals, je…
4. Quand les grandes vacances seront arrivées, je…
5. Lorsque j'aurai terminé mes études, je…
6. Quand j'aurai trouvé un bon travail, je…
7. Quand j'aurai rencontré le/la partenaire idéal/e, je…
8. Quand j'aurai eu des enfants, je…

A2-2 Allons au musée. Complétez chaque phrase logiquement en employant le **futur antérieur**.

MODÈLE   Il y aura des critiques dans le journal dès que l'exposition…
    ➤ Il y aura des critiques dans le journal dès que l'exposition aura commencé.

1. Il y aura des critiques dans le journal dès que l'exposition…
2. J'obtiendrai mon billet avec une réduction aussitôt que je…
3. Nous achèterons le programme quand nous…
4. Nous sortirons dans le jardin dès qu'on…
5. Vous pourrez entrer dans le musée lorsque vous…
6. Vous pourrez visiter librement les salles quand la visite guidée…
7. On prendra un café dès qu'on…
8. Je mettrai ma nouvelle affiche au mur dès que…
9. On achètera des cartes postales lorsqu'on…

a. arriver dans la boutique du musée
b. arriver devant la cafétéria
c. terminer
d. montrer ma carte d'étudiant
e. visiter toutes les salles
f. acheter des billets à l'entrée
g. rentrer à la maison
h. commencer
i. arriver à la caisse

A2-3 En l'an 2015. Qu'est-ce que vous aurez fait en l'an 2015 ? Parlez de votre avenir avec un/e partenaire.

When each pair has finished, compare answers among the whole class. Who has the most interesting plans for the future? the most realistic? the most ambitious?

MODÈLE   É1   En l'an 2015, j'aurai terminé mes études et je serai médecin. Je me serai marié et j'habiterai à New York avec ma femme.

      É2   Et moi, en l'an 2015, j'aurai gagné un million de dollars avec ma propre société et je serai très riche. J'aurai acheté un appartement à Paris, une grande maison à Long Island et une maison en Floride pour les vacances.

Appendice 3 *Le passé du conditionnel*

- Use the past conditional to express a hypothetical action or event in the past. In this case, the past conditional is often used with such expressions as **à ta place**, **à votre place**, or with the stressed pronouns **moi**, **nous**.

À ta place, je n'**aurais** pas **dépensé** 60 euros pour une place à l'opéra.	*If I were you, I wouldn't have spent 60 euros for an opera ticket.*
Moi, je **serais sortie** quand même.	*I still would have gone out.*

- To express what should have or could have been done in the past, use the past conditional of **devoir** or **pouvoir**.

Il s'est trompé pendant le concert. Il **aurait dû** répéter plus.	*He made a mistake during the concert. He should have practiced more.*
Je ne suis pas allée au théâtre parce que j'avais du retard, mais j'**aurais pu**.	*I didn't go to the theater because I was late, but I could have.*

Although standard English employs the same sequence of tenses, colloquial American usage often differs, for example: "If I would have known, I would not have come." Students should be aware of this and be careful to use the appropriate tenses in French.

- You have learned that the conjunction **si** is used in clauses expressing a condition followed by another clause expressing the result. To express a past hypothetical situation, use **si** plus the **plus-que-parfait** followed by the result in the past conditional.

Si j'**avais su**, je ne **serais** pas **venu**.	*If I had known, I would not have come.*
Si on **avait eu** de l'argent, on **aurait acheté** des places pour l'opéra.	*If we had had money, we would have bought tickets for the opera.*

- To form the past conditional, use the conditional of **avoir** or **être** plus the past participle. The forms of the past conditional are illustrated with the verbs **devoir** and **partir**.

Point out to students that the final *s* on *partis* in the form *on serait partis* reflects the fact that *on* is used here as the equivalent of *nous*. In actual fact, this usage is variable.

Grammatical agreement can be made with *on* as either a singular or plural subject, even though the subject is semantically plural when used as the equivalent of *nous*.

j'**aurais** dû	je **serais** parti/e
tu **aurais** dû	tu **serais** parti/e
il	il **serait** parti
elle } **aurait** dû	elle **serait** partie
on	on **serait** partis
nous **aurions** dû	nous **serions** parti/e/s
vous **auriez** dû	vous **seriez** parti/e/s
ils	ils **seraient** partis
elles } **auraient** dû	elles **seraient** parties

À vous la parole

A3-1 Pour être un grand artiste. Dites ce que ces gens auraient dû faire ou auraient pu faire pour être un grand artiste.

MODÈLE Sophie n'a pas pris de leçons de chant.
➤ Elle aurait dû prendre des leçons de chant.
OU Elle aurait pu prendre des leçons de chant.

1. Hélène n'a pas beaucoup joué de violon quand elle était petite.
2. Ces peintres n'ont pas utilisé beaucoup de couleurs.
3. Je ne suis pas allée à toutes les répétitions (*rehearsals*).
4. Les garçons n'ont pas bien appris leurs rôles.
5. Suzanne n'a pas considéré l'opinion des critiques.
6. Elle n'a pas eu le temps de se concentrer.
7. Nous n'avons pas trouvé d'inspiration.

A3-2 Des conseils tardifs. Vos amis n'ont pas de chance. Ils ont raté un bon spectacle pour des raisons diverses. Dites ce qu'ils auraient pu faire pour pouvoir y aller.

MODÈLE J'avais perdu les billets pour le spectacle.
➤ Tu aurais pu les garder dans un endroit sûr.

1. Elle ne savait pas à quelle heure le spectacle commençait.
2. Nous n'avions pas assez d'argent.
3. Janique avait trop de devoirs à faire.
4. Mes amis ne savaient pas où se trouvait le théâtre.
5. Mon père ne voulait pas que j'y aille un mardi soir.
6. Nous sommes arrivés en retard pour le premier acte.
7. On n'aimait pas le premier groupe.
8. Elles ne savaient pas le prix des billets.

A3-3 Des regrets. Ce week-end ne s'est pas bien passé. Avec un partenaire, dites ce que ces personnes auraient pu faire selon les cas suivants.

MODÈLE S'il avait fait beau ce week-end…

É1 … j'aurais joué au tennis avec ma copine.
É2 … et moi, j'aurais fait de la planche à voile.

1. Si j'avais eu de l'argent…
2. Si j'avais eu plus de temps libre…
3. Si je n'avais pas eu cet examen de philosophie à préparer…
4. Si mes parents étaient venus ce week-end…
5. Si mes copains avaient voulu aller à ce concert avec moi…
6. Si mon prof de français avait été plus raisonnable…
7. Si l'examen n'avait pas duré si longtemps…

Begin practice by having students transform the conditional to the past conditional in short sentences: *À ta place, je prendrais le bus.* —*À ta place, j'aurais pris le bus,* etc.

A3-1, A3-2 These exercises offer limited practice with the conditional past by limiting students to the commonly used verbs *pouvoir* and *devoir* in the conditional past. Ex. A3-3 offers more varied, open-ended practice.

A3-3 All of these hypothetical situations in the past could have more than one answer. Begin by brainstorming as a class possible answers to a few of the situations. Then put students in pairs or small groups to compare their reactions to each situation. You could vary the activity by providing the result clause and have students suggest a plausible reason, for example, *j'aurais dansé jusqu'à trois heures du matin.* —*si je n'avais pas eu mal aux pieds ; si je n'avais pas porté des nouvelles chaussures ; si le club n'était pas fermé à deux heures du matin,* etc.

Appendice 4 Verbes réguliers

VERBE INFINITIF	PRÉSENT DE L'INDICATIF	PRÉSENT DU SUBJONCTIF	IMPARFAIT	PASSÉ COMPOSÉ	FUTUR	CONDITIONNEL	IMPÉRATIF
verbes -er							
regarder *to look at*	je regarde tu regardes il regarde nous regardons vous regardez ils regardent	que je regarde que tu regardes qu'il regarde que nous regardions que vous regardiez qu'ils regardent	je regardais tu regardais il regardait nous regardions vous regardiez ils regardaient	j'ai regardé tu as regardé il a regardé nous avons regardé vous avez regardé ils ont regardé	je regarderai tu regarderas il regardera nous regarderons vous regarderez ils regarderont	je regarderais tu regarderais il regarderait nous regarderions vous regarderiez ils regarderaient	regarde regardons regardez
verbes -ir							
dormir *to sleep*	je dors tu dors il dort nous dormons vous dormez ils dorment	que je dorme que tu dormes qu'il dorme que nous dormions que vous dormiez qu'ils dorment	je dormais tu dormais il dormait nous dormions vous dormiez ils dormaient	j'ai dormi tu as dormi il a dormi nous avons dormi vous avez dormi ils ont dormi	je dormirai tu dormiras il dormira nous dormirons vous dormirez ils dormiront	je dormirais tu dormirais il dormirait nous dormirions vous dormiriez ils dormiraient	dors dormons dormez
verbes -ir / -iss							
choisir *to choose*	je choisis tu choisis il choisit nous choisissons vous choisissez ils choisissent	que je choisisse que tu choisisses qu'il choisisse que nous choisissions que vous choisissiez qu'ils choisissent	je choisissais tu choisissais il choisissait nous choisissions vous choisissiez ils choisissaient	j'ai choisi tu as choisi il a choisi nous avons choisi vous avez choisi ils ont choisi	je choisirai tu choisiras il choisira nous choisirons vous choisirez ils choisiront	je choisirais tu choisirais il choisirait nous choisirions vous choisiriez ils choisiraient	choisis choisissons choisissez
verbes -re							
attendre *to wait for*	j'attends tu attends il attend nous attendons vous attendez ils attendent	que j'attende que tu attendes qu'il attende que nous attendions que vous attendiez qu'ils attendent	j'attendais tu attendais il attendait nous attendions vous attendiez ils attendaient	j'ai attendu tu as attendu il a attendu nous avons attendu vous avez attendu ils ont attendu	j'attendrai tu attendras il attendra nous attendrons vous attendrez ils attendront	j'attendrais tu attendrais il attendrait nous attendrions vous attendriez ils attendraient	attends attendons attendez
verbes pronominaux							
se laver *to wash oneself*	je me lave tu te laves il se lave nous nous lavons vous vous lavez ils se lavent	que je me lave que tu te laves qu'il se lave que nous nous lavions que vous vous laviez qu'ils se lavent	je me lavais tu te lavais il se lavait nous nous lavions vous vous laviez ils se lavaient	je me suis lavé/e tu t'es lavé/e il s'est lavé/elle s'est lavée nous nous sommes lavé/e/s vous vous êtes lavé/e/s ils/elles se sont lavés/lavées	je me laverai tu te laveras il se lavera nous nous laverons vous vous laverez ils se laveront	je me laverais tu te laverais il se laverait nous nous laverions vous vous laveriez ils se laveraient	lave-toi lavons-nous lavez-vous

Comme **dormir** : *s'endormir, partir, ressentir, se sentir, servir, sortir.*   *Comme* **choisir** : *désobéir à, finir, grandir, grossir, maigrir, obéir à, pâlir, punir, réfléchir à, réussir à, rougir.*
Comme **attendre** : *descendre, se défendre, (s')entendre, perdre, rendre à, rendre visite à, répondre à, vendre.*

Verbes irréguliers en -er

VERBE INFINITIF	PRÉSENT DE L'INDICATIF	PRÉSENT DU SUBJONCTIF	IMPARFAIT	PASSÉ COMPOSÉ	FUTUR	CONDITIONNEL	IMPÉRATIF
verbes -er							
acheter to buy	j'achète tu achètes il achète nous achetons vous achetez ils achètent	que j'achète que tu achètes qu'il achète que nous achetions que vous achetiez qu'ils achètent	j'achetais	j'ai acheté	j'achèterai	j'achèterais	achète achetons achetez
appeler to call	j'appelle tu appelles il appelle nous appelons vous appelez ils appellent	que j'appelle que tu appelles qu'il appelle que nous appelions que vous appeliez qu'ils appellent	j'appelais	j'ai appelé	j'appellerai	j'appellerais	appelle appelons appelez
commencer to call	je commence tu commences il commence nous commençons vous commencez ils commencent	que je commence que tu commences qu'il commence que nous commencions que vous commenciez qu'ils commencent	je commençais nous commencions	j'ai commencé	je commencerai	je commencerais	commence commençons commencez
s'essuyer to wipe, to dry oneself	je m'essuie tu t'essuies il s'essuie nous nous essuyons vous vous essuyez ils s'essuient	que je m'essuie que tu t'essuies qu'il s'essuie que nous nous essuyions que vous vous essuyiez qu'ils s'essuient	je m'essuyais	je me suis essuyé/e	je m'essuierai	je m'essuierais	essuie-toi essuyons-nous essuyez-vous
manger to eat	je mange tu manges il mange nous mangeons vous mangez ils mangent	que je mange que tu manges qu'il mange que nous mangions que vous mangiez qu'ils mangent	je mangeais nous mangions	j'ai mangé	je mangerai	je mangerais	mange mangeons mangez
préférer to prefer	je préfère tu préfères il préfère nous préférons vous préférez ils préfèrent	que je préfère que tu préfères qu'il préfère que nous préférions que vous préfériez qu'ils préfèrent	je préférais	j'ai préféré	je préférerai	je préférerais	préfère préférons préférez

Comme **acheter** : amener, geler, (se) lever, (se) promener.   Comme **appeler** : épeler, jeter, se rappeler.   Comme **commencer** : recommencer.   Comme **s'essuyer** : s'ennuyer, essayer, essuyer, nettoyer, payer.
Comme **manger** : (s')arranger, exiger, loger, nager, partager, protéger, ranger, voyager.   Comme **préférer** : compléter, espérer, s'inquiéter, posséder, protéger, répéter, suggérer.

D'autres verbes irréguliers

VERBE INFINITIF	PRÉSENT DE L'INDICATIF	PRÉSENT DU SUBJONCTIF	IMPARFAIT	PASSÉ COMPOSÉ	FUTUR	CONDITIONNEL	IMPÉRATIF
aller to go	je vais / tu vas / il va / nous allons / vous allez / ils vont	que j'aille / que tu ailles / qu'il aille / que nous allions / que vous alliez / qu'ils aillent	j'allais	je suis allé/e	j'irai	j'irais	va / allons / allez
avoir to have	j'ai / tu as / il a / nous avons / vous avez / ils ont	que j'aie / que tu aies / qu'il ait / que nous ayons / que vous ayez / qu'ils aient	j'avais	j'ai eu	j'aurai	j'aurais	aie / ayons / ayez
boire to drink	je bois / tu bois / il boit / nous buvons / vous buvez / ils boivent	que je boive / que tu boives / qu'il boive / que nous buvions / que vous buviez / qu'ils boivent	je buvais	j'ai bu	je boirai	je boirais	bois / buvons / buvez
connaître to know, be acquainted with	je connais / tu connais / il connaît / nous connaissons / vous connaissez / ils connaissent	que je connaisse / que tu connaisses / qu'il connaisse / que nous connaissions / que vous connaissiez / qu'ils connaissent	je connaissais	j'ai connu	je connaîtrai	je connaîtrais	connais / connaissons / connaissez
courir to run	je cours / tu cours / il court / nous courons / vous courez / ils courent	que je coure / que tu coures / qu'il coure / que nous courions / que vous couriez / qu'ils courent	je courais	j'ai couru	je courrai	je courrais	cours / courons / courez
croire to believe	je crois / tu crois / il croit / nous croyons / vous croyez / ils croient	que je croie / que tu croies / qu'il croie / que nous croyions / que vous croyiez / qu'ils croient	je croyais	j'ai cru	je croirai	je croirais	crois / croyons / croyez
devoir must, to have to; to owe	je dois / tu dois / il doit / nous devons / vous devez / ils doivent	que je doive / que tu doives / qu'il doive / que nous devions / que vous deviez / qu'ils doivent	je devais	j'ai dû	je devrai	je devrais	
dire to say	je dis / tu dis / il dit / nous disons / vous dites / ils disent	que je dise / que tu dises / qu'il dise / que nous disions / que vous disiez / qu'ils disent	je disais	j'ai dit	je dirai	je dirais	dis / disons / dites
se distraire to amuse oneself	je me distrais / tu te distrais / il se distrait / nous nous distrayons / vous vous distrayez / ils se distraient	que je me distraie / que tu te distraies / qu'il se distraie / que nous nous distrayions / que vous vous distrayiez / qu'ils se distraient	je me distrayais	je me suis distrait/e	je me distrairai	je me distrairais	distrais-toi / distrayons-nous / distrayez-vous
écrire to write	j'écris / tu écris / il écrit / nous écrivons / vous écrivez / ils écrivent	que j'écrive / que tu écrives / qu'il écrive / que nous écrivions / que vous écriviez / qu'ils écrivent	j'écrivais	j'ai écrit	j'écrirai	j'écrirais	écris / écrivons / écrivez
envoyer to send	j'envoie / tu envoies / il envoie / nous envoyons / vous envoyez / ils envoient	que j'envoie / que tu envoies / qu'il envoie / que nous envoyions / que vous envoyiez / qu'ils envoient	j'envoyais	j'ai envoyé	j'enverrai	j'enverrais	envoie / envoyons / envoyez

Comme **devoir** : recevoir (passé composé : j'ai reçu).   Comme **écrire** : décrire.

VERBE INFINITIF	PRÉSENT DE L'INDICATIF	PRÉSENT DU SUBJONCTIF	IMPARFAIT	PASSÉ COMPOSÉ	FUTUR	CONDITIONNEL	IMPÉRATIF
être to be	je suis tu es il est nous sommes vous êtes ils sont	que je sois que tu sois qu'il soit que nous soyons que vous soyez qu'ils soient	j'étais	j'ai été	je serai	je serais	sois soyons soyez
faire to do, make	je fais tu fais il fait nous faisons vous faites ils font	que je fasse que tu fasses qu'il fasse que nous fassions que vous fassiez qu'ils fassent	je faisais	j'ai fait	je ferai	je ferais	fais faisons faites
falloir to be necessary	il faut	qu'il faille	il fallait	il a fallu	il faudra	il faudrait	
s'instruire to educate oneself	je m'instruis tu t'instruis il s'instruit nous nous instruisons vous vous instruisez ils s'instruisent	que je m'instruise que tu t'instruises qu'il s'instruise que nous nous instruisions que vous vous instruisiez qu'ils s'instruisent	je m'instruisais	je me suis instruit/e	je m'instruirai	je m'instruirais	instruis-toi instruisons-nous instruisez-vous
lire to read	je lis tu lis il lit nous lisons vous lisez ils lisent	que je lise que tu lises qu'il lise que nous lisions que vous lisiez qu'ils lisent	je lisais	j'ai lu	je lirai	je lirais	lis lisons lisez
mettre to put, put on	je mets tu mets il met nous mettons vous mettez ils mettent	que je mette que tu mettes qu'il mette que nous mettions que vous mettiez qu'ils mettent	je mettais	j'ai mis	je mettrai	je mettrais	mets mettons mettez
mourir to die	je meurs tu meurs il meurt nous mourons vous mourez ils meurent	que je meure que tu meures qu'il meure que nous mourions que vous mouriez qu'ils meurent	je mourais	je suis mort/e	je mourrai	je mourrais	meurs mourons mourez
naître to be born	je nais tu nais il naît nous naissons vous naissez ils naissent	que je naisse que tu naisses qu'il naisse que nous naissions que vous naissiez qu'ils naissent	je naissais	je suis né/e	je naîtrai	je naîtrais	nais naissons naissez
ouvrir to open	j'ouvre tu ouvres il ouvre nous ouvrons vous ouvrez ils ouvrent	que j'ouvre que tu ouvres qu'il ouvre que nous ouvrions que vous ouvriez qu'ils ouvrent	j'ouvrais	j'ai ouvert	j'ouvrirai	j'ouvrirais	ouvre ouvrons ouvrez
peindre to paint	je peins tu peins il peint nous peignons vous peignez ils peignent	que je peigne que tu peignes qu'il peigne que nous peignions que vous peigniez qu'ils peignent	je peignais	j'ai peint	je peindrai	je peindrais	peins peignons peignez
pleuvoir to rain	il pleut	qu'il pleuve	il pleuvait	il a plu	il pleuvra	il pleuvrait	
pouvoir to be able to	je peux tu peux il peut nous pouvons vous pouvez ils peuvent	que je puisse que tu puisses qu'il puisse que nous puissions que vous puissiez qu'ils puissent	je pouvais	j'ai pu	je pourrai	je pourrais	
prendre to take	je prends tu prends il prend nous prenons vous prenez ils prennent	que je prenne que tu prennes qu'il prenne que nous prenions que vous preniez qu'ils prennent	je prenais	j'ai pris	je prendrai	je prendrais	prends prenons prenez

Comme **lire** : relire. Comme **mettre** : permettre, promettre, remettre. Comme **ouvrir** : couvrir, découvrir, offrir. Comme **peindre** : éteindre. Comme **prendre** : apprendre, comprendre, surprendre.

VERBE INFINITIF	PRÉSENT DE L'INDICATIF	PRÉSENT DU SUBJONCTIF	IMPARFAIT	PASSÉ COMPOSÉ	FUTUR	CONDITIONNEL	IMPÉRATIF
réduire to reduce	je réduis tu réduis il réduit / nous réduisons vous réduisez ils réduisent	que je réduise que tu réduises qu'il réduise / que nous réduisions que vous réduisiez qu'ils réduisent	je réduisais	j'ai réduit	je réduirai	je réduirais	réduis réduisons réduisez
savoir to know	je sais tu sais il sait / nous savons vous savez ils savent	que je sache que tu saches qu'il sache / que nous sachions que vous sachiez qu'ils sachent	je savais	j'ai su	je saurai	je saurais	sache sachons sachez
suivre to follow	je suis tu suis il suit / nous suivons vous suivez ils suivent	que je suive que tu suives qu'il suive / que nous suivions que vous suiviez qu'ils suivent	je suivais	j'ai suivi	je suivrai	je suivrais	suis suivons suivez
valoir to be worth	il vaut	qu'il vaille	il valait	il a valu	il vaudra	il vaudrait	
venir to come	je viens tu viens il vient / nous venons vous venez ils viennent	que je vienne que tu viennes qu'il vienne / que nous venions que vous veniez qu'ils viennent	je venais	je suis venu/e	je viendrai	je viendrais	viens venons venez
vivre to live	je vis tu vis il vit / nous vivons vous vivez ils vivent	que je vive que tu vives qu'il vive / que nous vivions que vous viviez qu'ils vivent	je vivais	j'ai vécu	je vivrai	je vivrais	vis vivons vivez
voir to see	je vois tu vois il voit / nous voyons vous voyez ils voient	que je voie que tu voies qu'il voie / que nous voyions que vous voyiez qu'ils voient	je voyais	j'ai vu	je verrai	je verrais	voyons
vouloir to want	je veux tu veux il veut / nous voulons vous voulez ils veulent	que je veuille que tu veuilles qu'il veuille / que nous voulions que vous vouliez qu'ils veuillent	je voulais	j'ai voulu	je voudrai	je voudrais	veuillez

Comme **réduire** : *construire, produire.*   *Comme* **venir** : *devenir, maintenir, obtenir, revenir, soutenir, (se) souvenir, tenir.*   *Comme* **voir** : *revoir.*

Appendice 5 *Lexique français-anglais*

This glossary lists most French words found in the text. The vocabulary can be divided into two types: productive vocabulary and receptive vocabulary. Productive vocabulary words appear in the **Points de départ** and **Formes et fonctions** sections and occasionally in the **Vie et culture** sections; these words reappear periodically. You are expected to recognize these words when you read and hear them and to use them yourself in exercises and conversational activities. All other words, including those presented in readings and realia, are receptive vocabulary; you are expected only to recognize them and to know their meanings when you see them in written form or hear them in context.

- For all productive vocabulary items, the numbers following an entry indicate the chapter and lesson in which that vocabulary item is first introduced. Since verbs in their infinitive form are occasionally introduced as vocabulary items before their conjugation is presented, refer to the Index to locate where the conjugation is introduced.

- To find the meaning of an expression, try to locate the main word in the expression and look that up. For example, the expression **Je vous en prie** is found with the entry for the verb **prier**; the expression **faire du sport** is found under the entry for the noun **sport**.

- The gender of nouns is indicated by the abbreviations *m.* for masculine and *f.* for feminine. Feminine and masculine nouns that are closely related in meaning and identical or similar in pronunciation are listed under a single entry: **architecte** *m./f.*; **étudiant** *m.*, **étudiante** *f.* Nouns that occur only in the plural form are followed by the gender indication and *pl.*: **beaux-arts** *m. pl.*, **vacances** *f. pl.*. Nouns and adjectives that show no agreement and do not change in the plural or feminine are indicated by the abbreviation *inv.*

- Adjectives with differing masculine and feminine written forms are shown in the masculine form followed by the feminine ending: **allemand/e, ambitieux/-euse, canadien/ne**. For adjectives whose masculine and feminine forms vary considerably, both forms are listed: **cher/chère**. Special prenominal forms of adjectives are given in parentheses: **beau (bel), belle**. When necessary for clarity, adjectives and adverbs are indicated by *adj.* and *adv.*, respectively.

- An asterisk (*) before a word indicates that the initial **h** is aspirate.

- The hashmark (†) appears after productive verbs showing some irregularity in conjugation; these verbs appear in their full conjugation in the verb charts, Appendix 4. Verbs showing irregularities in conjugation that are considered part of receptive vocabulary are not always indicated in the glossary, since you are only expected to recognize and not produce these verbs. The conjugations of many of these verbs are similar to conjugations you will find in Appendix 4. For example, the verb **admettre** is conjugated just like the verb **mettre**. For verbs that require a preposition under certain conditions, the latter appears in parentheses: **commencer (à)**, (**il commence son travail**, **il commence à travailler**); for verbs that always require a preposition, the preposition is indicated without parentheses: **s'occuper de** (**il s'occupe de moi**).

A

à to, at, in, on, P-1
abbaye *f.* abbey, 9-3
abîmé/e worn, worn out, 6-3
abstrait/e abstract, 12-2
abominable abominable
abonnement *m.* subscription
s'abonner (à) to subscribe (to), 11-2
d'abord first (of all), 5-2
absence absence
absent/e absent, missing, 7-1
absolument absolutely
abstrait/e abstract
accent accent
accepter (de) to accept, 4-3
accès *m.* access
accessoire *m.* accessory
accident *m.* accident
accompagner to accompany, 5-3
    Tu veux/vous voulez m'accompagner ? Would you like to come with me?, 5-3
d'accord agreed, OK
    être d'accord to agree, 10-2
    Je suis d'accord… I agree . . . , 11-3
    Je ne suis pas d'accord… I disagree . . . , 11-3
accordéon *m.* accordion
accueillir to welcome
achat *m.* purchase, 5-2
    faire des achats to shop, 5-2
acheter † to buy, 4-3
acteur *m.*, **actrice** *f.* actress/actor, 3-3
action *f.* action
actif/-ive active
activités *f.* activities, 1-3
actuel/le current
addition *f.* bill, 6-1
adjectif *m.* adjective
admettre † to admit
administratif/-ive administrative, 3-1
administration *f.* administration

admirer to admire
adolescent/e adolescent
adorable adorable
adorer to adore, love, 2-1
adresse *f.* address
adulte *m.* adult
adulte *adj.* adult
adverbe *m.* adverb
aérobic *f.* aerobics
aéroport *m.* airport, 9-1
aérosol *m.* aerosol
affaires *f. pl.* belongings, things, 5-2; business, 11-3
    faire des affaires to be in business
affectueux/-euse affectionate, warm-hearted
affiche *f.* poster, P-2
affirmatif/-ive affirmative
afin de + *inf.* in order to + *verb*
africain/e African
Afrique *f.* Africa, 9-2
âge *m.* age, P-2
    Quel est ton/votre âge ? What is your age?, P-2
    Quel âge as-tu/avez-vous ? How old are you?, P-2
    d'un certain âge middle-aged, 1-1
âgé/e aged, elderly, old, 1-1
agence *f.* agency
    agence de voyage travel agency
    agence immobilière real estate agency
agenda *m.* datebook
agent de police *m.* police officer, 3-3
agent immobilier *m.* real estate agent
s'agir de to be about
    il s'agit de… it's about . . .
agneau *m.* lamb, 8-3
agréable pleasant, 5-2
agricole agricultural
agriculteur *m.*, **agricultrice** *f.* farmer
aider (à) to help, 3-3
ail *m.* garlic

aimable lovable
aimer to like, to love, 1-3
    aimer beaucoup to like or love a lot, 3-2
    aimer bien to like fairly well, 3-2
    aimer mieux to prefer, 10-2
aîné/e older (brother/sister)
ainsi (que) thus, in such a way
air *m.* air, 10-3
    air frais fresh air, 8-3
    avoir l'air (bon/mauvais) to appear/seem (good/bad), 8-3
    avoir l'air (d'être) + *adj.* to seem/to appear (to be) + *adj.*, 7-3
    en plein air outdoors, 3-3
aisance *f.* ease
aisé/e easy, well off
ajouter to add
alarme *f.* alarm
album *m.* album
alcool *m.* alcohol, 10-2
alcoolisé/e *adj.* containing alcohol, 8-1
alerte *adj.* alert
Algérie *f.* Algeria, 9-2
algérien/ne Algerian, 9-2
alimentaire *adj.* relating to food
aliments *m. pl.* food, 8-2
Allemagne *f.* Germany, 9-2
allemand/e *adj.* German, 9-2
allemand *m.* German (language)
aller † to go, 2-3
    aller sur Internet to go on-line, 11-3
    Ça ne va pas. Things aren't going well., P-1
    Ça va, et toi ? Fine, and you?, P-1
    Comment allez-vous ? How are you?, P-1
    On y va ? Shall we go?, 4-3
allô hello (telephone only)
allumer to turn on (an appliance), 11-1
alors so, 2-3; then
alphabet *m.* alphabet

alpinisme *m.* mountain climbing, 5-2
    faire de l'alpinisme to go mountain climbing, 5-2
ambassadeur *m.*, **ambassadrice** *f.* ambassador
ambitieux/-euse ambitious, 1-1
améliorer to improve
amener † to bring (along) a person, 4-3
américain/e American, 9-2
Amérique *f.* **du Nord** North America, 9-2
Amérique *f.* **du Sud** South America, 9-2
ami *m.*, **amie** *f.* friend, P-1
amoureux/-euse in love, 7-3
    tomber amoureux/-euse (de) to fall in love (with)
amphithéâtre *m.* amphitheater, lecture hall, 3-1
amusant/e funny, 1-1
s'amuser to have fun, 7-3
an *m.* year, 1-2
    J'ai 39 ans. I am 39 years old., 1-2
analyse *f.* analysis
analytique analytical
anchois *m.* anchovy
ancien/ne old, antique, 6-2; former, 7-1
angine *f.* strep throat, tonsillitis, 10-1
anglais/e *adj.* English, 9-2
anglais *m.* English (language), 3-2
Angleterre *f.* England, 9-2
angoisse *f.* anguish
angoissé/e anguished
animal *m.* animal, 1-1
    animal familier pet, 1-1
animateur *m.*, **animatrice** *f.* organizer
animation *f.* animation, excitement
animé/e animated, excited
année *f.* year, 2-3
    l'année dernière last year, 5-1
    l'année prochaine next year, 2-3
anniversaire *m.* birthday, 1-2
    Joyeux anniversaire ! Happy Birthday!, 7-2
annonce *f.* advertisement
annoncer to announce
annuaire *m.* phone book
anorak *m.* parka with hood, 4-3
anthropologie *f.* anthropology, 3-2
antibiotique *m.* antibiotic, 10-1
anxiété *f.* anxiety
anxieux/-euse anxious, 7-3
août August, 1-2
apéritif *m.* **(un apéro)** before-meal drink, 8-2
appareil (photo) *m.* camera, 9-1
appareil (photo) numérique *m.* digital camera, 9-1
appartement *m.* apartment, 6-1
    appartement sous le toit attic apartment, 6-2
appartenir † to belong

appel *m.* call
appeler † to call, 5-3
    s'appeler to be called, 7-3
    Je m'appelle… My name is . . . , P-1
appliquer to apply (sthg)
apporter to bring (an object), 6-2
apprécier to appreciate
apprendre (à) † to learn, 7-1
apprentissage *m.* apprenticeship, learning
approprié/e appropriate
après after, after that, 3-1
    après avoir/être… after having . . . , 11-2
    après-midi *m.* afternoon, 1-3
    après tout after all, 11-3
    d'après vous according to you
    de l'après-midi in the afternoon, P.M., 4-2
aquarelle *f.* watercolor
aquarium *m.* aquarium
arabe *m.* Arabic
arbre *m.* tree, 8-3
archéologie *m.* archaeology
archipel *m.* archipelago
architecte *m./f.* architect, 3-3
architecture *f.* architecture
argent *m.* money, 3-1
argentin/e Argentinian, 9-2
Argentine *f.* Argentina, 9-2
argot *m.* slang
argotique *adj.* slang
argument *m.* argument
armoire *f.* armoire, 6-2
s'arranger † to be all right, to work out, 7-3
arrêt *m.* stop
arrêter (de) to stop, 12-1
    Arrête ! Stop it!, 2-1
s'arrêter to stop oneself
arrière back, rear
    arrière-grand-parent great-grandparent
arriver to arrive, 1-3
arrondissement *m.* Parisian city district
arroser to water; to celebrate with wine or champagne
art *m.* art, 11-2
article *m.* article
    articles de toilette *m. pl.* toiletries, 4-1
articulatoire *adj.* articulatory
artifice *f.* artifice
artificiel/le artificial
artisan *m.* craftsman
artisanat *m.* arts and crafts
artiste *m./f.* artist, 3-3
artistique artistic
asiatique Asiatic
ascenseur *m.* elevator, 6-1
Asie *f.* Asia, 9-2
aspect *m.* aspect

asperge *f.* asparagus, 8-2
aspiré/e aspirated
aspirine *f.* aspirin, 10-1
s'asseoir to sit down
    Asseyez-vous ! Sit down!, P-2
assez rather, 1-1; enough, 4-1
assiette *f.* plate, 8-3
assistant social *m.*, **assistante sociale** *f.* social worker, 3-3
assister à to attend, 2-3
association (étudiante) *f.* (student) association, 3-1
associé/e associate(d)
astrologie *f.* astrology
astrologue *m./f.* astrologer
astronomie *f.* astronomy, 3-2
athlète *m./f.* athlete
atlas *m.* atlas, 11-2
atmosphérique atmospheric
attendre to wait (for), to expect, 5-1
attention *f.* attention
    faire attention (à) to pay attention (to); to be careful
attentivement attentively
attraper to catch
au (à + le) 2-2
    au revoir good-bye, P-1
auberge *f.* inn, 9-3
    auberge de jeunesse youth hostel, 9-3
augmenter to increase
aujourd'hui today, 1-3
auprès de next to, close to
aussi also
    aussi … que as . . . as, 3-3
    moi aussi me too
aussitôt que as soon as
Australie *f.* Australia, 9-2
australien/ne Australian, 9-2
autant (de) … que as many/much . . . as, 3-3
auteur *m.* author, 11-2
(auto)bus *m.* city bus, 9-1
automatique automatic
auto(mobile) *f.* car
automne *m.* fall, 5-1
autonome independent, 3-3
autonomie *f.* autonomy
autoritaire authoritarian, 7-1
autorité *f.* authority
autoroute *f.* highway
autour around
autre other, another, 2-1
autrefois in the past
autrement otherwise
aux (à + les) 2-2
avance: (être) en avance (to be) early, 4-3
avant de + *inf.* before . . . , 11-2
avant-hier the day before yesterday, 5-1
avantage *m.* advantage
avec with, 1-3

avenir *m.* future
aventure *f.* adventure, 11-1
aventurier *m.*, **aventurière** *f.* adventurer
avenue *f.* avenue, 9-3
avion *m.* plane, 9-1
avis *m.* opinion, 11-3
   à mon avis, ... in my opinion, ..., 11-3
avocat *m.*, **avocate** *f.* lawyer, 3-3
avoir † to have, 1-2
avril April, 1-2

B

bac(calauréat) *m.* high-school leaving exam (France), 3-2
bacc(alauréat) (en) *m.* B.A. or B.S. degree (in) (Can.), 3-2
bacon *m.* bacon, 8-2
bagage *m.* luggage
baguette *f.* French bread (long, thin loaf), 8-3
baignoire *f.* bathtub
bain *m.* bath
   maillot *m.* **de bain** bathing suit, 4-3
   prendre un bain to take a bath
baisser to lower
bal *m.* ball, dance
   bal populaire *m.* street dance, 7-2
balade *f.* walk, stroll
baladeur *m.* Walkman
balcon *m.* balcony, 6-1
ballet *m.* ballet, 2-3
banaliser to make commonplace
banane *f.* banana, 8-2
bande dessinée *f.* **(une BD)** comic, comic strip, 11-2
banlieue *f.* suburbs
banque *f.* bank
baptême *m.* baptism, 9-2
bar *m.* bar
bas low
   en bas downstairs
base de données *f.* database, 11-3
basilic *m.* basil
basket(-ball) *m.* basketball, 2-2
bateau (à voile) *m.* (sail)boat, 6-3
bâtiment *m.* building, 6-1
batterie *f.* percussion, drum set, 2-2
battu/e beaten
beau (bel), belle beautiful, handsome, 2-1
   Il fait beau. It's beautiful weather., 5-1
beaucoup a lot, 1-1
beau-frère *m.* brother-in-law, 7-1
beau-père *m.* stepfather, father-in-law, 1-1
beaux-arts *m. pl.* fine arts, 3-2
beige beige, 4-3
belge Belgian, 9-2
Belgique *f.* Belgium, 9-2
belle-mère *f.* stepmother, mother-in-law, 1-1
belle-sœur *f.* sister-in-law, 7-1

besoin *m.* need, 9-1
   avoir besoin de to need, 9-1
bête stupid, 2-1
beurre *m.* butter, 8-2
bibliothèque *f.* library, 2-3
   bibli *f.* (Can.) library, 3-1
   bibliothèque universitaire *f.* **(la BU)** university library, 3-1
bien well, fine, P-1
   faire du bien to do (someone) good
   bien sûr of course, 2-1
bien-être *m.* well-being
bientôt soon, 2-3
   à bientôt see you soon, P-1
bienvenu/e *adj.* welcome
bienvenue *f.* welcome; you're welcome (Can.)
bière *f.* beer, 8-1
bifteck *m.* beefsteak, 8-3
   bifteck haché ground beef, 8-3
bijou *m.* piece of jewelry
bilingue bilingual
billet (d'entrée) *m.* ticket, 5-2
billet (d'avion) *m.* (airplane) ticket, 9-1
biodégradable biodegradable, 10-3
biographie *f.* biography, 11-2
biologie *f.* biology, 3-2
biscuit *m.* cookie, 8-2
bise *f.* kiss
   faire une/la bise to kiss hello/ good-bye on the cheeks
blanc/blanche white, 4-3
bleu/e blue, 4-3
blond/e blond, 2-1
bloquer to block
blouson *m.* heavy jacket, 4-3
boire † to drink, 8-1
bois *m.* woods, 6-3; wood
boisson *f.* drink, 8-1
   boisson alcoolisée alcoholic beverage, 8-1
   boisson chaude hot drink, 8-1
   boisson rafraîchissante cold drink, 8-1
boîte *f.* can; box 8-3
   boîte postale post box
bol *m.* bowl, 8-2
bonbon *m.* piece of candy
bon/ne good, 3-1
   Bon anniversaire ! Happy birthday!, 9-2
   bonjour hello, P-1
   bon marché *adj.* cheap, 4-3
   Bonne année ! Happy New Year!, 9-2
   Bonnes vacances ! Have a good vacation!, 9-2
   bonsoir good evening, P-1
   Bon voyage ! Have a good trip!, 9-2
Il fait bon. It's nice weather., 5-1
bonheur *m.* happiness
bord *m.* edge, shore

   au bord (du lac) at the shore (of the lake), 6-3
   bord de la mer seashore
borgne one-eyed
bosser (*colloq.*) to work
botanique *f.* botany, 3-2
botte *f.* boot, 4-3
boubou *m.* African robe, dress
bouche *f.* mouth, 10-1
boucher *m.*, **bouchère** *f.* butcher
boucherie *f.* butcher shop, 8-3
bougie *f.* candle, 7-2
bouillabaisse *f.* seafood stew
bouillir to boil
boulanger *m.*, **boulangère** *f.* baker
boulangerie *f.* bakery, 8-3
boulevard *m.* boulevard, 9-3
boulot *m.* work (*colloq.*)
bout *m.* tip, end
bouteille *f.* bottle, 8-2
boutique *f.* boutique, shop
branché/e plugged in, connected with, 11-3
bras *m.* arm, 10-1
bravo ! great! well done!, 5-2
bref/brève brief
Brésil *m.* Brazil, 9-2
brésilien/ne Brazilian, 9-2
Bretagne *f.* Brittany
breton/ne Breton
bricolage *m.* puttering around, odd jobs, 2-2
   faire du bricolage to do odd jobs around the house, 2-2
bricoler to do odd jobs around the house, 2-2
brin *m.* sprig, strand
   brin de muguet sprig of lily of the valley, 7-2
brochure *f.* brochure, pamphlet
brodé/e embroidered
bronchite *f.* bronchitis, 10-1
brosse *f.* chalkboard eraser, P-2; brush, 4-1
   brosse à cheveux hairbrush, 4-1
   brosse à dents toothbrush, 4-1
se brosser to brush one's —, 4-1
   se brosser les cheveux to brush one's hair, 4-1
   se brosser les dents to brush one's teeth, 4-1
brouillard *m.* foggy, 5-1
   Il y a du brouillard. It's foggy., 5-1
brouillon *m.* rough draft
bruit *m.* sound, noise, 10-3
brûlé/e burned
brun/e brunette, 2-1
bruyant/e noisy
budget *m.* budget
bureau *m.* desk, office, P-2; office, 3-3
bus *m.* (city) bus, 9-1

C

ça that
    Ça va ? How are things?, P-1
    Ça va. It's going fine., P-1
    C'est ça. That's right., 4-3
    Comment ça va ? How's it going?, P-1
cabinet *m.* office (doctor's)
câble *m.* cable (television)
caché/e hidden, 7-2
cacher to hide, 7-2
cadeau *m.* present, gift, 7-2
cadre *m.* business executive; frame (for a picture)
café *m.* café, 2-3; coffee, 8-1
    café au lait with milk, 8-2
    café crème with cream, 8-1
caféine *f.* caffeine
cafétéria *f.* cafeteria, 3-1
cahier *m.* notebook, P-2
caisse *f.* cash register
caissier *m.*, **caissière** *f.* cashier
calcul *m.* calculus, 3-2
calculatrice *f.* calculator, P-2
calendrier *m.* calendar
calme calm, 1-1
se calmer to calm down, 7-3
camarade *m./f.* friend, buddy
    camarade de classe classmate, P-1
Cameroun *m.* Cameroon, 9-2
camerounais/e Cameroonian, 9-2
campagne *f.* countryside, 5-2
    à la campagne in the country, 5-2
camping *m.* campground, 9-3
    faire du camping to camp, to go camping, 5-2
camping-car *m.* RV, 9-3
campus *m.* campus
Canada *m.* Canada, 9-2
canadien/ne Canadian, 9-2
canapé *m.* couch, 6-2
candidat *m.* candidate
canne *f.* cane
canoë *m.* canoe
capacité *f.* ability
car *m.* excursion bus, intracity bus, 9-1
caractère *m.* nature, disposition, 1-1
carafe *f.* **(d'eau)** carafe (of water), 8-2
caravane *f.* camper (vehicle), 9-3
cardinal/e cardinal
carnet *m.* small notebook
    carnet d'adresses address book, 9-1
carrière *f.* career, 3-3
carte *f.* map, P-2; playing card, 2-2
    à la carte from the menu; cafeteria-style
    carte bancaire debit card, 9-1
    carte de crédit credit card, 9-1
    carte météorologique weather map
    carte postale postcard, 5-2
    jouer aux cartes to play cards, 2-2

cas *m.* case
casquette *f.* baseball cap, 4-3
casse-croûte *m. inv.* snack, 8-1
casser to break
cassette *f.* cassette tape
catégorie *f.* category
cathédrale *f.* cathedral, 9-3
catholicisme *m.* Catholicism
catholique Catholic
cause *f.* cause
    à cause de due to, because of, 5-3
causer to cause
cave *f.* wine cellar, 9-3
CD *m. inv.* CD, compact disk, P-2
ce (c') it, that
    c'est... this/it is . . . , P-1
    c'est-à-dire that is to say
    ce sont... these/they are . . . , P-1
    ce (cet), cette this, that, 7-2
    ces these, those, 7-2
céder to relinquish
ceinture *f.* belt
cela that
célèbre famous, 11-1
célébrer to celebrate
célébrité *f.* celebrity
céleste celestial
célibataire single, 1-1
    mère/père célibataire single mother/father, 7-1
cendre *f.* ash
cendrier *m.* ashtray
cent hundred, 2-3
centre *m.* center
    centre des sports sports complex, 3-1
    centre étudiant student center, 3-1
    centre informatique computer center, 3-1
    centre-ville downtown, 6-2
cependant however
céramique ceramic
céréales *f. pl.* cereal, 8-2
cérémonie *f.* ceremony, 7-2
    cérémonie civile civil wedding, 7-2
certain/e certain
certainement certainly
ces *see* ce
chacun/e each one
chaîne *f.* chain; TV (or radio) station, 11-1
chaise *f.* chair, P-2
chambre *f.* bedroom, 6-1
champ *m.* field, 6-3
champignon *m.* mushroom, 8-3
champion *m.*, **championne** *f.* champion
championnat *m.* championship
chance *f.* luck
    avoir de la chance to be lucky
changement *m.* change
changer to change

chanson *f.* song
chant *m.* singing
chanter to sing, 4-2
chanteur *m.*, **chanteuse** *f.* singer, 3-3
chapeau *m.* hat, 2-1
chapelle *f.* chapel
chaque each, 6-1
charcuterie *f.* pork butcher shop; cooked pork meats, 8-3
charmant/e charming
charges *f. pl.* utilities, 6-1
chariot *m.* shopping cart
chasse *f.* hunting
chat cat, 1-1
châtain *adj. inv.* chestnut colored, auburn, 2-1
château *m.* castle, 9-3
    château fort fortress, 9-3
chaud hot, 5-1
    Il fait chaud. It's hot (weather)., 5-1
    J'ai chaud. I'm hot/cold., 5-1
chauffeur *m.* driver
chausser to put shoes on
chaussette *f.* sock, 4-3
chausson *m.* slipper
chaussure *f.* shoe, 4-3
    chaussure à talon high-heeled shoe, 4-3
chef *m.* boss; chef
chef d'œuvre *m.* **(chefs-d'œuvre** *pl.*) masterpiece, 12-3
chemin *m.* way, 9-3; path
    indiquer le chemin to give directions, 9-3
cheminée *f.* chimney
chemise *f.* man's shirt, 4-3
chemisier *m.* blouse, 4-3
chêne *m.* oak, oak tree
cher/chère expensive, 4-3
chercher to look for, 2-3
chéri/e *m./f.* love, darling
cheval *m.* horse, 5-2
    faire du cheval to go horseback riding, 5-2
cheveux *m. pl.* hair, 4-1
cheville *f.* ankle, 10-1
chez at the home of, at the place of, 1-1
    chez nous at our place, 1-1
chic chic, stylish, 6-2
chien *m.* dog, 1-1
chiffre *m.* numeral, digit
chimie *f.* chemistry, 3-2
Chine *f.* China, 9-2
chinois/e *adj.* Chinese, 9-2
chinois *m.* Chinese (language)
chocolat chaud *m.* hot chocolate, 8-1
chœur *m.* chorus, 12-1
choisir to choose, 6-1
choix *m.* choice
cholestérol *m.* cholesterol
chômage *m.* unemployment

choquant/e shocking
chorale *f.* choir
chose *f.* thing, 2-2
chou *m.* cabbage
choucroute *f.* sauerkraut
chouette ! neat!, 5-2
chute *f.* fall
ci-dessous below
ci-dessus above
cidre *m.* cider
ciel *m.* sky, 5-1
   Le ciel est couvert. The sky is overcast., 5-1
cigarette *f.* cigarette
cimetière *m.* cemetery
cinéaste *m.* filmmaker
cinéma *m.* cinéma, the movies, 2-3
cinématographe *m.* cinematographer
cinq five, 1-2
cinq-pièces *m.* three-bedroom apartment/house, 6-1
cinquante fifty, 1-2
cinquième fifth, 6-1
circulation *f.* traffic
citer to cite
citoyen *m.*, **citoyenne** *f.* citizen
citron *m.* lemon, 8-1
   citron pressé lemonade, 8-1
civil/e civil
clair/e clear
clarinette *f.* clarinet, 12-1
classique classic; classical (music)
clavier *m.* computer keyboard, 11-3; musical keyboard, 12-1
clé/clef *f.* key, 9-1
climat *m.* climate
clinique *f.* private hospital, 2-1
coca(-cola) *m.* cola, 8-1
cocher to check off
code *m.* code
   code postal postal code
cœur *m.* heart, 10-1
   avoir mal au cœur to be nauseated, 10-1
se coiffer to fix one's hair, 4-1
coin *m.* corner
   au coin de at the corner (of)
   avec coin cuisine with a kitchenette, 6-2
colère *f.* anger, 7-3
   en colère angry, 7-3
collant *m.* pantyhose, 4-3
collège *m.* middle school, 2-1
collier *m.* necklace
colline *f.* hill, 6-3
coloc(ataire) *m./f.* roommate, housemate, 2-1
colocation *f.* renting a house or an apartment together
Colombie *f.* Colombia, 9-2
colombien/ne Colombian, 9-2

colonie *f.* colony
   colonie de vacances summer camp
colonne *f.* column
combattre to combat
combien how much, 2-1
   combien de how many, 2-1
combinaison *f.* combination
combiner to combine
comédie *f.* comedy, 11-1
   comédie musicale musical, 11-1
commander to order, 8-1
comme like, as
   Comme-ci, comme-ça. So-so., P-1
commencer † to begin, to start, 4-2
comment how, 2-1
   Comment ça va ? How's it going?, P-1
   Comment dit-on… ? How do you say . . . ?, P-2
   Comment tu t'appelles ? What is your name?, P-1
   Comment vous appelez-vous ? What is your name?, P-1
commentaire *m.* comment
commerçant *m.*, **commerçante** *f.* merchant, 8-3
communauté *f.* community
communément communally, in common
communication *f.* communication, 4-1
communiquer to communicate
compagnie *f.* company
comparaison *f.* comparison
comparatif/-ive comparative
comparer to compare, 4-3
compliment *m.* compliment
compliqué/e complicated
comportement *m.* behavior
composé/e composite
composition *f.* in-class essay exam, 3-2; composition, 12-2
compréhension *f.* comprehension
comprendre † to understand, 8-1
   Je ne comprends pas. I don't understand., P-2
compris/e *adj.* included, 8-1
comptabilité *f.* accounting, 3-2
comptable *m./f.* accountant, 3-3
compte *m.* account
compter to count
comptine *f.* nursery rhyme
concept *m.* concept
concerner to concern
concert *m.* concert, 2-2
concierge *m./f.* caretaker, manager
concombre *m.* cucumber, 8-3
condamner to condemn
condiments *m.* condiments, 8-3
conditionnel *m.* conditional tense
conduire to drive
confiture *f.* jam, 8-2
conflit *m.* conflict

conformiste conformist, 1-1
confort *m.* comfort
confortable comfortable (material objects), 6-2
congé *m.* leave
   prendre congé to take leave, say good-bye
congélateur *m.* freezer
conjonction *f.* conjunction
conjugaison *f.* conjugation
conjugué/e conjugated
connaissance *f.* knowledge, understanding, 7-1
connaître † to know, be familiar with, 7-3
connecté/e connected
connu/e known
conquête *f.* conquest
consacrer to devote
conseil *m.* piece of advice
   demander un conseil to ask for advice, 10-1
conseiller to advise
conseiller *m.*, **conseillière** *f.* advisor
conséquence *f.* consequence
conservateur/-trice conservative
conservation *f.* conservation
conserver to store
consister to consist
consommateur *m.*, **consommatrice** *f.* consumer
consommation *f.* drink
consonne *f.* consonant
construire † to construct, build
consultation *f.* visit with a health professional
consulter to consult
   consulter le médecin to see a doctor, 10-2
contaminer to contaminate, 10-3
contempler to contemplate
contenir † to contain
content/e happy, 7-3
continent *m.* continent, 9-2
continuer to go on/keep going, 9-3
continuer (à) to continue, 12-1
contraire *m.* opposite
   au contraire,… to the contrary, . . . , 11-3
contraste *m.* contrast
contribuer to contribute
contrôle *m.* inspection, control, test
convaincre to convince
convenir † to suit
   Cela vous convient ? Does this suit you?, 9-3
copain *m.*, **copine** *f.* friend, 2-1
copieux/-euse copious, hearty, 8-2
corps *m.* body, 10-1
correspondance *f.* correspondance
correspondant/e *m./f.* penfriend

correspondre to correspond
corriger to correct
costume *m.* man's suit, 4-3
   costume-cravate *m.* suit and a tie
côte *f.* coast
côté *m.* side
   à côté de next to, 3-1
   de l'autre côté,... on the other hand, . . . , 12-3
Côte-d'Ivoire *f.* Ivory Coast, 9-2
côtelette *f.* **d'agneau** lamb chop, 8-3
coton *m.* cotton, 4-3
côtoyer to rub shoulders with
cou *m.* neck, 10-1
se coucher to go to bed, 4-1
coude *m.* elbow, 10-1
couler to flow, to run (a liquid), 10-1
   avoir le nez qui coule to have a runny nose, 10-1
couleur *f.* color, 4-3
   de quelle couleur est... ? what color is . . . ?, 4-3
couloir *m.* hallway, 6-1
coup *m.* blow, strike, punch
   ça vaut le coup it's worth it, 12-3
   coup de soleil sunburn, 10-1
couper to cut
couple *m.* couple
couplet *m.* verse of a poem
cour *f.* courtyard, 6-1
courant/e current
   au courant up-to-date (for a person)
   courant d'air draft, breeze
courir to run, 4-2
couronne *f.* crown
courriel *m.* e-mail message, 11-3
courrier électronique *m.* e-mail, 11-3
cours *m.* course, class, 3-1
course *f.* errand, 2-2
   faire des courses to run errands, 2-2
   faire les courses to go grocery/food shopping, 8-3
court/e short, 4-3
cousin *m.*, **cousine** *f.* cousin, 1-1
coussin *m.* cushion
coussinet *m.* small cushion
coûter to cost
coutume *f.* custom
couture *f.* sewing, dressmaking
   haute couture *f.* designer fashion
couturier *m.* fashion designer
couturière *f.* dressmaker, seamstress
couvert: le ciel est couvert The sky is overcast., 5-1
couvrir † to cover
craie *f.* stick of chalk, P-2
cravate *f.* tie, 4-3
crayon *m.* pencil, P-2
créer to create
crème *f.* cream, 8-1

crémerie *f.* dairy store
crevette *f.* shrimp, 8-3
crier to yell, 7-3
crime *m.* crime
crise *f.* crisis
cristal *m.* crystal
critère *m.* criterion
critique *f.* critique, criticism
critique *m.* critic (person)
croire † **(à, en)** to believe, 11-1
   Je crois/Je crois que oui. I think so., 11-1
Je crois que... I believe that . . . , 11-1
Je ne crois pas/Je crois que non. I don't think so., 11-1
croissant *m.* croissant, 8-2
croque-monsieur *m.* grilled ham and cheese sandwich, 8-1
croustillant/e crusty
crudités *f. pl.* cut-up raw vegetables, 8-1
cubiste cubist
cuiller, cuillère *f.* spoon, 8-1
cuir *m.* leather, 4-3
cuisine *f.* kitchen, 6-1
   avec coin cuisine with a kitchenette, 6-2
   faire la cuisine to cook, 2-2
cuisinière *f.* stove, 6-2
culturel/le cultural

D

d'accord OK, agreed
dame *f.* lady, P-2
danger *m.* danger
dans in, into, inside, P-2
danse *f.* dance, 3-2
   faire de la danse to dance, to study dance, 2-2
danser to dance
d'après... according to . . .
date *f.* date, 1-2
   Quelle est la date ? What is the date?, 1-2
davantage more
de (d') from, of, about, P-1
débarquer to disembark
debout standing, on one's feet
   être debout to be up, 4-1
début *m.* beginning
décédé/e deceased, 1-1
décembre December, 1-2
déception *f.* disappointment
décharge (municipale) *f.* (municipal) dump, 10-3
déchet *m.* waste, refuse, 10-3
   déchets domestiques *pl.* household garbage, 10-3
   déchets industriels *pl.* industrial waste
décider (de) to decide, 12-1
se décider to make up one's mind, 12-3

déclaration *f.* declaration
décontracté/e relaxed
décorer to decorate
découverte *f.* discovery
découvrir † to discover
décrire † to describe, 7-1
déçu/e disappointed, 10-3
déduire to deduce
défaire † to undo
défaite *f.* defeat, loss
défilé *m.* parade, 7-2
définir to define
déforestation *f.* deforestation
degré *m.* degree; step
   Il fait vingt degrés. It's 20 degrees (Celsius)., 5-1
dehors outside
   en dehors de outside of
déjà already, 4-1
déjeuner *m.* lunch, 8-2
déjeuner to have lunch, 1-3
délicieux/-euse delicious, 8-3
demain tomorrow, 2-3
   à demain see you tomorrow, P-1
demander to ask, request, 6-2
démarrer to begin, to start
demi/e half
   demi-frère *m.* half-brother, 7-1
   demi-kilo *m.* half-kilo, 8-3
   demi-sœur *f.* half-sister, 7-1
   demi-tour *m.* U-turn
   et demi/e and a half, 4-2
   faire demi-tour to make a U-turn
démodé/e old-fashioned, out-of-date, 4-3
démonstratif/-ive demonstrative
dent *f.* tooth, 4-1
   se brosser les dents to brush one's teeth, 4-1
   se laver les dents to brush one's teeth
dentifrice *m.* toothpaste, 4-1
dentiste *m./f.* dentist, 3-3
départ *m.* departure
département *m.* department, regional, administrative unit in France
dépasser to exceed
se dépêcher to hurry up, 4-1
dépense *f.* expenditure
dépenser to spend
depuis since, when, 11-3
   depuis combien de temps... ? for how long . . . ?, 11-3
   depuis quand... ? since when . . . ?, 11-3
dernier/-ière last, behind, 3-1
derrière behind, 3-1
des *pl.* some, P-2
dès que as soon as
désagréable disagreeable, 1-1
désastre *m.* disaster
descendant (de) *m.* descendant (of)

descendre to go down, 5-1
descente *f.* descent
désert *m.* desert
se déshabiller to undress, 4-1
désignation *f.* name, designation
désirer to desire, to want, 10-2
désobéir à to disobey, 6-1
désolé/e sorry, 5-3
    Je suis désolé/e... I am sorry . . . ?, 5-3
dessert *m.* dessert, 8-2
desservir to serve, to stop at
dessin *m.* drawing, 3-2
    dessin animé *m.* cartoon, animated film, 11-1
dessinateur/-trice *f.* draftsman/woman, 12-2
dessiner to draw
destination *f.* destination, 5-2
se détendre to relax, 6-3
détente *f.* relaxation; release (of a consonant)
détester to detest, 3-2
deux two, 1-2
deuxième *m.* second, 6-1
devant in front of, 3-1
développement *m.* development
développer to develop
devenir † to become, 5-2
deviner to guess
devoir † must, to have to, should, 3-3
devoir *m.* essay, 3-2
devoirs *m. pl.* homework, P-2
    faire des devoirs *m.* to do homework
diagnostic *m.* diagnosis, 10-1
dialecte *m.* dialect
dialogue *m.* dialogue
dictionnaire *m.* (**un dico**) dictionary, 3-2
différent/e different
différer to differ
difficile difficult, 3-2
dimanche Sunday, 1-3
dîner *m.* dinner, 8-2
dîner to have dinner, 1-3
diplomate *m./f.* diplomat
diplôme *m.* degree, 3-2
    avoir un diplôme to have a degree
dire † to say, 7-1
    Ça (ne) me dit rien I'm not interested in that., 12-3
discipliné/e disciplined, 1-1
discuter to have a discussion, to talk, 3-3
disjoint/e disjointed, stressed (pronouns)
disparaître to disappear
disparition *f.* disappearance
disponible available
se disputer to argue, 7-3
disquette *f.* diskette, 11-3
distractions *f. pl.* amusements/diversions, 5-3
se distraire to amuse oneself, 11-2

divers/e various
diversité *f.* diversity
divertissement *m.* variety show, 11-1
divisé/e divided, split
divorcé/e divorced, 1-1
divorcer to divorce, 7-1
dix ten, 1-2
dixième tenth, 6-1
dix-huit eighteen, 1-2
dix-huitième eighteenth, 6-1
dix-neuf nineteen, 1-2
dix-neuvième nineteenth, 6-1
dix-sept seventeen, 1-2
dix-septième seventeenth, 6-1
doctorat *m.* doctorate, Ph.D.
documentaire *m.* documentary, 11-1
dodo (*colloq.*) sleep, 4-1
    faire dodo (*colloq.*) go to sleep, 4-1
doigt *m.* finger, 10-1
    doigt de pied toe, 10-1
domaine *m.* area, field
dommage : C'est dommage... It's too bad. It's a pity., 5-3
donc then, therefore, 2-1
donnée *f.* data, 11-3
    base de données database, 11-3
donner to give, P-2
    donner sur to look onto or lead out to, 6-1
dormir to sleep, 4-2
dos *m.* back, 10-1
dossier *m.* file, case, folder
double double
doublé/e dubbed, 11-1
doubler to dub, 11-1
doucement gently, softly
douche *f.* shower
    prendre une douche to take a shower, 4-1
se doucher to shower, 4-1
doué/e to be talented, 3-3
douleur *f.* pain
doute *m.* doubt
    douter que... to doubt that . . .
    sans aucun doute without a doubt
    sans doute probably
doux/douce gentle
douzaine *f.* dozen, 8-3
douze twelve, 1-2
douzième twelfth, 6-1
drame psychologique *m.* psychological drama, 11-1
dresser (une liste) to make (a list)
se droguer to take drugs, to be on drugs
droit *m.* law, 3-2; straight, 9-3
    tout droit straight ahead, 9-3
droite *f.* right
    à droite (de) to the right (of), 3-1
drôle amusing, funny, strange, 2-1
du (de + le) 2-2

dur/e hard
durer to endure, last
DVD *m. inv.* DVD, P-2
dynamique dynamic, 1-1

E

eau *f.* water, 8-1
    eau minérale mineral water, 8-1
    eau potable drinkable water, 10-3
échange *f.* exchange
échanger to exchange
échappement *m.* exhaust, 10-3
échapper to escape
écharpe *f.* scarf, 4-3
échecs *m. pl.* chess, 2-2
échelle *f.* ladder
éclair *m.* lightning, 5-1
    Il y a des éclairs. There is lightning., 5-1
école *f.* school, 1-3
    école maternelle preschool
    école primaire elementary school
    école secondaire secondary school
écologie *f.* ecology
écologique ecological
économie *f.* economics, 3-2
économique economical
économiser to save, economize, 10-3
écotourisme *m.* ecotourism
écouter to listen, P-2
    écouter de la musique to listen to music, 1-3
écran *m.* screen, 11-1
écrire † to write, 7-1
    Écrivez votre nom ! Write down your name!, P-2
écrivain *m.* writer, 3-3
écureuil *m.* squirrel
éducatif/-ive educational
effacer to erase, P-2
effet *m.* effect
    en effet yes, indeed, 6-3
efficace efficient
effort *m.* effort
égal/e equal
église *f.* Catholic church, 2-3
égoïste selfish, 2-1
élaborer to elaborate
électricité *f.* electricity
électrique electric
électronique electronic
élégance *f.* elegance
élégant/e elegant, 2-1
éliminer to eliminate
elle *f.* she, her, it, P-1
    elle-même *f.* herself
elles *f. pl.* they, them, P-1
    elles-mêmes *f. pl.* themselves
emballage *m.* packaging, 10-3
embarrassé/e embarrassed, 7-3

embarquement *m.* boarding dock
embarquer to embark, to board a boat
embarras *m.* trouble
s'embrasser to kiss, 7-3
émission *f.* program, 11-1
    émission de télé-achat infomercial, 11-1
    émission de télé-réalité reality show, 11-1
emmener to bring someone along
émotion *f.* emotion
empêcher to prevent
emploi *m.* use; job
employer to use
emporter to bring something, to take with
emprunter to borrow, 6-2
en in, to, at, P-1; some, any, 8-3
enchaînement *m.* linking
enchanté/e delighted (to meet you), P-1
encore still, yet, again, another, 4-2
    encore un quart d'heure another fifteen minutes, 4-2
encyclopédie *f.* encyclopedia, 11-2
s'endormir to fall asleep, 4-1
endroit *m.* place, 6-3
énergique energetic, 2-1
énervé/e irritable
s'énerver to become irritated/worked up
enfance *f.* childhood
enfant *m.* child, 1-1
enfin finally, 5-2
s'ennuyer † to become bored, 7-3
ennuyeux/-euse boring, tedious, 3-2
enquête *f.* poll
enseignant/e *m./f.* teacher, instructor
enseignement *m.* teaching, 11-3
enseigner to teach
ensemble together, 1-3
ensuite next, then, 5-2
entendre to hear, 5-1
s'entendre (avec) to get along (with), 7-3
entendu: C'est entendu. It's understood. 12-1
enthousiaste enthusiastic
entourer to surround
entraîneur *m.* trainer, coach
entre between, 4-2
entrée *f.* entrance, foyer, 6-1; appetizer or starter, 8-2
entreprise *f.* firm, place of business
entrer to go/come in, 5-2
entretien *m.* interview
énumérer to enumerate, to list
envie *f.* : **avoir envie de** (+ *nom*, + *inf.*)... to want, desire (sthg, to do sthg) . . . , 4-3
environ about, approximately
environnement *m.* environment, 10-3
environs *m. pl.* surroundings
envoyer † to send, 11-3

épaule *f.* shoulder, 10-1
épeler † to spell, 5-3
épice *f.* spice, 8-2
épicerie *f.* grocer's shop, 8-3
épinards *m. pl.* spinach, 8-3
épisode *m.* episode
époque *f.* era, time
époux *m.*, **épouse** *f.* spouse
épreuve *f.* test, 7-1
éprouver to feel, to experience
équilibré/e balanced, 10-2
équipe *f.* team
équipé/e equipped, 6-2
équivalent *m.* equivalent
erreur *f.* mistake, error
escalier *m.* staircase, stairs, 6-1
espace *m.* place, space
Espagne *f.* Spain, 9-2
espagnol/e *adj.* Spanish, 9-2
espagnol *m.* Spanish (language), 3-2
espion *m.* spy
espionnage *m.* spying, 11-1
est *m.* east
en espèces in cash
espérer † to hope, 12-1
essai *m.* essay
essayer (de) † to try, 10-3
essuyer † to dry
s'essuyer † to dry one self off, towel off, 4-1
estomac *m.* stomach, 10-1
et and, P-1
établir to establish
établissement *m.* establishment
étage *m.* floor, 6-1
    premier étage second floor, 6-1
étape *f.* stage, step (in a process)
état *m.* state
    état civil marital status, 1-1
États-Unis *m. pl.* the United States, 9-2
éteindre † to turn off, 10-3
    éteindre les lumières to turn off the lights, 10-3
étendu/e extended, 7-1
été *m.* summer, 2-3
    l'été prochain next summer, 2-3
étoile *f.* star, 9-3
étonnant/e surprising, 10-3
étonné/e surprised, 10-3
étranger/-ère foreign, 3-2
être † to be, P-1
    être d'accord to agree, 10-2
    être en train de + inf. to be busy doing something, 4-1
être humain *m.* human being
étude *f.* study, 3-2
    faire des études to study
étudiant *m.*, **étudiante** *f.* student, P-2
étudier to study
Europe *f.* Europe, 9-2

européen/ne European
eux *m. pl.* they, them, P-1
    eux-mêmes *m. pl.* themselves
événement *m.* event, 7-2
éventuel/le probable
éventuellement probably, perhaps
évident obvious, 11-3
évier *m.* (kitchen) sink, 6-2
éviter to avoid, 10-2
exacte exact
exactement exactly
exagérer to exaggerate
examen *m.* exam, 3-2
    passer un examen to take an exam
    préparer un examen to study for an exam, 3-2
    réussir un examen to pass an exam
excès *m.* excess
exercer to exercise, exert
exercice *m.* exercise
    faire de l'exercice to exercise, 10-2
exigeant/e demanding, 7-1
exiger † to require, to demand, 10-2
exotique exotic
expérience *f.* experience; experiment
expliquer to explain, 6-2
exposé *m.* report, talk
exposition *f.* exhibition, 2-3
expression *f.* expression
exprimer to express
s'exprimer to express one self
extrait *m.* exerpt, extract
extraterrestre *m.* extraterrestrial, alien
extrême extreme
extrêmement extremely

F

fabriquer to make, to produce
fac = faculté
face *f.*: **en face (de)** facing, across from, 3-1
fâché/e angry, upset, 7-3
se fâcher (contre) to get angry (at, with), 7-3
facile easy, 3-2
facilement easily
façon *f.* way
    de toute façon in any case
facture *f.* bill
faculté *f.* college, university, 2-1
faible weak
faim *m.* hunger, 8-1
    avoir faim to be hungry, 8-1
faire † to do, to make, 2-2
    Ça (ne) fait rien. That doesn't matter., 12-3
    deux et deux font quatre 2 + 2 = 4 (equals)
    faire partie de to belong to, 7-1

faire *(continued)*

Ne t'en fais pas !/Ne vous en faites pas ! Don't worry!, 7-3

se faire du souci to worry, 7-3

se faire un petit plaisir to treat oneself, 12-3

Il fait beau. It's beautiful weather., 5-1

faire-part *m. inv.* (birth, wedding) announcement

falloir † to be necessary, 10-1

Il faut que… It is necessary that/ You must . . . , 10-1

Il ne faut pas que… You must not . . . , 10-1

fameux/-euse famous

familial/e familial, related to family

familier/-ière familiar

famille *f.* family, 1-1

famille étendue extended family, 7-1

famille monoparentale single-parent family, 7-1

famille nombreuse big family, 1-1

famille recomposée blended family, 7-1

fanatique *m.* fan, fanatic

être fanatique de to be a fan of, 12-3

fantaisiste fantastic (not based in reality)

fantastique fantastic (great, wonderful); fantasy

fantôme *m.* phantom, ghost

farine *f.* flour

fariné/e floured

fasciné/e fascinated

fatigué/e tired, P-1

faune *f.* wildlife, fauna

faut *see* **falloir**

faute *f.* mistake

faire une faute to make a mistake

fauteuil *m.* armchair, 6-2

faux/-sse false

favoriser to favor

Félicitations ! Congratulations!, 7-2

féminin/e feminine

féminisation *f.* to make feminine (esp. names of professions)

femme *f.* wife, woman, 1-1

femme au foyer *f.* housewife, 7-1

fenêtre *f.* window, P-2

férié : jour *m.* **férié** public holiday, 7-2

ferme *f.* farm, 6-3

fermer to close, P-2

fête *f.* party, 2-2; holiday, 7-2

fête religieuse *f.* religious holiday, 7-2

fêter to celebrate

feu *m.* fire

feu d'artifice *m.* fireworks, 7-2

feu rouge *m.* stoplight

feuille *f.* sheet of paper; leaf

feuilleton *m.* series, soap opera, 11-1

feutre *m.* felt-tip pen, marker

fève *f.* broad bean, favor baked in **la Galette des rois**

février February, 1-2

fiançailles *f. pl.* engagement

fiancé/e engaged, 1-1

se fiancer to get engaged, 7-3

fichier *m.* computer file, 11-3

fidèle faithful

fièvre *f.* fever, 10-1

avoir de la fièvre to have a temperature, to run a fever

figure *f.* face, 4-1

fille *f.* daughter, girl, 1-1

film *m.* film, 11-1

fils *m.* son, 1-1

fin/e thin, elegant, delicate, 4-3

final/e final, 3-2

finalement finally, 11-2

finir to finish, 6-1

flamand *m.* Flemish (language)

fleur *f.* flower, 7-2

fleuve *m.* river, 10-3

flore *f.* flora, plant-life

flûte *f.* recorder

flûte traversière *f.* flute, 12-1

foie *m.* liver, 10-1

fois *f.* time

x fois par semaine x times a week

une fois once, one time, 2-3

folklorique folkloric, 12-1

foncé/e dark

fonction *m.* function

fonctionner to function

fond *m.* bottom, end

à fond deeply; loudly

fondre to melt

fondu/e melted

fontaine *f.* fountain

football (foot) *m.* soccer, 1-3

football américain *m.* American football, 2-2

foraine : fête foraine *f.* fair

forcément inevitably, necessarily

forêt *f.* forest, 6-3

formation *f.* formation; training

avoir une formation to have training

forme *f.* shape, form

être en forme to be fine, P-1

être en pleine forme to be in good shape, 10-2

former to form

formidable great

fort *adv.* loudly, 7-3

fort/e *adj.* strong, stout, 2-1

forum *m.* forum

forum de discussion discussion forum, newsgroup

foulard *m.* silk scarf, 4-3

foule *f.* crowd

four *m.* oven, 6-2

fourchette *f.* fork

fourrure *f.* coat, fur

foyer *m.* household, 7-1

frais/fraîche fresh, 8-3

Il fait frais. It's cool (weather)., 5-1

fraise *f.* strawberry, 8-3

français/e *adj.* French, 9-2

français *m.* French (language), 2-2

faire du français to study French, 2-2

France *f.* France, 9-2

francophone French-speaking

francophonie *f.* French-speaking world

fréquence *f.* frequency, 4-1

frère *m.* brother, 1-1

frigo *m.* (*colloq.*) fridge

frite *f.* French fry, 8-1

froid cold, 5-1

Il fait froid. It's cold (weather)., 5-1

J'ai froid. I'm hot/cold., 5-1

fromage *m.* cheese, 8-2

frontière *f.* border, 9-2

fruit *m.* fruit, 8-2

fruits de mer *m. pl.* seafood

fruitier/fruitière *adj.* fruit, 6-3

fumé/e *adj.* smoked

fumée *f.* smoke

fumer to smoke, 10-2

fumet *m.* aroma

furieux/-euse furious, 7-3

futur *m.* future tense

futur proche *m.* immediate future

G

gagner de l'argent to earn money, 3-3

galérie *f.* (art) gallery

galette *f.* cake for the Epiphany, 7-2; savory dinner crepe made with buckwheat flour

gant *m.* glove, 4-3

gant de toilette wash mitt, 4-1

garage *m.* garage, 3-1

garantir to guarantee

garçon *m.* boy, 1-1

gare *f.* train station, 2-3

garer to park, 6-1

gaspiller to waste, 10-3

gâteau *m.* cake, 7-2

gauche *f.* left, 3-1

à gauche (de) to the left (of), 3-1

gaz *m.* gas, 10-3

gaz d'échappement *m. pl.* exhaust fumes, 10-3

gazeux/-euse carbonated

geler † to freeze, 5-1

Il gèle. It's freezing (weather)., 5-1

gêné/e bothered, embarrassed, 7-3

général/e general

généralement generally

généreux/-euse generous, warm-hearted, 2-1

générique *m.* screen credits

genou *m.* knee, 10-1

genre *m.* (grammatical) gender; kind, type

gens *m. pl.* people, 3-3

gentil/le kind, nice, 2-1

    C'est gentil à toi/vous. That's kind (of you)., 5-3

géographie *f.* geography

géologie *f.* geology

gestion *f.* business, 3-2; management

gilet *m.* cardigan sweater, 4-3

gîte (rural) *m.* (rural) bed and breakfast, 9-3

glace *f.* ice cream, 8-1

    glace au chocolat chocolate ice cream, 8-1

glaçon *m.* ice cube, 8-1

golf *m.* golf, 1-3

gomme *f.* eraser, P-2

gorge *f.* throat, 10-1

    avoir mal à la gorge to have a sore throat, 10-1

goût *m.* taste, liking

    avoir le goût du travail to have a strong work ethic, 7-1

goûter *m.* afternoon snack, 8-2

goûter to have a snack, to taste

goutte *f.* drop, 10-1

    gouttes pour le nez/les yeux *f. pl.* nose/eye drops, 10-1

gouvernement *m.* government

grâce à thanks to, 11-3

graisse *f.* fat, grease, 10-2

graissé/e greased

gramme *m.* (*abbr.* **gr**) gram

grand-chose *m. inv.* : **pas grand-chose** not very much, not a great deal, 2-2

    ne pas faire grand-chose to not do much, 2-2

grand/e tall, 2-1

grande surface *f.* superstore, 8-3

grandir to grow taller, to grow up (for children), 6-1

grand magasin *m.* department store, 4-3

grand-mère *f.* grandmother, 1-1

grand-père *m.* grandfather, 1-1

grand-parent *m.*, (**grands-parents** *pl.*) grandparent, 1-1

grave serious, 7-3

    Ce n'est pas grave. It's not serious., 7-3

graveur CD *m.* CD burner, 11-3

gravité *f.* gravity, seriousness

grignoter to snack, 10-2

grillé/e grilled, toasted, 8-2

grimper to climb up

grippe *f.* flu, 10-1

gris/e gray, 4-3

gros/se fat, 2-1

grossir to gain weight, 6-1

grotte (préhistorique) *f.* (prehistoric) cave, 9-3

groupe *m.* group

    groupe de consonnes *m.* consonant cluster

guerre *f.* war

gueule *f.* jaws, jowls (of an animal)

guide *m.* guide (tour guide or guidebook), 9-3

guidé/e guided

guitare *f.* guitar, 1-3

    guitare basse base guitar, 12-1

    guitare électrique electric guitar, 12-1

gymnase *m.* gym, 2-3

H

s'habiller to get dressed, 4-1

habitation *f.* dwelling, housing

habiter to live (in a physical sense), 1-3

d'habitude usually, 6-3

habituel/le habitual

s'habituer à to get used to

*haché/e chopped, ground, 8-3

*hamburger *m.* hamburger, 8-1

*haricot *m.* bean, 8-3

    *haricot vert *m.* green bean, 8-2

harmonica *m.* harmonica, 2-2

harmonie *f.* harmony

*haut high

hebdomadaire *adj.* weekly, 11-2

*hein ! huh!, understood?

heure *f.* hour, 4-2

    être à l'heure to be on time, 4-2

Il est une heure. It's one o'clock., 4-2

    Quelle heure est-il ? What time is it?, 4-2

    Vous avez l'heure ? Do you have the time?, 4-2

heureusement luckily, 7-1

heureux/-euse happy, 7-1

*heurter to strike

hier yesterday, 5-1

histoire *f.* history, 3-2; story

    histoire drôle joke, 2-1

historique historical, 11-1

hiver *m.* winter, 5-1

*hockey *m.* hockey, 2-2

*hollandais/e Dutch, hollandaise (sauce)

*Hollande *f.* Holland

*homard *m.* lobster

homme *m.* man

    homme au foyer house husband, 7-1

hôpital *m.* public hospital, 3-3

horloge *f.* clock, 4-2

horreur *f.* horror, 11-1

    Quelle horreur ! How awful!, 8-1

*hors except; outside

hôte *m.* guest or host

hôtel *m.* hotel, 2-3

huile *f.* oil, 8-3

    huile d'olive *f.* olive oil

    huile usée *f.* wasted or used oil, 10-3

*huit eight, 1-2

*huitième eighth, 6-1

huître *f.* oyster

humain/e human 10-1

I

ici here, 3-1

idéal/e ideal

idée *f.* idea

idéaliste idealistic, 1-1

identité *f.* identity

idiomatique idiomatic

il *m.* he, it, P-1

île *f.* island

ils *m. pl.* they, P-1

il y a there is/are, P-2; ago, 5-1

    il y a deux jours two days ago, 5-1

    il n'y a pas de… there isn't/aren't . . . , P-2

    Il n'y a pas de quoi. You're welcome., P-2

    il y a … que it's been . . . , for . . . , 11-3

illogique illogical

illustre illustrious

imaginaire imaginary

imaginer to imagine

imbécile *m./f.* idiot

immense huge, immense

immeuble *m.* building, 6-1

immigré/e immigrant

immobilier *m.* real estate business

immunodéficitaire immunodeficient

imparfait *m.* imperfect tense

impatience *f.* impatience

impératif *m.* imperative

imper(méable) *m.* raincoat, 4-3

importance *f.* importance

important important, 10-1

impression *f.* impression

impressionnisme *m.* Impressionism

impressionniste Impressionist, 12-2

imprimante *f.* printer, 11-3

imprimer to print, 11-3

inclure to include

inclus/e included

inconvénient *m.* disadvantage, inconvenience

Inde *f.* India, 9-2

indéfini/e indefinite

indication *f.* sign, indication

indien/ne Indian, 9-2

indifférence *f.* indifference

indigestion *f.* indigestion

indiquer to indicate

indiscipliné/e undisciplined, 1-1

indiscret/-ète indiscreet

indispensable necessary

individualiste individualistic, 1-1
individu *m.* individual
individuel/le individual
indulgent/e indulgent, lenient, 7-1
industriel/le industrial, 10-3
infection *f.* infection, 10-1
infinitif *m.* infinitive
infirmerie *f.* health center/clinic, 3-1
infirmier *m.*, **infirmière** *f.* nurse, 3-3
informaticien *m.*, **informaticienne** *f.* programmer, 3-3
information *f.* information
informations *f. pl.* **(les infos)** news, 11-1
informatique *f.* computer science, 3-2
s'informer to get information, 11-2
ingénieur *m.* engineer, 3-3
innovateur/-trice innovative
innovation *f.* innovation
inquiet/-ète worried, uneasy, anxious, 7-3
s'inquiéter † to worry, 7-3
inscription *f.* registration, enrollment
  bureau *m.* **des inscriptions** registrar's office, 3-1
insensible insensitive
instable unstable
installer to put in, to install
instant *m.* moment, instant
instituteur *m.*, **institutrice** *f.* elementary teacher, preferred term is **professeur des écoles** *m.*
s'instruire † to educate oneself, to improve one's mind, 11-2
instrument *m.* instrument, 12-1
insulter to insult
insupportable unbearable
intégrer to incorporate, integrate
intelligent/e intelligent, smart, 2-1
intensité *f.* intensity
interactif/-ive interactive
interdiction *f.* ban
interdire to ban, to forbid
intéressant/e interesting, 3-2
s'intéresser (à) to be interested (in), 3-3
intérieur *m.* inside, interior
interlocuteur *m.* partner in dialogue, interlocutor
internaute *m.* Internet user
Internet *m.* Internet
  aller sur Internet to go on the Internet
  surfer sur Internet to surf the Internet
interpréter to interpret
interrogatif/-ive interrogative
interrogation *f.* quiz
interviewer to interview
intime intimate
s'intituler to be titled, 12-2
intrigue *f.* plot, scheme
invariable invariable
invitation *f.* invitation, 5-3
invité/e *m./f.* guest

inviter to invite, 1-3
irrégularité *f.* irregularity
irrégulier/-ière irregular
Italie *f.* Italy, 9-2
italien/ne *adj.* Italian, 9-2
italien *m.* Italian (language)
ivoirien/ne Ivorian, 9-2

J
jalousie *f.* jealousy
jaloux/-ouse jealous, 7-3
jamais ever
  ne … jamais never, 4-1
jambe *f.* leg, 10-1
jambon *m.* ham, 8-1
janvier January, 1-2
Japon *m.* Japan, 9-2
japonais/e *adj.* Japanese, 9-2
japonais *m.* Japanese (language)
jardin *m.* garden, yard, 1-3
jardinage *m.* gardening, 2-2
  faire du jardinage to garden, to do some gardening, 2-2
jaser to chatter, prattle (Can.)
jaune yellow, 4-3
jazz *m.* jazz, 2-2
je (j') I, P-1
jean *m.* jeans, 4-3
jet *m. sg.* spurt, spray; jet
jeter † to throw/throw out, 5-3
jeu *m.* game, 2-2
  jeu de société board game, 2-2
  jeu électronique video game
  jeu télévisé game show, 11-1
jeudi Thursday, 1-3
jeune *adj.* young, 2-1
jeune *m./f.* young person
jeûne *m.* fast
jeûner to fast
jeunesse *f.* youth, young people
job (d'été) *m.* (summer) job
jogging *m.* jogging, 2-2
  faire du jogging to go jogging, to jog, 2-2
joie *f.* joy
joli/e pretty, 2-1
jouer to play, 1-3
  jouer une pièce to perform a play, 5-3
  jouer à to play (a sport), 1-3
  jouer de to play (an instrument), 1-3
jour *m.* day, 1-3
  ce jour-là that day, 5-1
  jour férié public holiday, 7-2
journal *m.* newspaper, 11-2
  journal télévisé (le JT) news broadcast, 11-1
journalisme *m.* journalism, 3-2
journaliste *m./f.* journalist, 3-3
journée *f.* day, 4-1
Joyeux Noël ! Merry Christmas!, 7-2

juger to judge
juif *m.*, **juive** *f.* Jewish, 7-1
juillet July, 1-2
juin June, 1-2
jumeau *m.*, **jumelle** *f.* twin, 1-1
jupe *f.* skirt, 4-3
jus d'orange *m.* orange juice, 8-1
jusqu'à until, 4-2
juteux/-euse juicy

K
kayak *m.* kayak
kilo *m.* kilo, 8-3
kiosque *m.* newsstand, 11-2

L
la (l') *f.* the, P-1; her, it, 6-1
là there, 6-3
là-bas there, over there, 6-3
labo(ratoire) *m.* laboratory, 3-1
  labo(ratoire) de chimie chemistry lab, 3-1
  labo(ratoire) de langues language lab, 3-1
lac *m.* lake, 6-3
laid/e ugly
laine *f.* wool, 4-3
laisser to leave (alone)
  laisser les lumières allumées to leave the lights on, 10-3
lait *m.* milk, 8-2
lampe *f.* lamp, 6-2
lancer to throw
langage *m.* language
langagier/-ière linguistic, of language
langue *f.* language, 3-2; tongue
  langue étrangère foreign language, 3-2
  langue maternelle native language, 9-2
laquelle *f.* which one
lapin *m.* rabbit
large big, large, loose-fitting, roomy, 4-3
lavabo *m.* bathroom sink, 4-1
laver to wash
se laver to wash oneself, 4-1
  se laver les cheveux to wash one's hair, 4-1
  se laver les dents to brush one's teeth
  se laver la figure to wash one's face, 4-1
  se laver les mains to wash one's hands, 4-1
le (l') *m.* the, P-1; him, it, 6-1
leçon *f.* lesson, 1-3
  leçon de chant singing lesson, 1-3
lecteur *m.*, **lectrice** *f.* reader
lecteur CD *m.* CD player, P-2
lecteur CD-ROM, DVD *m.* CD-ROM, DVD drive, 11-3

lecteur DVD *m.* DVD player, P-2
lecture *f.* reading
légende *f.* caption; legend; key
leger/-ère light
légume *m.* vegetable, 8-2
lequel *m.* which one
les *pl.* the, P-2
lesquels, lesquelles *m. pl./f. pl.* which ones
lettre *f.* letter
lettres *f. pl.* humanities, 3-2
leur their, 1-2; to them, 6-2
leurs *pl.* their, 1-2
lever † to raise, 5-3
    lever le doigt to raise one's hand
se lever † to get up, 4-1
    Levez-vous ! Get up/Stand up!, P-2
lèvre *f.* lip, 10-1
liaison *f.* link, liaison
librairie *f.* bookstore, 2-3
libre free (a person), available, 5-3
    Je ne suis pas libre. I'm not free., 5-3
    Tu es/vous êtes libre(s) ? Are you free?, 5-3
lieu *m.* place
    au lieu de instead of
    avoir lieu to take place, 7-2
    lieu de travail *m.* workplace
ligne *f.* line
    en ligne online, 11-3
limonade *f.* lemon-lime soft drink, 8-1
linguistique *f.* linguistics
lire † to read, 7-1
    Lisez les mots… ! Read the words . . . !, P-2
lit *m.* bed, 6-2
litre *m.* liter, 8-3
littérature *f.* literature, 3-2
livre *m.* book, P-2
locataire *m.* tenant, renter, 6-1
location *f.* renting
logement *m.* lodgings, accommodation, 9-3
loger † to stay temporarily, 9-3
logiciel *m.* software program, 11-3
logique logical
loin (de) far from, 3-1
lointain *adj.* distant, faraway
loisir *m.* leisure time, 2-2
long/longue long, 4-3
longtemps a long time, 10-1
    il y a longtemps a long time ago, 5-1
lorsque when
loto *m.* lottery, 2-2
louer to rent, 6-1
louisianais/e from Louisiana
lourd/e heavy, 5-1
    Il fait lourd. It's humid., 5-1
loyer *m.* rent, 6-2
lui *m.* him, P-1; to him, to her, 6-2
    lui-même *m.* himself
luisant/e gleaming, shining

lumière *f.* light, 10-3
    éteindre les lumières to turn off the lights, 10-3
lunaire lunar, pertaining to the moon
lundi Monday, 1-3
    le lundi every Monday, on Mondays, 6-3
lune (Lune) *f.* moon (the Moon), 10-3
    être dans la lune to have one's head in the clouds
    lune de miel *f.* honeymoon
lunettes *f. pl.* eyeglasses, 4-3
    lunettes de soleil pair of sunglasses, 4-3
lutte *f.* struggle; wrestling
lutter to struggle, fight
luxe *f.* luxury
luxueux/-euse luxurious
lycée *m.* high school, 3-3

M

ma *f.* my, 1-1
McDo *m.* McDonald's restaurant
machine *f.* machine
macroéconomique *f.* macroeconomics
madame (Mme) Mrs., Ms, P-1
mademoiselle (Mlle) Miss, P-1
magasin *m.* store, 3-3
magazine *m.* news show, 11-1; magazine, 11-2
    magazine télé listing of TV programs, 11-1
maghrébin/e North African, 7-1
magnétophone *m.* tape player
magnétoscope *m.* videocassette recorder, P-2
magnifique magnificent
mai May, 1-2
maigre skinny, thin, 6-1
maigrir to lose weight, 6-1
maillot (de bain) *m.* swimsuit, 4-3
main *f.* hand, 4-1
maintenant now, 1-3
maintenir † to maintain
maire *m.* mayor
mairie *f.* city hall, 2-3
mais but, 1-1
maison *f.* house, home, 1-3
    rester à la maison to stay home
maître *m.* master
maîtrise *f.* mastery; M.A. or M.S. degree in former French academic system
majeur/e *adj.* principal, major
majeure (en) *f.* academic major (in), (Can.), 3-2
majoritairement predominantly
mal *adv.* badly
mal *m.* (**maux** *pl.*) pain, ache, 10-1
    avoir du mal à respirer to have difficulty breathing, 10-1
    avoir mal to hurt, 10-1

    avoir mal à la tête to have a headache, 10-1
    avoir mal au cœur to be nauseated, 10-1
    avoir mal partout to hurt all over, 10-1
    mal au cœur nausea, 10-1
malade *adj.* sick, P-1
malade *m./f.* sick person, 10-1
    malade imaginaire *m./f.* hypochondriac
maladie *f.* sickness, disease, 10-1
malgré in spite of
malheureux/-euse unhappy, unfortunate, 7-3
manière de vivre *f.* way of life
manifestation *f.* protest, demonstration
manger † to eat, 2-3
manque *m.* lack
manquer to miss, to be lacking, 11-3
manteau *m.* overcoat, 4-3
manuel *m.* manual, handbook
maquillage *m.* makeup, 4-1
se maquiller to put on makeup, 4-1
marché *m.* market, 2-3
    bon marché *adj.* cheap
    marché en plein air open-air market
mardi Tuesday, 1-3
mari *m.* husband, 1-1
mariage *m.* wedding, 7-2; marriage
marié *m.*, **mariée** *f.* bridegroom/bride, 7-2
marié/e married, 1-1
se marier to get married, 7-3
marin/e related to the sea
maritime coastal, seaside, maritime
Maroc *m.* Morocco, 9-2
marocain/e Moroccan, 9-2
marraine *f.* godmother, 9-2
marron *adj. inv.* brown, 4-3
marquant/e *adj.* outstanding
mars March, 1-2
masse *f.* group, mass
master: diplôme de master *m.* M.A. or M.S. degree in current French academic system
match *m.* (**matchs** *pl.*) game (sports), 2-2
mathématiques *f. pl.* (**les maths**) mathematics, 3-2
matière *f.* matter, material, subject
matin *m.* morning, 1-3
    dix heures du matin ten o'clock in the morning, 4-2
    du matin in the morning; A.M., 4-2
mauvais/e bad, 3-1
    Il fait mauvais. The weather's bad., 5-1
maux *see* **mal**
mazurka *f.* Mazurka, Polish folk dance
me (m') me, to me, P-1
mécanicien *m.*, **mécanicienne** *f.* mechanic, 3-3

méchant/e mean, naughty, 2-1
médecin *m.* doctor (M.D.), 3-3
médecine *f.* medicine, 3-2
médias *m. pl.* media, 11-1
médical/e medical
médicament *m.* medicine, drug, 10-1
médiocre mediocre, 3-2
se méfier to be suspicious
meilleur/e *adj.* better, best, 4-3
   meilleur/e ami/e *m./f.* best friend
   Meilleurs vœux ! Best wishes!, 7-2
mél *m.* e-mail address (France)
mélanger to mix
melon *m.* cantaloupe, 8-3
membre *m.* member, limb
même same, 4-3; even, 6-1
mémoire *m.* long essay, M.A. thesis
mémoire *f.* memory
ménacé/e threatened
ménacer to threaten, 10-3
mensuel/le monthly, 11-2
mental/e mental
menthe *m.* mint
   thé *m.* à la menthe mint tea
   tisane *f.* à la menthe herbal mint tea, 10-1
mentionner to mention
mer *f.* sea, 5-2
   au bord de la mer at the seashore
merci thank you, P-2
mercredi Wednesday, 1-2
mère *f.* mother, 1-1
mériter to earn, merit
merveilleux/-euse marvelous, wonderful
mes *pl.* my, 1-1
mésaventure *f.* misfortune
message *m.* message
messagerie instantanée *f.* instant messaging
messe *f.* Catholic mass
mesure *f.* measurement
mesurer to measure
métaphore *f.* metaphor
météo(rologie) *f.* weather forecast, 5-1
métier *m.* occupation, job, 3-3
métro *m.* subway, 9-1
metteur en scène *m.* film or stage director, 11-1
mettre † to put on, 4-3
   mettre la musique à fond to turn the music up loud, 10-3
   mettre la table to set the table
meublé/e furnished, 6-2
meuble *m.* piece of furniture, 6-2
mexicain/e Mexican, 9-2
Mexique *m.* Mexico, 9-2
midi noon, 4-2
mieux better, 4-2
   mieux ... que better . . . than, 4-2
militaire military

mille thousand, 2-3
milliard billion, 2-3
million million, 2-3
mince *adj.* thin, slender, 2-1
   Mince ! Shoot!, 4-2
mineure *f.* (en) minor (Can.), 3-2
ministre *m.* minister, secretary
Minitel *m.* minitel, French sytem of computer networking
minorité *f.* minority
minuit midnight, 4-2
minute *f.* minute, 4-1
mobylette *f.* moped, motor scooter, 9-1
mocassin *m.* loafer, 4-3
moche ugly, 2-1
modalité *f.* form, modality
mode *f.* fashion, 4-3
   à la mode fashionable, 4-3
mode *m.* form, mode
   mode articulatoire articulatory mode
   mode d'emploi directions
modèle *m.* style, 4-3; model
moderne modern, 6-2
modeste modest
modifier to modify
moelle *f.* marrow
moi me, P-1
   moi-même myself
moins less, 4-2
   moins ... que less . . . than, 4-2
   moins le quart a quarter to, 4-2
   moins vingt twenty to, 4-2
mois *m.* month, 1-2
   le mois prochain next month, 2-3
moitié *f.* half
moment *m.* moment, 5-1
   à ce moment-là at that moment, 5-1
mon *m.* my, 1-1
monde *m.* world
   tout le monde everyone, everybody
mondial/e worldwide
moniteur *m.* monitor, 11-3
moniteur *m.*, monitrice *f.* camp counselor
monnaie *f.* currency; change
mononucléose *f.* mononucleosis
monoparental/e single-parent, 7-1
monotone monotonous
monsieur (M.) Mr., P-1
monsieur *m.* man, P-2
monstre *m.* monster
montagne *f.* mountain, 5-2
montée *f.* climb
monter to go up, 5-2
montre *f.* watch, 4-2
montrer to show, P-2
monument *m.* monument, 2-3
   monument aux morts veterans' memorial, 2-3
se moquer to tease, mock
morceau *m.* piece, 8-3

mortel/le mortal
mot *m.* word, P-2
   mot apparenté cognate
   mot-clé keyword
   mot juste right word
moteur *m.* engine, 10-3
   moteur de recherche search engine, 11-3
moto *f.* motorcycle, 9-1
mouche *f.* fly (insect)
   bateau-mouche Paris river boat
mourir † to die, 5-2
moutarde *f.* mustard, 8-3
moyen de transport *m.* means of transportation, 9-1
muet/te silent, mute
muguet *m.* lily of the valley, 7-2
   brin *m.* de muguet sprig of lily of the valley, 7-2
multiculturel/le multicultural, 7-1
multiethnique multiethnic
multimédia multimedia
multiple multiple
municipal/e municipal, 2-3
mur *m.* wall, 6-2
mûr/e ripe, 8-3
musée *m.* museum, 2-3
musical/e *adj.* musical, 11-1
musicien *m.*, musicienne *f.* musician, 3-3
musique *f.* music, 1-3
   faire de la musique to play music, 3-3
musulman/e Muslim
mystérieux/-euse mysterious
mythe *m.* myth

N

nager † to swim, 2-3
naissance *f.* birth
naître † to be born, 5-2
narratif/-ive narrative
narration *f.* narrative, account
nasal/e nasal
natation *f.* swimming, 2-2
   faire de la natation to swim, 2-2
nationalité *f.* nationality, 9-2
nature *f.* nature, 6-3
   nature morte still life, 12-2
ne ... jamais never, 4-1
ne ... pas not, 1-3
ne ... personne no one, 8-2
ne ... rien nothing, 8-2
nécessaire necessary, 10-1
nécessité *f.* need, necessity
néerlandais/e Dutch, 9-2
néerlandais *m.* Dutch (language)
négatif/-ive negative
neiger to snow, 5-1
   Il neige. It's snowing, 5-1
nettoyer † to clean, 10-3
neuf nine, 1-2

neuf/ve *adj.* brand new, 6-2
neuvième ninth, 6-1
neveu *m.* nephew, 1-1
    neveux *m. pl.* nieces and nephews, 1-1
nez *m.* nose, 10-1
nièce *f.* niece, 1-1
Noël *m.* Christmas
noir/e black, 4-3
nom *m.* last name, P-2
nombre *m.* number, 1-2
nombreux/-euse numerous, 1-1
nommer to name
non non, P-1
    non plus neither
    moi non plus me neither
non biodégradable nonbiodegradable, 10-3
nord *m.* north, 9-2
normalement normally
nos *pl.* our, 1-2
note *f.* grade, 3-2
    avoir une note to have/receive a grade, 3-2
notre *m./f.* our, 1-2
nourricier/-ière nourishing
nourrir to nourish
nourriture *f.* food, nourishment
nous we, P-1; us, to us, 6-2
    nous-mêmes ourselves
nouveau (nouvel), nouvelle new, 3-1
    de nouveau again, 4-1
nouvelle *f.* piece of news, 7-3
nouvelles *f. pl.* news
novembre November, 1-2
nuage *m.* cloud, 5-1
    Il y a des nuages. It's cloudy., 5-1
nucléaire nuclear
nuisance *f.* something harmful, environmental problem, 10-3
nuit *f.* night, 4-1
numéro *m.* number

O

obéir à to obey, 6-1
obligatoire required, 3-2
observer to observe
obtenir † to obtain, 9-2
occasion *f.* chance, opportunity, occasion
    avoir l'occasion de to have the opportunity to
Occident *m.* the West
occupé/e busy, P-1
s'occuper de to take care of, 6-3
Océanie *f.* Pacific, 9-2
octobre October, 1-2
odeur *f.* odor
œil *m.* (**yeux** *pl.*) eye, 10-1
œuf *m.* egg, 8-2
    œuf en chocolat chocolate egg, 7-2
    œufs sur le plat/au plat fried eggs, 8-2

œuvre *f.* work (esp. literary or artistic)
    oeuvre d'art work of art, 12-2
office du tourisme *m.* tourism office, 9-3
officiel/le official
offrir † to give (a gift), 6-2
oignon *m.* onion, 8-3
oiseau *m.* bird, 1-1
olive *f.* olive
omelette *f.* omelet
omniprésent/e omnipresent
on one, people in general, 1-3
oncle *m.* uncle, 1-1
onze eleven, 1-2
onzième eleventh, 6-1
opéra *m.* opera, 12-1
opinion *f.* opinion
optimiste optimistic, 1-1
orage *m.* (thunder) storm, 5-1
    Il y a un orage. There is a (thunder)storm., 5-1
oral/e oral
orange *adj. inv.* orange, 4-3
orange *m.* orange (fruit), 8-1
Orangina *m.* Orangina orange soda, 8-1
orchestre *m.* orchestra, 12-1
ordinaire ordinary
ordi(nateur) *m.* computer, P-2
    ordinateur portable laptop computer, 11-3
ordonnance *f.* prescription, 10-1
ordre *m.* order
ordure *f.* trash, waste, 10-3
oreille *f.* ear, 10-1
organiser to plan, to organize, 2-2
origine *f.* origin
orphelin/e orphaned
ou or, P-1
où where, 2-1
ouest *m.* west
oublier(de) to forget, 9-1
Ouf ! Whew!, 4-2
oui yes, P-1
ouvrage de référence *m.* reference book, 11-2
ouverture *f.* opening
ouvrier *m.*, **ouvrière** *f.* worker, laborer, 3-3
ouvrir † to open, P-2

P

pagne *m.* wrap, piece of (African) cloth
pain *m.* bread, 8-2
    du pain avec du chocolat bread with chocolate, 8-2
    pain au chocolat chocolate croissant, 8-2
    pain de campagne round loaf of bread, 8-3
    pain de mie loaf of sliced bread, 8-3
    pain grillé toast, 8-2
    petit pain roll, 8-3

paire *f.* pair
paix *f.* peace
pâle pale, 6-1
pâlir to become pale, 6-1
panier *m.* basket, 10-3
pantalon *m. sg.* slacks, 4-3
pantouflard/e homebody, 2-1
paquet *m.* package, 8-3
par by, through
    par terre on the floor, 6-2
parapluie *m.* umbrella, 4-3
parc *m.* park, 2-3
parce que because, 2-1
pardon excuse me, P-2
parent *m.* parent, relative, 1-1
paresseux/-euse lazy, 2-1
parfaitement perfectly, completely, 10-3
parfois sometimes
parler to speak, P-2
    parler au telephone to talk on the phone, 1-3
    Parlez plus fort ! Speak louder!, P-2
parmi among
paroisse *f.* parish, county in Louisiana
parrain *m.* godfather, 7-2
partager † to share, 7-2
partenaire *m./f.* partner
participer à to participate in
particulier/particulière particular, specific, exceptional, special
partie *f.* part
    faire partie de to belong to, 7-1
partir to leave, 4-2
    à partir de from
    partir en vacances to go on vacation, 5-2
partitif/-ive partitive
partout everywhere, all over, 10-1
pas not, P-1
    ne … pas not, 1-3
    pas du tout not at all
    pas mal not bad, P-1
    pas si vite not so fast, 12-3
    pas tout à fait not quite, 5-2
passage *m.* passage
passager *m.*, **passagère** *f.* passenger
passant *m.*, **passante** *f.* passerby, 10-3
passé *m.* past
    passé composé compound past tense
passeport *m.* passport, 9-1
passer to go/come by, 5-2; to spend time, 5-3
    passer une soirée tranquille to spend a quiet evening, 5-3
se passer to happen, 7-3
passion *f.* passion
passionné/e passionate
pastel *m.* pastel, 12-2
pâte *f.* pasta, dough, 8-2
pâté *m.* pâté, 8-3

patience f. patience
patin m. **à glace** ice skate
patin m. **à roulettes** roller skate
patinage m. skating
pâtissier/-ère m. pastry chef
pâtisserie f. pastry shop, 8-3
patron m., **patronne** f. boss
pauvre poor
pavillon m. building, 3-1
payer † to pay
pays m. country, 9-2
paysage m. landscape, 12-2
Pays-Bas m. The Netherlands, 9-2
PDA m. PDA, 11-3
peau f. skin
    être bien dans sa peau to have confidence in oneself, 7-1
pêche f. peach, 8-3
pêche f. fishing, 5-2
    aller à la pêche to go fishing, 5-2
peigne m. comb, 4-1
peindre to paint, 12-2
peintre m. painter, 3-3
peinture f. painting, 3-2
pellicule f. roll of film
pendant during, for, 4-2
    pendant que while, 12-2
pénicilline f. penicillin
pensée f. thought
penser (à, de) to think, 7-1
    Je pense que non. I don't think so.
    Je pense que oui. I think so.
    Je pense que… I think that . . . , 11-3
perdre to lose, to waste, 5-1
    perdre son sang-froid to lose one's composure, 7-3
père m. father, 1-1
période f. period
perle f. pearl
permettre † **(à, de)** to permit, 7-1
permis de conduire m. driver's license, 9-1
persan/e adj. Persian
persil m. parsley
personnage m. character
    personnage principal main character, 11-1
personnalisé/e personalized
personne f. person, P-1
    ne … personne no one, nobody, 8-2
personnel/le personal
perspective f. perspective
persuader to persuade
perte f. loss
pessimiste pessimistic, 1-1
petit-déjeuner m. breakfast, 8-2
petit/e short, small, little, 2-1
petite annonce f. classified ad
petit-enfant m. grandchild, 1-1
petite-fille f. granddaughter, 1-1
petit-fils m. grandson, 1-1

petit pois m. pea, 8-3
peu m. a little, 1-1
peur f. fear, 11-3
    avoir peur to be afraid, 11-3
peut-être maybe, 2-1
phare m. lighthouse, beacon
pharmacie f. pharmacy
pharmacien m., **pharmacienne** f. pharmacist, 3-3
phénomène m. phenomenon
philosophie f. philosophy, 3-2
photographe m./f. photographer, 12-2
photo(graphie) f. photograph, photography, 2-1
phrase f. sentence
physiologie f. physiology, 3-2
physique adj. physical
physique f. physics, 3-2
physique m. physical traits, 2-1
piano m. piano, 1-3
pièce f. play, 2-3; room 6-1
    un cinq-pièces m. three-bedroom apartment, 6-1
    pièce f. **de monnaie** coin
    pièce jointe f. (e-mail) attachment, 11-3
pied m. foot, 10-1
    à pied on foot, 9-1
pierre f. stone
piétonnier/-ière for pedestrians
piquant/e spicy, hot
pique-nique m. picnic, 5-2
    faire un pique-nique to have a picnic, 5-2
piquer to sting
pire worse
piscine f. a swimming pool, 2-3
pizza f. pizza, 8-1
placard m. cupboard, kitchen cabinet, 6-2
place f. (city) square, 2-3; seat, place, 5-3
plage f. beach, 5-2
se plaindre to complain
plaisanter to joke
    Tu plaisantes ! You're joking!
plaisir m. pleasure, 5-3
    avec plaisir with pleasure, 5-3
plan m. map, blueprint
    plan de ville city map, 9-1
    plan du campus map of campus, 3-1
planche f. board
planche à voile f. windsurfing, windsurfing board, 5-2
    faire de la planche à voile to windsurf, 5-2
planète f. planet
planifier to plan
plastique plastic, 10-3
plat m. dish or course, 8-2
    plat préparé prepared dish, 8-3
    plat principal main dish, 8-2
plein/e (de) full (of), 11-1

plein air open air
pleurer to cry, 7-3
pleuvoir † : **Il pleut.** It's raining., 5-1
pluie f. rain, 5-1
plupart f. majority, most
plus more; plus
    non plus neither
    moi non plus me neither
    plus … que more . . . than, 4-2
plusieurs several
plutôt more, rather, 12-3
pneumonie f. pneumonia, 10-1
poche f. pocket
poêle f. pan
poème m. poem
poésie f. poetry, 11-2
poète m./f. poet
poignet m. wrist, 10-1
point m. point, period
poire f. pear, 8-2
poirier m. pear tree
poison m. poison
poisson m. fish, 8-2
poissonnerie f. seafood shop, 8-3
poitrine f. chest, 10-1
poivre m. pepper, 8-2
poivron m. (bell) pepper
policier : film policier m. detective/police film, 11-1
polluer to pollute, 10-3
pollution f. pollution, 10-3
    pollution atmosphérique air pollution, 10-3
    pollution sonore noise pollution, 10-3
polo m. polo shirt, 4-3
pommade f. ointment, salve, 10-1
pomme f. apple, 8-2
pomme de terre f. potato, 8-2
populaire popular
popularité f. popularity
porc m. pork
portable m. laptop computer 11-3; cell phone
porte f. door, P-2
portée f. reach
portefeuille m. wallet, 9-1
porte-monnaie m. inv. change purse, 9-1
porter to wear, 4-3; to carry
portrait m. portrait, 12-2
portugais/e adj. Portuguese, 9-2
Portugal m. Portugal, 9-2
poser to place, put
    poser une question to ask a question, 2-1
posséder † to possess, 6-3
posséssif/-ive possessive
possibilité f. possibility
possible possible
postal/e postal
poste m. job, position

poster *m.* poster
pot *m.* jar, 8-3
potable *adj.* drinkable
potager *m.* vegetable garden, 6-3
poubelle *f.* trash can, 10-3
poudre *f.* powder
   poudre à pâte baking powder (Louisiana)
poule *f.* hen
poulet *m.* chicken, 8-2
pouls *m.* pulse
poumon *m.* lung, 10-1
pour for, 2-1
   pour + inf. in order to
pourboire *m.* tip
pourcentage *m.* percentage
pourquoi why, 2-1
   pourquoi pas ? why not?, 12-3
pousser to push, encourage
pouvoir *m.* power
pouvoir † to be able to, 3-3
poux *m. pl.* lice
pratiquant/e practicing (esp. for religion), 7-1
pratique *adj.* practical
pratique *f.* practice
pratiquer to do, to engage in, 2-3
pré *m.* meadow
précis/e precise
prédécesseur *m.* predecessor
prédiction *f.* prediction
préfecture *f.* **(de police)** prefecture (police headquarters)
préférence *f.* preference, 3-2
préférer † to prefer, 3-2
préhistorique prehistoric, 9-3
premier/-ière first, 1-1
   C'est le premier mai. It's May first., 1-2
prendre † to take; to have a meal, 8-1
   prendre congé to take leave, say good-bye
   prendre le petit-déjeuner to have breakfast, 8-2
   prendre un bain to take a bath
   prendre une douche to take a shower, 4-1
   Prenez un stylo ! Take a pen!, P-2
prénom *m.* first name, P-2
prénominal/e prenominal, before the noun
préparer to prepare, 1-3
   préparer le dîner to fix dinner, 1-3
   préparer un diplôme (en) to do a degree (in), 3-2
   préparer un examen to study for an exam, 3-2
   préparer une leçon to prepare for a lesson/class, 1-3
préposition *f.* preposition

près (de) near to, 3-1
   tout près very near
présent *m.* present, present tense
présentateur *m.*, **présentatrice** *f.* presenter; newscaster
présenter to introduce, présent, P-1
   Je te/vous présente Guy. Let me introduce Guy to you., P-1
se présenter to introduce oneself
préservation *f.* conservation, preservation
préserver to preserve, 10-3
président/e *m./f.* president
presque almost
presse *f.* press, 11-2
pressé/e squeezed; in a hurry
   citron pressé *m.* lemonade, 8-1
prestige *m.* prestige, 3-3
prêt/e ready
prêter to lend, 6-2
prétexte *m.* excuse
prêtre *m.* priest
prévenir to prevent, to avoid; to warn someone
prier to beg, to pray
   Je vous/t'en prie. You're welcome., P-2
prière *f.* prayer
primaire primary
primitif/-ive primitive, 12-2
principal/e main, principal, 3-1
printemps *m.* spring, 5-1
   au printemps in the spring
priorité *f.* priority
pris/e : Je suis pris/e. I'm busy. I have a previous engagement., 5-3
privé/e private
privilégier to favor
prix *m.* price, 4-3; prize
probable probable
probablement probably
problème *m.* problem
   sans problème no problem, 8-1
prochain/e next, 2-3
proche close
producteur *m.*, **productrice** *f.* producer
produit *m.* product
   produit chimique *m.* chemical product, 10-3
prof *m.* = **professeur**
professeur *m.* professor, P-2; teacher, 3-2
   professeur des écoles *m.* elementary school teacher, 3-3
professeure *f.* professor, teacher (Can)
profession *f.* profession, 3-3
profond/e deep
programme d'études *m.* course of study
projet *m.* (future) plan
   projets de vacances *m. pl.* vacation plans, 5-2

promenade *f.* walk, stroll, 2-2
   faire une promenade to go for a walk, 2-2
se promener † to take a walk, 7-3
promettre † to promise
pronom *m.* pronoun
   pronom complément d'objet direct direct-object pronoun
   pronom complément d'objet indirect indirect-object pronoun
   pronom disjoint stressed pronoun
   pronom réfléchi reflexive pronoun
   pronom relatif relative pronoun
   pronom sujet subject pronoun
pronominal/e pronominal
prononcer to pronounce
prononciation *f.* pronunciation
prophétique prophetic
propos *m.* remark
   à propos de on the subject of, about
proposer to propose, to sugest
propre one's own, 6-1; clean
propriétaire *m./f.* landlord/landlady; homeowner, 6-1
protéger † to protect, 10-3
proverbe *m.* proverb
province *f.* province
provisions *f. pl.* food supplies
provoquer to provoke
proximité *f.* nearness, closeness, proximity
prune *f.* plum
psychologie *f.* psychology, 3-2
psychologique psychological
public *m.* public, 3-3
   avoir un contact avec le public to have contact with the public, 3-3
publicitaire *adj.* promotional, advertising
publicité *f.* **(pub)** advertisement, 11-2
puce *f.* flea
   marché *m.* **aux puces** flea market
puis then, 5-2
pull(-over) *m.* pullover sweater, 4-3
punir to punish, 6-1

Q

qualification *f.* label, description, qualification
quand when, 2-1
   quand même anyway, just the same
quantité *f.* quantity, 8-3
quarante forty, 1-2
quart *m.* quarter, 4-2
   et quart a quarter after, 4-2
   moins le quart a quarter to, 4-2
quartier *m.* neighborhood, 6-1
quatorze fourteen, 1-2
quatorzième fourteenth, 6-1
quatre four, 1-2
quatrième fourth, 6-1

quatre-vingts eighty, 1-2

quatre-vingt-dix ninety, 1-2

quatre-vingt-onze ninety-one, 1-2

que (qu') what, whom, which, that, 5-3

    qu'est-ce que/qui... ? what . . . ?, 5-3

    Qu'est-ce que tu as ? What's wrong?, 7,3

quel/le which, 5-2

    Quel âge as-tu/avez-vous ? How old are you?, 1-2

    Quel est ton/votre âge ? What's your age?, 1-2

    Quelle est la date ? What's the date?, 1-2

    Quelle heure est-il ? What time is it?, 4-2

    Quel temps fait-il ? What's the weather like?, 5-1

quelque some

quelque chose something, 8-2

quelquefois sometimes, 4-1

quelqu'un someone, P-2

question *f.* question, 2-1

    poser une question to ask a question, 2-1

questionnaire *m.* questionnaire, survey of questions

queue *f.* line (of people)

qui who, which, whom, 2-1

quinze fifteen, 1-2

quinzième fifteenth, 6-1

quitter to leave, 4-2

quoi what, 5-3

    n'importe quoi anything, no matter what

    Quoi de neuf ? What's new?

quotidien *m.* daily publication, 11-2

quotidien/ne daily, 11-2

R

racine *f.* root, origin, 7-1

    avoir des racines to have roots/origins, 7-1

raconter to tell a story, 11-1

radio *f.* radio, 1-3

    écouter la radio to listen to the radio, 1-3

radio reveil *m.* clock radio, 4-2

rafraîchissant/e refreshing, 8-1

raisin *m.* grape, 8-3

raison *f.* reason

    avoir raison to be right

raisonnable reasonable, 1-1

rajouter to add (some) more

randonnée *f.* hike, 5-2

    faire une randonnée to take a hike, 5-2

ranger † to arrange, to tidy up, 6-2

rap *m.* rap music

rapide quick, rapid

rapidement quickly, rapidly

rappel *m.* reminder

se rappeler † to remember, 7-3

rapport *m.* relationship, 7-1; report

    avoir des bons rapports avec qqn to get along well with sb, 7-1

rare rare

rarement rarely, 4-1

se raser to shave, 4-1

rasoir *m.* razor, 4-1

rater to miss, 7-1

ravi/e delighted, 7-3

rayon *m.* supermarket section, aisle, 8-3

    rayon boucherie meat counter, 8-3

    rayon boulangerie-pâtisserie bakery/pastry aisle, 8-3

    rayon charcuterie deli counter, 8-3

    rayon crémerie dairy aisle

    rayon fruits et légumes produce aisle, 8-3

    rayon poissonnerie fish counter, 8-3

    rayon surgelés frozen foods, 8-3

réagir to react

réalisateur *m.*, **réalisatrice** *f.* film director

réaliste realistic, 1-1

rebelle rebellious, 7-1

récemment recently

récent/e recent

réception *f.* welcome; reception (room)

réceptionniste *m./f.* receptionist

recette *f.* recipe

recevoir † to receive

réchauffer to reheat

recherche *f.* research, 11-3

    à la recherche de in search of

    faire de la recherche to do research

récipient *m.* container

réciprocité *f.* reciprocity

récit *m.* narrative, 5-2

réciter to recite

recommandation *f.* recommendation, 11-2

recommander to recommend

recommencer (à) † to begin again, 10-2

récompense *f.* reward, award

recomposé/e blended, put together again, 7-1

reconstitué/e reconstituted

recyclage *m.* recycling, 10-3

recycler to recycle, 10-3

rédaction *f.* composition, short essay

rédiger to compose, write

réduire † to reduce, 10-2

réfléchi/e reflexive; thoughtful

réfléchir à to think of/about, 6-1

reflet *m.* reflection, 12-2

refléter to reflect

réflexion *f.* reflection

réforme *f.* reform

refrain *m.* chorus, refrain

réfrigérateur *m.* **(frigo)** refrigerator, 6-2

refuser (de) to refuse, 5-3

regarder to watch, 1-3

    regarder la télé to watch TV, 1-3

    Regardez le tableau ! Look at the board!, P-2

    regarder un film to watch a film on TV, 1-3

régime *m.* diet, 10-2

    être au régime to be on a diet

    faire/suivre un régime to diet, 10-2

région *f.* area, region

régional/e regional

règle *f.* ruler, P-2

regret *m.* regret

regretter to be sorry, to regret, 5-3

régulier/-ière regular

régulièrement regularly

reine *f.* queen

relation *f.* relation, relationship

    relation familiale *f.* family relation, 1-1

relier to join, link together

religieux/-euse religious

religion *f.* religion

relire † to reread

remarié/e remarried, 1-1

rembourser to reimburse

remède *m.* remedy, 10-1

remercier to thank, P-2

remettre † to hand in/over, 6-2

remplacer to replace

remue-méninges *m. inv.* brainstorming

se rencontrer to meet, 7-3

rendez-vous *m.* meeting, date, appointment, 5-3

rendre (à) to hand in, P-2; to give back, 5-1

rendre visite à to visit someone, 5-1

rénové/e renovated, 6-2

renseignement *m.* information, 9-3

renseigner to inform

se renseigner to get information, 9-3

rentrée *f.* back-to-school, P-2

rentrer to return home, 4-1; to go/come back, 5-2

répandu/e widespread

réparer to repair

repartir to leave again

repas *m.* meal, 8-2

    repas équilibré well-balanced meal, 10-2

répéter † to repeat, P-2; to rehearse

replanter to replant

répondre (à) to answer, 5-1

    Répondez en français ! Answer in French!, P-2

répondeur (automatique) *m.* answering machine

reportage *m.* report (esp. news), 11-1

repos *m.* rest, 5-2

se reposer to rest, 7-3

reprendre † to take back

représentant *m.*, **représentante** *f.* **de commerce** sales representative, 3-3
représentation *f.* (theatrical) production, 12-1; representation
réputation *f.* reputation
RER *m.* commuter train from Paris to suburbs, 9-1
réseau *m.* network, 11-3
réservation *f.* reservation
réservé/e reserved, 1-1
réserver to reserve
résidence *f.* dormitory, 3-1
résidentiel/le residential, 6-1
résoudre to resolve, to solve
respirer to breathe, 10-3
responsabilité *f.* responsibility, 3-3
ressentir to feel, be affected by, 7-1
ressource *f.* resource
    ressource naturelle natural resource
restaurant *m.* restaurant, 2-3
    restaurant universitaire (resto U) dining hall, 3-1
restauration *f.* restaurant business, catering
rester to stay, 1-3
    rester à la maison to stay home, 1-3
    rester à la résidence to stay in the dorm, 2-2
    rester en pleine forme to stay in shape, 10-2
résultat *m.* result
résumé *m.* summary
résumer to summarize
résurrection *f.* resurrection
retard : être en retard to be late, 4-2
retenir † to retain
retomber to fall again
retour *m.* return
retourner to go back, 5-2
retraite *f.* retirement
    prendre la retraite to retire
retrouver (qqn) to meet up with (sb), 3-1
se retrouver to meet, 5-3
réunion *f.* meeting, 9-2
se réunir to get together, 6-1
réussir (à) to succeed/pass, 8-2
rêve *m.* dream
    faire un rêve to have a dream
réveil *m.* alarm clock, 4-2
se réveiller to wake up, 4-1
réveillon *m.* Christmas or New Year's Eve
revenir † to return, 5-2
rêver (de) to dream, 12-1
réviser to review, 1-3
revoir † to see again
    au revoir good-bye, P-1
revue *f.* review, journal
rez-de chaussée *m.* (**RdeCh**) ground floor, 6-1
rhume *m.* cold, 10-1

rideau *m.* curtain, 6-2
rien *m.* nothing
    De rien. Not at all. You're welcome., P-2
    ne … rien nothing, 8-2
rire *m.* laugh
rire to laugh
ris de veau *m. pl.* veal sweetbreads
risque *m.* risk
risquer (de) to risk, run the risk of, 12-3
rite *m.* rite, ritual
rituel *m.* ritual
rivière *f.* large stream or river (tributary), 6-3
riz *m.* rice, 8-2
robe *f.* dress, 4-3
robot *m.* robot
rock *m.* rock music, 2-2
roi *m.* king
rôle *m.* role, part
roman *m.* novel, 11-2
romanche *f.* Romansch (language spoken in Switzerland)
rond/e round
rosbif *m.* roast beef, 8-3
rose pink, 4-3
rose *f.* rose (flower)
rosé *m.* rosé wine, 8-1
rôti *m.* roast, 8-3
rôtie *f.* piece of toast (Can.), 8-2
rouge red, 4-3
rougir to blush, 6-1
routine *f.* routine, 4-1
roux/-sse redhead, redheaded, 2-1
rue *f.* street, 6-1
rugby *m.* rugby, 2-2
rupture *f.* break, rupture
rural/e rural, 9-3
rythme *m.* rhythm

S

sa *f.* his, her, 1-1
sac *m.* purse, 4-3; sack, bag, 10-3
    sac à dos *m.* backpack, 9-1
    sac en plastique *m.* plastic bag, 10-3
sage wise; well-behaved (for children)
saison *f.* season, 5-1
salade *f.* salad, lettuce, 8-1
    salade verte *f.* green salad, 8-1
salaire *m.* salary, 3-3
salle *f.* room, P-2
    salle à manger dining room, 6-1
    salle de bains bathroom, 6-1
    salle de classe classroom, P-2
    salle de séjour living room, 6-1
saluer to greet, P-1
salut hi, bye, P-1
samedi Saturday, 1-2
    samedi dernier last Saturday, 5-1
sandale *f.* sandal, 4-3

sandwich *m.* (**sandwichs** *pl.*) sandwich, 8-1
    sandwich au jambon ham sandwich, 8-1
    sandwich au fromage cheese sandwich, 8-1
sang *m.* blood
sang-froid *m.* composure, 7-3
sanglot *m.* sob
sans without, P-2
    sans doute undoubtedly
sapin *m.* pine tree, Christmas tree, 7-2
satellite *f.* satellite
sauce *f.* sauce
saumon *m.* salmon, 8-3
sauter to jump, to skip
    sauter un repas to skip a meal, 10-2
sauvage wild, savage
sauvegarder (un fichier) to save (a file), 11-3
sauver to protect, 10-3
savane *f.* savannah
savoir † to know (how), 7-3
savon *m.* bar soap, 4-1
saxophone *m.* saxophone, 2-2
scanner *m.* scanner, 11-3
scénario *m.* screenplay, script, scenario
science *f.* science, 3-2
    science-fiction *f.* science fiction, 11-1
    sciences de l'éducation *f. pl.* education, 3-2
    sciences économiques *f. pl.* economics, 3-2
    sciences humaines *f. pl.* social sciences, 3-2
    sciences naturelles *f. pl.* natural sciences, 3-2
    sciences physiques *f. pl.* physical sciences, 3-2
    sciences politiques *f. pl.* political science, 3-2
scientifique scientific
sculpteur *m.* sculptor, 12-2
sculpture *f.* sculpture, 3-2
sec/seche dry
secondaire secondary
secrétaire *m./f.* secretary, 3-3
sécurisant/e reassuring, 7-1
sécurité *f.* security
sédentaire unmoving, sedentary
seize sixteen, 1-2
seizième sixteenth, 6-1
séjour *m.* living room, 6-1; stay (abroad)
sel *m.* salt, 8-2
selon according to
semaine *f.* week, 1-3
    la semaine prochaine next week, 2-3
    par semaine per week
semblable *adj.* similar
sembler to appear
    il me semble it seems to me, 6-3

semestre *m.* semester, 3-2
semi-voyelle *f.* semivowel, glide
semoule *f.* semolina
Sénégal *m.* Senegal, 9-2
sénégalais/e Senegalese, 9-2
sensible sensitive, 7-3
sentimental/e sentimental
sentiment *m.* feeling, 7-3
se sentir to feel, 10-1
se séparer to separate, 7-3
sept seven, 1-2
septembre September, 1-2
septième seventh, 6-1
série *f.* TV serial, 11-1; series
sérieux/-euse serious, 2-1
se serrer la main to shake hands
serveur *m.*, **serveuse** *f.* server (in restaurant), 3-3
service *m.* service, tip
    Le service est compris ? Is the tip included?, 8-1
    service compris gratuity included
services *m. pl.* service sector, 3-3
serviette *f.* **(de toilette)** towel, 4-1
servir to serve, 4-2
    se servir de (qqch) to use (sthg), 11-3
ses *pl.* his, her, 1-1
seulement only, 6-2
shampooing *m.* shampoo, 4-1
short *m.* shorts, 4-3
si yes, 1-3; if, whether, 7-3
SIDA *m.* AIDS
siècle *m.* century
sieste *f.* nap
    faire la sieste to take a nap
sigle *m.* initials, acronym
signaler to indicate, to be a sign of
signe *m.* sign
silence *m.* silence
s'il vous/te plaît please, P-2
similaire alike, similar
similarité *f.* likeness, similarity
singulier/-ière singular
sinon *adv.* otherwise, or else
sirène *f.* siren
sirop *m.* cough syrup 10-1
site *m.* site, 9-3
    site culturel cultural site, 9-3
    site historique historical site, 9-3
    site Web Web site
situé/e located, situated, 6-1
situer to situate
six six, 1-2
sixième sixth, 6-1
ski *m.* skiing, 5-2
    faire du ski (nautique) to (water) ski, 5-2
    ski nautique water skiing
slogan *m.* slogan
snack-bar *m.* snack bar

sociable outgoing, 1-1
socialisme *m.* socialism
sociologie *f.* sociology, 3-2
sœur *f.* sister, 1-1
se soigner to take care of oneself, 10-1
soie *f.* silk, 4-3
soif *f.* thirst, 8-1
    avoir soif to be thirsty, 8-1
soir *m.* evening, 1-3
    ce soir tonight, 2-3
    du soir in the evening, P.M., 4-2
soirée *f.* evening, 5-3
    Bonne soirée ! Have a good evening!
soixante sixty, 2-1
soixante et un sixty-one, 2-1
soixante-dix seventy, 2-1
soixante et onze seventy-one, 2-1
sol *m.* ground, earth, 10-3
solde *f.* sale, 4-3
    en solde on sale
soldé/e *adj.* on sale
soleil *m.* sun, 5-1
    Il y a du soleil. It's sunny., 5-1
solution *f.* solution
sombre somber, dark, 12-2
sommaire *m.* brief table of contents
somme *f.* amount, sum
sommet *m.* top, summit
son *m. adj.* his, her, 1-1
son *m.* sound, volume
    baisser le son turn down the volume
sondage *m.* survey, poll
sonner to ring, 4-2
sonore resonant, sonorous
    pollution *f.* **sonore** noise pollution, 10-3
sophistiqué/e sophisticated
sortie *f.* outing, trip
sortir to go out, 4-2
souci *m.* worry, concern
    se faire du souci to worry, 7-3
souhaiter to hope, to wish, 10-2
soumettre to submit
soupe *f.* soup, 8-2
souper *m.* supper
souper to have supper
source *f.* source, credit
souris *f.* mouse, 11-3
sous under, below, 6-2
    sous les toits in the attic, 6-2
sous-sol *m.* basement, 6-1
sous-titre *m.* subtitle, 11-1
sous-titré/e subtitled
soutenir † to support, uphold
souvenir *m.* memory, recollection ; souvenir, memento
se souvenir de † to remember
souvent often, 4-1
spécial/e peculiar, special
spécialisation *f.* **(en)** major (in), 3-2
spécialité *f.* speciality

spectacle *m.* show, 12-3
    spectacle sons et lumières sound and light historical production, 9-3
sport *m.* sport, 2-2
    faire du sport to do/play sports, 2-2
    sport d'hiver winter sport, 5-2
sportif/-ive athletic, 2-1
stade *m.* stadium, 2-3
standardiste *m./f.* telephone operator, receptionist
station de métro *f.* subway stop, 3-1
statistique *f.* statistic
stéréotype *m.* stereotype
stress *m.* stress
stressé/e stressed, P-1
strophe *f.* stanza
studio *m.* studio apartment, 6-1
style *m.* style, 12-2
stylo *m.* pen, P-2
subjonctif *m.* subjunctive mood
subventionné/e subsidized
succès *m.* success
succession *f.* sequence, succession
sucre *m.* sugar, 8-1
sucré/e sweet (for food)
sud *m.* south
suggérer † to suggest, 3-2
suisse *adj.* Swiss, 9-2
Suisse *f.* Switzerland, 9-2
suivant/e *adj.* following, next
suivi/e *adj.* consistent, continuous
suivre † to follow, 3-2
    suivre un cours to take a course, 3-2
    suivre un régime to be on a diet, 10-1
sujet *m.* subject, 12-2
super super, 4-2
superbe superb
superlatif *m.* superlative
superstition *f.* superstition
supplément *m.* extra or additional part
supplémentaire extra or additional
sur over, on, 6-2
surconsommation *f.* overconsumption
sûr/e sure
    bien sûr of course, 2-1
surf *m.* surfing, 5-2
    faire du surf to surf, 5-2
    faire du surf des neiges to snowboard, 5-2
surface : grande surface *f.* large (department) store, 8-3
surfer to surf (the Internet)
surgelé/e *adj.* frozen, 8-3
surgelés *m. pl.* frozen foods, 8-3
surmédicalisation *f.* overmedication
surpopulation *f.* overpopulation
surprenant/e surprising
surprendre † to surprise
surpris/e surprised, 7-3
surtout above all, 6-2

surveiller to oversee

survol *m.* overview, survey

sympa(thique) nice, 1-1

symptôme *m.* symptom, 10-1

syncopé/e syncopated, irregular (rhythm)

syndicat *m.* (trade) union

système *m.* system

T

ta *f.* your, 1-1

tabac *m.* specialty shop for tobacco products, newspapers, magazines

table *f.* table

    table basse coffee table, 6-2

tableau *m.* board, P-2; painting 12-2; chart, table

taille *f.* waist, 10-1; size

    de taille moyenne average height, 2-1

tailleur *m.* women's suit, 4-3

talon *m.* heel

    chaussure *f.* **à talons** high-heeled shoe, 4-3

    talons hauts *m. pl.* high heels

    talons plats *m. pl.* flat heels

tante *f.* aunt, 1-1

taper to type

tapis *m.* rug, 6-2

tapisserie *f.* tapestry, 12-2

tard late, 4-1

tarte *f.* pie, 8-3

    tarte aux pommes apple pie, 8-2

tartelette *f.* small pie or tart

tartine *f.* slice of bread, 8-2

tasse *f.* cup, 8-2

taxi *m.* taxi, 9-1

te (t') you, to you, P-1

technicien *m.*, **technicienne** *f.* lab technician, 3-3

tee-shirt *m.* T-shirt, 4-3

télé *f.* = **télévision**

télé-achat *m.* infomercial, 11-1

télécommande *f.* TV remote control, 11-1

télécours *m.* distance learning

télématique *n.* data communications

téléphoner (à qqn) to phone (sb), 1-3

se téléphoner to phone one another, 7-3

télé-réalité *f.* reality TV, 11-1

télétravail *m.* telecommuting (for work)

télévisé/e televised

télévision TV, television (monitor), P-2

tempérament *m.* disposition, temperament

température *f.* temperature, 5-1

tempéré/e temperate

temps *m.* weather, 5-1; time; tense

    depuis combien de temps... ? for how long . . . ?, 11-3

    de temps en temps from time to time, 10-2

Quel temps fait-il ? What's the weather like?, 5-1

tendance *f.* tendency

tendre tender, affectionate

tendresse *f.* tenderness

Tenez ! [from **tenir**] Here!, 4-3

tenir † to hold

tennis *m.* tennis, 1-3; tennis shoe, 4-3

tension *f.* tension; blood pressure

tente *f.* tent

terminer to end, to finish

terrain de sport *m.* playing field, court, 3-1

terrasse *f.* terrace, 6-1

terre (Terre) *f.* earth (the Earth), 10-3

    par terre on the floor, 6-2

terrine *f.* loaf made of ground meats, fish, and/or vegetables

territoire *m.* territory

tes *pl.* your, 1-1

tête *f.* head, 10-1

têtu/e stubborn, 1-1

thé *m.* tea, 8-1

    thé au citron with lemon, 8-1

    thé au lait with milk

théâtre *m.* theater, 2-3

    théâtre romain Roman theater, 9-3

thème *m.* theme

thèse *f.* thesis

thon *m.* tuna, 8-3

ticket *m.* subway ticket, 9-1

timide shy, 1-1

tirage *m.* printing, circulation in print

tirer (une conclusion) to draw (a conclusion)

tisane *f.* herbal tea, 10-1

    tisane à la menthe mint herbal tea, 10-1

tissu *m.* fabric, 4-3

titre *m.* title

toilettes *f. pl.* toilets, restroom, 6-1

    articles de toilette *m. pl.* toiletries, 4-1

toi you, P-1

    toi-même yourself

toit *m.* roof, 6-2

    sous les tois in the attic, 6-2

tomate *f.* tomato, 8-3

tomber to fall, 5-2

    tomber amoureux/-euse (de) to fall in love (with)

ton *m.* shade, tone

tonnerre *m.* thunder, 5-1

    Il y a du tonnerre. There is thunder., 5-1

tôt early, 4-1

toujours always, 4-1

tour *f.* tower

tour *m.* trip, outing, visit

    faire un tour dans le quartier to tour the neighborhood, 5-2

    faire un tour au parc to go around the park, 5-2

tourisme *m.* : **faire du tourisme** *m.* to go sightseeing, 5-2

tourner to turn, 9-3

    tourner un film to shoot a film, 11-1

tous *m. pl.* all, 3-1

tout *m.* everything, 9-1

tout, tous, toute, toutes all, 4-1

    tous/toutes les... every . . . , 4-1

    tous les jours every day, 4-1

    tout à fait completely, 11-3

    tout de suite right away, immediately

    tout droit straight ahead, 9-3

    tout le monde everyone, everybody, 11-3

tousser to cough, 10-1

toux *f.* cough, 10-1

toxique toxic, 10-3

trace *f.* trace

tradition *f.* tradition

traditionnel/le traditional, 7-1

traduire translate

tragédie *f.* tragedy

train *m.* train, 9-1

    être en train de + *inf.* to be busy doing sthg, 4-1

traitement de texte *m.* word processing, editing, 11-3

tranche *f.* slice, 8-2

tranquil/le calm, tranquil, 6-1

transfert *m.* transfer

transport en commun *m.* public transportation, 10-3

travail *m.* work, 3-3

    avoir le goût du travail to have a strong work ethic, 7-1

travailler to work, to study, 1-3

    travailler dans le jardin to work in the garden/yard, 1-3

travailleur/-euse hard-working, 7-1

traverser to cross, 10-3

treize thirteen, 1-2

treizième thirteenth, 6-1

trente thirty, 1-2

trente et un thirty-one, 1-2

très very, P-1

    Très bien, merci. Very well, thank you., P-1

triangle *m.* triangle

trier to sort, 10-3

trimestre *m.* trimester, quarter, 3-2

trio *m.* trio, 12-1

triste sad, 7-3

trois three, 1-2

troisième third, 6-1

trombone *m.* trombone, 12-1

trompette *f.* trumpet, 12-1

trop too much, 1-1

troupe *f.* troop

trouver to find, 4-2

    Je trouve que... I find that . . . , 11-3

se trouver to be located, 3-1

truite *f.* trout

tu you, P-1

typique typical, 1-3

U

un one, 1-2

un/e a, an, one, P-2

    -unième: vingt et unième twenty-first, 6-1

uni/e united

uniforme *adj.* regular, uniform

uniforme *m.* uniform

union libre *f.* cohabitation, 7-1

universel/le universal

universitaire related to the university

université *f.* university, 3-1

urbain/e related to the city, urban

urgence *f.* emergency

urgent urgent, 10-1

usé/e waste, used, 10-3

usine *f.* factory, 3-3

utile useful, 10-1

utilisation *f.* use

utiliser to use, 10-3

V

vacances *f. pl.* vacation, 5-2

    grandes vacances summer vacation, 7-2

vaisselle *f.* dishes

    faire la vaisselle to do the dishes

valise *f.* suitcase, 9-1

vallée *f.* valley, 6-3

valoir † to be worth

    ça vaut le coup it's worth it, 12-3

    Il vaut/vaudrait mieux que... It is/would be better (best) that . . . , 10-1

valse *f.* waltz

vaste vast

vaut *see* **valoir**

vedette *f.* movie star, 11-1

vélo *m.* bicycle, 2-2

    faire du vélo *m.* to ride a bicycle, to go bike riding, 2-2

vendeur *m.*, **vendeuse** *f.* sales clerk, 3-3

vendre to sell, 5-1

vendredi Friday, 1-3

venir † to come, 5-2

    venir de + inf. to have just (done sthg), 9-2

vent *m.* wind, 5-1

    Il y a du vent. It's windy., 5-1

ventre *m.* belly, abdomen, 10-1

verbal/e verbal

verbe *m.* verb

verglas *m.* sleet, ice on the ground, 5-1

    Il y a du verglas. It's icy, slippery., 5-1

vérifier to check, verify

verre *m.* glass, 8-2

vers toward, around, 8-2

vers *m.* line of verse

verser to pour, 10-3

version originale (v.o.) *f.* in the original language, 11-1

vert/e green, 4-3; unripe

veste *f.* jacket, suit coat, 4-3

vêtement *m.* clothing, 4-3

viande *f.* meat, 8-2

vidéocassette *f.* videotape, P-2

vie *f.* life, 6-3

vieux (vieil), vieille old, 3-1

Vietnam *m.* Vietnam, 9-2

vietnamien/ne *adj.* Vietnamese, 9-2

vif/vive *adj.* bright, vivid, 12-2

villa *f.* house in a residential area, villa, 6-3

village *m.* village, 9-3

    village médiéval medieval village, 9-3

    village perché village perched on a hillside, 9-3

ville *f.* city, 2-1

vin *m.* wine, 8-1

    vin blanc white wine, 8-1

    vin rosé rosé wine, 8-1

    vin rouge red wine, 8-1

vinaigre *m.* vinegar, 8-3

vingt twenty, 1-2

vingt et un twenty-one, 1-2

vingt-deux twenty-two, 1-2

vingtième twentieth, 6-1

violon *m.* violin, 12-1

violoncelle *m.* cello, 12-1

virus *m.* virus

visage *m.* face, 10-1

vision *f.* vision

    avoir une vision du monde to have a world view, 7-1

visite *f.* visit, 5-2

    rendre visite à to visit a person, 5-1

visiter to visit a place, 5-2

vitesse *f.* speed

vitrine *f.* display window, 4-3

vive... (les Seychelles) ! hurray for . . . (the Seychelles)!, 5-2

vivre † to live, 7-1

vœu *m.* wish, 7-2

    Meilleurs vœux ! Best wishes!, 7-2

voici... here is/are . . . , P-1

voilà... here/there is/are . . . , P-2

voile *m.* veil

voile *f.* sail, sailing

    faire de la voile to go sailing, 5-2

voilé/e veiled

voir † to see, 2-3

    voir une exposition to see an exhibit, 2-3

    voir un film to see a film, 2-3

    voir une pièce to see a play, 2-3

    Voyons ! See here!, 7-3

    Voyons... Let's see . . . , 9-1

voisin *m.*, **voisine** *f.* neighbor, 6-1

voiture *f.* automobile, car, 3-1

voix *f.* voice

    à voix haute out loud

vol *m.* flight, 9-1

voler to fly; to steal

volley(-ball) *m.* volleyball, 2-2

volonté *f.* wish, will

    de bonne volonté *adv.* willingly

Volontiers. With pleasure, gladly., 5-3

vomir to vomit

vos *pl.* your, 1-2

votre *m./f.* your, 1-2

vouloir † to want, to wish, 3-3

    je voudrais I would like

vous you, P-1; to you, 6-2

    vous-même yourself

    vous-mêmes yourselves

voyage *m.* trip, voyage, 9-1

voyager † to travel, 3-3

Voyons *see* **voir**

voyelle *f.* vowel

vrai true

    c'est vrai. that's true.

    c'est pas vrai ! it can't be!, 5-2

vraiment really, 1-1

vue *f.* view

    vue d'ensemble overview

W

W.-C. *m. pl.* toilets, restroom (*lit.* water closet), 6-1

week-end *m.* weekend, 1-3

    ce week-end this weekend, 2-3

    le week-end on weekends, every weekend, 6-3

western *m.* western (film), 11-1

Y

y there, 9-1

yaourt *m.* yogurt, 8-2

yeux *m. pl. see* **œil**

Z

zapper to channel surf, 11-1

zéro zero, 1-2

zoologie *f.* zoology, 3-2

Zut (alors) ! Darn!, 4-2

Appendice 6 Lexique anglais-français

A

a, an un/e
abdomen ventre *m.*
able: to be able to pouvoir †
about de, environ
    it is about . . . il s'agit de…
absent, missing absent/e
accountant comptable *m./f.*
accounting comptabilité *f.*
ache mal (des maux) *m.*
active actif/-ive
activity activité *f.*
actor/actress acteur *m.*, actrice *f.*
address book carnet d'adresses *m.*
to adore adorer
adventure movie film d'aventures *m.*
advertisement annonce *f.*, publicité *f.*
    (pub)
to be affected by ressentir
affectionate affectueux/-euse, tendre
afraid: to be afraid avoir peur
Africa Afrique *f.*
after après
    after having . . . après avoir/ être +
    part. passé…
afternoon après-midi *m.*
    in the afternoon, P.M. de l'après-midi
age âge *m.*
    What is your age? Quel est ton/votre
    âge?, Quel âge as-tu/avez-vous?
aged, old âgé/e
ago il y a…
    two days ago il y a deux jours
to (not) agree (ne pas) être d'accord
air pollution pollution atmosphérique *f.*
air air *m.*
airplane avion *m.*
airport aéroport *m.*
Algeria Algérie *f.*
Algerian algérien/ne
all tout, tous, toute, toutes
along: to get along (with) s'entendre
    (avec)
already déjà
also aussi
always toujours
ambitious ambitieux/-euse
American américain/e
amphitheater amphithéâtre *m.*
to amuse oneself se distraire
amusements distractions *f. pl.*

amusing drôle
anger colère *f.*
angry fâché/e, en colère
    to be angry être fâché/e, en colère
    to become angry se fâcher
animated film dessin animé *m.*
ankle cheville *f.*
announcement (public) annonce *f.*
    birth announcement faire-part *m. inv.*
    de naissance
    wedding announcement faire-part
    m. inv. de mariage
to answer répondre (à)
    to answer the phone répondre au
    téléphone
    to answer a question répondre à une
    question
answer réponse *f.*
anthropology anthropologie *f.*
antibiotic antibiotique *m.*
anxious anxieux/-euse ; inquiet/-ète
anyway quand même
apartment appartement *m.*
to appear (good) avoir l'air (bon)
appetizer entrée *f.*
apple pomme *f.*
April avril
Arabic language arabe *m.*
architect architecte *m./f.*
Argentina Argentine *f.*
Argentinian argentin/e
to argue se disputer
arm bras *m.*
armchair fauteuil *m.*
armoire armoire *f.*
around vers, autour de
to arrange ranger
to arrive arriver
art book livre d'art *m.*
as comme
    as . . . as aussi … que
    as much . . . as autant … que
    as soon as dès que/aussitôt que
Asia Asie *f.*
to ask demander
    to ask a question poser une question
asleep endormi/e
asparagus asperge *f.*
aspirin aspirine *f.*
astronomy astronomie *f.*
athletic sportif/-ive

atlas atlas *m.*
to attend assister à
attention attention *f.*
August août
aunt tante *f.*
Australia Australie *f.*
Australian australien/ne
author auteur *m./f.*
authoritarian autoritaire
away: right away tout de suite
automobile voiture *f.*

B

back dos *m.*
    to come back revenir †
backpack sac *m.* à dos
bacon bacon *m.*
bad mauvais/e
    Not bad. Pas mal.
    It's too bad. C'est dommage.
bag sac *m.*
bakery/pastry aisle rayon boulangerie-
    pâtisserie *m.*
balcony balcon *m.*
banana banane *f.*
baptism baptême *m.*
bar soap savon *m.*
basement sous-sol *m.*
basket panier *m.*
basketball basket(-ball) *m.*
bathroom salle de bains *f.*
to be être †
beach plage *f.*
    to go to the beach aller à la plage
bean *haricot *m.*
    green bean *haricot vert *m.*
beautiful beau (bel), belle
    It's beautiful weather. Il fait beau.
because parce que
    because of à cause de
to become devenir †
bed lit *m.*
    to get out of bed se lever †
    to go to bed se coucher
    (rural) bed and breakfast
    gîte (rural) *m.*
bedroom chambre *f.*
beef boeuf *m.*
    ground beef bifteck haché *m.*
beer bière *f.*
to beg prier

before avant

    before (doing something). . . avant de + inf.

to begin commencer †

behind derrière

beige beige

Belgian belge

Belgium Belgique *f.*

to believe croire † (à, en)

    I believe that . . . Je crois que…

    I don't believe so Je ne crois pas.

belly ventre *m.*

to belong to faire partie de, appartenir à

belongings affaires *f. pl.*

best le/la meilleur/e

    Best wishes! Meilleurs vœux !

better meilleur/e *adj.*, mieux *adv.*

    better . . . than mieux … que

    it is better (to) il vaut mieux…

    it would be better (to) il vaudrait mieux…

bicycle vélo *m.*

    to go for a bike ride faire du vélo

big grand/e, gros/se, large

bill (restaurant) addition *f.*

bill utility facture *f.*

biography biographie *f.*

biology biologie *f.*

bird oiseau *m.*

birthday anniversaire *m.*

    Happy Birthday! Joyeux anniversaire !

black noir/e

blackboard tableau *m.*

blond blond/e

blouse chemisier *m.*

blue bleu/e

to blush rougir

board planche *f.*

board game jeu de société *m.*

boat bateau *m.*

    sailboat bateau à voile

book livre *m.*

bookstore librairie *f.*

boot botte *f.*

border frontière *f.*

bored ennuyé/e

    to become bored s'ennuyer †

boring ennuyeux/-euse

born: to be born naître †

to borrow emprunter

botany botanique *f.*

bothered gêné/e

bottle bouteille *f.*

bowl bol *m.*

box boîte *f.*

boy garçon *m.*

brand new neuf/neuve

Brazilian brésilien/brésilienne

Brazil Brésil *m.*

bread pain *m.*

round loaf of bread pain de campagne

sliced bread pain de mie

breakfast petit-déjeuner *m.*

    to have breakfast prendre le petit-déjeuner

to breathe respirer

bride mariée *f.*

bridegroom marié *m.*

to bring (along) a person amener †

to bring (something) apporter, emporter

brochure brochure *f.*

bronchitis bronchite *f.*

brother frère *m.*

    half-brother demi-frère *m.*

    brother-in-law beau-frère *m.*

brown marron *adj. inv.*

brunette brun/e

to brush se brosser

    to brush one's teeth se brosser les dents, se laver les dents

    to brush one's hair se brosser les cheveux

building bâtiment *m.*, immeuble *m.*

business gestion *f.*, les affaires *f. pl.*

to be busy doing something être en train de…

    I'm busy. Je suis pris/e. Je suis occupé/e.

but mais

butter beurre *m.*

to buy acheter †

by par

bye salut

C

cake gâteau *m.*

calendar calendrier *m.*

    (calendar) planner agenda *m.*

call appel *m.*

to call appeler †

    to be called s'appeler †

calm calme

    to calm down se calmer

camera appareil photo *m.*

    digital camera appareil (photo) numérique *m.*

    video camera caméscope *m.*

Cameroon Cameroun *m.*

Cameroonian camerounais/e

campground camping *m.*

to camp/go camping faire du camping

camper (vehicle) caravane *f.*

campus campus *m.*

can boîte *f.*

can (to be able to do something) pouvoir †

Canada Canada *m.*

Canadian canadien/ne

candle bougie *f.*

cantaloupe melon *m.*

car voiture *f.*

carafe carafe *f.*

card carte *f.*

    to play cards jouer aux cartes *f. pl.*

care: to take care of s'occuper de

    to take care of oneself se soigner

career carrière *f.*

carrot carotte *f.*

cartoon dessin animé *m.*

cash register caisse *f.*

cashier caissier *m.*, caissière *f.*

cassette tape cassette *f.*

cat chat/te *m./f.*

CD, compact disk CD *m. inv.*

    CD burner graveur *m.* CD

    CD player lecteur *m.* CD

CD-ROM CD-ROM *m.*

    CD-ROM drive lecteur *m.* CD-ROM

cell phone portable *m.*

cereal céréales *f. pl.*

chair chaise *f.*

    armchair fauteuil *m.*

    rocking chair fauteuil *m.* à bascule

    wheelchair fauteuil *m.* roulant

chalk (stick of) craie *f.*

change purse porte-monnaie *m.*

to channel-surf zapper

character personnage *m.*

    main character personnage principal

cheap bon marché

cheese fromage *m.*

chemical product produit chimique *m.*

chemistry chimie *f.*

chemistry lab labo(ratoire) *m.* de chimie

chess échecs *m. pl.*

chest poitrine *f.*

chicken poulet *m.*

child enfant *m.*

    grandchild petit-enfant *m.*

China Chine *f.*

Chinese chinois/e

choir chorale *f.*

chorus chœur *m.*

to choose choisir

church (Catholic) église *f.*

city ville *f.*

    in the city en ville

    city bus bus *m.*

    city hall mairie *f.*

    city map plan de ville *m.*

civil wedding cérémonie civile *f.*

class (subject) cours *m.*

    chemistry class cours de chimie

    elective class cours facultatif

    required class cours obligatoire

class (group of people) classe *f.*

    French class classe de français

classified ad petite annonce *f.*

classmate camarade de classe *m./f.*

classroom classe *f.*, salle *f.* de classe

to clean nettoyer †
clear clair/e
clothing vêtement *m.*
cloud nuage *m.*
    It's cloudy. Il y a des nuages.
coat manteau *m.*
    fur coat fourrure *f.*
    rain coat imperméable *m.*
    (suit coat) veste *f.*
    winter coat anorak *m.*
coffee café *m.*
    coffee with cream café crème *m.*
    coffee with milk café au lait *m.*
coffee table table basse *f.*
cohabitation union libre *f.*
coin pièce (de monnaie) *f.*
cola coca(-cola) *m.*
cold froid/e ; rhume *m.*
    I have a cold. J'ai un rhume. Je suis
    enrhumé/e.
    I'm cold. J'ai froid.
    It's cold (weather). Il fait froid.
college fac(ulté) *f.*
Colombia Colombie *f.*
Colombian colombien/colombienne
color couleur *f.*
comb peigne *m.*
to comb se peigner
to come venir †
    to come back revenir †
    to come by passer
    to come home rentrer
    to come in entrer
comedy comédie *f.*
comfortable (material objects) confortable
comic strip bande dessinée (BD) *f.*
communications communication *f.*
commuter train from Paris to suburbs
    RER *m.*
completely tout à fait
composition rédaction *f.*
computer ordinateur *m.*
    computer center centre
    informatique *m.*
    computer file fichier *m.*
    computer science informatique *f.*
    laptop computer (ordinateur)
    portable *m.*
concert concert *m.*
condiments condiments *m.*
conformist conformiste
Congratulations! Félicitations !
to contaminate contaminer
continent continent *m.*
to cook faire la cuisine, cuisiner
cookie biscuit *m.*
cool: It's cool weather. Il fait frais.
confidence: to have confidence in oneself
    être bien dans sa peau

contrary: To the contrary, . . .
    au contraire, …
copious copieux/-euse
corner coin *m.*
    at the corner (of) au coin de
to cost coûter
cotton coton *m.*
couch canapé *m.*
cough toux *f.*
    cough syrup sirop *m.*
to cough tousser
country pays *m.*
    foreign country pays étranger
    in this country dans ce pays
country(side) campagne *f.*
    in the country à la campagne
course cours *m.*
    to take a course suivre † un cours
    of course bien sûr
courtyard cour *f.*
cousin cousin *m.*, cousine *f.*
credit card carte de crédit *f.*
critic (person) critique *m.*
criticism critique *f.*
critique critique *f.*
croissant croissant *m.*
    chocolate croissant pain au chocolat *m.*
to cross traverser
to cry pleurer
cucumber concombre *m.*
cup tasse *f.*
cupboard placard *m.*
curtain rideau *m.*

D

dairy aisle rayon crémerie *m.*
dance danse *f.*
to dance faire de la danse, danser
Darn! Zut (alors) !
database base *f.* de données
datebook agenda *m.*
daughter fille *f.*
day jour *m.*, journée *f.*
    day before yesterday avant-hier
    that day ce jour-là
dear cher/chère
debit card carte bancaire *f.*
December décembre
to decide décider
deep profond/e
degree (in) diplôme *m.* (en)
    to do a degree (in) préparer un
    diplôme (en)
    to have a degree avoir un diplôme,
    une formation
deli counter rayon charcuterie *m.*
delicious délicieux/-euse
delighted enchanté/e, ravi/e
dentist dentiste *m./f.*
department store grand magasin *m.*

to describe décrire †
desert désert *m.*
to desire désirer, vouloir †
desk bureau *m.*
dessert dessert *m.*
detective movie film policier *m.*
to detest détester
dictionary dictionnaire *m.*
to die mourir †
diet régime *m.*
    to be on a diet suivre un régime, faire
    un régime
difficult difficile
difficulty: to have difficulty avoir du mal
    à + inf.
dining hall restaurant universitaire *m.*
    (resto U)
dining room salle à manger *f.*
dinner dîner *m.*, souper *m.*
    to have dinner dîner
    to fix dinner préparer le dîner
disagreeable désagréable
disappointed déçu/e
disciplined discipliné/e
to discuss discuter
dish assiette *f.*, plat *m.*
    to do the dishes faire la vaisselle
diskette disquette *f.*
to disobey désobéir à
disposition caractère *m.*
display window vitrine *f.*
to divorce divorcer
divorced divorcé/e
to do faire †
    to not do much ne pas faire
    grand-chose
doctor (M.D.) médecin *m.*
documentary documentaire *m.*
dog chien/ne *m./f.*
door porte *f.*
dormitory résidence *f.*
to doubt (that) douter (que)
    without a doubt sans doute
downtown centre-ville *m.*
    to go downtown descendre en ville
dozen douzaine *f.*
draftsman/woman dessinateur *m.*,
    dessinatrice *f.*
drawing dessin *m.*
dream rêve *m.*
to dream rêver
dress robe *f.*
    to get dressed s'habiller
    to get undressed se déshabiller
drink boisson *f.*
    alcoholic beverage boisson alcoolisée
    cold drink boisson rafraîchissante **hot**
    drink boisson chaude
to drink boire †
driver's license permis de conduire *m.*

drum set batterie f.
to dry essuyer †
to dry oneself off s'essuyer
to dub doubler
dubbed doublé
due to à cause de
during pendant
dynamic dynamique

E

ear oreille f.
early tôt
    to be early être en avance
to earn money gagner de l'argent
earth (the Earth) terre (la Terre) f.
to eat manger †
    to eat breakfast prendre le petit-déjeuner
    to eat dinner dîner
    to eat lunch déjeuner
    to eat a snack goûter
economics sciences économiques f., économie f.
edge bord m.
to educate oneself s'instruire
education sciences de l'éducation f.
egg œuf m.
    fried egg œuf sur le plat m. œuf au plat m.
elbow coude m.
elegant élégant/e
elementary school école f. primaire
    elementary school teacher professeur des écoles m.
elevator ascenseur m.
e-mail courrier électronique m., mél m.
    e-mail address mél m.
    e-mail message courriel m.
embarrassed embarrassé/e, gêné/e
to encourage encourager
encyclopedia encyclopédie f.
energetic énergique
engaged fiancé/e
    to get engaged se fiancer
engine moteur m.
engineer ingénieur m.
England Angleterre f.
English anglais/e
enough assez
    enough of assez de
entrance (foyer) entrée f.
environment environnement m.
equipped équipé/e
eraser (pencil) gomme f.
eraser (board) brosse f.
essay essai m.
    in-class essay exam composition f.
Europe Europe f.
European européen/-enne
evening soir m., soirée f.

eventually finalement
every chaque ; tout, toute, tous, toutes
    every day tous les jours
    every evening tous les soirs
    everyone tout le monde
    everything tout
    everywhere partout
exam examen m.
    pass an exam réussir un examen
    study for an exam préparer un examen
    take an exam passer un examen
excursion bus car m.
exhaust gases gaz d'échappements m. pl.
exhibition exposition f.
expensive cher/chère
to explain expliquer
eye (eyes) œil m. (yeux)

F

face visage m., figure f.
facing face f. : en face de
factory usine f.
    factory worker ouvrier m., ouvrière f.
fair juste
    to be fair être juste
    it's not fair ! ce n'est pas juste !
fairly assez
faithful fidèle
fall automne m.
to fall tomber
    to fall asleep s'endormir
    to fall in love (with) tomber amoureux/-euse (de)
family famille f.
    big family famille nombreuse
    blended family famille recomposée
    extended family famille étendue
    single-parent family famille monoparentale
    family relation relation familiale
fan fanatique m.
    to be a fan of être fanatique de
fanatic fanatique adj.
far (from) loin (de)
farm ferme f.
farmer fermier m., fermière f.
fashion mode f.
    to be in fashion être à la mode
    fashion designer couturier m.
    high fashion haute couture f.
    out of fashion démodé/e
fashionable à la mode
fat adj. gros/se
fat graisse f.
father père m.
    father-in-law beau-père
    single father père célibataire
    step-father beau-père
fear peur f.
to fear avoir peur de

February février
to feel se sentir, toucher
to feel ressentir
feminine féminin/e
fever fièvre f.
field champ m.
to fill remplir
film film m.
    film or stage director metteur en scène m.
final final/e
finally finalement
to find trouver
    I find that . . . Je trouve que…
fine arts beaux-arts m. pl.
to be fine être en forme
    Fine, also. Bien aussi.
    Fine, and you? Ça va, et toi ?
finger doigt m.
to finish finir
first of all d'abord
first premier/-ière
fish counter rayon poissonnerie m.
fish poisson m.
    fishing pêche f.
    to go fishing aller à la pêche
to fix réparer
    to fix one's hair se coiffer
flight vol m.
floor étage m.
    first floor rez-de-chaussée m.
    second floor premier étage m.
    on the floor par terre
flour farine f.
to flow couler
flower fleur f.
flu grippe f.
fog brouillard m.
    It's foggy. Il y a du brouillard.
food aliment m., nourriture f.
foot pied m.
    on foot à pied
football football américain m.
    football game match m. de football américain
    football stadium stade m.
for pour; depuis (temps); pendant (temps)
foreign étranger/-ère
forest forêt f.
to forget oublier
former ancien/ne
France France f.
free (a person) libre ; **(a thing)** gratuit/e
    I'm not free. Je ne suis pas libre.
to freeze: It's freezing. geler ; † Il gèle.
French français/e
    French bread (long, thin loaf) baguette f.
    French fries frites f.

fresh frais/fraîche
Friday vendredi
friend ami/e, camarade *m./f.*, copain *m.*, copine *f.*
    best friend meilleur/e ami/e *m./f.*
from de (d')
front: in front of devant
frozen foods surgelés *m. pl.*
fruit fruit *m.*
fun: to have fun s'amuser
funny amusant/e, drôle
furious furieux/-euse
furnished meublé/e
furniture meuble *m.*
future avenir *m.*

G

to gain weight grossir
game jeu *m.*; **(sports)** match *m.*
game show jeu télévisé *m.*
garage garage *m.*
garden jardin *m.*
    to do some gardening faire du jardinage, travailler dans le jardin
gas gaz *m.*
generous généreux/-euse
gentle doux/douce
geography géographie *f.*
geology géologie *f.*
German allemand/e
Germany Allemagne *f.*
to get obtenir
    to get a grade avoir une note
    to get a degree obtenir † un diplôme
to get up se lever †
    Get up/stand up! Levez-vous !
gift cadeau *m.*
girl fille *f.*
to give donner, offrir †
    to give advice conseiller
    to give back rendre
glass verre *f.*
glasses lunettes *f. pl.*
glove gant *m.*
to go aller †
    to go around faire un tour
    to go back retourner
    to go down descendre
    to go home rentrer
    to go in entrer
    to go on/keep going continuer
    to go out sortir
    to go to bed se coucher
    to go up monter
godfather parrain *m.*
godmother marraine *f.*
golf golf *m.*
    to play golf jouer au golf
good bon/ne
    goodbye au revoir

Good evening. Bonsoir.
Good morning. Bonjour.
Have a good evening. Bonne soirée.
grade note *f.*
    to have/get a grade avoir une note
grandchild petit-enfant *m.*
granddaughter petite-fille *f.*
grandmother grand-mère *f.*
grandparents grands-parents *m. pl.*
grandson petit-fils *m.*
grape raisin *m.*
gray gris/e
grease graisse *f.*
great! chic (alors) !
green vert/e
    green bean *haricot vert *m.*
    green salad salade *f.*
grilled grillé/e
    grilled ham and cheese sandwich croque-monsieur *m.*
ground sol *m.*
    ground floor rez-de chaussée *m.*
to grow pousser
    to grow larger grossir
    to grow old vieillir
    to grow taller grandir
    to grow up (for children) grandir
to guarantee garantir
guide (tour guide or guidebook) guide *m.*
guitar guitare *f.*
    base guitar guitare basse
    electric guitar guitare électrique
    to play the guitar jouer de la guitare
gym gymnase *m.*

H

hair cheveux *m. pl.*
    to do one's hair se coiffer
half demi/e
    half-brother demi-frère *m.*
    half-kilo demi-kilo *m.*
    half-past et demi/e
    half-sister demi-sœur *f.*
hallway couloir *m.*
hamburger *hamburger *m.*
hand main *f.*
    to hand in/over remettre †
    On the other hand, . . . De l'autre côté, en revanche
    to raise your hand lever le doigt, lever la main
handsome beau (bel), belle
to happen se passer, avoir lieu
happy heureux/-euse, content/e
    Happy birthday! Joyeux anniversaire !
    Happy New Year! Bonne année !
harmonica harmonica *m.*
hat chapeau *m.*

to have avoir †
    to have just (done something) venir de + inf.
    to have to (do something) devoir †
he il
head tête *f.*
health center/clinic infirmerie *f.*
hear entendre
heart cœur *m.*
    heart attack crise *f.* cardiaque
hearty copieux/-euse
heavy jacket blouson *m.*
height taille *f.*
    of average height de taille moyenne
Hello. Bonjour.
    hello (telephone only) allô
to help aider (à)
her elle ; la ; son, sa, ses
    to her lui
herbal tea tisane *f.*
here is/are . . . voici…
here ici
here/there is/are . . . voilà…
herself elle-même
hi salut
high school lycée *m.*
high *haut/e
hike randonnée *f.*
    to go on a hike faire une randonnée
hill colline *f.*
him le ; lui
    to him lui
himself lui-même
his son, sa, ses
history histoire *f.*
hockey *hockey *m.*
holiday fête *f.*
    public holiday jour férié *m.*
    religious holiday fête religieuse
home maison *f.*
    homeowner propriétaire *m./f.*
homebody pantouflard/e
homework devoirs *m.*
    to do homework faire des devoirs *m.*
to hope espérer †, souhaiter
horror movie film d'horreur *m.*
horse cheval *m.*
    to go horseback riding faire du cheval
hospital (public) hôpital *m.*
    private hospital clinique *f.*
hostel (youth) auberge de jeunesse *f.*
hot chaud
    hot chocolate chocolat chaud *m.*
    I'm hot. J'ai chaud.
    It's hot. (weather) Il fait chaud.
hotel hôtel *m.*
hour heure *f.*
    for an hour pendant une heure, pour une heure, depuis une heure
    in an hour dans une heure

house maison *f.*
    at the home of chez
    housemate colocataire *m./f.*
housewife/househusband femme *f.*,
    homme *m.* au foyer
how comment
    how many combien de
    how much combien
    How's it going? Comment ça va ?
human being être humain *m.*
human body corps humain *m.*
humanities lettres *f.*
humid lourd/e
    It's humid. Il fait lourd.
hunger faim *m.*
    to be hungry avoir faim
hurray for . . . ! vive… !
to hurry up se dépêcher
to hurt (somewhere) avoir mal à
to hurt (someone) faire mal à
husband mari *m.*

I
I je (j')
ice on the ground verglas *m.*
ice cream glace *f.*
ice cube glaçon *m.*
icy: It's icy Il y a du verglas.
idealistic idéaliste
if si
important important/e
in à, dans, en
independent autonome
India Inde *f.*
Indian indien/ne
individualistic individualiste
indulgent indulgent/e
industrial industriel/le
infection infection *f.*
information renseignement *m.*
to get information se renseigner
inn auberge *f.*
instant messaging messagerie instantanée *f.*
instead of au lieu de
intelligent intelligent/e
intensity intensité *f.*
interesting intéressant/e
to be interested (in) s'intéresser (à)
internet Internet *m.*
    connect to the internet se connecter
    sur l'Internet
    to go on the internet aller sur l'Internet
    internet access accès à l'Internet
    internet browser browser *m.*
    on the internet sur l'Internet
into dans
to introduce présenter
    Je vous/te présente X. This is X.
invitation invitation *f.*
to invite inviter

irritable énervé/e
irritated: to become irritated s'énerver
it ce (c') ; il ; elle ; le ; la
it is . . . c'est…
Italian italien/ne
Italy Italie *f.*
Ivorian ivoirien/ne
Ivory Coast Côte-d'Ivoire *f.*

J
jacket blouson *m.*
    (suit coat) jacket veste *f.*
jam confiture *f.*
January janvier
Japan Japon *m.*
Japanese japonais/e
jar pot *m.*
jazz jazz *m.*
jealous jaloux/-ouse
jeans jean *m. sg.*
job poste *m.*, travail *m.*, métier *m.*
    summer job job d'été *m.*
    a full-time job un travail à plein temps
    a part-time job un travail à mi-temps
to jog faire du jogging
to joke plaisanter, blaguer
joke histoire drôle *f.*, blague *f.*,
    plaisanterie *f.*
journalism journalisme *m.*
journalist journaliste *m./f.*
July juillet
June juin

K
keyboard clavier *m.*
key clé *f.*, clef *f.*
    key word mot clé *m.*
kilo kilo *m.*
kind gentil/le
    That's kind (of you). C'est gentil à
    toi/vous.
king roi *m.*
to kiss s'embrasser
kitchen cuisine *f.*
kitchen cabinet placard *m.*
(with) kitchenette (avec) coin cuisine *m.*
knee genou *m.*
to know (how to) savoir †
to know or be familiar with
    connaître †

L
lab(oratory) laboratoire *m.* (labo)
    lab technician technicien *m.*,
    technicienne *f.*
lady dame *f.*
lake lac *m.*
lamb chop côtelette *f.* d'agneau
lamp lampe *f.*
landlord/landlady propriétaire *m./f.*

language langue *f.*
    in the original language en version
    originale (v.o.) *f.*
    foreign language langue étrangère
    language lab labo(ratoire) de
    langues *m.*
    native language langue maternelle
last dernier/dernière
    last month le mois dernier
    last Saturday samedi dernier
    last week la semaine dernière
    last year l'année dernière,
    l'an dernier
late retard
    to be late être en retard
law droit *m.*
    law school faculté *f.* de droit
lawyer avocat *m.*, avocate *f.*
lazy paresseux/-euse
to learn apprendre (à) †
leather cuir *m.*
to leave partir, **(someone, something)**
    quitter
    to leave the lights on laisser les
    lumières allumées
lecture conférence *f.*
lecture hall amphithéâtre *m.*
left gauche *f.*
    left-overs restes *m. pl.*
    to the left à gauche
leg jambe *f.*
lemon citron *m.*
lemonade citron pressé *m.*
lemon-lime soft drink limonade *f.*
to lend prêter
lenient indulgent/e
less moins
    less . . . than moins… que, moins de…
    que
library bibliothèque *f.* (bibli)
    public (city) library bibliothèque
    municipale (BM)
    university library bibliothèque
    universitaire (BU)
light (color) clair/e
light lumière *f.*
    turn out the lights éteindre les
    lumières
    leave the lights on laisser les lumières
    allumées
lightning éclair *m.*
    There's lightning. Il y a des éclairs.
like comme
to like aimer
    to like fairly well aimer bien
    to like or love a lot aimer beaucoup
line ligne *f.*
    on-line en ligne
linguistics linguistique *f.*
lip lèvre *f.*

to listen écouter
    to listen to music écouter de la musique
listing of TV programs magazine télé *m.*
liter litre *m.*
literature littérature *f.*
little petit/e
little bit peu *m.*
to live habiter ; vivre
liver foie *m.*
living room séjour *m.*, (une salle de séjour)
loaf of sliced bread pain *m.* de mie
to locate trouver
    located situé/e
    to be located se trouver
long long/ue
    a long time longtemps
    a long time ago il y a longtemps
    for how long . . . ? depuis combien de temps… ?
to look (seem) avoir l'air
    to look after soigner
    to look at regarder
    to look for chercher
    to look like ressembler
to lose perdre
    to lose one's composure perdre son sang-froid
    to lose weight maigrir
a lot beaucoup (de)
lottery loto *m.*
    to play the lottery jouer au loto
loudly fort
lovable aimable
to love aimer
    to be in love (with) être amoureux/-euse (de)
    to fall in love (with) tomber amoureux/-euse (de)
    in love amoureux/-euse
luck chance *f.*
    luckily heureusement
    to be lucky avoir de la chance
luggage bagages *m. pl.*
    to carry up luggage monter les bagages
lunch déjeuner *m.*
    to eat lunch déjeuner
lung poumon *m.*

M

magazine magazine *m.*
    monthly magazine mensuel *m.*
    weekly magazine hebdomadaire *m.*
main character personnage principal *m.*
main dish plat principal *m.*
major (in) spécialisation *f.* (en), majeure *f.* (en) (Can.)
majority plupart *f.*

to make faire †
    to make a mistake faire une faute
makeup maquillage *m.*
    to put on makeup se maquiller
man homme *m.*, monsieur *m.*
March mars
marital status état civil *m.*
married marié/e
    to get married se marier
mathematics mathématiques *f.*, (les maths)
May mai
maybe peut-être
mayor maire *m.*
me moi
    to me me (m')
meal repas *m.*
    before-meal drink apéritif *m.*
    well-balanced meal repas équilibré
mean méchant/e
to mean vouloir † dire
meat viande *f.*
    meat counter rayon boucherie *m.*
mechanic mécanicien *m.*, mécanicienne *f.*
medicine (field of study) médecine *f.*
medicine (drug) médicament *m.*
mediocre médiocre
to meet se rencontrer, se retrouver, se connaître, faire la connaissance de quelqu'un
to meet up with (se) retrouver, se réunir
meeting rendez-vous *m.*
Merry Christmas! Joyeux Noël !
Mexico Mexique *m.*
Mexican mexicain/e
middle: in the middle au milieu de
    middle school collège *m.*
    middle-aged d'un certain âge
midnight minuit
milk lait *m.*
minor (in) mineure *f.* (en) (Can.)
mint menthe *f.*
    mint tea thé à la menthe *m.*
    herbal mint tea tisane à la menthe *f.*
minute minute *f.*
Miss mademoiselle (Mlle)
to miss manquer, rater
    I miss him/her. Il/Elle me manque.
    I miss them. Ils/elles me manquent.
    I miss you. Tu me manques, Vous me manquez.
missing absent/e
mistake faute *f.*
    to make a mistake faire une faute, se tromper
modern moderne
moment moment *m.*
    at that moment à ce moment-là
Monday lundi
money argent *m.*
monitor moniteur *m.*

month mois *m.*
    last month le mois dernier
    next month le mois prochain
moon (the Moon) lune (la Lune) *f.*
moped mobylette *f.*
more . . . than plus… , que, plus de… que
morning matin *m.*
Moroccan marocain/e
Morocco Maroc *m.*
most plupart *f.*
mother mère *f.*
    mother-in-law belle-mère
    single mother mère célibataire
    step-mother belle-mère
motorcycle moto *f.*
motorscooter mobylette *f.*
mountain montagne *f.*
    to go mountain climbing faire de l'alpinisme *m.*
mouse souris *f.*
mouth bouche *f.*
to move (an object) bouger
to move (one's home) déménager
movie star vedette *f.*, star *f.*
Mr. monsieur (M.)
Mrs. madame (Mme)
museum musée *m.*
mushroom champignon *m.*
music musique *f.*
musical comédie musicale *f.*
musician musicien *m.*, musicienne *f.*
must devoir †
    You (one) must . . . Il faut…
    You (one) must not . . . Il ne faut pas…
mustard moutarde *f.*
my mon, ma, mes
myself moi-même

N

to name nommer
name (last) nom *m.*
    first name prénom *m.*
    nickname surnom *m.*
    My name is . . . Je m'appelle…
    What is your name? Comment vous appelez-vous/tu t'appelles ?
natural sciences sciences *f.* naturelles
nature nature *f.*, caractère *m.*
nausea mal au cœur *m.*
near (to) près (de)
    very near tout près (de)
neat! chouette !
necessary nécessaire
    to be necessary falloir : il faut
neck cou *m.*
to need avoir besoin de
need besoin *m.*
neighbor voisin/e *m./f.*
neighborhood quartier *m.*

neighboring voisin/e
nephew neveu *m.*
Netherlands Pays-Bas *m.*
network réseau *m.*
never ne... jamais
new nouveau (nouvel), nouvelle
   brand new neuf, neuve
news informations *f. pl.*, (infos) nouvelles *f. pl.*
   news broadcast journal télévisé *m.*
newspaper journal *m.*
newsstand kiosque *m.*
next prochain/e
next to à côté de
nice sympa(thique), gentil/le
niece nièce *f.*
   nieces and nephews neveux *m. pl.*
nighttime nuit *f.*
no non
   no longer ne... plus
   no matter what n'importe quoi
   no more ne... plus
   no one ne... personne
noise bruit *m.*
   to make noise faire du bruit
   noise pollution pollution *f.* sonore
nonbiodegradable non-biodégradable
noon midi
normally normalement
North America Amerique *f.* du nord
nose nez *m.*
   nose drops gouttes *f. pl.* pour le nez
   to have a runny nose avoir le nez qui coule
not pas, ne... pas
   not at all pas du tout
   not bad pas mal
notebook cahier *m.*
nothing ne... rien
novel roman *m.*
November novembre
now maintenant
nurse infirmier *m.*, infirmière *f.*

O

to obey obéir à
to obtain obtenir †
obvious évident
occupation métier *m.*
October octobre
odd jobs: to do odd jobs around the house bricoler, faire du bricolage
of de (d')
office bureau *m.*
often souvent
oil huile *f.*
   olive oil huile d'olive
ointment pommade *f.*
OK d'accord
old: to be X years old avoir X ans

How old are you? Quel âge avez-vous/as-tu ?
old vieux (vieil), vieille ; ancien/ne
old-fashioned démodé/e
olive olive *m.*
on à, sur
one un/e
onion oignon *m.*
on-line en ligne
   to go on-line aller sur Internet
only seulement ; ne... que
to open ouvrir †
opinion: In my opinion, à mon avis, d'après moi
opposite contraire *m.* ; en face (de)
optimistic optimiste
optional facultatif/-ive
or ou
orange (color) orange *adj. inv.*
   orange fruit orange *m.*
   orange juice jus *m.* d'orange
   Orangina orange soda Orangina *m.*
other autre
our notre, nos
ourselves nous-mêmes
outdoors en plein air
outgoing sociable
out-of-date démodé/e
outside dehors
oven four *m.*
over sur
overcast: It's overcast. Le ciel est couvert.
overcoat manteau *m.*
to owe devoir †
to own posséder †, avoir †

P

Pacific Océanie *f.*
   Pacific Ocean océan *m.* Pacifique
package paquet *m.*
packaging emballage *m.*
pain mal (des maux) *m.*
to paint peindre †
painter peintre *m.*
painting peinture *f.*, tableau *m.*
pale pâle
   to become pale pâlir
pants pantalon *m. sg.*
pantyhose collant *m.*
parent parent *m.*
to park garer
parka with hood anorak *m.*
to participate in participer à
partner partenaire *m./f.*
part-time à mi-temps
party fête *f.*, soirée *f.*
to pass (an exam/a course) réussir
passerby passant *m.*, passante *f.*
passport passeport *m.*
pastry pâtisserie *f.*

pastry chef pâtissier *m.*, pâtissière *f.*
pâté pâté *m.*
pay payer †
to pay attention faire † attention
peach pêche *f.*
pear poire *f.*
peas petits pois *m. pl.*
pedestrian piéton *m.*
   pedestrian street rue *f.* piétonne
pen stylo *m.*
pencil crayon *m.*
penicillin pénicilline *f.*
people gens *m. pl.*
pepper poivre *m.*
   green pepper poivron vert *m.*
   red pepper poivron rouge *m.*
percussion batterie *f.*
perfectly parfaitement
person personne *f.*
pessimistic pessimiste
pet animal familier *m.*
pharmacist pharmacien *m.*, pharmacienne *f.*
philosophy philosophie *f.*
to phone one another se téléphoner
to phone téléphoner
physical sciences sciences *f.* physiques
physics physique *f.*
physiology physiologie *f.*
piano piano *m.*
picnic pique-nique *m.*
   to have a picnic faire † un pique-nique
pie tarte *f.*
   apple pie tarte aux pommes
piece morceau *m.*
   piece of news nouvelle *f.*
   piece of toast (Can.) rôtie *f.*
pineapple ananas *m.*
pink rose
pizza pizza *f.*
place endroit *m.*, lieu *m.*
   at the place (home) of chez
   to take place avoir lieu
to plan organiser, planifier
plan projet *m.*
   already have plans être pris/e, avoir des projects
   to make plans faire des projets
plane avion *m.*
plastic plastique
plate assiette *f.*
to play jouer
   to play an instrument jouer (de)
   to play a sport jouer (à)
   to play sports faire du sport
playing field terrain *m.* de sport
pleasant agréable
please s'il te plaît, s'il vous plaît
poetry poésie *f.*
police officer agent de police *m.*

political science sciences *f.* politiques
to pollute polluer
pork porc *m.*
Portugal Portugal *m.*
Portuguese portugais/e
possibly éventuellement
poster affiche *f.*, poster *m.*
potato pomme de terre *f.*
position (job) poste *m.*
to pour verser
to practice répéter †
to prefer préférer †, aimer mieux
prepared dish plat préparé *m.*
prescription ordonnance *f.*
present cadeau *m.*
to present présenter
to press presser
    to press (a button) appuyer sur un
    bouton
press presse *f.*
prestige prestige *m.*
pretty joli/e
to prevent empêcher
price prix *m.*
printer imprimante *f.*
produce aisle rayon fruits et légumes *m.*
profession profession *f.*
professor professeur *m.*, professeure *f*
    (Can.)
program (TV) émission *f.*
programmer informaticien *m.*,
    informaticienne *f.*
to promise promettre †
to protect protéger †, sauver
psychological drama drame
    psychologique *m.*
psychology psychologie *f.*
public public *m.*
    public transportation transport en
    commun *m.*
pullover sweater pull(-over) *m.*
to punish punir
to push pousser
    to push (a button) appuyer sur
to put (on) mettre †; **(away)** ranger
to putter around the house faire du
    bricolage, bricoler
puttering around bricolage *m.*

Q

quantity quantité *f.*
quarter quart *m.* ; trimestre *m.*
    quarter past et quart
    quarter to moins le quart
queen reine *f.*
quiz interrogation *f.*

R

racquetball racket-ball *m.*
rain pluie *f.*

to rain pleuvoir †
    It's raining. Il pleut.
raincoat imper(méable) *m.*
to raise lever †
    to raise one's hand lever le doigt,
    lever la main
rarely rarement
rather assez, plutôt
razor rasoir *m.*
to read lire †
ready prêt/e
real vrai/e
realistic réaliste
reality show émission *f.* de télé-réalité
really vraiment
reason raison *f.*
reasonable raisonnable
rebellious rebelle
receptionist réceptionniste *m./f.*
recommendation recommandation *f.*
recycle recycler
recycling recyclage *m.*
red rouge
redhead, redheaded roux/-sse
reference book ouvrage *m.* de référence
refrigerator réfrigérateur *m.*, frigo *m.*
to rehearse répéter †
relax se détendre, se décontracter, se relaxer
relative parent *m.*
remarried remarié/e
remedy remède *m.*
remember se rappeler †, se souvenir † de
renovated renové/e
rent loyer *m.*
to rent louer
to repeat répéter †
    to repeat a grade redoubler
report rapport *m.*, reportage *m.*
to request demander (à, de)
to require exiger
required obligatoire
reservation réservation *f.*
to reserve réserver, faire une réservation
reserved réservé/e
residential résidentiel/le
    residential neighborhod quartier *m.*
    résidentiel
resource ressource *f.*
responsibility responsabilité *f.*
rest repos *m.*
to rest se reposer
restroom toilettes *f. pl.*, W.C. *m. pl.*
to return revenir †
    to return home rentrer
rice riz *m.*
to ride a bicycle faire du vélo *m.*
right droite *f.*
    to the right à droite
    to be right avoir raison
    to be all right s'arranger

to ring sonner
ripe mûr/e
river fleuve *m.*
    river tributary rivière *f.*
roast rôti *m.*
roast beef rosbif *m.*
rock music rock *m.*
role rôle *m.*
roll of film pellicule *f.*
roll petit pain *m.*
roommate colocataire *m./f.*
routine routine *f.*
rug tapis *m.*
rugby rugby *m.*
ruler règle *f.*
run courir †
    to run errands faire des courses *f.*
RV camping-car *m.*

S

sad triste
sailboat bateau *m.* à voile
    to go sailing faire de la voile
salary salaire *m.*
sales clerk vendeur *m.*, vendeuse *f.*
sales representative représentant *m.*,
    représentante *f.* de commerce
salmon saumon *m.*
    smoked salmon saumon fumé
salt sel *m.*
salve pommade *f.*
same même
    just the same quand même
sandal sandale *f.*
sandwich (ham, cheese) sandwich *m.* (au
    jambon, au fromage)
Saturday samedi
to save (money) économiser
    to save a file sauvegarder un fichier
saxophone saxophone *m.*
to say dire †
scanner scanner *m.*
scarf écharpe *f.*
    silk scarf foulard *m.*
schedule emploi du temps *m.*
school école *f.*
    elementary school école primaire
    middle school collège *m.*
    high school lycée *m.*
    school within a university faculté *f.*
science science *f.*
science-fiction science-fiction *f.*
screen écran *m.*
sculpture sculpture *f.*
seafood fruits de mer *m. pl.*
search engine moteur de recherche *m.*
seashore bord *m.* de la mer
season saison *f.*
seat place *f.*, siège *m.*
second floor premier étage *m.*

secretary secrétaire *m./f.*
to see voir †
    Let's see . . . Voyons…
    see you soon à bientôt
    see you tomorrow à demain
to seem (good) avoir l'air (bon)
selfish égoïste
to sell vendre
semester semestre *m.*
Senegal Sénégal *m.*
Senegalese sénégalais/e
sensitive sensible
to separate se séparer
separated séparé/e
September septembre
series feuilleton *m.* ; série *f.*
serious sérieux/-euse ; grave
to serve servir
service sector services *m. pl.*
set the table mettre la table
several plusieurs
shampoo shampooing *m.*
to share partager †
to shave se raser
she elle
shirt (man's) chemise *f.*
shoe chaussure *f.*
to shop for groceries faire les courses *f. pl.*
shore bord *m.*
short petit/e ; court/e
shorts short *m. sg.*
shoulder épaule *f.*
show spectacle *m.*, représentation *f.*
to show montrer
to shower se doucher, prendre une douche
shrimp crevette *f.*
shy timide, réservé/e
sick malade
sick person malade *m./f.*
sickness maladie *f.*
side côté *m.*
sightseeing: to go sightseeing faire du tourisme *m.*
silk soie *f.*
since (because) puisque
since (time) depuis
    since when . . . ? depuis quand…?
to sing chanter
singer chanteur *m.*, chanteuse *f.*
singing lesson leçon *f.* de chant
single célibataire
sink (bathroom) lavabo *m.*
sink (kitchen) évier *m.*
sister sœur *f.*
    half-sister demi-sœur
    sister-in-law belle-sœur
to sit down s'asseoir †
to situate situer
    to be situated at être situé/e à
size taille *f.*

to ski faire du ski *m.*
skin peau *f.*
skinny maigre
to skip (a meal) sauter (un repas)
skirt jupe *f.*
sky ciel *m.*
slacks pantalon *m. sg.*
to sleep dormir
    to be asleep être endormi/e
    to fall asleep s'endormir
sleet verglas *m.*
slice tranche *f.*
small petit/e
smart intelligent/e
smoke fumée *f.*
to smoke fumer
smoked fumé/e
to snack grignoter ; goûter
    afternoon snack goûter *m.*
    snack casse-croûte *m. inv.*
    snack bar snack-bar *m.*
snow neige *f.*
to snow neiger
    It's snowing. Il neige.
to snow-board faire du surf des neiges
so alors
soap opera feuilleton *m.*
soccer football (foot) *m.*
    soccer game match *m.* de football
social sciences sciences *f.* humaines
social worker assistant *m.*, assistante *f.* social/e
sociology sociologie *f.*
sock chaussette *f.*
software (program) logiciel *m.*
some des ; en
someone quelqu'un
something quelque chose
sometimes quelquefois
son fils *m.*
song chanson *f.*
soon bientôt
sorry désolé/e
    to be sorry être désolé/e, regretter
to sort trier
so-so comme ci, comme ça
sound bruit *m.*
soup soupe *f.*
South America Amerique *f.* du sud
Spain Espagne *f.*
Spanish espagnol/e
to speak parler
    Speak louder! Parlez plus fort !
to spell épeler †
to spend (money) dépenser
to spend (time) passer
to spend a quiet evening passer une soirée tranquille
spice épice *f.*
spinach épinards *m. pl.*

sport sport *m.*
    sports show émission *f.* sportive
    to do sports faire du sport
spring printemps *m.*
spouse époux *m.*, épouse *f.*
spy movie film *m.* d'espionnage
square (in a city) place *f.*
stadium stade *m.*
staircase escalier *m.*
stairs escalier *m.*
to start commencer †
    to start exercising again se remettre † à faire de l'exercice
to stay rester
    to stay in a hotel loger † dans un hôtel
steak biftek *m.*, steak, *m.*
stepfather beau-père *m.*
stepmother belle-mère *f.*
stomach estomac *m.* ; ventre *m.*
    stomach ache mal au ventre *m.*
to stop (s')arrêter
    Stop it! Arrête !
stoplight feu rouge *m.*
stout fort/e
stove cuisinière *f.*
straight ahead tout droit
strange bizarre, drôle
strawberry fraise *f.*
stream (large) rivière *f.*
street rue *f.*
strep throat angine *f.*
strong fort/e
stubborn têtu/e
student étudiant *m.*, étudiante *f.*
studies études *f. pl.*
studio apartment studio *m.*
to study étudier
    to study for an exam préparer un examen
    to study (French) faire du (français)
stupid bête
stylish chic, à la mode
to subscribe (to) s'abonner (à)
suburb banlieue *f.*
subway métro *m.*
to succeed réussir à
sugar sucre *m.*
to suggest suggérer †
suit (man's) costume *m.*
suit (woman's) tailleur *m.*
suitcase valise *f.*
summer été *m.*
    summer vacation grandes vacances *f. pl.*
sun soleil *m.*
    It's sunny. Il y a du soleil.
sunburn coup *m.* de soleil
Sunday dimanche
sunglasses lunettes *f. pl.* de soleil
super super

supermarket aisles rayons *m. pl.* du supermarché
sure sûr/e
surfing surf *m.*
to surf faire du surf
    to surf the web surfer sur Internet
surprised étonné/e, surpris/e
swim nager †, faire † de la natation
swimming la natation *f.*
swimming pool piscine *f.*
swimsuit maillot (de bain) *m.*
Swiss suisse
Switzerland Suisse *f.*
symptom symptôme *m.*

T

table table *f.*
    to set the table mettre la table
take prendre †
    to take courses suivre des cours †
talented doué/e
to talk parler
tall grand/e
tape player (cassette) magnétophone *m.*
taste goût *m.*
to taste goûter
taxi taxi *m.*
tea thé *m.*
teacher (elementary level) professeur des écoles ; (*formerly*) instituteur *m.*, institutrice *f.*
teacher professeur *m.*, enseignant/e *m./f.*
to tease plaisanter
tedious ennuyeux/-euse
television télévision *f.*, (télé)
tender tendre
tennis tennis *m.*
    to play tennis jouer au tennis
tennis shoes tennis *m. pl.*
tent tente *f.*
terrace terrasse *f.*
thank you merci
theater théâtre *m.*
their leur/s
them eux ; elles ; les
    to them leur
themselves eux-mêmes ; elles-mêmes
then alors, ensuite, puis
there là ; y
there is/are … voilà ; il y a…, voici
therefore donc
these ces
they ils, elles
thin fin/e, mince
think penser, réfléchir à
    I don't think so. Je pense que non. Je (ne) pense pas.
    I think so. Je pense que oui.
    I think that … Je pense que…
thirst soif *f.*

to be thirsty avoir soif
this ce (cet), cette
this is … c'est/ce sont… ; voici
throat gorge *f.*
through par
to throw (out) jeter †
thunderstorm orage *m.*
thunder tonnerre *m.*
    There is thunder. Il y a du tonnerre.
Thursday jeudi
ticket billet *m.*
tie cravate *f.*
time temps *m.* ; l'heure *f.*
    What time is it? Quelle heure est-il ?
    full-time plein temps
    part-time mi-temps
    long time longtemps
tip pourboire *m.* ; service *m.*
    Is the tip included? Le service est compris ?
tired fatigué/e
to tidy up ranger †
to à, en
today aujourd'hui
toe doigt *m.* de pied
together ensemble
toilet toilette *f.*
toiletries articles *m. pl.* de toilette
tomato tomate *f.*
tomorrow demain
tonight ce soir
too aussi
too much trop
tooth dent *f.*
toothbrush brosse *f.* à dents
toothpaste dentifrice *m.*
tourism office office *m.* du tourisme
toward vers
towel serviette *f.* (de toilette)
to towel off s'essuyer
town hall mairie *f.*
toxic toxique
traffic circulation *f.*
    traffic circle rond-point *m.*
    traffic jam embouteillage *m.*
train train *m.*
    train station gare *f.*
transportation (means of) moyen *m.* de transport
    mass transportation transports *m. pl.* en commun
trash ordures *f. pl.*
    trash can poubelle *f.*
to travel voyager †
tree arbre *m.*
    Christmas tree sapin *m.* de Noël
    fir tree sapin *m.*
    fruit tree arbre fruitier *m.*
tremendous formidable
trimester trimestre *m.*

trip voyage *m.*
    to go on a trip faire un voyage, voyager, partir †
    Have a good trip! Bon voyage !
trousers pantalon *m. sg.*
true vrai/e
    That's true. C'est vrai.
to try essayer † (de)
t-shirt tee-shirt *m.*
Tuesday mardi
tuna thon *m.*
to turn tourner
    to turn off (the lights) éteindre † (les lumières)
    to turn on (an appliance) allumer
TV télévision *f.*, (télé)
    TV (or radio) station chaîne *f.*
    TV remote control télécommande *f.*
    TV serial série *f.*
twin jumeau *m.*, jumelle *f.*
typical typique

U

ugly moche, laid/e
umbrella parapluie *m.*
uncle oncle *m.*
under sous
to understand comprendre †
undisciplined indiscipliné/e
to undress se déshabiller
uneasy inquiet/e
unhappy malheureux/-euse
United States États-Unis *m. pl.*
university université *f.*, faculté *f.* (*fac*)
    university dining hall restaurant universitaire (resto U) *m.*
    university library bibliothèque universitaire (BU, bibli) *f.*
until jusqu'à
up: to be up être debout
    to get up se lever †
    to go up monter
to be upset être fâché/e, en colère
urgent urgent
us nous
to use (something) se servir de (quelque chose), employer, utiliser
useful utile
usually d'habitude, habituellement
utilities charges *f. pl.*

V

vacation vacances *f. pl.*
    vacation plans projets de vacances *m. pl.*
    to go on vacation partir en vacances
valley vallée *f.*
variety show divertissement *m.*
VCR magnétoscope *m.*

vegetable légume *m.*
    vegetable garden potager *m.*
    cut-up raw vegetables crudités *f. pl.*
very très
video games jeux électroniques *m. pl.*
videotape vidéocassette *f.*
Vietnam Vietnam *m.*
Vietnamese vietnamien/ne
vinegar vinaigre *m.*
to visit someone rendre visite à
to visit (someplace, something) visiter
volleyball volley(-ball) *m.*
    to play volleyball jouer au volley (-ball)

W

waist taille *f.*
to wait (for) attendre
waiter/waitress serveur *m.*, serveuse *f.*
to wake up se réveiller
to walk marcher
    to take a walk se promener †, faire † une promenade
wall mur *m.*
wallet portefeuille *m.*
to want vouloir †, avoir envie de, désirer
warm-hearted affectueux/-euse
to wash se laver
    to wash one's face se laver la figure
    to wash one's hands se laver les mains
wash mitt gant de toilette *m.*
waste ordures *f. pl.* ; déchets *m. pl.*
to waste gaspiller
    to waste time laisser passer des heures, perdre du temps
watch montre *f.*
to watch regarder, voir
    to watch a game voir un match
    to watch a game on TV regarder un match
    to watch a movie voir un film
    to watch a play voir une pièce (de théâtre)
    to watch TV regarder la télé
water eau *f.*
    drinkable water eau potable
    mineral water eau minérale
    sparking water eau gazeuse
    tap water l'eau du robinet

water skiing ski nautique *m.*
    to go water skiing faire du ski nautique
way of life manière *f.* de vivre
we nous
to wear porter
weather temps *m.*
    weather forecast météo *f.*
    What's the weather like? Quel temps fait-il ?
    The weather's bad. Il fait mauvais.
    It's nice weather. Il fait bon.
wedding mariage *m.*
Wednesday mercredi
week semaine *f.*
weekend week-end *m.*
welcome bienvenu/e ; bienvenue *f.*
    you're welcome je t'en prie/je vous en prie ; bienvenue (Can.)
    welcome to . . . soyez la bienvenue !
well bien
well done! bravo !
western western *m.*
what . . . ? qu'est-ce que/qui… ? ; quoi
what color is . . . ? de quelle couleur est… ?
what? quoi ?
when quand, lorsque, où
where où
whether si
which quel/le ; que (qu'), qui
while pendant que
white blanc/blanche
who qui
why pourquoi
wife femme *f.*
willingly volontiers
to win gagner
    the winner le/la gagnant/e ; le vainqueur
wind vent *m.*
    It's windy. Il y a du vent.
window fenêtre *f.*
    shop window vitrine *f.*
to windsurf faire de la planche à voile
wine vin *m.*
winter hiver *m.*
    winter sports sports d'hiver *m. pl.*
to wish vouloir †, souhaiter
wish(es) vœu(x) *m.*

with avec
without sans
woman femme *f.*
wood bois *m.*
woods bois *m.*
wool laine *f.*
word mot *m.*
word processing traitement de texte *m.*
work travail *m.*
to work travailler
    hard-working travailleur/euse
    to work (colloq.) bosser
    to work in the garden travailler dans le jardin
    to work at the computer travailler à l'ordinateur
    workplace lieu de travail *m.*
    It'll work out. Ça va s'arranger
    to work out faire du sport
world monde *m.*
worn, worn out (objects) abîmé/e
worried inquiet/-ète
    to worry s'en faire † (du souci), s'inquiéter †
wrist poignet *m.*
to write écrire †, rédiger
writer écrivain *m.*

Y

yard jardin *m.*
year an *m.*
    I am 19 years old. J'ai 19 ans.
    Happy New Year! Bonne année !
to yell crier
yellow jaune
yes oui ; si (*after negative question*)
yesterday hier
yet encore
    not yet pas encore
yogurt yaourt *m.*
young jeune
you tu ; vous ; toi
    to you te (t') ; vous
your ton, ta, tes ; votre, vos
yourself toi-même ; vous-même
yourselves vous-mêmes

Z

zero zéro *m.*
zoology zoologie *f.*

Appendice 7 L'alphabet phonétique international

a	la	b	le **b**ureau
e	écout**ez**	k	le **c**ahier, **q**ui
ɛ	**e**lle	ʃ	la **ch**aise
i	**i**l, styl**o**	d	**d**ans
o	le styl**o**, bient**ô**t, le tabl**eau**	f	la **f**emme
ɔ	**go**mme	g	le **g**arçon
u	n**ou**s	ɲ	espa**gn**ol
y	d**u**	ʒ	**j**our, **g**entil
ø	d**eu**x	l	**l**a
œ	l**eu**r, s**œu**r	m	**m**al
ɑ̃	**en**f**an**t	n	**n**euf
ɛ̃	le cous**in**	ŋ	campi**ng**
õ	b**on**jour	p	**p**ère
œ̃	**un**	r	la **r**ègle
j	n**i**èce, la f**i**lle, le cra**y**on	s	**s**alut, cin**q**
ɥ	l**u**i	t	**t**ante
w	m**oi**, j**ou**er	v	**v**oici
		z	**z**éro, cou**s**ine

Sources

Text Credits

Page 15: FCB pour MONOPRIX/Catalogue Rentrée 2003; **page 25: (1)** Extrait du journal "Le Soir" (Bruxelles, Belgique) du 20 février, 1993; **(2)** Extrait de l'hebdomadaire "Haïti en marche" vol. 4, no. 44; **(3)** "Dossier beauté" 20ANS no. 67, mars 1992, page 68; **(4)** "L'Express" Neuchâtel; **(5)** "Le Devoir," Gilles Lesage, 11 mars 1992; **(6)** Titre paru dans "Le Nouvel Observateur," no. 1447 (30.7.1992); **page 62:** Adapted from: Statistics Canada's Internet Site, http://www12.statcan.ca/francais/census01/products/highlight/PrivateHouseholds/Page.cfm?Lang=F&Geo=PR&View=1b&Code=0&Table=3&StartRec=1&Sort=2&B1=Change http://www12.statcan.ca/francais/census01/products/highlight/PrivateHouseholds/Page.cfm?Lang=F&Geo=PR&View=1b&Table=1&StartRec=1&Sort=2&B1=Counts, June 28, 2004; **pages 97–98:** © ASO; **page 99:** © La Croix, no. 36892, le 26 juillet 2004; **page 137:** Courtesy of Moving to Magazines Ltd., Toronto, Canada, www.movingto.com; **page 154:** Jacques Prévert, *Paroles*, © Éditions GALLIMARD; **page 175:** Laurence Benaïm & Jean-Louis Arnaud, *Label France*; **page 186:** En avril, ne te découvre pas d'un fil Michel Barelli, Nice-Matin, 9 avril 2003, Tous droits réservés; **page 200:** © Copyright Agenda Quoi Vadis 2004; **page 208:** Pratiques culturelles des Français. Enquête 1997 Olivier Donnat, Ministère de la culture; **page 209:** Extrait du site www.centrepompidou.fr, Copyright Centre Pompidou, 2003; **page 217:** Textes issues de "Guide Pratique" Martinique édité par l'O.D.T. de la Martinique; **page 248:** Extrait du « Memento du Tourisme-édition 2004 », source : enquête SDT Direction du Tourisme/SOFRES; **page 254:** J.M.G. Le Clézio « Zinna », *Printemps et autres saisons.* © Éditions GALLIMARD; **page 257:** Henriette Walter, *Le Français dans tous les sens.* © Éditions Robert Laffont, 1988; **page 260:** Office du Tourisme et des Congres; **pages 273–75:** (Editions Perce-Neige): Je suis Cadien (suite poétique); **page 299:** Camara Laye, *l'Enfant noir* © Éditions PLON; **page 315:** Jacques Prévert, *Paroles*, © Éditions GALLIMARD; **pages 324–25:** Courtesy of Laurent Beauvallet, Le Petit Villiers; **page 347:** Courtesy of la SNCF; **page 374:** Albert Camus, *Journaux de voyage*, © Éditions GALLIMARD; **pages 379–81:** Eugène Ionesco, *La Leçon*, © Éditions GALLIMARD; **page 418:** (illustration) Troy Leleux; **page 425:** Télérama no. 2829 du 7 avril 2004; **page 428:** © le Nouvel Observateur; **page 437:** François Truffaut, *Préface, Le cinéma de l'occupation* d'André Bazin; **page 439:** © Etude Audience AEPM. France; **page 449:** Courtesy of France Télécom; **page 457:** Logo du Festival Panafricain du Cinéma et de la télévision de Ouagadougou (FESPACO); **page 459 (top and middle):** Extrait du site CineKritik - www.cinekritik.com; courtesy of Matthieu Granacher; **page 459 (bottom):** Extrait de la critique du film « Les Invasions Barbares », parue sur le site Web « Spirale d'Amour » : http://giridhar.free.fr; **page 461:** Survey/Hachette Filipachi Presse; **page 467:** © lmcommuniquer.com; **page 481:** © Musée national des beaux-arts du Québec. Contenu : Musée national des beaux-arts du Québec. Réalisation (design graphique et programmation) : Telus MD; **page 483:** *Pariscope* numéro: 1881, du mercredi 9 au mardi 15 juin 2004 sommaire, p. 3; **page 484:** adopted from *Pariscope*, numéro 1881, du mercredi 9 au mardi 15 juin 2004; **page 497:** Babette Gazeau, Danseuse Chorégraphe de danse africaine http://www.danse-africaine.net.

Photo Credits

Page 2: Simon Harris/Robert Harding World Imagery; **page 5 (top):** R. Lucas/The Image Works; **page 5 (bottom):** Owen Franken/Stock Boston; **page 15:** GoldPitt LLC; **page 23 (top):** Dennis, Lisl/Getty Images Inc. - Image Bank; **page 23 (bottom):** Kathleen Campbell/Getty Images Inc. - Stone Allstock; **page 24 (top):** Owen Franken/Stock Boston; **page 24 (middle):** Owen Franken/Stock Boston; **page 24 (bottom):** P. Quittemelle/Stock Boston; **page 26 (all):** GoldPitt LLC; **Page 30:** Stuart Cohen/The Image Works; **page 33 (left):** Hazel Hankin/Stock Boston; **page 33 (right):** Syndey Byrd; **page 36 (all):** Mary Ellen Scullen; **page 57:** Mary Ellen Scullen; **page 61:** GoldPitt LLC; **page 64 (top):** Susan Kuklin/Photo Researchers, Inc.; **page 64 (bottom left):** Dannielle Hayes/Omni-Photo Communications, Inc.; **page 64 (bottom right):** GoldPitt LLC; **page 68:** Alexandra & Pierre Boulat/Alexandra Boulat; **page 69:** Mary Ellen Scullen; **page 71:** Owen Franken/Stock Boston; **page 74:** Robert Fried/Robert Fried Photography; **page 77 (all):** Courtesy of the Library of Congress; **page 87 (left):** Andrew D. Bernstein/Getty Images, Inc.; **page 87 (middle):** Getty Images, Inc.; **page 87 (right):** Harry How/Getty Images, Inc.; **page 89:** Jean-Marc Charles/AGE Fotostock America, Inc.; **page 96:** Jacques Demarthon/Agence France Presse/Getty Images; **page 98:** Graham Chadwick/Getty Images Inc. -Stone Allstock; **page 99 (right):** Joel Saget/Agence France Presse/Getty Images; **page 100 (left):** Jac Verheul; **page 100 (right):** Philippe Desmazes/Agence France Presse/Getty Images; **page 104:** Ulrike Welsch/PhotoEdit; **page 107 (top):** Guy Schiele/

Publiphoto, Inc.; **page 107 (bottom)**: GoldPitt LLC; **page 110**: Mary Ellen Scullen; **page 111**: GoldPitt LLC; **page 112**: Mary Ellen Scullen; **page 113 (left)**: Beryl Goldberg; **page 113 (right)**: Peter Cade/Getty Images Inc. - Stone Allstock; **page 114**: GoldPitt LLC; **page 116**: GoldPitt LLC; **page 120**: Will & Deni McIntyre/Getty Images Inc. - Stone Allstock; **page 134 (top)**: Ed Simpson/Getty Images Inc. - Stone Allstock; **page 134 (bottom)**: Lee Snider/The Image Works; **page 138**: Nik Wheeler; **page 144**: © Owen Franken/CORBIS; **page 157 (top)**: GoldPitt LLC; **page 157 (bottom left and right)**: Cathy Pons; **page 162 (all)**: Mary Ellen Scullen; **page 165 (top)**: © Robert Holmes/CORBIS; **page 165 (bottom)**: J. P. FRUCHET/Getty Images, Inc. - Taxi; **page 173 (left)**: Mary Ellen Scullen; **page 173 (middle and right)**: GoldPitt LLC; **page 174**: Cary Wolinsky/Aurora & Quanta Productions Inc.; **page 176**: Noel Quidu/Getty Images, Inc - Liaison; **page 178**: Max Alexander © Dorling Kindersley; **page 179 (top)**: PricewaterhouseCoopers LLP; **page 179 (bottom left)**: GoldPitt LLC; **page 179 (bottom right)**: Werner Otto/AGE Fotostock America, Inc.; **page 180 (top)**: Mary Ellen Scullen; **page 180 (bottom)**: Robert Fried/Stock Boston; **page 181**: Max Alexander © Dorling Kindersley; **page 184**: Mary Ellen Scullen; **page 188 (top left)**: Mark Junak/Getty Images Inc. - Stone Allstock; **page 188 (top right)**: Arv Diesendruck/Getty Images Inc. - Stone Allstock; **page 188 (bottom left)**: Esbin-Anderson/The Image Works; **page 188 (bottom right)**: Lawrence Migdale/Stock Boston; **page 189 (top)**: Mary Ellen Scullen; **page 189 (bottom)**: Mary Ellen Scullen; **page 195**: Corbis/Bettmann; **page 206 (top)**: David Cassidy; **page 206 (bottom)**: La Poste; **page 215**: Patrick Aventurier/Getty Images, Inc - Liaison; **page 216**: Guy Thouvenin/Robert Harding World Imagery; **page 219**: Jess Stock/Getty Images Inc. - Stone Allstock; **page 220 (bottom)**: Robert Harding/Robert Harding World Imagery; **page 221**: GoldPitt LLC; **page 224**: Michael Busselle/Getty Images Inc. - Stone Allstock; **page 225**: Mary Ellen Scullen; **page 228**: Beryl Goldberg/Beryl Goldberg; **page 238**: Mary Ellen Scullen; **page 239**: GoldPitt LLC; **page 247**: Beryl Goldberg; **page 252 (top)**: Patrick Ingrand/Getty Images Inc. - Stone Allstock; **page 252 (bottom)**: Mary Ellen Scullen; **page 256 (left)**: Mary Ellen Scullen; **page 258**: GoldPitt LLC; **page 261 (all)**: Simeone Huber/Getty Images Inc. - Stone Allstock; **page 264**: GoldPitt LLC; **page 265**: Stuart Cohen/The Image Works; **page 266**: David Simson/Stock Boston; **page 273**: Philip Gould Photography; **page 275**: John Elk, III/John Elk III; **page 276 (all)**: Virginie Cassidy/Michele Delefortrie; **page 277 (top left)**: Beryl Goldberg; **page 277 (top right)**: Mary Ellen Scullen; **page 277 (bottom)**: Cathy Pons; **page 284**: Owen Franken/Stock Boston; **page 295**: Mary Ellen Scullen; **page 297 (top left)**: Daninielle Hayes/Omni-Photo Communications, Inc.; **page 297 (top right)**: Owen Franken/Stock Boston; **page 297 (bottom)**: Chris Brown/Stock Boston; **page 300 (top)**: Mary Ellen Scullen; **page 300 (bottom)**: Frank Siteman/Omni-Photo Communications, Inc.; **page 304**: David R. Frazier/David R. Frazier Photolibrary, Inc.; **page 305**: Richard Passmore/Getty Images Inc. - Stone Allstock; **page 308 (top)**: Cathy Pons; **page 308 (bottom)**: Mary Ellen Scullen; **page 310**: Mary Ellen Scullen; **page 318 (top)**: Mary Ellen Scullen; **page 318 (bottom)**: R. Lucas/The Image Works; **page 319**: Mary Ellen Scullen; **page 325**: Mary Ellen Scullen; **page 328 (top and bottom left)**: Mary Ellen Scullen; **page 328 (bottom right)**: GoldPitt LLC; **page 329 (top)**: Dannielle Hayes/Omni-Photo Communications, Inc.; **page 329 (bottom)**: Mary Ellen Scullen; **page 332**: Mary Ellen Scullen; **page 336 (top and middle)**: Envision Stock Photography, Inc.; **page 336 (bottom)**: Becky Luigart-Stayner/Corbis; **page 337 (left and middle)**: Beryl Goldberg; **page 337 (right)**: EyeWire Collection/Getty Images - Photodisc-; **page 338**: GoldPitt LLC; **page 340**: GoldPitt LLC; **page 341 (left and right)**: Jean Marie DG Perrin/Recette de Jean Perrin, Z.A. 25330, Cléron, France; **page 344**: Hubert Raguet/Getty Images, Inc - Liaison; **page 355 (all)**: GoldPitt LLC; **page 356 (top)**: Owen Franken/Stock Boston; **page 356 (bottom left)**: Fotografia Productions/Julie Houck/Stock Boston; **page 356 (bottom right)**: J.C. Francolon/Getty Images, Inc - Liaison; **page 361**: Mary Ellen Scullen; **page 364**: Kim Sayer © Dorling Kindersley; **page 366**: David Simson/Stock Boston; **page 367 (left)**: Ray Stott/The Image Works; **page 367 (right)**: John Elk III; **page 368**: Mary Ellen Scullen; **page 372**: Getty Images, Inc - Liaison; **page 375 (left)**: Chad Ehlers/AGE Fotostock America, Inc.; **page 375 (right)**: GoldPitt LLC; **page 377**: Mary Ellen Scullen; **page 379 (left)**: Mary Ellen Scullen; **page 379 (right)**: DE MALGLAIVE ETIENNE/Gamma Press USA, Inc.; **page 382 (left)**: Hulton Getty/Getty Images, Inc - Liaison; **page 382 (right)**: Getty Images Inc. - Hulton Archive Photos; **page 386**: GoldPitt LLC; **page 389**: Mary Ellen Scullen; **page 397**: National Library of Medicine; **page 398**: Richard Pasley/Stock Boston; **page 400**: GoldPitt LLC; **page 405**: GoldPitt LLC; **page 406 (all)**: Mary Ellen Scullen; **page 407**: Beryl Goldberg; **page 411**: Virginie Cassidy; **page 415**: Mary Ellen Scullen; **page 417 (all)**: Frans Lanting/Minden Pictures; **page 424**: GoldPitt LLC; **page 426 (top)**: Photo by Pathe Films/ZUMA Press. (©) Copyright 2002 by Courtesy of Pathe Films; **page 426 (bottom)**: Micheline Pelletier/CORBIS-NY; **page 436**: French Film Office Unifrance Film U.S.A.; **page 438**: Thomas Craig/Index Stock Imagery, Inc.; **page 439**: Mary Ellen Scullen; **page 449 (bottom)**: Max Alexander © Dorling Kindersley; **page 454**: Mary Ellen Scullen; **page 455 (left)**: Picture Desk, Inc./Kobal Collection; **page 457 (bottom left)**: Getty Images, Inc.; **page 457 (bottom right)**: François Roy/The Canadian Press; **page 458**: Picture Desk, Inc./Kobal Collection; **page 464**: © Gail Mooney/CORBIS; **page 465**: George Haling/AGE Fotostock America, Inc.; **page 467 (left)**: © lmcommuniquer.com/Photo Stéphanie Lacombe; **page 467 (right)**: Mary Ellen Scullen; **page 471**: Cathy Pons; **page 472**: Mary Ellen Scullen; **page 474 (bottom right)**: Art Resource/Reunion des Musees Nationaux/The Magpie, 1869, Claude Monet, Musee d'Orsay, Paris, Photo RMN; **page 475**: Mary Ellen Scullen; **page 477 (top)**: Corbis/Bettmann; **page 477 (bottom)**: National Gallery of Art, Washington D.C.; **page 482 (all)**: GoldPitt LLC; **page 485**: Mary Ellen Scullen; **page 488**: Office du tourisme d'Avenches; **page 493**: Erica Lansner/Getty Images Inc. - Stone Allstock; **page 495 (top)**: John Elk III; **page 495 (bottom)**: Connie Coleman/Getty Images Inc. - Stone Allstock; **page 496 (left)**: Ken Gillham/Robert Harding World Imagery; **page 500**: © 2001 Jack Vartoogian.

Index

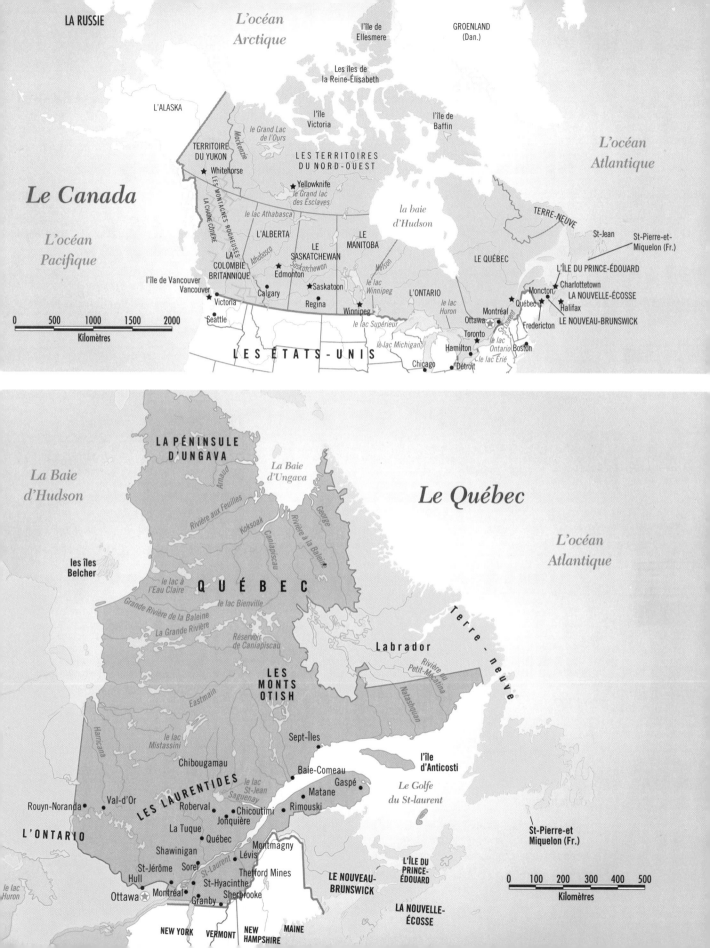

Le Canada

LA RUSSIE

L'océan Arctique

l'île de Ellesmere

GROENLAND (Dan.)

Les îles de la Reine-Élisabeth

L'ALASKA

l'île Victoria

l'île de Baffin

L'océan Atlantique

le Grand Lac de l'Ours

TERRITOIRE DU YUKON

LES TERRITOIRES DU NORD-OUEST

★ Whitehorse

★ Yellowknife

le Grand lac des Esclaves

la baie d'Hudson

TERRE-NEUVE

Mackenzie

le lac Athabasca

St-Jean

St-Pierre-et-Miquelon (Fr.)

LA COLOMBIE BRITANNIQUE

L'ALBERTA

LE SASKATCHEWAN

LE MANITOBA

LE QUÉBEC

L'ÎLE DU PRINCE-ÉDOUARD

Athabasca

Saskatchewan

LA CHAÎNE CÔTIÈRE

LES MONTAGNES ROCHEUSES

★ Edmonton

Nelson

Charlottetown

Moncton

LA NOUVELLE-ÉCOSSE

l'île de Vancouver

Vancouver

★ Calgary

★ Saskatoon

le lac Winnipeg

L'ONTARIO

Montréal

Québec

Halifax

LE NOUVEAU-BRUNSWICK

★ Victoria

Regina

★ Winnipeg

le lac Huron

Ottawa

Fredericton

Seattle

le lac Supérieur

Toronto

le lac Ontario

Boston

L'océan Pacifique

Hamilton

le lac Michigan

le lac Érié

| 0 | 500 | 1000 | 1500 | 2000 |

Kilomètres

LES ÉTATS-UNIS

Chicago

Détroit

St-Laurent

Le Québec

La Baie d'Hudson

LA PÉNINSULE D'UNGAVA

La Baie d'Ungava

L'océan Atlantique

Arnaud

Rivière aux Feuilles

Koksoak

George

Rivière à la Baleine

les îles Belcher

Caniapiscau

QUÉBEC

le lac à l'Eau Claire

Grande Rivière de la Baleine

le lac Bienville

Terre-neuve

La Grande Rivière

Réservoir de Caniapiscau

Labrador

Rivière du Petit-Mécatina

LES MONTS OTISH

Eastmain

Natashquan

Harricana

le lac Mistassini

Sept-Îles

l'île d'Anticosti

Chibougamau

Baie-Comeau

Le Golfe du St-laurent

LES LAURENTIDES

le lac St-Jean

Gaspé

Rouyn-Noranda

Val-d'Or

Roberval

Saguenay

Matane

St-Pierre-et-Miquelon (Fr.)

Chicoutimi

Rimouski

L'ONTARIO

Jonquière

La Tuque

Québec

Shawinigan

Montmagny

Lévis

le lac Huron

St-Jérôme

Sorel

St-Laurent

Thetford Mines

L'ÎLE DU PRINCE-ÉDOUARD

Hull

St-Hyacinthe

Sherbrooke

LE NOUVEAU-BRUNSWICK

Ottawa

Montréal

Granby

LA NOUVELLE-ÉCOSSE

| 0 | 100 | 200 | 300 | 400 | 500 |

Kilomètres

NEW YORK   VERMONT   NEW HAMPSHIRE   MAINE

La France